Direct Social Work Practice
Theory and Skills

Direct Social Work Practice

Theory and Skills

Third Edition

Dean H. Hepworth
Arizona State University

Jo Ann Larsen
Private Practitioner
Salt Lake City, Utah

Wadsworth Publishing Company
Belmont, California
A Division of Wadsworth, Inc.

Social Work Editor: Peggy Adams
Production: Ruth Cottrell
Print Buyer: Martha Branch
Designer: Harry Voigt
Copy Editor: Sheryl Rose
Compositor: Carlisle Communications, Ltd.
Cover: Harry Voigt

Printed in the United States of America

3 4 5 6 7 8 9 10——94 93 92 91 90

Library of Congress Cataloging-in-Publication Data

Hepworth, Dean H.
    Direct social work practice : theory and skills / Dean H.
Hepworth, Jo Ann Larsen. — 3rd ed.
        p.   cm.
    Includes bibliographical references.
    ISBN 0-534-12366-X
    1. Social service.   I. Larsen, Jo Ann.   II. Title.
HV40.H53   1989
361.3'2—dc20   89-24771
                                                  CIP

Contents in Brief

v

Contents in Detail

Chapter 12
Enhancing Motivation with Involuntary and Ambivalent Clients / 318

Chapter 13
Negotiating Goals and Formulating a Contract / 336

Part 3
The Change-Oriented Phase / 373

Chapter 14
Planning and Implementing Change-Oriented Strategies / 374

Chapter 15
Enhancing Clients' Problem Solving, Social Skills, and Assertiveness / 404

Preface

Eight years have elapsed since the birth of the first edition of this book. As with that birth, this third edition also entailed severe labor pains and culminated with an enormous sense of relief. The product of that labor, we hope, will be rewarding to faculty members and to undergraduate and graduate students in social work who use it as a textbook.

As with the previous editions we have endeavored to achieve a balance between social work theory and practice skills that translate theory into action. Our original motivation to write a textbook, in fact, was to respond to students' persistent pleas for learning experiences that would equip them to cope with the *concrete* challenges encountered in direct work with various clients. In addition to presenting theory, then, we have continued to delineate many basic skills essential to effective practice and have included relevant skill development exercises and modeled responses, many adapted from actual clinical situations we have encountered during our combined 62 years of direct social work practice.

Before undertaking the revision of the book, we received many suggestions from reviewers of the previous edition who were selected because of their emi-

nence in the field. We incorporated many of their suggestions and express our gratitude to them for their thoughtful recommendations.

Structural Changes

Revisions for this edition are more extensive than were those for the second edition. In addition to updating content, we have eliminated the old Chapter 17, transferring the content on authenticity and assertiveness of practitioners to the new Chapter 5 (now entitled "Relationship Building Skills") and the content on assertiveness training to Chapter 15 (newly entitled, "Enhancing Clients' Problem Solving, Social Skills, and Assertiveness"). These changes, we believe, enhance the coherence of the book.

Other structural changes involve the reordering of chapters in the beginning of Part 2 and in Part 3. Chapters 5–7 have been reordered to introduce students to vital skills in the beginning phase of the helping process (new Chapters 5 and 6) before focusing on counterproductive patterns of communication (new Chapter 7). These changes engage students in learning skills earlier and foster a more positive perspective by beginning with skills to be mastered rather than patterns to be avoided.

In Part 3, we have shifted the contents of the old Chapter 21 to Chapter 16. Feedback from reviewers and instructors indicated they focused on this content (the revised chapter is entitled "Modifying Environments, Developing Resources, and Planning") earlier than on the content embodied in the succeeding chapters. The revised content from the previous Chapter 20 has been shifted to Chapter 17 for the same reason (the revised chapter title is "Enhancing Interpersonal Relationships"). Chapters 16, 18, and 19 from the previous edition thus have become Chapters 18, 19, and 20 respectively in the new edition.

Major Changes in Content

Content for Generalist Practice

In addition to the structural changes just detailed, we have added major new sections and reorganized content within several chapters. The most significant revisions in content were made *to enhance the utility of the book for generalist practice courses.* For example, we have discussed generalist practice in Chapter 2 and have broadened the definition of direct practice to include pertinent roles practitioners perform (or should perform) in areas of administration and social planning. We have also included (in Chapter 16) a new section concerned with social planning and have expanded content related to resource development. To further augment content germane to generalist practice, we

have incorporated content related to organizational barriers to change, as reflected in the title to the new Chapter 20, "Managing Individual, Relational, and Organizational Barriers to Change."

Both Chapters 1 and 2 have been extensively revised. Chapter 1 introduces students to social work, focusing on its purposes, objectives, ethics, values, methods of practice, and various practice roles. Chapter 2 now focuses exclusively on direct (clinical) practice, beginning with a new section that traces the evolution of direct practice. This chapter also addresses generalist practice and embodies new content that reflects the latest thinking about direct practice roles. Other new sections in this chapter clarify terms used to refer to direct practitioners, including caseworker, clinical social worker, and psychotherapist.

Content on Ethnocultural Factors and Vulnerable Populations

Numerous additions to the already extensive content related to minority groups and ethnocultural factors have been included in this new edition. These additions include material on the use of interpreters in transcultural relationships and critical factors that foster building relationships with minority clients.

Other new areas of content deal with problems and vulnerable populations that have moved to the forefront of social workers' concerns since the previous edition. Empowering people with AIDS, developing resources to meet the needs of this highly vulnerable population, and dealing with the impact of homophobia on helping relationships with people with AIDS are new topics addressed. Also focused upon are the problem of homelessness in America, vital factors to be considered in assessing homeless clients, and resources needed to meet the diverse needs of this heterogeneous population.

We have expanded sections that deal with case management, a role increasingly assumed by direct practitioners in response to the needs of homeless people and other vulnerable groups. Emerging knowledge about case management in relationship to the needs of chronic mentally ill persons, physically and developmentally disabled persons, foster children, pregnant adolescents, and immigrants is also presented.

Other Major Additions

Other new sections include the application of reactance theory to work with involuntary clients and content related to assessing developmental needs, wants, and problems associated with life transitions. Related to assessment we have also added a section concerned with the use of computers and have made reference to other instruments used for assessment.

Still other new or expanded sections deal with methods of empowering various client groups (in Chapter 16), new approaches to working through the resistance of multideficit families (in Chapter 20), and relapse prevention (Chapter 21). Many other minor changes, too numerous to mention, have also been made.

Theoretical Orientation

In this book we address human problems from an ecological systems framework. A major feature of the book thus is the inclusion of content germane to various systems and subsystems typically implicated in problems encountered by social workers. These systems include individuals, couples, families, groups, and various environmental systems.

To equip students with a broad range of skills, we have adopted and presented a systematic-eclectic (pluralistic) perspective of practice. Both demanding and rigorous, this perspective enables practitioners to draw from various theories, practice models, and interventions those that best match the unique needs of each client. To the extent possible, we have included models, interventions, and techniques that are empirically grounded. Moreover, we have included interventions and techniques applicable to modifying environments, improving interpersonal relationships, and enhancing individuals' biophysical, cognitive, emotional, and behavioral functioning. The text thus incorporates a truly multidimensional approach to both assessment and interventions.

Organization of the Book

Despite the reorganization the book retains its basic structure, consisting of four parts. The first part introduces the reader to the profession and to direct practice and provides an overview of the helping process. Part 1 concludes with Chapter 4, which is concerned with the cardinal values of social work and how they are operationalized in practice.

Part 2, which is devoted to the beginning phase of the helping process, begins with a chapter that focuses on relationship-building skills. Chapter 6 shifts the focus to theory and skills entailed in eliciting vital information from clients, exploring problems in depth, and providing direction, focus, and continuity to sessions. The content in Chapter 7 deals with barriers in communication, followed by Chapters 8–13, which are concerned with assessing problems of individuals, families, and groups; enhancing motivation; and formulating goals and negotiating contracts.

Devoted to the middle phase (goal attainment) of the helping process, Part 3 begins with Chapter 14, which is concerned with planning strategies and implementing general change-oriented strategies (the task-centered approach and crisis intervention). Chapter 15 delineates numerous interventions and skills, including teaching independent problem-solving skills, social skills, and assertiveness. In Chapter 16 the focus changes to modifying environments, developing resources, empowering clients, serving as a case manager, employing advocacy, and engaging in social planning. Chapter 17 deals at length with methods of enhancing interpersonal relations, emphasizing family and group relationships. The focus of Chapter 18 is on biophysical and cognitive interventions, which include relaxation training, cognitive restructuring, stress inoculation, and self-instruction. This is followed by content in Chapter 19 concerned with implementing additive empathy, interpretation, confrontation, and related interventions. Part 3 concludes with Chapter 20, which discusses manifestations of and methods of dealing with relational reactions and other obstacles to change, methods of coping with resistances of multideficit families, and strategies for overcoming organizational resistances to change.

Part 4 consists of Chapter 21, which deals with the terminal phase of the helping process. This chapter focuses on five different types of termination, evaluating outcomes, consolidating and maintaining gains and preventing relapse, and employing skills entailed in making referrals.

We would like to thank the following reviewers for their helpful comments: Thomas J. Blakely, Western Michigan University; Judith Cingolani, Southern Illinois University; John A. Gabriel, Fordham University; and Wallace J. Gingerich, University of Wisconsin, Milwaukee.

Finally, we express our deep appreciation to Patricia Hepworth, who encouraged us and willingly and cheerfully devoted long and painstaking hours to the typing of the manuscript (as she did with the two previous editions).

Dean H. Hepworth

Jo Ann Larsen

Part 1
Introduction

1 ■ Social Work: An Overview

The Challenges of Social Work

Social work has a rich heritage and has achieved distinction as *the* profession that advocates for the poor, the disadvantaged, the disenfranchised, and the oppressed. Social work, in fact, can take pride in being referred to as the profession that serves as the nation's conscience. Although the profession historically has been committed to serving the poor and the disadvantaged, its domain has steadily expanded, and today social workers serve in such diverse settings as governmental agencies, schools, health care centers, family and child welfare agencies, mental health centers, business and industry, correctional settings, and private practice, to name just a few. People served by social workers range in age from infants to the elderly and include those of all races, ethnic groups, socioeconomic levels, and religions.

Groups of people whom social workers commonly serve include:

- People who are homeless.
- Families, including single-parent families and those that have serious conflicts manifested by runaways, delinquency, violence, learning difficulties, and the like.
- Couples and families that have problems of child or spouse abuse.
- Couples that have serious marital conflicts.
- Individuals and families whose income is inadequate due to unemployment, absence of a wage earner, physical incapacity, lack of job skills, and other such factors.
- Individuals and families whose lives have been disrupted by punishment for violations of the law.
- Unwed, pregnant teenagers.
- Individuals or families whose lives are disrupted by physical or mental illness or disability.
- Substance abusers and their families.
- Foster parents and children whose parents are deceased or who have abandoned or neglected them.
- Immigrants and minority persons who lack essential resources or opportunities or who have been victims of racism, sexism, or other forms of discrimination.
- Developmentally disabled (mentally retarded) persons and their families.
- Aging persons no longer able to function adequately.
- Migrants and transients who lack essential resources.
- Children (and their families) who have school-related difficulties.
- Persons who experience extreme stress related to traumatic events or to major life transitions such as retirement, death of loved ones, children who leave home, and the like.

3

Social workers themselves variously describe their work as rewarding, frustrating, satisfying, discouraging, stressful, and most of all, *challenging.* Consider, for example, the magnitude and challenge of working with a family that manifests several of the problems included in the preceding list. For example, a family may have an alcoholic father who fails to provide adequately for the family and who abuses his wife and children. In addition, the wife may be depressed and unable to parent the children adequately. One child may be truanting from school, another involved in delinquent behavior, and a third pregnant out of wedlock. Direct social work practitioners encounter many such multiproblem families.

ments can be subsumed under the four following conceptual domains:

1. The purpose and objectives of the profession.

2. Values, ethics, and a philosophy of direct practice.

3. Knowledge base of direct practice.

4. Methods and processes employed.

In this chapter we consider each of the first three dimensions. The fourth dimension, which warrants separate treatment, is discussed in Chapter 3. That chapter draws the big picture of the helping process, thus setting the stage for the remainder of the book.

Toward a Definition of Social Work

Given the diversity and complexity of social work activities, it is small wonder that defining social work practice has proven to be an elusive task. Numerous definitions of social work have been developed, but we have chosen to cite part of the definition adopted by the National Association of Social Workers (NASW), the professional social work organization:

Social work is the professional activity of helping individuals, groups, or communities to enhance or restore their capacity for social functioning and to create societal conditions favorable to their goals.

(NASW, 1973, pp. 4–5)

Rather than to quote the definition in its entirety or to engage in a lengthy explanation of it, we shall delineate core elements that lie at the heart of social work, irrespective of where it is practiced. These core ele-

Overall Purposes of Social Work

In serving clients, social work practitioners work toward particular objectives that are (or should be) defined at a high level of specificity. These specific objectives and the means of accomplishing them vary appropriately according to the unique circumstances of each problematic situation. Despite the uniqueness of each situation encountered, the activities of all practitioners, stated at a high level of abstraction, share common goals that constitute the purpose and objectives of the profession. It is important to become knowledgeable about these goals, for they serve to unify the profession and to assist members to avoid developing perspectives that are limited in scope to particular practice settings. To accomplish the purpose of the profession, practitioners must therefore be committed to it and willing to assume responsibilities and engage in actions that go beyond the functions of specific social agencies and their designated individual roles as staff members.

Since the beginning of social work, members of the profession have engaged in discussions of the purpose and objectives of the profession. The latest discussion that occurred in 1979 under the auspices of the NASW Publication Committee involved eminent social workers who had previously been involved in a similar effort, the results of which were published in 1977.[1] As a result of the deliberations in 1979, a working statement on the purpose of social work was formulated. This document consisted of two parts: (1) a statement of purpose together with three major beliefs and (2) a statement of six major objectives. For purposes of discussion, we shall separate the two parts of the working statement, the first part of which is as follows:

The purpose of social work is to promote or restore a mutually beneficial interaction between individuals and society in order to improve the quality of life for everyone. Social workers hold the following beliefs.

> The environment (social, physical, organizational) should provide the opportunity and resources for the maximum realization of the potential and aspirations of all individuals, and should provide for their common human needs and for the alleviation of distress and suffering.

> Individuals should contribute as effectively as they can to their own well-being and to the social welfare of others in their immediate environment as well as to the collective society.

> Transactions between individuals and others in their environment should enhance the dignity, individuality, and self-determination of everyone. People should be treated humanely and with justice.

> A client may be an individual, a family, a group, a community, or an organization.
>
> (*Social Work*, 1981, *26*, p. 6)

Enhancing Social Functioning

Inherent in the preceding statement of purpose is the definition of social work we quoted earlier in the chapter to the effect that the profession's activities involve helping individuals, groups, or communities to enhance their capacity for social functioning and to improve the quality of life for everyone by working toward the enhancement of the social and physical environments. Toward these ends social workers perform functions related to the following:

- *Prevention*—involves the timely provision of services to vulnerable persons before dysfunction develops and includes programs and activities such as family planning, well-baby clinics, parent education, premarital and preretirement counseling, and marital enrichment programs.

- *Restoration*—is aimed at rehabilitating clients whose functioning has been impaired by physical or mental difficulties.

- *Remediation*—entails the elimination or amelioration of existing problems such as marital dysfunction, delinquency, educational maladjustment, social isolation, child abuse, substance abuse, and many problems of living.

Enhancing social functioning involves addressing common human needs that must be adequately met to enable individuals to achieve a reasonable degree of

---

[1]Readers who desire to study in depth the results of both of these efforts are strongly encouraged to read the following issues of *Social Work* (the journal of NASW), 1977, *22* (5), and 1981, *26* (1). These issues are devoted to conceptual frameworks on social work practice and consist of articles that present varying viewpoints of eminent social workers.

fulfillment and to function as productive and contributing members of society. It follows that to meet human needs, essential resources and opportunities must be available; and social workers, therefore, are vitally involved in activities that involve resource utilization and development. Rosenfeld (1983), in fact, defines the domain of social work practice as constituted by incongruities or discrepancies between needs and resources that various systems and social institutions have not dealt with adequately, a view first posited by Gordon (1962) and later reaffirmed by Gordon and Schutz (1977). The aim of social work, according to Rosenfeld, "is to match resources with needs to increase the 'goodness of fit' between them, largely by harnessing potential provider systems to perform this function" (p. 187).

Tapping resources essential to meeting human needs generally involves enhancing transactions between people and their environments—social or physical. To further clarify the transactions between individual needs and environmental resources, consider certain basic needs and the loci of resources that correspond to those needs. These interactions are graphically demonstrated in Table 1-1, from which it is apparent that human beings are extremely dependent upon the environment for the fulfillment of basic needs. Social work practice thus is directed to the interface between people and their environments.

Remedying Personal Dysfunction

It is important to recognize that problems at the interface between people and these environments are not exclusively caused by environmental deficiencies. Many clients whom practitioners serve manifest *personal dysfunction* that impairs their

ability to utilize resources that *are* available. For example, people who manifest dysfunction in interpersonal relationships by being withdrawn are likely to experience difficulties in meeting their needs for companionship and love from others. Practitioners, therefore, often must focus their efforts on reducing clients' fears and inhibitions or helping them to gain interpersonal skills (resources) to reduce the mismatch between their clients' needs and environmental resources.

Table 1-1   Human Needs and Related Loci of Resources

Human Needs	Loci of Resources
Positive self-concept: Identity Self-esteem Self-confidence	Nurturance, acceptance, love and positive feedback provided by significant others (parents, relatives, teachers, peer group)
Emotional: Feeling needed and valued by others Companionship Sense of belonging	Parents, marital partner, friends, siblings, cultural reference groups, social networks
Personal fulfillment: Education Recreation Accomplishment Aesthetic satisfaction Religion	Educational, recreational, religious, employment, and other social institutions
Physical needs: Food, clothing, housing Health care Safety Protection	Economic, legal, and health care institutions; formal social welfare systems, law enforcement, and disaster relief organizations

Promoting Social Justice

Also inherent in the purpose of social work is the goal of promoting social justice, for if resources and opportunities are to be available to all members of society, laws, governmental policies, and social programs must assure equal access of citizens to resources and opportunities. Social workers in direct practice, however, must devote the bulk of their time to providing services and obtaining resources on behalf of their clients. Their actions to promote social justice are therefore generally limited to advocacy for their clients and social action conducted in concert with other social workers through the professional organization.

Objectives of Social Work

In the following sections, we consider the six objectives as presented in the earlier cited working statement. The objectives appear in italics, and the content that follows each is our commentary. The objectives are introduced by the following preface: "Social workers focus on person-and-environment in *interaction*. To carry out their purpose, they work with people to achieve the following objectives."

1. *Help people enlarge their competence and increase their problem-solving and coping abilities.* People who employ social work services are typically overwhelmed by their difficulties and have exhausted their coping resources. Practitioners intervene in the following ways: assist clients to view their difficulties from a fresh perspective, consider various remedial alternatives, foster awareness of strengths and mobilize both active and latent coping resources, enhance self-awareness, and teach problem-solving strategies and interpersonal skills. Consistent with this objective, we have presented in this book a strength-oriented perspective to working with clients. We have further devoted Chapter 15 to a modality that enhances clients' problem-

solving capacities and have included in this and other chapters content that delineates ways of assisting clients to expand their interpersonal and other coping skills.

2. *Help people obtain resources.* People often have little knowledge about various available resource systems, so practitioners often perform the role of *broker* in referring people to resource systems, such as public legal services, health care agencies, child welfare divisions, mental health centers, centers for elderly persons, and family counseling agencies. In some instances, individual clients or families may require goods and services from many different providers, and may lack the language facility, physical or mental capacity, experience, or skill in availing themselves of essential goods and services. Practitioners then may assume the role of *case manager,* which involves not only providing direct services but also assuming responsibility for linking the client to diverse resources and ensuring that the client receives needed services in a timely fashion. Both the broker and case manager roles are discussed in the next chapter, and in later chapters.

Clients sometimes need resource systems that are not available, and in these cases, practitioners must carry out the role of *program developer* by assisting in creating and organizing new resource systems. Examples of such efforts include the following: working with citizens and public officials to arrange transportation to health care agencies for elderly, disabled, and indigent people; developing neighborhood organizations to campaign for better educational and recreational programs; organizing tenants to assert rights to landlords and housing authorities for improved housing and sanitation; and organizing support groups, skill development groups, and self-help groups to assist people to cope with difficult problems of living.

3. *Make organizations responsive to people.* To accomplish this objective, practitioners must assume the role of *expediter* or *troubleshooter* by scrutinizing the policies and procedures of their own and other organizations to determine if clients have ready access to resources and if services are delivered in ways that enhance the dignity of clients. Complex application procedures, needless delays in providing resources and services, discriminatory policies, inaccessible sites of agencies, inconvenient hours of service delivery, dehumanizing procedures or behaviors by staff—these and other factors may deter clients from utilizing resources or subject them to demeaning experiences. Systematically obtaining input from consumers is a method of monitoring an organization's responsiveness to clients. Advocacy actions with and on behalf of clients are sometimes required to secure services and resources to which clients are entitled. We discuss these matters at greater length in Chapter 20.

4. *Facilitate interactions between individuals and others in their environment.* The quality of life for people is determined in large measure by the quality of their interactions with people in their social environment. To accomplish this objective, social workers perform the role of *facilitator* or *enabler* in carrying out the following functions: enhance communication among family members; coordinate efforts of teachers, school counselors, and social workers in assisting troubled students; assist groups to provide maximal support to members; open channels of communication between co-workers; include patients or inmates in the governance of institutions; facilitate teamwork among members of different disciplines in hospitals and mental health centers; and

provide for consumer input into agency policy-making boards. Later chapters deal specifically with content intended to assist students and practitioners to accomplish this objective.

5. *Influence interactions between organizations and institutions.* To accomplish this objective, practitioners perform roles as *coordinator, mediator,* or *disseminator of information.* For example, as a case manager, a practitioner may coordinate medical, educational, mental health, and rehabilitative services provided a given family by multiple resource systems. Mediational activities may be required to resolve conflicts between agencies, minority and majority groups, and neighborhood groups. Dissemination of information regarding legislation or the availability of new funding sources that potentially affect the relationships between public and private agencies may strengthen interactions between these resource systems. Practitioners must also maintain liaison with key organizations to facilitate mutual awareness of changes in policies and procedures that affect ongoing relationships and the availability of resources.

6. *Influence social and environmental policy.* Although direct practitioners work primarily in providing direct service, they also have a responsibility to work toward improving the quality of life by promoting policies and legislation that enhance physical and social environments. Problems of individuals, families, groups, and neighborhoods can often be prevented or ameliorated by laws and policies that prohibit contamination of the physical environment and that promote enrichment of both physical and social environments. Therefore, direct social workers should not limit themselves to remedial activities but should also seek to discover environmental causes of problems and to

sponsor or support efforts aimed at enhancing the environments of people. We discuss this topic at greater length in Chapters 16 and 20.

The part of the working statement concerned with objectives concludes with the following: "To achieve these objectives, social workers work with other people. At different times, the target of change varies—it may be the client, others in the environment, or both."

Values and Ethics

All professions have value preferences that give purpose, meaning, and direction to people who practice within them. Indeed, the purpose and objectives of social work and other professionals emanate from their respective value systems. Professional values, however, do not exist separate and apart from societal values; rather, professions espouse and champion selected societal values, and society in turn gives sanction and recognition to professions through supportive legislation, funding, delegation of responsibility for certain societal functions, and mechanisms for assuring that those functions are adequately discharged. Because a profession is linked to certain societal values, it tends to serve as society's conscience with respect to those particular values.

Values of a profession refer to strongly held beliefs about people, preferred goals for people, preferred means of achieving those goals, and preferred conditions of life. Stated simply, values represent selected ideals as to how the world should be and how people should normally act. Social work has a myriad of values stated at varying levels of abstraction. Not all

social workers support all values of the profession (in fact, one social work value is that people should have the freedom to make choices for themselves); however, all likely subscribe to the following cardinal values:

1. People should have access to the resources they need to meet life's challenges and difficulties as well as access to opportunities to realize their potentialities throughout their lives.

2. Every person is unique and has inherent worth; therefore, interactions with people as they pursue and utilize resources should enhance their dignity and individuality.

3. People have a right to freedom insofar as they do not infringe on the rights of others; therefore, transactions with people in the course of seeking and utilizing resources should enhance their independence and self-determination.

4. Realization of the above values should be the mutual responsibility of individual citizens and of society. Society should foster conditions and provide opportunities for citizens to participate in the democratic process. Citizens should fulfill their responsibilities to society by actively participating in the democratic process.

Considered individually, the preceding values, mission, and objectives are not unique to social work. Their unique combination, however, differentiates social work from other professions. Considered in their entirety, these ingredients make it clear that social work's identity derives from its connection with the institution of social welfare, which, according to Gilbert (1977), represents a special helping mechanism devised to aid those who suffer from the variety of ills found in industrial society. "Whenever other major institutions, be they familial, religious, economic, or educational in nature, fall short in their helping and resource-providing functions, social welfare spans the gap" (p. 402).

Of the four cardinal values listed above, access to resources and opportunities is most important in defining the mission and identity of the profession. All four cardinal values represent the ultimate values or prized ideals of the profession and, as such, are stated at high levels of abstraction. As Siporin (1975) and Levy (1973, 1979) have noted, however, there are different levels of professional values. At an intermediate level, values pertain to various segments of society, as for example, characteristics of a strong community. At a third level, values are more operational, referring to preferred behaviors and instrumentalities. The ideal social work practitioner, for example, is a warm, caring, open, and responsible person who safeguards the confidentiality of information disclosed by clients and participates actively in the professional organization.

Because you, the reader, have chosen social work, it is probable that most of your personal values coincide with those espoused by the majority of social work practitioners. But at the intermediate and third levels of values, you may not always be in harmony with value positions taken by the majority of social workers. During the Vietnam War, the majority of social workers favored withdrawal from Vietnam, but support of that position by members of the profession was by no means unanimous. The same might be said of other controversial issues, such as the right to work, legalization of marijuana, tax-supported abortion, and capital punishment.

Issues such as these may pose value dilemmas for individual practitioners be-cause of conflicts between personal and professional values. Indeed, conflicts or antinomies between two professional values and/or principles are far from rare. For example, when considered in relationship to the issue of legalized marijuana, the value of the right to self-determination and the value that it is good to promote the health and well-being of others collide.[2] Public positions taken by the profession that emanate from its values also sometimes stand in opposition to attitudes of a large segment of society. Consonant with its value that all people should have adequate economic resources to assure a minimal standard of living, the professional organization has supported legislation for guaranteed annual income for all citizens. Yet such legislation has not been supported by the majority of representatives in Congress.

With respect to diverse value preferences among social workers, we advocate the value that social workers should be sufficiently flexible to accommodate differing value positions on most moral and political issues. Different value positions do not necessarily reflect divergence among social workers on the ultimate values delineated earlier. Rather, such differences reflect that there are many possible means of achieving given ends, and rigid assumptions about preferred means to an end often crumble when put to the test of hard experience. Consistent with our value preference for flexibility, we reaffirm our commitment to the value that social workers, whatever their beliefs, should assert them in the forum of the professional organization. We maintain further that social workers should accord colleagues who differ on certain value

---

[2]Self-determination refers to the right of people to exercise freedom of choice in making decisions.

positions the same respect, dignity, and right to self-determination that would be accorded clients. Issues are clarified, and the cohesiveness among professionals is fostered by debate in a climate of openness and mutual respect. By contrast, when aggressive and vociferous people, however noble their intentions, attempt to force their value positions upon others by efforts to intimidate or to employ economic pressure, as has unfortunately happened at times in the past, they do violence to the ultimate values of the profession.

Although you may regard the foregoing discussion of values as academic, mundane, and dull, it is likely that you will be confronted with value dilemmas early on in the real world of direct practice. Such dilemmas often result from conflict between personal and/or professional values on one hand and the personal values of a client or group on the other. Not infrequently, students (and even seasoned practitioners) experience conflict over value-laden problematic situations, such as incest, infidelity, rape, child neglect and/or abuse, spouse abuse, and criminal behavior. Because direct practitioners encounter these and other problems typically viewed by the public as appalling and because personal values inherently shape attitudes, perceptions, feelings, and responses to clients, it is vital that you be flexible, open, and nonjudgmental in your work. It is equally vital that you be aware of your own values, how they fit with the profession's values, and the impact they may have on clients whose values differ from your own or whose behavior offends you. Because values are critical determinants of behavior in interaction with clients and other professional persons, we have devoted Chapter 4 to practice situations involving potential value dilemmas, including exer-cises to assist you in expanding your awareness of your personal values. Chapter 4 also deals at length with the relationship-enhancing dimension of respect and contains exercises to assist you in responding respectfully to value-laden situations that are potentially painful for both you and your clients.

Social Work's Code of Ethics

One essential attribute of a legitimate profession is that it have a code of ethics, which consists of an aggregate of principles that define expectations of its members. A code of ethics specifies rules of conduct to which members must adhere to remain in good standing within a professional organization. A code of ethics thus defines expected responsibilities and behaviors as well as proscribed behaviors. Central to the purposes of a code of ethics is its function as a formalized expression of accountability of (1) the profession to the society that gives it sanction, (2) constituent practitioners to consumers who utilize their services, and (3) practitioners to their profession. Consequent to its function in promoting accountability, a code of ethics serves additional vital purposes, including the following:

1. Safeguards the reputation of a professional by providing explicit criteria that can be employed to regulate the behavior of members.

2. Furthers competent and responsible practice by its members.

3. Protects the public from exploitation by unscrupulous or incompetent practitioners.

To accomplish the above objectives, the National Association of Social Workers provides mechanisms for reviewing allegations of unethical conduct. Local and state chapters of NASW establish committees of inquiry to investigate alleged violations of the profession's Code of Ethics, and national committees provide consultation to local committees and consider appeals of decisions made by local chapters. Because your practice as a social worker must conform to this Code of Ethics, we have included it in its entirety in the Appendix, and we recommend that you study it carefully.

Knowledge Base of Social Work Practice

One of the core elements of social work practice is its undergirding knowledge base. Although much of the knowledge base is borrowed from other disciplines in the social and behavioral sciences, that knowledge is packaged in unique ways; moreover, many of the profession's basic concepts are unique to social work. The profession's universe of knowledge can be subsumed under the following categories, which are regarded as core curriculum areas by the Council on Social Work Education, a body that provides leadership in social work education and serves as the official accrediting body of schools of social work.

1. *Human behavior in the social environment.* Knowledge about human growth and development with particular emphasis on the life tasks encountered by individuals during different developmental stages is essential to practitioners. To assess and to work with human problems, practitioners must be aware of needs and resources associated with each developmental phase. Knowledge of ecological systems theory is also essential as is

knowledge about the forces that motivate behavior in groups and organizations. Because of its mission in enhancing the social functioning of people, social work is particularly concerned with knowledge of factors that contribute to developmental difficulties. Knowledge of these factors, which commonly involve inadequate physical and emotional resources, is essential to planning and implementing effective preventive and remedial programs.

2. *Social policy.* The emphasis accorded by social work to the body of knowledge concerned with social policy most sharply differentiates social work curricula from those of related disciplines. This broad body of knowledge embodies the complex factors involved in the formulation of social policies that shape and guide planning of human service systems at all levels of government and in the private sector as well. To practice in full accordance with the mission and ethics of the profession, social workers have a responsibility to participate in the development of and to utilize social policies that enhance the social functioning of individuals, families, groups, and communities. Because of social work's commitment to social justice, knowledge of inequities in the distribution in America of opportunities, resources, goods, and services, and the impact of these inequities on minority and disadvantaged groups is essential to social work practitioners.

3. *Social work practice methods.* To accomplish the mission and objectives of the profession, practitioners need knowledge and practice skills that enable them to enhance the social functioning of clients. Knowledge of and skills in practice methods vary according to the level of populations served by practitioners. The levels have been designated as *micro, mezzo,* and *macro.* Effective practice requires knowl-

edge related to all three levels of practice, but schools of social work commonly offer "concentrations" in either micro or macro practice and require less preparation in the other methods. Curricula of schools vary, of course, and some schools have "generalist" practice curricula, which require students to achieve balanced preparation in all three levels of practice. Undergraduate programs often have generalistic practice curricula, which are aimed at preparing students for working with all levels of populations.

The practice methods that correspond to the three levels of practice are:

1. *Micro level practice.* At this level, the population served by practitioners is various client groups, including individuals, couples, families, and groups. Practice at this level is designated as *direct* practice (or clinical practice) because practitioners deliver services directly to clients in face-to-face contacts. Direct practice, however, is by no means limited to such face-to-face contacts, as we discuss in Chapter 2, which is devoted to direct practice, the primary focus of this book.

2. *Mezzo level practice.* In contrast to direct practice, mezzo and macro levels generally involve minimal face-to-face contact with clients and hence are referred to as *indirect* practice. Mezzo level practice involves the process of *administration,* which entails assuming leadership in human service organizations directed to enabling the effective delivery of services in accordance with the values and laws of society. Definitions of administration vary, but according to Sarri (1987), ". . . administration is the sum of all the processes involved in:

1. Formulation of policy and its translation into operative goals.

2. Program design and implementation.

3. Funding and resource allocation.

4. Management of internal and interorganizational operations.

5. Personnel direction and supervision.

6. Organizational representation and public relations.

7. Community education.

8. Monitoring, evaluation, and innovation to improve organizational productivity" (pp. 29–30).

Direct practitioners are necessarily involved to some degree in administrative activities, as we discuss in the next chapter. Further, many direct practitioners become supervisors or administrators later in their professional careers. Knowledge of administration, therefore, is vital to direct practitioners, and courses in administration are typically part of the required foundation courses in schools of social work.

3. *Macro level practice.* Still further removed from face-to-face delivery of services, macro practice involves the processes of *social planning* and *community organization.* On this level social workers serve as professional change agents who assist community action systems composed of individuals, groups, or organizations to deal with social problems. Practitioners at this level may work with citizen groups or with private, public, or governmental organizations. Activities of practitioners at this level include the following:

1. Development of and work with community groups and organizations.

2. Program planning and development.

3. Implementation of programs.

Although most direct practitioners engage in little or no macro level practice, those who work in rural areas where practitioners are few and specialists in social planning are not available may work in concert with concerned citizens and community leaders in planning and developing resources to prevent or combat social problems. For a brief but informative overview of social planning and community organization, see the article by Gilbert and Specht (1987), the source of the foregoing information.

4. *Research.* Increasingly, research is receiving emphasis as a vital dimension of the knowledge base essential to social work practitioners. Knowledge of research is indispensable to scientific and scholarly inquiry, which in turn is the driving force behind rigorous advancement of knowledge. To keep abreast of knowledge, practitioners must be able to utilize information gained from research studies. This requires some knowledge of research designs and the ability to discriminate between conclusions based on empirical data and others that are subjective and unwarranted. Moreover, practitioners require knowledge of single-subject experimental designs to be able to evaluate the effectiveness of their own practice from time to time.

Practicing Competently: An Ethical Requirement

As reflected in the profession's Code of Ethics (I, B) attaining and maintaining competence in practice is an ethical requirement of social workers. To meet this requirement aspiring social workers must achieve proficiency in a broad range of activities.[3] The rationale for this require-

ment is compelling because much is at stake for consumers of social work services. Furthermore, who would question that clients have the right to expect competent services from those who represent themselves to the public as experts in their field of practice? What then does competent practice actually mean? The dictionary defines *competent* simply as "fitting, suitable for the purpose; adequate; properly qualified; having legal capacity or qualification." To assess professional competency, however, is far from simple because competency in practice embodies knowledge, values, skills, and attitudes essential to fulfill one's professional role skillfully. Ingredients essential to perform one's role adequately vary according to the demands of each situation. A practitioner may thus be competent in providing certain types of service, such as marital or family therapy, and not in others, such as correctional services or protective services to children who have been abused or neglected. Furthermore, the elements of competent practice in various settings are in a constant state of flux as a result of expanding knowledge, emerging skills, and the changing demands of practice. Competency must thus be viewed within a temporal context, for a practitioner may achieve competence at one time only to suffer steady erosion of that competence by failing to keep abreast of ever-expanding knowledge and skills.

Our primary aim in writing this book was to assist students and practitioners to achieve and to advance their professional competence. This is not a modest objective, as social work practice theory has been in a state of vigorous ferment for the past 20 years. This ferment has

---

[3]Because of the broad scope of social work activities embodied in the three levels of practice, it is highly doubtful that, without extensive study beyond the master's level, practitioners can achieve advanced expertise in all levels of practice. This reality is reflected in the curricula of schools of social work, which typically require master's level students to select one level of practice or "concentration" for intensive study.

resulted from three major sources: (1) analyses of earlier research studies that cast doubt on the effectiveness of traditional social work interventions; (2) emerging theories and empirically proven interventions developed by researchers in the helping professions, including social work; and (3) ever-constricting sources of funding for social work programs, which has produced strident demands for accountability and cost effectiveness of services.

The knowledge base of social work practice has expanded rapidly, and empirical research has infused the profession with welcome stimulation and scientific vitality. Whereas students of the 1970s entered the profession during a time when earlier research findings had cast serious doubt on the efficacy of social work interventions, subsequent research studies have demonstrated convincingly that direct social work practice is effective in helping the majority of clients (Reid & Hanrahan, 1982; Rubin, 1985; Thomlison, 1984). Moreover, practitioners have available an ever-widening array of interventions they can employ for many different human problems.

Our objective of assisting students and practitioners to achieve competence presented a formidable challenge. We responded by including principles of effective practice identified by prominent theoreticians, researchers, and educators. Our task was further complicated by the fact that competence embodies much more than possessing knowledge of practice theory; *competent practitioners must be able to transform that knowledge into action.* Indeed, in recent years social work educators have been increasingly occupied with identifying and defining competencies (skills) in explicit terms and with developing technologies of assisting students to master these skills. We have incorporated these technologies in this book. In fact, the most significant contribution of this book, in our judgment, is its thrust in assisting students *to gain mastery of specific skills essential to competent practice.*

Evolving Theory and Competence

Possessing skills alone does not assure competence, for without an undergirding knowledge base a practitioner would be little more than a technician. To analyze problems, persons, and situations; to plan remedial interventions; and to implement appropriate techniques requires an adequate grasp of practice theory and knowledge about human behavior in the social environment. Direct practice theory involves a broad and complex domain within which rapid expansion in recent years has supplied much needed vigor, but not without painful growing pains. Much of the new theory has not expanded the margins of preexisting theory but has tended to be incompatible with and to replace the older theory. Incorporating new theory, therefore, has posed some challenging dilemmas to schools of social work, responses to which are discussed in the following section.

Trend Toward Integrating Practice Models

Because human beings present a broad array of problems of living, no single theory or practice model is sufficiently comprehensive to adequately address them all. Moreover, techniques associated with one practice model may be applied equally effectively by practitioners who espouse other models. Indeed, although some practitioners identify largely with only one practice model, few if any are purists in a strict sense; that is, few apply interventions and techniques that originated from only one practice model. Practitioners who do commit themselves to only one practice model do a disservice to themselves and to many of their clients, for they limit their range of effectiveness by attempting to fit all clients and problems into their chosen model. Logic dictates that the opposite should be the case; practitioners should select interventions and techniques that best fit certain types of problems and clients.

Practice theories vary widely in their world views, targets of intervention, specifications of techniques, methods of assessment, length of interventions, and other important dimensions. Some interventions are thus more relevant to and cost effective for certain problems than are others. Moreover, except for a limited number of problems, no single theory has proven to be more effective than other practice theories, although some interventions have proven to be effective and others ineffective in treating certain problems. All theories may thus be viewed as possessing some part of the universe of truth—but not more than just a part.

The proliferation of theories in the social sciences, social work, and allied disciplines has ushered in a new era that offers the potential of enabling practitioners to select specific interventions proved effective for specific problem situations. To achieve this potential presents a formidable challenge, however, for although an abundance of knowledge is available, that knowledge is fragmented. To integrate the plethora of theories and interventions, a generic framework capable of encompassing such theories and interventions is essential. Fortunately, such a unifying framework, the ecological systems model (Germain, 1979, 1981; Meyer, 1983; Siporin, 1980), is available.

Ecological Systems Model   This model is a natural extension of the "person-in-environment" perspective that was dominant in social work until the mid-1970s. Although that perspective accorded recognition to the impact of environmental factors upon human functioning, an inordinate emphasis had been accorded to psychodynamic factors in assessing human problems. This heavy emphasis, which resulted from the prominence and wide acceptance of Freud's theories in the 1920s and '30s, reached its zenith in the 1940s and '50s. With the emergence of ego psychology, systems theory, theories of family therapy, expanded awareness of the importance of ethnocultural factors, and emphasis on ecological factors in the 1950s and 1960s, increasing importance was accorded to environmental factors and to understanding ways in which people interact with their environments. Ecological systems theory thus evolved as a natural outgrowth and synthesis of these trends.

Ecological systems theory posits that individuals are engaged in constant transactions with other human beings and with other systems in the environment and that these various persons and systems reciprocally influence each other. Further, each system is unique, varying in characteristics and ways of interacting (e.g., no two individuals, families, groups, or neighborhoods are the same).

People thus are not mere reactors to environmental forces. Rather, they act on their environments, thereby shaping the responses of other people, groups, institutions, and even the physical environment. For example, people make choices about where to live, whether to upgrade or to neglect their living arrangements, and whether or not to initiate or support policies that combat urban decay, safeguard the quality of air and water, provide adequate housing for the elderly poor, and the like. Adequate assessments of human problems and plans of interventions, therefore, must consider the reciprocal impact of people and environmental systems.

The importance of considering the reciprocal interaction between people and their environments in formulating assessments has been reflected in changing views over the past decade of various human problems. Disability, for example, is now defined in psychosocial terms rather than in medical or economic terms, as had previously been the case. As Roth (1987) has clarified, "What is significant can be revealed only by the ecological framework in which the disabled person exists, by the interactions through which society engages a disability, by the attitudes others hold, and by the architecture, means of transportation, and social organization constructed by the able-bodied" (p. 434). Disability is thus minimized by goodness of fit between needs of people with physical or mental limitations and environmental resources that correspond to their special needs (e.g., rehabilitation programs, special physical accommodations, education and social support systems). In this regard, the critical importance of environmental resources to rehabilitation of patients with major paralyses caused by severe spinal cord injuries has been illustrated and documented in a study reported by Mackelprang and Hepworth (1987).

From the ecological systems perspective, it is clear that the satisfaction of human needs and mastery of developmental tasks require the availability of adequate resources in the environment and positive transactions between persons and their environments (e.g., effective learning by a student requires adequate schools, competent teachers,

parental support, adequate perception and intellectual ability, motivation to learn, and positive relationships between teachers and students). Gaps in the environmental resources, deficiencies in individuals who need or utilize these resources, or dysfunctional transactions between individuals and environmental systems block the fulfillment of human needs and lead to stress or impaired functioning. Reduction or removal of the stress requires coping efforts aimed at gratifying the needs, or stated another way, achieving adaptive fit between person and environment. People, however, often do not have access to adequate resources, or they lack effective coping methods. Social work, of course, involves assisting such people to find ways to meet their needs by linking them with or developing essential resources or by enhancing their capacities for utilizing resources or coping with environmental forces.

Assessment from an ecological systems perspective obviously requires knowledge of the diverse systems involved in interactions between people and their environments. These systems include the following: subsystems of the individual (biophysical, cognitive, emotional, behavioral, motivational); interpersonal systems (parent-child, marital, family, kin, friends, neighbors, cultural reference groups, and others in people's social networks); organizations, institutions, and communities; and the physical environment (housing, neighborhood environment, buildings, other artificial creations, water, and weather and climate). These various systems and their interactions are considered in Chapters 8–11.

A major advantage of the ecological systems model is that it is so broad in scope that typical human problems involving health care, family relations, inadequate income, mental health difficulties, conflicts with law enforcement agencies, unemployment, educational difficulties, and so on can all be subsumed under this model, enabling the practitioner to analyze the complex variables involved in such problems. Assessing the sources of problems and determining the focuses of interventions are the first steps in applying the ecological systems model. The next step is to determine what is to be done vis-à-vis the pertinent systems involved in the problem situation. In this step, the practitioner surveys the broad spectrum of available practice theories and interventions. To be maximally effective, interventions, of course, must be directed to all systems that are critical in a given problem system. These and other principles of ecological systems theory are discussed at greater length in an informative article by Allen-Meares and Lane (1987).

Criteria for Selecting Theories and Interventions. To make judicious choices and to implement chosen interventions skillfully requires knowledge of numerous practice theories and techniques and a rigorous approach to selecting those that are most appropriate for a given client. Systematic eclecticism (Beutler, 1983; Fischer, 1978; and Siporin, 1979) is such a rigorous approach to practice. A systematic eclectic practitioner adheres exclusively to no single theory but rather selects models and theories that best match a given problem situation and accords highest priority to techniques that have been empirically demonstrated to be effective and efficient. Systematic eclecticism is thus most demanding, requiring the practitioner to keep abreast of emerging theories and research findings. In our judgment, this approach to practice holds the highest promise of being efficacious with a broad range of clients and prob-

lems. The theoretical base of this book, therefore, is systematic eclecticism practiced under the umbrella of ecological systems theory.

The systematic eclectic approach to practice would be fairly straightforward if clear guidelines for selecting theories and interventions were available, but as Ivanoff, Blythe, and Briar (1987) and Thomlison (1984) have noted, the state of the art in social work has not advanced to this point. How then does one decide which theories and interventions to study in depth? The most important criterion to consider is *the extent to which a given theory has been supported by empirical research.* Obviously, theories whose tenets have been affirmed through research and whose efficacy have likewise been established are preferable to theories that have not been subjected to rigorous empirical testing.

A number of writers have stressed the importance of basing direct practice upon empirical research. This has prompted controversy over a period of several years, with other writers cautioning that adherents of empirically based practice have taken an extreme position that discounts the importance of other approaches to expanding knowledge. For a discussion of issues involved and of a rationale for empirically based practice see Ivanoff, et al. (1987).

The second criterion for selecting theories and interventions is that if two interventions have both been proven effective, *the intervention that produces results with the least expenditure of time, money, and effort is the more efficient and is preferable to the other.*

Another important factor to be considered in evaluating the value of a theory for practice situations is the *extent to which interventions and techniques subsumed under the theory are specifically delin-*

eated. Theories that are largely composed of abstractions fail to inform practitioners as to how to implement theory in actual practice situations and therefore have limited value. Psychoanalytic theory has been criticized for that reason. Behavior modification, by contrast, is characterized by the high degree of specificity with which its procedures are delineated.

Two other criteria that should be carefully considered in selecting interventions are *ethical implications and the practitioner's level of knowledge and skill with respect to given interventions.* With regard to the former, practitioners should avoid interventions that subject the client to emotional trauma or humiliation, that violate confidentiality, or that otherwise conflict with the profession's code of ethics. With respect to knowledge and skill, it is vital that the practitioner be well grounded in knowledge of interventions, including the rationale of an intervention, indications and contraindications for em-

ploying it, cautions to be observed, guidelines for appropriate timing, and specific procedures for implementing it. Interventions are best learned under careful supervision, and practitioners have an ethical responsibility not to apply them in a haphazard manner or to subject clients to the risk of trial-and-error learning.

Because this book rests on a systematic eclectic approach to direct practice, we have drawn from and integrated numerous behavioral theories and models of practice extant in social work and other helping professions. These theories and models include the task-centered system, cognitive therapy, behavior modification, client-centered therapy, ego psychology, role theory, social learning theory, decision theory, crisis intervention, existential theory, and several models of family therapy. We refer to these theories and models in the book and you will study some of them in depth during your professional education.

2 ■ Direct Practice: Domain, Philosophy, and Roles

Domain

The terms *direct practice* and *clinical practice* are relatively new in social work nomenclature. In fact, even the term *social work practice* was not used before 1970. Earlier, practice was defined by methodologies or by fields of practice. Social workers were thus variously identified as caseworkers, group workers, community organizers, child welfare workers, psychiatric social workers, school social workers, medical social workers, public welfare workers, and so on.

With the unification of the profession in 1955 and the inauguration of its journal, *Social Work,* the gradual transformation from the earlier and more narrow views of practice to the current broad view connoted in the title *social work practice* was under way. This transformation accelerated during the 1960s and '70s when social unrest in the United States led to challenges and criticisms of all institutions, including social work. Minority groups, organized groups of poor people, and other oppressed groups accused the profession of being irrelevant to their pressing needs. In large degree these accusations were justified because most social workers were engaged in narrowly focused and therapeutically oriented ac-

tivities that, in fact, did not address the social problems of concern to oppressed groups.

Until this era of unrest, *casework* had been the predominant social work method. Casework involved the activities of a caseworker, in widely varying types of settings, aimed at assisting individuals, couples, or families to cope more effectively with any of the many types of problems that commonly impair social functioning. Group work had also evolved as a practice method and group workers were practicing in settlement houses, neighborhoods, on the streets with youth gangs, in hospitals, and in other settings. Although the target units served by group workers were larger, the objectives did not address broad social problems. It thus became apparent that urgent needs for broadly defined social services could not be met through the narrowly defined remedial (therapeutic) efforts of the casework and group work methods.

The efforts of Gordon (1965) and Bartlett (1970) to formulate a framework or common base for social work practice comprised of purpose, values, sanction, knowledge, and common skills resulted in a broadened perspective of practice in social work. This new perspective was not oriented to methods of practice and fostered the use of the presently employed generic term *social work practice.*

In light of the foregoing discussion, it is understandable that the Council on Social Work Education responded by adopting a curriculum policy statement stipulating that to meet accreditation standards educational programs in social work must have a curriculum containing foundation courses that embody the common knowledge base of social work practice. It is also understandable that many educational programs are now designed to prepare students for *generalist* practice. The curricula of these programs eschew specialization in practice methods. A number, in fact, do not use method-oriented terms such as casework, group work, direct practice, and community organization but instead use generic terminology in referring to discrete practice courses (e.g., "Social Work Practice with Individuals and Families," "Social Work Practice with Groups," and so on).

The rationale for generalist programs, as we discussed in Chapter 1, is that practitioners should view problems holistically and be prepared to plan interventions that address all systems implicated in clients' problems (also referred to as client systems). Client systems are also broad in scope, ranging from micro systems (individuals, couples, families, and groups) to macro systems (organizations, institutions, communities, regions, and nations). Because method specialization requires completion of a number of courses in a given method, most undergraduate programs have generalist curricula.

Some graduate programs also are generalist but the majority offer specializations or concentrations in a micro or macro "track," with less preparation required in the track not selected as a concentration. Micro tracks are typically identified as *direct practice, clinical practice,* or *direct/clinical practice.*

Direct practice typically embodies casework, group work, and marital and family therapy. Direct practitioners thus focus their efforts primarily on work with individuals, couples, families, and groups. In serving these groups of clients, however, they work in collaboration with other professionals, organizations, and institutions, and in advocacy actions that may involve contacts with landlords, agency administrators, various policy-making boards and legislatures, to name just a few. The direct practitioner thus performs many roles besides delivering face-to-face service, as we discuss later.

The term *clinical practice* is commonly used interchangeably with *direct practice,* but the terms may have different meanings for different people. Some people think of clinical practice as limited to psychotherapy done in mental health settings, private practice settings, or similar settings. Direct practice is usually thought of as encompassing the full range of roles, including doing psychotherapy. Subsequently in this book we use the terms direct practice or clinical practice in the broad sense to refer to practice done in any of the diverse settings in which micro services are delivered. Services delivered by direct practitioners may be addressed to most of the troubling situations encountered by human beings and may be delivered in any of the diverse settings listed at the beginning of Chapter 1.

Central to assisting people with difficulties is knowledge of and skill in implementing the problem-solving process. Entailed in this process are knowledge and skills in assessing human problems and in locating, developing, or utilizing appropriate resource systems. Skills in engaging clients, mutually planning relevant goals, and defining roles of the participants are also integral parts of the problem-solving process. Similarly, the practitioner must possess knowledge of interventions and skills in implementing them. A somewhat more extensive review of the helping process is contained in the next chapter, and the entire book, of course, is devoted to explicating theory and skills related to direct practice with clients.

Direct practitioners of social work must be knowledgeable and highly skilled in interviewing and in assessing and intervening in dysfunctional interactions that involve individuals, couples, families, and groups. Knowledge related to group process and skill in leading groups are also essential, as are skills in forming natural helping networks, functioning as a member of an interdisciplinary team, and negotiating within and between systems. The negotiating function entails skills in mediating conflicts and advocating and obtaining resources, both of which embody high levels of interpersonal skills.

Questions as to whether direct practitioners do or should engage in psychotherapy are still raised by some social workers, who regard psychotherapy as the exclusive province of psychiatry. These individuals argue that only psychiatrists or psychoanalysts are trained to work with the unconscious mind and that social workers should limit their function to casework or counseling. In our opinion the debate is moot. To be sure, the large majority of direct practitioners do not attempt to work directly with the unconscious. The same can be said of many psychiatrists. The reality, however, is that unconscious forces may intrude into the helping process, irrespective of a practitioner's intentions, and that practitioners must deal with such forces when they affect the helping process. Perhaps an even more compelling argument in support of the view that many direct practitioners do psychotherapy is the fact that more social workers are employed in

mental health centers (which deal in psychotherapy) than members of any other core profession (Taube & Barrett, 1983). We might add (with tongue in cheek) that clients, too, seem not to differentiate casework from psychotherapy.

A Philosophy of Direct Practice

As a profession evolves, its knowledge base expands and practitioners gain experience in applying abstract values and knowledge to specific practice situations. Instrumental values thus gradually evolve, and as they are adopted, they become *principles* or guidelines to practice. Such principles express preferred beliefs and attitudes about the nature and causes of human problems, the capacity of humans to deal with problems, desirable goals, desired qualities in helping relationships, vital elements of the helping process, roles of the practitioner and client, characteristics of effective group leaders, the nature of the human growth process, and so on.

Although no widely accepted philosophy of direct practice per se has generally been promulgated in social work, a number of principles have been generally accepted. Although these principles involve value preferences, it is important to recognize that some of them also have been validated by empirical research. Over many years, we have evolved a philosophy of practice from a synthesis of principles gained from sources too diverse to acknowledge, including our own value preferences. We thus offer as our philosophy of direct practice the following principles:

1. People are capable of making their own choices and decisions. Although controlled to some extent by their environment, they are able to direct their lives more than they realize. They always have freedom and responsibility to exercise freedom in shaping their own lives.

2. Helping persons have a responsibility to assist people to achieve maximal independence. Clients grow in strength as social workers promote independent action.

3. Helping persons have a responsibility to work toward changing environmental influences that adversely impact upon clients.

4. Human behavior is purposive and goal directed, although the purpose and goals are often not readily discernible.

5. People are capable of learning new behaviors. Helping professionals have a responsibility to assist people to discover and employ their strengths and to affirm their capacity to grow and change.

6. Although problems of living may stem from past relationships and events and although limited focus on the past may be beneficial in some instances, most difficulties can be resolved by focusing on present choices and by mobilizing extant and latent strengths and coping patterns.

7. Problems of living are often produced by inadequate knowledge and/or coping mechanisms. By gaining knowledge and learning new skills, people often not only resolve difficulties, but also achieve personal growth in the process.

8. Many problems of living are societal and systemic rather than personal or interpersonal. By learning to implement effective strategies, people can effect changes in various types of systems.

9. Adversity is an inherent part of the human condition, but human beings grow in strength through meeting adversities. Life's crises therefore represent opportunities for growth and mastery as well as sources of strain.

10. Human beings want and need to have self-esteem. To gain and maintain self-esteem, people need confirmation of their worth from significant others (spouses, parents, children, other relatives, and friends). Many interpersonal conflicts are indirect expressions of not feeling loved and esteemed.

11. Human growth occurs in the context of relationships with other human beings. Growth in helping relationships is fostered by the power of love, as manifested by acceptance, respect, concern, encouragement, and affirmation of clients' self-worth.

12. A prized aspect of human growth is becoming an open, authentic person. Open, authentic behavior by social workers fosters like behavior in clients.

13. Another prized aspect of human growth is becoming attuned to, concerned about, and responsive to the needs of loved ones and other people.

14. To live in the reality of the present moment is to exercise potentialities more fully.

15. Means to an end are equally important as the ends themselves. Any means of assisting clients to achieve goals should safeguard dignity, self-esteem, self-determination, and confidentiality.

16. Awareness of self is the first step to self-realization; astute and sensitive understanding by social workers facilitates self-understanding by clients. A genuine desire to understand is a gift of the self.

17. People's right to their own values and belief systems are inviolate. Nevertheless, certain values and beliefs lead to dysfunc-

tional and self-defeating behavior. When such is the case, social workers have a responsibility to assist clients to face these aspects of their difficulties.

Roles of Direct Practitioners

During very recent years increasing attention has been devoted to the various roles that direct practitioners perform (or should perform) in discharging their responsibilities. In Chapter 1 we referred to a number of these roles. In this section we summarize these and other roles and refer to sections of the book where we discuss certain roles at greater length. We have categorized the roles based in part on a schema presented by Lister (1987).

I. Direct Provision of Services

Roles subsumed under this category are those in which practitioners meet face-to-face with clients or consumer groups in providing services. These include:

1. *Individual casework or counseling.*

2. *Marital and family therapy* (may include sessions with individuals, conjoint sessions, and group sessions).

3. *Group work services* (may include support groups, therapy groups, self-help groups, and skill development groups).

4. *Educator/disseminator of information.* The practitioner may provide essential information in individual, conjoint, or group sessions or may make educational presentations to consumer groups or to the public. For example, practitioners may conduct educative sessions concerned with parenting skills, marital enrichment, stress management, or various aspects of mental health or health care.

Roles involved in the direct provision of services are primary in the work of most practitioners, especially roles 1–3 listed above. Because this book is aimed at preparing practitioners to provide such direct services, we shall not elaborate on these roles in this section.

II. System Linkage Roles

Because clients often need resources not provided by a given social agency and lack knowledge of or ability to utilize other available resources, social workers often perform roles in linking people to other resources. System linkage roles include the following:

1. *Broker.* To perform the role of broker (i.e., an intermediary who assists in connecting people with resources), practitioners must have a thorough knowledge of community resources so that they can make appropriate referrals. Familiarity with the policies of resource systems and working relationships with key contact persons are essential to successful referrals.

Before some people will avail themselves of resources they may require the practitioner's assistance in overcoming fears and misconceptions. Practitioners also have responsibilities in developing simple and effective referral mechanisms and ways of monitoring whether clients actually follow through on referrals. To assist you in gaining skills in referring clients to needed resources, we have presented relevant guidelines in Chapter 21.

2. *Case manager/coordinator.* Some clients lack the ability to follow through on referrals to other resource systems. In such instances, social workers may serve as a case manager, a person designated to assume primary responsibility for assessing the needs of a client, arranging and coordinating the delivery of essential goods and services provided by other re-

sources, and working directly with the client to ensure that the goods and services are provided in a timely manner. Case managers must maintain close contact with clients and with other service providers to ensure that plans for service delivery are in place and are subsequently delivered as planned. It is noteworthy that in the case manager role, practitioners function at the interface between the client and the environment more than in any other role.

Because of dramatic increases in recent years in the numbers of people needing case management services (e.g., homeless, elderly, and chronically mentally disabled people), numerous articles have appeared in the literature concerned with those who need such services, issues related to case management, and various functions of case managers. Because we discuss these topics at some length in Chapter 16, we defer discussion of them to that chapter.

3. *Mediator/arbitrator.* Occasionally breakdowns occur between clients and service providers so that clients do not receive needed services to which they are entitled. For example, a client may be denied badly needed public assistance, food stamps, or health care. Service may be denied, however, because of arbitrary decisions of a provider, because clients did not adequately represent their eligibility for services, or because of strains that sometimes develop between clients and service providers that precipitate withdrawals of requests for services by clients or withholding of services by providers.

In such instances practitioners may serve as mediators with the goal of eliminating obstacles to service delivery. Mediation is a process that "provides a neutral forum in which disputants are encouraged to find a mutually satisfactory resolution to their problems" (Chandler, 1985, p. 346). In serving as a mediator you must carefully listen to and draw out facts and feelings from both parties to determine the cause of the breakdown. It is important not to take sides with either party until you are confident you have accurate and complete information. When you have determined the nature of the breakdown, you can plan appropriate remedial action aimed at removing barriers, clarifying possible misunderstandings, and working through negative feelings that have impeded service delivery. This process entails the use of communication skills that are delineated in subsequent chapters of this book.

In recent years knowledge of mediation skills has evolved to a high level of sophistication, and a small but increasing number of practitioners are working independently or in tandem with attorneys to mediate conflicts between divorcing partners regarding child custody, visitation rights, and property settlements. These same skills can be used to mediate personnel disputes and labor-management conflicts. To discuss skills in mediation, however, is beyond the scope of this book. In fact, numerous articles and books have been written concerning mediation. For a concise overview of mediation we recommend Chandler's (1985) article; for detailed discussion books by Folberg and Milne (1988) and Lemmon (1985) are excellent resources.

4. *Client advocate.* Serving as an advocate for a client or group of clients has been a role assumed by social workers since the inception of the profession. The obligation to assume this role has since been reaffirmed many times, the most recent being in the Code of Ethics adopted in 1979. With respect to linking clients with resources, advocacy is the process of working with and/or on behalf of clients to obtain services and resources that would not otherwise be provided. We

discuss circumstances under which this might occur and appropriate remedial measures at length in Chapter 20. We also discuss skills involved in advocacy (including social action for groups of clients) in Chapter 16.

III. System Maintenance and Enhancement

As staff members of social agencies, practitioners bear responsibility for evaluating structures, policies, and functional relationships within agencies that impair effectiveness in service delivery. Roles that relate to fulfilling this responsibility include:

1. *Organizational diagnostician.*[1] Discharging this role entails pinpointing factors in agency structure, policy, and procedures that have a negative impact on service delivery. Knowledge of organizational and administrative theory are essential to performing this role effectively, but detailed content related to these topics lies outside the scope of this book. Most schools of social work have required courses in other segments of their curricula that deal specifically with these topics.

2. *Facilitator/expediter.* After pinpointing factors that impede service delivery, practitioners have a responsibility to plan and implement ways of enhancing service delivery. This may involve providing relevant input to agency administrators, recommending staff meetings to address problems, working collaboratively with other staff members to bring pressure to bear on resistant administrators, encouraging and participating in essential in-service training sessions, and other similar activities.

3. *Team member.* In many agency and institutional settings (e.g., mental health,

health care, and rehabilitation settings) practitioners function as members of clinical teams that collaborate in assessing clients' problems and delivering services. Teams commonly consist of a psychiatrist or physician (usually the team leader), a psychologist, a social worker, a nurse and perhaps a rehabilitation counselor, occupational therapist, and/or a recreational therapist, depending upon the setting. Members of the team have varying types of expertise that are tapped in formulating assessments and planning and implementing therapeutic interventions.

As team members, social work practitioners often contribute knowledge related to family dynamics and engage in therapeutic work with family members. Social workers also are expected to apply their knowledge of community resources in planning for discharge of patients and facilitating their reentry into the community following periods of hospitalization. As team members, social workers also often serve as case managers in coordinating discharge planning for patients who would otherwise be unable to function adequately in the community.

IV. Researcher/Research Consumer

Practitioners have a responsibility to evaluate the effectiveness of their interventions, to systematically monitor the progress of their clients, and to keep abreast of and evaluate relevant findings reported in the research literature. Implementing these processes requires practitioners to don the mantle of researcher.

Actual research conducted by direct practitioners usually involves single-subject (also denoted as single-system) designs. Although we briefly discuss single-subject research in Chapters 13 and 21, adequate treatment of this topic is beyond the scope of this book. Most stu-

---

[1]We have borrowed this term from the following article: Weissman, H. H., Epstein, I. E., and Savage, A. (1987). Expanding the role repertoire of clinicians. *Social Casework, 68,* 150–155.

dents of direct practice learn the role of researcher in research courses, especially courses in clinical research, for which several excellent textbooks are available.

V. System Development

Direct practitioners sometimes have opportunities to improve or to expand agency services based on assessment of unmet client needs, gaps in service, needs for preventive services, or findings of one's own or other research studies that indicate more promising results achieved by interventions other than those currently employed. Roles that relate to system development include:

1. *Program developer.* As we noted earlier, practitioners often have opportunities to develop services in response to emerging needs of clients. Such services may include educative programs (e.g., for immigrants or unwed pregnant teenagers), support groups (e.g., for rape victims, adult children of alcoholics, and victims of incest), and skill development programs (e.g., stress management, parenting, and assertiveness training groups).

2. *Planner.* In small communities, rural areas, and boom towns that lack access to community planners, direct practitioners may need to assume a planning role, usually in concert with community leaders. In this role the practitioner works both formally and informally with influential people to plan programs in response to unmet and emerging needs. Varying from one area to another, such needs may include child care programs, transportation for the elderly and disabled, and recreational and health care programs, to name just a few.

3. *Policy and procedure developer.* Participation of direct practitioners in formulating policies and procedures typically is limited to agencies in which they provide direct services to clients. The degree of participation is largely determined by the style of administration within a given agency. Able administrators generally solicit and invite input from professional staff as to how the agency can more effectively respond to consumers of services. Because practitioners serve in the "front lines" they are in a strategic position to evaluate clients' needs and how policies and procedures serve or fail to serve the best interests of clients. It is important, therefore, that practitioners seek to be actively involved in decision-making processes related to policies and procedures.

In rural areas and small communities, direct practitioners often participate in policy development concerned with the needs of a broad community rather than the needs of a circumscribed target group. In such instances practitioners must draw from knowledge and skills gained in courses in social welfare policy and services and community planning.

4. *Advocate.* Just as practitioners may advocate for an individual client, they may also join client groups and other social workers and allied professionals in advocating for legislation and social policies aimed at providing needed resources and enhancing social justice. We discuss skills in advocacy and social action in the concluding section of Chapter 16.

As we have indicated previously, knowledge and skills related to some of the foregoing roles are taught in segments of the curriculum that lie outside of direct practice courses. To do justice in one volume to the knowledge and skills entailed in all these roles is an impossible task; consequently we have limited our focus primarily to the roles subsumed under I, providing direct service. Weissman, Epstein, and Savage (1983) have written an excellent book concerned with many of the administrative roles involved in direct practice.

3 ■ Overview of the Helping Process

Common Elements among Diverse Theorists and Practitioners

In working with individuals, couples, families, groups, and other systems, direct practitioners espouse contrasting theories of human behavior, draw from different models of practice, implement diverse interventions, and serve widely varying clients who are struggling with problems. Despite these many and varied factors, all direct practitioners work toward social work's common objective—improving the quality of life for people. In pursuing this objective, they largely focus their efforts on assisting clients to cope more effectively with problems of living. People are impelled (from either internal or external sources) to secure social work services because of disequilibrium in their lives that stems from unsuccessful coping with problems. The helping process thus is aimed at assisting people to regain equilibrium and to achieve growth in coping capacity by developing new resources or employing untapped resources in ways that reduce tension and achieve mastery of problems.

Whatever their approach to assisting clients, direct practitioners in a global sense employ essentially the same problem-solving process.[1] Further, as they seek to enhance the functioning of different systems involved in clients' problems, they primarily employ the vehicle of interviewing. (In work with families and groups, of course, practitioners also extensively use group process.)

In this chapter, then, the first portion is devoted to an overview of the helping process and to its three distinct phases. (Subsequent portions of the book are organized to correspond to these phases.) The latter part of this chapter focuses on the structure and processes involved in interviewing. Later chapters deal with the structure, processes, and skills involved in modifying the processes of families and groups.

The Helping Process

Virtually all social work theorists agree that the helping process consists of three major phases. Each of the phases has distinct objectives, and the helping process generally proceeds successively through these phases. It is important to keep in mind, however, that these phases are not sharply demarcated by activities and skills employed. Rather, the activities and skills differ more in frequency and intensity than in kind. The processes of exploration and assessment, for example, are central during Phase I, but these processes continue throughout the helping

---

[1] As used in this book, the terms *helping process* and *problem-solving process* have identical meanings and are used interchangeably.

process, although in somewhat diminished significance during subsequent phases. The three major phases are:

Phase I   Exploration, assessment, and planning.

Phase II   Implementation and goal attainment.

Phase III   Termination and evaluation.

Phase I: Exploration, Assessment, and Planning

This phase lays the groundwork for subsequent implementation of interventions and strategies aimed at resolving clients' problems and promoting coping skills. Processes involved and tasks to be accomplished during Phase I include the following:

1. Establishing rapport.

2. Exploring clients' problems by eliciting comprehensive data about the person(s), the problem, and environmental factors.

3. Formulating a multidimensional assessment of the problem, systems that play a significant role in the difficulties, and relevant resources that can be tapped or must be developed.

4. Enhancing motivation of client(s) when inadequate.

5. Mutually negotiating goals to be accomplished in remedying or alleviating the problem and formulating a contract.

In the following sections, we briefly discuss each of the preceding processes and refer to portions of the book that include extensive discussions of these processes.

Establishing Rapport Effective communication in the helping relationship is crucial, for unless practitioners succeed in engaging clients, they may be guarded in revealing vital information and feelings and, even worse, may not return after the initial session. Engaging clients successfully means establishing rapport, which involves reducing the level of threat and gaining the trust of clients in the practitioner's helpful intent. A condition of rapport is that clients perceive a practitioner as understanding and genuinely interested in their well-being. In groups, the task for clients is twofold, for they must not only develop trust in the practitioner but in other group members as well.

Establishing rapport requires that practitioners manifest the values and attitudes identified in Chapter 1 and discussed at length in Chapter 4. These are (1) nonjudgmental attitude, (2) acceptance, (3) clients' right of self-determination, and (4) respect for clients' worth and dignity, uniqueness and individuality, and problem-solving capacities. And finally, practitioners foster rapport when they relate with *empathy* and *authenticity*, which involve facets of both attributes and skill. Both of these skills are considered in later chapters of this book.

Exploring the Problem Situation Establishing rapport and exploring clients' problems are processes that practitioners implement concurrently. Moreover, these processes mutually reinforce each other. Careful and astute exploration not only yields rich data but also cultivates rapport by inspiring confidence in the practitioner. Similarly, *empathic communication* is employed not only to convey understanding and foster rapport but also to elicit expanded expressions of feelings, thereby enabling practitioners to evaluate the role clients' emotions play in their difficulties. Certain responses thus serve dual functions, and the process of relationship building and problem exploration not only proceed concurrently but also over-lap to some extent.

Problem exploration is a critical process, for comprehensive information must be gathered before all the dimensions of a problem and their interaction can be understood. Exploration begins by attending to the emotional states and immediate concerns manifested by clients. Gradually, the practitioner broadens the exploration to encompass relevant systems (individual, interpersonal, and environmental) and explores in depth aspects of the problem that appear salient. During the process of exploration, the practitioner is also alert to and highlights strengths manifested by clients, realizing that these strengths represent a vital resource to be identified and tapped later during the goal-attainment phase.

Skills that are employed in the exploratory process with individuals, couples, families, and groups are delineated later in this chapter and at length in subsequent chapters. To explore problematic situations thoroughly, practitioners must also be knowledgeable about the various systems commonly involved in human difficulties, topics considered at length in Chapters 8–11.

Formulating a Multidimensional Assessment Assessment is an ongoing process that begins from the first contact with clients. During interviews, practitioners weigh the significance of clients' behavior, emotions, and of course, information revealed. These moment-by-moment assessments guide the practitioner in deciding what aspects of the problem to explore in depth, when to explore emotions more deeply, and so on, as we discuss at greater length later in this chapter. In addition to this ongoing process of assessment, the practitioner must formulate a working assessment from which flow the goals and contract upon which Phase II of the problem-solving process is based.

An adequate assessment includes analysis of the problem, the person(s), and the ecological context. Analysis of the problem specifies the nature of the difficulties, which may involve inadequate resources; decisions about a crucial aspect of one's life; dysfunction in individual, interpersonal, or societal systems; or interactions between any of the preceding factors. Analysis of the problem also involves judgments about the duration and severity of a problem as well as the extent to which the problem is susceptible to change, given the clients' potential coping capacity and the permeability of the problematic situation to change. In considering the nature and severity of problems, practitioners must also weigh these factors against their own competencies and the types of services provided by the agency. If the problems call for services that are beyond the agency's function, such as prescribing medication or rendering speech therapy, referral to another professional person or agency may be indicated.

Analysis of the individual system includes assessment of the client's needs, coping capacity, strengths and limitations, and motivation to work on the problem(s). In evaluating the first two dimensions, the practitioner must assess such factors as flexibility, judgment, emotional characteristics, degree of responsibility, capacity to tolerate stress, ability to reason critically, and interpersonal skills. These factors, which are critical in selecting appropriate and attainable goals, are discussed at length in Chapter 9.

Assessment of ecological factors entails consideration of the adequacy or deficiency, success or failure, and strengths or weaknesses of salient systems in the environment that bear on the client's problem. Ecological assessment thus is aimed at identifying systems that must be strengthened, mobilized, or developed in response to the client's unmet needs. Systems that often bear on clients' needs include marital, family, and social support systems (e.g., kin, friends, neighbors, coworkers, peer groups, and ethnic reference groups); child care, health care, and employment systems; various institutions; and the physical environment.

Cultural factors are also vital in ecological assessment, for personal and social needs and means of satisfying them vary widely from culture to culture. Moreover, resources that can be tapped to meet clients' needs also vary according to cultural contexts. Some cultures have indigenous helping persons, such as folk healers, religious leaders, and relatives from extended family units who have been invested with authority to assist clients in times of crises. These persons can often provide valuable assistance to practitioners.

Assessment of the client's situational context further involves consideration of the circumstances as well as actions and reactions of participants in problematic interaction. Knowledge of circumstances and specific behavior of participants before, during, and after troubling events is crucial to understanding the forces that shape and maintain dysfunctional behavior. Assessment, therefore, requires that practitioners elicit detailed information about actual transactions between people.

Whether making assessments of individuals per se or of individuals as subsets of marital dyads, families, or groups, it is important to assess the functioning of these larger systems. These systems have unique properties including power distribution, role definitions, rules, norms, channels of communication, and repetitive interactional patterns. Such systems also manifest both strengths and dysfunctions that strongly impact upon and shape

the behavior of constituent members. It follows that individual dysfunction tends to be a product of systemic dysfunction, and interventions must therefore be directed to the system as well as to the individual.

Assessments of systems are based on varied data-gathering procedures. With couples and families, practitioners may or may not conduct individual interviews, depending upon their theoretical biases, practice styles, and impressions gained during preliminary contacts with family members. If exploration and assessment are implemented exclusively in conjoint sessions, the processes are similar to those of individual interviews except that interaction between the participants assumes major significance. Whereas information gained in individual interviews is limited to reports and descriptions by clients, requiring the practitioner to make inferences about actual interaction within relevant systems, in conjoint interviews and group sessions, practitioners view interaction directly. The practitioner is alert to strengths and dysfunction in communication and interaction and to the properties of the system (see Chapters 10 and 11). Assessment therefore focuses heavily on styles of communication employed by individual participants, interactional patterns among members, and the impact of individual members on processes that occur in the system. These factors are weighed in selecting interventions aimed at enhancing functioning at these different levels of the larger systems.

Finally, a working assessment involves synthesizing all relevant information gained in the exploration process. To enhance the validity of the assessment, it is desirable to involve clients in the process by sharing impressions with them as to the nature of the problems, thus inviting their affirmation or disconfirmation of the impressions, and by seeking additional input. It is also beneficial to further highlight their strengths and to identify other relevant resource systems that can be tapped or need to be developed to accomplish remediation of the difficulties. When the practitioner and client(s) reach agreement about the nature of the problems involved, they are ready to enter the process of negotiating goals, assuming that clients are adequately motivated to advance to Phase II of the helping process.

Enhancing Motivation   Indispensable to success in the helping process are acknowledgment of a problem and adequate motivation on the part of clients to actively work toward its solution. A substantial percentage of clients initially lack one or both of these essential ingredients. Motivation is not static, of course, and practitioners, therefore, must possess skills for enhancing motivation of such clients and of those who readily acknowledge a problem but lack willingness to expend the required effort or to bear the discomfort generally involved in effecting essential change.

Involuntary or captive clients—so called because services are imposed upon them by legal authority (e.g., protective child welfare services or court-imposed supervision while on probation) or because services are an integral part of an institution's program (e.g., correctional center or mental hospital)—frequently manifest initial negativism toward social workers and resist efforts to engage them in the helping process. Many of these clients, as well as others who come to agencies in acquiescence to ultimatums issued by spouses, parents, employers, or other significant persons, either disavow having a problem or attribute the source of difficulties to another person or to untoward circumstances. Such clients confront practitioners with the challenging task of (1) neutralizing negative feelings, (2) attempting to penetrate the client's refusal to acknowledge ownership of a problem, and (3) creating an incentive to work on acknowledged problems. Skillful practitioners often succeed in motivating negativistic clients, thus affirming that motivation is substantially influenced by the interaction between clients and practitioners.

In still other instances, clients freely acknowledge problems and do not lack incentive for change but assume a passive role, expecting practitioners to magically work out their difficulties for them. Practitioners must be able to avoid taking on the impossible role that some clients would ascribe to them and instead impart a belief in clients' abilities to work as partners in searching for remedial courses of action and to mobilize clients' energies in implementing tasks essential to successful problem resolution.

Negotiating Goals and Formulating a Contract   When the practitioner and the individual client, couple, family, or group have reached agreement concerning the nature of the difficulties and the systems that are involved, the participants are ready to negotiate individual and/or group goals. This is a mutual process aimed at identifying what needs to be changed and what related actions need to be taken to resolve or ameliorate the problematic situation. We briefly discuss the process of goal selection in this chapter and at length in Chapter 13.

After goals have been negotiated, participants undertake the final task of Phase I—formulating a contract. The contract (see Chapter 13), which is also mutually negotiated, consists of a formal agreement or understanding between the practitioner and client that specifies the goals to be accomplished, relevant strategies to be implemented, roles and responsibilities of participants, practical arrangements, and other factors. When the client system is a couple, family, or group, the contract also specifies group goals that tend to accelerate group movement and to facilitate accomplishment of group goals.

Mutually formulating a contract is a vital process because it divests the helping process of mystery and clarifies for clients what they may realistically expect from the practitioner and what is expected of them; what they will mutually be seeking to accomplish and in what ways; and what the problem-solving process entails. Comprehending these factors is significant to the majority of clients, many of whom have lacked accurate knowledge about what social workers do and have stereotyped fears of being analyzed or controlled.

Phase II: Implementation and Goal Attainment

After mutually formulating a contract, the practitioner and client(s) enter the heart of the problem-solving process—the implementation and goal-attainment phase, also denoted as the *action-oriented* or *change-oriented* phase (terms that are used interchangeably in this book). Phase II involves translating into action plans formulated between the practitioner and individual clients, couples, families, or groups. The participants thus combine their efforts in working toward the goal accorded highest priority. This process begins by dissecting the goal into subgoals that consist of discrete actions or tasks that are integral units of the overall goal. Tasks may relate to the individual's personal functioning or to interaction with others in the client's environment, or they

may involve interaction with other resource systems, such as schools, hospitals, or law enforcement agencies. The processes of negotiating goals and tasks are discussed in Chapter 13.

After mutually formulating goals with clients, practitioners have the responsibility of selecting and implementing interventions that will assist clients in accomplishing their goals and subsidiary tasks. In selecting interventions, it is vital that practitioners observe the principle that *interventions should directly relate to the problems and to the consequent goals that were mutually negotiated with clients and that were derived from accurate assessment.* This principle may seem so elementary that it is unworthy of mention. The contrary is true. Helping efforts can fail when social workers employ global interventions without considering clients' views of their problems and without attending to the uniqueness of such problems.

Enhancing Self-Efficacy   Research findings (Bandura, 1977; Kazdin, 1979; Zeiss, Lewinsohn, & Munoz, 1979) have strongly indicated that a major source of gain in the helping process is an increased sense of self-efficacy on the part of clients. *Self-efficacy* refers to an expectation or belief that one can successfully accomplish tasks or perform behaviors associated with specified goals. The most powerful means of enhancing self-efficacy is to assist clients in actually performing certain behaviors prerequisite to accomplishing their goals. Another potent technique is to draw awareness of clients to their strengths and to accredit incremental progress of clients toward goal attainment. Moreover, family and group members represent potent resources for enhancing self-efficacy. Practitioners can develop and tap these resources by assisting families and groups to accomplish tasks that involve perceiving and accrediting strengths and progress of group and family members. We consider other sources of self-efficacy and relevant techniques in Chapter 14 and to a lesser extent in other chapters.

Monitoring Progress As work toward goal attainment proceeds, it is important to monitor progress on a regular basis. The reasons for this are fourfold:

1. To evaluate the effectiveness of change strategies and interventions. If an approach or intervention is not producing desired effects, practitioners should determine the reasons for this and/or consider negotiating a different approach.

2. To guide clients' efforts toward goal attainment. Evaluating movement toward goals enhances continuity of focus and efforts and promotes efficient use of time.

3. To keep abreast of clients' reactions to progress or lack of progress. When they believe they are not progressing, clients tend to become discouraged and may lose confidence in the helping process. By evaluating progress periodically, practitioners will be alerted to negative client reactions that might otherwise undermine progress.

4. To enhance clients' motivation and confidence in the helping process. Concentrating on goal attainment and evaluating progress tend to sustain clients' motivation to work on their problems. Moreover, clients tend to respect practitioners who do not passively permit them to expend time in unproductive and fruitless excursions unrelated to the task at hand.

Methods of evaluating progress vary from eliciting subjective opinions to using various types of measurement. These and other matters related to evaluating progress on an ongoing basis are discussed in Chapter 13.

Barriers to Goal Accomplishment As clients strive to accomplish goals and related tasks, progress is rarely smooth and uneventful. Rather, clients experience anxiety, uncertainties, fears, and other untoward reactions as they struggle to give up self-defeating behaviors and to master new behavior or to confront situations that they have previously shunned. Furthermore, family or group members or other significant persons may undermine clients' efforts to change by opposing such changes, by ridiculing the client for seeing a practitioner, by making derisive comments about the practitioner, or otherwise making change even more difficult for the client. (For this reason, it is vital to involve significant others in the problem-solving process whenever feasible.) Because of the potency of barriers to change, practitioners must be perceptive to manifestations of clients' struggles and skillful in assisting them to surmount these obstacles.

Barriers to goal accomplishment are frequently encountered in work with families and groups. Such barriers include personality factors that limit participation of certain group members, dysfunctional behaviors of group members, or dysfunctional processes within the group that impede progress. These matters are addressed in later chapters.

Still other barriers may involve *organizational resistance* within systems whose resources are essential to goal accomplishment. Denial of resources or services (e.g., health care, rehabilitation services, and public assistance) by organizations, or policies and procedures that unduly restrict clients' access to resources may require the practitioner to assume the role of mediator or advocate. A major portion of a chapter in Part 3 of this book is devoted to ways of overcoming organizational resistance.

Relational Reactions As practitioners and clients work together in solving problems, emotional reactions on the part of either party toward the other may impair the effectiveness of the working partnership and pose an obstacle to goal accomplishment. Clients, for example, may have unrealistic expectations or may misperceive the intent of the practitioner. Consequently, clients may experience disappointment, discouragement, hurt, anger, rejection, longings for closeness, or many other possible emotional reactions that may seriously impede progress toward goals. Marital partners, parents, and group members may also experience relational reactions to other members of these larger client systems, resulting in dysfunctional interactional patterns within these systems. Not uncommonly, such relational reactions are manifestations of inappropriate attitudes and beliefs learned from relationships with parents or significant others; in many other instances, however, the practitioner or members of clients' systems may unknowingly behave in ways that understandably foster unfavorable relational reactions on the part of individuals or family or group members. In either event, it is critical to explore and resolve the relational reaction. Otherwise, clients' efforts may be diverted from working toward goal accomplishment, or even worse, clients may prematurely withdraw from the helping process.

Practitioners are also susceptible to relational reactions, and they may experience dislike, disinterest, annoyance, tender feelings, boredom, and other similar reactions. Social workers, after all, are fallible human beings and are not immune to making blunders and experiencing emotions and desires in relationships with clients. It is vital that practitioners be aware of unfavorable reactions to clients and be knowledgeable about how to manage them. Otherwise, they may be working on their own problems rather than the client's, placing the helping process in severe jeopardy. Chapter 20 is designed to assist practitioners in coping with potential relational reactions residing with the client(s), the practitioner, or both.

Enhancing Clients' Self-Awareness As clients interact in a novel relationship with a practitioner and risk new interpersonal behaviors in marital, family, or group therapy, they commonly experience emotions (or physical manifestations of emotions) that may be pleasing, frightening, confusing, and even overwhelming. Though managing such emotional reactions may require a temporary detour from goal-attainment activities, such activities frequently represent rich opportunities for growth in self-awareness. Self-awareness, you will recall from the principles of our working philosophy, is the first step to self-realization. Many clients wish to understand themselves more fully, and they can benefit from being more aware of feelings that have previously been buried or denied expression. Practitioners can facilitate the process of self-discovery by employing *additive empathic responses* during the goal-attainment phase. Additive empathic responses focus on deeper feelings than do reciprocal empathic responses (referred to earlier in the discussion of Phase I). This technique can be appropriately applied in individual and conjoint interviews as well as in group sessions. Additive empathy, explicated at length in

Chapter 19, is of particular value in assisting clients to get in touch with their emotions and to express them clearly to significant other persons.

Another technique that can be employed in fostering self-awareness is *confrontation,* a major topic of Chapter 19. This technique is employed to assist clients to become aware of growth-defeating discrepancies in perceptions, feelings, communications, behavior, values, and attitudes; and to examine such discrepancies in relation to stated goals. Confrontation must be offered in the context of goodwill, and it requires the utmost skill. This skill is particularly useful in assisting clients to become aware of and to resolve intrapersonal barriers to change and untoward relational reactions.

Use of Self As helping relationships become strong during the implementation and goal-attainment phase, practitioners increasingly use themselves as tools to facilitate growth and accomplishment. Relating spontaneously and appropriately disclosing one's feelings, views, and experiences provide for clients an encounter with an open and authentic human being. Modeling authentic behavior encourages clients to reciprocate by risking authentic behavior themselves, thereby achieving significant growth in self-realization and in interpersonal relations. Indeed, when practitioners model authentic behavior in groups, members usually follow suit by assuming like behavior. Practitioners who relate in an authentic manner provide clients with experience that is transferable to the real world of the client's social relationships. A contrived, detached, and sterile "professional" relationship, by contrast, lacks transferability to other relationships.

Practitioners can also use themselves to enhance progress by being facilitatively *assertive.* Assertiveness involves dealing tactfully but firmly with dysfunctional behaviors that impinge on the helping relationship or impede progress toward goal attainment. For example, when clients are habitually tardy, behave irresponsibly, fail to apply themselves actively in the problem-solving process, or neglect to pay fees, the practitioner must deal with these situations. Further, practitioners must relate assertively to larger client systems at times; for example, to focus on the behavior of group members that hinders the accomplishment of goals. To passively permit dysfunctional behavior to continue is tantamount to contributing to that same behavior. Using oneself to relate authentically and assertively is a major focus of Chapter 5.

Phase III: Termination and Evaluation

The terminal phase of the helping process involves four major aspects: (1) assessing when individual and group goals have been satisfactorily attained and planning termination accordingly, (2) effecting successful termination of the helping relationship, (3) planning for maintenance of change and continued growth following termination, and (4) evaluating the results of the helping process. Deciding when to terminate is relatively straightforward when time limits are specified in advance as part of the initial contract, as is done with the task-centered approach. Decisions about when to terminate are also simple when individual or group goals are clear-cut (e.g., to get a job, obtain a prosthetic device, arrange for nursing care, secure tutoring for a child, implement a specific group activity, or hold a public meeting).

In other instances, however, goals involve growth or changes that have no limits, and judgments must be mutually made about when a satisfactory degree of change has been attained. Examples of such goals include increasing self-esteem, communicating more effectively, becoming more outgoing in social situations, and resolving conflicts more effectively. Actually, judgments about termination that involve such goals are much less difficult when goals have been explicitly specified in terms of behavioral indexes of desired levels of growth, a matter discussed in Chapters 13 and 21.

Successfully Terminating Helping Relationships As clients share personal problems and are accompanied through rough emotional terrain by a warm, understanding, and caring practitioner, it is common for them to develop feelings of closeness to the practitioner. Consequently, termination tends to produce mixed feelings for clients. They are likely to feel strong gratitude to the practitioner. They are also likely to experience a sense of relief over no longer having to go through the discomfort associated with exploring problems and making changes (not to mention the relief from paying fees when fees are charged). Although clients are usually optimistic about the prospects of confronting future challenges independently, they often experience a sense of loss over terminating the relationship with the practitioner. Moreover, uncertainty about their ability to cope independently often is mixed with their optimism.

When engaged in the helping process over a lengthy period of time, clients sometimes develop a strong attachment to a practitioner, especially if the practitioner has fostered dependency. For such individuals, termination involves a painful process of letting go of a relationship that has met significant emotional needs. Moreover, these clients often experience apprehension about facing the future without the reassuring strength represented by the practitioner. Group members often similarly experience painful reactions as they face the loss of supportive relationships with the practitioner and group members as well as a valued resource that has assisted them to cope with their problems. To effect termination with individuals or groups that minimizes psychological stress requires both perceptiveness to manifestations of emotional reactions and skills in helping clients to work through such reactions. This subject is discussed in Chapter 21.

Planning Change-Maintenance Strategies In recent years, practitioners have been increasingly concerned over the need to develop strategies that maintain change and continue growth after formal service is terminated. These concerns have been prompted by disconcerting findings to the effect that a significant portion of clients revert to previous dysfunctional behavior patterns following termination. Consequently, strategies for maintaining change are receiving increasing attention (see Chapter 21).

Evaluating Results The final aspect of the problem-solving process is to evaluate the results. Evaluation is important because it enables practitioners and agencies to respond to demands for accountability from funding sources and consumers of service. Furthermore, by evaluating results, practitioners are able to test the efficacy of interventions employed and to monitor their own successes, failures, and progress in achieving favorable outcomes.

Until recent years, practitioners were unable to evaluate outcomes because research studies required large numbers of clients, substantial expense, and sophistication in both research design and statistical analysis. Moreover, group research designs are of little value in assessing individual outcomes. Fortunately, a new approach to outcome research (single-subject design) has evolved in recent years, making it feasible for practitioners to go far beyond subjective evaluation of outcomes. Single-subject research is convenient, involves little or no expense, appeals to most clients, and can be employed with minimal research expertise. Although research methodology is beyond the scope of this book, a brief discussion of single-subject research is included in Chapter 13.

Ideally, evaluation should not end with termination. Planning for follow-up sessions not only makes it possible to evaluate the durability of results, but also facilitates the termination process by indicating the practitioner's continuing interest in clients, a matter we discuss in Chapter 21.

Interviewing Process: Structure and Skills

In direct practice, social workers employ interviewing as the primary vehicle of influence, although administrators and social planners also rely heavily on interviewing skills to accomplish their objectives. Interviews vary according to purpose, types of setting, characteristics, and number of participants. For example, interviews may involve interaction between a practitioner and individuals, couples, or family units. Interviews are conducted in offices, homes, hospitals, prisons, automobiles, and other diverse settings. Despite the numerous variables that affect interviews, certain factors are essential to *all* effective interviews. The following discussion identifies and discusses these essential factors and highlights relevant skills.

Physical Conditions

The physical climate in which an interview is conducted determines in part the attitudes, feelings, and degree of cooperation and responsiveness of people during interviews. Conditions conducive to productive interviews include:

1. Adequate ventilation and light.
2. Comfortable room temperature.
3. Ample space (to avoid a sense of being confined or crowded).
4. Attractive furnishings and decor.
5. Chairs that adequately support the back.
6. Privacy.
7. Freedom from distraction.
8. Open space between participants.

The first five items obviously are concerned with providing a pleasant and comfortable environment and need no elaboration. Privacy is vital, of course, because people are likely to be guarded in revealing personal information and expressing feelings if other people can see or hear them. Interviewers also find it awkward and have difficulty in concentrating or expressing themselves when others can hear them. In certain settings, of course, it may be impossible to assure complete privacy. Even when interviewing a patient in a hospital bed, however, privacy can be maximized by closing doors, drawing curtains that separate beds, and requesting nursing staff to avoid nonessential interruptions. Privacy during home interviews may be even more difficult to arrange, but people will often take measures to reduce unnecessary intrusions if interviewers stress that privacy enhances the productivity of sessions.

Because interviews often involve intense emotional involvement by participants, freedom from distraction is a critical requirement. Telephone calls, knocks on the door, and external noises can impair concentration and disrupt important dialogue. Moreover, clients are unlikely to feel important and valued if practitioners permit avoidable intrusions. Still other sources of distraction are crying, attention seeking, and restless behavior of clients' infants or children. Small children, of course, cannot be expected to sit quietly for more than short periods of time; hence it is advisable to encourage parents to make arrangements for the care of children during interviews (except when it is important to observe interaction between parents and their children).

Having a desk between an interviewer and interviewee(s) tends to emphasize the authority of the practitioner and creates a barrier and a sense of formality that is not conducive to open communication. Although there may be instances in which an interviewer believes that maximizing authority will promote therapeutic objectives, most practitioners strive to foster a sense of equality. Hence, they arrange their desks so that they can rotate their chairs to a position where there is open space between them and their clients. Others prefer to leave their desks entirely and use other chairs in the room when interviewing.

The Structure of Interviews

Interviews in social work have purpose, structure, direction, and focus. The purpose is to exchange information systematically with a view toward illuminating and solving problems, promoting growth, or planning strategies or actions aimed at improving the quality of life for people. The structure of interviews varies somewhat from setting to setting, client to client, and from one phase of the helping process to another. Indeed, skillful interviewers adapt flexibly both to different contexts and to the ebb and flow of each individual session. Thus, each interview is unique. Still, effective interviews conform to a general structure, manifest certain properties, and reflect use of certain basic skills by interviewers. In considering these basic factors, we shall begin by focusing on the structure and processes involved in initial interviews.

Establishing Rapport A cardinal feature of effective social work interviews is open and free communication. Essential to open communication is rapport between the participants, as we explained earlier. Achieving rapport requires that clients gain trust in the helpful intent and goodwill of the practitioner to the extent they are willing to risk revealing personal and sometimes painful feelings and information. Some clients readily achieve trust and confidence in a practitioner, particularly when they have the capacity to form relationships easily.

Establishing rapport begins with introductions. In making introductions and addressing clients by their names, practitioners are prudent to use surnames or to determine by what name clients prefer to be addressed. Although some clients prefer the informality involved in using first names, practitioners should be discreet in using first-name introductions with all clients because of their diverse ethnic and social backgrounds. For example, adult blacks interpret being addressed by their first names as indicative of a lack of respect (Edwards, 1982; McNeely & Badami, 1984).

With many clients, practitioners must surmount formidable barriers before establishing rapport. It is important to bear in mind that the majority of clients have had little or no experience with social work agencies and enter initial interviews or group sessions with uncertainty and apprehension. Many view having to seek assistance with their problems as evidence of failure, weakness, or inadequacy. Moreover, revealing personal problems is embarrassing and even humiliating for some people, especially those who have difficulty in confiding in others.

Cultural factors compound potential barriers to rapport even further. For example, Asian-Americans who retain strong ties to cultural traditions have been conditioned not to discuss personal or family problems with outsiders. Revealing problems to others may be perceived as a reflection of personal inadequacy and as a stigma upon an entire family. The resultant fear of shame may thus impede the development of rapport with clients from this ethnic group (Kumabe, Nishida, & Hepworth, 1985; Tsui and Schultz, 1985). Blacks, Native Americans, and Hispanics may also experience difficulty in developing rapport because of distrust that derives from a history of being exploited or discriminated against by other ethnic groups.

Clients' difficulties in communicating openly tend to be even more severe when their problems involve socially unacceptable behavior, such as child abuse, moral infractions, or criminal behavior. In groups, the pain is further compounded by having to expose one's difficulties to other group members, especially in early sessions when the reactions of other members represent the threat of the unknown.

One means of fostering rapport with clients is to employ a "warm-up" period. This is particularly important with ethnic minority clients for whom such openings are the cultural norm, including Native Americans, persons with strong roots in the cultures of Asia and the Pacific basin, and Hispanics. Aguilar (1972), for example, has stressed the importance of warm-up periods in work with Mexican-Americans:

When Mexican-Americans meet to negotiate or arrange affairs, the first step is to set the climate or ambience. A preliminary period of warm, informal, personal conversation precedes the discussions of the concerns that brought them together. Jumping into the middle of serious and controversial affairs—as many persons in the United States are inclined to do—seems confusing and even discourteous to most Mexican-Americans.

(p. 67)

Native Hawaiians and Samoans also typically expect to begin new contacts with outside persons by engaging in "talk story," which also involves warm, informal, and light personal conversation similar to that described by Aguilar. To plunge into discussion of serious problems without a period of talk story would be regarded by members of these cultural groups as rude and intrusive. Practitioners who neglect to engage in a warm-up period are likely to encounter passive-resistant behavior from members of these cultural groups.

A warm-up period and a generally slower tempo are also critically important with Native Americans, as Hull (1982) has emphasized:

The social worker who is all business and who attempts to deal with an Indian family as she or he might with a non-Indian family may be rebuffed, since forcing or hurrying relationships with Native-Americans does not work. A variety of casual behaviors including small talk, comments addressed to all family members regardless of age, and patience are important if the Indian is to feel comfortable with the worker.

(p. 346)

Consistent with this recommendation, Palmer and Pablo (1978) suggest that practitioners who are most successful with Native-Americans are low-key, nondirective individuals.

Warm-up periods are also important in gaining rapport with adolescents, many of whom are in a stage of emancipating themselves from adults. Consequently, they may be wary of practitioners, and this is a particularly strong tendency among those who are delinquent or who are otherwise openly rebelling against authority. Moreover, adolescents who have had little or no experience with social workers have an extremely limited grasp of practitioners' roles. Many adolescents initially perceive social workers as adversaries, fearing that their role is to punish or to exercise power over them in some vague manner.

With the majority of clients, a brief warm-up period is usually sufficient. When barriers discussed in the preceding do not apply, introductions and a brief discussion of a timely topic (unusual weather, a widely discussed local or national event, or a topic of known interest to the client) adequately fosters a climate conducive to exploring clients' concerns. Most clients, in fact, expect to plunge into discussion of their problems early on, and their anxiety level heightens if practitioners delay getting to the business at hand. With these clients, rapport often develops rapidly if practitioners respond sensitively to their feelings and skillfully give direction to the process of exploration.

An attitude that is critical to establishing rapport is respect for clients. Early in this chapter and in Chapter 1, we stressed the importance of respecting clients' dignity and worth, uniqueness, capacities to solve problems, and other factors. An additional aspect of respect is common courtesy. Being punctual, attending to clients' comfort, listening attentively, remembering clients' names, assisting clients who have limited mobility—these and other similar behaviors convey the message that the practitioner values the client and esteems the client's dignity and worth. Courtesy should never be taken lightly.

Verbal and nonverbal messages from practitioners that convey understanding and acceptance of clients' feelings and views are another vital factor that facilitates the development of rapport. (This does not mean agreeing with or condoning clients' views or problems but rather apprehending and affirming clients' rights to their own views, attitudes, and feelings.) Attentiveness and perceptiveness to feelings that clients manifest both verbally and nonverbally and empathic responses to these feelings convey understanding in a form that clients readily discern. Empathic responses clearly convey the message, "I am with you. I understand what you are saying and experiencing." The "work-horse" of successful helping persons, empathic responding is important not only in Phase I but in subsequent phases as well. Mastery of this vital skill (discussed extensively in Chapter 5) requires consistent and sustained practice.

Authenticity, or genuineness, is still another quality of practitioners that facilitates rapport. Being authentic during Phase I of the helping process involves relating as a genuine person rather than assuming a prescribed, contrived, and sterile professional role. Authentic behavior by practitioners also models openness, the effect of which is to encourage clients to reciprocate by lowering their defenses and relating more openly (Doster & Nesbitt, 1979). Further, encounters with authentic practitioners provide clients with a relationship experience that more closely approximates relationships in the real world than do relationships with people who conceal their real selves behind a professional facade.

A moderate level of authenticity or genuineness during early interviews fosters openness most effectively (Giannandrea & Murphy, 1973; Mann & Murphy, 1975; Simonson, 1976). At this level, the practitioner is not phony but is spontaneous and relates openly to the extent of being nondefensive and congruent. In other words, the practitioner's behavior and responses match her/his inner experiencing. Being authentic also permits the constructive use of humor. Relating with a moderate level of authenticity, however, precludes a high level of self-disclosure. Rather, the focus is on the client, and the practitioner reveals personal information or shares personal experiences judiciously. During the change-oriented phase of the helping process, however, practitioners engage in self-disclosure when they believe that doing so may facilitate growth of clients. Self-disclosure is discussed at length in Chapter 5.

Rapport is also fostered by *not* employing certain types of responses that block communication. To avoid responses that hinder communication, practitioners must be knowledgeable about such types of responses and must eliminate them from their communication repertoires. Toward this end we have devoted Chapter 7 to identifying various types of responses and interviewing patterns that inhibit communication and to describing strategies for eliminating them.

Starting Where the Client Is   A concept that guides practitioners in establishing and sustaining rapport and in maintaining psychological contact with clients is *starting where the client is.* Applying this concept to interviewing involves focusing attention on the immediate concerns and emotional states of clients. If, for example, a client appears in emotional distress at the beginning of an initial interview, the practitioner focuses attention on the client's distress before proceeding to explore the client's problematic situation. An example of an appropriate focusing response would be: "I can sense you're having a difficult time. Could you share with me what you're experiencing at this moment?" Discussion of the client's emotions and related factors tends to reduce

the distress, which might otherwise impede the process of exploration. Moreover, responding sensitively to clients' emotions fosters rapport as clients begin to regard practitioners as concerned, perceptive, and understanding persons.

Language also poses a barrier with many ethnic minority clients who may have a limited grasp of the English language that could cause difficulty in understanding even commonplace expressions. With ethnic minority clients and others whose educational backgrounds have been limited, practitioners must slow down the pace of communication and be especially sensitive to nonverbal indications that clients are confused. To avoid embarrassment, ethnic minority clients sometimes indicate they understand messages when, in fact, they are perplexed.

Use of Interpreters   When ethnic minority clients have virtually no command of the English language, effective communication requires the use of an interpreter of the same ethnicity as the client, making it possible to bridge both cultural value differences and language differences. To work effectively together, however, both the practitioner and interpreter must possess special skills. Interpreters must be carefully selected and trained to understand the importance of the interview and their role in the process, and to interpret cultural nuances to the practitioner. Skilled interpreters thus assist practitioners by translating far more than verbal content, including nonverbal communication, cultural attitudes and beliefs, subtle expressions, emotional reactions, and expectations of clients. To achieve rapport it is also essential for practitioners to convey empathy and establish an emotional connection with the ethnic minority client. The interpreter thus "must have the capacity to act exactly as the interviewer acts—express the same feelings, use the same intonations to the extent possible in another language, and through verbal and nonverbal means convey what the interviewer expresses on several levels" (Freed, 1988, p. 316).

The practitioner should explain the interpreter's role to the client and assure the client of neutrality and confidentiality on the part of both the practitioner and the interpreter. Obviously these factors should also be covered in the training process for interpreters.

Successful transcultural work through an interpreter requires that the practitioner be acquainted with the history and culture of the client's and the interpreter's country of origin. Practitioners must also adapt to the slower pace of interviews. When practitioners and interpreters are skilled in working together in interviews, effective working relationships can evolve and many clients experience the process as beneficial and therapeutic. As implied in this brief discussion, interviewing through an interpreter is a complex process requiring careful preparation of practitioners and interpreters. We recommend Freed's (1988) article, which addresses the complexities and cites many useful references.

Involuntary Clients With involuntary clients, the concept of starting where the client is has critical significance. Because these clients are compelled by external sources to see practitioners, they generally enter initial interviews with negative and perhaps hostile feelings. Practitioners, therefore, should begin by eliciting these feelings and focusing on them until they have subsided. By responding empathically to negative feelings and conveying understanding and acceptance of them, skillful practitioners often succeed in neutralizing these feelings, which enhances clients' receptivity to exploring their problem situations. If practitioners fail to deal with cli-

ents' negativism, they are likely to encounter persistent sullenness, recalcitrance, and other forms of resistance. Skills involved in working with involuntary clients are discussed in a number of chapters in the book.

Process of Exploration

When clients manifest readiness to discuss their problem situations, it is appropriate to begin the process of problem exploration. *Open-ended* responses typically employed to initiate the process are:

- "Could you tell me about your situation?"

- "I'm interested in hearing about what brought you here and how you think I might be helpful."

- "Tell me about the difficulties you've been having, and we can think about them together."

Clients will generally respond by beginning to relate their problems. The practitioner's role at this point is to draw out the client(s), to respond in ways that convey understanding, and to seek elaboration of information needed to gain a clear picture of factors involved in clients' difficulties. Some clients spontaneously provide rich information with little assistance. Others may be hesitant, struggle with emotions, or have difficulty finding words to express themselves.

To facilitate the process of exploration, practitioners employ a number of skills, often blending two or more in a single response. One type of skill, *furthering responses,* encourages clients to continue verbalizing. Furthering responses include *minimal prompts* (both verbal and nonverbal) and *accent responses.* Furthering responses, which convey attention, interest, and an expectation that the client continue verbalizing, are discussed in Chapter 6.

Other responses facilitate communication (and rapport) by providing immediate feedback that assures clients that practitioners have not only heard but also understood their messages. *Paraphrasing* is employed to provide feedback that the practitioner has grasped the *content* of a client's message. In using paraphrasing, the practitioner rephrases (with different words) what the client has expressed. *Empathic responding,* by contrast, provides feedback that the practitioner is aware of *emotions* the client has experienced or is currently experiencing.

Both paraphrasing and empathic responding, which are discussed in Chapters 5 and 6, are especially crucial with clients who have limited language facility, including ethnic minority and developmentally disabled clients. When language barriers exist, practitioners should be careful not to assume they correctly understand the client or that the client understands the practitioner. Further, with ethnic clients who have been culturally conditioned not to discuss personal or family problems with outsiders, practitioners need to make special efforts to grasp intended meanings. Many of these clients are not accustomed to participating in interviews and tend not to discuss their concerns openly. Rather, they may send covert (hidden) messages and expect practitioners to discern their problems by reading between the lines. Practitioners thus need to use feedback more extensively with these clients to determine if their perceptions of intended meanings are on target. Using feedback to ascertain that the practitioner has understood the client's intended meaning and vice versa can avoid unnecessary misunderstandings. Further, clients generally appreciate efforts of practitioners to reach shared understanding, and they interpret patience and persistence in seeking to understand as evidence that the practitioner respects and values them.

During the entire process of exploration, practitioners assess the significance of information revealed as clients discuss problems and interact with the practitioner, group members, or significant others. Indeed, judgments about the meaning and significance of fragments of information guide practitioners in deciding which aspects of a problem are salient and warrant further exploration, how ready a client is to explore certain facets of a problem more deeply, what patterned behaviors of the client or system interfere with effective functioning, when and when not to draw out intense emotions, and so on.

The direction of problem exploration proceeds from general to specific. Clients' initial accounts of their problems are typically general in nature (e.g., "We fight over everything," "I don't seem to be able to make friends," or "We just don't know how to cope with Scott. He won't do anything we ask.") Clients' problems, however, typically have a number of facets, and accurate understanding requires careful assessment of each one. Whereas open-ended responses, such as those illustrated earlier, are effective in launching problem explorations, other types of responses are used to probe for the detailed information needed to identify and unravel the various factors and systems that contribute to and maintain the problem. *Responses that seek concreteness* are employed to elicit such detailed information. There are many different types of such responses, each of which is considered at length in Chapter 6. Another type of response needed to elicit detailed factual information (also discussed in Chapter 6) is a *closed-ended question.*

In addition to possessing discrete skills to elicit detailed information, practitioners must be able to *maintain focus* on manifest problems until they have elicited comprehensive information. Adequate assessment of problems is not possible until a practitioner possesses detailed information concerning the various forces (involving individual, interpersonal, and environmental systems) that interact to produce the problems. Focusing skills (discussed at length in Chapter 6) involve blending the various skills identified thus far as well as *summarizing responses.*

During the course of exploration, practitioners should elicit information that will enable them to answer numerous questions, the answers to which are crucial in understanding various factors that bear on the clients' problems, including ecological factors. These questions (discussed in Chapter 8) serve as guideposts to practitioners and provide direction to interviews.

In addition to answering questions that are relevant to virtually all interviews, practitioners may need to elicit data that will answer questions pertinent to the function of specific practice settings. Outlines that embody essential questions to be answered can be extremely helpful to beginning practitioners. It is important, however, to use outlines flexibly and to focus on the client, not the outline. An example of an outline and suggestions for using such are contained in Chapter 6.

During the process of exploration, practitioners must be keenly sensitive to clients' moment-to-moment emotional reactions and to the part that emotional patterns (e.g., inadequate control of anger, depression, and widely fluctuating moods) play in their difficulties. Emotional reactions during the interview (e.g., crying, intense anxiety, anger, and hurt feelings) often impede problem exploration and require detours aimed at assisting clients to regain equanimity. Emotional patterns that powerfully influence behavior in other contexts may also be problems in and of themselves that warrant careful exploration. Empathic communication is a major skill employed to work through emotional reactions and to explore emotional patterns.

Exploring Expectations

After exploring problems to the satisfaction of both the client(s) and the practitioner, it is important to determine clients' expectations, which vary considerably and are influenced by socioeconomic level, cultural background, level of sophistication, and previous experience with helping professionals. In some instances, clients' expectations diverge markedly from what practitioners can realistically provide. Unless practitioners are aware of and deal successfully with such unrealistic expectations, clients may be keenly disappointed and disinclined to continue beyond the initial interview. By exploring expectations, however, practitioners create an opportunity to clarify the nature of the helping process and to work through clients' feelings of disappointment. Being aware of clients' expectations also assists practitioners to vary their approaches and interventions according to clients' needs and expectations, a matter discussed at greater length in Chapter 13.

Negotiating Goals and a Contract

When practitioners and clients believe they have adequately explored the problems, they are ready to enter the process of planning. By this point (if not sooner), it should be apparent whether other resources and/or services are needed. If it appears other resources are needed or are more appropriate, the practitioner may initiate the process of referring clients elsewhere. If clients' problems match the function of the agency and clients express readiness to proceed further in the helping process, it is appropriate to begin negotiating a contract. Goals specify the end results that will be attained if the problem-solving efforts are successful. Generally, after participating together in the process of exploration, practitioners and clients share common views as to end results or changes that are desirable or essential. In some instances, however, practitioners may recognize the importance of accomplishing certain goals that clients have overlooked and vice versa.

Practitioners introduce the process of negotiating goals by explaining the rationale for formulating them. If formulated in explicit terms, goals give direction and purpose to the problem-solving process; moreover, they serve as guideposts of progress and as criteria of the outcome of the helping efforts. To employ goals effectively, practitioners need skills in involving clients in selecting goals, in formulating both global and specific goals, and in selecting attainable goals.

When more than one goal is entailed in resolving a problematic situation, as is usually the case, practitioners assist clients to assign priorities to goals so that immediate efforts can be directed to the most burdensome aspects of the problem. Giving clients major responsibility for selecting goals enhances their commitment to actively participate in the problem-solving process by assuring that goals are of maximal relevance. Essential elements of the goal selection process are delineated in Chapter 13.

Both initial interviews and the contracting process conclude with discussion of "housekeeping" arrangements and an agreement about next steps. During this final portion, practitioners focus on the matters of length and frequency of sessions, who will participate, means of accomplishing goals, duration of the helping period, fees, date and time of next appointment, pertinent agency policies and procedures, and other relevant matters. The contracting process is discussed at length in Chapter 13.

Goal Attainment

During Phase II of the helping process, interviewing skills are used to help clients accomplish their goals. Much of the focus during this phase thus is on identifying and carrying out actions or tasks clients must implement to accomplish their goals. Preparing clients to carry out actions is crucial to successful implementation. Fortunately, effective strategies of preparations are available (see Chapter 14).

As clients undertake the challenging process of making changes, it is important that they maintain focus on a selected goal until they have made sufficient progress to warrant shifting to another goal. Otherwise, they may jump from one concern to another, dissipating their energies without achieving significant progress. The burden, therefore, falls on the practitioner to provide structure for and direction to the client. Toward this end, skills in maintaining focus during single sessions and continuity between sessions are critical (see Chapter 6).

As noted earlier, barriers to goal attainment commonly occur during the helping process. Typical individual barriers include unrecognized or unresolved fears associated with change and/or behavior and thought patterns that are highly resistant to change efforts because they serve a protective function (usually at great psychological cost to the individual). With couples and families, barriers include entrenched dysfunctional interactional patterns that resist change because they perpetuate power or dependence, maintain safe psychological distance, or foster independence (at the cost of intimacy). In groups, common barriers involve dysfunctional processes that persist despite repeated efforts by leaders to replace these patterns with others that are conducive to group goals and to group maturation.

Additive empathy, a skill referred to earlier, is used with individuals, couples, and groups to recognize and to resolve emotional barriers that are blocking growth and progress. Confrontation is a high-risk

Table 3-1   Phases of the Helping Process
and Constituent Activities and Processes

Phases		
Phase I (Exploration, Assessment, and Planning)	Phase II (Implementation and Goal Attainment)	Phase III (Termination and Evaluation)
Establishing rapport (using appropriate warm-up period)	Partializing goals into subgoals and tasks	Evaluating readiness for termination
Starting where the client is	Selecting and implementing interventions	Mutually planning termination
Exploring the client's problem and the ecological context: exploring problem in depth, maintaining focus, eliciting information needed to answer critical questions	Planning task implementation Enhancing self-efficacy Maintaining focus within sessions	Effecting positive termination of relationship Planning strategies to maintain change and continued growth Evaluating results
Responding to clients' emotional reactions	Maintaining continuity between sessions	Conducting follow-up evaluation
Determining if problems match agency's function	Monitoring progress	
Making referrals when indicated	Resolving barriers to change: enhancing awareness by employing additive empathy, managing relational reactions, resolving resistances to change by employing confrontation and other techniques	
Exploring clients' expectations		
Enhancing deficient motivation		
Formulating a multidimensional assessment		
Negotiating goals and ranking them by priority	Employing self-disclosure and assertiveness to facilitate change	
Defining roles		
Formulating a contract		

skill used to assist clients in recognizing and resolving resistant patterns of thought and behavior. Because of the sophistication involved in using these techniques effectively, we have devoted Chapter 19 to them and have provided relevant skill-development exercises. Additional techniques for managing barriers to change (including relational reactions) are discussed in Chapter 20.

Termination

During the final phase of the helping process, the focus shifts to consolidating gains that clients have achieved, planning maintenance strategies, and evaluating results. The same basic skills employed earlier in the helping process, however, are employed during the terminal phase.

Use of these skills during this phase is discussed in Chapter 21.

Summary

In this chapter, we have viewed the three phases of the helping process from a global perspective and have briefly considered the structure and processes involved in interviewing. Table 3-1 depicts in summary form constituent parts of the helping process and their interrelationships with various interviewing processes.

The remaining parts of the book focus in detail on the three phases of the helping process and on various subsidiary interviewing skills and interventions.

4 ■ Operationalizing the Cardinal Social Work Values

The Interaction between Personal and Professional Values

In this chapter, we present a more thorough exposition of the cardinal values of the profession and demonstrate how these values apply to specific clinical situations. As you read this chapter, you will have opportunities to place yourself in complex clinical situations that challenge you to analyze your values and to assess their compatibility with social work values. You will also be presented with situations that present value dilemmas even to seasoned practitioners.

Your personal values have far-reaching effects on what you actually do in the helping process, for your beliefs and attitudes inevitably influence your feelings and behavior with your clients. For this reason, it is critical that you develop an appreciation of the significant role your values play in your daily encounters with clients. To the extent that you are unaware of these values, you are likely to attempt, sometimes unknowingly, to impose them on your clients. There are four major ramifications associated with imposing values on clients, the first of which is that *imposing values is antithetical to the client's right to self-determination,* which we discuss at length later in this chapter.

The second ramification is that *until clients have internalized new values, behaving contrary to deeply held values may create intense feelings of guilt,* as illustrated in the following example.

Mr. R., a single man, age 35, who lived with his aging parents and was very devoted to them, sought counseling because of conflicts between his personal needs and those of his parents. He had recently become interested in a widow but could tell that his parents were hurt because of the considerable amount of time he was spending with her. They had said nothing, as was typical, but they related coolly to him. He didn't wish to hurt them but felt they should understand that he needed to live his own life. The practitioner appropriately supported his thrust for independence but, in addition, pushed Mr. R. to confront his parents directly with their unrealistic expectations and to express his intentions of living his own life, irrespective of how they behaved. The practitioner further indicated that, in devoting himself to his parents, Mr. R. had done himself a strong injustice, and the practitioner suggested it was high time he rectified the situation. Upon the strong urging of the practitioner, Mr. R. agreed to confront his parents, although he manifested considerable apprehension and misgiving. In the confrontation, his parents responded with unexpected understanding. Mr. R. could sense their hurt and disappointment, however, and felt extremely guilty. Attempts to relieve his guilt failed and he rapidly became depressed and preoccupied with thoughts that life was not worth living.

The third ramification is that *many clients resent and oppose attempts to impose values upon them*—some to the extent that they discontinue seeing a practitioner, as in the following instance reported by a student who had been a participant observer in an interview conducted by an experienced practitioner.

Mrs. W., a widow, had sought professional help for depression that had persisted following her husband's death one year earlier. In this, the fifth interview, Mrs. W. expressed a deep sense of loss associated with her husband's death. She said that she and Mr. W. had been very close and had enjoyed a mutually fulfilling sexual relationship. She missed their sexual relationship and was frustrated because she believed only married people should engage in sexual relations. She had dated several men, most of whom had made sexual overtures. She was inclined to respond positively on a few occasions but believed to do so would be wrong. The practitioner responded that she was an adult and that there was nothing wrong with sex between consenting adults. The practitioner further suggested she needed to discard her outmoded ideas and enjoy herself more. Mrs. W. hesitantly replied that she wasn't sure she could or wanted to do that. She subsequently canceled her next appointment and did not return for additional interviews.

The final ramification of imposing values is that *practitioners must be aware of their own values in order to assist clients who themselves are having value conflicts.* Otherwise, they may unwittingly impose their own values rather than engage clients in careful exploration and analysis of issues and consequences involved in various courses of action associated with differing value preferences. Of course, clients' problems may derive from self-defeating behaviors associated with dysfunctional values, and practitioners have a responsibility to assist them to come to this realization so that they can make choices, having awareness of the values involved and of the probable outcomes of those choices. In such instances, the practitioner's motivation is constructive, for it is based on the client's needs. By contrast, attempting to convert clients to one's values because of a conviction that these values are right meets the needs of the practitioner, not the client.

The Cardinal Values of Social Work

To assist you to operationalize the cardinal values of social work and to reflect those values in your responses to specific practice situations, we delineate in the subsequent sections the following values and concepts that flow from the profession's cardinal values.

1. Developing and utilizing resources.

2. Affirming the worth and dignity of clients.

3. Affirming uniqueness and individuality.

4. Affirming problem-solving capacities and self-determination.

5. Safeguarding confidentiality.

In this chapter, we have included *value clarification exercises* designed to expand your awareness of your personal values and of the implications of these values for you as a social work practitioner. Finally, we have provided *skill development exercises* in the latter portion of the chapter to give you practice in formulating responses to specific situations that involve implementing the values and concepts discussed earlier.

Developing and Utilizing Resources

Perhaps the paramount value of social work is the belief that human beings should have access to the resources they need to cope with life's stresses and to the opportunities to develop their potentialities. This value is reflected in the Code of Ethics (VI, P. 2; see Appendix), which reads as follows: "The social worker should act to ensure that all persons have access to the resources, services, and opportunities which they require." To implement this value requires that you develop the following:

1. Commitment to the value.

2. Knowledge of and skill in employing community resources.

3. Willingness to develop, actively support, and implement policies and programs that effectively meet human needs.

Social workers generally express firm commitment to this value; yet when applied to certain situations, that commitment sometimes dwindles to little more than lip service. In these situations, conflicting beliefs and personal biases come into play, and ultimate attitudes may indicate that a competing belief supersedes one's commitment to assist a client in obtaining resources.

To enhance your awareness of the extent to which you meet the three conditions listed above, we describe several situations in the following. We suggest that you explore your personal feelings and attitudes regarding these situations by engaging in the following activity. Imagine yourself in interviews with the clients involved in each of the following situations. Try to picture yourself and your client as vividly as possible. Imagine the client making the request for the resource described and think of the response you would make. Be aware of your feelings and of possible discomfort or conflict. Then contemplate how your response is or is not consistent with the social work value in question. If the client has not requested a resource, but the need for one is apparent, consider what resource might be developed and how you might go about developing it.

Situation 1 You are a practitioner in a public assistance agency that has a policy of making special funds available to assist clients to purchase essential eyeglasses, dentures, hearing aids, and other prosthetic items. Your client, Mr. Y., who lives in a large apartment complex for single persons, is disabled by a chronic psychiatric disorder. He requests special aid in purchasing new glasses. He says he accidentally dropped his old glasses and they were stepped on by a person passing by. However, you know from talking to his landlord earlier that Mr. Y. broke his glasses while in a drunken stupor.

Situation 2 During a home visit to a large impoverished family in the central city, you observe Eddy, a teenage boy, drawing pictures of animals. The quality of the drawings reveals an exceptional talent. When you compliment him, he appears shy, but his faint smile expresses his delight over your approval. Eddy's mother then complains that he spends most of his time drawing, which she thinks is a waste of time. Eddy's face registers pain and discouragement at her remarks.

Situation 3 During a routine visit to an elderly couple who are recipients of public assistance, you discover that the roof on their home leaks. They have had small repairs on several occasions, but the roof is old and worn out. They have had bids for reroofing, and the lowest bid was over $2,500. They ask if your agency can assist them with funding. State policies permit expenditures for such repairs under exceptional circumstances, but much red tape is involved, including securing special approval from the county director of social services, the county advisory board, and the state director of social services.

Situation 4 A number of low-income families in your community have been forced to move to housing beyond their means by real estate development companies that have been demolishing older apartment houses to construct high-rise condominiums. In the last session of the state legislature, a bill to provide low-interest mortgage funds for low-income families was defeated by a narrow margin. The legislature will be convening next month.

Situation 5 Mr. M. sustained a severe heart attack three months ago. His medical report indicates that he must limit future physical activities to light work. Mr. M. has worked as a freight handler for trucking firms and has no other special skills. Not working, he feels useless and worried about how he can provide adequately for his wife and three children.

Situation 6 During the course of an interview with Laurie, a teenage girl in foster care, you learn that her younger sister, age 15, has been having serious difficulties with her parents and has confided in Laurie that she plans to run away and support herself through prostitution. An older male has promised to set her up in an apartment and refer customers to her.

Represented in the preceding vignettes are needs of clients for resources or for opportunities to develop potentials or needed skills. Possible obstacles to responding positively to these needs, according to the sequence of the vignettes, are as follows: (1) judgmental attitude by a practitioner, (2) failure of significant others or of a practitioner to recognize a potential that might be developed, (3) unwillingness to support a request because of the red tape and effort required, (4) unwillingness by practitioners and others to actively support needed legislation, (5) ignorance of both practitioner and client of potential rehabilitation services, and (6) judgmental attitude or failure to intervene assertively in a timely manner. As you read the vignettes, you may have experienced some of these reactions or additional ones. Such reactions, which are not uncommon among learners, may result from personal values that you have not scrutinized. If you experienced negative reactions to these situations, you need not be unduly alarmed. However, these reactions are indications of your need for expanded self-awareness and additional experience.

Affirming the Worth and Dignity of Clients

One of the cardinal social work values is that all human beings have intrinsic worth, irrespective of their past or present behavior, beliefs, lifestyle, race, or status in life. As they perform their responsibilities, practitioners should affirm the dignity and self-worth of those whom they serve. Universally accepted among the helping professions, this value embodies several related concepts, which have been variously denoted as *unconditional positive regard, nonpossessive warmth, acceptance, nonjudgmental attitude,* and *respect.*

Although this value derives largely from Judeo-Christian and humanistic moral beliefs, it also has pragmatic implications associated with the helping process. Before people will risk sharing personal problems and expressing deep emotions, they must first feel fully accepted and experience the goodwill and helpful intent of practitioners. Keep in mind that many people feel highly vulnerable in requesting or accepting assistance, fearing they may be perceived as inadequate or as failures. Vulnerability is even greater when clients' problematic behavior involves moral infractions, cruelty, child neglect, dishonesty, and other behaviors generally regarded by society as offensive. Such clients enter helping relationships with their antennas finely attuned to possible condemning reactions by practitioners. Usually these clients have been criticized, rebuked, and condemned previously by others, and their anticipation and fear of being judged by the practitioner are readily understandable.

The social worker's role, of course, is not to judge but to seek to understand clients and their difficulties and to assist them to search for solutions. The role of judging falls under the purview of legal and ecclesiastical authorities. Social workers thus should eschew making judgments as to whether clients are good, bad, evil, worthy, guilty, or innocent. Similarly, it is inappropriate for social workers to seek to determine the extent to which clients are to blame for their difficulties. In this regard, it has been our observation that experienced practitioners who have rendered service to many people with diverse problems are less judgmental than are neophytes. This difference can be attributed to the fact that seasoned practitioners have learned through experience that the more one understands the life experience of others, however appalling their behavior may be, the more understanding and accepting one becomes of them.

As you work with clients, therefore, seek to view them as persons in distress and avoid perceiving them according to labels, such as lazy, irresponsible, immoral, delinquent, rapist, child abuser, alcoholic, or prostitute. As you learn more about your clients, you will find that many of them have suffered various forms of deprivation and have themselves been victims of harsh, abusive, rejecting, or exploitative behavior. Remember also that many clients lacked sustained love and approval during critical periods of development, the result of which is a diminutive sense of self-worth. Consistent respect and acceptance on your part tends to exert a corrective influence in assisting them to gain self-esteem, which is vital to sound mental health.

Withholding judgments does not mean that social workers condone or approve of illegal, immoral, abusive, exploitative, or irresponsible behavior. Social workers have their own values and moral codes and are offended by child neglect, rape, brutal crimes, and like behaviors to much the same extent as are other persons. Moreover, social work as a profession and social workers as individuals have responsibilities to assist people to live according to the laws and moral codes of society and to contribute to the common good of society. Indeed, the profession has been entrusted with these responsibilities.

The objective of not blaming people for their difficulties should not be construed to mean that social workers do not assist clients to take responsibility for the part they play in their difficulties. Indeed, change is possible in many instances only as clients gain awareness of the part they play and seek to modify their behavior accordingly. The difference between blaming and defining ownership of responsibilities lies in the fact that the former tends to be negative and punitive whereas the latter emanates from understanding and positive intentions to ameliorate difficulties.

The implication of the preceding discussion is that you as a practitioner are confronted with the challenges of maintaining your own values (except those that hinder relating effectively to people) without imposing them and of divesting yourself of possible tendencies to judge people whose behavior may be highly offensive to you and to others. Still another challenge is to develop composure and equanimity to the extent that you do not manifest embarrassment, shock, dismay, or other discomfort when people discuss value-laden or emotionally charged problems associated with socially unacceptable behavior. The value clarification exercises provided below will assist you in identifying particular areas of vulnerability.

To the extent that you fall short of the goal of developing an openness and ability to accept people whose behavior runs counter to your values, your range of effectiveness will be diminished, for it is difficult if not impossible to conceal negative feelings toward others. Even if you are able to mask negative feelings toward certain clients, you likely will be unsuccessful in helping them, for clients are quick to discern insincerity. In seeking to expand your capacity for openness and acceptance, you may find it helpful to view association with others whose beliefs, lifestyles, and behaviors differ strikingly from your own as an opportunity to enrich yourself as you experience their uniqueness. Truly open people relish such

opportunities, viewing differentness as refreshing and stimulating. Furthermore, gaining understanding of the forces that motivate people can also be intriguing and enlightening. By prizing the opportunity to relate to all types of people and by seeking to understand them, you will gain a deeper appreciation of the diversity and complexity of human beings. In so doing, you will become disinclined to pass judgments and will achieve personal growth in the process.

Value Clarification Exercises

The following exercises will assist you in expanding awareness of values and attitudes that may impair your effectiveness in working with certain clients. In each situation, imagine yourself in an interview or group session with the client(s). If appropriate, you can role-play the situation with a fellow student, changing roles so that you can benefit by playing the client's role as well. As you engage in imagination or role-playing, be aware of your feelings, attitudes, and behavior. After *each* situation, contemplate or discuss the following:

1. What feelings and attitudes did you experience? Were they based on what actually occurred or did they emanate from preconceived beliefs about such clients?

2. Were you comfortable or uneasy with the client? What were your partner's perceptions of your attitudes as reflected in your behavior?

3. What values were reflected in your feelings, attitudes, and behavior?

Situation 1 Your client is a 35-year-old married male who was ordered by the court to secure mental health services following his arrest for making obscene telephone calls. He appears uncomfortable and blushes as you introduce yourself.

Situation 2 You are just starting your first group session with a group of males being treated for AIDS in a health center.

Situation 3 You are a child welfare worker, and your client is a 36-year-old father whose 13-year-old daughter ran away from home after he enticed her into having sexual intercourse on several occasions during the past two months. She reported to you earlier that he has been molesting her since she was six years of age.

Situation 4 Your 68-year-old client has been receiving chemotherapy for terminal cancer at your hospital for the past month. Appearing drawn and dramatically more emaciated than last month, she reports she has been increasingly suffering with pain and believes her best course of action is to take an overdose of sleeping pills.

Situation 5 You are a probation officer, and the judge has ordered you to complete a presentence investigation of a woman arrested for being an accomplice in a con game employed to bilk elderly people out of their savings.

Situation 6 You have been working for eight weeks with Mr. X., who initially sought help for marital difficulties. His wife left him four weeks ago, and he has continued seeing you for anxiety and depression. He confides he has been pushing drugs for 18 months and has wanted to stop but doesn't know how he could produce a comparable income.

Situation 7 You are interviewing parents for inclusion in a group formed to help the members control violent outbursts toward their children. You introduce yourself to Mr. O., who was referred by the hospital following admission of Isabel, his four-year-old daughter. Isabel sustained a broken leg and rib injuries when Mr. O. threw her against the wall in a fit of rage.

If you experienced discomfort or negative feelings as you read or role-played any of the above situations, your reactions were not unusual. Most people (even social work students) are repulsed by some of the problematic behaviors embodied in the situations described. Trying to look beyond the repugnant behaviors to see clients as individuals in distress is a formidable challenge. However, by striving to focus selectively on the person rather than the behavior, you can gradually overcome inclinations to label people negatively and learn to see them in full perspective.

When practitioners warmly accept clients as they are, consistently manifesting care and concern, they increase the likelihood that the clients will gradually lower their defenses.[1] A climate of trust and mutual respect usually evolves, and clients increasingly sense and keenly appreciate practitioners' goodwill. Acceptance is conveyed by listening attentively; by responding sensitively to feelings manifested by the client; by facial expressions, voice intonations, and gestures that convey interest, care, and concern; and by extending courtesies and attending to the client's comfort.

Acceptance is probably conveyed most strongly by consistent efforts to understand clients and their difficulties. Verbal following by the practitioner, especially in the form of empathic responding, conveys a commitment to understand. Though you may not always fully understand all of your client's messages, genuine efforts on your part to do so will be discerned and

---

[1]Some clients, of course, remain distant and hostile irrespective of how practitioners relate.

appreciated. Careful efforts to explore the client's problems also convey interest, commitment to understand, and a desire to assist clients with difficulties.

As we have noted, acceptance is also conveyed through warmth, an elusive but important attribute of the practitioner. Although the element of warmth is difficult to define, it is generally agreed that a warm person is attentive, yet calm and relaxed, and speaks with a well-modulated voice that reflects the nuances of feeling manifested by a client. Monotonic speech, by contrast, tends to be interpreted as indicating boredom, whereas rapid and staccato speech has an excited quality that fosters tension.

Although you likely can do little to modify the pitch of your voice, you can increase your warmth by listening to recordings of your interviews and identifying both positive and negative patterns in your speech. If, for example, you wished to convey genuine concern for a client at a particular point in a session and your voice intonations failed to adequately convey that concern, you may benefit by engaging in practice that involves varying your voice inflections until you attain the desired intonation. Feedback from colleagues after role-playing exercises can also help you to identify strengths as well as areas for improvement in reflecting warmth.

With respect to warmth, a caveat is in order. Excessive efforts to be warm may achieve effects opposite to those desired. Some clients, especially those who habitually maintain considerable distance from others to protect themselves from imagined hurt, are frightened by lavish friendliness and warmth. Other people may view effusive warmth as inappropriate, insincere, or seductive. Clients vary in the extent to which they welcome or tolerate emotional closeness, and it is vital to avoid pressuring for a degree of intimacy that exceeds their level of tolerance. A warm, pleasant demeanor, augmented by genuine demonstrations of interest and concern, fosters a positive helping relationship and is appreciated by clients; gushy friendliness, by contrast, offends some people.

Other Threats to Acceptance and Respect

In addition to differences in values between you and your clients and possibly stereotypes and prejudices that you may have toward certain client groups (we discuss stereotypes and prejudices more fully later), other threats in the form of certain behavioral patterns of clients may severely test your tolerance and your capacity to affirm the dignity and worth of clients. These types of behaviors, of course, are by no means limited to clients, and when confronted in other walks of life, such behaviors tend to produce negative interactions and to strain relationships. Because acceptance of and respect for clients are indispensable to the helping process, it is important that you develop awareness of your reactions to these behaviors and evolve patterns of response that safeguard the helping relationship.

Because practitioners vary widely in their personalities, each will be vulnerable to responding negatively to certain types of behavior and not to others. We have not attempted to identify all the kinds of behavior that pose threats to acceptance and respect but have limited our focus to those most commonly encountered. These include the following, each of which is discussed subsequently:

1. Helplessness and excessive dependency.

2. Silence and withdrawal.

3. Aggressive and sullen behavior.

4. Manipulative and exploitative behavior.

5. Self-effacing behavior.

6. Passive noncompliant behavior.

Helplessness and Excessive Dependency

The threat posed by helpless and excessively dependent behavior is that a practitioner will underestimate the strengths and capacities of clients and thereby foster and reinforce dependency by assuming responsibility for solving a client's difficulties. The following are typical examples of bids for dependency:

MOTHER OF ADOLESCENT SON: I just don't know what to do with Larry. He's so demanding and loses his temper when I don't let him have his way. I'm just lost in knowing what to do. He's a good boy, but he's so strong willed [*cries and wrings hands*]. Please talk with him and help him see how he's just killing his poor mother. I'm at my wit's end.

WIFE, AGE 38: I've talked to my friends, my doctor, and my lawyer about my marriage. But I still don't know what to do. I've been told you're tops as a marriage counselor. Tell me what you think I should do.

In such instances, taking the initiative in response to pressure from clients manifests disrespect for their strengths and fosters unrealistic expectations that you are all-powerful and capable of dispensing ready-made solutions to their difficulties. Moreover, by unrealistically assuming the burden of solving clients' problems, you negate the cardinal value of self-determination.

After failing to cope successfully with problems, many clients, of course, seek help precisely because they feel helpless and overwhelmed. Rather than inviting dependency, however, your tasks in such instances are to engender hope, enhance motivation, and enlist active participation in the search for remedial courses of action. For example, responding to the message of the married woman cited previously who implores the practitioner to give her answers to her problems, the worker might say:

"I sense you're saying, 'I'm desperate. I've talked to others about my marriage, but it hasn't seemed to help. I'm hoping that you can give me the answers.' I do wish that solving problems were that easy, but it has been my experience that there are no easy solutions. If I were to give you answers now, they wouldn't be helpful because I know very little about what you're really struggling with. Further, I would be cheating you by taking over your problems and presuming that I know what is best for you. In the long run you'll benefit more by our exploring your difficulties together and discovering resources you have for solving them."

Clients who participate actively in the problem-solving process are much more likely to be committed to follow through on mutually selected courses of action than are those who passively depend on practitioners. Adopting a strength-oriented perspective and conveying expectations of responsible, independent behavior also foster hope, self-respect, and commitment to implement strategies for change.

Practitioners should be aware of the special threat to acceptance and respect involved in work with immigrants and ethnic minority groups who remain closely tied to their cultures of origin. Handicapped by inability to communicate in English and overwhelmed by the alien and complex bureaucracies of American society, many of these people manifest dependency and helplessness that reflect their situational context rather than personality deficiencies. It is important to keep in mind that most of these clients functioned adequately and were productive citizens in their native lands. Their seeming helplessness thus belies latent strengths that can be mobilized by according them respect, assisting them through the maze of bureaucratic procedures, and linking them with support systems that can enable them to gain greater language facility and knowledge of available resources and their rights.

Unduly catering to dependency that is a realistic response to an alien environment may foster or prolong dependency. Aiding such clients to mobilize their coping capacities, teaching them new skills, working in partnership with them to develop support networks, and providing direct assistance as needed strengthens their adaptation to their new environment.

Silence and Withdrawal   The threat represented by silence and withdrawal is similar to that posed by excessive dependency and helplessness. When confronted with silence or withdrawal, beginning practitioners tend to respond by assuming inordinate responsibility for maintaining verbalization. Although silence tends to produce a certain amount of tension, to cope with that tension by consistently taking the initiative tends to result in nonproductive monologue by the practitioner and to produce a sense of frustration. Moreover, constantly assuming the initiative for conversation establishes a pattern in sessions that may be difficult to change, since clients will understandably assume that this is the norm and will passively wait for you to break periods of silence. With other clients, your assuming the initiative provides them with leverage to control the interview. Still other clients may deliberately use silence in a hostile manner, realizing early on that they can produce

anxiety in the practitioner by remaining silent.

For the above reasons, it is important that you learn to tolerate silence without undue discomfort. Although few pauses occur in successful interviews, it is not realistic to expect constant verbalization. Pauses naturally occur when either clients or practitioners need a moment to reflect on an idea or feeling or when clients have exhausted a given topic and need to gather thoughts before proceeding to a different one. Such natural pauses usually are short-lived and do not warrant interruption on your part. Moreover, clients vary in levels of verbalization and in verbal facility. Some clients reveal rich information with minimal prompting, whereas others lack verbal skills or find it difficult to reveal personal information. With the latter type of client, you will need to be active in eliciting information, as silence may engender acute anxiety, especially with clients who are insecure and hypersensitive. These clients may misinterpret silence as indicative of lack of interest or rejection on your part. Passivity is no more desirable than is constantly assuming the initiative. It should be noted, however, that there are instances when it is appropriate to give a client permission to be silent (e.g., when the client is discussing painful material or pondering an issue) by employing a message such as "Take your time—I know this is painful for you to discuss."

In addition to the meanings cited above, silence may also be a manifestation of resistance to change or of strong emotions (positive or negative) experienced toward the practitioner. These dynamics generally occur later in the helping process; skills needed to manage these phenomena are discussed in Chapter 20. For the present, it is sufficient to point out that prominent silence is a signal that you need to shift the focus to exploring underlying thoughts and feelings that, if not resolved, may become a major barrier to progress.

In the final analysis, decisions about breaking silence must be made according to the type of client and the situational context. Our point is that you must be sufficiently flexible to remain silent or to break silence according to the client's best interest. Otherwise, you may unwittingly deprive clients of opportunities to assume an appropriate measure of responsibility for maintaining verbalization in individual and group sessions. Equally important, you may undermine the helping relationship by establishing communication patterns that foster dependency and passivity.

Aggressive and Sullen Behavior Perhaps the greatest threats to relating to clients with acceptance and respect are aggressive and sullen behavior, which are often encountered with delinquent youth and inmates of correctional institutions but are by no means limited to these populations. Aggressive behavior may consist of verbal attacks in the form of challenges to your integrity, competence, or motives, or it may involve insults directed at your status, appearance, speech, or other aspects of personal demeanor. Clients' anger may emanate from many sources. Some clients tend to be angry people, and little or no provocation is required to trigger angry outbursts. To avoid responding defensively to such persons, it is helpful to recognize that their aggressive behavior, though directed at you, usually derives from other sources. Some clients have harbored lifelong resentment toward persons in authority and may be reacting to your role as an authority rather than to you as a person. In other instances, an angry outburst may be an

expression of displaced frustration over being confined to an institution. For example, one of our graduate students, after introducing herself to an adolescent in a state correctional center, was greeted with the following: "You mean I've got *another* student for a counselor. Crap! I just got rid of one. How long are you going to be here?"

Involuntary clients who are coerced to see social workers also frequently enter initial interviews bristling with anger and resentment—not toward the social worker, although the practitioner becomes the target of those hostile feelings. Other clients respond angrily when the practitioner is unable or chooses not to respond to unrealistic requests, such as granting unearned privileges or permitting them to violate rules of an institution. Whatever the source, the natural reaction to provocative messages is to feel defensive and to counter anger with anger or to set the other person straight. Similarly, when an involuntary client sits sullenly, avoiding eye-to-eye contact except for an occasional glare, the natural reaction is to express irritation or to admonish the client to shape up. Such defensive reactions or counterattacks only tend to inflame the situation and empower the client with the ability to control the tone of the interview and thus avoid having to deal with the problems at hand. It is important to recognize that such clients sometimes deliberately bait practitioners and take delight when the latter rise to the bait. Often these clients later boast to their peers of their prowess in getting their practitioner's goat.

When confronted with aggressive behavior, you must explore and resolve the hostile feelings, or they will undermine the helping relationship. Responding defensively or counterattacking merely repeats reaction patterns that the client has typically experienced from others in the past, and hence, it is counterproductive.

Moreover, such reactions on your part tend to validate feelings of some clients that others are against them and are not to be trusted.

How then should you respond to aggressive and provocative behavior? First, it is vital to master your natural tendency to respond defensively. Recognizing that the client's hostility may be displaced from other sources can assist you *not to personalize verbal attacks or sullen behavior,* thus freeing you from feeling threatened and enabling you to respond facilitatively. To resolve the hostility, it is important to assist clients to drain off angry feelings. This is best accomplished by employing empathic responses, which not only foster expanded expression of feelings but also convey respect and understanding for the client. Clients' anger may also emanate from their understandably perceiving certain social work roles or functions as threatening (e.g., investigating a complaint of child neglect). In such instances, practitioners must be empathically responsive to such feelings. By fostering a release of hostile feelings, empathic responses tend to defuse anger, permitting a more rational exploration of the factors associated with the client's feelings.

It is important to recognize that you are not expected to become a perpetual target for client abuse. If responding empathically for a period of time fails to mellow the client or if the situation is otherwise timely, you may wish to authentically (but unabrasively) describe the impact of the client's provocative or abusive behavior upon you (see Chapter 5). It is vital that clients receive descriptive feedback about their aggressive and provocative behavior, particularly if it seems to be an ongoing, repetitive style of behavior that is also manifested in significant relationships with others. One of the reasons why provocative behavior is often maintained in the client's repertoire is that others have responded defensively rather than authentically describing the negative reaction the client's behavior causes in them and the damaging effect it has upon the relationship. Further, if rapport between the practitioner and client is sufficiently developed and the client is amenable, the practitioner may wish to explore with the client the possibility of modifying the provocative behavior through subsequent change efforts.

To respond openly and nondefensively to expressions of angry feelings is difficult for practitioners who have not as yet evolved effective ways of coping with their own angry feelings. Research (Bandura, Lipsher, & Miller, 1960) has indicated that practitioners who avoid expressing their own negative feelings in social interactions tend to avoid aggressive expressions of clients by ignoring them, changing the subject, or by employing other avoidance behaviors. In such instances, unfortunately, clients are left to struggle with negative feelings by themselves, often to the detriment of the helping process. Self-awareness is thus essential to responding facilitatively to aggressive behavior. If you tend to suppress or to avoid expressing anger, you may wish to consider joining an assertiveness training group, seeking personal therapy, or enlisting peers and/or supervisors in giving you periodic feedback related to changes you are trying to implement in becoming more expressive of your feelings. You will find exercises for dealing with aggressive behavior, as well as modeled responses, in the last portion of this chapter.

Manipulative and Exploitative Behavior

Similar to aggressive behavior in their effect on practitioners are manipulative and exploitative behaviors on the part of certain clients—usually those disposed to antisocial behavior. These behaviors also engender natural reactions of anger at being deceived or ripped off. In some instances, the anger also stems in part from disgust with oneself for being gullible or for making errors in judgment that lead to exploitation. One beginning practitioner, for example, went to some lengths to provide a positive experience for a delinquent who was permitted temporary leave from a state correctional institution. The practitioner took the youth shopping for new clothes, to the movies, and generally extended himself in the youth's behalf. When they returned to the institution, the youth expressed profuse gratitude. Shortly thereafter, the social worker's sense of satisfaction and dedication turned to bitterness and near fury when he discovered his "grateful" client had stolen his keys to the institutional facilities.

In other instances, practitioners in correctional settings have staunchly defended clients who have indignantly protested their innocence to charges of possessing marijuana or committing other infractions only to learn to their later chagrin that their clients had indeed committed the infractions. Even canny and experienced practitioners occasionally succumb to the oily tongues of clients who excel as con artists.

To affirm the worth and dignity of clients who engage in such brazen and manipulative behavior severely strains the capacity for acceptance of even the most altruistic and patient practitioners. (Social workers, after all, are human beings subject to the full spectrum of human passions.) But accept such clients you must, for the alternative is to consign them to the scrap heap of hopelessness. Accepting the person, however, does not mean condoning or disregarding the exploitative behavior. Indeed, to do so would

involve a dereliction of responsibility. In such instances, practitioners can and should confront the client in an open and genuine manner, expressing their feelings of disappointment and resentment with tact and restraint. This involves relating authentically and employing confrontation and other skills judiciously.

Rather than jeopardizing the helping relationship, facilitative confrontations ultimately strengthen it, for they demonstrate that clients are of sufficient worth and importance that the practitioner will not passively permit them to engage in behavior that can result in their loss of freedom and engender condemnation and social ostracism from others as well. Moreover, manipulative clients respect persons who see through their ploys and deal firmly with them.

Self-Effacing Patterns of Behavior Dominated by feelings of inadequacy and worthlessness, some clients tear themselves down, constantly apologize for themselves, and attempt to win the approval of others, including practitioners, by ingratiating behavior and flattery. Because they continually attempt to please others, they unwittingly foster being taken for granted.

When clients harbor negative opinions of their self-worth, their attitudes may be manifested in the form of placating behavior as they relate to the practitioner and other family or group members who may be involved in sessions. Furthermore, the tendency of clients to "discount" themselves is an inherent theme that will be reflected in discussions of problems they are experiencing in relating to significant others. For example, Mrs. A. came to a family agency seeking help in coping with myriad pressures related to a recent divorce and her new role as single parent of five children. In the first few minutes of the initial interview, Mrs. A. apologized several times for taking the practitioner's time and profusely thanked him for seeing her, even though she was paying for the interview. She spoke several times of her feelings of failure and worthlessness as a parent and expressed her doubts that she had the capacity to adequately parent her children. She further indicated that she "always seemed to foul up her life" and that she could "never seem to do anything right." A common thread in her discussion of current problems with her ex-husband, with whom she was still deeply psychologically involved, was the consistency with which she discounted her own judgment and rights in numerous transactions with him (e.g., negotiating visitation privileges with the children) and repeatedly acquiesced to his demands.

When the timing is appropriate, it is important to assist clients to observe their own self-effacing behavior, its repetitive nature, and the impact of their actions on themselves and others. The practitioner does this with the objective of helping clients to take action to alleviate such self-defeating behaviors and to assume more functional and assertive ways of relating.

Because of their miniscule self-respect, it is also crucial that you respond to clients such as Mrs. A. by affirming their worth and dignity as well as their strengths and problem-solving capacities. The threat to implement these values is that the practitioner may also take such clients for granted because of their lack of assertiveness and self-depreciating behavior. When they must juggle their schedules, it is not uncommon for practitioners to be tardy for appointments, to cut interviews short, or to change the appointment times of such clients rather than others. It is important to recognize that although these clients typically acqui-

esce when inconvenienced, they nevertheless experience hurt, disappointment, and resentment. Moreover, they tend to interpret being taken advantage of as evidence of their lack of worth.

Being aware of the diminutive self-esteem of self-effacing clients, practitioners can convey respect for them (thereby fostering self-respect) by helping them to believe in their right to expect more from others, including the practitioner. Moreover, practitioners can nurture assertive behavior by tuning in to and empathizing with negative feelings that lie beneath the client's manifest obsequious behavior. Such empathic responding validates negative feelings and enables clients to get in touch with these emotions that have previously been suppressed or denied expression. Gradually, as clients risk expressing negative feelings without being rebuked or rejected, they learn that the practitioner and others can value them quite apart from their complying with the real or imagined expectations of others. And finally, if practitioners are courteous and empathic, conveying the expectation that clients have a perfect right to respect, clients will gradually gain self-respect.

Passive Noncompliant Behavior   Still another pattern of behavior that poses a threat to responding to clients with acceptance and respect is passive noncompliant behavior. Clients, for example, may fail to keep agreed-upon appointments with practitioners, physicians, or prospective employers, or they may fail to follow through in carrying out vital actions they have agreed to perform (e.g., following a prescribed medical regimen for a child). Such passive noncompliance can tax the patience of practitioners and lead them to conclude that these clients are undependable, irresponsible, and unworthy of continued efforts on their behalf. Although it is true that some clients are not responsible in carrying out actions on behalf of themselves or others, prematurely labeling them as irresponsible and hopeless may result in underestimating their potentialities for growth and failing to consider negotiating with them the goal of modifying the pattern itself. Before clients will be receptive to embracing such a goal, of course, they must first be tactfully assisted to acknowledge the pattern and to realize its detrimental impact on themselves and others.

Passive noncompliance in certain cultural contexts, however, has an entirely different meaning. For example, among some groups of Filipino extraction, it is common to regard openly disagreeing with another person or declining an invitation to another's home as rude and offensive. Consequently, persons of these cultural orientations may overtly agree to comply with certain arrangements or planned courses of action but express their actual intentions through passive noncompliance.

Noncompliant behavior can be both puzzling and vexing to social workers. Further, failure to understand the cultural significance of such behavior can lead to inaccurate assessments and to lack of respect for these clients. However, practitioners who are knowledgeable about culturally mediated behavior carefully and sensitively explore clients' beliefs about causes of problems and are keenly alert to nonverbal negative reactions that signal the need to explore feelings further and to defer making plans or suggestions until clients are likely to be genuinely receptive. As clients gain trust, practitioners also assist them to resolve inhibitions about expressing themselves more openly by clarifying for the clients that they welcome disagreement and open expression of feelings and views, rather than being

offended by such behavior. By thus clarifying the cultural differences in expectations, practitioners assist these clients to risk new behaviors. Changes in actual behavior, of course, occur gradually because such values and beliefs are deeply embedded.

Affirming Uniqueness and Individuality

Intertwined with acceptance and nonjudgmental attitude is the equally important value that every person is unique and that social workers should both prize and affirm the individuality of those whom they serve. Human beings, of course, are endowed with widely differing physical and mental characteristics; moreover, their life experiences are infinitely diverse. Consequently, people differ from one another in appearance, beliefs, physiological functioning, interests, talents, motivation, goals, values, emotional and behavioral patterns, and many other factors.

To affirm the uniqueness of another person, you must not only be committed to the value just discussed but must also enter the other person's world, endeavoring to understand how that person experiences life, including thoughts, feelings, world view, daily stresses, joys, hopes, longings, disappointments, hurts, and all of the myriad facts of human experience. Only through attempting to walk in the shoes of another person can you gain a full appreciation of the rich and complex individuality of that person. Affirming the individuality of another, of course, goes far beyond gaining an appreciation of the other person's manifold perspectives of life. One must be able to convey awareness of what the other is experiencing moment by moment and affirm the validity of that experience.

Affirming the validity of another's experience does not mean agreeing with or condoning that person's views and feelings. To be sure, part of your role as a practitioner is to help people to disentangle their confusing, conflicting, and otherwise dysfunctional thoughts and feelings; to align distorted perceptions with reality; and to differentiate irrational reactions from reality. To fulfill this role, you must retain your own separateness and individuality. Otherwise, you may overidentify with clients, thereby losing your potential for providing fresh and objective input. Affirming the experiences of another person, then, means understanding and confirming or validating those experiences, thus fostering and reinforcing that person's sense of personal identity and self-esteem.

Opportunities for affirming individuality and sense of self-worth are lost when practitioners are blinded to the uniqueness of clients by prejudices and stereotyped perceptions. Although prejudices may be either favorable or unfavorable, we are using the term to refer to unfavorable judgments or feelings toward persons or groups that are made on the basis of preconceived opinions rather than actual experience. Prejudices commonly are directed toward people who differ from one's own reference group on dimensions such as race, ethnicity, gender, religion, sexual orientation, socioeconomic level, political persuasion, and lifestyle. Such prejudices generally are associated with misconceptions caused by limited and inaccurate information and little or no interaction with members of a particular group. We have observed various social work students, for example, who manifest irrational fears of talking with delinquents, elderly clients, or mental patients, perceiving them as strange, different, or otherwise vaguely threatening. Interestingly, social workers themselves have been the objects of stereotyping, being labeled by some people as do-gooders or flaming liberals.

Prejudices tend to diminish or to disappear altogether when people have frequent personal contacts with members of a particular group. As they are subjected to the test of actual experience, supposed or even real differences among people tend to shrink to a level of insignificance due in large measure to the fact that people become more aware of how much greater are their similarities than their differences. Thus liberated from their prejudices, people are able to see others formerly regarded as members of an alien group as worthwhile and interesting individuals in their own right.

Stereotypical perceptions are closely related to prejudices in that they also derive from preconceived fixed opinions about other people on the basis of their membership in particular groups. For example, some people view long-haired males as rebellious, irresponsible, immoral, and addicted to drugs. While these labels may well be applicable to some such individuals (and to short-haired males and females as well), they are entirely inappropriate for others.

As such, stereotypes are also antithetical to the value of affirming the uniqueness and individuality of other people. Although stereotypes do not necessarily involve negative judgments about others, they do involve conventional views and inaccurate perceptions that may obscure practitioners' awareness of clients' potentialities. Consequently, practitioners may unwittingly restrict efforts to assist clients to actualize these potentials or, even worse, may block clients' efforts to develop themselves more fully.

Stereotypes of greatest significance to social workers involve perceptions of ethnic minority groups, sex roles, the elderly, people with disabilities, and various groups whose lifestyles diverge markedly from the cultural norm. Stereotypical perceptions of minority groups are endemic in our culture, as attested to by the popularity of ethnic jokes that typically degrade and demean people of African, Mexican, Italian, Polish, Irish, Native American, and Jewish extraction. Further, stereotypical attitudes are often reflected unknowingly and perpetuated in everyday language as, for example, in the following statements: "You really jewed him down!"; "Is that white man's time or Indian time you're speaking of?"; or "Let's go nigger-fishing."

You may counter the detrimental effects of stereotypes by seeking to gain extensive knowledge about the culture of your clients. If you manifest a genuine interest in and respect for a culture, members of that culture will usually be receptive to your efforts to expand your knowledge. Conducive to this objective and to working effectively in cross-cultural relationships is the same value cited earlier—namely, affirming the worth and uniqueness of other cultures. If you work extensively with a cultural group that speaks another language, it is highly desirable to learn to speak that language. The ability to converse in the client's language facilitates developing of a working relationship and enhances understanding of clients and their cultures. By being open to and prizing the differences among cultures, you will be broadened and enriched. You may even internalize certain values of other cultures that appear more valid than your own.

Research findings further emphasize the importance of affirming the worth and uniqueness of other cultures. In an outcome study of casework with Chicano clients, Gomez, Zurcher, Farris, and Becker (1985)

found that the factor that correlated most highly ($r = .43$) with clients' satisfaction with services was the practitioner's skill in "... the development and reinforcement of positive feelings about clients' self-concept as Mexican-Americans" (p. 481). Probably this finding is also applicable to work with other ethnic minority groups.

You may have little opportunity to learn about other cultures firsthand, but you can gain knowledge by reaching out to fellow students who are members of different ethnic groups and by studying the substantial literature pertaining to different cultures. (Many universities devote portions of their libraries to ethnic literature.) You might also participate in programs related to specific minorities, such as black studies programs. Opportunities for developing resources also exist within your student body, as, for example, organizing a program for cultural enrichment within your student organization.

Sex-role stereotypes have been a major concern to social workers in recent years, and the professional organization has vigorously attempted to abolish discriminatory practice associated with these stereotypes.[2] Sex-role stereotypes may also have a detrimental impact on the helping process. Research findings concerning the extent to which social work students and practitioners have stereotypical sex-role perceptions have generally indicated that the profession (females particularly) have made substantial strides in supplanting traditional, anachronistic role perceptions with egalitarian views. The findings are not conclusive, however, and the challenge remains to foster the individuality of both men and women rather than to view them in fixed,

---

[2]For those interested in studying sex discrimination in social work in depth, two issues of *Social Work* are largely devoted to this topic: 1976, *21* (6); and 1977, *22* (6).

sex-linked ways. To meet this challenge, you will need to make individual efforts, for as Davenport and Reims (1978) stress, "Clinicians also must be aware that their attitudes are influenced by factors external to their training, and they cannot assume that professional training in and of itself will address or correct potential bias" (p. 308).

Stereotypical perceptions of elderly persons may also distort assessment, limit goals, and restrict helping efforts with this neglected group of Americans. Individual problems in social functioning may incorrectly be attributed to the infirmities of age. Similarly, reversible health problems associated with inadequate nutrition or need for medication may be dismissed as merely symptomatic of advanced age. Depression associated with unfulfilled common human needs for affection, meaningful activities, companionship, and sexual gratification may likewise be overlooked. Considering the many losses (energy, health, employment, loved ones, status, reduced income) and stresses commonly associated with old age, it is a sad commentary that only 2 to 3 percent of all persons seen in community mental health centers in our country are over age 65 (Butler, 1975).

Strengths of elderly persons are also frequently overlooked, resulting in faulty assessment and restricted goal planning. Common stereotypes held by many Americans tend to relegate elderly persons to a rocking-chair status or to playing bingo in senior citizens' centers. The capacity to grow, to develop new skills, and to be productive, however, does not abruptly cease when people reach retirement age. Toseland (1977), for example, has reported research findings that document the capacity of elderly persons to master problem-solving skills and to enhance social skills. Elderly couples also frequently

need and can benefit from marital therapy and from sex therapy (Sander, 1976).

Stereotypes about people with physical and developmental disabilities also skew perceptions of practitioners toward clients' incapacities rather than toward their capacities, strengths, and potentialities. Many people still view those with disabilities as objects of curiosity and pity. Haney and Rabin (1984), for example, characterize negative societal attitudes as *the* major obstacle to resocialization of persons paralyzed by severe spinal cord injury. Some of these persons report that others stare at them, continually causing them to feel they are on display. Intrusive questions about their disabilities, unsolicited help, and comments made within earshot, such as "I'd rather be dead than like that" abridge the rights of these and others with disabilities (Weinberg, 1983). Yuker (1988) has edited a volume concerned with societal attitudes toward people with disabilities.

Societal attitudes toward the developmentally disabled (research findings reveal these people feel stigmatized and demeaned by the term "mentally retarded") are perhaps even more negative than toward the physically disabled. Moreover, the public holds misconceptions that this group of people has little or no awareness of their handicaps and are indifferent to the terms used to refer to them. The fact is that this group, like people with severe disabilities, experience anguish when stared at and asked intrusive questions. The effects of stigmas toward this group and implications for overcoming them have been discussed by Dudley (1987).

Social workers and other health care professionals can join people with disabilities in seeking to overcome negative societal attitudes toward them (it is important to work *with* them, which manifests respect for their capacities and fosters development of the same). Practitioners, of course, should begin by taking inventory of their own perceptions and attitudes. Beyond this they should advocate for policies that provide opportunities for people with disabilities and that bring them into the mainstream of American society. Social policy implications related to this goal have been discussed by Coudroglou and Poole (1984).

Social workers must also be aware of and rectify prejudices and stereotypes associated with groups of people whose lifestyles and sexual orientations diverge from cultural norms. In our pluralistic society, many people also have fixed ideas about the desirable type of family unit—the traditional nuclear family (consisting of father, mother, and children)—and look askance at other types of living arrangements. Social workers must avoid such preconceived judgments, for they work with many different types of family structures and must render services impartially.

Prejudices toward and stereotypical views of homosexuals are especially rampant in our society. Research findings (Wisniewski & Toomey, 1987), unfortunately, reveal "preliminary empirical support" (p. 455) that a substantial percentage of social workers manifest signs of homophobia (i.e., fear and anxiety and perhaps disgust toward homosexuals). One-third of 77 clinical social workers surveyed in Columbus, Ohio earned scores on the Index of Attitudes Toward Homosexuals (Hudson & Ricketts, 1980) that classified them as homophobic. Obviously these findings are of concern because practitioners with fears of or negative attitudes toward homosexuals are unlikely to be effective in work with such clients or with others who hold similar negative attitudes. Further, it is highly probable that homophobic attitudes are

intensified toward homosexuals who are afflicted with AIDS, a group that may feel isolated from society at the very time when their need for social and emotional support is greatest.[3]

Discriminated against both legally and socially, many homosexuals choose to remain "in the closet" rather than risk losing their jobs, friends, and status and subjecting themselves to ostracism and abuse. Such prejudices create serious difficulties for families with a homosexual parent, and these families therefore have particular needs for social services (Hall, 1978; Lewis, 1980; Wyers, 1987). The challenge to social workers has been aptly stated by Hall, who defines the first step that social workers must take in assisting these families as that of acknowledging the existence of the homosexual family and recognizing it "as a special group with a special identity and special needs" (p. 384). Hall's challenge is equally applicable to homosexual male and female parents.

Hall's challenge should be preceded by still another step—being aware of one's prejudices or stereotypes. It is natural to have biases or stereotypes regarding certain groups of people within our society; in fact, it is probably impossible to be entirely free of preconceived attitudes toward certain groups of people. If you are open to considering that you have certain biases, however, you are in a position to strive to overcome them.

Value Clarification Exercises

The following exercises will assist you in expanding your awareness of prejudices or stereotypes you may have that could impair your effectiveness in working with

_____
[3]An entire issue of *Social Casework* (*69*, June 1988) and a portion of *Social Work* (*33*, May–June, 1988) are devoted to the topic of AIDS and implications for social workers.

certain clients. In each situation, imagine yourself in an interview or group session with the client(s). Try to picture the client as vividly as possible. As you engage in imagination be aware of your feelings, attitudes, and behavior. After each situation contemplate or discuss with peers the following:

1. What feelings and attitudes did you experience? Did you experience any visceral or muscular reactions as you pictured the client(s)? Did you experience any feeling of repulsion, disgust, annoyance, or uneasiness?

2. Have you experienced like reactions to similar persons in the past?

3. What possible prejudices or stereotypes were reflected in your body reactions, feelings, or attitudes?

Most students discover they do have some active or residual biases, and thus it is no cause for alarm. It is a basis of concern, however, for if you do not alter such negative attitudes, they will impair your effectiveness in working with related practice situations.

Situation 1 A young couple have come to your family counseling agency for help with sexual problems. The female has long, straggly hair, wears no makeup, and is attired in a wrinkled blouse, patched, cut-off jeans with holes in them, and sandals. The male has long, unkempt hair, an untrimmed beard, and wears a gold earring in his left ear. His attire is similar to his partner's. Both have pronounced body odor. You learn they are unmarried and have been living together for five months.

Situation 2 Two women in their mid-20s request help in resolving difficulties in their relationship. One complains the other is jealous and overly possessive. The other replies that her partner is insensitive to her needs and feelings. They have lived together in a lesbian relationship for two years.

Situation 3 As an adoption worker in a children's service agency, you have just learned that Mr. and Mrs. Y., a Caucasian couple in their 30s, have applied for adoption of a black infant.

Situation 4 You are a social worker in a large university hospital that pioneered surgical techniques for changing males into females. After learning that many patients who have undergone such operations have difficult problems in adjusting socially, the director of social services has requested that you lead a group of such individuals.

Situation 5 You have been invited to participate in a student encounter group formed to enhance cultural awareness. The group will consist of Anglos, blacks, and Hispanics.

Unfortunately, many people lack awareness of their prejudices and stereotypes, deceiving themselves into believing they are entirely free of such unfavorable attitudes. Indeed, some practitioners mistakenly pride themselves on possessing no traces of racism, sexism, ageism, or other biases, and their naiveté in this regard limits their openness to experiencing themselves, let alone other people who are strikingly different from them. Never really able to come to terms with their prejudices, they tend to alienate others who perceive and respond negatively to subtle manifestations of their prejudices. Still others perceive themselves as champions of victims of discrimination and, blinded by their zeal, erroneously attribute problems rooted in other sources to the effects of discrimination. Such zeal often emanates from unconscious overcompensation for guilt about living in a racist society. Overcompensation and overidentification with the oppressed can result in offering special privileges and relaxing standards of behavior beneath those expected by minorities themselves. As such, overidentification can impair effective work with minorities as much as prejudices and stereotypes.

It is thus clear that self-awareness is key to liberating oneself from prejudices and stereotypical perceptions. Self-awareness notwithstanding, practitioners occasionally encounter situations in which a client's behaviors or goals evoke such negative reactions that a positive helping relationship cannot be attained. For example, practitioners who have extreme feelings about rape or who are intensely opposed to abortions may be unable to accept a rapist as a client or to offer help to a person seeking an abortion. In such instances, it is important to acknowledge such feelings to oneself and to sensitively prepare a client for transfer to another practitioner who can accept both the client and the goals. It is vital to clarify for clients that the reason for transfer is not personal rejection of them but that they deserve the best service possible and that the practitioner cannot provide that service because of value conflicts. Such an explanation conveys goodwill and safeguards the self-esteem of clients. Practitioners who frequently encounter difficulties in accepting clients probably tend to be inflexible and consequently have a limited range of effectiveness. Such practitioners owe it to themselves and to future clients to seriously consider if they have chosen the appropriate profession.

Affirming Problem-Solving Capacities and Self-Determination

Basic social work values embody the beliefs that clients have the capacity to grow and change and to see and develop solutions to their difficulties, as well as the right and capacity to exercise free choice responsibly. These values are magnified when practitioners adopt a strength-oriented perspective, looking for positive qualities and undeveloped potentialities rather than limitations and past mistakes. Such a positive perspective engenders hope and courage on the client's part and nurtures self-esteem as well. These factors, in turn, enhance the client's motivation, which is indispensable to a successful outcome.

The positive effects of accrediting strengths and highlighting increments of progress were manifested in a fourth interview with a client who had entered counseling because of frequent periods of depression. She began the interview by complaining she had been depressed over the weekend. Her depressed mood during the interview, in part, seemed to derive from discouragement over being unable to control the feelings of depression. After carefully reviewing the events that occurred over the weekend and the client's response to them, the practitioner made several observations that reflected improvement in the client's coping with her depressed feeling. The client had not deemed it necessary to call the practitioner for support, as she had done previously. The depression was also less intense and of a shorter duration than usual. Further, rather than going to bed as she typically did when depressed, the client had actively tried to ward off the depression by taking a walk, going to a movie, and going for a ride with her husband. Accrediting these efforts, the practitioner expressed the impression that the client appeared to be moving from the position of feeling helpless about coping with her depressed mood to a position of actively taking steps to counter it. The client was pensive for a few moments and then replied she hadn't thought of it that way, but it was true. Her mood brightened perceptively as she realized the progress she had made.

Belief in the capacity of others to change is critically needed, for people's perceptions of themselves and their problems are strongly influenced by feedback from others. Thus, if you view clients positively and express the belief that they can work out their problems, they are likely to adopt a similar outlook. Of course, your view must be realistic in the sense that clients' situations are susceptible to change and that clients possess the capacity to implement whatever actions are required. Otherwise you may engender false hope that ultimately will lead to discouragement, disillusionment, a sense of failure, and perhaps to justifiable resentment toward you. Most problem situations can be remedied to some extent, however, and the large majority of clients have the capacity to take constructive actions on their problems.

Self-Determination

Before considering how social workers affirm self-determination, a definition is in order. Biestek (1957) has defined self-determination as "the practical recognition of the right and need of clients to freedom in making their own choices and decisions" (p. 103). Self-determination is a value accorded high priority by social

work, as attested to by the following section from the NASW Code of Ethics, which is subsumed under Major Principle II pertaining to the social worker's ethical responsibility to clients.

G. Rights and prerogatives of clients—the social worker should make every effort to foster maximum self-determination on the part of clients.
   1. When the social worker must act on behalf of a client who has been adjudged legally incompetent, the social worker should safeguard the interests and rights of that client.
   2. When another individual has been legally authorized to act in behalf of a client, the social worker should deal with that person always with the client's best interest in mind.
   3. The social worker should not engage in any action that violates or diminishes the civil or legal rights of clients.

The extent to which you affirm self-determination rests in large measure on your perceptions of the helping role and of the helping process. If you consider your major role to be that of providing solutions or dispensing advice freely, you may foster dependency, demean clients by failing to recognize and affirm their strengths, and relegate them to a position of passive cooperation—or passive resistance, as often occurs under such circumstances.[4] Such domineering behavior is counterproductive; not only does it discourage open communication but, equally important, it denies clients the opportunity to gain strength and self-respect as they actively struggle with their difficulties. Fostering dependency generally leaves people weaker rather than stronger and is a disservice to clients.

---

[4]After goals have been mutually identified and roles in the helping relationship clarified, practitioners need not be hesitant to offer advice, for their expertise and input give impetus and direction to change efforts. Our point is that giving advice should not be the primary means of assisting clients.

The type of relationship that affirms self-determination and fosters growth is a partnership wherein practitioner and client (whether individual, couple, or group) are joined in a mutual effort to search for solutions to problems or to promote growth. As enablers, practitioners assist clients to view their problems realistically, to consider various solutions and their consequences, to implement change-oriented strategies, to understand themselves and others more fully, to gain awareness of previously unrecognized strengths and opportunities for growth, and to resolve obstacles to change and growth. Although these facilitative functions often prove invaluable to clients, the ultimate determinant of the outcome of the shared venture resides, as it should, with the client.

Just as fostering self-determination enhances client autonomy, paternalism (i.e., depriving a person from exercising choice to act or to be acted upon) infringes on autonomy. Paternalistic behavior rests on the assumption that a practitioner has a right to interfere with a client's right to choose because she/he knows better than the client what is for the client's good. As Abramson (1985) clarifies, however, a practitioner who takes paternalistic actions for a client should be obliged to justify such actions and carries responsibility for the burden of proof. Abramson acknowledges four conditions in which paternalism may be justifiable:

1. When the client is a child and is assumed to lack the capacity to make an informed decision.

2. When the client is considered mentally incompetent or lacking in rationality to the extent of being unable to comprehend the results of decision making.

3. When the consequences of an act are far reaching and are irreversible (e.g., a suicide attempt).

4. When temporary interference with liberty ensures future freedom and autonomy.

Abramson cautions practitioners to be judicious in employing paternalistic actions and builds a strong philosophical and pragmatic case for encouraging self-determination. From an existential stance, Weick and Pope (1988) have taken an even stronger position about the hazards of permitting erosion of the principle of self-determination.

Some people, of course, partially forfeit their right to freedom of choice by violating laws, infringing on the rights of others, or failing to adequately discharge responsibilities in providing for others. Illustrated in the following list are a few acts of commission or omission that may constrain self-determination:

1. Criminal acts that result in incarceration.

2. Child abuse that results in loss of custody.

3. Status offenses, such as running away from home or habitual truancy, that require court intervention.

4. Unethical acts that result in loss of the privilege to practice one's profession.

5. Physical or emotional neglect of a child, including exposing the child to immoral acts.

6. Refusal to secure medical services vital to a child's health, requiring court intervention to assure that services are provided.

7. Violations of moral laws resulting in excommunication from religious organizations.

Self-determination may also be constrained by the incapacity to exercise one's freedom of choice. In such instances, people lose the *opportunity* rather than the *right* to exercise self-determination. Typical constraints include physical or mental incapacity (e.g., being unable to function autonomously because of hospitalization), immobility because of unavailable transportation, or mental incompetence caused by organic brain disease or other forms of trauma to the brain. In such instances, social workers have an obligation to reduce the losses of self-determination to a minimum by mobilizing resources that restore opportunity (e.g., arranging transportation so that immobile people can exercise their right to vote or to participate in social activities) or providing a proxy who can represent the client's interests or make essential decisions. This obligation, together with guidelines for selecting proxies, has been amply clarified by Salzberger (1979).

Value Implementation Exercises

To challenge your thinking about how you might affirm the value of self-determination in practical situations, we have provided exercises that consist of problematic situations actually encountered by the authors or colleagues. As you read each exercise, analyze alternate courses of action that are available. Consider how you would work with the client to maximize self-determination, taking care also to promote the best interests of the client. You may also wish to suggest discussion of these situations in class.

Situation 1 In your work for the state welfare department, you oversee the care of numerous nursing home residents whose expenses are funded by the state. Two of your clients, both in their 20s, reside in the same nursing home and have told you that they are eager to get married. The administrator of the home strenuously protests that the two are retarded and, if they marry, might produce a child they could not properly care for. Further, she has stressed that she has no private room for a couple and that if the two marry, they will have to leave the nursing home.

Situation 2 A runaway 15-year-old adolescent who is four months pregnant has contacted you several times in regard to planning for her child. In her last visit, she confided to you that she is habituated to heroin. You have expressed your concern that the drug may damage her unborn child, but she does not seem worried nor does she want to give up use of the drug. You also know that she obtains money for heroin through prostitution and is not attending school.

Situation 3 While making a visit to Mr. F., an elderly recipient of public assistance, you discover that his health is failing and that his memory and thinking are impaired, suggesting advanced senility. Although he has two married daughters in the community, it is apparent from his apartment that he has been living in deplorable conditions and is in need of supervision and care. You discuss with him your concern that he receive proper care, but he strongly opposes any suggestions about moving.

Situation 4 As a rehabilitation worker, you have arranged for a young woman to receive training as a beautician in a local technical college, a vocation in which she expressed intense interest. Although initially enthusiastic, she now tells you that she wants to discontinue the program and go into nursing, indicating that her supervisor at the college is highly critical of her work and that the other trainees tease her and talk about her behind her back. You are torn about what to do, knowing that your client tends to antagonize other people with her quick and barbed remarks.

Rather than changing programs, you wonder if your client needs to learn more appropriate ways of communicating and relating to her supervisor and co-workers.

Safeguarding Confidentiality

Another way in which social workers convey respect and affirm the worth of clients is by preserving the confidentiality of private information disclosed during the course of the helping process. Confidentiality is vital to the helping process for practical, ethical, and legal reasons. Practitioners, therefore, must be knowledgeable about the various facets of this critical value.

From a practical standpoint, confidentiality is a sine qua non of the helping process, for without assurance of confidentiality, it is unlikely that clients would risk disclosing private aspects of their lives that, if revealed, could damage their reputations and statuses as employees, spouses, friends, public officials, and so forth. This is especially true when clients' problems involve marital infidelity, deviant sexual practices, illicit activities, child abuse, and the like. Implied confidentiality, if not explicitly requested by clients, is an assurance that such personal revelations will never be revealed to others by the practitioner.

Social workers are bound by the NASW Code of Ethics to safeguard confidentiality, as indicated in the following:

H. Confidentiality and privacy—the social worker should respect the privacy of clients and hold in confidence all information obtained in the course of professional service.

1. The social worker should share with others confidences revealed by clients, without their consent, only for compelling professional reasons.
2. The social worker should inform clients fully about the limits of confidentiality in a given situation, the purposes for which the information is obtained, and how it may be used.
3. The social worker should afford clients reasonable access to any official social work records concerning them.
4. When providing clients with access to records, the social worker should take due care to protect the confidences of others contained in those records.
5. The social worker should obtain informed consent of clients before taping, recording, or permitting third-party observation of their activities.

Social workers thus have a profound responsibility to safeguard confidentiality. An unjustified breach of confidentiality is a violation of justice and is tantamount to theft of a secret with which one has been entrusted (Biestek, 1957). Maintaining strict confidentiality requires a strong commitment, for clients sometimes reveal information that is shocking, humorous, bizarre, or "juicy." To fulfill your responsibility in maintaining confidentiality, it is vital to guard against disclosing information in inappropriate situations, the most common of which include the following:

1. Discussions with family and friends.

2. Bull sessions with colleagues.

3. Conversations with other workers.

4. Dictating within the listening range of others.

5. Cocktail parties.

6. Discussing client situations within earshot of repairmen.

7. Inappropriately sharing information with one's personal secretary.

8. Remarks about clients made in elevators or hallways.

Violation of the client's right to confitiality could result not only in loss of right to practice but also in a malpractice suit.

The right to confidentiality is not absolute, however, for confidential information is often stored in case records that are typed by stenographers. Moreover, case situations are sometimes discussed with supervisors and consultants and may be presented at staff conferences. Disclosing information in these instances, however, is for the purpose of enhancing service to clients, who will generally consent to these uses when the purposes are clarified. The client has a right to be informed that such disclosures may occur, and practitioners have a responsibility to conceal the identity of the client to the fullest extent possible and also to reveal no more personal information than is absolutely necessary.

Practitioners are often requested by other social workers, members of other disciplines, or other agencies to provide confidential information pursuant to the client's contacts with these other parties or agencies. In these instances, it is important that such information be provided only with the written, informed consent of clients, which releases the practitioner and agency from liability in disclosing the requested information. Even when informed consent is obtained, however, it is important that information be revealed selectively according to the essential needs of the other party. There are exceptions when information can be revealed without informed consent, such as a bona fide emergency in which a client's life appears at stake. In other instances, however, it is prudent to obtain legal counsel before disclosing confidential information without a written consent for release of information.

Others who have access to confidential information are similarly obligated to preserve confidentiality. Such persons include supervisors, administrators, volunteers, members of other disciplines, secretarial and clerical staff, consultants, board members, researchers, legal counsel, and outside persons who may review records for purposes of quality assurance, peer review, or accreditation. It is thus essential that social workers promote policies that assure stringent measures to protect confidentiality and carefully orient and hold employees of the agency to their ethical responsibilities.

In certain instances, the client's right to confidentiality may be less compelling than the rights of other people who could be severely harmed or damaged by actions planned by the client and confided to the practitioner. For example, if a client plans to commit kidnapping, injury, or murder, the practitioner is obligated to disclose these intentions to the intended victim and to law enforcement officials so that timely preventative action can be implemented. Indeed, if practitioners fail to make appropriate disclosure under these circumstances, they are extremely liable to civil prosecution for negligence. In recent years, for example, practitioners have lost court cases in which they have been tried for negligence in failing to warn intended victims of harmful actions threatened by clients.

Confidentiality in Child Abuse

Rights of others also take precedence over the right to confidentiality in instances of child abuse and/or neglect. In fact, all 50 states now have statutes making it mandatory for professionals to report suspected or known child abuse. Moreover, all statutes governing the mandatory reporting of child abuse contain a criminal clause for failure to report. As of 1985, however, there had been no reported cases of successful prosecution for failure to report. It is noteworthy that practitioners are protected from both civil and criminal liability for breach of confidentiality resulting from the legal mandate to report (Butz, 1985). Without such immunity, as Butz indicates, involved professionals would be placed in a double bind.

Although afforded immunity from prosecution for reporting, practitioners are still confronted with the difficult challenge of preserving the helping relationship after having breached confidentiality. Butz discusses related issues at length and makes a number of recommendations. To do justice to his discussion, however, would exceed space limitations, and we therefore refer you to his article.

When child abusing parents are being treated by a social worker for substance abuse, conflicting state and federal statutes place professionals in a quandary. On one hand, they are mandated by state law to report child abuse under threat of penalty; on the other hand, if they report cases involving parents who are substance abusers they may be prosecuted either criminally or civilly by *federal* authorities for breaching federal confidentiality requirements set forth in the federal alcohol and drug abuse confidentiality acts. In her discussion of the complex issues involved, which are far from resolved, Saltzman (1986) cites a federal policy statement that authorizes substance abuse workers covered by the federal acts to report child abuse parents who are also substance abuse patients *if they first obtain a court order.* Although seeking a court order may be cumbersome and time consuming, Saltzman concludes:

Based on the court cases and advisory legal opinions . . . social workers who make reports of child abuse involving their substance abuse clients without a court order do so at their peril. Although it is unlikely that these workers would be held criminally or civilly liable (or even be brought to court), they could be violating federal law by making such reports.

Social workers are thus advised to seek court orders before reporting incidents of child abuse involving a substance abuse client.

(p. 475)

Social workers and other professionals may also find themselves in a different sort of quandary involved in reporting child abuse that occurs in rural subcultures. As Long (1986) reports, ". . . on Indian reservations and in small rural towns it is often impossible to prevent community awareness of abuse victims, abuse perpetrators, and abuse informants. Despite the best efforts of health care professionals involved, abuse perpetrators may learn of an informant through informal channels or through tribal court procedures" (p. 133). Further, the sense of loyalty to one's clan members may take precedence over the commitment to protect an informant and the need to protect an abused child. Consequently tribal sanctions may be more severe in relation to the informant than to the abuser. Long provides documentation of case situations in which both informant and victim were physically beaten, verbally abused, and harassed by clan members. Definitions of abuse also differ from culture to culture and within certain subcultures even severe abuse (according to common standards) may not be considered a problem by the victim or other family members.

Subcultural differences are by no means limited to members of ethnic minority groups. Long provides additional documentation of how closely knit Anglo health care practitioners discounted reports of child abuse perpetrated by a colleague and hindered effective intervention. Clearly, loyalty to the professional "clan" protected a member of the clan and hampered efforts to protect the child.

What course of action should practitioners take when community (subcultural) definitions of child abuse diverge from generally accepted standards, and when clan loyalties may result in punishment to informants and victim rather than perpetrators? We concur with Long's (1986) recommendations that we

". . . must look beyond legal guidelines and discipline-specific prescriptions. . . . If professionals are to be both genuinely helpful and realistically effective, there is often a need to make compromises related to treatment ideals. Thoughtful evaluation is required to allow for treatment strategies that can fit and be useful within a given subcultural context, and which still maintain the ethical and legal principles.

(p. 136)

Privileged Communication

Still another constraint on clients' rights to confidentiality is the fact that this right does not necessarily extend into courts of law. Unless social workers are practicing in one of the states that grant privileged communication, they may be compelled by courts to reveal confidential information and to produce confidential records.[5] Bernstein (1977) therefore recommends that social workers practicing in states without statutes that grant privileged communication explain to clients that practitioners "can be subpoenaed in court, records in hand, and forced under penalty of contempt to testify full and completely, under oath, as to what was said between the parties and what was recorded concerning such exchanges (p. 264). Bernstein further recommends that, "To avoid even a hint of malpractice, the social worker should explain the problem of privileged communication . . . and should have in each

---

[5]Privileged communication is a legal right that protects clients from having confidences revealed publicly from the witness stand during legal proceedings. Statutes that grant privileged communication exempt certain professions from being legally compelled to reveal content disclosed in the context of a confidential relationship.

client's file a document carefully drafted by an attorney and signed by the client acknowledging the possibilities" (p. 268).

Privileged communication for social work clients is allowed in fewer states than it is for clients of psychologists. Whereas 47 states and the District of Columbia have statutes that grant privileged communication to psychologists, only one state (California) includes social workers in its privileged communication statute (VandeCreek, Knapp, & Herzog, 1988). Social workers, however, may be covered in 16 other states that have a broader psychotherapist-patient privilege.

The authors just cited and Levick (1981) argue that the need for privileged communication laws for social workers is more important than ever before because of expanded social work roles and the fact that social workers provide more mental health services than do any other professionals. These writers recommend that social workers lobby their state legislators for a statute that grants the same protection to psychotherapy clients of *all* mental health professionals.

It is important to note that the right to invoke privileged communication resides with the client, not the practitioner. In other words, if the practitioner were called on to take the witness stand, the attorney for the client could invoke the privilege to prohibit testimony of the practitioner (Bernstein, 1977). The client's attorney can also waive this privilege, in which case the practitioner would be obligated to disclose information as requested by the court.

Another important factor regarding privileged communication is that the client's right is not absolute (Levick, 1981). If, in a court's judgment, disclosure of confidential information would produce benefits that outweigh the injury that might be incurred by revealing that information, the presiding judge may waive the privilege. In the final analysis, then, courts make decisions on privilege on a case-by-case basis.

It is also important to recognize that not only practitioners, but group members as well may be subpoenaed to testify in legal proceedings that involve another group member. Group members, of course, have the same obligation to preserve confidentiality of information revealed by other group members and should be so informed early in the process of group development. Because of the nature of group therapy, each member becomes a therapeutic agent for other group members. Unfortunately, privileged communication has not been extended to group members even in states that grant such privileges to social workers (Bernstein, 1977). The group practitioner thus has a responsibility to inform group members that their right to confidentiality does not extend into legal courts. It would be inimical to group process, however, to place heavy emphasis on this constraint, for as Bernstein notes, group members could hardly be expected to interact freely "with a judicial cloud hanging over their heads" (p. 267). Therefore, in explaining the matter to group members, it is desirable to emphasize that the possibility of being subpoenaed is remote. Indeed, the authors are unaware of a single instance in which this has occurred.

Confidentiality in Various Types of Recording

Because case records can be subpoenaed and because clients and other personnel have access to them, it is essential that practitioners work toward the development and implementation of policies and practices that provide maximal confidentiality. To this end, practitioners should observe the following:

1. Record no more than is essential to the functions of the agency.

2. Omit details of clients' intimate lives from case records; describe intimate problems in general terms.

3. Do not include verbatim or process recordings in case files.

4. Employ private and soundproof dictation facilities.

5. Keep case records in locked files and issue keys only to those who require frequent access to the files.

6. Do not remove case files from the agency except under extraordinary circumstances with special authorization.

7. Do not leave case files on desks where janitorial personnel or others might have access to them.

8. Use in-service training sessions to stress confidentiality and to monitor observance of agency policies and practices instituted to safeguard confidentiality.

Practitioners sometimes record live interviews or group sessions so that they can later analyze dynamics, interactional patterns, or group process, as well as scrutinize their own performance with a view toward improving skills and techniques. Recording is also used extensively for training purposes, particularly for instructional sessions between students and practicum instructors. Still another use of recordings is to provide firsthand feedback to clients by having them listen to or view their actual behavior in live sessions.

Before recording sessions for any of the preceding purposes, practitioners should obtain written consent from clients on a form that explicitly specifies how the recording will be used, who will listen to or view the recording, and when it will be erased. *In no instance* should a recording be made without the knowledge and consent of the client. Clients vary widely in their receptivity to having sessions recorded, and if they manifest reluctance, their wishes should be respected. Practitioners who tape sessions assume a heavy burden of responsibility in safeguarding confidentiality, for live sessions are extremely revealing. Such recordings should be guarded with utmost caution to assure that copies cannot be made and that unauthorized persons do not have access to them. When they have served their designated purpose, tapes should be promptly erased. Failure to heed these guidelines may constitute a breach of professional ethics.

Used for training purposes, tapes of live interviews are extremely valuable, enabling instructors and trainees to analyze moment-by-moment transactions. Such learning experiences are indispensable in developing mastery of specific skills. To avail yourself of this rich learning opportunity, you must, of course, first gain consent from clients to tape sessions. The chances of gaining consent are enhanced by discussing the matter openly and honestly, taking care to explain the client's right to decline. If approached properly, the majority of clients consent to taping. Indeed, it has been our experience that students are more uncomfortable with taping than are clients. The following is an example of an interchange that involves a practitioner's request for taping an interview. Obviously, not all requests proceed as smoothly as this example, but in our experience, students' hesitancy to introduce the matter is usually the biggest obstacle.

PRACTITIONER: Mrs. F., to be as helpful to you as possible, I'd like, with your permission, to tape-record our interviews so that I can review them with my supervisor, who may have suggestions as to other ways I can be helpful. How do you feel about that possibility?

MRS. F.: Gee, I don't know [*laughs uncomfortably*]. I think I'd probably be a little self-conscious. Uh—What do you do with the tape?

PRACTITIONER: I'm sensing some concern on your part and assure you you're in no way obligated. In answer to your question, after my supervisor and I have gone over the tape together, I erase it. We're very careful with the tape, and if you agree to the taping, I'd want to have a written agreement with you that specifies how the tape will be used and when it will be erased. But before we go any further, I'm wondering about your feeling self-conscious. I don't want to create a problem for you.

MRS. F.: I'm sure I'd get over being self-conscious. If it'd help you, I'm agreeable.

PRACTITIONER: I appreciate your honesty and willingness [*laughs*]. You know, I'm a little self-conscious myself at first. But I have found that taping is very helpful to me. Most important, though, is that you feel good about it.

MRS. F.: It's no problem for me. Let's go ahead.

PRACTITIONER: Good. I have the consent form right here. I'll go over it with you.

Exercises in Confidentiality

The following exercises will give you practice in applying the concept of confidentiality to specific practice situations, which include some of the most difficult ones that we and our colleagues have encountered in practice. You will note that in few of the situations is the appropriate response or course of action cut and dried. After reading each situation, consider the following:

1. How can you best discharge your ethical responsibility in the situation?

2. Do you experience conflicting pulls regarding possible courses of action?

3. In situations that involve legal ramification, how would you handle it with the client in the event your planned action would be contrary to the client's request?

Situation 1   A male client confided in an individual marital therapy session several weeks ago that he is a practicing homosexual, although his wife does not know this. The client's wife, whom you have also seen conjointly with him, calls you today, troubled over the lack of progress in solving marital problems, and asks you point-blank whether you think her husband could be homosexual.

Situation 2   You are forming a group for youth in a state correctional facility. You know from past experience that youth sometimes makes references in the group to previous offenses that they have committed without being apprehended. You also know that they may talk about plans to run from the institution or about indiscretions or misdemeanors they (or others) may have committed or plan to commit within the institution, such as smoking marijuana or stealing institutional supplies or property from peers or staff.

Situation 3   In conducting an intake interview with a client in a family agency, you observe that both of her young children are withdrawn. Further, one of the children is badly bruised, and the other, an infant, appears malnourished. Throughout the interview, the client seems defensive and suspicious and also

ambivalent about having come for the interview. At one point, she states that she feels overwhelmed with her parenting responsibilities and is having difficulty in coping with her children. She also alludes to her fear that she may hurt them but then abruptly changes the subject. As you encourage her to return to the discussion of her problems with the children, your client says she has changed her mind about wanting help, takes her children in hand, and leaves the office.

Situation 4   You have seen a husband and wife and their adolescent daughter twice regarding relationship problems between the parents and the girl. The parents are both extremely negative and blaming in their attitudes toward their daughter, believing their troubles would be over if she would just "shape up." Today, during an individual interview with the girl, she breaks into tears and tells you that she is pregnant and plans to "go somewhere" with her boyfriend this weekend to get an abortion. She pleads with you not to tell her parents, who she feels would be extremely angry if they knew.

Situation 5   In a mental health agency, you have been working with a male client who has a past history, when angered, of becoming violent and physically abusive. He has been under extreme psychological pressure lately because of problems relating to a recent separation from his wife. In an interview today, he is extremely angry, clenching his fists as he tells you that he has heard that his wife has initiated divorce proceedings and plans to move to another state. "If this is true," he loudly protests, "she is doing it to take the kids away from me, and I'll kill her rather than let her do that."

Legal Implications for Keeping Case Records

Although social work has historically embraced clients' rights to confidentiality, implementation of this ethical principle has been more stringent in recent years as a result of the federal Privacy Act of 1974, which was enacted to safeguard people against "harmful disclosures of information whether through inaccurate information being used in irrelevant circumstances or through inaccurate information being used in important decisions affecting individuals" (Schrier, 1980, p. 452). Although this act applies only to the federal government, many states have passed corresponding statutes or have used provisions of the law as criteria in adjudicating civil cases that involve alleged violations of people's rights to privacy. The act specifies duties for agencies that maintain record-keeping systems, including the following:

(1) maintaining only information relevant and necessary to the agency's purposes, (2) collecting as much information as possible from the client directly, (3) informing clients of the agency's authority to gather information, whether disclosure is mandatory or voluntary, the principal purpose of the use of the information, the routine uses and effects, if any, of not providing part or all of information, (4) maintaining and updating records to assure accuracy, relevancy, timeliness and completeness, (5) notifying clients of the release of records owing to compulsory legal actions, and (6) establishing procedures to inform clients of the existence of their records, including special measures if necessary for disclosure of medical and psychological records and a review of requests to amend or correct the records.

(Schrier, 1980, p. 453)

You will note that the professional's Code of Ethics reflects most of these provisions.

Item 6 in the preceding list establishes clients' rights of access to their records, which is consistent with provisions of the federal Freedom of Information Act of 1966. Where federal funds are involved and where states have enacted similar legislation, agencies and institutions are obligated to grant clients access to their case records. These statutes, of course, have major implications for record-keeping procedures, which Schrier (1980) discusses at length. (We strongly recommend you read Schrier's article.)

Social workers have reacted to the right-to-access law in mixed ways. Many strongly resisted making records available to clients, arguing they could no longer be candid in recording and could include only innocuous information. Some private agencies that were not subject to the laws responded positively by modifying recording procedures and inviting clients to review their records. According to Freed (1978), "The few agencies, hospitals, and clients that have tried sharing social work records with clients have found that the practice contributes favorably to the casework process and promotes the therapeutic goal by enhancing the client's trust and the openness of the relationship" (p. 460). Others similarly reported favorable results from sharing case records with clients whose problems involved marital and family difficulties. Interestingly, the experience of most agencies is that clients do *not* wish to see their records.

Because case recording procedures have been tightened and to avoid strains with clients and even a possible lawsuit, Freed (1978) recommends that practitioners carefully distinguish objective from subjective information, use descriptive terms rather than professional jargon, and avoid using psychiatric and medical diagnoses that have not been verified. Further, information gained in confidence from other sources should not be made a part of the record unless permission is obtained from parties who provided the information. And finally, if there is reason to believe the client may be harmed by knowing what is in the record, the practitioner is obligated to share this opinion with the client. In our opinion, the changes that have resulted from both of the acts cited have enhanced the rights of clients by avoiding misuse of records and have compelled practitioners to be more prudent, rigorous, and scientific in keeping case records.

Managing Ethical Dilemmas

Social workers frequently experience quandaries in making choices as to which ethic should take precedence in situations that involve conflicts of duty. For example, a practitioner may recognize that a certain agency policy is detrimental to clients but may be torn about exercising the ethical responsibility to advocate change in the policy because doing so poses a threat to relationships with certain staff members or to continued employment. Moreover, clients may confide information that indicates their behavior or threatened behavior places in jeopardy the health or safety of other persons. Taking preventive action, however, may involve revealing to others information that was disclosed in confidence.

Conflicts involving ethics often pose difficult and painful challenges to social workers, as you likely discovered in the "Exercises in Confidentiality" presented earlier. In some instances, the appropriate action is relatively clear-cut; in others, however, decisions are agonizingly difficult. Fortunately, Reamer (1982a) has presented a general guideline to assist social workers in

making the hard decisions they typically encounter. According to Reamer, "one's actual duty in instances where prima facie duties conflict should be based on a determination of which duty is most necessary for the performance of action and represents the least threat to the well-being of individuals" (p. 583). The principle also assists social workers in determining priorities in that "it is based on a ranking of goods and resources according to the extent to which they are necessary for individual well-being and the extent to which their absence threatens the opportunities and abilities of individuals to fulfill their intentions" (p. 583). Reamer clarifies that "goods and resources can be ranked, qualitatively ranging from, on one hand, those which are necessary for the performance of any and all human action (life, physical health, food, shelter, and basic mental equilibrium) to, on the other, goods and resources which may enhance an individual's ability to fulfill his or her goal but are not, in the strict sense, necessary for human action (excessive wealth, recreational facilities, and artistic artifacts)" (pp. 583–584).

Reamer's general guideline takes on additional meaning when applied to specific conflictual situations as in the following:

The duty to save a human life would take precedence over the duty to keep information shared by a client confidential . . . because the former is more necessary for the possibility of human action (that is, represents a greater threat to basic human well-being) than is the latter. Thus, if conflicts force practitioners to make hard choices, protecting individuals from threats to life itself . . . is more important than, for example, keeping information confidential, telling the truth, keeping promises, and avoiding deception.

(p. 584)

Although Reamer's guideline contributes to social work practice, applying it to the myriad situations that social workers encounter still involves uncertainties and ambiguities, a reality that practitioners must accept. For example, it is often extremely difficult to assess the degree of risk a client's behavior poses to the health and safety of the client or others. Simple and clear-cut guidelines for solving ethical dilemmas are not available, but Biggs and Blocher (1987), Reamer (1982b), Rhodes (1986), and Wells and Masch (1986) have written books specifically aimed at assisting practitioners with ethical dilemmas.

Skill Development Exercises in Operationalizing Cardinal Values

To assist you in developing skill in operationalizing the cardinal values in specific practice situations, we have provided a number of exercises with modeled responses. As you read each one, note which of the values is (are) germane to the situation and whether one of the six threats to acceptance and respect is involved in the client's messages. To refresh your memory, the values and threats are as follows:

Values	Threats to Acceptance and Respect
1. Access to needed resources.	1. Helplessness and excessive dependency.
2. Acceptance of and belief in the worth and dignity of human beings.	2. Silence and withdrawal.
3. Uniqueness and individuality of clients.	3. Aggressive and sullen behavior.
	4. Mainpulation and exploitative behavior.

4. Belief in self-determination and problem-solving capacities of clients.

5. Confidentiality.

5. Self-effacing behavior.

6. Passive noncompliant behavior.

Next, assume you are the client's practitioner and formulate a response that implements the relevant social work value. After completing each exercise, compare your response with the modeled response that follows the exercises. Bearing in mind that the modeled response is only one of many possible acceptable responses, analyze it and compare it with your own. By carefully completing these exercises, you will improve your competence in operationalizing the cardinal values in the varied and challenging situations encountered in direct social work practice.

Client Statements

1. Group member [*in first group session*]: Before I really open up and talk about myself, I need to be sure what I say isn't blabbed around to other people. [*Turning to practitioner.*] What assurance is there that won't happen?

2. Rural mother [*living in dilapidated but neatly kept home; her children are shabbily dressed but appear healthy*]: You city folk don't seem to understand that you don't have to have a fancy home and heaps of luxuries to have a good life and raise healthy kids.

3. Adolescent delinquent in correctional institution [*after practitioner introduces self*]: So you want to help me, huh? I'll tell you how you can help. You can get me out of this damn place—that's how!

4. Female client, age 21 [*to mental health practitioner*]: Yeah, I know that kicking the habit was a victory of sorts. But I look at my life and I wonder what's there to live for. I've turned my family against me. I've sold my body to more rotten guys that I can count—just to get a fix. I've had VD three times. What do I have to offer anyone? I feel like my life has been one big cesspool.

5. Teenage male [*in a group session in a correctional setting*]: [*Takes off shoes and sprawls in his chair. His feet give off a foul odor, and other members hold noses and make derisive comments. He responds defensively.*] Hey, get off my back, you creeps. What's the big deal about taking off my shoes?

6. Female [*initial interview in family counseling center*]: Before I talk about my marital problems, I need to let you know I'm a Seventh Day Adventist. Do you know anything about my church? I'm asking because a lot of our marital problems involve my religion.

7. Client [*as interview ends and time of next appointment is discussed*]: Oh, just work me into your schedule where it's convenient for you. Just let me know when you want me to come, and I'll get here somehow.

8. Female client [*sixth interview*]: Maybe it sounds crazy, but I've been thinking this last week that you're not really interested in me as a person. I have the feeling I'm just someone for you to analyze or to write about.

9. Mexican-American male client [*in fifth group session, the members of which are largely Anglos*]: I have the feeling that you people look down on my people—like we're all just Frito-Banditos. It really gripes me.

10. Teenage female delinquent [*caught with contraband in her possession to supervisor-counselor in correctional institution*]: Please don't report this, Mrs. Wilson.

I've been doing better lately, and I've learned my lesson. You won't need to worry about me. I won't mess with drugs anymore.

11. Client [*observing practitioner taking notes during initial interview*]: I'm dying to know what you're writing down about me. But I guess I'm afraid too—wondering if you think I'm a nut.

12. Single female client, age 29 [*in mental health center*]: I just heard about a job that opened up on the outskirts of town. It'd be right down my alley, but I'd have to drive because there's no bus service that comes within three miles. I don't drive, and I don't want to learn. I've always been afraid I might have an accident and kill someone. Everyone tells me I should learn to drive.

13. Male parolee, age 27, who has a reputation as a con artist [*in mandatory weekly visit to parole officer*]: Man, you've really got it made. Your office is really cool. I admire your tastes in furnishing it. But then you deserve what you've got. You've probably got a terrific wife and kids, too. Is that their picture over there?

14. Male client, age 34 [*in third interview*]: I'm really uptight right now. I've got this tight feeling I get in my chest when I'm nervous. [*Pause.*] Well, I guess I'll have to tell you if I expect to get anything out of this. [*Hesitantly.*] You know the marital problems we've talked about. Well, Janice doesn't know this, but I've been a practicing homosexual since I was 19. [*Blushes.*] I've tried—I've really tried, but Janice doesn't turn me on. I have to think about men to even get an erection. She thinks something's wrong with her, but it's not her fault. [*Chin quivers.*]

15. Female, age 68 [*to geriatric worker in county-sponsored housing complex*]: It's been hard since Ralph died a year ago. I didn't know how many things I depended on him for. Like taking me places. I just feel like I'm chained down now because I don't drive. I still have our car, and it's only three years old—just sitting in storage. Ralph always prodded me to learn to drive, and I wish I had now. Do you think I'm too old to learn? I'm no spring chicken, you know.

16. Black male probationer [*to white therapist*]: You're so damn smug. You say you want to help me, but I don't buy that jive. You don't know the first thing about black people. Man, I grew up where it's an accomplishment just to survive. What do you know about life in the ghetto, man?

Modeled Responses

1. "Ginny raises a good point that concerns all of you. So that you can feel more comfortable about sharing personal feelings and experiences with the group, we need an understanding that each of you will keep what is shared in the strictest confidence. I can assure you that I'll keep information confidential myself, but I am interested in hearing from the rest of you regarding the question that Ginny is asking."

2. "Sounds like you're concerned I might look down on you because I'm from the city. I can tell it's important to you to take good care of your children. I want you to know too that rather than being critical, I'm impressed with how clean you keep your house. You know, I don't see us as being all that different because I live in the city and you live in the country. We're a lot more alike than different, and I want you to know I respect you as a person."

3. "I guess that's what I'd want also if I were in your situation. As a matter of fact, that's what I want for you, too. But we both know the review board won't release you until they feel you're prepared to make it on the outside. I can't get you out,

but with your cooperation I can help you to make changes that will get you ready for release."

4. "I can see you're really down on yourself and feel pretty worthless. While it's true you've done a lot that you feel bad about, it's important not to let your past ruin your future. Where you're going is a lot more important than where you've been. I'm impressed you kicked the habit. That's a giant step in the right direction. If you just hang in there, you can gradually rebuild your life, and with that you'll feel a lot better about yourself."

5. "I think we need to look as a group at how we can give Jim some *helpful* feedback rather than making fun of him. Let's talk about what just happened. Maybe you could begin, Jim, by sharing with the group what you're feeling just now."

6. "I have to confess I know just a little bit about your religion. Understandably you're wondering if I can appreciate your problems. I can assure you I'll do my best to understand if you're willing to take a chance with me. You might have to educate me a little bit, but I'm a willing learner. The most important thing, though, is your feelings about it. How do you feel about sharing your problems with me under these circumstances?"

7. "I appreciate that, but your time's important too. Let's see if we can find a mutually convenient time. I have openings at _____ and _____ . Would any of those times be convenient for you?"

8. "That sounds like a painful feeling to have—that I'm not personally concerned with you as an individual. I'd like to explore that with you further because that's not at all how I feel about you, and I'm uncomfortable being seen that way. I'd like to understand more how I've come across to you and how you've reached that conclusion."

9. "Arturo, I'm pleased you could share those feelings because I've noticed you've been pretty quiet in our sessions and I have wondered why. I'd like to know more about you as a person. Perhaps you could tell the group a little more about what you've been experiencing."

10. "I'm sorry you're still involved with drugs, Joy, because of the trouble it's caused you. I don't like to see you get into trouble but I have no choice—I have to report this. If I didn't, I'd be breaking a rule myself by not reporting you. That wouldn't help you in the long run. Frankly, I'm going to keep worrying about you until I'm satisfied you're really sticking to the rules."

11. [*Chuckling.*] "So you're wondering what I think of you. Well, you surely don't come across like a nut. Actually what I'm writing down is what we're talking about. What you tell me is important, and notes help to refresh my memory. You're welcome to look at my notes if you like. Actually, I would be interested in hearing a little more about your thoughts about what I might think of you."

12. "I can understand your desire not to harm anyone, but it sounds as though you have to pass up some choice opportunities because of your fear. I respect your right to decide for yourself about learning to drive. But it strikes me that you're letting yourself be at the mercy of that fear. Fears like that can be mastered, and if you're inclined to work on your fear of driving, I'd be happy to explore it with you."

13. "As a matter of fact it is, and I think they're pretty terrific. But we're here to talk about you, Rex. I'd like to hear how your job interview went at _____ ."

14. "This has been very painful for you—sharing this problem with me. You've kept this inside for a long time, and I gather you've been afraid I'd condemn you. I'm pleased you brought it up so that we can work on it together. And rest assured I won't sit in judgment. It took some real courage on your part to talk about this, and I respect you for that."

15. "If you have the determination, I see no reason why you couldn't learn. There are some excellent instructors available in the adult education program. To be honest, I'm delighted you're considering it. You'd feel more independent, and it would open up a lot of possibilities. But what *you* feel is most important. What goes on inside of you when you think about it?"

16. "I'd be phony if I said I understood all about being black and living in a ghetto. But you're wrong about my being smug or trying to jive you. I am interested in you, and I'd like to understand more about your life. How have you come to the conclusion that I've been jiving you?".

Part 2

Exploring, Assessing, and Planning

Part 2 of this book deals with processes and skills involved in the first phase of the helping process. To introduce this part we focus in this chapter on skills essential to building effective working relationships with clients, one of the two major objectives of initial interviews. In Chapter 6 we shift our focus to skills entailed in accomplishing the other major objective, namely, to thoroughly explore clients' difficulties. In Chapter 7 we identify verbal and nonverbal patterns of communication that impede the development of effective working relationships.

5 | Relationship-Building Skills: Communicating with Empathy and Authenticity

The Facilitative Conditions

The present chapter is concerned with two of the three skills embodied in what have been variously referred to as the facilitative conditions, core conditions, or central ingredients in helping relationships. These conditions or skills, deemed by Carl Rogers (1957) the "necessary and sufficient conditions of personality change," were originally denoted as empathy, unconditional positive regard, and congruence. Other terms have since evolved and we shall refer to the conditions as empathy, respect, and authenticity or genuineness. Although no longer considered *sufficient,* the facilitative conditions have been demonstrated empirically to be associated with positive outcomes.

The two skills upon which we focus in this chapter entail communicating with empathy and with authenticity. The third skill (or condition) is respect or nonpossessive warmth, which embodies the social work concepts of acceptance, nonjudgmental attitude, respect for the dignity and worth of the individual, and individualization of the client. We discussed these concepts at length and provided related exercises in Chapter 4; therefore we do not address the condition of respect in this chapter.

Empathic Communication

This skill involves the ability of the practitioner to *perceive* accurately and sensitively inner feelings of the client and to *communicate* understanding of these feelings in language attuned to the client's experiencing of the moment. The first dimension of empathy, that of empathic recognition, is a precondition of the second dimension, that is, demonstrating through accurate reflection of feelings that the practitioner comprehends the client's inner experiencing.

Empathic communication plays a vital role in nurturing and sustaining the helping relationship and providing the vehicle through which the practitioner becomes emotionally significant and influential in the client's life. Furthermore, conveying empathic understanding reduces threat and defensiveness, conveys interest and helpful intent, and creates an atmosphere conducive to behavior change.

In responding to clients' feelings, practitioners must avoid being misled by conventional facades used to conceal emotions. Thus, the empathic communicator responds to feelings that underlie such messages as "Oh, no, it doesn't really matter," or "I don't care what he does!" These messages likely mask disappointment or hurt as do such messages as "I don't need anyone" when experiencing painful loneliness, or "I don't let anyone hurt me" when one is finding rejection hard to bear. To enter the client's private world of practical experience, the practitioner must also avoid making personal interpretations and judgments of the client's private logic and feelings that, in superficial contacts, might appear as weak, foolish, or undesirable.

Being empathically attuned involves not only grasping the client's immediately evident feelings but, in a mutually shared, exploratory process, identifying underlying emotions and discovering the meaning, purposiveness, and personal significance of feelings and behavior. In getting in touch with camouflaged feelings and meanings, the practitioner must tune in not only to verbal messages but to more subtle cues, including facial expressions, tone of voice, tempo of speech, and postural and gestural cues that amplify and sometimes contradict verbal meanings. Such nonverbal cues as blushing, crying, pausing, stammering, changing voice intonation, clenching jaws or fists, pursing the lips, lowering the head, or shifting the posture often reveal the presence of distressing feelings and thoughts.

Empathic communication also involves "stepping into the shoes of another," in the sense of attempting to perceive the world of experience of the other person. The listener, however, must remain outside, avoiding being overwhelmed by the fears, anger, joys, and hurts of that person, though deeply sensing the meaning and significance of these feelings for the other. "Being with" the client involves the practitioner's focusing intensely on the client's affective state without losing perspective or taking on the emotions experienced by the client.

When a person experiences feelings in common with another person and is similarly affected by whatever the other person is experiencing, the former usually responds *sympathetically* rather than empathically. Sympathetic responding, which depends on emotional and intellectual accord, involves supporting and condoning the other person's feelings (e.g., "I'd feel the same way you do if I were in your position" or "I think you're right"), whereas empathic responding involves *understanding* the other person's feelings and circumstances without taking that person's position (e.g., "I sense you're feeling..." or "You seem to be saying..."). When practitioners support clients' feelings, clients may feel no need to examine their behavior or circumstances and may not engage in the process of self-exploration so vital to growth and change; rather, in such instances, clients look to the practitioner to change the behavior of other persons who play a significant role in their problems. Retaining separateness and objectivity thus is a critical dimension in the helping process, for when practitioners assume the client's feelings and positions, they lose not only vital perspective but the ability to be helpful as well.

Being empathic involves more than recognizing clients' feelings. Practitioners must also respond verbally and nonverbally in ways that affirm their understanding of clients' inner experiencing. It is not unusual for a person to experience empathic feelings for another without conveying them in any way to the second party. High-level empathy requires skill in verbally and nonverbally *demonstrating* understanding. A common mistake made by practitioners is to tell the client, "I understand how you feel." Rather than producing a sense of being understood, such a response often creates doubts in the client's mind about the practitioner's perceptiveness because specific demonstration of understanding is lacking. Indeed, use of this response may mean that the practitioner has *not* explored the client's feelings sufficiently to fully grasp the significance of the problematic situation. To convey unmistakably, "I am with you; I understand," the practitioner must respond empathically. Use of this skill creates an ambience of acceptance and understanding in which the client is more likely to risk sharing deeper and more personal feelings.

Later in the chapter, we present theory and exercises for developing skill in empathic responding. Initially, we provide a list of affective words and phrases to assist you in expanding your vocabulary so that you can meet the challenge of responding to the wide range of emotions experienced by clients. We also provide exercises to assist you to refine your ability to perceive the feelings of others—a prerequisite to the mastery of empathic communication. To assist you to discern levels of empathy, a rating scale for empathic responding is included, accompanied by examples of varying levels of practitioner responses and exercises. These exercises will assist you to gain mastery of empathic communication at an effective working level.

Developing Perceptiveness to Feelings

A vital and universal aspect of human experiencing, feelings or emotions exert a powerful influence on behavior and usually play a central role in the problems of clients. Responding to the broad spectrum of emotions and feeling states presented by clients requires that the practitioner be fully aware of the diversity of human emotion. Further, the practitioner

needs a rich vocabulary of words and expressions that not only reflect client feelings accurately but also capture the intensity of those feelings. For example, there are dozens of descriptive feeling words to express anger, including furious, aggravated, vexed, provoked, put out, irritated, impatient—all of which express different shades and intensities of this feeling. When used judiciously, such words serve to give sharp and exact focus to the feelings of clients.

Possessing and utilizing a rich vocabulary of affective words and phrases that accurately reflect client feelings is a skill that often is not developed by even experienced practitioners. It is important to realize that high-level empathic responding involves first a *thinking* process and, second, a *responding* process. A deficient vocabulary of feelings limits practitioners' ability to conceptualize and hence to reflect the full intensity and range of feelings experienced by clients.

It has been our experience that beginning practitioners have a limited range of feeling words from which to draw in conveying empathy. Although there are literally hundreds of feeling words that may be used to capture feelings, learners often limit themselves to, and use to excess, a few catch-all terms, such as *upset* or *frustrated,* losing much of the richness of client messages in the process.

The accompanying lists illustrate the wide range of expressions available for practitioners' use in responding to clients' feelings. It must be noted that using feeling words discriminately is important not only in empathic responding but indispensable in relating authentically as well. Becoming a competent professional involves a maturing process whereby practitioners develop not only the capacity to deeply share the inner experiencing of others, but also to express their own personal feelings in constructive ways.

AFFECTIVE WORDS AND PHRASES
Competence, Strength

convinced you can	committed
confident	sense of accomplishment
sense of mastery	daring
powerful	feeling oats
potent	effective
courageous	sure
resolute	sense of conviction
determined	trust in yourself
strong	self-reliant
influential	sharp
brave	able
impressive	adequate
forceful	firm
inspired	capable
skillful	on top of it
successful	can cope
secure	important
in charge	up to it
in control	ready
well-equipped	equal to it

Happiness, Satisfaction

elated	elevated
superb	happy
ecstatic	lighthearted
on cloud nine	wonderful
on top of the world	glowing
organized	gay
fantastic	neat
splendid	glad
exhilarated	fine
jubilant	pleased
terrific	good
euphoric	contented

delighted	hopeful
marvelous	mellow
excited	satisfied
enthusiastic	gratified
thrilled	fulfilled
great	tranquil
super	serene
in high spirits	calm
joyful	at ease
cheerful	

Caring, Love

adore	respect
loving	admire
infatuated	concern for
enamored	taken with
cherish	turned on
idolize	trust
worship	close
attached to	esteem
devoted to	hit it off
tenderness toward	value
affection for	warm toward
hold dear	friendly
prize	like
caring	positive toward
fond of	accept
regard	

Depression, Discouragement

anguished	sorrowful
in despair	demoralized
dreadful	pessimistic
miserable	tearful
dejected	weepy
disheartened	down in the dumps
rotten	deflated

awful

horrible

terrible

hopeless

gloomy

dismal

bleak

depressed

despondent

grieved

grim

brokenhearted

forlorn

distressed

downcast

blue

lost

melancholy

in the doldrums

lousy

kaput

unhappy

down

low

bad

blah

disappointed

sad

below par

clumsy

overwhelmed

ineffective

uncertain

weak

inefficient

Anxiety, Tension

terrified

frightened

intimidated

horrified

desperate

panicky

terror-stricken

paralyzed

frantic

stunned

shocked

threatened

afraid

scared

stage fright

dread

vulnerable

fearful

apprehensive

jumpy

shaky

alarmed

distrustful

butterflies

awkward

defensive

uptight

tied in knots

rattled

tense

restless

fidgety

jittery

on edge

nervous

anxious

unsure

hesitant

timid

shy

worried

uneasy

bashful

embarrassed

ill at ease

doubtful

uncomfortable

self-conscious

insecure

Inadequacy, Helplessness

utterly worthless

good for nothing

washed up

powerless

helpless

impotent

crippled

inferior

emasculated

useless

finished

like a failure

impaired

inadequate

whipped

defeated

stupid

incompetent

puny

inept

like a klutz

lacking

awkward

deficient

unable

incapable

small

insignificant

like a wimp

unfit

unimportant

over the hill

incomplete

immobilized

like a puppet

at the mercy of

inhibited

insecure

lacking confidence

unsure of self

Confusion, Troubledness

bewildered

puzzled

tormented by

baffled

perplexed

disconcerted

frustrated

floored

flustered

in a bind

overwhelmed

trapped

confounded

in a dilemma

befuddled

in a quandary

at loose ends

going around in
circles

mixed-up

disorganized

in a fog

troubled

adrift

lost

torn

ambivalent

disturbed

conflicted

stumped

feeling pulled apart

mixed feelings about

uncertain

unsure

bothered

uncomfortable

undecided

uneasy

discredited

disparaged

laughed at

maligned

mistreated

unappreciated

taken for granted

taken lightly

underestimated

Rejection, Offensiveness

crushed

destroyed

ruined

degraded

pained

wounded

devastated

tortured

cast off

betrayed

discarded

knifed in the back

discounted

hurt

belittled

shot down

abused

depreciated

criticized

censured

ridiculed

devalued

scorned

mocked

scoffed at

used

exploited

debased

slammed

slandered

impugned

cheapened

mistreated

put down

slighted

neglected

overlooked

minimized

let down

disappointed

Anger, Resentment

furious

enraged

livid

seething

could chew nails

infuriated

fighting mad

burned up

violent

hateful

bitter

galled

vengeful

resentful

indignant

irritated

hostile

pissed off

have hackles up

had it with

annoyed

upset with

bent out of shape

agitated

annoyed

got dander up

bristle

dismayed

uptight

disgusted

bugged

turned off

put out

miffed

ruffled

irked

perturbed

ticked off

teed off

chagrined

griped

cross

impatient

Loneliness

isolated

all alone in the
universe

abandoned

totally alone

forsaken

rejected

remote

alone

apart from others

shut out

cut off	left out
forlorn	excluded
lonely	lonesome
alienated	distant
estranged	aloof

Guilt, Embarrassment

sick at heart	lost face
unforgivable	demeaned
humiliated	foolish
disgraced	ridiculous
degraded	silly
horrible	stupid
mortified	egg on face
exposed	regretful
branded	wrong
could crawl in a hole	embarrassed
like two cents	at fault
ashamed	in error
guilty	responsible for
remorseful	blew it
crummy	goofed
really rotten	lament

Use of the Lists of Affective Words and Phrases

The lists of affective words and phrases may be used with the exercises at the end of the chapter to assist you in formulating responses that capture the nature of feelings expressed by clients. After you have initially responded to "feeling messages," check the lists to determine if there are other words and phrases that might more accurately capture the client's feelings. Also, scan the lists to see if the client's message involves feelings in addition to those you identified. The lists may similarly assist you in checking out the accu-

racy of your reflective responses as you review taped sessions.

We suggest you read the lists aloud several times to aid you in making the feeling words and phrases part of your working vocabulary. We further recommend that you memorize five or six words or phrases in each category to further your mastery of feeling language. Developing an alertness to affective words used in the communication media, in conversations with acquaintances, or in reading material and repeating them to yourself will also assist you in expanding your feeling vocabulary. You will increasingly employ words that you rarely, if ever, used before. As you broaden your vocabulary you will experience growing confidence in your ability to formulate feeling responses in sessions. A further benefit will be that your feeling responses will assist your clients to experience their emotions more keenly, thereby pinpointing some of the distress they are feeling.

Although the lists of affective words and phrases are not exhaustive, they encompass many of the feelings and emotions frequently encountered in the helping process. Feeling words are subsumed under 11 categories, running the gamut from emotions that express intense anguish and pain, such as *grieved, terrified, bewildered, enraged, powerless,* to such positive feeling states as *joy, elation, ecstasy, bliss,* and *pride in accomplishment.* Given the emphasis on clients' strengths in this book, care has been taken to include a grouping of terms to assist practitioners in capturing clients' feelings related to growth, strengths, and competence.

Feeling words in each category are roughly graduated by intensity, with words conveying strong intensity grouped toward the beginning of each category and words denoting moderate to mild intensity toward the end. In responding to client messages, the practitioner should choose feeling words that accurately match the intensity of the feelings the client is experiencing. To illustrate, picture a client who, seething with anger, describes an incident in which a man much larger than he crowded in front of him during a lengthy wait in line to purchase movie tickets: "I was so mad I could have killed him. But what do you do when the other guy's twice your size and looks like a gorilla?" Such a response appropriately calls for an intense response by the practitioner: "Sounds like you were so furious you'd like to have plowed him under. Still, you realized you might take an awful beating. It must have been humiliating—being pushed around and not being able to do anything about it." In addition to using words that accurately reflect the intensity of the client's feelings, it is important to respond with a tone of voice and nonverbal gestures and expressions that similarly reflect the intensity of feelings conveyed by the verbal response. Further, the proper intensity of affect may also be conveyed by using appropriate qualifying words. For example, "You feel (somewhat) (quite) (very) (extremely) discouraged by your low performance on the entrance test."

Clients' messages may also contain multiple feelings. Consider, for instance, the following client message: "I don't know what to do about my teenage daughter. I know that she's on drugs, but she shuts me out and won't talk to me. All she wants is to be out with her friends, to be left alone. There are times when I think she really dislikes me."

Feeling words that would capture the various facets of this message include: *confused, bewildered, alarmed, troubled, overwhelmed, lost, desperate, worried, frightened, alienated, rejected,* and *hurt.* A response that included all of these feeling words would be extremely lengthy and overwhelming to the client; however, a well-rounded empathic response should embody at least several of the surface feelings, such as *worried* and *confused,* and with appropriate timing, the practitioner might also bring deeper-level feelings in focus, as explained in the following paragraphs.

Notice in the preceding client message that many feelings were implied but not explicitly expressed by the client. Some of these emotions would likely be just beyond the client's level of awareness but could easily be recognized if they were drawn to the client's attention. For example, the client might emphatically confirm a practitioner response that sensitively identifies the hurt, rejection, and even anger inherent in the client's message. Yet without the practitioner's assistance, the client might not develop full awareness of those deeper-level feelings.

In responding to client messages, you must be able to distinguish between readily apparent feelings and probable deeper feelings. In the early phase of the helping process, the practitioner's objectives of developing a working relationship and creating a climate of understanding are best accomplished by using a reciprocal level of empathy—that is, focusing on the client's immediately evident feelings. As the client perceives your genuine effort and commitment to understand, that experience of being "empathically received" gradually creates a low-threat environment that obviates the need for self-protection. The resultant climate of trust sets the stage for self-exploration, a prerequisite to self-understanding, which in turn facilitates behavior change. This positive ambience prepares the way for the use of "additive" or "expanded" levels of empathy to reach for underlying feelings, as well as hidden meanings and goals of behavior. However, attempting to explore underlying feelings during the early phase of the helping process is counterproductive. Uncovering feelings beyond the client's awareness before a working relationship is firmly established tends to mobilize resistance and may precipitate premature termination.

Exercises in Identifying Surface and Underlying Feelings

In the following exercise, attempt to identify both the apparent surface feelings and the probable underlying feelings embodied in the client's message. Remember that most of the feelings in the messages are only implied, as clients often do not use feeling words. As you complete the exercise, read each message and write down the feelings involved. Then scan the lists of affective words and phrases to see if you can improve your response. After you have responded to all three messages, check the feeling words and phrases you identified with those given by the authors at the end of the chapter. If the feelings you identified were similar in meaning to those of the authors, consider your responses accurate. If they were not, review the client messages again to see if you can identify clues about the client's feelings that you overlooked.

Client Statements

1. **Elderly client:** I know my children are busy, but I haven't seen them for ages. They don't even bother to call.
Apparent feelings:
Probable deeper feelings:

2. **Client:** I don't know if my husband loves me or not. He says he cares, but he doesn't pay much attention to me, particularly when we're with other people. Sometimes he even seems ashamed of me.
Apparent feelings:
Probable deeper feelings:

3. **Client:** When I was a teenager, I thought that when I was married and had my own children, I would never yell at them like my mother yelled at me. Yet, here I am doing the same things with Sonny. (*Tearful.*)
Apparent feelings:
Probable deeper feelings:

Exercises at the end of this chapter for formulating reciprocal empathic responses will also assist you in increasing your perceptiveness to feelings. In subsequent chapters, particularly Chapter 19, other exercises are provided for identifying feelings and formulating responses.

Accurately Conveying Empathy

Empathic responding is a fundamental yet complex skill that requires systematic practice and extensive effort to achieve competency. Skill in empathic communication has no limit or ceiling; rather, this skill is always in the process of "becoming." In listening to their taped sessions, even highly skilled professionals discover feelings they overlooked. Many practitioners, however, do not fully utilize or selectively employ empathic responding, failing to grasp the versatility of this skill and its potency in influencing clients and fostering growth in moment-by-moment transactions.[1] In fact, some practitioners dismiss the need for training in empathic responding mistakenly believing themselves to be empathic in contacts with clients.

Research findings indicate that beginning social work students relate at empathic levels considerably lower than the levels necessary to work facilitatively with clients (Fischer, 1978; Larsen, 1975). These findings are not totally unexpected, for comparatively few people are inherently helpful in the sense of relating naturally with high levels of empathy or any of the other core conditions. Although people achieve varying degrees of empathy, respect, and genuineness through life experiences, to attain high levels of these skills appears to require rigorous training.

Research scales that operationalize empathy conditions have been developed and validated in extensive research studies (Truax & Carkhuff, 1967). These scales, which specify levels of empathy along a continuum ranging from high- to low-level skills, represented a major breakthrough not only in operationalizing essential practitioner skills but also in establishing a relationship between these skills and successful outcomes in therapy.

The empathic communication scale has been particularly helpful to social work educators in assessing pre- and post-levels of empathy of trainees in laboratory classes (Larsen & Hepworth, 1978; Wells, 1975). The scale has been further employed to assist students to distinguish between high- and low-level empathic responses and has been used by peers and instructors in group training to assess levels of students' responses. Students then receive guidance in reformulating low-level responses to bring them to higher levels.

The Carkhuff (1969) empathy scale, which consists of nine levels, has been widely used in training and research, and similar versions of this scale can be found in the literature. Although we have found nine-point scales valuable as training aids, they have proven somewhat confusing to students, who have difficulty in making the fine distinctions between levels. For this reason, we have adapted the nine-level scale described by Hammond, Hepworth & Smith (1977) by collapsing it to the five-level scale reproduced below.

On the following empathic communication scale, level 1 responses are generally made by practitioners who are preoccupied with their own rather than the client's frame of reference and as such completely fail to match the client's feelings. At this low level of responding, practitioners' responses are usually characterized by the ineffective communication styles identified in Chapter 7. Responses at level 2 convey an effort to understand but are partially inaccurate or incomplete. At level 3, the midpoint, practitioners' responses are essentially interchangeable in affect with the surface feelings and expressions of the client. This midpoint, widely referred to as "interchangeable" or "reciprocal" responding in the literature, is considered the "minimally facilitative level" at which an effective and viable process of helping can take place. Above the midpoint, the practitioner's responses add noticeably to the surface feelings and, at the highest level, add significantly to client expressions. At these higher levels of empathic responding, the practitioner accurately responds to clients' full range of feelings at their exact intensity and is "with" clients in their deepest moments. Level 4 and 5 empathic responses, which require the practitioner to infer underlying feelings, involve mild to moderate interpretations.

---

[1]The selective use of this skill to achieve specific therapeutic objectives is discussed briefly later in this chapter and in Chapter 19.

Empathic Communication Scale

Level 1: Low-Level Empathic Responding   At this level, the practitioner communicates little or no awareness or understanding of even the most conspicuous of the client's feelings; practitioners' responses are irrelevant and often abrasive, hindering rather than facilitating communication. Operating from a personal frame of reference, the practitioner changes the subject, argues, gives advice prematurely, lectures, or uses other ineffective styles that block communication, often diverting clients from their problems and fragmenting the helping process. Furthermore, the practitioner's nonverbal responses are not appropriate to the mood and content of the client's statement.

When practitioners relate at this low level, clients often become confused or defensive, reacting by discussing superficialities, arguing, disagreeing, changing the subject, or withdrawing into silence. Thus, the client's energies are diverted from exploration and/or work on problems.

Level 2: Moderately Low-Level Empathic Responding   The practitioner responds to the surface message of the client but erroneously omits feelings or factual aspects of the message. At this level, the practitioner may also inappropriately qualify feelings (e.g., "somewhat," "a little bit," "kind of") or may inaccurately interpret feelings (e.g., "angry" for "hurt," "tense" for "scared"). Responses may also emanate from the practitioner's own conceptual formulations, which may be diagnostically accurate but not empathically attuned to the client's expressions. Although level 2 responses are only partially accurate, they do convey an effort to understand and, for this reason, do not completely block the client's communication or work on problems.

Level 3: Interchangeable or Reciprocal Level of Empathic Responding   Practitioner's verbal and nonverbal responses at this level convey understanding and are essentially interchangeable with the obvious expressions of the client, accurately reflecting factual aspects of the client's messages and surface feelings or state of being. Reciprocal responses do not appreciably add affect or reach beyond the surface feelings, nor do they subtract from the feeling and tone expressed. Factual content of the client's message, though desirable, is not required; if included, this aspect of the message must be accurate. Level 3 responses facilitate further exploratory and problem-focused responses by the client. The beginner does well in achieving skill in reciprocal empathic responding, which is an effective working level.

Level 4: Moderately High-Level Empathic Responding   Responses at this level are somewhat additive, accurately identifying implicit underlying feelings and/or aspects of the problem. The practitioner's response illuminates subtle or veiled facets of the client's message, enabling the client to get in touch with somewhat deeper-level feelings and unexplored meanings and purposes of behavior. Level 4 responses thus are aimed at enhancing self-awareness.

Level 5: High-Level Empathic Responding   Reflecting each emotional nuance, and using voice and intensity of expressions finely attuned to the client's moment-by-moment experiencing, the practitioner accurately responds to the full range and intensity of both surface and underlying feelings and meanings. The practitioner may connect current feelings and experiencing to previously expressed experiences or feelings, or may accurately identify implicit patterns, themes, or purposes. Responses may also identify implicit goals embodied in the client's message, which point the direction for personal growth and pave the way for action.

Responding empathically at this high level facilitates the client's exploration of feelings and problems in much greater breadth and depth than at lower levels.

Examples of Levels of Empathic Responding

Client Statement (Teenage Girl to School Social Worker) "I didn't get invited to the dance. I don't know what's wrong with me. I try hard to be friendly, but the boys just don't pay much attention. Maybe I'm just plain ugly."

Level 1 Responses "You'll just have to be patient. The next dance is girls' choice, and you can be sure of going to that one."(Giving advice.)

"But let's think for a moment about all of the dances you have been invited to this year. You're blowing this way out of proportion." (Persuading with logical argument; negatively evaluating client's actions.)

"Oh, by the way, have you seen the decorations for the dance? I'm really impressed with them." (Changing the subject.)

"Don't you think there's still time for you to get asked to the dance?" (Leading question, untimely reassurance.)

"Why, that's ridiculous. You have a lot of attractive qualities. You just have to wait for the right guy to come along." (Reassuring, consoling, giving advice.)

The preceding examples illustrate various ineffective styles of communication used at this low level. Notice that messages reflect the practitioner's own formulations concerning the client's problem, rather than capture the client's inner experiencing. Such responses stymie clients, blocking their flow of thought and producing negative feelings toward the practitioner.

Level 2 Responses "I can see you're upset."

The word *upset* only vaguely defines the client's feelings, whereas feeling words such as *left out, rejected, disappointed, hurt,* or *inadequate* more accurately reflect the inner experiencing of the client.

"You feel left out because you haven't been invited to the dance, but perhaps you care too much about going. There will be other dances."

In this case, the listener begins to accurately capture the client's feelings but then moves to an evaluative interpretation ("you care too much") and inappropriate reassurance.

"You didn't get invited to the dance?"

This response focuses on external, factual circumstances to the exclusion of the client's feelings or perceptions regarding the event in question.

"You didn't get invited to the dance and you wonder what is wrong with you. You think perhaps it is because you may be ugly."

This stilted response merely parrots the client's statement.

"You feel like going to the dance."

This response contains no reference to the client's immediately apparent feelings. Beginning practitioners often use the lead-in phrase "You feel like . . . ," without noticing that, in employing it, they have not captured the client's feelings.

"You're disappointed that you haven't been asked to go to the dance?"

This response, although partially accurate, fails to capture the client's worry about her attractiveness, which is an important surface feeling in the message.

"I can see you're hurt that you haven't been asked to the dance, but I think it's probably because boys at your age are still shy about asking girls to dances."

Although the message has a strong beginning, the empathic nature of the response is negated by the listener's explanation of the reason for the client's difficulties. This response represents a form of sidetaking, that is, justifying the actions of other persons involved in the client's problems.

The preceding responses illustrate many of the common errors made by practitioners in responding empathically to client messages. Although some part of the messages may be accurate or helpful, notice that all the responses in some way ignore or subtract from the client's experiencing.

Level 3 Responses   "You're really disappointed over not being asked to the dance and wondering if it's because the boys find you unattractive."

"I can tell you feel very let down and are asking yourself, 'Is there something wrong with me?' "

Essentially interchangeable, these responses express accurately the immediately apparent emotions in the client's message. The content of the responses is also accurate, but deeper feelings and meanings are not added. The second also illustrates a technique for conveying empathy that involves changing the reflection from the third to the first person, and speaking as if the practitioner were the client.

Level 4 Responses   "I gather you're feeling really hurt and left out, perhaps even rejected, in not getting asked to the dance. You wonder if it is because something is wrong with you."

This response conveys not only immediately apparent feelings and content, but also is noticeably additive in reflecting the client's deeper feelings of hurt and rejection.

Level 5 Responses   "Not getting asked to the dance has been a keen disappointment to you. I'm sensing that you're unsure of yourself and fearing the worst—maybe thinking, 'I just don't have it; fellows just aren't going to get interested in me.' It's important to you to be accepted by boys, and you want to understand what's wrong."

Significantly additive, this response goes well beyond the surface feelings in reflecting the keen disappointment of the client and her underlying fear that she may not be adequate. In addition, the latter part of the response includes an action or goal statement that paves the way for further exploration of the problem.

Exercises to Discriminate Levels of Empathic Responding

The following exercises in rating varied responses for their level of empathy are designed to assist you in refining your ability to determine the helpfulness of responses. These exercises will prepare you for subsequent practice in formulating empathic messages. Three client statements are given, followed by a number of possible responses. Using the empathic scale, rate each response. Rating messages will be less difficult if, using the list of affective words and phrases, you first identify the feelings contained in the client's message. After you have rated each response, compare your rating with those of the authors at the end of the chapter. Referring to the rating scale, analyze the responses you rated inaccurately, trying to pinpoint the reason for the authors' ratings.

Client Statements

1. **Female public assistance recipient, age 80** [*to social worker concerning her request to move to a special apartment complex provided for ambulatory elderly persons*]: Goodness, the more I think of moving, the more scared I get. I have neighbors here who look after me, and I won't know a soul there. I'm afraid I'll be all alone.

Level   Responses:

____   1. "It's pretty scary to you, leaving your neighbors and familiar surroundings. But there will be a lot of friendly people there and things to do. Besides, they fix one hot meal for you every day."

____   2. "Don't worry, you'll make friends in no time, and you'll wish you'd moved sooner."

____   3. "Did you sign those application papers I left with you a few days ago?"

____   4. "Just thinking about moving worries you because you'll be leaving your own neighborhood and friends. Even though your life would be much easier, you're unsure you'll be better off in other ways."

____   5. "So I gather in some ways you'd rather stay right where you are rather than gamble on a change."

____   6. "Lots of other people in the new apartments were just as scared as you before they moved, but I don't know a single one who's sorry now."

____   7. "It sounds as though you have some pretty mixed feelings about moving. Part of you wants to go because you could live more comfortably, but another part of you is afraid you'll feel alone and lost and wants to cling to people you know care about you."

____   8. "Are you saying we just ought to forget the whole thing?"

2. **Male, age 16** [*in weekly visit to social work probation officer*]: I don't see the sense in having to come here every lousy week. I haven't been in a jam now since I went to court a month ago. You should know by now you can trust me.

Level   Responses:

____   1. "A month isn't very long, you know. And how can I be sure you're staying out of trouble?"

____   2. "I gather you resent having to see me. I can understand that, but the judge ordered it and you'd be in a jam with him if you didn't meet the conditions of your probation."

____   3. "Has it been a month since you went to court? I didn't think that it had been that long."

____   4. "You'd prefer not coming here and feel you've earned my trust."

____   5. "Having to come here each week gripes you, and I gather you're feeling some irritation with me for insisting you follow the judge's order."

____   6. "Look, you got yourself into this predicament so don't complain to me if you don't like it. Maybe you'd like to talk the judge into changing his mind."

_____ 7. "It's pretty irritating to you to have to come here each week. You'd like me to get off your back."

_____ 8. "You're confused about why you have to come here and wish you didn't have to."

3. **Group member** [*in hesitant, quiet voice*]: It's really hard for me to say what I want to say in this group. When I do start to talk, I get tongue-tied, and my heart starts beating faster and faster. I think it has partly to do with feeling that some of you are critical of me.

Level   Responses by group members or group leader:

_____ 1. "Yeah, I feel that same way sometimes, too."

_____ 2. "It is frightening to you to try to share your feelings with the group. Sounds like you find yourself at a loss for words and wonder what others are thinking of you."

_____ 3. "I know you're timid, but I think it's important that you make more of an effort to talk in the group, just like you're doing now. It's actually one of the responsibilities of a group member."

_____ 4. "You get scared when you try to talk in the group."

_____ 5. "I sense that you're probably feeling pretty tense and tied up inside right now as you talk about the fear you've had in expressing yourself. Although you've been frightened of exposing yourself, I gather there's a part of you that wants to overcome that fear and become more actively involved with the rest of the group."

_____ 6. "What makes you think we're critical of you? You come across as a bit self-conscious, but that's no big deal."

_____ 7. "You remind me of the way I felt the first time I was in a group. I was so scared, I just looked at the floor most of the time."

_____ 8. "I wonder if we've done anything that came across as being critical of you."

Developing Skill in Responding with Reciprocal Empathy

Reciprocal or interchangeable empathic responding (level 3) is a basic skill used throughout the helping process to acknowledge client messages and to encourage exploration of problems. In the initial phase, empathic responding serves the vital purpose in individual, conjoint, and group sessions of facilitating the development of a working relationship and fostering the climate of understanding necessary to communication and self-disclosure, thereby setting the stage for deeper exploration of feelings during subsequent phases. Additive empathic responses, that is, those rated as a 4 or 5 on the empathic scale, exceed the level of feelings and meanings expressed by clients and are thus reserved, in large part, for the later phases of the helping process.

Since reciprocal responding is an essential skill used frequently to meet objectives of the first phase of the helping process, we recommend you first seek beginning mastery of responding at level 3; extended practice of this skill should significantly increase your effectiveness in establishing viable helping relationships, interviewing, and gathering data. In the remainder of this chapter, we provide guidelines and practice exercises that will help you in mastering reciprocal responding. Although responding at additive levels is an extension of the skill of reciprocal responding, the former is an advanced skill that can be used in varied ways to achieve specific therapeutic objectives and, for this reason, has been grouped with other change-oriented or "action" skills presented in Part 3 of the book.

Constructing Reciprocal Responses

To reach level 3 on the empathic scale, you must be able to formulate responses that accurately capture the content and the surface feelings in the client message. It is also important to frame the message so that you do not merely parrot or restate the client's message. The following paradigm, which identifies the various elements of an empathic or reflective message, has proven useful for conceptualizing and mastering the skill of empathic responding:

	about or
You feel _____	because _____
(Accurately identifies feelings of client)	(Accurately describes situation or event referred to by client.)

As shown, the response focuses exclusively on the *client's* message and does not reflect the practitioner's conceptualizations. The following excerpt from a session involving a practitioner and a 17-year-old female illustrates the use of the preceding paradigm in constructing an empathic response:

CLIENT: I can't talk to my father without feeling scared and crying. I'd like to be able to express myself and to disagree with him, but I just can't.

PRACTITIONER: Sounds as though you just feel panicky when you try to talk to your father. I gather you're discouraged because you'd like to feel comfortable with your dad and able to talk openly with him without falling apart.

Many times client messages contain conflicting or contrasting emotions, such as the following: "I like taking drugs, but sometimes I worry about what they might do to me."

In such cases, each contrasting feeling should be highlighted: You feel _____, yet you also feel _____. For example: "I sense that you feel torn because while you find taking drugs enjoyable, you have nagging thoughts that they might be harmful to you."

Remember that in order to respond empathically at a reciprocal level, you must use language clients will readily understand. Abstract, intellectualized language, sophisticated terminology, and professional jargon are barriers to communication that should be avoided. It is also important to vary the language you use in responding. Many professionals tend to respond with stereotyped, repetitive speech patterns, commonly using a limited variety of communication leads to begin their empathic responses. Such leads as "you feel . . ." and "I hear you saying . . ." repeated over and over not only are distracting to the client but also seem phony, unnatural, and contrived. Such stereotyped responding draws more attention to technique than to message.

The list of varied introductory phrases will help you expand your repertoire of possible responses. We encourage you to read the list aloud several times and to review the list frequently while practicing the empathic communication training exercises in this chapter and in Chapter 19 on additive empathic responding. The reciprocal empathic response format ("You feel _____ because _____") is merely a training aid to assist you in focusing on the affect and content of client messages. The leads list will help you respond more naturally.

Leads for Empathic Responses

Could it be that you're feeling . . .

I wonder if . . .

I'm not sure if I'm with you but . . .

What I guess I'm hearing is . . .

Correct me if I'm wrong, but I'm sensing . . .

You appear to be feeling . . .

It appears you feel . . .

Perhaps you're feeling . . .

Maybe you feel . . .

Sometimes you think . . .

Do you feel . . .

Maybe this is a long shot, but . . .

I'm not sure that I'm with you; do you mean . . .

I'm not certain I understand; you're feeling . . .

It seems that you . . .

As I hear it, you . . .

Is that what you mean?

If I'm hearing you correctly . . .

To me it's almost like you are saying . . .

So, you're feeling . . .

So, as you see it . . .

You feel . . .

I'm picking up that you . . .

It sounds as though you are saying . . .

I wonder if you're saying . . .

I hear you saying . . .

So, it seems to you . . .

So, from where you sit . . .

Sometimes you think . . .

Right now you're feeling . . .

I sense that you're feeling . . .

You must have felt . . .

Your message seems to be, "I _____"

Listening to you, it seems as if . . .

I gather you're feeling . . .

Is that the way you feel?

What I think I'm hearing is . . .

Let me see if I'm with you; you . . .

I get the impression that . . .

The message I'm getting is that . . .

As I get it, you felt that . . .

You convey a sense of . . .

If I'm catching what you say . . .

As I think about what you say, it occurs to me you're feeling . . .

What you're saying comes across to me as . . .

From what you say, I gather you're feeling . . .

Exercises designed to help you to respond to clients with level 3 reciprocal empathic responses are found at the end of the chapter. Contained in the exercises are a variety of client statements taken from actual work with individuals, groups, couples, and families in diverse settings.

In addition to completing the skill development exercises, we also recommend that you keep a record of the number of empathic responses you employ in sessions over several weeks to determine the extent to which you are applying this skill. We also suggest that either you or a knowledgeable associate rate your responses and determine the mean level of empathic responding for each session. If you find (as most beginning practitioners do) that you are underutilizing empathic responses or responding at low levels, you may wish to set a goal to improve your skill.

Employing Empathic Responding

In early sessions, empathic responding should be used frequently as a method of developing rapport and "staying in touch" with the client. Responses should be couched in a tentative manner to allow for inaccuracies in the practitioner's perception. Further, checking out the accuracy of responses with appropriate lead-in phrases, such as "Let me see if I understand . . ." or

"Did I hear you right?" is helpful in communicating a desire to understand and a willingness to correct misperceptions.

In initially using empathic responses, learners are often leery of the flood of emotions that sometimes occurs as the client, experiencing none of the usual barriers to communication, releases a Niagara of feelings often pent up for months or years. It is important to understand that empathic responses have not "caused" such feelings but rather have facilitated their expression, thus clearing the way for the client to explore and to consider such feelings more rationally and objectively.

You may worry, as do many beginning practitioners, about whether you will "damage" the client or the helping relationship if your empathic responses do not always accurately reflect the client's feelings. Perhaps even more important than accuracy, however, is the "commitment" to understand conveyed by genuine efforts to perceive the client's world of experience. If you consistently demonstrate your goodwill, caring, and intent to help through attentive verbal and nonverbal responding, occasional lack of understanding or faulty timing will not damage the relationship. In fact, efforts to clarify the client's message will usually enhance rather than detract from the helping process, particularly if you respond to corrective feedback in an open, nondefensive, and empathic manner.

Multiple Uses of Empathic Communication

Earlier in the chapter, we referred to the versatility of empathic communication. In this section, we delineate a number of ways in which you can employ reciprocal empathic responding.

1. Establishing Relationships with Clients in Initial Sessions As discussed previously, the use of empathic responding actively demonstrates the practitioner's keen awareness of clients' feelings and creates an atmosphere wherein the latter will risk and explore personal thoughts and feelings. Numerous researchers have established that when practitioners relate empathically, clients are more likely to continue in treatment than when little empathy is conveyed.

Over a span of many years, a plethora of publications have emphasized the critical nature of empathic communication to successful work with virtually every type of client. Recently, for example, Miller (1983) has stressed the vital nature of empathy in work with problem drinkers, and Zingale (1985) has focused on the importance of empathy with a broad spectrum of clients.

Research studies (e.g., Banks, Berenson, & Carkhuff, 1967; Cimbolic, 1972; Santa Cruz & Hepworth, 1975) also indicate that empathic communication, along with respect and genuineness, facilitate the development of effective working relationships when practitioners and client are from different ethnic or cultural backgrounds. These findings are particularly meaningful in view of the fact that social workers typically work with diverse populations that include ethnic minorities and clients from low socioeconomic backgrounds. To employ empathy with maximal effectiveness in transcultural relationships, practitioners must be aware of and sensitive to cultural factors.

The importance of knowledge of cultural factors was perhaps first documented by the research findings of Mayer and Timms (1969), who studied clashes of perspectives between clients and social workers. Based on their findings they concluded: "It seems that social workers start where the client is psychodynamically but they are insufficiently empathic in regard to cultural components" (p. 38).

Although empathic communication is important in bridging cultural gaps, it can be used to excess with Asian-Americans and American Indians. Both of these groups tend to be lower in emotional expressiveness than other client groups and may react with discomfort and confusion if a practitioner relies heavily on empathic communication. Still, it is important to "read between the lines" and to sensitively respond to troubling emotions that these clients do not usually express directly. Like other clients, they are likely to appreciate sensitive awareness by a practitioner to painful emotions associated with their difficulties.

We again emphasize the importance of assuming a more directive, active, and structured stance with Asian-Americans. As Tsui and Schultz (1985) have clarified, "A purely empathetic, passive, nondirective approach serves only to confuse and alienate the [Asian] client" (p. 568). The same can be said of the American Indian client.

2. Staying in Touch with Clients Reciprocal empathic responding operationalizes the social work principle of "starting where the client is" and keeps practitioners attuned to clients' current feelings. Although employing many other skills and techniques, the practitioner utilizes and returns to empathic responding to keep in touch with the client. In that sense, empathic communication is a fundamental intervention prerequisite to the use of other interventions. Writing to this point, Gendlin (1974) uses the analogy of driving a car to refer to the vital role of empathy in keeping in touch with clients. Driving involves much more than watching the road. A driver does many things, including steering, operating the brakes, signal-

ing, and watching signs. One may glance at the scenery, visit with others, and think private thoughts, but watching the road must be accorded highest priority. When visibility becomes limited or hazards appear, all other activities must cease and one must attend exclusively to observing the road and conditions that may pose hazards. Just as some drivers fail to maintain proper lookout and become involved in accidents, some practitioners also fail to attend sufficiently to changes in clients' moods and reactions, mistakenly assuming they know their frame of mind. As a consequence, practitioners may fail to discern important feelings of clients, who may perceive them as disinterested or insensitive and subsequently disengage from the helping process.

3. Accurately Assessing Client Problems Extensive evidence indicates that the levels of empathy offered by practitioners correlate with levels of self-exploration by clients. High-level empathic responding thus increases clients' exploration of self and problems. As the practitioner moves "with" clients by frequently using empathic responses in initial sessions, clients begin to unfold their problems and to reveal events and relevant data. Figuratively speaking, clients then take practitioners where they need to go by providing information crucial to making an accurate assessment. Such an approach contrasts sharply with sessions in which history-taking is emphasized and where practitioners, following their own agendas rather than the clients', spend unnecessary time asking hit-or-miss questions and gathering information often extraneous to the problem.

4. Responding to the Nonverbal Messages of Clients Clients often convey through their facial features, gestures, and body postures feelings they do not express verbally. In the course of a session, for instance, a client may become pensive, or show puzzlement, pain, or discomfort. In such instances, the practitioner may convey understanding of the client's feeling state and verbalize the feeling explicitly through a reflective response that attends to the emotion suggested in the client's nonverbal expressions. For instance, in response to a client who has been sitting dejectedly with her head down for several minutes after having reported some bad grades, a practitioner might say: "At this moment you seem to be feeling very sad and discouraged, perhaps even defeated." Further, in group or conjoint sessions, the practitioner might reflect the nonverbal messages of several, or all, of the members—for example: "I sense some restlessness today, and we're having a hard time staying on our topic. I'm wondering if you're saying, 'We're not sure we want to deal with this problem today.' Am I reading the group correctly?" Empathic responses that accurately tune into clients' nonverbal experiencing will usually prompt clients to begin exploring feelings they have been experiencing. Making explicit the nonverbal messages of clients is an important skill discussed in several chapters in the book.

5. Making Confrontations More Palatable

Confrontation is employed in the change-oriented phase to expand clients' awareness and to motivate them to action. However, even well-timed confrontations may be met with varying degrees of receptivity. Concern as well as prudence dictate that the practitioner determine the impact of confrontations upon clients and implement a process of making these interventions more palatable. This may be accomplished by employing empathic responses attuned to client reactions im-

mediately following confrontations. As practitioners listen attentively and sensitively to client expressions, defensiveness abates, and clients often begin to engage in processing new information and thinking through and testing the validity of ideas, embracing those that fit and rejecting others that seem inapplicable. Blending confrontation and empathic responses is a particularly potent technique for managing group processes when the practitioner must deal with a controversial issue or distractive behavior that is interfering with the work of the group.

6. Handling Obstacles Presented by Clients

Client resistance to what is happening in a session is sometimes healthy. What is often interpreted as unconscious resistance may be a negative reaction to poor interviewing and intervention techniques or to client confusion, misunderstanding, or even inertia. It is thus important to carefully monitor client reactions and to deal directly and sensitively with their related feelings. Instances frequently occur in sessions in which clients' verbal or nonverbal actions indirectly comment on what is occurring in the helping process. For instance, the client may look at her watch and ask how long the session is going to take, shift body position away from the practitioner, begin tapping a foot, or stare out the window. In such cases, when it appears the client is disengaging from the session, an empathic response that reflects the client's verbal and/or nonverbal message may be used effectively to initiate discussion of what is occurring. Shifting to what is happening in the here-and-now is an important skill that we further elaborate in later chapters.

Practitioners are also often confronted with excessively verbal clients who talk rapidly and move quickly from one topic to another. Overly verbal clients present a particular challenge to beginning practitioners, who must often overcome the misconception that interrupting clients is rude. Because of this misconception, novice interviewers sometimes spend most of an initial session listening passively to verbal clients without providing any form or direction to the helping process. Further, beginning practitioners may also allow clients to talk incessantly because they mistakenly view this as constructive work on problems. Quite the contrary, verbosity often keeps the session on a superficial level and interferes with problem identification and exploration.

It is important that practitioners take charge of sessions by providing structure and direction, thereby conveying an expectation that specific topics will be considered in depth. Much more will be said about this in later chapters. However, for the present, it is important to underscore the necessity of using empathic responses with verbal clients as a preliminary effort to slow the process and to provide some depth to the discussion. For example, a practitioner might interject or intervene with: "I'd like to interrupt to check if I'm understanding what you mean. As I get it, you're feeling . . . ," or "Before you get into talking about that, I would like to make sure I'm with you. You seem to be saying . . . " or "Could we hold off discussing that for just a minute? I'd like to be sure I understand what you mean. Would you expand on the point you were just making?"

7. Managing Anger and Patterns of Violence
During individual or group sessions, clients often experience surges of intense and conflicting feelings, such as anger, hurt, or disappointment. In such instances, empathic responding is a key tool for assisting them to work through those feelings. As empathic responses facilitate expanded expression of these feelings, clients engage in a process of ventilating, thinking through, clarifying, relinquishing, and experiencing different feelings, gradually achieving a mellowing of emotions and a more rational and thoughtful state of being. Employed to focus sharply on clients' feelings, empathic responding thus efficiently manages and modifies strong emotions that represent obstacles to progress. As the practitioner successfully handles such moments and clients experience increased self-awareness and cathartic benefits, the helping relationship is strengthened.

Empathic responding is particularly helpful in dealing with hostile clients and is indispensable when clients are angry with the practitioner, as illustrated in the following example: "What you're doing to help me with my problems doesn't seem to be doing me any good. I don't know why I keep coming."

At such moments, the practitioner must resist the temptation to react defensively, for such responses further antagonize the client and exacerbate the situation. Responding by challenging the client's perception, for instance, would be destructive to the helping relationship. The purpose of the practitioner's responses should be to *understand* the client's experiencing and feelings and to engage the client in fully exploring those feelings. Keeping this in mind, consider the impact of the following reciprocal empathic response: "You're very disappointed that things aren't better, and are irritated with me, feeling that I should have been more helpful to you."

This response accurately and nondefensively acknowledges the client's frustration with the situation and with the practitioner. By itself, the preceding response would not be sufficient to mellow the client's ire and to free the client to consider the problem more fully and rationally. Carefully following feelings and remaining sensitively attuned to the client's experiencing by employing empathic responses for several minutes usually assists both the practitioner and client to understand more clearly the strong feelings that prompted the client's message and to adequately assess the source of those feelings.

When faced with angry clients in group and conjoint sessions, it is critical that the practitioner empathically reflect not only the negative feelings and positions of the clients who are manifesting the anger but also reach for and reflect the feelings or observations of members who may be experiencing the situation differently. Utilizing empathic responses in this manner assists the practitioner to gather information that will elucidate the problem, to help angry members air and examine their feelings, and to put other points of view before the group for consideration. Further, employing empathic responding at such moments also encourages a more rational discussion of issues involved in the problem and thus sets the stage for possible problem solving.

The principles just discussed also apply to clients who are prone to violent behavior. Such clients often come to the attention of social workers because they have abused their children and/or spouses. People who engage in violence often do so because of underlying feelings of helplessness and frustration and because of deficiencies in coping with troubling situations in more constructive ways. Some have short fuses and weak emotional controls, often coming from backgrounds in which they vicariously learned violence as a mechanism of coping. Using empathy to defuse their intense anger and to tune in to their frustrations is an important first step in work with such clients. In this regard, Lane (1986) has written an informative article. Assisting clients to control anger, of course, involves use of other interventions, some of which we discuss in Chapters 15 and 18.

8. *Utilizing Empathic Responses to Facilitate Group Discussions* Practitioners may facilitate discussion of specific issues in conjoint or group sessions by first identifying a desired topic and then utilizing empathic (or paraphrasing) responses to reflect the observations of various group members in relation to that topic. The practitioner may also reach for responses from members who have not contributed and then employ empathic responses (or paraphrases) to acknowledge their observations. Utilized frequently in this manner, empathic responding encourages (and reinforces) clients' participation in group discussions.

Teaching Clients to Respond Empathically

Clients often have difficulties in relationships because their styles of communication include many barriers that prevent them from accurately hearing messages or conveying understanding to others. An important task of the practitioner thus involves teaching clients to respond empathically, a task accomplished in part by modeling, which is generally recognized as a potent technique for promoting client change and growth. People who manifest problems associated with distorting or ignoring messages of others (as frequently occurs in marital, family, and other close relationships) vicariously benefit by observing the practitioner listen effectively and respond empathically. Moreover, clients who are hard to reach or who have difficulties in expressing themselves gradually learn to recognize their own emotions and to express themselves more fully as a result of the practitioner's empathic responding.

Practitioners' roles as educators require them to intervene actively at opportune moments to enable clients to respond empathically, particularly when they have ignored, discounted, or attacked the contributions of others in a session. With respect to this role, we suggest that practitioners consider taking the following actions:

1. Teach clients the paradigm for empathic responding introduced in the chapter. If appropriate, ask them to engage briefly in a paired practice exercise similar to the one recommended for beginning practitioners at the end of the chapter. Utilizing topics neutral to the relationship, have each person in turn carefully listen to the other for several minutes, and afterwards evaluate with participants the impact of the exercise on them.

2. Introduce clients to the list of affective words and phrases and to the leads list contained in this chapter. If appropriate, you may wish to have clients assume tasks during the week to broaden their feeling vocabulary similar to those recommended for beginning practitioners.

3. Intervene in sessions when clients ignore or fail to validate messages, a situation that occurs frequently in work with couples, families, and groups. At those moments, facilitatively interrupt the process to ask the sender to repeat the message and the receiver to paraphrase or capture the essence of the former's message with fresh words, as illustrated in the following example:

16-YEAR-OLD DAUGHTER: I don't like going to school. The teachers are a bunch of jerks, and most of the kids just laugh and make fun of me.

MOTHER: But you've got to go. If you'd just buckle down and study, school wouldn't be half so hard for you. I think . . .

PRACTITIONER: [*Interrupting and speaking to mother.*] I can see that you have some real concerns about Janet's not going to school, but for a moment, I'm going to ask you to get in touch with what she just said to you by repeating it back to her.

MOTHER: [*Looking at practitioner.*] She said she doesn't like school.

PRACTITIONER: That's close, but turn and talk to Janet. See if you can identify what she's *feeling*.

MOTHER: [*Turning to daughter.*] I guess it's pretty painful for you to go to school when you don't like your teachers and you feel shut out and ridiculed by the kids.

JANET: [*Tearfully.*] Yeah, that's it . . . it's really hard.

Notice that the mother did not respond empathically to her daughter's feelings until the practitioner intervened and coached her. This example thus illustrates the importance of persevering in teaching clients to "hear" the messages of others, a point we cannot overemphasize. Clients often have considerable trouble mastering listening skills because habitual dysfunctional responses are difficult to discard. This is true even when clients are highly motivated to communicate more effectively and when practitioners actively intervene to assist them.

4. Give positive feedback when you observe clients listening to each other or, as in the preceding example, when they

respond to your coaching. In the example cited, for instance, the practitioner might have responded to the mother as follows: "I liked the way you responded because your message accurately reflected what your daughter was experiencing. I think she felt you really understood what she was trying to say." It is also helpful to ask participants to discuss what they experienced during the exchange and to highlight positive feelings and observations.

Authenticity

Although theoreticians generally agree that empathy and respect are vital to developing effective working relationships, they do not agree about the amount of openness or self-disclosure practitioners should offer. Theorists who espouse traditional psychoanalytically oriented theory have advocated that practitioners should relate to clients in a professionally detached manner, although one psychoanalyst, Bernstein (1972), contends that psychoanalysts have gone to an undesirable extreme in emotionally detaching themselves from their patients. He adds "... if an analyst is a healthy, mature, gentle human being, his human response to the expression of a need for help ... is a feeling of compassion" (p. 163). The findings of a study by Grunebaum (1986) further indicate that emotional detachment by practitioners can actually be harmful to clients. In a study of 47 patients who believed they had been harmed by psychotherapy, 18 attributed the harm to coldness, distance, and rigidity by the therapist. It is noteworthy that the patients in this study were all mental

health professionals who had sought psychotherapy for themselves.

Taking an opposing position to the traditional view, humanistic writers maintain that practitioners should relate openly and authentically as "real" persons. These writers argue that relating in a prescribed "professional" role presents clients with a sterile, contrived relationship that fails to model openness and authenticity, inhibits clients' growth, and fails to provide clients with an experience in relating that is transferable to the real world.

With respect to empirical evidence, numerous research studies cited by Truax and Mitchell (1971) and Gurman (1977) indicated that empathy, respect, and genuineness were correlated with positive outcomes. Critical analyses of these studies and conflicting findings from other research studies have led experts to question these earlier findings and to conclude that "a more complex association exists between outcome and therapist 'skills' than originally hypothesized" (Parloff, Waskow, & Wolfe, 1978, p. 251). However, authenticity or genuineness and the other facilitative conditions are still viewed as central to the helping process.

Authenticity is defined as the sharing of self by relating in a natural, sincere, spontaneous, open, and genuine manner. Being authentic, or genuine, involves relating personally so that expressions are spontaneous rather than contrived. Practitioners' verbalizations are also congruent with their actual feelings and thoughts. Authentic practitioners thus relate as real persons, expressing their feelings and assuming responsibility for them rather than denying the feelings or blaming the client for causing them. Authenticity also involves being nondefensive and human enough to admit errors to clients. Realizing that they expect clients to lower their defenses and to relate openly (thereby increasing their vulnerability), practitioners themselves must model humanness and openness and avoid hiding behind a mask of "professionalism."

Relating authentically does not mean that practitioners indiscriminately disclose feelings. Indeed, authentic expressions can be abrasive and destructive. Yalom and Lieberman (1971), for example, found in a study of encounter groups that attacks or rejections of group members by leaders or other members produce many psychological casualties. Practitioners should thus relate authentically only when doing so is likely to further therapeutic objectives. This qualification provides considerable latitude and is only intended to, constrain practitioners from (1) relating abrasively (even though the practitioner may be expressing genuine feelings) and (2) meeting their own needs by focusing on personal experiences and feelings rather than those of the client.

With respect to the first constraint, practitioners must avoid misconstruing authenticity as granting free license to do whatever they wish, especially with respect to expressing hostility. The second constraint reiterates the importance of practitioners' responding to clients' needs rather than their own. Moreover, when practitioners share their feelings or experiences for a therapeutic purpose, they should immediately shift the focus back on the clients. Keep in mind that the purpose of relating authentically, whether with individuals, families, or groups, is to facilitate growth of clients, not to demonstrate one's own honesty or authenticity.

Types of Self-Disclosure

The aspect of authenticity denoted as self-disclosure has been variously defined by different authors (Chelune, 1979). For this discussion we define it as the conscious and intentional revelation of information about oneself through both verbal expressions and nonverbal behaviors (e.g., smiling, grimacing, or shaking one's head in disbelief). Viewed from a therapeutic perspective, self-disclosure encourages clients to reciprocate with trust and openness. In fact, numerous studies (Doster & Nesbitt, 1979) document that client self-disclosure is correlated with practitioner self-disclosure.

Danish, D'Augelli, and Hauer (1980) have identified two types of self-disclosure, *self-involving statements* and *personal self-disclosing*. The former type includes messages that express the practitioner's personal reaction to the client during the course of a session. Examples of this type would be:

"I'm impressed with the progress you've made this past week. You applied what we discussed last week and have made another step toward learning to control angry feelings."

"I want to share my reaction to what you just said. I found myself feeling sad for you because you put yourself down unmercifully. I see you so differently from how you see yourself and find myself wishing I could somehow spare you the torment you inflict on yourself."

"You know, as I think about the losses you've experienced this past year, I marvel you've done as well as you have. I'm not at all sure I'd have held together as well as you have."

Personal self-disclosing messages, by contrast, center on struggles or problems the practitioner is currently experiencing or has experienced that are similar to the client's problems. The following are examples of this type of self-disclosure:

(*To couple*) "As you talk about your problems with your children, it reminds me of similar difficulties I had with mine when they were that some age" (goes on to relate his experience).

(*To individual client*) "I think all of us struggle with that same fear to some degree. Earlier this week I . . ." (goes on to relate events in which she experienced similar fears).

Research findings comparing the effects of different types of self-disclosure have been mixed (Dowd & Boroto, 1982; McCarty & Betz, 1978; Reynolds & Fischer, 1983). Given the sparse and inconclusive findings, practitioners should use personal self-disclosure judiciously. Logic suggests that self-disclosures of current problems may undermine confidence of clients, who may well wonder how practitioners can presume to help others when they haven't successfully resolved their own problems. Moreover, focusing on the practitioner's problems diverts attention from the client, who may conclude the practitioner prefers to focus on his/her own problems. Self-involving disclosures, by contrast, appear to be low risk and relevant to the helping process.

Timing and Intensity of Self-Disclosure

Still another aspect of self-disclosure involves timing and level of intensity, ranging from superficial to highly personal statements. Giannandrea and Murphy (1973) found that moderate self-disclosing by practitioners, rather than high or low levels, resulted in a higher rate of returns by clients for second interviews. Simonson (1976) has reported similar findings. It is thus logical to assume that practitioners should avoid sharing personal feelings and experiences until rapport and trust have been achieved and clients have demonstrated readiness to engage on a more personal level. The danger in premature self-disclosure is that such responses can threaten clients and lead to emotional retreat at the very time when it is vital to reduce threat and defensiveness. The danger is especially great with clients from other cultures who are unaccustomed to relating on an intense personal basis. For example, in a study comparing the reactions of American and Mexican undergraduate students to self-disclosure, Cherbosque (1987) found that the Mexican students perceived counselors who did *not* engage in self-disclosure as *more* trustworthy and expert than those who did. This researcher concluded, therefore, that practitioners who work with Mexican-Americans need to maintain a degree of formality that is unnecessary with Anglo clients. We believe that this caution is also applicable to American Indian clients. Formality, however, should not preclude honesty, for Gomez et al. (1985) have reported that manifesting honesty and respect and communicating genuine concern were positively correlated with satisfaction levels of Chicano clients treated as outpatients in a mental health system.

With respect to Asian-Americans, Tsui and Schultz (1985) indicate that self-disclosure by practitioners may facilitate the development of rapport:

Personal disclosure and an *appropriate* [italics ours] level of emotional expressiveness are often the most effective ways to put Asian clients at ease. Considering the generally low level of emotional expressiveness in Asian families, the therapist is, in effect, role modeling for the client and showing the client how the appropriate expression of emotion facilitates the treatment process.

(p. 568)

As clients manifest trust, practitioners can appropriately relate with increased openness and spontaneity, assuming, of course, that authentic responses are relevant to clients' needs and do not shift the focus from the client for more than brief periods. Even when trust is strong, practitioners should exercise moderate self-disclosure, for beyond a certain level authentic responses no longer facilitate the helping process (Truax & Carkhuff, 1964). Practitioners must exercise discretion in employing self-disclosure with severely mentally ill clients. Shimkunas (1972) and Doster, Surratt, and Webster (1975) report higher levels of symptomatic behavior (e.g., delusional ideation) by paranoid schizophrenic patients following personal self-disclosure by practitioners. Superficial self-disclosure, by contrast, did not produce increases in disturbed behavior.

A Paradigm for Responding Authentically

Beginning practitioners (and clients) learn the skill of relating authentically more readily if they have a paradigm for formulating effective messages. Note in the following paradigm that there are four elements of an authentic message:

(1) "I" ( )	About	Because
(2) Specific feelings or wants.	(3) Neutral description of event.	(4) Impact of situation upon sender or others.

The following example (Larsen, 1980), involving a social work student's response to a message from an institutionalized youth, illustrates the use of the paradigm. The student describes the situation: "Don and I had a tough go of it last week. I entered the living unit only to find that he was angry with me for some reason, and he proceeded to abuse me verbally all night long. This week, Don approached me to apologize."

DON: I'm really sorry about what happened the other night. I didn't mean nothing by it. You probably don't want nothing more to do with me.

STUDENT: Well, you know, Don, I'm sorry it happened, too. I was really hurt and puzzled that night because I didn't understand where all your anger was coming from. You wouldn't talk to me about it, so I felt frustrated and I didn't quite know what to do or make of it. And you know, one of my real fears that night was that this was going to get in the way of our getting to know each other. I didn't really want to see that happen.

In the preceding message, note that the student uses all the elements of the paradigm, identifying specific feelings (hurt, puzzlement, frustration, fear), describing the events that occurred in a neutral, nonblaming manner, and identifying the *impact* she feared these events might have upon their relationship.

As you consider the paradigm, note that we are not recommending that you use it in a mechanistic and undeviating "I-feel-this-way-about . . ." response pattern. Rather, we suggest you learn and combine the elements of the paradigm in various ways as you practice constructing authentic messages. Later, as you incorporate authentic relating within your natural conversational repertoire, you will no longer need to refer to the paradigm.

This paradigm is also applicable in teaching clients to respond authentically.

We suggest that you present the paradigm to clients and guide them through several practice messages, assisting them to include all the elements of the paradigm in their responses. For example:

"I"	Specific Feelings	Description of Event	Impact
I	get frus-trated	when you keep reading the paper while I'm speaking to you	because I feel discounted and very unimportant to you.

It is important to stress with clients the need to use conversational language when they express authentic messages. Also emphasize, however, that they should talk about their *own* feelings and opinions. Otherwise, they may slip into accusative forms of communication as they vary their messages.

Guidelines for Responding Authentically

As you practice authentic responding and teach clients to respond authentically in their encounters with others, we suggest you keep in mind the following guidelines that relate to the four elements of an authentic message.

1. Personalize messages by using the pronoun "I." When attempting to respond authentically, both practitioners and clients commonly make the mistake of starting their statements with "You . . ." This introduction tends to focus a response on the other person rather than on the sender's experiencing. Beginning messages with "I," however, encourages senders to own responsibility for their feelings and to personalize their statements.

Efforts by practitioners to employ "I" statements when responding can profoundly affect the quality of group processes, increasing the specificity of communications and the frequency of "I" statements by clients. As a general rule, groups (including couples and families) are likely to follow a practitioner's communication style.

Just as groups tend to follow suit when practitioners frequently use "I" messages, they also imitate counterproductive behavior of the practitioner, including communicating in broad generalities, focusing on issues external to the individual, or relating to the group in an interrogative or confrontational manner.

The behavior of practitioners thus may not necessarily be a good model for clients to emulate in real life. Practitioners must be careful to model the skills they wish clients to acquire. Practitioners should master relating authentically to the extent that they automatically personalize their messages and constructively share their inner experiencing with clients. To facilitate personalizing messages, practitioners can negotiate an agreement with individuals or groups specifying that clients will endeavor to incorporate the use of "I" statements in their conversational repertoires. Thereafter, it is critical to intervene consistently to assist clients to personalize their messages when they have not done so.

2. Share feelings that lie at varying depths. To achieve this, practitioners must reach for feelings that underlie their immediate experiencing. Doing so is particularly vital when practitioners experience strong negative feelings (dislike, anger, repulsion, disgust, boredom) toward a client, for an examination of the deeper aspects of feelings often discloses more positive feelings toward the client. Expressing these feelings preserves the client's self-esteem, whereas expressing superficial negative feelings often poses a threat to the client, creating defensiveness and anger. In expressing anger (and perhaps disgust) toward a client who is chronically late for appointments, the practitioner may first connect his feelings of anger to feeling inconvenienced. In reaching for deeper feelings the practitioner may discover that the annoyance derives from disappointment that the client is not fully committed to the helping process. At an even deeper level may lie hurt in not being more important to the client. Further introspection may also discover a concern that the client may be manifesting similar behavior in other areas of life that could adversely affect relationships with others.

Utilizing an example of boredom, Gendlin (1967) illustrates the process a practitioner might go through to analyze feelings toward a client and to discover positive aspects of this experiencing that can be safely and beneficially shared with the client. Rather than just blurting out, "You bore me" or "Why do you never say anything important?" Gendlin recommends that practitioners advance their own experiencing for a few moments in a chain of "content mutation and explication":"I am bored. . . . This isn't helping him. . . . I wish I could help. . . . I'd like to hear something more personal. . . . I really would welcome him. . . . I have more welcome on my hands for him than he lets me use . . . but I don't want to push away what he does express. . . ." The resulting therapist expression now will make a personal interaction, even if the client says nothing in return. The therapist will say something like: "You know, I've been thinking the last few minutes, I wish I'd hear more from you, more of how you really feel inside. I know you might not want to say, but whenever you can or want, I would like it" (p. 90).

By employing the process just described, the practitioner may discover multiple (and sometimes conflicting) feelings that may be beneficially shared with the client, as illustrated in the following message:

[*To mother.*] "I've been experiencing some feelings in the session I want to share with you because it may shed some light on what others may experience with you. I was wanting to tell you that it appears you often come to Robert's [*son's*] rescue in the session and that at times you seem to protect him from the consequences of his own actions, but I held back and began to feel a slight knotting in my stomach. Then it hit me that I was afraid you'd be hurt and offended and that it might have a negative impact on our relationship. As I think about it just now, I'm aware that sometimes I feel I'm walking on eggshells with you , and I don't like that because it puts distance between us. Another reason I don't like it is because I think I'm underestimating your ability to handle constructive feedback. I think you're stronger than you come across at times. [*Slight pause.*] Could you share what you're feeling just now about what I said?"

Sharing multiple emotions also assists practitioners to manage situations in which they experience frustration or anger with clients. Dyer (1969) cites an example of feeling extremely angry at a client and simultaneously feeling guilty about having that feeling. Rather than sharing just the anger, Dyer shared the multiple emotions he was experiencing, including his wish *not* to feel angry and his desire to discuss and resolve his feelings. In such instances, a practitioner could also express underlying caring for the client and highlight the importance of understanding the dynamics involved so that both might learn from the situation. It is critical, of course, to analyze what changes need to be made by the client and/or practitioner to prevent future recurrences.

Like prospective practitioners, clients are prone to focus on one aspect of their experiencing to the exclusion of deeper and more complex emotions. Clients often have difficulty, in fact, pinpointing *any* feelings they are experiencing. In either case, practitioners should persevere to help clients broaden their awareness of their emotions and to express them openly, as illustrated in the following excerpt. The practitioner speaks to the husband:

PRACTITIONER: When you told your wife you didn't want to take her to a movie and she said you were a "bump on a log"— that you never seemed to want to do anything with her—what feelings did you experience?[2]

HUSBAND: I decided that if that's what she thought of me, that's what I'd be.

PRACTITIONER: Can you get in touch with what you were feeling? You told me a little bit about what you thought, but what about what's happening inside? Try to use feeling words to describe what you're experiencing.

HUSBAND: [*Pause.*] I felt that if she was going to get on my back . . .

PRACTITIONER: [*Gently interrupting.*] Can you use a feeling word like "bad," or "hurt," or "put down"? What did you *feel*?

HUSBAND: OK. I felt annoyed.

PRACTITIONER: So you experienced a sense of irritation. Good. I'm pleased you could get in touch with that feeling. Now see if you can get to an even more basic feeling. Remember, as we've talked about

before, anger is usually a surface feeling that camouflages other feelings. What was under your annoyance?

HUSBAND: Uhhh, I'd say frustrated. I just didn't want to sit there and listen to her harp at me. She never quits.

PRACTITIONER: I would like to check out something with you. Right now, as you're talking about this, it seems you're experiencing a real sense of discouragement and perhaps even hopelessness about things ever changing. It's as though you've given up. Maybe that's part of what you were feeling Saturday.

HUSBAND: Yeah, I just turn myself off. Doesn't seem to be anything I can do to make her happy.

PRACTITIONER: I'm glad that you can recognize the sense of despair you're feeling. I also appreciate your hanging in there with me for a minute to get in touch with some of your feelings. You seem to be a person whose feelings run deep, and at times expressing them may come hard for you. I'm wondering how you view yourself in that regard.

In the preceding excerpt, the practitioner engaged in extensive coaching to assist the client to get in touch with his underlying feelings. Deeper than the feelings of annoyance and frustration the client identified lay the more basic emotions of hurt and being unimportant to his wife.[3] By providing other spontaneous "training sessions," the practitioner can help him to identify his feelings more readily, to find the feeling words to express them, and to begin formulating "I" statements.

---

[2]In categorizing her husband as a "bump on a log," the wife makes a sweeping generalization that fits her husband's behavior into a mold. Although the practitioner chose to keep the focus momentarily on the husband, it is important that he help the couple to avoid labeling each other. Strategies for intervening when clients use labels are delineated in a later chapter.

[3]We suggest that you teach clients the concept that anger usually overlays other feelings and systematically assist them to identify the multiple emotions they are experiencing when they express anger, an approach that is illustrated in the above excerpt.

3. Describe the Situation or Targeted Behavior in Neutral or Descriptive Terms. In their messages, clients often omit reference or make only vague reference to situations that prompted their responses. Moreover, they may convey their messages in a blaming manner, engendering defensiveness that overshadows other aspects of self-disclosure. In either event, self-disclosure is minimal and respondents do not receive information that could otherwise be of considerable value. Consider, for example, the low yield of information in the following messages:

- "You're a neat person."
- "You should be more conscientious."
- "You're progressing well in your work."
- "You have a bad attitude."

All the preceding messages lack supporting information that respondents need to identify specific aspects of their behavior that is competent and warrants recognition or is substandard or dysfunctional. Practitioners should thus assist parents, spouses, or others to provide higher-yield feedback by including behavioral references. Examples of such messages are as follows:

[*Parent to six-year-old girl*]: "I've really appreciated all that you've done tonight by yourself. You picked up your toys, washed your hands before dinner, and ate dinner without dawdling. I'm so pleased."

"I'm very disappointed with your behavior right now. You didn't change your clothes when you came home from school; you didn't feed the dog; and you haven't started your homework."

Note in the last example that the parent sent an "I" message and owned the feelings of disappointment rather than attacking the child for being undependable. When responding authentically, practitioners should also carefully describe specific events that prompted their responses, particularly when they wish to bring clients' attention to some aspect of their behavior or to a situation of which they may not be fully aware. The following practitioner's message illustrates this point:

"I need to share something with you that concerns me. Just a moment ago, I gave you feedback regarding the positive way I thought you handled a situation with your husband. [*Refers to specific behaviors manifested by client.*] When I did that, you seemed to discount my response by [*mentions specific behaviors*]. Actually, this is not the first time I have seen this happen. It appears to me that it is difficult for you to give yourself credit for the positive things you do and the progress you are making. This, in fact, may be one of the reasons that you get so discouraged at times. I wonder how you view your behavior in this regard."

Practitioners constantly need to assess the specificity of their responses to assure that they give clients the benefit of behaviorally specific feedback and provide positive modeling experiences for them. It is also vital to coach clients in giving specific feedback whenever they make sweeping generalizations and do not document the relationship between their responses and specific situations.

4. Identify the specific impact of the problem situation or behavior on others. Authentic messages often stop short of identifying the specific impact of the situation upon the sender or others, even though such information would be very appropriate and helpful. This element of an "I" message also increases the likelihood that the receiver will adjust or make changes, particularly if the sender demonstrates that the receiver's behavior is having a tangible effect on him/her. Consider a practitioner's authentic response to a male member of an adult group:

"Sometimes I sense some impatience on your part to move on to other topics. [*Describes situation that just occurred, documenting specific messages and behavior.*] At times I find myself torn between responding to your urging us "to get on with it" or staying with a discussion that seems beneficial to the group. It may be that others in the group are experiencing similar mixed feelings and some of the pressure I feel."

Note that the practitioner first clarifies the tangible effects of the client's behavior upon himself and then suggests that others may experience the behavior similarly. Given the practitioner's approach, it is likely that others in the group will also give feedback. The client is then free to draw his own conclusions about the cause-effect relationship between his behaviors and the reactions of others and to decide whether he wishes to alter his way of relating in the group.

In addition to documenting the impact of specific behaviors of clients on themselves, practitioners can also identify the negative impact of a client's behavior on the *client* (e.g., "I'm concerned about [*specific behavior*] because it keeps you from achieving your goal"). Further, they may document the impact of a client's behavior on *others* (e.g., wife) or the *relationship* between the client and another person (e.g., "It appears that your behavior creates distance between you and your son").

Clients often have difficulty in clarifying the impact of others' behavior on themselves. A mother's message to her child, "I want you to play someplace else," establishes no reason for the request nor does it specify the negative impact of the behavior on her. If the mother responds in the following authentic manner, she clearly identifies the tangible effect of her child's behavior: "I'm having a hard

time getting through the hallway because I keep stumbling over toys and having to go around you. *I've almost fallen several times, and others might also. I'm worried that someone might get hurt*, so I'm asking you to move your toys to your room."

The preceding illustration underscores our point that when clients clarify how a situation affects them, their requests do not appear arbitrary and are more persuasive; hence, others are likely to make appropriate accommodations. We suspect that an important reason why many clients have not changed certain self-defeating behaviors before entering the helping process is that others have previously attacked, blamed, cajoled, put down, intimidated, threatened, or pressured them to change, rather than authentically and unabrasively imparting information that highlights how the clients' behavior strikes them. Others have also often attempted to prescribe behavioral changes that appear to be self-serving (e.g., "Come on, stop that sulking") instead of relating their feelings (e.g., "I'm concerned that you're down and unhappy. I'd like to help but I'm not sure how"). Such responses do not strike a responsive chord in clients, who may equate making changes with putting themselves under the control of others (by following their directives), thereby losing their autonomy.

In the following excerpt, note how the practitioner assists Carolyn, a group member, to personalize her statements and to clarify her reaction to the behavior of another member who has been consistently silent throughout the first two sessions:

CAROLYN: We've talked about needing to add new guidelines for the group as we go along. I think we ought to have a guideline that everyone should talk in the group. [*Observe that the member has not personalized her message but has proposed a solution to meet a need she has not identified.*]

PRACTITIONER: [*To Carolyn.*] The group may want to consider this guideline, but for a minute, can you get in touch with what you're experiencing and put it in the form of an "I" statement?

CAROLYN: Well, all right. Janet hasn't talked at all for two solid weeks, and it's beginning to really irritate me.

PRACTITIONER: I'm wondering what else you may be experiencing besides irritation? [*Assists member to identify feelings besides mild anger.*]

CAROLYN: I guess I'm a little uneasy because I don't know where Janet stands. Maybe I'm afraid she's sitting in judgment of us—I mean, me. And I guess I feel cheated because I'd like to get to know her better, and right now I feel shut out by her.

PRACTITIONER: That response helps us to begin to get to the heart of the matter. Would you now express yourself directly to Janet? Tell her what you are experiencing and, particularly, *how her silence is affecting you.*

CAROLYN: [*To Janet.*] I did wonder what you thought about me since I really opened up last week. And I do want to get to know you better. But, you know, underneath all this, I'm concerned about you. You seem unhappy and alone, and that makes me uncomfortable—I don't like to think of your feeling that way. Frankly, I'd like to know how you feel about being in this group, and if you're uneasy about it, as you seem to be, I'd like to help you feel better somehow.

In the preceding example, the practitioner assisted Carolyn to experience a broader range of feelings and to identify her reaction to Janet's silence. In response to the practitioner's intervention,

Carolyn also expressed more positive feelings than were evident in her initial message—a not infrequent occurrence when practitioners encourage clients to explore deeper-level emotions.

Engaging one member in identifying specific reactions to the behavior of others provides a learning experience for the entire group, and members often expand their conversational repertoires to incorporate such facilitative responding. In fact, there is a correlation between the extent to which practitioners assist clients to acquire specific skills and the extent to which clients acquire those same skills.

Cues for Authentic Responding

The impetus for practitioners to respond authentically may emanate from (1) clients' messages that request self-disclosure or (2) practitioners' decisions to share perceptions and reactions they believe will be helpful. In the following section, we consider authentic responding that emanates from these two sources.

Authentic Responding Stimulated by Clients' Messages

Requests from Clients for Personal Information Clients often confront students and practitioners with questions aimed at soliciting personal information such as "How old are you?" "Do you have any children?" "What is your religion?" "Do you and your wife ever fight?" and "Are you a student?" It is natural for clients to be curious and to ask questions about a practitioner in whom they are confiding, especially when their well-being and future are at stake.

Self-disclosing responses may or may not be appropriate, depending on the practitioner's assessment of the client's motivation for asking a particular question. When questions appear to be prompted by a natural desire for information, such responses are often very appropriate. Seemingly innocuous questions, however, may camouflage deep concerns or troubling feelings. In such instances, providing an immediate answer may be countertherapeutic because doing so may close the door to exploring and resolving clients' concerns and feelings. Clients are thus left to struggle with their feelings alone, which may seriously impair progress or cause premature termination. To illustrate, consider the following excerpt taken from an initial session involving a 23-year-old student and a 43-year-old woman who requested help for marital problems:

CLIENT: Are you married?
STUDENT: No, but I'm engaged. Why do you ask?
CLIENT: Oh, I don't know. I just wondered.

Given the context of an older adult with a much younger student, the client's question was likely motivated by the concern that the student might lack life experience essential to understand her marital difficulties or the competence needed to assist her in resolving them. In this instance, immediate authentic disclosure by the student was inappropriate because it did not facilitate exploration of the feelings underlying the client's inquiry.

An exchange such as the preceding may yield information vital to the helping process if the practitioner avoids premature self-disclosure. It is sometimes very difficult to distinguish between situations in which questions of clients are motivated by a natural desire for information or by hidden concerns or feelings. As a rule of thumb, when you have questions about clients' motivation for making personal inquiries, *precede disclosures of views or feelings with either open-ended* (see Chapter 6) *or empathic responses.* Responding in this manner significantly increases the probability that clients will reveal their real concerns. Notice what happens when the practitioner utilizes an empathic response before responding authentically:

CLIENT: Are you married?
STUDENT: I gather you're wondering if I can understand and help you with your difficulties in light of the fact that I'm much younger than you.
CLIENT: Well, I guess I was thinking that. I hope that doesn't offend you.
STUDENT: To the contrary—I appreciate your frankness. It's natural that you want to have confidence in your counselor. I know there's a lot at stake for you. Tell me more about your concerns.

In the preceding excerpt the student responded to the probable concern of the client and struck pay dirt. Such astuteness tends to foster confidence by clients and greatly facilitates the development of a therapeutic partnership. The fact that the student "leans into" the situation by inviting further exploration rather than skirting the issue may also be read by the client as an indicator of the student's own confidence in his/her ability to help. After fully exploring the client's concerns, the student can respond with an authentic response identifying personal qualifications, as illustrated in the following message:

"I do want you to know that I believe I can be helpful to you. I have studied marriage counseling at some length, and I have counseled other clients whose difficulties were similar to your own. I also consult with my supervisor regularly. However, the final judgment of my competence will rest with you. It will be important for us to discuss any feelings you may still have at the end of the interview as you make a decision about returning for future sessions."

Questions That Solicit the Practitioner's Perceptions   Clients may also pose questions that solicit the practitioner's opinions, views, or feelings. Typical questions include, "How do I compare to your other clients?" "Do you think I need help?" "Am I crazy?" or "Do you think there's any hope for me?"Such questions can be challenging, and practitioners must again consider the motivation behind the question and judge as to whether to disclose their views or feelings immediately or to employ either an empathic or open-ended response. As practitioners do disclose their perceptions, however, their responses must be congruent with their inner experiencing. In response to the question, "Do you think there's any hope for me?" the practitioner may congruently respond with a message that blends elements of empathy and authenticity:

"Your question tells me you're probably afraid you're beyond help. Although you do have some difficult problems, I'm optimistic that if we work hard together things can improve. You've shown a number of strengths that should help you make changes, including [*reviews strengths*]. A lot, of course, will depend on whether you're willing to commit to making changes *you* think would improve your situation and to invest the time and effort necessary to achieve your goals. In that respect, you're in control of the situation and whether things change for the better. That fact is something that many people find encouraging to know."

It is not necessary to answer all questions of clients in the service of authenticity. If you feel uncomfortable about answering a personal question or deem it inadvisable to do so, you should feel free to decline answering. In so doing, it is important to explain your reason for not answering directly, again utilizing an authentic response. If a teenage client, for example, asks whether the practitioner had sexual relations before she married, the practitioner may respond as follows:

"I need to share with you some thoughts I have about answering your question. Frankly, I'd rather not reveal that information to you inasmuch as that area is a very personal and private part of my life. Too, I'm doubtful that knowing that personal information about me would be helpful to you in the long run. However, I'm also aware of feeling apprehensive that you might feel embarrassed or put down by my response, and I don't want that to happen. Asking me that took some risk on your part. I have an idea that your question probably has to do with a struggle you're having, although I could be wrong. I would appreciate your sharing your thoughts about what I've said and telling me what sparked your question." The practitioner should then utilize empathic responding and open-ended questions to explore the client's reaction and motivation for asking her question.

Authentic Responding Initiated by Practitioners

Authentic responding initiated by practitioners may take several forms, which are considered separately in the following sections.

Disclosing Past Experiences   As we previously indicated, such responses should be used sparingly, be brief, relevant to the client's concerns, and well timed. In relating to a particular client's struggle, a practitioner may indicate, "I remember I felt very much like that when I was struggling with. . . ." Practitioners may also cite personal perceptions or experiences as reference points for clients, as, for example, "I think that is very normal behavior for a child. For instance, my five-year-old. . . ." A fundamental guideline that applies to such situations is that practitioners should be certain they are focusing on themselves to meet the therapeutic needs of clients.

Sharing Perceptions, Ideas, Reactions, and Formulations

A key role of the practitioner in the change-oriented phase of the helping process is to act as a "candid feedback system" by revealing personal thoughts and perceptions relevant to client problems (Hammond et al., 1977). The function of such responding is to further the change process in one or more of the following ways:

1. To heighten clients' awareness of dynamics that may play an important part in problems.

2. To offer a different perspective regarding issues and events.

3. To aid clients in conceptualizing the purposes of their behavior and feelings.

4. To enlighten clients on how they affect others (including the practitioner).

5. To bring clients' attention to cognitive and behavioral patterns (both functional and dysfunctional) that operate at either an individual or group level.

6. To share here-and-now affective and physical reactions of the practitioner to clients' behavior or to processes that occur in the helping relationship.

7. To share positive feedback concerning clients' strengths and growth.

After responding authentically to achieve any of these purposes, it is vital to invite clients to express their own views and draw their own conclusions. *Owning* perceptions rather than using under-the-table methods to influence clients to adopt particular views or to change in ways deemed desirable by the practitioner (e.g., "Don't you think you ought to consider . . .") relieves clients of the need to behave deviously or to defend themselves from the tyranny of views with which they do not agree.

Sharing perceptions with clients involves some risk that clients may misinterpret the practitioner's motives and thus feel criticized, put down, or rebuked. Clarifying helpful intent before responding diminishes the risk somewhat. Nevertheless, it is vital to be observant of clients' reactions that may indicate a response has struck an exposed nerve.

To avoid damaging the relationship (or to repair it), the practitioner should be empathically attuned to the client's reaction to candid feedback, shifting the focus back to the client to determine the impact of the self-disclosure. If the client appears to have been emotionally wounded by the practitioner's authentic response, the practitioner can use empathic skills to elicit troubled feelings and to guide subsequent responses aimed at restoring the relationship's equilibrium. Expressions of concern and clarification of the goodwill intended by the response are also usually facilitative: "I can see that what I shared with you hit you pretty hard—and that you're feeling put down right now. [*Client nods but avoids eye contact.*] I feel badly about that because the last thing I'd want is to hurt you. Please tell me what you're feeling."

Openly (and Tactfully) Sharing Reactions When Put on the Spot

Clients sometimes create situations that put practitioners under considerable pressure to respond to messages that bear directly on the relationship, such as when they accuse a practitioner of being uninterested, unfeeling, irritated, displeased, critical, inappropriate, or incompetent. Clients may also ask pointed questions (sometimes before the relationship has been firmly established) that require immediate responses. The first statement of one female client in an initial interview, for example, was, "I'm gay. Does that make any difference to you?" In the opening moments of another session, a pregnant client asked the practitioner, "How do you feel about abortion?"

Over the years, students have reported numerous such situations that sorely tested their ability to respond facilitatively. In one instance, a male member of a group asked a female student leader for her photograph. In another, an adolescent boy kept taking his shoes off and putting his feet (which smelled very bad) on the practitioner's desk. By reflecting on your practice experience, you too can no doubt pinpoint instances in which the behavior of clients caused you to squirm or produced butterflies in your stomach. Experiencing discomfort in sessions (sometimes *intense* discomfort) may be an indication that something is going awry that needs to be addressed. It is thus important to reflect on your discomfort, seeking to identify events that seem to be causing or exacerbating that discomfort (e.g., "I'm feeling very uneasy because I don't know how to respond when my client says things like, 'You seem to be too busy to see me,' or 'I'm not sure I'm worth your trouble.' "). After privately exploring the reason for the discomfort, the practitioner might respond:

"I'd like to share some impressions about several things you've said in the last two sessions. [*Identifies client's state-ments.*] I sense you're feeling pretty unimportant—as though you don't count for much—and that perhaps you're imposing on me just by being here. I want you to know that I'm pleased you had the courage to seek help in face of all the opposition from your family. It's also important to me that you know that I *want* to be helpful to you. I am concerned, however, that you feel you're imposing on me. Could you share more of those feelings with me?"

Notice that in the preceding response the practitioner specifically identifies the self-defeating thoughts and feelings and blends elements of empathy and authenticity in the response.

Situations that put practitioners on the spot also include clients' angry attacks, as we discuss later in the chapter. Practitioners must learn to respond authentically in such situations. Consider a situation in which an adolescent attacks a practitioner in an initial interview, protesting, "I don't want to be here. You counselors are all losers." In such instances, practitioners should share their reactions, as illustrated in the following:

"It sounds as though you're really ticked off about having to see me and that your previous experiences with counselors have been bummers. I respect your feelings and don't want to pressure you to work with me. I am concerned and uncomfortable, however, because you apparently have lumped all counselors together and that makes *me* a loser in your eyes. If you close your mind to the possibility that we might accomplish something together, then the chances are pretty slim I can be helpful. I want you to know that I *am* interested in you and that I would like to know what you're up against."

Intertwining empathic and authentic responses in this manner often defuses clients' anger and encourages them to think more rationally about a situation.

Sharing Feelings When Clients' Behavior Is Unreasonable or Distressing Although practitioners should be able to take most client behaviors in stride, there are times when they experience justifiable feelings of frustration, anger, or even hurt. In one case, a client acquired a practitioner's home phone number from another source and began calling frequently about daily crisis situations, although discussions of these events could easily have waited until the next session. In another instance, a tipsy client called the practitioner in the middle of the night "just to talk." In yet another case, an adolescent client let the air out of a practitioner's automobile tires. In such situations, practitioners should share their feelings with clients—*if they believe they can do so constructively*. In the following recorded case example, note that the student interweaves authentic and empathic responses in confronting a Chicano youth in a correctional institution who had maintained he was innocent of hiding drugs that staff had found in his room. Believing the youth's story, the student went to bat for him, only to find out later he had lied. Somewhat uneasy at her first real confrontation, the student tries to formulate an authentic response; ironically, the youth helps her to be "up-front" with him:

STUDENT: There's something I wanted to talk to you about, Randy . . . [*Stops to search for the right words.*]

RANDY: Well, come out with it, then. Just say it straight.

STUDENT: Well, remember last week when you got that incident report? You know, I really believed you were innocent. I was ready to go to the hearing and tell staff I was sure you were innocent and that the charge should be dropped. I guess I'm feeling kind of bad because when I talked to you, you told me you were innocent, and, well, that's not exactly the way it turned out.

RANDY: You mean I lied to you. Go ahead and say it.

STUDENT: Well, yes, I guess I felt kind of hurt because I was hoping that maybe you had more trust in me than that.

RANDY: Well, Susan, let me tell you something. Where I come from, that's not lying, that's what we call survival. Personally, I don't consider myself a liar. I just do what I need to do to get by. That's an old ghetto trick, but it just didn't work.

STUDENT: I hear you, Randy. I guess you're saying we're from two different cultures, and maybe we both define the same thing in different ways. I guess that with me being Anglo, you can't really expect me to understand what life has been like for you.

Several minutes later in the session, after the student has further explored the client's feelings, the following interchange occurs:

STUDENT: You know, Randy, there are two things I want you to know. One is that when social workers work with clients they have what they call confidentiality, just like lawyers and doctors. Everything we talk about is confidential. The other thing is that I don't expect you to share everything with me. I know there are certain things you don't want to tell me, so rather than lying about something that I ask you about, maybe you can just tell me you don't want to tell me. Would you consider that?

RANDY: Yeah, that's OK. [*Pause*] Listen, Susan, I don't want you to go around thinking I'm a liar now. I'll tell you this, and you can take it for what it's worth, but this is the truth. That's the first time I've ever lied to you. But you may not believe that.

STUDENT: I do believe you, Randy. [*He seemed a little relieved and there was a silence.*]

RANDY: Well, Susan, that's a deal, then. I won't lie to you again, but if there's something I don't want to say, I'll tell you I don't want to say it.

STUDENT: Sounds good to me. [*Both start walking away.*] You know, Randy, I really want to see you get through this program and get out as fast as you can. I know it's hard starting over because of the incident with the drugs, but I think we can get you through. [*This seemed to have more impact on Randy than anything I had said to him in a long time. The pleasure was visible on his face, and he broke into a big smile.*]

Noteworthy in this exchange is that the practitioner relied almost exclusively on the skills of authenticity and empathy to bring the incident to a positive conclusion. Ignoring her feelings would have impaired the student's ability to relate facilitatively to the client and would have been destructive to the relationship; focusing on the situation, on the other hand, was beneficial for both.

Sharing Feelings When Clients Give Positive Feedback Practitioners sometimes have difficulty responding receptively to clients' positive feedback about their own attributes and/or performance. We suggest that practitioners model the same receptivity to positive feedback they ask clients to demonstrate in their own lives, as illustrated in the following exchange between a client and a practitioner:

CLIENT: I don't know what I would have done without you. I'm just not sure I would have made it if you hadn't been there when I needed you. You've made such a difference in my life.

PRACTITIONER: I can sense your appreciation. I'm touched by your gratitude and pleased you are feeling so much more capable of coping with your situation. I want you to know, too, that even though I was there to help, your efforts have been the deciding factor in your growth.

Positive Feedback: A Form of Authentic Responding

Because positive feedback plays such a vital role in the change process, we have allocated this separate section to do justice to the topic. Practitioners often employ (or should employ) this skill in supplying information to clients about positive attributes or specific areas in which they manifest strengths, effective coping mechanisms, and incremental growth. In so doing, practitioners enhance motivation to change and foster hope for the future. Many opportune moments occur in the helping process when practitioners experience warm or positive feelings toward clients because of the latter's actions or progress. When appropriate, practitioners should share such feelings spontaneously with clients, as illustrated in the following messages:

"I'm pleased you have what I consider exceptional ability to 'self-observe' your own behavior and to analyze the part you play in relationships. I think this strength will serve you well in solving the problems you've identified."

"I've been touched several times in the group when I've noticed that, despite your grief over the loss of your husband, you've reached out to other members who needed support."

[*To newly formed group*]: "In contrast to our first session, I've noticed that this week we haven't had trouble getting down to business and staying on task. I've been pleased as I've watched you develop group guidelines for the past 20 minutes with minimal assistance from me, and I had the thought, 'This group is really moving.' "

The first two messages accredit strengths of individuals, and the third lauds a behavioral change the practitioner has observed in a group process. Both types of messages sharply focus clients' attention on specific behaviors that facilitate the change process, ultimately increasing the frequency of such behaviors. Given consistently, positive messages also have the long-range effect of helping clients who have low self-esteem to develop a more positive image of self. When positive feedback is utilized to document the cause-effect relationship between their efforts and positive outcomes, clients also experience satisfaction, accomplishment, and control over their situation. Positive feedback can have the further effect of increasing clients' confidence in their ability to cope. We have occasionally had experiences with clients who were on the verge of falling apart when they came to a session but left feeling able to manage their problems for a while longer. We attribute their increased ability to function in part to authentic responses that documented and highlighted areas in which they *were* coping and successfully managing problems.

Taped sessions of students and practitioners often reflect a dearth of authentic responses that underscore clients' strengths or incremental growth, which is unfortunate because, in our experience,

clients' rates of change often correlate with the extent to which practitioners focus on these two vital areas. As practitioners consistently focus on clients' assets and the subtle positive changes that often occur in early sessions, clients invest more effort in the change process. As the rate of change accelerates, practitioners can focus more extensively on clients' successes, identifying and reinforcing their strengths and functional coping behaviors.

Practitioners face several challenges in accrediting clients' strengths and growth, including enhancing their ability to recognize and express fleeting positive feelings when clients manifest strengths or progress. Practitioners must also learn to document events so that they can provide information about specific positive behaviors. Still another challenge *and* responsibility is to teach clients to give positive feedback to each other, strategies for which we discuss in Chapter 17.

To increase your ability to discern client strengths, we recommend you and your clients construct a profile of their resources. This may be done with individuals, couples, families, or groups, preferably early in the helping process. In individual sessions, the practitioner should ask the client to identify and list all the strengths she or he can think of. The practitioner also shares observations of the client's strengths, adding them to the list, which is kept for ongoing review to add further strengths as they are discovered.

With families, couples, or groups, practitioners may follow a similar procedure in assessing the strengths of individual members, but they should ask other group members to share their perceptions of strengths with each member. The practitioner may also wish to ask couples, families, or groups to identify the strengths and incremental growth of the group per se periodically throughout the helping process. After clients have identified their strengths or those of the group, the practitioner should elicit observations regarding their reactions to the experience. Often they may mutually conclude that clients have many more strengths than they have realized. The practitioner should also explore discomfort experienced by clients as they identify strengths, with the goal of having them acknowledge more comfortably their positive attributes and personal resources.

We further suggest that you carefully observe processes early on in sessions and note subtle manifestations of strengths and positive behavioral changes, systematically recording these in your progress records. The following observations are taken from the progress records of a practitioner regarding the strengths of several members of a group formed for young adults with cerebral palsy:

- *Lorraine*: Expresses caring and concern for feelings of other members; acts as "interpreter" between myself and members with difficult speech patterns; speaks for herself when appropriate; exhibits leadership in the group; can carry out tasks both in the group and outside; open to change.

- *Ken*: Accepts his physical limitations; is concerned for members' feelings and problems; expresses love and affection freely; has many friends; gets along remarkably well with father and sister; is patient and easygoing; sense of humor; encourages group members to participate; actively involved in every session; listens attentively.

- *Dale*: Helps keep group on designated topic when one member strays or focuses too much on self; expresses opinion and feelings somewhat openly and freely; can present positive aspects of situations, sometimes in a different light than oth-

ers; can be persistent, even patient; is able to "hear" another's honest, sincere response to his behavior (positive and negative); at times can be very open and nondefensive; can admit to mistakes and has the ability to keep to tasks when he wants to accomplish things.

In your progress records, note not only the strengths and incremental growth of clients but also whether you (or group members) focused on those changes. Keep in mind that changes often occur very subtly within a single session. For instance, clients may begin to discuss problems more openly during the later part of a session, tentatively commit to work on a problem they refused to tackle earlier, show growing trust in the practitioner by confiding high-risk information about themselves, or own responsibility for the first time for their part in problems. Groups and families may likewise manifest growth within short periods of time. It is thus vital to keep your antenna finely attuned to such changes so that you do not overlook clients' progress.

Relating Assertively to Clients

Still another aspect of relating authentically entails relating assertively to clients when a situation warrants such behavior. Reasons for relating assertively are manifold. To inspire confidence and influence clients to follow their lead, practitioners must relate in a manner that projects competence and "expert authority." This is especially important in the initial phase of the helping process in which clients usually covertly test or check out practitioners to determine whether they can understand their problems and appear competent to help them.

In conjoint or group sessions, clients may also entertain the question of whether the practitioner is strong enough to protect them from destructive interactional processes that may occur in sessions. (Family or group members, in fact, generally will not fully share, risk, or commit to the helping process until they have answered this question affirmatively through consistent observation of assertive actions by the practitioner.) If practitioners are relaxed and demonstrate through decisive behavior that they are fully capable of handling clients' problems and of providing the necessary protection and structure to control potentially chaotic or volatile processes, clients generally relax, muster hope, and begin to work on problems. If the practitioner appears incapable of curtailing or circumventing dysfunctional processes that render clients vulnerable, clients will have justifiable doubts as to the advisability of placing themselves in jeopardy and, consequently, may disengage from the helping process.

Skill in relating assertively is also prerequisite to implementing confrontation, a major technique that practitioners employ to surmount resistances to change. But practitioners must employ confrontation with sensitivity and finesse, as the risk of alienating clients by using this technique is high. All forms of assertiveness, in fact, must be conveyed in a context of goodwill and empathic regard for clients' feelings and self-esteem.

In the following discussion, we identify guidelines that can assist you to intervene assertively with clients:

Making Requests and Giving Directives

To assist clients to relate more facilitatively and to solve problems, practitioners frequently must make requests of them, some of which involve relating in new ways during sessions. These requests may include asking clients to do any of the following:

1. Speak directly to each other rather than through the practitioner.

2. Give feedback to others in the session.

3. Respond by checking out meanings of others' messages, take a listening stance, or personalize messages.

4. Change the arrangement of chairs.

5. Role-play.

6. Make requests of others.

7. Assume tasks to respond in specified ways within sessions.

8. Agree to carry out defined tasks during the week.

9. Identify strengths or incremental growth of themselves or others in the group or family.

In making requests, it is important to express them firmly and decisively and to deliver them with assertive nonverbal behavior. Practitioners often err by couching their requests in tentative language, thus conveying doubt to clients as to whether they expect them to comply with requests. The contrast between messages couched in tentative language and those couched in firm language can be observed in the illustrations that follow.

Tentative Requests	Firm Requests
Would you mind if I interrupted . . .	I would like to pause for a moment . . .
Is it OK if we role-play?	I'd like you to role-play with me for a moment.
Excuse me, but don't you think you're getting off track?	I think we're getting off track. I'd like to return to the subject we were discussing just a minute ago.
Could we talk about something Kathy just said?	Let's go back to something Kathy just said. I think it's very important . . .

Many times practitioners' requests of clients are actually *directives,* as are those under the column, "Firm requests." In essence, directives are declarative statements that place the burden on clients to object if they are uncomfortable, as the following message illustrates: "Before you answer that question, please turn your chair toward your wife. [*Practitioner leans over and helps client to adjust chair. To wife.*] Will you please turn your chair, also, so that you can speak directly to your husband? Thank you. It's important that you be in full contact with each other while we talk."

If the practitioner had given clients a choice (e.g., "Would you like to change your chairs?"), they might not have responded affirmatively. We thus suggest that when you want clients to behave differently in sessions, you simply state what you would like them to do. If clients verbally object to directives or manifest nonverbal behavior that may indicate reservations, it is vital to respond empathically and to explore the basis of their opposition. Such exploration often resolves fears or misgivings, freeing clients to engage in requested behavior.

Maintaining Focus and Managing Interruptions Maintaining focus is a vital task that takes considerable skill and assertiveness on the practitioner's part. It is often essential to intervene verbally to focus or refocus processes when interruptions or distractions occur. At times, practitioners also respond assertively on a nonverbal level to prevent members from interrupting important processes that may need to be brought to positive conclusion, as illustrated in the following excerpt from a family session:

KIM [14 YEARS OLD]: [*In tears, talking angrily to her mother.*] You hardly ever listen. At home, you just always yell at us and go to your bedroom.

MRS. R: I thought I was doing better than that . . .

MR. R: [*Interrupting his wife to speak to practitioner.*] I think it's hard for my wife because . . .

PRACTITIONER: [*Holds up hand to father in a "halt" position, while continuing to maintain eye contact with mother and daughter. To Kim.*] I would like to stay with your statement for a moment. Kim, please tell your mother what you're experiencing right now.

Interrupting Dysfunctional Processes Unseasoned practitioners often permit dysfunctional processes to continue for long periods either because they lack knowledge of how to intervene or because they think they should wait until clients have completed a series of exchanges. In such instances, practitioners fail to fulfill one of their major responsibilities, that is, to *guide* and *direct* processes and to influence participants to interact in more facilitative ways. Remember that clients often seek help because they cannot manage their destructive interactional processes, and permitting them to engage at length in their usual dysfunctional patterns of arguing, cajoling, threatening, accusing, attacking, blaming, criticizing, and labeling each other only exacerbates their problems. Rather, the practitioner should intervene, teaching them more facilitative behaviors and guiding them to implement such behaviors in subsequent interactions.

If you decide to interrupt ongoing processes, do so decisively so that clients listen to you or heed your directive. If you intervene nonassertively, your potential to influence clients (particularly aggressive clients) will suffer, since being able to interrupt a discussion successfully manifests your power or influence in the relationship (Parlee, 1979). If you permit clients to ignore or to circumvent your interventions to arrest dysfunctional processes, you yield control and assume a "one-down" position in relationship to the client.

With respect to interrupting or intervening in processes, we are advocating assertive, not aggressive behavior. You must thus be sensitive to vested interests of clients, for even though you may regard certain processes as unproductive or destructive, clients may not. The timing of interruptions is thus vital. If it is not critical to draw clients' attention to what is happening immediately, you can wait for a natural pause. If such a pause does not occur shortly, you should then interrupt. You should *not* delay interrupting destructive interactional processes, however, as illustrated in the following excerpt:

WIFE: [*To practitioner.*] I feel the children need to mind me, but every time I ask them to do something, he [*husband*] says they don't have to do it. I think we're just ruining our kids, and it's mostly his fault.

HUSBAND: Oh—well—that shows your lack of intelligence.

PRACTITIONER: I'm going to interrupt you because finding fault with each other will only lead to mutual resentment.

Observe that the practitioner intervenes to refocus the discussion after only two dysfunctional responses on the clients' part.[4] If participants do not disengage immediately, the practitioner will need to use body movements that interfere with communication pathways or, in extreme instances, a whistle or loud exclamation to interrupt behavior. When practitioners have demonstrated their intent to intervene quickly and decisively, clients will usually comply immediately when asked to disengage.

"Leaning into" Clients' Anger We cannot overstate the importance of openly addressing clients' anger and complaints. Unless practitioners are able to handle themselves assertively and competently in the face of such anger, they lose the respect of most clients and thus their ability to help them. Further, clients may use their anger to manipulate practitioners just as they have done with others. To help you respond assertively in managing clients' anger, we offer the following suggestions:

- Respond empathically to reflect clients' anger and, if possible, other underlying feelings (e.g., "I sense you're angry at me for _____ and perhaps disappointed about _____").

- Continue to explore the situation and the feelings of participants until you understand the nature of the events that have caused the angry feelings. As you do so, you may find that anger toward you dissipates and that clients begin to focus on themselves, assuming appropriate responsibility for their part in the situation at hand. The "real problem," as often happens, may not directly involve you.

- As you explore clients' anger, authentically express your feelings and reactions if it appears appropriate (e.g., "I didn't know you felt that way. . . . I want to hear how I might have contributed to this situation. There may be some adjustments I'll want to make in my style of relating. . . . I'm pleased that you shared your feelings with me").

---

[4]Many practitioners do not immediately intervene when clients engage in heated arguments, erroneously believing that ventilating anger serves a therapeutic purpose. They thus allow participants to play out the escalating sequence. Research reviewed by Saunders (1977) fails to support this belief, indicating instead that engaging in aggressive communication tends to produce greater subsequent levels of aggression.

■ Apply a problem-solving approach (if appropriate) so that all concerned make adjustments to avoid similar occurrences or situations in the future. If a particular client expresses anger frequently and in a dysfunctional manner, you may also focus on the client's style of expressing anger, identify problems this may cause him/her in relationships with others, and negotiate a goal of modifying this response pattern.

Saying No and Setting Limits

In contracting with clients, practitioners must occasionally decline requests or set limits. This is sometimes difficult for beginning practitioners, who may be zealous in their desires to render service and to demonstrate willingness to help others. Commitment to helping others is a desirable quality, but it must be tempered with judgment as to when acceding to clients' requests is in the best interest of both practitioner and client. There are instances when clients grow more by carrying out actions themselves than by having practitioners act for them. Moreover, certain clients are manipulative, and if practitioners permit themselves to be manipulated, they may unwittingly reinforce exploitive or irresponsible behavior.

Being tactfully assertive is no easier for practitioners who have excessive needs to please others than it is for clients. These practitioners have difficulty declining requests or setting limits when doing so is in the best interests of clients. We therefore recommend that such practitioners engage in introspection and study carefully the section of Chapter 15 that deals with cognitive factors involved in nonassertive behavior. Further, such practitioners may benefit by setting tasks for themselves related to increasing their assertiveness. Participating in an assertiveness training group and delv-

ing into the popular literature on assertiveness may also be highly beneficial.

Following are a few of the many situations in which you may need to decline requests of clients:

1. When clients invite you to participate with them socially.

2. When clients ask you to grant them preferential status (e.g., set lower fees than specified by policy).

3. When clients request physical intimacy.

4. When clients ask you to intercede in a situation they should handle themselves.

5. When clients request a special appointment after having broken a regular appointment for an invalid reason.

6. When clients make requests to borrow money.

7. When clients request that you conceal information about violations of probation, parole, or institutional policy.

8. When spouses request that you withhold information from their partners.

9. When clients disclose plans to commit crimes or acts of violence against others.

10. When clients ask you to report false information to a draft board, employer, or other party.

In addition to declining requests, you may need to set limits with clients in situations such as the following:

1. Making excessive telephone calls to you at home or the office.

2. Canceling appointments without advance notice.

3. Expressing emotions in abusive or violent ways.

4. Habitually seeking to go beyond designated ending points of sessions.

5. Continuing to fail to abide by contracts (e.g., not paying fees or missing appointments excessively).

6. Behaving inappropriately in reception room or in institution.

7. Making sexual overtures toward you or other staff members.

8. Coming to sessions when intoxicated.

Part of maturing professionally involves being able to decline requests, set limits, and feel comfortable in so doing. As you gain experience, you will realize increasingly that in holding clients to reasonable expectations you help as much as when you provide a concrete action for them. Modeled responses for refusing requests and for saying no to clients are found among the exercises to assist practitioners to relate authentically and assertively.

Situations also occur in which it is important that practitioners assert themselves with other social workers and members of other professions. Lacking experience and sometimes confidence, beginning practitioners often tend to be in awe of physicians, lawyers, psychologists, and more experienced social workers. Consequently, they may relate passively or may acquiesce to plans or demands that appear unsound or unreasonable. Although it is critical to be open to ideas of other professionals, beginning practitioners should also risk expressing their own views and asserting their own rights. Otherwise, they may know more about a given client than other professionals but fail to contribute valuable information in joint case planning.

Beginning practitioners should also set limits and assert their rights in refusing to accept unreasonable referrals and inappropriate assignments. Assertiveness may also be required when other professionals deny resources to which clients are entitled, refer to clients with demeaning labels, or engage in unethical conduct. Assertiveness, indeed, is critical in assuming the role of client advocate—a role we discuss at length in Chapter 16.

Exercises in Responding Authentically and Assertively

The following exercises will assist you in gaining skill in responding authentically and assertively. Read each situation and client message and formulate a written response as though you are the practitioner in the situation presented. Then compare your written responses with the modeled responses provided in the following section, keeping in mind that the modeled responses are only examples of many appropriate responses.

You will find additional exercises that involve authentic and assertive responding under exercises in confrontation in the final portion of Chapter 19 and in exercises concerned with managing relational reactions and resistance in the final section of Chapter 20.

Client Statements and Situations

1. Marital partner [*in third conjoint marital therapy session*]: It must be really nice being a marriage counselor—knowing just what to do and not having problems like ours.

2. Female client, age 23 [*in first session*]: Some of my problems are related to my church's stand on birth control. Tell me, are you a Catholic?

3. Client [*fifth session*]: You look like you're having trouble staying awake. [*Practitioner is drowsy from having taken an antihistamine for an allergy.*]

4. Adult group member [*to practitioner in second session—group members have been struggling to determine the agenda for the session*]: I wish you'd tell us what we should talk about. Isn't that a group leader's function? We're just spinning our wheels.

5. Male client [*sixth session*]: Say, my wife and I are having a party next Wednesday, and we thought we'd like to have you and your wife come.

6. Client [*calls three hours before scheduled appointment*]: I've had the flu the past couple of days, but I feel like I'm getting over it. Do you think I should come today?

7. Client [*Scheduled time for ending appointment has arrived, and practitioner has already moved to end session. In previous sessions, client has tended to stay beyond designated ending time*]: What we were talking about reminded me of something I wanted to discuss today but forgot. I'd like to discuss it briefly, if you don't mind.

8. Client [*has just completed behavioral rehearsal involving talking with employer and played role beyond expectations of practitioner*].

9. Female client [*10th interview*]: I've really felt irritated with you during the week. When I brought up taking the correspondence course in art, all you could talk about was how some correspondence courses are rip-offs and that I could take courses at _____ for less money. I knew that, but I've checked into this correspondence course, and it's well worth the money. You put me down, and I've resented it.

10. Client [*seventh session*]: You seem uptight today. Is something bothering you? [*Practitioner has been under strain associated with recent death of a parent and assisting surviving parent, who has been distraught.*]

11. Client [*sends the following message as the final session of successful therapy draws to a close*]: I really want to thank you for your help. You'll never know just how much help you've been. I felt like a sinking ship before I saw you. Now I feel I've got my head screwed on straight.

12. Male delinquent on probation, age 15 [*first session*]: Before I tell you much, I need to know what happens to the information. Who else learns about me?

13. Public assistance recipient [*during home visit*]: You've told me in the past I should report any income I receive. Well, I've been doing some part-time work for the past six months and making about $25 a week. I was hoping you wouldn't report it, though, because they'll cut my monthly check if you do. It's too small now.

14. Male welfare recipient, age 47 [*with problem of alcoholism*]: I was wondering if you could lend me five bucks to get my coat out of hock. I'll pay you back when I get my check.

15. Practitioner [*forgot to enter an appointment in daily schedule and, as a result, failed to keep a scheduled appointment with a client. Realizing this the next day, she telephones her client*].

Modeled Responses

1. [*Smiling.*] "Well, I must admit it's helpful. But I want you to know that marriage is no picnic for marriage counselors either. We have our rough spots, too. I have to work like everyone else to keep my marriage alive and growing."

2. "I gather you're wondering what my stand is and if I can understand and accept your feelings. I've worked with many Catholics before and have been able to understand their problems. Would it trouble you if I weren't Catholic?"

3. "You're very observant. I have been struggling with drowsiness these past few minutes, and I apologize for that. I had to take an antihistamine before lunch, and a side effect of the drug is drowsiness. I want you to know my drowsiness has nothing to do with you. If I move around a little, the drowsiness passes."

4. "I can sense your frustration and your desire to firm up an agenda. If I made the decision, though, it might not fit for a number of you and I'd be assuming the group's prerogative. Perhaps it would be helpful if the group followed the decision-by-consensus approach we discussed in our first session."

5. "Thank you for the invitation. I'm complimented you'd ask me. Although a part of me would like to come because it sounds like fun, I must decline your invitation. If I were to socialize with you while you're seeing me professionally, it would dilute my role, and I couldn't be as helpful to you. I hope you can understand my not accepting."

6. "I appreciate your calling to let me know. I think it would be better to change our appointment until you're sure you've recovered. Quite frankly, I don't want to risk being exposed to the flu, which I hope you can understand. I have a time open day after tomorrow. I'll set it aside for you if you'd like in the event you're fully recovered by then."

7. "I'm sorry I don't have the time to discuss the matter today. Let's save it for next week, and I'll make a note that you wanted to discuss it. We'll have to stop here today because I'm scheduled for another appointment."

8. "I want to share with you how impressed I was with how you asserted yourself and came across so positively. If you'd been with your boss, he'd have been impressed too."

9. "I'm glad you shared those feelings with me. And I can see I owe you an apology. You're right, I didn't explore whether you'd checked into the program, and I made some unwarranted assumptions. I guess I was overly concerned about your not being ripped off because I know others who have been by taking correspondence courses. But I can see I goofed because you had already looked into the course."

10. "Thank you for asking. Yes, I have been under some strain this past week. My mother died suddenly, which was a shock, and my father is taking it very hard. It's created a lot of pressure for me, but I think I can keep it from spilling over into our session. If I'm not able to focus on you, I'll stop the session. Or if you don't feel I'm fully with you, please let me know. I don't want to shortchange you."

11. "Thank you very much. As we finish, I want you to know how much I've enjoyed working with you. You've worked hard, and that's the primary reason you've made so much progress. I'm very interested in you and want to hear how your new job works out. Please keep in touch."

12. "Your question is a good one. I'd wonder the same thing if I were in your situation. I keep the information confidential as much as I can. We keep a file on you, of course, but I'm selective about what I put in it, and you have the right to check the file if you wish. I do meet with a supervisor, too, and we discuss how I can be of greatest help to clients. So I might share certain

information with her, but she keeps it confidential. If you report violations of the law or the conditions of your probation, I can't assure you I'll keep that confidential. I'm responsible to the court, and part of my responsibility is to see that you meet the conditions of your parole. I have to make reports to the judge about that. Could you share with me your specific concerns about confidentiality?''

13. "I appreciate your sharing this information, knowing your check might be cut. I wish your check could remain the same because I know it's not a lot. I don't really have any choice about reporting the income, though, because I'd be putting my job in jeopardy. I *will* look into policies to see how we can keep your cut to a minimum and help you to realize as much benefit as possible from working.''

14. "Let's think about some other ways of your getting by until you get your check. It would complicate our relationship if I loaned you money, and I don't want that to happen. Sometimes the thrift store will lend a coat on credit. Have you considered that?''

15. "Mr. M., I'm very embarrassed calling you because I realized just a few minutes ago I blew it yesterday. I forgot to enter my appointment with you in my schedule book last week and completely forgot about it. I hope you can accept my apology. I want you to know it had nothing to do with you.''

Skill Development Exercises in Empathic Communication

The following exercises, including a wide variety of actual client messages, will assist you in gaining mastery of reciprocal empathic responding (level 3). Read the client message and compose on paper an empathic response that captures the client's surface feelings. You may wish to use the paradigm, "You feel _____ about (or because)_____" in organizing your response before phrasing it in typical conversation language. Strive to make your responses fresh, varied, and spontaneous. To expand your repertoire of responses, we strongly encourage you to continue using the lists of affective words and phrases.

After formulating your response, compare it with the modeled response provided at the end of the exercises. Analyze the differences, being particularly aware of the varied forms of responding and the elements that enhance the effectiveness of your own and/or the modeled responses.

Because 30 different exercises are included, we recommend that you not attempt to complete them in one sitting, but space them across several sittings. Consistent practice and careful scrutiny of your responses are essential in gaining mastery of this vital skill.

Client Statements

1. **Father of developmentally disabled child, age 14** [*who is becoming difficult to manage*]: We just don't know what to do with Henry. We've always wanted to take care of him, but we've reached the point where we're not sure it's doing any good for him or for us. He's grown so strong—we just can't restrain him anymore. He beat on my wife last week when she wouldn't take him to the 7–11 late at night—I was out of town—and she's still bruised. She's afraid of him now, and I have to admit I'm getting that way too.

2. **Chicano** [*living in urban barrio*]: Our children do better in school if they teach Spanish, not just English. We're afraid our

children are behind because they don't understand English so good. And we don't know how to help them. Our people been trying to get a bilingual program, but the school board pay no attention to us.

3. Female client, age 31: Since my husband left town with another woman, I get lonely and depressed a lot of the time. And I find myself wondering whether something is wrong with *me* or whether men just can't be trusted.

4. Mother [*to child welfare protective services worker on doorstep during initial home visit*]: Who'd want to make trouble for me by accusing me of not taking care of my kids? [*Tearfully.*] Maybe I'm not the best mother in the world, but I try. There are a lot of kids around here that aren't cared for as well as mine.

5. Male ninth-grade student [*to school social worker*]: I feel like I'm a real loser. In sports I've always had two left feet, and when they choose up sides, I'm always the last one chosen. A couple of times they've actually got into a fight over who doesn't have to choose me.

6. Member of abused-women's group at YWCA: That last month I was living in mortal fear of Art. He'd get that hateful look in his eyes, and I'd know he was going to let me have it. The last time I was afraid he was going to kill me—and he might have if his brother hadn't dropped in. I'm afraid to go back to him. But what do I do? I can't stay here much longer!

7. Male, age 34 [*to marital therapist*]: Just once I'd like to show my wife I can accomplish something without her prodding me. That's why I haven't told her I'm coming to see you. If she knew it, she'd try to take charge and call all the shots.

8. Black person [*in a group session*]: All I want is to be accepted as a person. When I get hired, I want it to be for what I'm capable of doing—not just because of my skin color. That's as phony and degrading as *not* being hired because of my skin color. I just want to be accepted for who I am.

9. Client in a state prison [*to rehabilitation worker*]: They treat you like an animal in here—herd you around like a damn cow. I know I've got to do my time, but there are some times I feel like I can't stand it any longer—like something's building up in me that's going to explode.

10. Client [*to mental health worker*]: I don't have any pleasant memories of my childhood. It seems like just so much empty space. I can remember my father watching television and staring at me with a blank look—as though I didn't exist.

11. Patient in hospital [*to medical social worker*]: I know Dr. Brown is a skilled surgeon, and he tells me not to worry—that there's very little risk in this surgery. I know I should feel reassured, but to tell you the truth, I'm just plain panic-stricken.

12. Female member, age 29 [*in marital therapy group*]: I'd like to know what it's like with the rest of you. Hugh and I get into nasty fights because I feel he doesn't help me when I really need help. He tells me there's no way he's going to do women's work! That really burns me. I get to feeling like I'm just supposed to be his slave.

13. Male college student, age 21: Francine says she's going to call me, but she never does—I have to do all the calling, or I probably wouldn't hear from her at all. It seems so one-sided. If I didn't need her so much, I'd ask her what kind of game she's playing. I wonder if she isn't pretty selfish.

14. Caucasian student, age 14 [*to school social worker*]: To be really honest, I don't like the black kids in our school. They pretty much stay to themselves, and they aren't friendly to whites. I don't know what to expect or how to act around them. I'm antsy when they're around and—well, to be honest—I'm scared I'll do something they won't like and they'll jump me.

15. Single female, age 27 [*to mental health worker*]: I've been taking this class on the joys of womanhood. Last time the subject was how to catch a man. I can see I've been doing a lot of things wrong. But I won't lower myself to playing games with men. If that's what it takes, I guess I'll always be single.

16. Married male, age 29 [*to marital therapist*]: Sexually, I'm unfulfilled in my marriage. At times I've even had thoughts of trying sex with men. That idea kind of intrigues me. My wife and I can talk about sex all right, but it doesn't get better. She just isn't responsive and admits she has a psychological problem. Her doctor told her that.

17. Married female, age 32 [*to family practitioner*]: I love my husband and children—don't know what I'd do without them. Yet on days like last Thursday, I feel I could just climb the walls. I want to run away from all of them and never come back.

18. Married blind female [*to other blind group members*]: You know, it really offends me when people praise me or make a fuss over me for doing something routine that anyone else could do. It makes me feel like I'm on exhibition. I want to be recognized for being competent—not for being blind.

19. Male teacher [*to mental health practitioner*]: I have this thing about not being able to accept compliments. A friend told me about how much of a positive impact I've had on several students over the years. I couldn't accept that and feel good. My thought was, "You must be mistaken. I've never had that kind of effect on anyone."

20. Lesbian, age 26 [*to private practitioner*]: The girls at the office were talking about lesbians the other day and about how repulsive the very thought of lesbianism was to them. How do you think I felt?

21. Male member of alcoholics group: I don't feel like I belong in this group. The rest of you seem to have better educations and better jobs. Hell, I only finished junior high, and I'm just a welder.

22. Patient [*to a medical social worker*]: Maybe it doesn't seem important to other people, but I don't like having to share a room with a heavy smoker. When I went through the admissions interview, I specifically requested that I not be put in a room with a smoker.

23. Male, age 30 [*to private practitioner*]: Sometimes I can't believe how bent out of shape I get over little things. When I lose a chess game, I go into orbit. First, I'm furious with myself for blundering. It's not like me to make rank blunders. I guess I feel humiliated, because I immediately want to start another game and get even with the other guy.

24. Male client, age 72 [*to medical social worker*]: Since I had my heart attack, I've just had this feeling of foreboding—like my life's over for all practical purposes. I feel like I'm just an invalid—of no use to myself or anyone else.

25. Male applicant [*to public assistance worker*]: This is a very hard thing for me to do. I never thought I'd have to turn to welfare for help. But what do you do when you're backed into a corner? I've looked for jobs everywhere, but there's none to be had.

26. Child, age 15, in foster care [*to child welfare worker*]: I've had it with them [*the foster parents*]. They want me to work all the time—like I'm a slave or something. If you don't get me out of here, I'm going to run.

27. Family member, age 13 [*in initial family group session*]: Yeah, I can tell you what I'd like to be different in our family. I'd like to feel that we care about each other, but it's not that way. Every time I go in the house, Mom nags me, and Dad doesn't say anything—he doesn't seem to care. Sometimes I feel there's no point in going home.

28. Married woman [*in initial interview with marital therapist*]: I think this is just a complete waste of time. I didn't want to come and wouldn't be here if my husband hadn't forced me. *He's* the one who should be here—not me.

29. Married woman [*in YWCA adult women's group*]: This past week I've felt really good about how things are going— like I've finally got my act together. I've handled my emotions better, and for the first time in a long time, I've felt like an intelligent human being.

30. Adoptive applicant [*to child welfare worker*]: After you left last week, I thought about some of the questions you asked, and I've been griped ever since. It seems to me you're sitting in judgment on our worthiness as prospective parents. And that just doesn't sit right with me. I don't have to prove myself to you or to anyone else. I'm long past the point of having to do that.

Modeled Responses

1. "So you're really on the horns of a dilemma. You've wanted to keep him at home, but in light of his recent aggressiveness and his strength, you're becoming really frightened and wonder if other arrangements wouldn't be better for both you and him."

2. "I can see you're worried about how your children are doing in school and believe they need a bilingual program."

3. "It's been a real blow—your husband leaving you for another woman—and you've just felt so alone. And you find yourself dwelling on the painful question, 'Is something wrong with me, or is it that you just can't trust men?' "

4. "This is very distressing to you. You seem to be saying that it's not fair being turned in when you believe you take care of your children. Please understand I'm not accusing you of neglecting your children. But I do have to investigate complaints. It may be I'll be able to turn in a positive report. I hope so. But I do need to talk with you further. May I come in?"

5. "So I gather you feel you really got shortchanged as far as athletic talents are concerned. It's humiliating to you to feel so left out and be the last guy chosen."

6. "It sounds as though you lived in terror that last month and literally feared for your life. You were wise to remove yourself when you did. A number of other women in the group have had similar experiences and are facing the same dilemma about what to do now. As group members, each of us can be helpful to other group members in thinking through what's best to do now. In the meantime, you have a safe place to stay and some time to plan."

7. "Sounds like you get pretty annoyed, thinking about her prodding and trying to take charge. I gather it's important right now that you prove to her and to yourself you can do something on your own."

8. "I gather you're fed up with having people relate to you as a color or a minority, instead of being accepted as an individual—as yourself."

9. "If I understand you, you feel degraded by the way you're treated—as though you're less than a human being. And that really gets to you—sometimes

you find yourself seething with resentment that threatens to boil over."

10. "From what you say, I get a picture of you just feeling so all alone as you were growing up—as though you didn't feel very important to anyone—especially your father."

11. "So intellectually, you tell yourself not to worry—that you're in good hands. Still, on another level you have to admit you're terrified of that operation. [*Brief pause.*] Your fear is pretty natural, though. Most people who are honest with themselves experience fear. I'd be interested in hearing more about your fears."

12. "So the two of you get into some real struggles over differences in your views as to what is reasonable of you to expect from Hugh. And you seem to be saying you very much resent his refusal to pitch in—like it's not fair to have to carry that burden alone. Hugh, I'd be interested in hearing your views. Then we can hear how other members deal with this kind of situation."

13. "Sounds like part of you is saying you have a right to expect more from Francine—that you don't feel good about always having to be the one to take the initiative. You also seem to feel you'd like to confront her with what she's doing, but you're uneasy about doing that because you don't want to risk losing her."

14. "So, you're uncomfortable around them and just don't know how to read them. I gather you kind of walk on eggs when they're around for fear you'll blow it and they'll climb all over you."

15. "If I understand you, you're saying you can see a lot of ways you've made mistakes with men in the past. But one of them wasn't playing games, and you're not about to start that now—whatever the price."

16. "Things don't get better despite your talks, and you get pretty discouraged. At times you find yourself wondering if you'd get sexual fulfillment with men, and that appeals to you in some ways."

17. "So even though you care deeply for them, there are days when you just feel so overwhelmed you'd like to buy a one-way ticket out of all the responsibility."

18. "Are you saying you feel singled out and demeaned when people flatter you for doing things anyone could do? It ticks you off, and you wish people would recognize you for being competent—not being blind."

19. "In a way you seem to be saying you don't feel comfortable with compliments because you feel you don't really deserve them. It's like you feel you don't do anything worthy of a compliment."

20. "You must have felt extremely uncomfortable and resentful wondering if they'd condemn you if they really knew. It must have been most painful for you."

21. "Ted, you seem to feel uncomfortable, like you don't fit with the other group members. I gather you're feeling the rest of the members are above you, and you're concerned they won't accept you."

22. "I can see you'd be pretty irritated then, ending up with a smoker, especially after making a specific request as you did. I can understand your feelings, and I'll look into having this corrected. Thanks for letting me know."

23. "When you lose, lots of feelings surge through you—anger and disappointment with yourself for goofing, loss of face, and an urgency to prove you can beat the other guy."

24. "So things look pretty grim to you right now. As though you have nothing to look forward to and are just washed up. And you're apprehensive that things might get worse rather than better."

25. "It sounds like you've struggled hard to make it on your own and that it's been painful to admit to yourself you needed help. I'm sensing you're feeling some embarrassment about having to ask for help."

26. "You sound pretty burned up right now, and I can sense you feel there has to be a change. I'd like to hear more about exactly what has been happening."

27. "Am I getting it right, that you feel picked on by Mom and ignored by Dad? And you'd like to feel they really care about you. You'd like more love shown by family members for each other."

28. "You're feeling pretty angry with your husband for forcing you to come. I gather you're pretty resentful right now at having to be here and just don't see the need for it."

29. "That sounds great. You seem delighted with your progress—like you're really getting on top of things. And most of all you're liking yourself again."

30. "So you've really been annoyed and felt demeaned by my asking questions, as though I was challenging you to prove you could be good parents."

Answers to Exercise in Identifying Surface and Underlying Feelings

1. *Apparent feelings:* unimportant, neglected, disappointed, hurt. *Probable deeper feelings*: rejected, abandoned, forsaken, deprived, lonely, depressed.

2. *Apparent feelings:* unloved, insecure, confused, embarrassed, left out or excluded. *Probable deeper feelings*: hurt, resentful, unvalued, rejected, taken for granted, degraded, doubting own desirability.

3. *Apparent feelings:* chagrined, disappointed in self, discouraged, letting children down, perplexed. *Probable deeper feelings:* guilty, inadequate, crummy, sense of failure, out of control, fear of damaging children.

Answers to Exercises to Discriminate Levels of Empathic Responding

Client Statement	
1	
Response	Level
1.	2
2.	1
3.	1
4.	3
5.	2
6.	2
7.	4
8.	1

Client Statement			
2		3	
Response	Level	Response	Level
1.	1	1.	1
2.	3	2.	4
3.	1	3.	2
4.	2	4.	2
5.	4	5.	5
6.	1	6.	1
7.	3	7.	2
8.	2	8.	2

Suggested Classroom Skill Development Exercises in Empathic Communication

1. The instructor presents a discrete client message to students who anonymously formulate responses on index

cards or slips of paper. The instructor then collects the written responses and reads the messages to the class. After reading each individual message, the instructor and group members, on the count of three, simultaneously indicate their rating of the message by all raising a hand and displaying the number of fingers that correspond to their respective ratings. Student and instructor then discuss the strengths and weaknesses of the response in question before moving to the next one.

2. Students pair off, and one shares a personal concern with the other for three to five minutes. The other assumes the role of social worker, practicing empathic responses that convey understanding of the feelings experienced by the other. It is important that the person who is sharing feelings give corrective feedback when the "practitioner" is off target. After the interaction is complete, the paired students can benefit from discussing their respective experiences and giving appropriate feedback to each other. Students should then reverse roles, again following the same instructions. After the paired practice, the instructor may wish to lead a group discussion of the students' collective experience.

3. (In the classroom or practicum, for students in units of five or six.) Ask one student in each unit to play the role of client. The "client" then proceeds to re-

late his/her difficulties message by message. After each message, the students take turns responding empathically as if each were the practitioner at a given moment. The other students rate the message given by raising an appropriate number of fingers to designate the level of response. Responses may be briefly discussed, and feedback from the client is particularly helpful. After a few minutes, rotate the client role to a different student so that all students have equal learning opportunities.

4. The instructor may wish to give the following assignments to students in the classroom or practicum one week and discuss student observations related to the assignments the following week:

a. As you interact with others and observe others interact during the week, notice how infrequently people send empathic messages. Also observe the types of messages that are sent and how these messages influence the course of conversations.

b. As you interact with your spouse, parents, children, friends, and fellow students, practice listening carefully and responding with empathic messages when appropriate. Be alert to how empathic messages draw others out and to the feeling tones that these responses create.

6 ▊ Verbal Following, Exploring, and Focusing Skills

Maintaining Psychological Contact with Clients and Exploring Their Problems

Researchers and theoreticians agree that *verbal following* by practitioners is a major activity that is critical in *communication with clients* (Finn & Rose, 1982; Katz, 1979; Mayadas & O'Brien, 1976; Schinke, Blythe, Gilchrist, & Smith, 1980). Verbal following involves the use of and, at times, blending of discrete skills that enable practitioners to maintain psychological contact on a moment-by-moment basis with clients and to convey accurate understanding of their messages. Moreover, embodied in verbal following behavior are two performance variables that are essential to satisfaction and continuance on the part of the client:

1. *Stimulus-response congruence:* the extent to which practitioners' responses provide feedback to clients that their messages are accurately received.

2. *Content relevance:* the extent to which the content of practitioners' responses is perceived by clients as relevant to their substantive concerns.

First conceptualized by Rosen (1972), who detailed empirical and theoretical support for their relationship to client continuance, these two variables received further validation as critical practitioner behavioral responses in findings of a study by Duehn and Proctor (1977). Analyzing worker-client transactions, these authors found that practitioners responded incongruently (i.e., with responses that did not provide immediate feedback affirming client messages had been accurately received) much more frequently in interviews with clients who prematurely discontinued treatment than with those who continued. Further, "discontinuers" received significantly fewer practitioner responses that were relevant to the content expectations than "continuers." These authors concluded that responses that are relevant and accurately attend to client messages gradually increase moment-by-moment client satisfaction with interactions in the interview. On the other hand, continued use of questions and other responses not associated with previous client messages and unrelated to the client's substantive concerns contribute to consistent client dissatisfaction. When content expectations of clients are not fulfilled, clients prematurely discontinue treatment. Employing responses that directly relate to client messages and concerns thus enhances client satisfaction, fosters continuance, and also greatly facilitates the establishment of a viable working relationship.

141

The importance of explaining the relevance of questions to Asian-Americans seen for mental health problems has been emphasized by Tsui and Schultz (1985):

The therapist must explicitly educate the client about the purpose of questions regarding clinical history, previous treatment information, family background, and psychosocial stressors. The linkage of these issues to their current symptoms is not clear to many Asian clients. Many Asian clients conceive of mental distress as the result of physiological disorder or character flaws. This issue must be dealt with sensitively before any sensible therapeutic work can be effected.

(pp. 567–568)

In addition to enabling practitioners to maintain close psychological contact with clients, verbal following skills serve two other important functions in the helping process. First, these skills yield rich personal information, allowing practitioners to *explore* clients' problems in depth. Second, these skills enable practitioners to *focus* selectively on facets of clients' experiencing and on dynamics in the helping process that facilitate positive client change.

In the following pages, we introduce you to skills for verbally following and exploring clients' problems. Several of these skills are easily mastered. Others require more effort to acquire. We provide exercises in the body of the chapter to assist you in acquiring proficiency. Although empathic responding is the most vital skill for verbally following clients' messages, we have not included it in this chapter since it was discussed in the preceding one. Later, however, we discuss the blending of empathic responses with other verbal following skills to advance your ability in focusing upon and fully exploring relevant client problems.

Verbal Following Skills

Briefly, the discrete skills highlighted in this chapter include the following types of responses:

1. Furthering.
2. Paraphrasing.
3. Closed-ended.
4. Open-ended.
5. Seeking concreteness.
6. Providing and maintaining focus.
7. Summarizing.

Furthering Responses

Furthering responses indicate practitioners are listening attentively and encourage the client to verbalize. They are of several types:

1. *Minimal prompts,* which signal the practitioner's attentiveness, include short but encouraging responses such as "Yes," "I see," "Mm-mmm," "And?" "But?" or "Then what?" Nonverbal counterparts include head nodding, facial expressions, and gestures that convey receptivity and commitment to understand.

2. *Accent responses.* (Hackney & Cormier, 1979) involve repeating, in a questioning tone of voice or with emphasis, a word or a short phrase. If, for instance, a client says, "I've really had it with the way my supervisor at work is treating me," the practitioner might use the short response, "Had it?" to prompt further elaboration by the client.

Paraphrasing Responses

Paraphrasing involves using fresh words to restate the client's message concisely.

Responses that paraphrase are more apt to focus on the *cognitive aspects* of client messages (i.e., emphasize situations, ideas, objects, persons) than on the client's affective state (Cormier & Cormier, 1979), although reference may be made to obvious feelings. Below are three examples of paraphrasing:

CLIENT: I wish I had studied for that test. I think I would have gotten a better grade.

PRACTITIONER: You think studying for your exam might have improved your grade.

CLIENT: I went to the doctor today for a final checkup, and she said that I was doing fine.

PRACTITIONER: She gave you a clean bill of health, then.

CLIENT: I just don't know what to think about the way my girlfriend treats me. Sometimes she seems so warm—like she really likes me—and at other times she acts really cold.

PRACTITIONER: Her hot and cold behavior really confuses you.

When employed sparingly, paraphrases may be interspersed with other facilitative responses to prompt client expression. Used to excess, however, paraphrasing produces a mimicking effect. Paraphrases may also be utilized when practitioners want to bring focus to an idea or situation for client consideration. However, paraphrasing is inappropriate when clients are preoccupied with feelings. In such cases, practitioners need to relate with empathic responses that accurately capture clients' affect and assist them to reflect on and sort through feelings. Sometimes practitioners may choose to direct discussion from feelings for therapeutic purposes. For instance, a practitioner may believe that a chronically depressed client who habitually expresses discouragement and disillusionment would benefit by focusing less on feelings and more on actions to alleviate distress. When the practitioner chooses to de-emphasize feelings, paraphrases that reflect content are helpful and appropriate.

Exercise in Paraphrasing In the following exercise, formulate written responses that paraphrase the messages of clients. Remember, paraphrases usually reflect the cognitive aspects of messages, rather than feelings. Modeled responses to these exercises are found at the end of the chapter.

Client Statements

1. Client: I can't talk to people. I just completely freeze up in a group.

2. Woman: I think that in the last few weeks I've been able to listen much more often to my husband and children.

3. Client: Whenever I get into an argument with my mother, I always end up losing. I guess I'm still afraid of her.

4. Husband: I just can't decide what to do. If I go ahead with the divorce, I'll probably lose custody of the kids—and I won't be able to see them very much. If I don't, though, I'll have to put up with the same old thing. I don't think my wife is going to change.

5. Wife: This week we haven't had much chance to work on our assignments. John [husband] has been out of town, and several of the kids went to camp.

6. Mother [speaking about daughter]: When it comes right down to it, I think I'm to blame for a lot of her problems.

Open- and Closed-Ended Responding

Generally used to elicit specific information, *closed-ended questions* define a topic and restrict the client's response to a few words or a simple yes or no answer. Typical examples of closed-ended questions are:

- "When did you obtain your divorce?"

- "Do you have any sexual difficulties in your marriage?"

- "When did you last have a physical examination?"

- "Are you taking any medications?"

Although closed-ended questions restrict the client and elicit limited information, many instances occur in which these responses are both appropriate and helpful. Later in the chapter we discuss how and when to use this type of response effectively.

In contrast to closed-ended responses, which circumscribe client messages, *open-ended responses* invite expanded expression and leave the client free to express what seems most relevant and important. For example:

PRACTITIONER: You've mentioned your daughter. Tell me how she enters into your problem.

CLIENT: I don't know what to do. Sometimes I think she is just pushing me so that she can go live with her father. When I ask her to help around the house, she won't, and says that she doesn't owe me anything. When I try to insist on her helping, it just ends up in an ugly scene without anything being accomplished. It makes me feel so helpless.

In the preceding example, the practitioner's open-ended response prompted the client to expand on the details of the problems with her daughter, including a description of her daughter's behavior, her own efforts to cope, and her present sense of defeat. The information contained in the message is typical of the richness of data obtained through open-ended responding.

Some open-ended responses are *unstructured,* leaving the topic to the client's choosing ("Tell me what you would like to discuss today," or "What else can you tell me about the problems that you're experiencing?"). Other open-ended responses are *structured* in that the practitioner defines the topic to be discussed but leaves clients free to respond in any way they wish ("You've mentioned feeling badly about the incident that occurred between you and your son. I'd be interested in hearing more about that.") Still other open-ended responses fall along a continuum between structured and unstructured in that they give the client leeway to answer with a few words or to elaborate with more information ("How do you feel about that?" or "How willing are you to do this?").

Practitioners may formulate open-ended responses either by asking a question ("What meaning do you make out of your husband's actions?") or by giving a *polite command* ("Would you tell me what meaning you make out of your husband's actions?"). Polite commands have the effect of direct questions in requesting information but are less forceful and involve greater finesse. Similar in nature are *embedded questions* that do not take the form of a question but embody a request for information. Examples of embedded questions are: "I'm curious about . . ." "I'm wondering if . . ." and "I'm interested in knowing . . .". Open-ended questions often start with *what* or *how. Why* questions are often unproductive inasmuch as they ask for reasons, motives, or causes that are either obvious, obscure, or unknown to the client. Asking *how* ("How did that happen?") rather than *why* ("Why did that happen?") often elicits far richer information regarding client behavior and patterns.

Exercises in Identifying Open- and Closed-Ended Responses The following exercises will assist you to differentiate between closed- and open-ended messages. Identify each statement with either a C for closed or O for open. Turn to the end of the chapter to check your answers.

1. _____ "Did your mother ask you to see me because of the problem you had with the principal?"

2. _____ "When John says that to you, what do you experience inside?"

3. _____ "You said you're feeling fed up and you're just not sure that pursuing a reconciliation is worth your trouble. Could you elaborate?"

4. _____ "When is your court date?"

Now read the following client messages and respond by writing open-ended responses. Avoid using *why* questions. Examples of open-ended responses to these messages can be found at the end of the chapter.

Client Statements

1. Client: Whenever I'm in a group with Ralph, I find myself saying something that will let him know that I have a good intellect.

2. Client: I always have had my parents telephone for me about appointments and other things. I might foul up.

3. Client: I am really excited about my new job. I started work today and everything went just perfect.

4. Teenager [*speaking of a previous probation counselor*]: He sure let me down. And I really trusted him. He knows a lot about me because I spilled my guts out.

In following sections we explain how you can blend open-ended and empathic responses to keep a discussion focused on a specific topic. In preparation for that, respond to the next two client messages by formulating an empathic response followed by an open-ended question that encourages the client to elaborate on the same topic.

5. Wife [*to practitioner in conjoint session*]: It really irritates me the way you take my husband's side when we talk about our problems with you. I feel like it's two against one in here.

6. Client: Life is such a hassle, and it doesn't seem to have any meaning or make sense. I just don't know whether I want to try figuring it out any longer.

The difference between closed-ended and open-ended responses may seem obvious to you, particularly if you completed the preceding exercises. It has been our experience, however, that beginning and even seasoned practitioners have difficulty in actual sessions in discriminating whether their responses are open- or closed-ended, in observing the differential effect of these two types of responses in yielding rich and relevant data, and in deciding which of the two types of responses is appropriate at a given moment. We recommend, therefore, that you complete the group exercises related to open- and closed-ended responding found in the concluding portion of the chapter. We also recommend that you use the form provided at the end of the chapter to assess both the frequency and the appropriateness of your closed- and open-ended responses in several taped client sessions.

Discriminate Use of Open- and Closed-Ended Questions

Beginning practitioners typically ask an excessive number of closed-ended questions, many of which block communication or are inefficient or irrelevant to the helping process. When this occurs, the session tends to take on the flavor of an interrogation, with the practitioner bombarding the client with questions and taking responsibility for maintaining verbalization. Notice what happens, for example, in the following excerpt from a recording of a practitioner interviewing an institutionalized youth:

PRACTITIONER: I met your mother yesterday. Did she come all the way from Colorado to see you?
CLIENT: Yeah.
PRACTITIONER: It seems to me that she must really care about you to take the bus and make the trip up here to see you. Don't you think so?
CLIENT: I suppose so.
PRACTITIONER: Did the visit with her go all right?
CLIENT: Fine. We had a good time.
PRACTITIONER: You had said you were going to talk to her about a possible home visit. Did you do that?
CLIENT: Yes.

When closed-ended responses are used to elicit information in lieu of open-ended responses, as in the preceding example, many more discrete interchanges will occur, but the client's responses will be brief and the yield markedly lower.

Occasionally, beginning practitioners also use closed-ended questions to explore *feelings,* but responses from clients typically involve minimal self-disclosure, as might be expected. Rather than en-

couraging expanded expression of feelings, closed-ended questions limit responses, as illustrated in the following example:

PRACTITIONER: Did you feel rejected when she turned down your invitation?
CLIENT: Yeah.
PRACTITIONER: Have there been other times when you've felt rejected that way?
CLIENT: Oh, yeah. Lots of times.
PRACTITIONER: When was the first time?
CLIENT: Gee, that's hard to say.

Had the practitioner employed empathic and open-ended responses to explore the feelings and thoughts associated with being rejected, the client would likely have revealed much more.

Open-ended responses often elicit the same data as closed-ended questions but in addition draw out much more information and elaboration of the problem from the client. The following two examples contrast open-ended and closed-ended responses that address the same topic with a given client. To appreciate the differences in the richness of information yielded by these contrasting responses, place yourself in the role of the client. Compare your likely responses to each of the contrasting messages:

1. *Closed-ended:* "How many children do you have?"
Open-ended: "Tell me about your children."

2. *Close-ended:* "Did your husband feel badly about that?"
Open-ended: "What impact did that have on your husband?"

Because open-ended responses elicit more information than closed-ended ones, frequent use of the former increases the efficiency of data gathering. The richness of information revealed by the client, in fact, is directly proportional to the frequency with which open-ended responses are employed. Frequent use of open-ended responses also fosters a smoothly flowing session; consistently asking closed-ended questions, by contrast, often results in a fragmented, discontinuous process.

Closed-ended questions are used chiefly to elicit essential factual information. Skillful practitioners use closed-ended questions sparingly, since clients usually reveal extensive factual information spontaneously as they unfold their stories, aided by the practitioners' open-ended and furthering responses. Employed little during the first part of a session, closed questions are used more extensively later to elicit data that may have been omitted by clients, such as names and ages of children, place of employment, date of marriage, medical facts, and data regarding family of origin.

In obtaining factual data such as the preceding, the practitioner can unobtrusively weave into the discussion closed-ended questions that directly pertain to the topic. For example, a client may relate certain marital problems that have existed for many years, and the clinician may ask parenthetically, "And you've been married how many years?" Similarly, a parent may explain that a child began to truant from school when the parent started to work six months ago, to which the practitioner may respond, "I see. Incidentally, what type of work do you do?" It is vital, of course, to shift the focus back to the problem. If necessary, the practitioner can easily maintain focus by using an open-ended response to pick up the thread of the discussion. For example, the practitioner may comment, "You mentioned that Ernie began truanting when you started to work. I'd like to hear more about what was happening in your family at that time."

Because open-ended responses generally yield rich information they are used throughout initial sessions. They are used most heavily, however, in the first portion of sessions to open up communication and to invite clients to reveal problematic aspects of their lives. The following open-ended polite command is a typical opening message: "Could you tell me what it is you wish to discuss, and we can think about it together." Because such responses convey interest in clients as well as respect for clients' abilities to relate their problems in their own way, they also contribute to the development of a working relationship.

As clients disclose certain problem areas, open-ended responses are also extensively employed to elicit additional relevant information. Clients, for example, may disclose difficulties at work or in relationships with other family members. Typical open-ended responses that will elicit clarifying information are:

- "Tell me more about your problems at work."

- "I'd like to understand more about your difficulties with your wife. Please tell me more about that."

It may sometimes be necessary to employ closed-ended questions extensively to elicit information if the client is unresponsive and withholds information or has limited conceptual and mental abilities. However, in the former case it is vital to explore the clients' immediate feelings about being in the session, which often are negative and impede verbal expression. Focusing on and resolving negative feelings, which we discuss in Chapter 12, may pave the way to using open-ended responses to good advantage. Using closed-ended messages as a major interviewing tool early in sessions may be appropriate with some children, but the use of open-ended responses should be consistently tested as the relationship develops.

When you incorporate open-ended responses into your repertoire, you will experience a dramatic positive change in interviewing style and confidence level. To assist you to develop skill in blending and balancing open-ended and closed-ended responses, we have provided a recording form that you may wish to use in examining your own interviewing style (see Figure 6-1 below). Utilizing the form, analyze several recorded individual, conjoint, or group sessions over a period of time to determine changes you are making in employing these two types of responses. The recording form will assist you in determining the extent to which you have used open- and closed-ended responses. In addition, however, you may wish to review your work for the following purposes:

1. To determine when relevant data are missing and whether the information might have been more appropriately obtained through an open- or a closed-ended response.

2. To determine when your use of closed-ended questions was irrelevant, ineffective, or distractive to the data-gathering process.

3. To practice formulating open-ended responses you might use in place of closed-ended responses to increase client participation and elicit richer data.

Seeking Concreteness

People (including clients and beginning practitioners) are inclined to think and talk in generalities and to use words that lack precision when speaking of their experiences. In order to communicate one's feelings and experiences so that they are fully understood, however, a person must be able to respond *concretely,* that is, with specificity. Responding concretely involves utilizing words that *describe* in explicit terms specific experiences, behaviors, and feelings. In the following message, the respondent expresses his experiencing in vague and general terms: "I thought you gave a good speech." By contrast, he might have described his experience in precise language: "As you delivered your speech, I was impressed with your relaxed manner and your clear articulation of the issues." To test your com-

Figure 6-1   Recording Form for Open- and Closed-Ended Responding

Practitioner's response	Open-ended responses	Closed-ended responses
1.		
2.		
3.		
4.		
5.		
6.		
7.		

Directions: Record your discrete open- and closed-ended responses and place a check (√) in the appropriate column. Retain a copy of the form so that you can monitor your progress in appropriately using open- and closed-ended responses from week to week.

prehension of the concept of concreteness, assess which of the following messages give descriptive information concerning a client's experiencing:

- "I'm uneasy right now because I don't know what to expect from counseling, and I'm afraid you might think that I really don't need it."

- "People don't seem to care whether other people have problems."

- "My previous experience with counselors was lousy."

- "I really wonder if I'll be able to keep from crying and to find the words to tell my husband that it's all over—that I want a divorce."

- "You did a good job."

Probably you could readily identify which of the preceding messages contained language that increased the specificity of the information conveyed by the client. In developing competency as a practitioner, one of your challenges is to consistently recognize clients' messages expressed in abstract and general terms and to assist them to reveal highly specific information related to feelings and experiences. Such information will assist you to make accurate assessments and, in turn, to plan interventions accordingly. The second challenge is to assist clients to learn *how* to respond more concretely in their relationships with others, a task you will not be able to accomplish unless you are able to model the dimension of concreteness yourself. Therein lies the third challenge—in addition to assisting clients to describe with specificity their own experiencing, you must be able to describe your own in language that is precise and descriptive. It is thus not enough to recognize concrete messages; you must familiarize yourself with and practice re-

sponding concretely to the extent that it becomes a natural style of speaking and relating to others. The remainder of our discussion on the skill of seeking concreteness is devoted to assisting you in meeting the three challenges.

Types of Responses that Facilitate Specificity of Expression by Clients Practitioners who fail to move beyond general and abstract messages often have little grasp of the specificity and meaning of a client's problem. Eliciting highly specific information that minimizes errors or misinterpretations, however, is a formidable challenge because clients typically present impressions, views, conclusions, and opinions that, despite efforts to be objective, are biased and distorted to some extent. Further, as we have already mentioned, clients are prone to speak in generalities and to respond with imprecise language, and thus their messages may be interpreted differently by different people. To help you to conceptualize various ways you may assist clients to respond more concretely, in the following sections we have identified, discussed, and illustrated different facets of responses that seek concreteness, including:

1. Checking out perceptions.

2. Clarifying the meaning of vague or unfamiliar terms.

3. Exploring the basis of conclusions drawn by clients.

4. Assisting clients to personalize their statements.

5. Eliciting specific feelings.

6. Focusing on the here and now, rather than on the distant past.

7. Eliciting details related to clients' experiences.

8. Eliciting details related to interactional behavior.

In addition to discussing the preceding categories, we have included 10 skill development exercises, the completion of which will further bring your comprehension of concreteness from the general and abstract to the specific and concrete.

Checking Out Perceptions   Responses that assist practitioners to clarify and to "check out" whether they have accurately heard clients' messages (e.g., "Do you mean . . ." or "Are you saying . . .") are vital in building rapport with clients and in communicating the desire to understand their problems. Such responses also minimize misperceptions or projections in the helping process. Benefits also accrue to clients from practitioners' efforts to understand, in that clarifying responses assist clients to sharpen and reformulate their thinking regarding feelings and other concerns and thus encourage self-awareness and growth.

At times, perception-checking is necessary because clients convey messages that are incomplete, ambiguous, or complex. Upon occasion, practitioners encounter clients who repetitively communicate in highly abstract, theoretical, or metaphorical styles, or other clients whose thinking is scattered and whose messages often just do not "track" or make sense. In such instances, practitioners must sometimes spend an inordinate amount of time sorting through clients' messages and clarifying perceptions.

At other times, the need for clarification is not because of confusing, faulty, or incomplete client messages but because the practitioner has simply not fully attended to a client's message or comprehended its meaning. It is important to realize that fully attending moment by moment throughout a session requires intense concentration and, as experienced practitioners will attest, is exhausting work. Further, it is impossible to fully focus on and comprehend the essence of every message in group and family meetings where myriad transactions occur and competing communications bid for the practitioner's attention. Thus, it is important that you develop skill in using clarifying responses to elicit ongoing feedback regarding your perceptions and to acknowledge freely your need for clarification when you are confused or uncertain. Rather than reflecting personal or professional inadequacy, your efforts to accurately grasp the client's meaning and feelings will most likely be perceived as signs of your genuineness and your commitment to understand.

Perception-checking may be accomplished by asking simple questions that seek clarification or by combining your request for clarification with a paraphrase or empathic response that reflects your perception of the client's message (e.g., "I think you were saying _____. Is that right?"). Examples of various clarifying messages include the following:

- "You seem to be really irritated, not only because he didn't respond when you asked him to help but because he seemed to be deliberately trying to hurt you. Is that what you are experiencing?"

- "I'm not sure I'm following you. Let me see if I understand the order of the sequence of events you described. . . ."

- "Would you expand on what you are saying so that I can be sure that I understand what you mean?"

- "Could you go over that again and perhaps give an illustration that might help me to understand?"

- "I'm confused. Let me try to restate what I think you're saying."

- "As a group, you seem to be divided in your approach to this matter. I'd like to summarize what I'm hearing, and I would then appreciate some input regarding whether I understand the various positions that have been expressed."

In addition to clarifying their own perceptions, practitioners need to assist clients in conjoint or group sessions to clarify their perceptions of the messages of others who are present. This may be accomplished in any of the following ways:

1. *By modeling* clarifying responses, which occurs naturally as practitioners seek to check out their own perceptions of clients' messages.

2. *By directing* clients to ask for clarification. Consider, for example, the following response by a practitioner in a conjoint session: "You [*mother*] had a confused look on your face, and I'm not sure that you understood your daughter's point. Would you repeat back to her what you heard and then ask her if you understood correctly?"

3. *By teaching* clients *how* to clarify perceptions and by reinforcing their efforts to "check out" the messages of others, as illustrated in the following responses:
[*To group*]: One of the reasons families have communication problems is that members don't hear accurately what others are trying to say, and therefore, they often respond or react on the basis of incorrect or inadequate information. I would like to encourage all of you to frequently use what I call "checking out" responses such as, "I'm not sure what you meant. Were you saying . . . ?" to clarify statements of others. As we go along, I'll point out instances in which I notice any of you using this kind of response.
[*To family*]: I'm wondering if you all noticed Jim "checking" out what his dad said. . . . As you may recall, we talked about the importance of these kinds of responses earlier. [*To dad*] I'm wondering, Bob, what you experienced when Jim did that?

Clarifying the Meaning of Vague or Unfamiliar Terms In expressing themselves, clients often employ terms that have multiple meanings or use terms in idiosyncratic ways. For example, in the message, "My husband is cruel to me," the word *cruel* may have different meanings to practitioner and client. Until establishing what this term means to a particular client, a practitioner cannot be certain whether the client is referring to physical abuse, criticism, nagging, withholding affections, or other like possibilities. The precise meaning can be clarified by employing one of the following responses:

- "In what way is he cruel?"
- "I'm not sure what you mean by cruel. Could you clarify that for me?"
- "I can tell that is painful for you. Could you give me some examples of times he has been cruel?"

Many other adjectives also lack precision, and it is therefore important to avoid assuming that the client means the same thing you mean when you employ a given term. The terms *oversexed, dependent, irresponsible, selfish, careless,* and a plethora of like terms conjure up meanings that vary according to the reference points of different persons. Exact meanings are best determined by asking for clarification or for examples of events in which the behavior alluded to actually occurred.

Exploring the Basis of Conclusions Drawn by Clients Clients often present views or conclusions as though they are established facts. For example, the messages, "I'm losing my mind," or "My wife doesn't love me anymore," involve views or conclusions that the client has drawn. To accurately assess the client's difficulties, additional information upon which the views or conclusions are based must be elicited. This information is valuable in assessing the thinking patterns of the client, which are powerful determinants of emotions and behavior. For example, a husband who believes his wife no longer loves him will behave as though his belief represents reality. The practitioner's role, of course, is to unravel distortions and to challenge erroneous conclusions in a facilitative manner.

Examples of responses that would elicit clarification of the basis of views and conclusions embodied in the messages cited earlier include the following:

- "How do you mean—losing your mind?"

- "How have you concluded you're losing your mind?"

- "What leads you to believe your wife no longer loves you?"

- "How have you come to the conclusion that your wife doesn't love you anymore?"

It should be noted that entire groups may hold in common erroneous conclusions or biased or distorted information about any variety of subjects, and in such instances, the practitioner has the challenging task of assisting members to reflect upon and to analyze their views. Examples of the conclusions or distortions that the practitioner may need to assist group members to assess include the following:

- "We can't do anything about our problems. We are helpless and others are in control of our lives."

- "We are innocent victims."

- "People in authority are out to get us."

- "Someone else is responsible for our problems."

- "They [*members of another race, religion, group, etc.*] are no good."

We further discuss the practitioner's role in challenging distortions and erroneous conclusions and identify relevant techniques that may be used for this purpose in several chapters of the book.

Assisting Clients to Personalize Their Statements The relative concreteness of a specific client message is related in part to the *focus* or subject of that message. Client messages fall into several different classes of topic focus (Cormier & Cormier, 1979), each of which emphasizes different information and leads into very different areas of discussion:

1. *Focus on self,* indicated by the subject "I" (e.g., "I'm disappointed that I wasn't able to keep the appointment").

2. *Focus on others,* indicated by subjects, such as "they," "people," "someone," or names of specific persons (e.g., "They haven't fulfilled their part of the bargain").

3. *Focus on the group or mutual relationship between self and others,* indicated by the subject "we" (e.g., "We would like to do that").

4. *Focus on content,* indicated by such subjects as events, institutions, situations, ideas (e.g., "School wasn't easy for me").

Clients are more prone to focus on others, on content, or to speak of themselves as a part of a group rather than to personalize their statements by using "I" or other self-referent pronouns, as illustrated in the following messages: "Things just don't seem to be going right for me," "They don't like me," or "It's not easy for people to talk about their problems." In the last example, the client means that it is not easy for *her* to talk about *her* problems; however, in talking about this concern, she uses the term *people,* thus generalizing the problem and obscuring her struggle.

In assisting clients to personalize statements, practitioners have a two-fold task:

1. To model, to teach, and to coach clients to use self-referent pronouns ("I," "me") in talking about concerns rather than using topic focuses that do not clearly show the affective relationship between individuals and their concerns. For example, in response to a vague client message that focuses on content rather than self ("Everything at home seems to be deteriorating"), the practitioner can gently ask the client to reframe the message by starting the response with "I" and giving specific information about what she is experiencing. It is also helpful to teach clients the difference between messages that focus on self—"I (think) (feel) (want) . . ."—and messages that are *other*-related ("You . . ." "they . . ." "we . . ." "it . . ." "someone . . .") or *subject*-related (objects, things, ideas, or situations). Although teaching clients to use self-referent pronouns when talking about their concerns is a substantive task, clients derive major benefits, since not owning or taking responsibility for feelings and speaking about problems in generalities and abstractions is perhaps one of the most prevalent causes of problems in communicating.

2. To focus frequently on the client, use the client's name or the pronoun "you." Beginning practitioners are apt to attend to client talk about other people, distant situations, the group at large, various escapades, or other events or content that give little information about self and the relationship between self and situations or people. Notice in the following illustration that the practitioner's response focuses on the situation rather than on the client:

CLIENT: My husband won't do anything to help around the house.

PRACTITIONER: What isn't he doing? [*or*] Why won't he help?

In contrast, consider the following message, which personalizes the client's concern and explicitly identifies the feelings she is experiencing:

PRACTITIONER: You're really irritated at your husband for not pitching in the way you feel he should. You'd like more help.

A practitioner may employ various techniques to assist clients to personalize messages; in the preceding example, however, the practitioner utilized an empathic response. In this instance, this skill is invaluable to the practitioner in helping the client to focus on self. Remember that personalizing feelings is an inherent aspect of the paradigm for responding empathically ("You feel _____ about/because _____"). Thus, a client can make a statement in which there are no self-referent pronouns, and by utilizing empathic responding, the practitioner may assist clients to "own" their feelings.

Eliciting Specific Feelings Even when clients personalize their messages and express feelings, practitioners often need to elicit information to clarify what they are experiencing, for certain "feeling words" denote *general feeling states* rather than *specific feelings*. For example, in the message, "I'm really upset that I didn't get a raise," the term *upset* helps to clarify the client's general frame of mind but fails to specify the precise feeling. "Upset" in this instance may refer to feeling disappointed, discouraged, unappreciated, devalued, angry, resentful, or even feeling incompetent or inadequate over not having been granted a raise. The point is that until practitioners have elicited additional information, they cannot be sure of how being "upset" is actually experienced by the client. Other feeling words that lack specificity include *frustrated, uneasy, uncomfortable, troubled,* and *bothered.* When clients employ such words, you can pinpoint their feelings by employing responses such as the following:

- "How do you mean, upset?"

- "I'd like to understand more about that feeling. Could you clarify what you mean by frustrated?"

- "In what way do you feel bothered?"

Focusing on the Here and Now   Still another aspect of concreteness embodies responses that shift the focus from the past to the present—the here and now. Messages that relate to the immediate present are high in concreteness, whereas those that center on the past are low. Some clients, however, are prone to discuss past feelings and events. Precious opportunities for promoting growth and understanding may slip through the fingers of practitioners who fail to focus on emotions and experiences that unfold in the immediacy of the interview. Focusing on feelings as they occur will enable you to observe reactions and behavior firsthand, thus eliminating bias and error caused by reporting feelings and experiences after the fact. Furthermore, the helpfulness of your feedback is greatly enhanced when this feedback relates to the client's immediate experiencing.

An example of concreteness in such situations is provided in the following excerpt:

CLIENT: [*Choking up.*] When she told me it was all over, that she was in love with another man—well, I just felt—it's happened again. I felt totally alone, like there just wasn't anyone.

PRACTITIONER: That must have been terribly painful. [*Client nods; tears well up.*] I

wonder if you're not experiencing the same feeling just now—at this moment. [*Client nods agreement.*]

Not only do such instances provide direct access to the client's inner experience, but they may also produce rich benefit as the client shares deep and painful emotions in the context of a warm, accepting, and supportive relationship. Here-and-now experiencing that involves emotions toward the practitioner (anger, hurt, disappointment, affectional desires, fears, and the like) is designated as *relational immediacy* or *immediacy in the relationship.* Skills pertinent to relational immediacy warrant separate consideration and are dealt with in Chapter 20.

Focusing on here-and-now experiencing with groups, couples, and families, discussed at length in Chapter 17, is a particularly potent technique for assisting members of these systems to clear the air of pent-up feelings. Further, interventions that focus on the immediacy of feelings bring covert issues to the surface, thus paving the way for the practitioner to assist members of these systems to clearly identify and explore their difficulties and (if appropriate) engage in problem solving.

Eliciting Details Related to Clients' Experiences   As previously mentioned, one of the reasons why concrete responses are essential is that clients often offer vague statements regarding their experiences. For example: "Some people in this group don't want to change bad enough to put forth any effort." Compare this to the following concrete statement in which the client assumes ownership of the problem and fills in details that clarify its nature:

"I'm concerned because I want to do something to work on my problems in this group, but when I do try to talk about them, you, John, make some sarcastic remark. It seems that then several of you [gives names] just laugh about it and someone changes the subject. I really feel ignored then and just go off into my own world."

Aside from assisting clients to personalize their messages and to "own" their feelings and problems, practitioners have the task of asking questions that elicit illuminating information concerning the client's experiencing, such as that illustrated in the preceding message. In this regard, questions that start with *how* or *what* are often helpful in assisting the client to give concrete data. To the client message, "Some people in this group don't want to change bad enough to put forth any effort," the practitioner might ask, "Specifically what has been happening in the group that leads you to this conclusion?"

Eliciting Details Regarding Interactional Behavior Concrete responses are also vital in accurately assessing interactional behavior. Such responses pinpoint what actually occurs in interactional events, that is, what circumstances preceded the events, what was said and done by the participants, what specific thoughts and feelings were experienced by the client, and what consequences followed the event. In other words, the practitioner elicits details of what happened, rather than settling for clients' views and conclusions. An example of a concrete response to a client message follows:

CLIENT: Well, Fred blew his cool as usual last night. He really read me the riot act, and I hadn't done one thing to deserve it.

PRACTITIONER: Could you recall exactly what happened—what led up to this situation and what each of you said and did.

To understand better what went wrong, I'd like to get the details as though I had been there and observed what happened.

In such cases, it is important to keep clients on topic by continuing to assist them to relate the events in question, using responses such as "Then what happened?" "What did you do next?" or "Then who said what?" If dysfunctional patterns become evident after exploring numerous events, practitioners have a responsibility to share their observations with clients, to assist them to evaluate the impact of the patterned behavior, and to assess their motivation to change it.

Specificity of Expression by Practitioners Seeking concreteness applies not only to the communication of clients but to that of practitioners as well. In this role, you will frequently explain, clarify, give feedback, and share personal feelings and views with clients. As a budding practitioner who has recently entered a formal professional educational program, you, too, may be prone to speak with the vagueness and generality that characterize much of the communication of the lay public. When such occurs, clients and others may understandably misinterpret, draw erroneous conclusions, or experience confusion about the meaning of your messages. Consider, for example, the lack of specificity in the following actual messages of practitioners:

- "You seem to have a lot of pent-up hostility."

- "You really handled yourself well in the group today."

- "I think a lot of your difficulties stem from your self-image."

Vague terms, such as *hostility, handled yourself well,* and *self-image,* tend to leave the client in a quandary as to what the practitioner actually means. Moreover, conclusions are presented without supporting information, thus requiring the client to accept them at face value, to reject them as invalid, or to speculate as to the basis of the conclusions. Fortunately, some clients are sufficiently perceptive, inquisitive, and assertive to request greater specificity, but many are not.

Contrast the preceding messages to the following in which the practitioner responds to the same situations but this time with messages that have a high degree of specificity:

- "I've noticed that you've become easily angered and frustrated several times as we've talked about ways you might work out child custody arrangements with your wife. This appears to be a very painful area for you. I would like to know just what you have been experiencing."

- "I noticed that you responded several times in the group tonight, and I thought you offered some very helpful insight to Marjorie when you said. . . . I also noticed you seemed to be more at ease than in previous sessions."

- "We've talked about your tendency to feel inferior to other members of your family and to discount your own feelings and opinions in your contacts with them. I think that observation applies to the problem you're having with your sister that you just described. You've said you didn't want to go on the trip with her and her husband because they fight all the time, and yet you feel you *have* to go because she is putting pressure on you. As in other instances, you appear to be drawing the conclusion that how you feel about the matter isn't important."

When practitioners speak with specificity, clarify meanings, personalize statements, and document the sources of conclusions, clients are much less likely to misinterpret, distort, or project their own feelings or thoughts. Misunderstandings are averted. Clients are clear about what is expected of them and how they are perceived, as well as how and why practitioners think and feel as they do about various matters discussed. Equally important, clients vicariously learn to speak with greater specificity as practitioners model sending concrete messages.

Both beginning and experienced practitioners face the additional challenge of avoiding the inappropriate use of jargon, which has pervaded professional discourse and has become rampant in social work literature and case records. The use of jargon confuses rather than clarifies meanings for clients. The careless use of jargon with colleagues also fosters stereotypical thinking and is therefore antithetical to the cardinal value of individualizing the client. Furthermore, labels tend to conjure up images of clients that vary from one practitioner to another, thus injecting a significant source of error into communication. Consider, for example, the lack of specificity in the following messages that are rich in jargonese:

- "Mrs. N. manifests strong *passive-aggressive* tendencies."

- "Sean displayed *adequate impulse control* in the group and *tested the leader's authority in a positive manner.*"

- "Hal needs assistance in gaining greater *self-control.*"

- "The group members were able *to respond to appropriate limits.*"

- "Ruth appears to be *emotionally immature* for an eighth-grader."

To accurately convey information about clients to your colleagues, you must explicitly describe their behavior and document the sources of your conclusions. Keeping in mind the preceding vague message, "Ruth appears to be emotionally immature for an eighth-grader," consider how much more accurately another practitioner could perceive your client if you conveyed information in the form of a concrete response: "The teacher says Ruth is quiet and stays to herself in school. She doesn't answer any questions in class unless directly called upon, and she often doesn't complete her assignments. She also spends considerable time daydreaming or playing with objects." By describing behavior, you avoid biasing your colleague's perceptions of clients through conveying either vague impressions or erroneous conclusions.

It has been our experience that mastery of the skill of communicating with specificity is gained only through extended and determined effort. The task is complicated by a typical lack of awareness by beginning practitioners of the vagueness and generality of their communication. We recommend that you carefully and consistently monitor your recorded sessions and your everyday conversations with a view toward identifying instances in which you did or did not communicate with specificity. Such monitoring will enable you to set relevant goals for yourself and to chart your progress. We also recommend that you enlist the assistance of your practicum instructor in providing feedback about your performance level on this vital skill.

Exercises in Seeking Concreteness In the preceding discussion, we identified guidelines for formulating concrete responses. To review, you achieve specificity by:

1. Checking out perceptions.

2. Clarifying the meaning of vague or unfamiliar terms.

3. Exploring the basis of conclusions drawn by clients.

4. Assisting clients to personalize their statements.

5. Eliciting specific feelings.

6. Focusing on the here and now.

7. Eliciting details related to clients' experiences.

8. Eliciting details related to interactional behavior.

In the following exercises, formulate written responses that will elicit concrete data regarding clients' problems. You may wish to combine your responses with either an empathic response or a paraphrase. Reviewing the above guidelines as you complete the exercise will assist you in formulating effective responses and will help you to clearly conceptualize the various dimensions of this skill as well. After you have finished the exercises, compare your responses with the modeled responses following the last client statement.

Client Statements

1. **Adolescent** [*speaking of his recent recommitment to a correctional institution*]: It really seems weird to be back here.

2. **Client:** You can't depend on friends; they'll stab you in the back every time.

3. **Client:** He's got a terrible temper—that's the way he is, and he'll never change.

4. **Client:** My supervisor is so insensitive, you can't believe it. All she thinks about is reports and deadlines.

5. Client: I was upset after I left your office last week. I felt you really didn't understand what I was saying and didn't care how I felt.

6. Client: My dad's 58 years old now, but I swear he still hasn't grown up. He always has a chip on his shoulder.

7. Teenager: Well, I finally asked Ann for a date, but it was a total disaster. I learned my lesson. She can rot in hell for all I care.

8. Client: I just have this uneasy feeling about going to the doctor. I guess I've really got a hang-up about it.

9. Black student [*to black practitioner*]: You ask why I don't talk to my teacher about why I'm late for school. I'll tell you why. 'Cause she's white, that's why. She's got it in for us blacks, and there's just no point talking to her. That's just the way it is.

10. Client: John don't give a damn about me. I could kick the bucket, and he wouldn't lose a wink of sleep.

Modeled Responses

1. "In what way does it seem weird?"

2. "I gather *you* feel that your friends have let you down in the past. Could you give me a recent example in which this has happened?"

3. "Could you tell me more about what happens when he loses his temper with you?" or "You sound like you don't have much hope that he'll ever get control of his temper. How have you concluded he will never change?" (A practitioner might explore each aspect of the message separately.)

4. "Could you give me some examples of how she is insensitive to you?"

5. "Sounds like you've been feeling hurt and disappointed over my reaction last week. I can sense you're struggling with those same feelings right now. Could you tell me what you're feeling at this moment?"

6. "That must make it difficult for you. Could you recall some recent examples of times you've had difficulties with him?"

7. "So it went really badly, I take it, and you're hurting right now. I'm interested in hearing what actually happened. Could you start at the beginning and give me the details of everything that happened, including what was going on inside of you and what you said and did; also, exactly what Ann said and did."

8. "Think of going to the doctor just now. Let your feelings flow naturally. [*Pause.*] What goes on inside you—your thoughts and feelings?"

9. "So you see it as pretty hopeless. You feel pretty strong about Ms. Wright. I'd be interested in hearing what's happened that you've come to the conclusion she's got it in for blacks."

10. "So you feel like you're nothing in his eyes. I'm wondering how you've reached that conclusion?"

Summarizing Responses

The technique of summarization embodies four distinct and yet related facets. Although employed at different times and in different ways, each facet serves the common purpose of tying together functionally related elements that are manifested in a fragmented fashion at different points in the helping process. These four facets include:

1. Highlighting salient aspects of discussions of specific problems before changing the focus of the discussion.

2. Making connections between relevant aspects of lengthy client messages.

3. Reviewing major focal points of a session and assignments clients plan to work on before the next session.

4. Recapitulating the highlights of a previous session and reviewing clients' progress on assignments during the week for the purpose of providing focus and continuity between sessions.

These facets of summarization are considered in the following sections.

Highlighting Salient Aspects of Problems During the phase of an initial session in which problems are explored in moderate depth, summarization can be effectively employed to tie together and highlight key aspects of a problem before proceeding to explore additional problems. The practitioner may summarize how the problem appears to be produced by the interplay of several factors, including external pressures, overt behavioral patterns, unfulfilled needs and wants, and covert thoughts and feelings. Connecting these key elements assists clients to gain a more accurate and complete perspective of their problems. Employed in this fashion, summarization involves fitting pieces of the problem together to form a coherent whole. Seeing the problem in a fresh and more accurate perspective is beneficial, as it expands clients' awareness and can generate hope and enthusiasm for tackling a problem that has hitherto seemed insurmountable.

Summarization that highlights problems is generally employed at a natural point in the session when the practitioner believes that relevant aspects of the problem have been adequately explored and clients appear satisfied in having had the opportunity to express personal concerns. The following example illustrates this type of summarization:

The client, a 38-year-old housewife, has been referred for persistent depression. One problem that has surfaced during the exploration involves dissatisfaction and discouragement with her marriage. According to her description, her husband is domineering, critical, and unaffectionate; consequently, she feels unloved, unappreciated, and hungry for approval and affection. Highlighting the salient factors, the practitioner summarizes:

"So the picture I get is that you're feeling very discouraged and want your marriage to be better. You want much more from your husband than you're getting, but you've kept your feelings inside and just end up hurting. It's as though you're unsure how much you have a right to expect from him. You also have difficulty expressing your needs and feelings to him, partly because you're afraid he wouldn't understand and partly because you have difficulty standing up for yourself. To deal with its means you have a task of learning to come to grips with thoughts and feelings that block you from expressing yourself more openly to your husband."

Summarizing responses of this type serve as a prelude to the process of formulating goals, as goals flow naturally from problem formulations. Moreover, highlighting various dimensions of the problem facilitates the subsequent delineation of subgoals and tasks that must be accomplished to achieve an overall goal. In the situation cited above, to improve her marriage the client would need to explore further and resolve her fears of standing up for herself, increase her self-esteem, and learn to express assertively her frustrations, hurts, and wants.

Summarizing salient aspects of problems is a valuable technique in sessions with groups, couples, and families, enabling the practitioner at timely moments to highlight the difficulties experienced by each member. In a family session with a depressed adolescent and her parents, for example, the practitioner might say:

[*To girl*]: You feel really labeled by the family. From your perspective, everyone sees you as the "sick one" and as the person responsible for the family problems. To you, it feels like no matter what you do, someone will criticize you for doing it. You feel very shut out, alone, and inferior to your brothers and sisters. I sense your deep discouragement—you seem to be saying, "why bother to try any more?" [*To mother*]: As you spoke, you seemed to feel very overwhelmed and perhaps helpless. You're saying, "I care about my daughter, I want to help, but I just can't seem to reach her. She won't let me in any more, and I just don't know what else to try." Like your daughter feels shut out of the family, you feel shut out of her life, and you wonder, "Has she shut me out because of something I've done? What went wrong?" You also seem to want more support from your husband in coping with the struggles you are having.

[*To father*]: You, too, seem to be throwing your hands up in despair and to be feeling that the situation is hopeless—that things won't change. You'd like to be more available to your wife and daughter, but pressures at work are interfering with that. When you do get involved, however, you sometimes feel caught between them when they disagree—sometimes defending your daughter and having your wife get angry at you as a result. I think you're saying "I don't like that position. I wish there wasn't so much tension between the three of us."

Such responses synthesize in concise and neutral language the needs, concerns, and problems of each participant for all other members of the session to hear.

When summarization of this type is employed frequently, it underscores the fact that *all* participants are struggling with and have responsibility for problems that are occurring, thus counteracting the tendency of families to view one person as the "identified patient," that is, the person who is the exclusive carrier and perpetuator of problems and is to blame for all of the family's ills.

Summarizing Lengthy Messages Clients' messages range from one word or one sentence to lengthy and sometimes rambling monologues. Although the meaning and significance of brief messages are often readily discernible, lengthy messages confront the practitioner with the challenge of encapsulating and tying together diverse elements that may possess marked complexity. Linking the elements together often highlights and expands the significance and meaning of the client's message. For this reason, such messages represent one form of additive empathy, a skill discussed in Chapter 19.

Because lengthy client messages typically include emotions, thoughts, and descriptive content, you will need to be perceptive to how these dimensions relate to the focal point of the discussion. To illustrate, consider the following message of a mildly brain-damaged and socially withdrawn 16-year-old female—an only child who is extremely dependent on her overprotective but subtly rejecting mother:

"Mother tells me she loves me, but I find that hard to believe. Nothing I do ever pleases her; and she yells at me when I refuse to wash my hair alone. But I can't do it right without her help. 'When are you going to grow up?' she'll say. And she goes bowling with her friends and leaves me alone in that creaky house. She knows how scared I get when I have to stay home alone. But she says, 'Nancy, I can't just baby-sit you all the time. I've got to do something for myself. Why don't you make some friends or watch TV or play your guitar? You've just got to quit pitying yourself all the time.' Does that sound like someone who loves you? I get so mad at her when she yells at me, it's all I can do to keep from killing her.''

Embodied in the preceding message are the following elements:

1. Wanting to be loved by her mother yet feeling insecure and rejected at times.

2. Feeling inadequate about performing certain tasks, such as washing her hair.

3. Feeling extremely dependent upon her mother for certain services and companionship.

4. Feeling afraid when her mother leaves her alone.

5. Feeling hurt (implied) and resentful when her mother criticizes her or leaves her alone.

6. Feeling intense anger and wanting to lash out when her mother yells at her.

The following is a summarizing response that ties these elements together:

"So you find your feelings toward your mother pulling you in different directions. You want her to love you, but you feel unloved and resent it when she criticizes you or leaves you alone. And you feel really torn because you depend on her in so many ways, and yet at times, you feel so angry you want to hurt her back for yelling at you. You'd like to have a smoother relationship without the strain."

In conjoint interviews or group sessions, summarization can also be used effectively to highlight and to tie together key elements and dynamics embodied in transactions, as illustrated in the following transaction and summarizing responses of a practitioner:

WIFE: [*To husband.*] You're just never home when I need you. I need your help making decisions about the children. We've got this big activity coming up with Susan this weekend. And where are you going to be? [*Said with animation and sarcasm.*] Deer hunting—of course.

HUSBAND: [*Bristling and defensive.*] You're damned right! You make it sound like a crime. I suppose you expect me not to go deer hunting just because you can't make a decision. Once a year I get to do something I really enjoy, and you bitch about it. Why shouldn't you make decisions? I didn't marry you to make your decisions for you. Making decisions about the children is your job. Why don't you learn to stand on your own two feet for a change?

PRACTITIONER: Let's stop here and think about what each of you is saying. [*To wife.*] You're feeling overwhelmed in coping with the children alone. I gather the bottom line of what you're saying is that your husband is very important to you, and you want to work together as a team in dealing with matters related to the children. [*Wife nods in agreement as husband listens attentively.*]

[*To husband.*] And I gather you're reading your wife's message as an attempt to pass the buck to you. You also sounded as though you felt attacked and read her message as an attempt to deny you an opportunity to enjoy yourself. [*He vigorously nods affirmatively.*]

[*To both.*] Each of you seems to be feeling a lack of caring and understanding by the other, but these needs get buried under your criticism and attempts to defend yourselves. Let's explore further what each of you is needing from the other.

The practitioner's summarization employs additive empathy in identifying needs that underlie the negative and destructive messages exchanged by the spouses. Going beyond the negative surface feelings, the practitioner summarizes implied messages and needs, the exploration of which may lead to increased understanding and to positive feelings rather than mutual recriminations.

On occasion, client messages may ramble to the extent that they contain numerous unrelated elements that cannot all be tied together. In such instances, your task is to extract and focus on those elements of the message that are most relevant to the thrust of the session at that point. Utilized in this manner, summarization provides focus and direction to the session and averts aimless wandering. With clients whose thinking is loose or who ramble to avoid having to focus on unpleasant matters, you will need to interrupt on occasions to assure some semblance of focus and continuity. Otherwise, the interview will be disjointed and unproductive. Skills in maintaining focus and continuity are discussed at length later in the chapter and in Chapter 14.

Reviewing Focal Points of a Session

During the course of an individual, conjoint, or group session, it is common to focus on more than one problem and to discuss numerous factors associated with each problem. Toward the end of the first or second session, therefore, depending on the length of the initial exploration, summarization is employed to review key problems that have been explored and to highlight themes and patterns that relate to these problems. Because summarizing themes and patterns expands the client's awareness of dysfunctional patterns and his or her role in the difficulties manifested (assuming the client affirms the

validity of the summarization), use of this skill opens up promising avenues for growth and change.

In fact, through summarizing responses, the practitioner can review problematic themes and patterns that have emerged in the session and test the client's readiness to consider goals aimed at modifying these dysfunctional patterns. The following is an example of such a message:

"As we explored the stresses that appear to precede your periods of depression, the theme of your discounting yourself by trying so hard to meet unreasonable demands of your family members struck me as very significant, and you seemed to agree. As we begin to consider goals, I wonder what you think about working toward the goal of giving your own needs higher priority and learning to say "No!" and feeling good about it when others make demands that conflict with your needs."

Providing Focus and Continuity

Summarization can also be utilized by the practitioner at the beginning of an individual, group, or conjoint session to review work that clients have accomplished in the last session(s) and to set the stage for work in the present session. At the same time, the practitioner may wish to identify a promising topic for discussion or to refresh clients' minds concerning work they wish to accomplish in that session. In addition, summarization can also be employed periodically to synthesize salient points at the conclusion of a discussion or utilized at the end of the session to review the major focal points. In so doing, the practitioner will need to place what was accomplished in the session within the broad perspective of the client's goals. By considering how the salient content and movement manifested in each session fit into the larger whole, both the practitioner and clients are more likely to maintain a sense of direction and to avoid needless delays caused by wandering and detours that commonly occur when continuity within or between sessions is weak.

Used as a "wrap-up" when the allotted time for a session is nearly gone, summarization also assists the practitioner to draw a session to a natural conclusion. In addition to highlighting and linking together the key points of the session, the practitioner reviews with clients plans for performing tasks that they have agreed to accomplish before the next session. Upon concluding the session in such a manner, all participants are clear about where they have been and where they are going in relation to the goals toward which their mutual efforts are directed.

Analyzing Your Verbal Following Skills

After taking frequency counts over a period of time of some of the major verbal following skills (empathy, concreteness, open-ended and closed-ended responses), as suggested in this chapter, you are ready to assess the extent to which you employ, blend, and balance these skills in relation to each other. Employing the form for verbal following (Figure 6-2) found below, categorize each of your responses from a recorded session. As you analyze your relative use and blending of responses alone or with your practicum instructor, determine whether you think certain types of responses were used either too frequently or too sparingly. Further, think of steps that you might take to correct any imbalances in your utilization of skills for future sessions.

Focusing: A Complex Skill

Skills in focusing are critical to effective social work practice for several reasons, the first of which is purely pragmatic. Clients and practitioners spend limited

Figure 6-2   Recording Form for Verbal Following Skills

Client message	Open-ended responses	Closed-ended responses	Empathic responses	Level of empathy	Concrete responses	Summarizing responses	Other types of responses
1.							
2.							
3.							
4.							
5.							
6.							
7.							

Directions: Categorize each of your responses from a recorded session. Where responses involve more than one category (blended responses), record them as a single response, but also check each category embodied in the response. Excluding the responses checked as "other," analyze whether certain types of responses were utilized too frequently or too sparingly. Set tasks for yourself to correct imbalances in future sessions. Retain a copy of the form so that you can monitor your progress in mastering verbal following skills over an extended period of time.

time together, and it is critical that they use that time fruitfully by focusing on topics and employing processes that produce maximal yield. Practitioners, therefore, are responsible for giving direction to the helping process and avoiding wandering that unnecessarily consumes valuable time. Indeed, one feature that differentiates effective helping relationships from general social relationships is that the former are characterized by sharp focus and continuity, whereas the latter are relatively unstructured.

Another reason why focusing skills are vital is that clients have limited perspectives of their problems and look to professionals for expertise and guidance in concentrating their efforts in areas likely to produce desired results. Moreover, a number of clients tend to be scattered in their thinking and dissipate their energies by rapidly shifting their focus from one topic to another. Practitioners perform a valuable role by assisting them to focus on problems in greater depth and to maintain focus until they accomplish desired changes.

Still another vital reason for developing focusing skills is that families and groups often engage in dysfunctional processes that not only cause interactional difficulties but also hinder groups from focusing effectively on their problems. To enhance family and group functioning, therefore, practitioners must be able to refocus the discussion any time dysfunctional processes cause families and groups prematurely to shift away from the topic at hand.

To assist beginning practitioners to learn how to focus effectively, we consider the various functions of focusing skills, which are as follows:

1. Selecting topics for exploration.

2. Exploring topics in depth.

3. Maintaining focus and keeping on topic.

Knowledge of these functions assists you to focus sharply on relevant topics and elicit sufficient data to formulate an accurate problem assessment—a prerequisite for competent practice.

Selecting Topics for Exploration

Areas relevant for exploration vary from situation to situation. However, clients who belong to the same populations, such as delinquents, unwed mothers, nursing home residents, mentally retarded persons, patients in psychiatric institutions, or families in the same stage of life development, generally share many problems in common. Before meeting with clients whose probable difficulties differ from client populations with which you are familiar, you can prepare yourself to conduct an effective exploration by developing (in consultation with your practicum instructor or an experienced practitioner) a list of relevant and promising problem areas to be explored. This preparation will assist you to avoid the tendency of beginning practitioners to focus on areas irrelevant to clients' problems and thus to elicit numerous bits of inconsequential information. In initially interviewing an institutionalized youth, for example, you could more effectively select questions and responses if you knew in advance that you might explore the following areas:

1. Client's perceived problem areas.

2. Details regarding client's relationships and problems with individual family members.

3. Brief family history.

4. School adjustment, including information about grades, problem subjects, areas of interest, and relationships with various teachers.

5. Reasons for being institutionalized and brief history of past problems related to legal authority and to use of drugs and alcohol.

6. Adjustment to institutional life, including relationships with peers and supervisors.

7. Peer relationships outside the institution.

8. Life goals.

9. Client's perceived strengths.

10. Reaction to previous experiences with counseling.

11. Motivation to engage in counseling relationship and to work on problems.

As noted previously, problem areas vary, and outlines of probable topical areas likewise vary accordingly. A list of areas for exploration in an initial session with a couple seeking marriage counseling or with a group of alcoholics will include a number of items that differ from those in the preceding list. Note, however, that items 1 and 9 through 11 would likely be included in all exploratory interviews with individual clients and would be equally applicable to preparatory interviews with prospective group members.

In using an outline, you should avoid following it rigidly or using it as a crutch, for you may otherwise destroy the spontaneity of sessions and block clients from relating their stories in their own way. Rather, you should encourage clients to discuss their problems freely and play a facilitative role in exploring in greater depth problems that emerge. You must use outlines flexibly, reordering the sequence of topics, modifying, adding, or deleting topics or abandoning the outline altogether if using it hinders communication.

You should note that you cannot always anticipate fruitful topical areas, for although clients from the same population share many commonalities, their problems also have unique aspects. It is thus important to review tapes of sessions with your practicum instructor or an experienced practitioner for the purpose of identifying other topical areas you should explore in future sessions.

Exploring Topics in Depth

A major facet of focusing involves centering discussions on relevant topics to assure that exploration moves from generality and superficiality to more depth and meaning. Practitioners must have skills that enable them to explore problems thoroughly, for success in the helping process depends on clear and accurate definitions of problems.

Selectively attending to specific topics is a challenging task for beginning practitioners, who often wander in individual or group sessions, repeatedly skipping across the surface of vital areas of content and feelings and eliciting largely superficial and sometimes distorted information. This is illustrated in the following excerpt from a first session with an adolescent in a school setting:

PRACTITIONER: Tell me about your family.
CLIENT: My father is ill and my mother is dead, so we live with my sister.
PRACTITIONER: How are things with you and your sister?
CLIENT: Good. We get along fine. She treats me pretty good.
PRACTITIONER: How about your father?
CLIENT: We get along pretty well. We have our problems, but most of the time things are okay. I don't really see him very much.

PRACTITIONER: Tell me about school. How are you getting along here?

CLIENT: Well, I don't like it very well, but my grades are good enough to get me by.

PRACTITIONER: I notice you're new to our school this year. How did you do in the last school you attended?

Notice that by focusing superficially on the topics of family and school, the practitioner misses opportunities to explore these potential problem areas in the depth necessary to illuminate the client's situation. The exploration thus yielded little information of value, in large part because the practitioner failed to employ responses that focus in depth on topical areas. In the following sections, we further delineate skills discussed earlier in the chapter that considerably enhance a practitioner's ability to maintain focus on specific areas.

Open-Ended Responses   Practitioners may employ open-ended questions or responses throughout individual, conjoint, and group sessions to focus unintrusively on desired topics. Earlier we noted that some open-ended responses leave clients free to choose their own topics and that others focus on a topic but encourage clients to respond freely to that topic. The following examples, taken from an initial session with a depressed mother of eight children, illustrate how practitioners can employ open-ended responses to define topical areas that may yield information vital in grasping the dynamics of the client's problems.[1]

---

[1]You will note that several of the following messages could also be categorized as seeking concreteness. Messages that seek concreteness and open-ended messages are not mutually exclusive and often overlap considerably.

1. "What have you thought that you might like to accomplish in counseling?"

2. "You've discussed many topics in the last few minutes. Could you pick the most important one and tell me more about it?"

3. "You've mentioned your husband isn't willing to come for help. I'd appreciate hearing more about that."

4. "Several times as you've mentioned your concern that your husband may leave you, your voice has trembled. I wonder if you could share what you are feeling."

5. "You've indicated that your husband won't help you with the children. You also seem to be saying that you feel overwhelmed and inadequate in managing the children by yourself. Tell me what happens as you try to manage your children."

6. "You indicate that you have more problems with your 14-year-old daughter than with the other children. Tell me more about Janet and your problems with her."

In the preceding illustrations, the practitioner's open-ended questions and responses progressively moved the exploration from the general to the specific. Note also that each response or question defined a new topic for exploration. To encourage in-depth exploration of the topics thus defined, the practitioner must blend open-ended questions with other facilitative verbal following responses that focus on and elicit expanded client expressions.

After having defined a topical area by employing an open-ended response, the practitioner may deepen exploration by weaving other open-ended responses into the discussion. If the open-ended responses shift the focus to another area, however, the exploration suffers a setback. Note in the following illustration that the practitioner's second open-ended response shifts the focus away from the client's message, which involves expression of intense feelings:

PRACTITIONER: You've said you're worried about retiring. I'd appreciate your sharing more about your concern. [*Open-ended response.*]

CLIENT: I can't imagine not going to work every day. I feel at loose ends already, and I haven't even quit work. I'm afraid I just won't know what to do with myself.

PRACTITIONER: What are your thoughts about doing some traveling? [*Open-ended response.*]

Even though open-ended responses elicit information about clients' problems, they may *not* facilitate the helping process if they *prematurely* lead the client in a different direction. If practitioners utilize open-ended or other types of responses that frequently change the topic, they will gain information that is disjointed and fragmented. As a result, assessments will suffer from large gaps in the practitioner's knowledge concerning clients' problems. As practitioners formulate open-ended responses, they must be acutely aware of the direction that responses will take.

Seeking Concreteness Earlier we discussed and illustrated the various facets of seeking concreteness. Because seeking concreteness enables practitioners to move from the general to the specific and to explore topics in depth, it is a key focusing technique. By focusing in depth on topical areas, practitioners are able to discern, and to assist clients to discern, dysfunctional thoughts, behavior, and interaction. We illustrate in subsequent sections how practitioners can effectively focus on topical areas in exploratory sessions by blending concreteness with other focusing skills. In actuality, the ma-

jority of responses that practitioners typically employ to establish and maintain focus are blends of various types of discrete responses.

Empathic Responding Empathic responding serves a critical function by enabling practitioners to focus in depth on troubling feelings, as illustrated in the next example:

CLIENT: I can't imagine not going to work every day. I feel at loose ends already, and I haven't even quit work. I'm afraid I just won't know what to do with myself.

PRACTITIONER: You seem to be saying, "Even now, I'm apprehensive about retiring. I'm giving up something that has been very important to me, and I don't seem to have anything to replace it." I gather that feeling at loose ends, as you do, you worry that when you retire, you'll feel useless.

CLIENT: I guess that's a large part of my problem. At times I feel useless now. I just didn't take time over the years to develop any hobbies or to pursue any interests. I guess I don't think that I can do anything else.

PRACTITIONER: It sounds like you regret not having developed other interests in the past and are afraid that now you may lack the ability to develop in other areas. Maybe you're wondering if it's too late.

CLIENT: Yes, that's right. But it isn't just that. I'm really dreading being at home with time on my hands. I can just see it now. My wife will want to keep me busy doing things around the house for her all the time. I've never liked to do that kind of thing.

Observe in the preceding example that the client's problem continued to unfold as the practitioner utilized empathic responding, revealing rich information in the process.

Blending Open-Ended, Empathic, and Concrete Responses to Maintain Focus

After employing open-ended responses to focus on a selected topic, practitioners should use other responses to maintain focus on that topic. In the following excerpt, observe how the practitioner employs open-ended and empathic responses to explore problems in depth, thereby enabling the client to move to the heart of her struggle. Notice also the richness of the client's responses elicited by the blended messages.

PRACTITIONER: As you were speaking about your son, I sensed some pain and reluctance on your part to talk about him. I'd like to understand more about what you're experiencing. Could you share with me what you are experiencing right now? [*Blended empathic and open-ended response that seeks concreteness.*]

CLIENT: I guess I haven't felt too good about coming this morning. I almost called and canceled. I feel I should be able to handle these problems with Jim [*son*] myself. Coming here is like having to admit I'm no longer capable of coping with him.

PRACTITIONER: So you've had reservations about coming [*paraphrase*]—you feel you're admitting defeat and that perhaps you've failed or that you're inadequate—and that hurts. [*Empathic response.*]

CLIENT: Well, yes, although I know that I need some help. It's just hard to admit it, I think. My biggest problem in this regard, however, is my husband. He

feels much more strongly than I do that we should manage this problem ourselves, and he really disapproves of my coming in.

PRACTITIONER: So even though it's painful for you, you're convinced you need some assistance with Jim, but you're torn about coming here because of your husband's attitude. I'd be interested in hearing more about that. [*Blended empathic and open-ended response.*]

In the preceding example, the practitioner initiated discussion of the client's here-and-now experiences through a blended open-ended and empathic response, following this with other empathic and blended responses to explore the client's feelings further. With the last response, the practitioner narrowed the focus to a potential obstacle to the helping process (the husband's attitude toward therapy), which could also be explored in a similar manner.

Open-ended and empathic responses may also be blended to facilitate and encourage discussion from group members about a defined topic. For instance, after using an open-ended response to solicit group feedback regarding a specified topic ("I'm wondering how you feel about..."), the practitioner can employ empathic or other facilitative responses to acknowledge the contribution of members who respond to the invitation to comment. Further, by utilizing open-ended responses, the practitioner can successively reach for comments of individual members who have not contributed ("What do you think about..., Ray?").

In the next example, the practitioner blends empathic and concrete responses to facilitate in-depth exploration. Notice how these blended responses yield behavioral referents of the problem. The empathic messages convey sensitive awareness and concern for the client's distress. The open-ended and concrete responses focus on details of a recent event and yield valuable clues that the client's rejections by women may be associated with insensitive and inappropriate social behavior, awareness of which is a prelude to formulating relevant goals. Goals thus formulated are highly relevant to the client.

CLIENT: [*Single male, age 20.*] There has to be something wrong with me, or women wouldn't treat me like a leper. Sometimes I feel like I'm doomed to be alone the rest of my life. I'm not even sure why I came to see you. I think I'm beyond help.

PRACTITIONER: You sound like you've about given up on yourself—as though you're utterly hopeless; but apparently part of you still clings to hope and wants to try. [*Empathic response.*]

CLIENT: What else can I do? I can't go on like this, but I don't know how many more times I can get knocked down and get back up.

PRACTITIONER: I sense you feel deeply hurt and discouraged at those times. Could you give me a recent example of when you felt you were being knocked down? [*Blended empathic and concrete response.*]

CLIENT: Well, a guy I work with got me a blind date for a dance. I took her, and it was a total disaster. I know I'm no Prince Charming, but you'd think she could at least let me take her home. After we got to the dance, she ignored me the whole night and danced with other guys. Then, to add insult to injury, she went home with one of them and didn't even have the decency to tell me. There I was, wondering what had happened to her.

PRACTITIONER: Besides feeling rejected, you must have been mad as blazes. When did you first feel you weren't hitting it off with her? [*Blended empathic and concrete response.*]

CLIENT: I guess it was when she lit up a cigarette while we were driving to the dance. I kidded her about how she was asking for lung cancer.

PRACTITIONER: I see. What was it about her reaction, then, that led you to believe you might not be in her good graces? [*Concrete response.*]

CLIENT: Well, she didn't say anything. She just smoked her cigarette. I guess I really knew then that she was upset at me.

In the next example, observe how the practitioner blends empathic and concrete responses to elicit details of interaction in an initial conjoint session. Such blending is a potent technique for eliciting specific and abundant information that bears directly on clients' problems. While responses that seek concreteness elicit details, empathic responses enable practitioners to stay attuned to clients' moment-by-moment experiencing, thereby focusing on feelings that may present obstacles to the exploration.

PRACTITIONER: You mentioned having difficulties communicating. I'd like you to give me an example of a time when you felt you weren't communicating effectively, and let's go through it step by step to see if we can understand more clearly what is happening.

WIFE: Well, weekends are an example. Usually I want to go out and do something fun with the kids, and John just wants to stay home. He starts criticizing me for wanting to go, go, go.

PRACTITIONER: Could you give me a specific example? [*Seeking concreteness.*]

WIFE: Okay. Last Saturday I wanted for us all to go out to eat and to a movie, and John wanted to stay home and watch TV.

PRACTITIONER: Before we get into what John did, let's stay with you for a moment. There you are, really wanting to go to a movie—tell me exactly what you did. [*Seeking concreteness.*]

WIFE: I think I said, "John, let's take the kids out to dinner and a movie."

PRACTITIONER: Okay. That's what you said. How did you say it? [*Seeking concreteness.*]

WIFE: I expected him to say no, so I might not have said it the way I just did.

PRACTITIONER: Turn to John, and say it the way you may have said it then. [*Seeking concreteness.*]

WIFE: Okay. [*Turning to husband.*] Couldn't we go out to a movie?

PRACTITIONER: There seems to be some doubt in your voice as to whether or not John wants to. [*Focusing observation.*]

WIFE: [*Interrupting.*] I knew he wouldn't want to.

PRACTITIONER: So you assumed he wouldn't want to go. It's as though you already knew the answer. [*To husband.*] Does the way your wife asked the question check out with the way you remembered it? [*Husband nods.*]

PRACTITIONER: After your wife asked you about going to the movie, what did you do? [*Seeking concreteness.*]

HUSBAND: I said, nope! I wanted to stay home and relax Saturday, and I felt we could do things at home.

PRACTITIONER: So your answer was short. Apparently you didn't give her information about why you didn't want to go but just said no. Is that right? [*Focusing observation.*]

HUSBAND: That's right. I didn't think she wanted to go anyway—the way she asked.

PRACTITIONER: What were you experiencing when you said no? [*Seeking concreteness.*]

HUSBAND: I guess I was just really tired. I have a lot of pressures from work, and I just need some time to relax. She doesn't understand that.

PRACTITIONER: You're saying, then, "I just needed some time to get away from it all," but I take it you had your doubts as to whether she could appreciate your feelings. [*Husband nods. Turning to wife.*] Now, after your husband said no, what did you do? [*Blended empathic and concrete response.*]

WIFE: I think that I started talking to him about the way he just sits around the house.

PRACTITIONER: I sense that you felt hurt and somewhat discounted because John didn't respond the way you would have liked. [*Empathic response.*]

WIFE: [*Nods.*] I didn't think he even cared what I wanted to do.

PRACTITIONER: Is it fair to conclude, then, that the way in which you handled your feelings was to criticize John rather than to say, "This is what is happening to me?" [*Wife nods.*] [*Seeking concreteness.*]

PRACTITIONER: [*To husband.*] Back, then, to our example, what did you do when your wife criticized you? [*Seeking concreteness.*]

HUSBAND: I guess I criticized her back. I told her she needed to stay home once in a while and get some work done.

Evaluating Use of Focusing and Exploring Skills

To gain mastery of focusing skills and other verbal following and exploring skills, it is important that you "track" the categories of your responses to determine the extent to which you are exploring problem areas in depth. By examining a portion of a session transcribed in verbatim form, you can diagram the session to identify topical areas, to determine the depth of exploration of each, and to analyze the categories of responses used. In an initial session you may find that your first attempts at interviewing take this form:

Fifteen-Minute Segment of Interview

t1	t2	t3	t4	t5	t6	t7	t8	t9	t10
CEQ	CEQ	CEQ	OER	CEQ	CEQ	OER	CEQ	CEQ	P
CEQ		CEQ	MP	P		MP	CEQ		OER
							MP		
							CEQ		

Key: t = Topical area.
      CEQ = Closed-ended question.
      OER = Open-ended response.
       MP = Minimal prompt.
        P = Paraphrase.

In the preceding diagram, note that the practitioner used a limited number of verbal following skills and changed topics frequently, thus exploring subjects only superficially. This type of interviewing explains why beginners sometimes complain that they "just couldn't get anywhere" in sessions or that clients discussed their problems in vague terms. Such difficulties, of course, may also result in part from behaviors of clients that interfere with practitioners' efforts to focus, as we discuss later. Often, however, the practitioner's interviewing style is largely responsible for the low yield of information and the sketchy picture of the client's situation.

If you use open-ended responses to focus on selected areas and employ verbal following skills to maintain focus on these topics, a profile of a 15-minute segment of an interview would likely resemble the following:

t1	t2	t3	t4	t5
OER	OER	ER/OER	OER	CEQ
MP	ER	CEQ	ER	OER
ER	ER	ER	OER/SC	ER
A	ER	ER	ER	A
ER		ER	ER	ER
SC		MP	CEQ	
ER		P	ER	
SR		SC	A	
			SR	

Key: t = Topical area.
      ER = Empathic response.
     CEQ = Closed-ended question.
     OER = Open-ended response.
      MP = Minimal prompt.
       P = Paraphrase response.
       A = Accent response.
      SC = Seeking concreteness.
      SR = Summary response.

A diagram of an actual initial session, of course, is unlikely to be as tidy as our illustration. Other types of responses (e.g., information-giving responses) might be intermixed with exploring and focusing responses. Further, practitioners expend some time and effort in sessions on activities such as negotiating goals and contracting.

We recommend that you diagram and analyze segments of actual and simulated sessions *many times,* with the goal of assessing your focusing patterns. Doing so will assist you to make appropriate modifications in style so that you achieve the second type of profile.

Although individual sessions are easier to diagram than group or conjoint sessions, it is possible to diagram the latter to determine the extent to which you focused and assisted members of the group to focus or to refocus on pertinent topics.

Managing Obstacles to Focusing

Occasionally you may find that your efforts to focus selectively and to explore topical areas in depth are unsuccessful in yielding pertinent information. Although you have a responsibility in such instances to assess the effectiveness of your own interviewing style, you should also analyze clients' styles of communicating to determine to what extent their behaviors are interfering with your focusing efforts. As we noted in an earlier chapter, a common reason why clients seek help is that they have, but are not aware of, patterned communications or behaviors that cause difficulties in relationships. Also manifested in their contacts with practitioners, these repetitive behaviors can impede communication; the pursuit of therapeutic objectives; and, pertinent to this discussion, exploration of problems. The following list includes common types of client communications that may challenge your efforts to focus in individual, family, and group sessions:

- Responding with "I don't know."

- Changing the subject or avoiding sensitive areas.

- Rambling from topic to topic.

- Intellectualizing or using abstract or general terms.

- Diverting focus from the present to the past.

- Responding to questions with questions.

- Interrupting excessively.

- Failing to express opinions when asked.

- Producing excessive verbal output.

- Using humor or sarcasm to evade topics or issues.

- Verbally dominating the discussion.

You can counter repetitive client behaviors and communications that divert the focus from exploring problems by tactfully drawing them to clients' attention and assisting clients to assume behaviors that are compatible with therapeutic objectives. It is important to recognize that until practitioners assist group members to modify behaviors that repetitively impede effective focusing and communication, groups will not move to the phase of group development wherein most of the work related to solving problems is accomplished.

Practitioners may use a number of different techniques for managing and modifying client behaviors that impede exploration. Some of these techniques include requesting the client to communicate or behave differently; teaching, modeling, and coaching clients to assume more effective communication styles; reinforcing facilitative responses; and selectively attending to functional behaviors.

Intervening to Help Clients Focus or Refocus Communications that occur in group or conjoint sessions are not only myriad and complex but may also be distractive or irrelevant. Consequently, the practitioner's task of assisting members to explore defined topics fully, rather than meander from subject to subject, is a challenging one. Related techniques that practitioners can employ are highlighting or clarifying issues or bringing clients' attention to a comment or matter that has been overlooked. In such instances, the objective is not necessarily to explore the topic (although that may subsequently occur) but, rather, to stress or elucidate important content. The practitioner thus focuses clients' attention on communications and/or events that occurred earlier in the session or immediately preceded the practitioner's focusing response, as illustrated in the following messages:

[*To wife in session with couple*]: Rayne, you made an important point a moment ago that I'm not sure that Larry heard. Would you please repeat your comment?

[*To individual*]: I would like to return to a remark you made several moments ago when you said. . . . I didn't want to interrupt then, but I think perhaps the remark was important enough that we should return to it now.

[*To family*]: Something happened just a minute ago as we were talking. [*Describes event.*] We were involved in another discussion then, but I made a mental note of it because of how deeply it seemed to affect all of you at the time. I think we should consider what happened for just a moment.

[*To group member*]: John, as you were talking a moment ago, I wasn't sure what you meant by. . . . Could you clarify that for me and for others in the group?

[*To group*]: A few minutes ago, we were engrossed in a discussion about . . . , yet we have moved away from that discussion to one that doesn't really seem to relate to our purpose for being here. I'm concerned about leaving the other subject hanging because you were working hard to find some solutions and appeared to be close to a breakthrough.

Because of the complexity of communications in group and family sessions, some inefficiency in the focusing process is inescapable; however, the practitioner can sharpen the group's efforts to focus and encourage more efficient use of time by teaching focusing behavior. We suggest that practitioners actually *explain* the focusing role of the group and identify behaviors, such as attending, active listening, and asking open-ended questions, emphasizing that by utilizing these skills members facilitate exploration of problems. Practitioners can also foster use of these skills by giving positive feedback to group or family members when they have adequately focused on a problem, thus reinforcing their efforts.

Traditionally, practitioners have not conceived of their roles as including the *teaching* of focusing and exploring behaviors but rather have used indirect approaches, that is, guidance and modeling to encourage groups to center on specific topics or problem areas. In the past, then, groups have gradually learned these behaviors by imitating practitioners' efforts to identify and explore problems and by responding to their encouragement. As a result, in group contexts focusing has often been inefficient and haphazard, typified by members neglecting important problem areas, exploring issues superficially, and allocating an inordinate amount of time to a few group members.

Although group members usually have difficulty in learning how to focus, they should be able to delve deeply into problems by the third or fourth session, given sufficient guidance *and* education by practitioners. Such efforts by practitioners tend to accelerate movement of groups to maturity, a phase in which members achieve maximum therapeutic benefits. A characteristic of a group in this phase, in fact, is that members explore issues in considerable depth rather than skim the surface of many topics.

Modeled Responses to Exercise in Paraphrasing

1. "You just get so uptight in a group you don't function."

2. "So you've made some real progress in tuning in to your husband and children."

3. "Because your fears really block you when you argue with your mother, you consistently come out on the short side."

4. "You're really torn and wonder if not seeing the children very often is too high a price to pay for a divorce. You seem pretty clear, though, that if you stay with her, there won't be any improvement."

5. "With all of you going different directions, your opportunities to work on your assignments have been almost nil."

6. "So the bottom line, as you see it, is that you're responsible for many of her problems."

Answers to Exercise in Identifying Closed- and Open-Ended Responses

Statement	Response
1.	C
2.	O
3.	O
4.	C

Modeled Open-Ended Responses

1. "Could you tell me more about your wanting to impress Ralph?"

2. "What are you afraid you'd do wrong?"

3. "I'm so pleased for you. Tell me more about your job."

4. "You wish now you hadn't trusted him. In what way did he let you down?"

5. "I gather you feel ganged up on and really resent it. I'd like to understand those feelings better. Could you tell me about when you last felt I took his side?"

6. "Sounds like you're feeling lost and confused about whether you want to try finding yourself. I gather you've been confused about what's been happening to you recently. I'd like to hear more about that."

Classroom Exercises for Developing Verbal Following Skills

1. (Open- versus closed-ended responses.) Instruct students to pair off and assign one member of each pair to play the role of social worker. Each "social worker" is then instructed to conduct a three-minute interview with the other student, who is to share a real-life problem, preferably one that is not deeply personal. Instruct the social worker to employ closed-ended responses exclusively during the interview. At the conclusion of the three-minute interval, ask the students to reverse roles and conduct another three-minute interview. When the role-playing is complete, invite students to share their reactions to the consistent closed-ended responses as they attempted to disclose their problems.

2. Follow the same instructions for (1) above, except that in this exercise instruct the student in the social worker role to employ *open-ended* responses while interviewing the other student concerning the same problem discussed previously. After the students have reversed roles, ask them to compare their reactions to the interviews conducted using open-ended and closed-ended interviewing techniques.

3. (Seeking concreteness.) Play a 15-minute segment of an actual or simulated interview, stopping the tape after each message of the client. Discuss the degree of specificity in each message and identify additional information that may be needed to achieve greater clarity. Evaluate the efficacy of the practitioner's responses in eliciting clarifying information and consider other responses that may have been more productive.

4. (Paraphrasing.) Have the students pair off and alternate playing social worker and client in five-minute role-playing situations. Instruct students to practice paraphrasing while playing the social worker role. Students in the client role may discuss actual stressful situations in their lives or in the lives of others with whom they are closely associated. Before having the students engage in practice, the instructor may model paraphrasing with a student volunteer in the client role.

5. (Recognizing and assessing verbal following skills.) Transcribe a 15-minute segment of an actual or simulated audiotaped initial interview. Make copies of the typed transcription and distribute to class members. (A taped interview may be substituted for a typewritten session if desired.) Using a list of the various types of following skills delineated in this chapter, have the students analyze each response of the interviewer, identifying the type of response employed. Discuss the appropriateness of each response, and analyze its effect as reflected in the client's subsequent response. Analyze whether responses facilitated the client's expression and yielded rich or limited data. Note instances in which other responses could have been used to greater advantage. (Not all of the interviewer's responses will be verbal following responses. Some, for example, may involve explanations or answers to questions.)

Classroom Exercises for Developing Skill in Focusing

1. After dividing the class into pairs, have each pair record role-played five-minute interviews, exchanging roles at the end of five minutes. Each student thus will play the roles of social worker and client discussing actual or simulated problems. In the practitioner's role, students are to explore one problem area in depth, employing open-ended, empathic, furthering, concrete, and closed-ended responses. After the role-playing, instruct students to review their tapes, identifying the types of responses used and ascertaining the extent to which they maintained focus and achieved depth in exploring one topical area.

2. Ask students to role-play and record actual or simulated problems in pairs for 15-minute interviews, exchanging roles so that both have opportunities to play the role of social worker. After the role-playing, instruct students to review their tapes, diagramming their focusing patterns as illustrated earlier in this chapter. Using the diagram, students should next determine the extent to which they explored topics in depth. Based on this anal-

ysis, students should be encouraged to set specific goals aimed at enhancing their skill in focusing by using certain techniques more frequently and eliminating the use of other counterproductive types of responses. Ask students to retain their diagrams for future comparisons.

3. After further practice in developing focusing skills over one week, ask students again to record 15-minute role-played interviews, exchanging roles as specified in (2) above. Students are to diagram their interviews and compare the present diagram with that completed one week earlier. Instruct students to determine the extent to which they have progressed in achieving their goals specified as part of exercise (2) and to specify additional goals that will enhance mastery of their skill.

4. Ask students to form groups according to the types of client populations they are working with in their practicum settings. Instruct the groups to develop interviewing guides that can be employed to assure that they explore relevant topical areas during initial interviews in these settings. Ask the students to compare their guidelines, citing similarities and differences.

5. Divide students into small groups and assign one student to be the leader of a five-minute taped discussion on a topic of the group's choosing. Ask the leader to facilitate discussion and to assist the group to stay on topic by utilizing empathic responding and the other verbal following skills delineated in this chapter. Ask each small group to review its tape and make observations related to the forces that occurred in the group that fostered or impeded focusing by the group. Further, ask group members to give leaders feedback as to their effective and ineffective use of skills. You may wish to do this exercise several times to give others in each group an opportunity to test their skills in focusing.

7 | Eliminating Counterproductive Communication Patterns

Impacts of Counterproductive Communication Patterns

In this chapter we focus on verbal and nonverbal communication patterns that inhibit the helping process. The communication repertoires of aspiring practitioners usually include response patterns that inhibit the free flow of information and negatively impact helping relationships. Such responses impede progress each time they occur, eliciting, for example, defensiveness, hostility, or silence. Consistent use of such responses can block growth, precipitate premature terminations, or cause deterioration in clients' functioning. Attaining competence, therefore, requires learning to avoid such messages and behaviors. This chapter will enable you to identify and eliminate from your repertoire such counterproductive verbal and nonverbal communications.

Eliminating Nonverbal Barriers to Effective Communication

Nonverbal behaviors strongly influence interactions between people. The impor-

tance of this medium of communication is underscored by numerous research findings that counselors' nonverbal interview behavior contributes significantly to ratings of counselor effectiveness. Nonverbal cues, which serve to confirm or to deny messages conveyed verbally, are in large part beyond the conscious awareness of participants. In fact, nonverbal cues may produce "leakage" by transmitting information the sender did not intend to communicate. Facial expressions, such as a blush, a sneer, or a look of shock or dismay, convey much more about the practitioner's attitude toward the client than what is said. In fact, if there is a discrepancy between the practitioner's verbal and nonverbal communication, the client is more likely to discredit the verbal, for people learn through myriad transactions with others that nonverbal cues more accurately indicate feelings than do spoken words.

Physical Attending

Beginning practitioners are often relatively unaware of their nonverbal behaviors, and they may not as yet have learned to consciously use these behaviors to advantage in conveying caring, understanding, and respect. Therefore, mastering *physical attending,* a basic skill critical to the helping process, is an initial learning task. Physical attentiveness to another person is communicated by receptive behaviors, such as facing the client squarely, leaning forward, maintaining eye contact, and remaining relaxed. Attending also requires practitioners to be fully present, that is, to keep in moment-to-moment contact with the client through disciplined attention.

Cultural Nuances of Nonverbal Cues

To consciously use nonverbal behaviors to full advantage in transcultural relationships, practitioners must be aware that different cultural groups ascribe varied meanings to certain nonverbal behaviors. Eye-to-eye contact, for example, is expected among communicating persons in mainstream American culture. People who avoid eye-to-eye contact, in fact, may be viewed as untrustworthy or evasive. Native Americans, however, regard direct gazing as an intrusion of privacy, and it is important, therefore, to employ minimal eye-to-eye contact with this cultural group. Blacks also tend to prefer minimal eye contact, particularly when they are in the listening role. Failure to understand this difference can result in misinterpretations of this nonverbal cue, as McNeely and Badami[1] (1984, p. 23) have explained:

The black person, when experiencing a direct gaze from a white listener, will not recognize that the listener's pattern signifies courteous

attention but will assume that the person is exhibiting hostility by intensive staring. A white person, on the other hand, will perceive a black listener's response as a discrepant reaction if the listener does not engage in the expected amount of direct gazing.

A practitioner's failure to understand the significance of the nonverbal behavior of Asian clients may pose a major barrier to effective communication. Asian clients tend to view helping professionals as authorities who can solve their problems (often presented as physical symptoms) by providing advice. Because Asian cultural patterns prescribe deference to authority, the Asian client may speak little unless spoken to by the practitioner, who may mistakenly perceive what the client regards as being respectful as being passive, silent, and ingratiating. Consequently, "Long gaps of silence may occur as the client waits patiently for the therapist to structure the interview, take charge, and thus provide the solution" (Tsui & Schultz, 1985, p. 565). Such gaps in communication engender anxiety in both parties that may undermine the development of rapport and defeat the helping process. Further, failure to correctly interpret the client's nonverbal behavior may lead the practitioner to conclude erroneously that the client has flat affect (i.e., little emotionality). Given these potential hazards, practitioners must be more active and directive with Asian clients, and they must focus on role expectations, a matter we discuss at more length in Chapter 13.

Other Nonverbal Behaviors

Barriers that prevent the practitioner from staying in psychological contact with

---

[1]McNeely and Badami also discuss several other significant factors that characterize verbal communication patterns of blacks. We recommend this informative article to readers.

the client can be caused by preoccupation with judgments or evaluations about the client or by inner pressures to find immediate solutions to the client's problems. Reduced focus on the client can also result from being preoccupied with oneself while practicing new skills. Further, extraneous noise, a ringing phone, an inadequate interviewing room, or lack of privacy can also interfere with the practitioner's being psychologically present.

Lack of concern for the client can also be conveyed by numerous undesirable behaviors and revealing postural cues. For example, staring vacantly, looking out the window, frequently glancing at the clock, cleaning a pipe, yawning, fidgeting, or clipping fingernails convey inattention; trembling hands or rigid posture may communicate anger or anxiety. These and a host of other behavioral cues that convey messages such as a lack of interest, disapproval, shock, or condemnation are readily perceived by most clients, many of whom are highly sensitive to criticism or rejection in any form.

Taking Inventory of Nonverbal Patterns of Responding

To assist you in taking inventory of your own styles of responding to clients, we have listed desirable and undesirable nonverbal behaviors in Table 7-1. You will probably find that you have a mixed bag of nonverbal responses, some of which have the potential to enhance therapeutic relationships and foster client progress and others that may block your clients from freely disclosing information and otherwise retard the work and flow of the helping process. You thus have a threefold task: (1) to assess your repetitive nonverbal behaviors; (2) to

TABLE 7-1 Inventory of Practitioner's Nonverbal Communication

Desirable	Undesirable
Facial expressions:	Avoidance of eye contact
Direct eye contact (except when culturally proscribed)	Eye level higher or lower than client's
Warmth and concern reflected in facial expression	Staring or fixating on person or object
Eyes at same level as client's	Lifting eyebrow critically
Appropriately varied and animated facial expressions	Nodding head excessively
Mouth relaxed; occasional smiles	Yawning
	Frozen or rigid facial expressions
	Inappropriate slight smile
	Pursing or biting lips
Posture:	Rigid body position; arms tightly folded
Arms and hands moderately expressive; appropriate gestures	Body turned at an angle to client
Body leaning slightly forward; attentive but relaxed	Fidgeting with hands (including clipping nails or cleaning pipe)
	Squirming or rocking in chair
	Slouching or placing feet on desk
	Hand or fingers over mouth
	Pointing finger for emphasis
Voice:	Mumbling or speaking inaudibly
Clearly audible but not loud	Monotonic voice
Warmth in tone of voice	Halting speech
Voice modulated to reflect nuances of feeling and emotional tone of client messages	Frequent grammatical errors
Moderate speech tempo	Prolonged silences
	Excessively animated speech
	Slow, rapid, or staccato speech
	Nervous laughter
	Consistent clearing of throat
	Speaking loudly
Physical proximity:	Excessive closeness or distance
Three to five feet between chairs	Talking across desk or other barrier

eliminate nonverbal styles that hinder effective communication; and (3) to sustain and perhaps increase desirable nonverbal behaviors.

At the end of this chapter is a checklist for use in training or supervision to obtain feedback on nonverbal aspects of attending. Given opportunity to review a videotape of your performance in actual or simulated interviews and/or to receive behaviorally specific feedback from supervisors and peers, you can adequately master physical aspects of attending in a relatively brief time. Review of your taped performance may reveal that you are already manifesting many of the desirable physical attending behaviors listed in Table 7-1. Further, you may possess personal nonverbal mannerisms that are particularly helpful to you in establishing relationships with others, such as a friendly grin or a relaxed, easy manner. As you take inventory of your nonverbal behaviors, elicit feedback from others regarding both your desirable and undesirable nonverbal behaviors. When appropriate, increase the frequency of positive behaviors that you have identified and especially cultivate the quality of warmth, which we discussed in Chapter 3.

As you review videotapes, pay particular attention to your nonverbal responses at those moments when you experienced pressure or tension, which will assist you to determine whether your responses were counterproductive. All beginning interviewers experience moments of discomfort in their first contacts with clients, and nonverbal behaviors are an index of their comfort level. As you review your work, you may notice that under pressure you respond with humor, fidget, change voice inflection, assume a rigid body posture, or manifest other nervous mannerisms. Making an effort to become aware of and to eliminate obvious signs of anxiety is an important step in achieving mastery of your nonverbal responding.

Eliminating Verbal Barriers to Communication

Many types of ineffective verbal responses prevent clients from exploring problems and sharing freely with the practitioner. Some responses are inherently destructive, that is, they invariably have a retarding or negative influence on the helping process. The destructive impact of ineffective communication can be seen in immediate client reactions to the practitioner's response, such as withdrawing, arguing, or moving to a superficial topic. The following list identifies common verbal barriers that usually have an immediate negative effect upon communications and thus prevent clients from revealing pertinent information and working on problems:

1. Moralizing.

2. Advising and giving suggestions or solutions *prematurely.*

3. Persuading or giving logical arguments, lecturing, instructing, arguing.

4. Judging, criticizing, or placing blame.

5. Analyzing, diagnosing, making glib or dogmatic interpretations.

6. Reassuring, sympathizing, consoling, excusing.

7. Using sarcasm or employing humor that is distractive or makes light of clients' problems.

8. Threatening, warning, or counterattacking.

The negative effect of certain types of responses is not always apparent because the client does not manifest untoward reactions at the time or because the retarding effect upon the helping process cannot be observed in a single transaction.

In order to assess the effect of responses, then, the practitioner must determine the *frequency* of detrimental responses and evaluate the overall impact of such responses on the helping process. Frequent use of some types of responses by the practitioner indicates the presence of counterproductive *patterns* of communication such as the following:

9. Using questions inappropriately.

10. Interrupting inappropriately or excessively.

11. Dominating interaction.

12. Fostering social interaction.

13. Responding infrequently.

14. Parroting or overusing certain phrases or clichés.

15. Dwelling on the remote past.

16. Using self-disclosure inappropriately.

Individual responses that fall within these patterns may or may not be ineffective when employed singularly; when employed extensively in lieu of varied response patterns, however, such responses inhibit the natural flow of a session and limit the richness of information revealed.

Verbal Barriers to Effective Communication

1. Moralizing and Sermonizing by Using "Shoulds" and "Oughts"

■ "You shouldn't have done that."

■ "You're too young to get married."

■ "You should try to understand your parents' position. They really have your welfare at heart."

■ "You ought to pay your bills."

Moralizing, sermonizing, admonishing, or otherwise passing judgment causes clients to respond defensively inwardly, if not outwardly. Should and ought messages, which imply that clients have a duty to some vague, external authority, have often been used effectively by significant others in clients' lives to make them feel guilty or obligated. (This, in fact, may be a significant cause of clients' problems.) Moralizing responses by practitioners have the same effect, eliciting feelings of guilt and resentment. Such messages also communicate lack of trust—"I'll tell you what to do because you're not wise enough to know." When experiencing such criticism and lack of confidence in their ability and judgment, clients are unlikely to be receptive to assessing their own positions or to considering others.

2. Advising and Giving Suggestions or Solutions Prematurely

■ "I suggest that you tell your husband you won't put up with his treating you that way."

■ "I think you need to try a new approach with your daughter. Let me suggest that . . ."

■ "I think it would be best for you to . . ."

■ "Since your boyfriend is such a loser, why don't you try to make some relationships with other men?"

Instead of assisting clients and enhancing helping relationships, untimely advice often has the opposite effect, eliciting resistance and even rebellion—"You don't really understand," or "I don't want to be told what to do." Such reactions are usually caused by the prematurity of proffered solutions. Interestingly, even when clients *solicit* advice in early phases of the helping process, they often react negatively when they receive such advice because recommended solutions based on superficial information often do not address their real needs. Further, because clients often are burdened and preoccupied with little-understood conflicts, feelings, and pressures, they are not ready to take action on their problems. For these reasons, after offering untimely advice, practitioners may observe clients replying with responses such as "Yes, but I've already tried that," or "That won't work."

Practitioners often dispense advice prematurely because they feel pressure to provide quick answers or solutions for clients who unrealistically expect magical answers and instant relief from problems that have plagued them for long periods of time. Beginning practitioners also experience inner pressure to dispense solutions to clients' problems, mistakenly believing that their new role demands that they, like physicians, prescribe a treatment regimen. They thus run the risk of giving advice before they have conducted a thorough exploration of the problem. Instead of dispensing wisdom, however, a major role of practitioners is to create and shape processes with clients in which they engage in mutual discovery of problems *and* solutions, work which will take time and concentrated effort.

In the helping process, the timing and form of recommendations are all important. Generally, advice should be offered sparingly, only after thoroughly exploring a problem and clients' ideas regarding possible solutions. At that point, practitioners may serve as consultants, tentatively sharing ideas regarding solutions to supplement those developed by clients. Pressures from clients to influence practitioners to dispense premature advice should be managed by stressing that problems are not simple and that advice based on superficial knowledge would deprive them of developing effective solutions to these problems. Practitioners should also stress clients' roles in helping to discover and to "tailor make" solutions that fit their unique problems.

Practitioners who clarify roles that lead to mutual participation in generating possible solutions further the growth and self-confidence of clients. Assuming a position of superiority and quickly providing solutions for problems without encouraging clients to formulate possible courses of action fosters dependency and stifles creative thinking. Freely dispensing advice also minimizes or ignores clients' strengths and potentials, and many clients may be expected to respond with inner resentment. In addition, clients who have not been actively involved in planning their own courses of action may lack motivation to implement the advice given by practitioners. Further, when advice does not remedy a problem, as it often doesn't, clients may blame practitioners and disown responsibility for an unfavorable outcome.

3. Persuading or Giving Logical Arguments, Lecturing, Instructing, Arguing, Intellectualizing

- "Let's look at the facts about drugs."
- "Remember that you have some responsibility for solving problems, too."
- "Taking that course of action will only get you in more difficulty."
- "That attitude won't get you anywhere."

Persuading with logic, arguing, instructing, and the like often provoke defensiveness and counterarguments from clients. Persuasive efforts by practitioners are futile, serving only to make clients defend their positions more strongly. For some clients, deferring to or agreeing with practitioners is tantamount to giving up individuality or freedom. In vigorously attempting to persuade clients to another point of view, practitioners also often foster power struggles, thereby perpetuating dynamics that have previously occurred in clients' personal relationships. By arguing, practitioners also ignore feelings and views of clients, focusing instead on "being right," which may engender feelings of resentment, alienation, or hostility.

4. Judging, Criticizing, or Placing Blame

- "You're wrong about that."

- "Running away from home was a bad mistake."

- "One of your problems is that you're not willing to consider another point of view."

- "You're not thinking straight."

Responses that evaluate and show disapproval are detrimental to clients and to the helping process. Clients usually respond defensively and sometimes counterattack when they experience criticism by practitioners; further, they often cut off any meaningful communication with practitioners. Intimidated by a practitioner's greater expertise, some clients also accept negative evaluations as accurate reflections of their poor judgment or lack of worth or value. In making such negative judgments about clients, practitioners violate the basic social work values of nonjudgmental attitude and acceptance.

5. Analyzing, Diagnosing, Making Glib or Dramatic Interpretations; Labeling Clients' Behavior

- "You're behaving that way because you're angry at your husband."

- "Your attitude may have kept you from giving their ideas a fair chance."

- "That is passive-aggressive behavior."

- "You are really hostile today."

Used sparingly and appropriately timed, interpretation of the dynamics of behavior is a potent change-oriented skill (see Chapter 19). However, even accurate interpretations that focus on purposes or meanings of behavior substantially beyond clients' levels of conscious awareness engender resistance and are doomed to failure. When stated dogmatically (e.g., "I know what's wrong with you," or ". . . how you feel," or ". . . what your real motives are"), interpretations also present a threat to clients, causing them to feel exposed or trapped. When a glib interpretation is thrust upon them, clients often expend their energies disconfirming the interpretation, explaining themselves, or making angry rebuttals rather than working on the problem at hand.

Using social work jargon, such as *fixation, transference, resistance, reinforcement, repression, passive,* or *neurotic,* and a host of other terms to describe the behavior of clients in their presence is also destructive to the helping process, often confusing or bewildering clients and creating resistance. These terms also oversimplify complex phenomena and psychic mechanisms and stereotype clients, thereby obliterating their uniqueness. In addition, these sweeping generalizations provide no operational definition of clients' problems, nor do they suggest avenues for modification of behavior. If clients accept practitioners' restricted definitions of their problems, they may then define themselves in the same terms as those used by practitioners (e.g., "I am a passive person," or "I have a schizoid personality"). This type of stereotypic labeling often causes clients to view themselves as "sick" and their situation as hopeless, thus providing them with a ready excuse for not working on problems.

6. *Reassuring, Sympathizing, Consoling, Excusing*

- "You'll feel better tomorrow."
- "Don't worry, things will work out."
- "You probably didn't do anything to aggravate the situation."
- "I really feel sorry for you."

When used selectively and with justification, well-timed reassurance can engender much needed hope and support.[2] In glibly reassuring clients that "things will work out," "everybody has problems," or "things aren't as bleak as they seem," however, practitioners avoid exploring clients' feelings of despair, anger, hopelessness, or helplessness. Situations faced by clients are often grim, with no immediate analgesics or relief at hand. Rather than glossing over clients' feelings and seeking to avoid discomfort, it is the task of practitioners to explore distressing feelings and to assist clients in acknowledging painful realities.

Reassuring clients prematurely or without genuine basis often serves the purposes of practitioners more than of clients and, in fact, may represent efforts by practitioners to dissuade clients from their troubling feelings. Such reassurance thus serves to restore the comfort level and equilibrium of practitioners rather than to help clients. Rather than fostering hope, glib reassurances also convey a lack of understanding of clients' feelings and raise doubts about the authenticity of practitioners, causing clients to react with thoughts such as "It's easy for you to say that, but you don't know how very fright-

---

[2]When utilized, reassurance is best directed to clients' *capabilities*. Appropriate reassurance can be effectively conveyed through the skill of positive feedback described in Chapter 5.

ened I really am," or "You're just saying that so I'll feel better." In addition, responses that excuse clients (e.g., "You're not to blame") or sympathize with their position (e.g., "I can see exactly why you feel that way; I think I would probably have done the same thing") often have the effect of unwittingly reinforcing inappropriate behavior or reducing clients' anxiety and motivation to work on problems.

7. *Using Sarcasm or Employing Humor That Is Distractive or Makes Light of Clients' Problems*

- "Get up on the wrong side of the bed?"
- "It seems to me that we've been all through this before."
- "You really fell for that line."
- "You think *you* have a problem. . . ."

Humor is an important therapeutic tool, bringing relief and sometimes perspective to work that may otherwise be tense and tedious. Excessive use of humor, however, is distractive, keeping the content of the session on a superficial level and interfering with therapeutic objectives. Sarcasm often emanates from unrecognized hostility that tends to provoke counterhostility in clients.

8. *Threatening, Warning, or Counterattacking*

- "You better . . . or else!"
- "If you don't . . . you'll be sorry."
- "If you know what's good for you, you'll. . . ."

These responses often produce active resistance, rebellion, and retaliatory communication, exacerbating an already strained situation. Recognizing the adverse effects of such harsh and antitherapeutic responses, skilled practitioners strive to refrain from using them with clients. Still, even the most well-intentioned practitioners may bristle or respond defensively under the pressure of verbal abuse, accusatory or blaming responses, or challenges to their integrity, competence, motives, or authority. Practitioners conducting group sessions with adolescents, for instance, can testify that provocative behavior of this client population may defeat even herculean efforts to respond therapeutically.

Whatever the dynamics behind provocative behavior, a defensive response by practitioners is counterproductive, often duplicating the destructive pattern of responses that clients have typically elicited and experienced from others. To achieve competence, therefore, it is important that you master your own natural defensive reactions and evolve effective ways of dealing with negative feelings. Empathic communication, for example, produces a cathartic release of negative feelings, defusing a strained situation, and permitting a more rational emotional exploration of factors that underlie clients' feelings.

9. Stacking Questions

In exploring problems, practitioners should use facilitative questions that assist clients to reveal detailed information about specific problem areas. However, when practitioners ask several questions in succession, they diffuse their focus on specific content areas, confusing and distracting clients, as illustrated in the following messages:

- "When you don't feel you have control of situations, what goes on inside of you? What do you think about? What do you do?"

- "How is your relationship with your husband? Is that one of your biggest concerns, or is there another that takes priority?"

Adequately answering even one of the foregoing questions would require an extended response by a client. Rather than focusing on one question, however, clients often respond superficially and nonspecifically to the practitioner's multiple inquiry, omitting important information in the process. Stacked questions thus have "low yield" and are unproductive and inefficient in gathering relevant information.

10. Asking Leading Questions

Leading questions are those with hidden or under-the-table agendas designed to induce clients to agree with a particular view or to adopt a solution that practitioners deem to be in clients' best interests. For example:

- "Do you think you've really tried to get along with your wife?"

- "You don't really mean that, do you?"

- "Aren't you too young to move out on your own?"

- "Don't you think that doing that will get in the way of your reconciling with your husband?"

In actuality, such leading questions often obscure legitimate concerns that practitioners should discuss with clients. Practitioners conceal their feelings and opinions about such matters, presenting them obliquely in the form of solutions (e.g., "Don't you think you ought to . . .") in hope that the leading questions will lead clients to desired conclusions. It is an error, however, to assume that clients will not see through such maneuvers. Clients, in fact, often discern the practitioner's motives and inwardly resist having views or directives imposed upon them under the guise of leading questions. Nevertheless, to avoid conflict or controversy with the practitioner, they may express feeble agreement or may simply divert the discussion to another topic.

By contrast, when practitioners authentically assume responsibility for concerns they wish clients to consider, they enhance the likelihood that clients will respond receptively.

11. Interrupting Inappropriately or Excessively To assure focus on relevant problem areas, practitioners must at times interrupt clients. To be effective, however, interruptions must be purposive, well timed, and smoothly executed. Interruptions are detrimental to the helping process when they are abrupt or divert clients from exploring pertinent problem areas. Frequent untimely interruptions tend to annoy clients, stifle spontaneous expression, and hinder exploration of problems.

12. Dominating Interaction At times, practitioners may dominate interaction by talking too much or by excessively asking closed-ended questions, thus assuming the initiative for discussions rather than placing this responsibility with clients. Domineering behaviors by practitioners also include frequently offering advice, pressuring clients to improve, presenting lengthy arguments to persuade clients, frequently interrupting, and so on. Some practitioners are also prone to behave as though they are omniscient, omnipotent, or infallible, failing to convey respect for clients' points of view or capacities to solve problems. Such dogmatic and authoritarian behavior discourages clients from expressing themselves and fosters a one-up, one-down relationship in which clients feel at a great disad-

vantage and resent the practitioner's supercilious demeanor.

Practitioners should monitor the relative distribution of participation by all persons (including themselves) who are involved in individual, family, or group sessions. Although clients naturally vary in their levels of verbal participation and assertiveness, all group members should have equal opportunity to share information, concerns, and views in the helping process. Practitioners have a responsibility to assure this opportunity.

As a general guideline, clients should consume more "speaking time" than practitioners in the helping process, although during initial sessions with Asian-American clients practitioners must be more directive than with Anglo clients, as we discussed earlier. Sometimes practitioners defeat therapeutic objectives in group or conjoint sessions by dominating interaction through such behaviors as speaking for members, focusing more on some members than others, or giving speeches.

Even practitioners who are *not* particularly verbal may dominate sessions that include reserved or nonassertive clients as a means of averting their own discomfort with silence and passivity. Although it is natural to be more active with reticent or withdrawn clients than with those who are more verbal, practitioners must avoid dominating the interaction. Using facilitative responses that draw clients out is an effective method of minimizing silence and passivity.

When review of one of your taped sessions reveals that you have monopolized interaction, it is important that you explore the reasons for your behavior. Identify the specific responses that were authoritarian or domineering and the situations that preceded those responses. Also examine the clients' style of relating for clues regarding your own reactions, and analyze the feelings you were experiencing at the time. Based on your review and assessment of your performance, plan a strategy to modify your own style of relating by substituting facilitative responses for ineffective ones. It may also be necessary to focus on and to explore the passive or nonassertive behavior of clients with the objective of contracting with them to increase their participation in the helping process.

13. *Fostering Social Interaction*   Channeling or keeping discussions focused on safe topics that exclude feelings and minimize self-disclosures is inimical to the helping process. Social chitchat about the weather, news, hobbies, mutual interests or acquaintances, and the like tends to foster a social rather than a therapeutic relationship. In contrast to the lighter and more diffuse communication characteristic of a social relationship, helpful, growth-producing relationships are characterized by sharp focus and specificity.

In the main, social interaction in the helping process should be avoided. It is important to note two qualifications to this general rule: (1) discussion of safe topics may be utilized to assist children or adolescents to lower defenses and risk increasing openness, thereby assisting practitioners to cultivate a quasi-friend role with such clients; (2) a brief discussion of conventional topics may be appropriate and helpful as part of the getting-acquainted or warm-up period of initial sessions or during early portions of subsequent sessions.[3] A warm-up period is particularly important when engaging cli-

ents from ethnic groups for which such informal openings are the cultural norm, as we discussed in Chapter 3.

Even when you try to avoid inappropriate social interaction, however, some clients may resist your attempts to move the discussion to a topic that is relevant to the problems they are experiencing and to the purposes of the helping process. Techniques for managing such situations are found in later chapters of the book.

14. *Responding Passively*   Monitoring the frequency of your responses in individual, conjoint, or group sessions is an important task. As a practitioner, you have an ethical responsibility to utilize fully the limited contact time you have with clients in pursuing therapeutic objectives and promoting their general well-being. Relatively inactive practitioners, however, usually ignore fruitful moments that could be explored to promote clients' growth and allow the focus of a session to stray to inappropriate or unproductive content. To be maximally helpful, practitioners must give structure to the helping process by developing contracts with clients that specify respective responsibilities of both participants, engaging clients in a process of identifying and exploring problems, formulating goals, and delineating tasks to alleviate clients' difficulties. To provide form and direction to the helping process, thereby maximizing change opportunities, you must be consistently active in structuring your work with clients.

Inactivity by practitioners contributes to counterproductive processes and failures in problem solving. One deleterious effect, for example, is that clients lose confidence in practitioners when practitioners fail to intervene by helping them with situations that are destructive to themselves or to others. Confidence is

---

[3]Although the relationship practitioners offer clients may have elements of friendship in it, practitioners must be careful to be more than a friend by channeling the focus to clients' problems.

particularly eroded by the failure of practitioners to intervene when clients communicate destructively in conjoint or group sessions.

Although practitioners' activity per se is important, the quality of their moment-by-moment responses is also critical. Practitioners significantly diminish their effectiveness by neglecting to utilize or by underutilizing facilitative responses.

15. Parroting or Overusing Certain Phrases or Clichés

Parroting a message often irritates clients, prompting at times a response of "Well, yes, I just said that." Rather than merely repeating clients' words, it is important that practitioners use fresh words that capture the essence of clients' messages and place them in sharper perspective. Practitioners generally should also refrain from punctuating their communications with superfluous phrases. The distracting effect of such phrases can be observed in the following message: "You know, a lot of people wouldn't come in for help. It tells me, you know, that you realize that you have a problem, you know, and want to work on it. Do you know what I mean?"

Frequent use of such phrases as "you know," "okay?" ("Let's work on this task, okay?"), and "stuff" ("We went to town, and stuff"), or "that's neat," can be very annoying to some clients (and practitioners, for that matter). Further, if used in excess, the same may be said of some of the faddish clichés that have permeated today's language, such as "far out," "super," "right on," "do your own thing," "getting it on," "turns you off," "let it all hang out," "that's a bad scene," "blows your mind," or "groovy."

Another mistake practitioners sometimes make is to "overrelate" to youth by using adolescent jargon to excess. Adolescents tend to perceive such communication as phony and the practitioner as inauthentic, which hinders rather than facilitates the development of a working relationship.

16. Dwelling on the Remote Past

Practitioners' verbal responses may focus on the *past, present,* or *future*. Helping professionals differ regarding the amount of emphasis they believe should be accorded to gathering historical facts about clients. Focusing largely on the present is vital, however, for clients can change only their present circumstances, behaviors, and feelings. Permitting individuals, groups, couples, or families to dwell on the past may reinforce diversionary tactics employed to avoid dealing with painful aspects of present difficulties and with the need for change. It is important to recognize that often implied in messages about the past are feelings the client is *currently* experiencing related to the past. For example:

CLIENT: [*With trembling voice.*] He used to make me so angry.

PRACTITIONER: There was a time when he really infuriated you. As you think about the past, even now it seems to stir up some of the anger and hurt you felt.

Thus, changing a client's statement from past to present tense often yields rich information about clients' present feelings and problems. The same may be said of bringing future-oriented statements of clients to the present (e.g., "How do you feel *now* about the future event you're describing?"). The point is that it is not only possible but also often productive to shift the focus to the present experiencing of clients even when historical facts are being elicited to illuminate client problems.

Gauging the Effectiveness of Your Responses

The preceding discussion should assist you in identifying ineffective patterned communications you may have been employing. Since most learners typically ask closed-ended questions excessively, frequently change the subject, and recommend solutions before completing a thorough exploration of clients' problems, you should particularly watch for these patterns. In addition, you will need to monitor your interviewing style for idiosyncratic counterproductive patterns of responding.

At the end of the chapter are exercises you can use informally with fellow students or in group training to assist you to recognize and eliminate ineffective responses. Further, since identifying ineffective styles of interviewing requires selective focusing upon the frequency and patterning of responses, you will find it helpful to analyze extended segments of taped sessions using the form, "Assessing Verbal Barriers to Communication," also found at the conclusion of the chapter.

One way of gauging the effectiveness of your responses is to carefully observe clients' reactions immediately following your response. Because of the number of clients involved in group and family sessions, you will often receive varied and nonverbal cues regarding the relative effectiveness of your responses to engage clients in these systems. As you assess your messages, keep in mind that a response is probably helpful if clients respond in one of the following ways:

- Continue to explore the problem or stay on the topic.
- Express pent-up emotions related to the problematic situation.

- Engage in deeper self-exploration and self-experiencing.
- Spontaneously volunteer more personally relevant material.
- Verbally or nonverbally affirm the validity of your response.

By contrast, a response may be too confrontive, poorly timed, or off target if clients respond in one of the following ways:

- Verbally or nonverbally disconfirm your response.
- Change the subject.
- Ignore the message.
- Appear mixed up or confused.
- Become more superficial, more impersonal, more emotionally detached, or more defensive.
- Argue or express anger rather than examining the relevance of the feelings involved.

In analyzing practitioner-client interactions, it is important to keep in mind that the participants mutually influence each other. Thus, a response by either person in an individual interview affects the following expressions of the other person. In group and conjoint sessions, the communications of each person, including the practitioner, also affect the responses of all other participants; in a group situation, however, the influence of messages on subsequent responses of other members is sometimes difficult to detect because of the complexity of the communications.

With respect to the mutual-influence process, beginning interviewers often reinforce unproductive client responses through responding indiscriminately or haphazardly or letting pass without comment positive responses that support therapeutic objectives or reflect growth.

Novice practitioners are also sometimes jolted as they realize the extent to which they have allowed clients to control sessions through dysfunctional or manipulative behaviors. As a beginning practitioner, then, it is extremely important that you monitor and review your moment-by-moment transactions with clients with a view toward avoiding getting caught in ongoing ineffective or destructive communication perpetuated by yourself and the client.

Although beginning practitioners encounter ineffective patterns of communication in individual interviews, they are even more likely to encounter recurring dysfunctional communications in groups or in conjoint sessions with spouses or family members. In fact, orchestrating an effective conjoint interview or group meeting often proves a challenge to even advanced practitioners because of clients' rampant use of ineffective communications, which may engender intense anger, defensiveness, and confusion among family or group members.

In summary, you have a twofold task of monitoring, analyzing, and eliminating your own ineffective responses while observing, managing, and modifying ineffective responses by clients—a rather tall order. Although modifying dysfunctional communication of clients requires advanced skill, you can eliminate your own barriers in a relatively short time. You can accelerate your progress by also eliminating ineffective styles of responding and testing out new skills in your private life. It is unfortunate that many practitioners compartmentalize and limit their helping skills to work with clients and continue to use ineffective styles with professional colleagues, friends, and families.

It is our experience that practitioners who have not fully integrated the helping skills in their private lives do not relate as effectively to their clients as do practitioners who have fully implemented and assimilated them as a part of their general style of relating in all situations. It is our conviction, in fact, that to adequately master essential skills and to fully tap their potential in assisting clients, practitioners must promote their own interpersonal competence and personality integration, thereby modeling for the client the self-actualized or fully functioning person. Pursuing this personal goal prepares practitioners for one of their major tasks or roles—teaching clients new skills of communicating and relating.

The Challenge of Learning New Skills

Because of the unique nature of the helping process, establishing and maintaining a therapeutic relationship requires highly disciplined efforts. Moment by moment, transaction by transaction, the practitioner must sharply focus on the needs and problems of clients. The success of each transaction is measured by the practitioner's adroitness in consciously applying specific skills to move the process toward therapeutic objectives.

Interestingly, one of the major threats to learning new skills emanates from student fear that in relinquishing old styles of relating they are giving up an intangible, irreplaceable part of themselves. Similarly, students who have previously engaged in social work practice may experience fear related to the fact that they have developed methods or styles of relating that have influenced and "moved" clients in the past; thus, giving up these response patterns may mean surrendering a hard-won feeling of competency. These fears are often exacerbated when the focus of instruction and supervision in the classroom and practicum is predominately upon eliminating errors and ineffective interventions and responses rather than on developing new skills or increasingly employing positive responses or interventions with clients. Learners may thus receive considerable feedback about their errors but receive inadequate input regarding their effective responses or styles of relating. Consequently, they may feel vulnerable and stripped of defenses (just as clients do) and experience more keenly the loss of something familiar.

Assessing Verbal Barriers to Communication

Directions: In reviewing each 15-minute sample of taped interviews, tally your use of ineffective responses by placing marks in appropriate cells.

	15-minute taped samples			
	1	2	3	4
1. Moralizing, sermonizing ("shoulds," "oughts")				
2. Advising prematurely				
3. Persuading, giving logical arguments, lecturing, instructing, arguing, intellectualizing				
4. Judging, criticizing, or blaming				
5. Analyzing, diagnosing, making glib interpretations; labeling behavior				
6. Reassuring, sympathizing, consoling, excusing				
7. Using sarcasm or employing distractive humor				
8. Threatening, warning, counterattacking				
9. Using excessive closed-ended questions				
10. Stacking questions				
11. Asking leading questions				

12. Using phrases repetitively (e.g., "OK," "you know," "that's neat"). List:				
Other responses that impede communication. List:				

Assessing Physical Attending Behaviors

	Comments
1. Direct eye contact 0 1 2 3 4	
2. Warmth and concern reflected in facial expression 0 1 2 3 4	
3. Eyes on same level as clients' 0 1 2 3 4	
4. Appropriately varied and animated facial expressions 0 1 2 3 4	
5. Arms and hands moderately expressive; appropriate gestures 0 1 2 3 4	
6. Body leaning slightly forward; attentive but relaxed 0 1 2 3 4	
7. Voice clearly audible but not loud 0 1 2 3 4	
8. Warmth in tone of voice 0 1 2 3 4	
9. Voice modulated to reflect nuances of feelings and emotional tone of client messages 0 1 2 3 4	
10. Moderate tempo of speech 0 1 2 3 4	
11. Absence of distractive behaviors (fidgeting, yawning, gazing out window, looking at watch) 0 1 2 3 4	
12. Other 0 1 2 3 4	

Rating scale:
0 = Poor, needs marked improvement.
1 = Weak, needs substantial improvement.
2 = Minimally acceptable, room for growth.
3 = Generally high level with few lapses.
4 = Consistently high level.

As a learner, it is important that you develop your capacity to openly and nondefensively consider constructive feedback regarding ineffective or even destructive styles of relating or intervening. However, it is also important that you assume responsibility for eliciting positive feedback from educators and peers regarding the positive moment-by-moment responses you make. Remember that supervision time is limited and that responsibility for utilizing that time effectively and for acquiring competency necessarily rests equally with you and your practicum instructor. It is also vital that you take steps to monitor your own growth systematically by reviewing audio and videotapes, by taking frequency counts of desired and undesired responses, and by comparing your responses against guidelines for constructing effective messages contained in the book. Perhaps the single most important requirement for you in furthering your competency is to assume responsibility for advancing your own skill level by consistently monitoring your responses and practicing proven skills.

Most of the skills delineated in this book are not easy to master. Competent practitioners have spent years in perfecting their ability to sensitively and fully attune themselves to the inner experiencing of clients, in furthering their capacity to share their own experiencing in an authentic, helpful manner, and in developing a keen sense of timing in employing these and other skills.

In the months ahead, as you forge new patterns of responding and test your skills, you will experience growing pains, that is, a sense of disequilibrium as you struggle to respond in new ways and, at the same time, to relate warmly, naturally, and attentively to your clients. You may also feel at times that your responses are mechanistic and experience a keen sense of transparency, that is, "The client will know that I'm not being real." If you work intensively over several months to master specific skills, however, your awkwardness will gradually diminish, and you will incorporate these skills naturally into your repertoire.

Suggested Classroom Exercises to Eliminate Barriers to Communication

1. Ask students to assume the role of practitioner and formulate written responses to the following client messages:

a. "I played hooky from school twice last week—all day long. I got a note to come to the principal's office tomorrow, and I'm scared to death. My parents will kill me. What can I do?"

b. "Since my divorce from my husband, I've just been at loose ends. There are so many things I have to do now that I'm not used to doing—taking care of the finances, the yard, the car, disciplining the kids by myself—I just don't know if I can handle all of the responsibilities."

c. "You don't really seem to understand my problems. I don't know why I keep coming every week. I don't seem to be getting anywhere."

Present the various categories of verbal communication barriers delineated in the body of the chapter to the group of students, and instruct the students to determine if their responses involved any of the identified barriers. Ask the group to share responses with each other and to evaluate the probable impact of these responses on the client. Identify and discuss facilitative responses that might be used in each instance.

2. Assign pairs of students to take turns role-playing a situation in which one of the students talks five minutes about a personal problem and the other plays the role of social worker. Ask the "social worker" to deliberately use ineffective verbal and nonverbal communication responses. Record on audio or video and instruct each pair of students to review their tape, identifying communication blocks on the part of the person playing the practitioner. Students may wish to review the "Inventory of Practitioner's Nonverbal Communication" found in the chapter as they discuss the nonverbal barriers used in each role-play. Discuss the exercise with the entire group.

3. Using the same situations role-played in (2) above, ask students again to take turns role-playing for five minutes and to tape their interviews. This time have each "social worker" avoid verbal and nonverbal barriers to communication and instead utilize physical attending behaviors (identified in the chapter) and paraphrase the statements of the other person. After each role-playing, have paired students review their tapes to determine the extent to which the social worker was able to assume more facilitative verbal interviewing behaviors. Also ask each student pair to discuss and mutually rate the physical attending behaviors of the social worker using the assessment form provided at the end of the chapter. After each student pair has switched roles, elicit feedback from the entire student group regarding their experiences with these two approaches as they played each role.

4. Ask students to review all or portions of their first interviews with clients, utilizing the form, "Assessing Verbal Barriers to Communication," to take frequency counts of ineffective responses. If students do not interview clients in the first weeks of the practicum, ask them to tape 15-minute role-played interviews with each other and assess these interviews with respect to barriers to communication.

8 ■ Multidimensional Assessment

The Critical Role of Assessment

Assessment is a critical process in social work practice, for the nature of goals and the selection of relevant interventions are largely based upon the assessment. Indeed, the effectiveness of selected interventions, and ultimately the case outcome, depend in large measure upon the accuracy of the assessment.

Historically, assessment was referred to as "diagnosis" or "psychosocial diagnosis" but we have chosen to eschew the term *diagnosis* because of its negative association with symptoms, disease, and dysfunction—in other words, what is wrong with a client. To be sure, an assessment does include what is wrong, but the broader meaning of the term leaves room for evaluating strengths, resources, healthy functioning, and other *positive* factors that can be tapped not only in resolving difficulties but also in promoting growth, enhancing functioning, actualizing potentials, and developing new resources.

Defining Assessment

Assessment is the process of gathering, analyzing, and synthesizing salient data into a formulation that encompasses the following vital dimensions: (1) the nature of clients' problems, including special attention to developmental needs and stressors associated with life transitions that require major adaptations; (2) coping capacities of clients and significant others (usually family members), including strengths, skills, personality assets, limitations and deficiencies; (3) relevant systems involved in clients' problems and the nature of reciprocal transactions between clients and these systems; (4) resources that are available or are needed to remedy or ameliorate problems; and (5) clients' motivation to work on their problems.

The nature of the assessment process varies according to the practitioner's specified role, which is largely determined by the setting in which the social worker practices. In many settings, social work is the primary (and often exclusive) profession, and in such settings the practitioner independently makes an assessment, at times consulting with colleagues or a member of another discipline. In other settings, the social worker may be a member of a clinical team (e.g., child guidance, mental health, medical and correctional settings), and the process of assessment may be a joint effort of a psychiatrist, social worker, psychologist, nurse, and perhaps members of other disciplines. In such settings, the social worker typically compiles a social history and contributes knowledge related to marital and family dynamics. The process of assessment in such settings ordinarily is longer because of the length of time required for team members to complete individual assessments and to meet as a group to reach a collective assessment. By contrast, in settings where social work is the primary or exclusive profession, practitioners may complete an assessment in one or two sessions. In this chapter, we consider assessment within the context of a social worker functioning as the primary helping professional.

Assessment as an Ongoing Process

At this point, it is important to differentiate between assessment as an ongoing process and as a product. Practitioners engage in the process of assessment from the time of an initial contact with clients to the terminal contact, which may be weeks, months, or even years later. Assessment thus is a fluid and dynamic process that involves receiving, analyzing, and synthesizing new information as it emerges during the entire course of a given case. In the first session, practitioners generally elicit abundant information and must assess its meaning and significance as it unfolds.[1] This moment-by-moment assessment guides practitioners in deciding which information is salient and merits deeper exploration. When they have gathered sufficient information to illuminate the problems, practitioners analyze it and, in collaboration with clients, integrate the data into a tentative formulation of the problem.

As the practitioners and clients move from the exploratory phase to the problem-solving phase, assessment continues, although on a somewhat diminished scale. Not uncommonly, clients disclose new information as problem solving progresses, casting the problems initially presented into an entirely different perspective. Some clients, for example, withhold vital information that they fear may evoke criticism or condemnation from the social worker until they are reasonably confident of the latter's goodwill and helpful intent. Many preliminary assessments thus prove inaccurate and must be discarded or drastically revised.

The process of assessment continues even during the terminal phase of service. During the final interviews, the practitioner carefully evaluates the client's readiness to terminate, assesses the presence of residual difficulties that may cause future difficulties, and identifies possible emotional reactions to termination. The practitioner also considers possible strategies to assist the client to maintain improved functioning or to achieve additional progress after formal social work service is concluded.

Assessment as a Product

As a product, assessment involves an actual formulation or statement at a given time regarding the nature of clients' problems and other related factors delineated earlier. A formal assessment thus involves analysis and synthesis of relevant data into a working definition of the problem that identifies various associated factors and clarifies how they interact to produce and maintain the problem. Because assessments must constantly be updated and revised, it is helpful to think of an assessment as a complex working hypothesis based on the most current data.

A formal assessment is generally made and recorded following an exploration of the client's problems, and tentative goals to be accomplished are based on this assessment. Another assessment could be made at any subsequent time during the course of service, but this is seldom done except in preparation for supervisory ses-

---

[1]It is also crucial to engage the client in the helping relationship while eliciting data; otherwise, you may gain data but lose the client in the process.

sions, consultations, or case presentations, or to complete an agency record. Rather, assessment thereafter consists of gradually reshaping and modifying the initial assessment as new information emerges.

Including Strengths in Assessments

The term *assessment* has been used in social work and related disciplines for many years. However, changes in practice have lagged far behind the change in terms from *diagnosis* to *assessment,* for social workers persist in formulating assessments that focus almost exclusively on the pathology and dysfunction of clients—despite the time-honored social work platitude that social workers work with strengths, not weaknesses.

The marked tendency of practitioners to focus on pathology has several important ramifications, the first of which is that to tap client strengths effectively, practitioners must be sensitive to them and skillful in utilizing them in the service of accomplishing case goals. The findings of at least one research study (Maluccio, 1979) strongly suggest that social workers are blind to or underestimate client strengths. In this study of comparisons between clients' and caseworkers' perceptions of the outcomes of interventions, Maluccio found that the former "presented themselves as *proactive,* autonomous, human beings . . . able to enhance their functioning and their competence . . . ," whereas the latter viewed them as *"reactive* organisms with continuing problems, underlying weaknesses, and limited potentialities" (p. 399). Given this finding, it is probable that the caseworkers studied focused their efforts extensively on perceived weaknesses.

The findings of this study also revealed that clients were more satisfied with the outcomes of service than were the caseworkers, who manifested concerns about residual pathology, especially with clients who terminated prematurely. These findings have been supported by the findings of Presley (1987) and Toseland (1987), both of whom found that clients who did not return after one session often terminated service "prematurely" for reasons other than dissatisfaction (often because they felt they had benefited from the session and needed no further help). Presley thus concluded that ". . . therapists may have a more fragile image of the client than appears warranted" (p. 607).

Again, one must wonder if preoccupation with dysfunction distorts social workers' perceptions and predisposes them to believe that clients should continue to receive service longer than is necessary. In this regard, Maluccio concluded: "there is a need to shift the focus in social work education and practice from problems or pathology to strengths, resources, and potentialities in human beings and their environments" (p. 401). We strongly concur!

A second ramification is that selectively attending to pathology impairs a social worker's ability to discern clients' potentials for growth. Although social workers fervently espouse the belief that human beings have the right and opportunity to develop their potentialities, their tendency to focus on pathology has the effect of undermining that very value commitment. To implement this value fully, social work practitioners must achieve more balanced perceptions of their clients by attuning themselves to strengths and potentialities as well as to dysfunction and pathology. By thus broadening their perspectives of clients, social workers may also enhance the efficacy of their interventive efforts.

The importance of discerning and focusing on strengths of Chicano clients has been documented by the findings of Gomez et al. (1985). A major finding of this outcome study was that supporting clients' strengths was one of the behaviors of practitioners that significantly correlated ($r = .33$) with helpfulness to clients. Concerning the impact of supporting strengths these authors concluded, "In supporting clients' strengths, workers project an honest belief in the clients' ability to deal with problems. This display of belief in the clients' potential strengthens their own belief of the possibilities in the undertaking" (p. 481).

A third ramification of attending excessively to pathology concerns the fact that a large proportion of clients need help in enhancing their self-esteem. Troubled by self-doubts, feelings of inadequacy, and even feelings of worthlessness, their lack of self-confidence and self-respect underlies many dysfunctional cognitive, emotional, and behavioral patterns, including fears of failure, depression, social withdrawal, alcoholism, and hypersensitivity to criticism—to name just a few. To assist clients to view themselves more positively, social workers themselves must first view their clients more positively. Indicative of the consequent challenge to helping professionals is Berwick's (1980) observation pertaining to work with parents of children who fail to thrive because of nonorganic reasons associated with inadequate parental nurturance. After cautioning practitioners to avoid the tendency to blame the parents, Berwick notes:

Self-esteem is already at a low ebb in many of the parents of these children, and the success of the hospital in nourishing a child when the mother has failed only serves to accentuate the pain of failure. . . . Even in the few cases that require foster care, the health care team's task is to seek strengths and to develop a sense of competence in both the parents and the child that will permit a synchronous nurturant relationship to emerge.

(p. 270)

Sources of Information

Information that is considered in the assessment process may derive from several sources, of which the following are the most common:

1. Background sheets or other forms that clients complete.

2. Verbal report of clients (i.e., accounts of problems, expressions of feelings, views, thoughts, events, and the like).

3. Direct observation of nonverbal behavior.

4. Direct observation of interaction between marital partners, family members, and group members.

5. Collateral information from relatives, friends, physicians, teachers, employers, and other professionals.

6. Psychological tests.

7. Personal experiences of the practitioner based on direct interaction with clients.

Verbal Report

Of these major sources, verbal report by clients is generally the primary source of information. Verbal report consists of descriptions of problems, expressions of feelings, reporting of events, presentation of views, and the like. Verbal report is an indirect source of information because it is provided "secondhand" or after the fact; that is, you do not *observe* the problematic behavior, events, feelings, or views firsthand but rely upon clients' reports. Though it is the primary source of information, verbal report is vulnerable to error because of possible faulty recall, distorted perceptions, biases, and limited self-awareness on the part of clients. It is thus vital to avoid the tendency to accept clients' views, descriptions, and reports as valid representations of reality. Similarly, it is important to recognize that feelings expressed by clients may emanate from faulty perceptions or may be altogether irrational.

Note that we are not suggesting that you challenge clients' constructions of reality or the rationality of their feelings. To do so would elicit defensiveness and would be counterproductive. Consequently, clients' feelings and reports should be respected as valid until additional information indicates otherwise. To minimize errors, however, it is essential that rather than settling for clients' views of problems and events, you elicit highly specific details of behavior and events. You will recall that focusing in depth and seeking concreteness are skills that enable you to achieve a high degree of specificity as you elicit information.

Direct Observation of Nonverbal Behavior

Far less subject to error is *direct observation of clients' nonverbal behavior,* for people generally lack awareness of their nonverbal behavior and it is therefore much less subject to conscious control than is verbal report. Nonverbal cues are valuable indicators of emotional states and reactions such as anger, hurt, embarrassment, and fear. It is thus vital to develop an acute perceptiveness to nonverbal cues, such as tone of voice, tears, clenched fists, voice tremors, quivering hands, tightened jaws, pursed lips, variations of countenance, and gesticulations. The doors to many rich discussions of emotional reactions have been opened by empathic responses directed to nonverbal cues (e.g., "Your eyes are telling me you feel very sad right now. Could you put into words what you're experiencing at this moment?").

Observation of Interaction

Direct observation of interaction between spouses, family members, and group members often is extremely enlightening. Students (as well as seasoned practitioners) frequently are amazed at the striking differences between impressions concerning interaction of clients gained from self-report and from subsequent direct observation of their actual interaction. A technique practitioners can employ to observe interaction firsthand rather than to rely on verbal report is *enactment.* Use of this technique involves having clients reenact a conflictual event during a live session. Participants are instructed to recreate the situation exactly as it occurred, using the same words, gestures, and tones of voice as in the actual event. Before giving the instructions, however, it is important to provide an explanation for making the request, such as the following:

"To understand what produced the difficulties in the event you just described, I'd like you to recreate the situation here in our session. By seeing what both of you do and say and how you do it, I can get an accurate picture of what actually happens. I'd like you to recreate the situation exactly as it happened. Use the same words, gestures, and tone of voice as you did. Now, where were you when it happened, and how did it start?"

Most clients are willing to engage in enactment, but encouragement is sometimes needed. Enactment can also be used in contrived situations to see how a couple or family interact in situations that involve decision making, planning, role negotiation, child discipline, or other like activities. Practitioners will need to exercise their creativity in designing situations likely to generate and clarify the types of interaction the practitioner desires to observe.

Direct observation of spontaneous behavior or of enacted situations is not without flaws, for clients may attempt to create a favorable impression and behave atypically. Practitioners can counter this possibility after enacted situations by asking to what extent the behaviors of participants corresponded with their behavior in actual situations. It is wise to elicit views of all participants to ascertain the authenticity of reported discrepancies. Reported discrepancies that are validated by participants are highly informative.

It is also important to recognize that an office setting is not a natural arena for family interaction and behavior of family members may be strongly influenced by this unnatural environment. As a corrective measure, it is desirable to visit clients in their homes, if possible. Observations of living conditions, incidentally, may also reveal problems that would otherwise not come to light.

Another flaw of direct observation is that it is subject to perceptual errors by the observer. A method to compensate for this error (often used in rigorous research) is to employ more than one observer and to determine the degree of congruence between observations made independently by different observers. This corrective measure, however, involves a heavy expenditure of time and is generally not feasible in practice. Despite the flaws of direct observation, information gained by this means is generally more valid than that gained from verbal report, although the latter has the considerable advantage of being more practicable.

Collateral Sources of Information

Information is also sometimes provided by relatives, friends, physicians, and others who possess essential information about relevant aspects of clients' lives. Information from such *collateral sources* is subject to the same limitations of other indirect sources. Nevertheless, persons who are not directly implicated in the problematic situation are not subject to the clients' blind spots and may provide information that illuminates otherwise obscure dynamics of problematic behavior. With seriously mentally disturbed clients, much of the information needed for assessment must be obtained from collateral sources because mental dysfunction may preclude the client from providing accurate information.

Unfortunately, practitioners often overlook collateral sources, thereby losing potentially valuable information. However, it is not necessary or even desirable to contact collateral sources routinely, and you must exercise prudence in deciding when such information is needed. Furthermore, it is axiomatic that you not contact other persons without consent of clients, except in the case of bona fide exigencies, for to do so would violate professional ethics. Although clients occasionally will request that you contact others to gain their views, you will often need to initiate such discussions. If you explain that you can best serve the client by gaining a well-rounded picture of the problematic situation and that others often can identify factors that may otherwise be overlooked, clients will often consent to and even welcome such collateral contacts.

Psychological Tests

Still another possible source of information consists of *psychological tests* including self-report inventories (e.g., personality inventories; fear, social skill, and depression inventories) and behavioral checklists, such as problem behavior, behavioral skills, and family verbal behavior checklists. Also an indirect source of information, psychological tests represent a useful and expedient way of quantifying data and behaviors. To use them effectively, however, practitioners must be well grounded in knowledge of test theory and specific tests. Many tests, for example, have low reliability and validity and should be used with extreme caution, if at all. In the hands of unqualified persons, psychological tests may be grossly misused. Because social workers generally have limited knowledge and experience in the realm of psychological testing, they are well advised to strictly observe the old caveat, "A little learning is a dangerous thing." If testing is needed or test results are available, social workers may wish to seek consultation from qualified psychologists in interpreting the results appropriately.

It is advantageous for social workers who practice in settings where psychological tests are extensively employed to gain knowledge of the testing. A valuable resource to those who would like to gain expertise in using a limited number of tests is the *Clinical Measurement Package* (CMP), which Hudson (1982) developed specifically for social workers. We briefly discuss the CMP and the nine scales that compose that package in Chapter 13. Another excellent resource is Corcoran's and Fischer's (1987) comprehensive review of instruments that can be used to assess various aspects of clients' functioning.

Computer-Assisted Assessment

Technological advances have led to still another promising aid in assessment. Nurius and Hudson (1988) have reported on the development of a microcomputer-based evaluation tool, the Clinical Assessment System (CAS), that was designed specifically for social workers and practitioners from allied professions. The program is user friendly and contains 20 clinical measures (including the nine scales of the CMP) that can be used immediately. Practitioners can also add any measure that is designed to assess the degree or severity of a client problem. Moreover, the CAS accommodates different types of scales including single-item, self-anchored, multi-item, multidimensional rating scales, checklists, and others.

Computer-aided assessment is a recent development that deserves the attention of practitioners. Clients reportedly respond well to use of this technology. The greatest potential for use of this tool derives from the computer's ability to process, integrate, and synthesize data from expanded sources of information. The objectivity of the computer also reduces evaluative errors caused by subjective interpretations of data by practitioners.[2]

Personal Experience Based on Direct Interaction

A final source of information is *personal experience* based on direct interaction with clients. You will react in varying ways to different clients, and your reactions may be useful in understanding how other people react to these clients. For example, you may experience certain clients as

---

[2]For more information on the CAS, contact Walter Hudson, Ph.D., at the School of Social Work, Arizona State University, Tempe, AZ 85287.

withdrawn, personable, dependent, caring, manipulative, seductive, assertive, overbearing, or determined. Because clients often manifest the same behavioral patterns in their general social relationships, your own reaction may be a vital clue to understanding their possible difficulties or successes in interpersonal relationships. For example, a client who reports that others take him for granted and make unreasonable demands upon him may make inordinate efforts to please a practitioner and manifest self-deprecating behavior. Similarly, a woman who complains that men frequently make sexual overtures and view her as a sexual object may wear revealing clothes and present herself seductively in an interview. In both these instances, the practitioner's experience with the clients provides clues to at least part of the source of their problems.

Initial impressions, of course, can be misleading and must be supported by additional contacts with clients. Moreover, such impressions are subjective and may be influenced by your own interpersonal patterns and perceptions. Before drawing even tentative conclusions, it is thus important that you scrutinize your reactions to identify possible biases, distorted perceptions, or behavior on your part that may have contributed to clients' behavior. If you tend to be domineering, for example, clients may respond with passivity or counteraggressiveness that is atypical. Similarly, overly challenging or confrontive behavior on your part may produce defensiveness or withdrawn behavior that is in part a natural reaction to your inappropriate behavior. Self-awareness thus is an essential prerequisite to drawing valid conclusions about the significance of your experiential reactions to clients.

The Multidimensionality of Assessment

Human problems, even those that appear to be simple, often involve a complex interplay of many factors. Rarely do sources of problems reside solely within an individual or within that individual's environment. Rather, reciprocal interaction occurs between a human being and the external world. One acts upon and responds to the external world, and the quality of one's actions affects reactions and vice versa. For example, a parent may complain about poor communication with an adolescent child, attributing the difficulty to the fact that the adolescent is sullen and refuses to talk about most things. The adolescent, however, may complain that it is pointless to talk with the parent because the latter consistently pries, lectures, or criticizes. Each participant's complaint about the other may be accurate, but each unwittingly behaves in ways that have produced and now maintain their dysfunctional interaction. Thus, the behavior of neither person is the sole cause of the breakdown in communication in a simple cause-effect (linear) fashion. Rather, it is their reciprocal interaction that produces the difficulty; the behavior of each is both cause and effect, depending upon one's vantage point.

The multidimensionality of human problems is also a consequence of the fact that human beings are social creatures, dependent upon other human beings and upon complex social institutions to meet their needs. Basic needs such as food, housing, clothing, and medical care require adequate economic means and the availability of goods and services. Educational, social, and recreational needs require interface with societal institutions.

Needs to feel close to and loved by others, to have companionship, to experience a sense of belonging, and to experience sexual gratification require satisfactory social relationships within one's marriage, family, social network, and community. The extent to which people experience self-esteem depends on certain individual psychic factors and the quality of feedback from other people.

To assess the problems of a client system (individual, couple, or family) thus requires extensive knowledge about that system as well as consideration of the multifarious systems (e.g., economic, legal, educational, medical, religious, social, interpersonal) that impinge upon the client system. Moreover, to assess the functioning of an individual entails evaluating various aspects of that person's functioning. For example, one must consider dynamic interactions among the biophysical, cognitive, emotional, cultural, behavioral, and motivational subsystems and the relationships of those interactions to problematic situations. With a couple or family client system, the social worker must also attend to communication and interactional patterns as well as to each member of the system. Although not all of the various systems and subsystems cited above are likely to play significant roles in the problems of any given client system, overlooking relevant systems results in assessment that is partial at best and irrelevant or erroneous at worst. Interventions based on incomplete or inaccurate assessments, therefore, are likely to have limited remedial effects, to be ineffective, or even to produce detrimental results. Conversely, interventions that are based on accurate and comprehensive assessments are more likely to be effective.

To assist you to formulate assessments that consider the many dimensions of human problems, in this chapter we consider in depth the problem system and major questions that you will need to answer in formulating an assessment. In the next chapter, we address multidimensional assessment of individuals and of the environment. In Chapter 10, we focus on assessment of interpersonal systems, with particular emphasis upon marriages and families. In Chapter 11, we consider assessment within the context of growth groups.

The Problem

In your initial contacts with clients, you take the first step in the challenging and fascinating task of uncovering the sources of their problems and engaging them in planning appropriate remedial measures. Clients typically seek help because they have exhausted their coping efforts and/or lack resources required for satisfactory living. Many of your clients will have struggled earnestly with their problems only to find that their coping efforts are futile or, even worse, seem to aggravate the problematic situation. In many such instances, clients have erred in defining their problems, and their solutions ironically have become problems in and of themselves. A client, for example, may make heroic efforts to please others—a spouse, parent, or employer—to no avail. The problem, however, may not be an inability to please others but rather a pattern of striving excessively to please others. Leaning over backwards to win approval of others tends to be self-defeating because one thereby devalues oneself in the eyes of others and invites being taken for granted. Having exhausted their coping efforts, clients turn to a professional person, expecting that the latter will somehow assist them to discover a solution to their problem.

Identifying the Problem

Early in a session, often after introductions have been made (or after a warm-up period), the practitioner invites clients to describe their problems or concerns. Clients typically respond to such overtures by giving a general account of their problems. The problem identified by clients typically involves a deficiency of *something needed* (e.g., health care, adequate income or housing, companionship, harmonious family relationships, self-esteem) or an excess of something that is not desired (e.g., fear, guilt, temper outbursts, marital or parent-child conflict, or addiction). In either event, clients are in a state of disequilibrium and experience both tension and troubled emotions. The emotions thus are often a prominent part of the problem configuration, which is one reason why empathic communication is such a vital skill.

The presenting problem (problem as viewed by the client) is highly significant because it reflects clients' immediate perceptions of the problem and is the focal point of clients' motivation for seeking help. This is a critical point, for *clients' motivation is the driving force behind the helping process.*

Consequently, problem definition is client centered; that is, the final authority for defining the problem resides with clients, not the practitioner. To be sure, clients generally modify their perceptions of their problems as they explore factors of which they previously had little or no awareness. Moreover, clients do not always initially reveal their most troubling

problems because to do so may be highly embarrassing or, from the client's perspective, may risk condemnation. Our point is that you must be carefully attuned to clients' definitions of their problems, for to proceed with work on problems they do not acknowledge is to risk losing their motivation, thereby precipitating premature discontinuance.

The presenting problem is also of vital significance because it suggests areas to be explored subsequently. If the presenting problem described by parents involves truancy and rebellious behavior of an adolescent, the exploration will include the family, school, and peer systems. As the exploration proceeds, it may also be necessary to explore the marital system if there is some indication that dysfunction in the marital relationship is negatively impacting on the parent-child relationship. If learning difficulties appear to contribute to the truancy, the cognitive and perceptual subsystems of the adolescent may also need to be assessed as part of the problem. The presenting problem thus identifies systems that are constituent parts of the problem.

Presenting Problems and Involuntary Clients To this point, we have assumed that clients come to agencies voluntarily seeking help with identified problems. Involuntary clients, who reluctantly "seek help" because of coercion from family members or some official power structure, often do not report presenting problems. Instead, such clients tend to deny having problems or portray the coercive referral source as the problem. Commonly, these clients manifest resentment toward the person who pressured them into coming and attribute problems to that person. Typically used by such clients is the following message, "I don't know why I should have to come. My wife is the one with the problems, and she's the one who should be here." When the source of motivation thus lies outside the client, the parameters of the problem are less readily identifiable. In such instances, after resolving the client's negativism about being forced to seek help, the practitioner engages the client in an exploration of the latter's life situation, the goals of which are to determine if wants or areas of dissatisfaction on the client's part can be identified and if motivation can be engendered to work toward enhancing the client's satisfaction in pertinent areas. When and if the client acknowledges a problem, the boundaries of the problem become clear, and the exploration then proceeds in a normal fashion. Skills in resolving negativism, engaging involuntary clients, and creating incentives for change are delineated in Chapter 12.

Clarifying Ecological Factors

As clients describe their difficulties, they identify other people and larger systems involved in their problematic situations. The configuration of the client(s), the social milieu, and relevant systems that interact to produce and maintain the problem constitute the ecological boundaries of the problem. To understand more fully how the client(s) and other involved systems interact to produce and maintain the problem, you must elicit specific information that pertains to the functioning and interaction of these various systems.

Systems with which clients commonly transact include:

1. The family and extended family or clan.
2. The social network (friends, neighbors, co-workers, religious leaders and associates, club members, and cultural groups).
3. Public institutions (educational, recreational, law enforcement and protection, mental health, social service, health care, employment, economic security, legal and judicial, and various governmental agencies).
4. Personal service providers (doctor, dentist, barber or hairdresser, bartender, auto mechanic, etc.).

Several authors have developed diagrams to depict interrelationships but we have found none that was wholly satisfactory nor have we succeeded in improving upon them. Depicting reciprocal interrelationships that change across time (as we discuss shortly) in one dimension is an impossible task. Suffice it to say that individuals have more or less ongoing transactions with the systems listed under (1) and (2) above and have less frequent transactions with other systems listed under (3) and (4), depending upon circumstances and the individual's stage of development. The challenge is including in the assessment those systems that reside in the ecological boundaries of the client's problem. Relevant systems are those that contribute to the client's difficulties or that can be tapped to resolve them.

Assessing Developmental Needs and Wants

As we noted earlier, clients' problems commonly involve unmet needs and wants that derive from lack of goodness of fit between these needs and resources in the environment. (Recall from Table 1-1 in Chapter 1 the close link between individual needs and sources of need gratification in the social milieu or in the environment.) Determining unmet needs, then, is the first step to identifying resources that must be tapped or developed. If resources are available but clients have been unable to avail themselves of the resources, it is important to determine the barriers to resource utilization. Some people, for example, may suffer from loneliness not because of an absence of support systems but because their interpersonal behavior alienates others and leaves them isolated. Still other clients may *appear* to have emotional support available from family or others but closer exploration may reveal that these potential resources are unresponsive to clients' needs. Reasons for the unresponsiveness typically involve reciprocal unsatisfactory transactions between the participants. The task in such instances is to assess the nature of the dysfunctional transactions and to attempt to modify them to the benefit of the participants—often a complex and difficult task.

Human needs include the universal necessities (adequate nutrition, clothing, housing, and health care). *Needs* are critical and must be met at least partially for human beings to survive and maintain sound physical and mental health and well-being. As we use the term, *wants* involve strong desires that motivate behavior and that, when fulfilled, enhance satisfaction and well-being. Although fulfillment of wants is not essential to survival, some wants develop a compelling nature, rivaling needs in their intensity, for example, people who are compelled to seek power, wealth, and prestige or people who are compelled to gain acceptance by others at any price. For illustrative purposes, we provide the following list of examples of typical wants involved in presenting problems.

Typical Wants Involved in Presenting Problems

To have less family conflict.

To feel valued by one's spouse.

To be self-supporting.

To achieve greater companionship in marriage.

To gain more self-confidence.

To have more friends.

To be included in decision making.

To improve social skills.

To gain release from an institution.

To stay out of trouble.

To have more freedom.

To handle conflict more effectively.

To control one's temper.

To overcome depression.

To gain more sexual satisfaction.

To make a difficult decision.

To master fear or anxiety.

To cope with children more effectively.

To achieve greater self-fulfillment.

In determining clients' unmet needs and wants it is essential to consider the *developmental stage* of the individual client, couple, or family. For example, the psychological needs of an adolescent for acceptance by peers, for sufficient freedom to develop increasing independence, for development of a stable identity, and for satisfactory relationships with the opposite sex are markedly different from the typical needs of elderly persons for health care, adequate income, social relationships, and meaningful activities. As with individuals, families go through developmental phases that also include both tasks to be mastered and needs that must be met if the family is to provide a climate conducive to the development and well-being of its members.

Different theorists conceptualize developmental stages for individuals in different ways and use different terms, but the following stages correspond with those generally identified:

Infancy	Late teenage
Preschool	Early adulthood
School age	Middle age
Early teenage	Old age

Families also have discrete stages of development but we defer discussion of them until Chapter 10, which is concerned with assessment of families. Although knowledge of the needs and tasks associated with each developmental stage is critical, we will not provide a detailed list of needs, for that content is germane to human behavior courses and textbooks. For those interested in reading more about the relationship between developmental needs and environmental resources we recommend an article by Vigilante and Mailick (1988).

Although clients' presenting problems often reveal obvious needs and wants (e.g., "Our unemployment benefits have expired and we have no income"), it is often necessary to infer what is lacking. Presenting problems may reveal only what is troubling clients on the surface and careful exploration and empathic "tuning in" are required to identify unmet needs and wants. Marital partners, for example, may initially complain that they disagree over virtually everything and fight constantly. From this information, one could safely conclude they want a more harmonious relationship; exploring their feelings on a deeper level, however, may reveal their ongoing disputes are actually a manifestation of unmet needs of both partners for expressions of love, caring, appreciation, or increased companionship.

Translating complaints and problems into needs and wants is often helpful to clients, many of whom have dwelled on the troubling behavior of other participants in the problem systems and have not thought in terms of their own specific needs and wants. The presenting problem of one client was that her husband was married to his job and spent little time with her. When the practitioner responded, "I gather then you're feeling left out of his life and want to feel important to him and valued by him," she replied, "You know, I hadn't thought of it that way, but that's exactly what I've been feeling." The practitioner then encouraged her to express this need directly to her husband, which she did. He listened attentively and responded with genuine concern. This was the first time she had expressed her needs directly. Previously, her messages had been complaints and his usual response had been defensive.

Identifying needs and wants also serves as a vital prelude to the process of negotiating goals. Goals, of course, often embody specified changes in problematic behavior on the part of participants that will enhance the degree of need gratification and satisfaction for those who are part of the problem system. Expressing goals in terms that address needs and wants also enhances the motivation of clients to work toward goal attainment, as the payoff for goal-oriented efforts is readily apparent to them.

Although goals generally relate to unmet wants and needs, clients' wants are sometimes unrealistic when assessed against the capacity of the client and/or opportunities in the social environment. (One mildly brain-damaged and slightly retarded young adult, for example, wanted to become a nuclear physicist.) Moreover, *wanting* to achieve a desired goal is not the same as being *willing* to expend the time and effort and to endure the discomfort required to attain that goal. These are matters that warrant extensive consideration and, as such, are central topics in Chapters 12 and 13.

Stresses Associated with Life Transitions

In addition to developmental stages that typically correspond to age ranges, individuals and families commonly must adapt to other major transitions that are less age-specific. Some transitions (e.g., geographical moves and immigrations, divorce, and untimely widowhood) can occur during virtually any stage of development. Many such transitions can be traumatic and the adaptations required may temporarily overwhelm the coping capacities of individuals or families. For example, losses or separations from a person, homeland, or familiar role are highly stressful for most persons and often temporarily impair social functioning.

Again the environment plays a crucial role in facilitating people's adaptation to major transitional events. People with strong support networks (e.g., close relationships with family, kin, friends, and neighbors) generally have less difficulty in adapting to traumatic changes than do those who lack strong support systems. Assessments and interventions related to transitional periods, therefore, should consider the availability or lack of essential support systems.

The following are major transitions that commonly beset *adults:*

Work, career choices and changes	Untimely widowhood
Marriage	Postparenthood years
Parenthood	Retirement

Geographic moves and migrations	Health impairment
Separation and divorce	Institutionalization
Single parenthood status	Death of a spouse and being single

Assessing whether clients are in the throes of a developmental phase or transitional period is vital because clients' presenting problems often involve "being stuck" as a result of failing to master tasks essential to adapting successfully to developmental or transitional periods of life. Practitioners can play a vital role in identifying essential tasks and assisting clients to master them, a role central to the modality of crisis intervention, which we discuss in Chapter 14.

Questions to Be Answered in Assessment

An accurate assessment should provide answers to a number of key questions, some of which have been implied earlier in this chapter. Using the questions delineated in this section will assist you in conducting thorough explorations and formulating accurate assessments. These questions, which are based in part on guidelines presented by Brown and Levitt (1979), are as follows:

1. What persons and systems are involved in the problems?

2. How or in what way are the participants involved?

3. What unmet *needs* or *wants* are involved in the problem?

4. What developmental stage or life transition is relevant to the problem?

5. What *meaning* do the clients ascribe to the problem?

6. *Where* does the problematic behavior occur?

7. *When* does the problematic behavior occur?

8. What is the *frequency* of the problematic behavior?

9. What is the *duration* of the problem?

10. What are the clients' *emotional reactions* to the problem?

11. How have the clients *attempted to cope* with the problem, and what are the *required skills* to resolve the problem?

12. What are the *skills and strengths of the clients?*

13. What *external resources* are needed?

We next consider the rationale of these questions, highlighting the answers to them in assessing more fully the various factors and forces that interact to produce and maintain problems.

1. What Persons and Systems Are Involved in the Problem(s)?

The presenting problem usually identifies key persons, and further exploration reveals other persons, groups, or organizations that are participants in the client's difficulties. An accurate assessment must consider all the elements and how they interact to produce difficulties. Furthermore, an effective plan of intervention should embody these same elements, recognizing that it is not always feasible to involve everyone who is a participant in a given problematic situation. Some participants, for example, may refuse to become involved.

2. How Are the Participants Involved?

To understand how the interplay of actors produces problems, it is essential to determine the role of each. This requires detailed information of their behavior, including what they say and do before, during, and after problematic events. Detailed information regarding these factors is vital, for analysis of them illuminates circumstances associated with the problematic behavior, how each person affects and is affected by others, and consequences of events that tend to perpetuate problematic behavior. In this regard, it is important to keep in mind that human behavior is purposive and can be understood by analyzing the forces that motivate people to behave as they do. Motivational forces consist of both external events (i.e., those that are visible to others) and covert forces (i.e., inner thoughts, beliefs, emotions, wishes, and images) as well as physiological and psychological states.

Question 2 is concerned with external (overt) events, whereas questions 3, 5, and 10 deal with covert forces. With regard to the former, certain events may typically precede problematic behavior. One family member may say or do something that precipitates an angry, defensive, or hurt reaction by another. Events that precede problematic behavior are referred to as *antecedents*. Antecedents often give valuable clues as to the behavior of one participant that may be provocative or offensive to another, thereby triggering a negative reaction, followed by a counter negative reaction, thus setting the problematic situation in motion.

What each participant does and says during the problematic event must also be determined, for the response of each participant is a stimulus to other participants, and the nature and intensity of these responses tend to intensify, perpetuate, or even to mitigate the dysfunctional interaction. One person may blame or insult another, and the latter may respond by yelling, making a counteraccusation, or calling the first party an unprintable name. We examine such dysfunctional interaction and patterns in depth in Chapter 10.

Determining the environmental consequences associated with problematic behaviors also may elucidate factors that perpetuate dysfunctional behaviors. It is common knowledge that certain actions or responses increase the frequency of (reinforce) behaviors that precede them, and effective intervention must therefore be aimed at modifying such consequences. Tantrum behavior may be unwittingly perpetuated by parents who yield to demands of their children. Pouting by a marital partner may similarly be reinforced by pleading with the pouter to talk or consistently apologizing even though apologies may not be warranted. Recognizing the dynamic significance (effects) of such response patterns often enables practitioners to assist clients in developing new response patterns that break dysfunctional cycles and gradually reduce the frequency of the problematic behaviors.

Analyzing the antecedents of problematic behavior, describing the behavior in specific terms, and assessing the consequences or effects of the problematic behavior provide a powerful means of identifying factors that motivate dysfunctional behavior and are appropriate targets of interventions. This straightforward approach to analyzing the functional significance of behavior has been designated by numerous authors as the ABC model (A = antecedent, B = behavior, C = consequence). Although it is far less simple than may seem apparent, the ABC model provides a coherent and practical approach to understanding behavior, particularly when it is supplemented by consideration of the factor described in item 5.

3. What Unmet Needs or Wants Are Involved in the Problem? Content related to this question was contained in the preceding section.

4. What Developmental Stage and/or Life Transition Is Relevant to the Problem? This was also discussed in the preceding section.

5. What Meaning Do the Clients Ascribe to the Problem? Despite the utility of the ABC model, assessments of the forces that motivate clients' behaviors are incomplete until the clients' perceptions and definitions of the problem are carefully considered. It is increasingly recognized that the meanings people attribute to events (*meaning attributions*) are as important as the events themselves, a fact recognized by the ancient Greek stoic philosopher Epictetus (first century A.D.) who asserted, "Men are disturbed not by the things which happen to them but by their opinions about the things." You, your clients, other participants in problems, and external observers thus may view problem situations in widely varying ways. Determining the views of the major actors will enhance your understanding of the motivation of each, for people behave according to the meaning a situation has for them. Moreover, to apply the principle of starting where the client is, you must first know clients' perceptions of the causes of problematic behavior (Goldstein, 1983).

Determining meaning attributions is also vital because clients' beliefs about factors that cause problems often represent barriers to changes that must be made if problems are to be ameliorated. Such meaning attributions thus tend to maintain problematic behavior and must also be regarded as targets of change (Hepworth,

1979). Hurvitz (1975, pp. 228–229) has categorized meaning attributions that pose obstacles to change, which in modified form with examples are as follows:

1. *Pseudoscientific explanations:*

"Our biorhythms don't mesh, and there's nothing we can do about it; we're just not good for each other."

"Jenny [an adopted child] just has bad blood. Her mother was a prostitute."

2. *Psychological labeling:*

"Mother is a paranoid; I've only lied to her a few times."

"I think Larry is just hyperactive."

3. *Beliefs that other major actors lack the ability or desire to make essential changes:*

"I know he says he wants our marriage to work, but I know better. He wants a divorce, and he's trying to provoke me into giving him a reason for it."

"She'll never change. She never has. I think we're wasting our time and money."

4. *Unchangeable external factors:*

"There's no point in talking to my teacher. She's got it in for me and doesn't even try to understand."

"As long as his father's alive, we don't have a chance of making it. His father just seems to have a hold on him."

5. *Misconceptions about innate qualities that cannot be changed:*

"I was born a loser. There's no point in talking about learning to be a mechanic. I'd just wash out."

"I know he has a right to expect me to be a better sexual partner. I wish I could be, but I've never had any sexual desires, and I never will."

6. *Unrealistic feelings of helplessness:*

"There's nothing I can do. Gloria is such a strong person that she defeats me at every turn."

"What can I do? I'm completely at the mercy of Hal. If I don't settle on his terms, he'll take the children away from me."

7. *Reference to "fixed" religious or philosophical principles, natural laws, or social forces:*

"Sure, I already have as many children as I want. But I don't really have a choice. The church says that birth control is evil."

"She calls all the shots because that's just how women are. They just see men as someone to bring home a paycheck."

8. *Assertion based upon presumed laws of human nature:*

"All children tell lies at that age. It's just natural. I did when I was a kid."

"Sure, I've had trouble with people in authority. When people get authority, they try to step on others. It's just human nature."

9. *Allegations about limitations of significant others involved in the problem:*

"He's just dense. I've tried every way I know how to get through to him, but he's too dense to understand my feelings."

"I think she must be a little stupid. Anyone with any brains would know how to balance a checkbook."

Fortunately, many clients manifest meaning attributions that are not inimical to change. Some clients are open and even eager to examine the part they play in problematic situations. Others readily acknowledge their parts and desire to modify their behavior. When obstacles such as those listed above are encountered, however, it is vital to explore them and to resolve them before attempting to negotiate change-oriented goals or to implement interventions. Until such barriers are removed, clients do not assume responsibility for their part in problems and typically and understandably resist having goals or interventions imposed upon them, for from their vantage point the practitioner is barking up the wrong tree.

To elicit meaning attributions from clients, you must employ appropriate exploratory responses following clients' accounts of their problems. Appropriate responses include the following:

- "What meaning do you make of his behavior?"

- "What were the reasons for your parents grounding you?"

- "What conclusions have you drawn about why your girlfriend dropped you?"

- "What are your views as to why you didn't get a promotion?"

6. Where Does the Problematic Behavior Occur? Answering this question may provide clues to understanding factors that trigger problematic behavior. Children may throw tantrums in certain locations and not in others. As a result of repeated experiences, they soon discriminate where certain behaviors are tolerated and where they are not. Adults may experience anxiety or depression in certain environmental contexts and not in others. One couple, for example, invariably experienced breakdown in communication in the home of one spouse's parents. Some children manifest problematic behavior at school but not at home, or vice versa. Determining where problematic behavior occurs will assist you in identifying areas that warrant further exploration aimed at pinpointing factors associated with the behavior in question.

Identifying where problematic behavior does *not* occur is also of value in some instances, for as Brown and Levitt (1979) explain, such understanding may identify sources available to the client for tempo-

rary relief of painful states, such as fear, anxiety, depression, loneliness, and insecurity. One client may be assisted to gain temporary respite from overwhelming anxiety by visiting a cherished aunt. In other instances, clients may actually gain permanent relief from intolerable stress by changing employment, discontinuing college, or moving out of relationships when tension or other unpleasant feeling states are experienced exclusively in these contexts.

7. When Does the Problematic Behavior Occur? Answers to this question often yield valuable clues to factors that play a critical role in clients' problems. Onsets of depressive episodes, for example, may coincide with the time of year when a loved one died or when a divorce occurred. Family problems may also occur, for example, when the father returns from work, at bedtime for the children, at mealtimes, or when children are (or should be) getting ready for school. Similarly, couples may experience severe conflict when one spouse is working the midnight shift, a few days before the wife's menstrual period, after participation by either spouse in activities that exclude the partner, or when one or both drink at parties. Clues such as the foregoing illuminate the nature of stresses associated with problems and suggest fruitful areas for detailed explorations of the behaviors of participants in the problem system.

8. Frequency of the Problematic Behavior The frequency of problematic behavior is an index to both the pervasiveness of a problem and its impact on the participants. Some couples or families live in constant turmoil because of continuous bickering among family members. Similarly, some clients may report constant feelings of depression, whereas others may experience depression only intermittently. Such a determination helps to clarify the degree of the dysfunctional behavior and the extent to which it impairs the daily functioning of the client.

Assessing the frequency of problematic behavior also enables you to determine the client's progress at a later time. By determining the baseline of behavior targeted for change before implementing interventions, you can also evaluate the efficacy of your interventions. Moreover, determining the frequency of both desired and dysfunctional behaviors is critical in single-subject design research, which we discuss briefly in Chapter 13.

9. What Is the Duration of the Problem?

Another important dimension vital to assessing problems relates to the history of the problem. Knowing when the problem developed and under what circumstances assists in further evaluating the degree of the problem, formulating psychosocial dynamic factors associated with the problem, determining the source of motivation to seek assistance, and planning appropriate interventions. Often significant changes in people's life situations, including even seemingly positive ones, disrupt their equilibrium to the extent that they are unable to adapt to changes. An unplanned pregnancy, loss of employment, job promotion, severe illness, birth of a first child, move to a new city, death of a loved one, divorce, retirement, severe disappointment—these and many other life events may cause severe stresses. Careful exploration of the duration of problems often discloses such antecedents to dysfunctional behavior. These antecedent events often are equally as significant as the immediate problematic situation and warrant careful exploration to determine residual emotions and problems that must be addressed.

Antecedent events that immediately precede decisions to seek help are particularly informative. Designated as *precipitating events,* these antecedents often give valuable clues to critical stresses that might otherwise be overlooked. Spouses and parents often report their problems have existed longer than a year. Why they chose to ask for help at a particular time is not readily apparent, but knowing why may cast their problems in a somewhat different light. For example, careful exploration revealed that a couple who identified their problem as fighting incessantly for the past four years did not decide to seek help until the wife began working outside the home for the first time, just two weeks before they called for an appointment. Similarly, parents who complained about their teenage daughter's long-standing rebelliousness did not seek assistance until they became aware (one week before calling the agency) that she was engaging in an affectional relationship with a woman six years her senior. In both these instances, the precipitating events would not have been disclosed had the practitioner not sought to answer the critical question of why they were seeking help at this particular time.

Precipitating events can usually be determined by asking clients to identify reasons for seeking assistance at a particular time. In some instances, clients themselves will not be fully aware of their reasons, and it may be necessary to explore what events or emotional experiences were occurring shortly before their decision to seek help.

Determining the duration of problems is also vital in assessing clients' levels of functioning and in planning appropriate interventions. Exploration may reveal that a client's adjustment has been marginal for many years and that the immediate problem is only an exacerbation of long-term multiple problems. In other instances, the onset of a problem may be acute and clients may have functioned at an adequate or high level for many years. In the first instance, modest goals and long-term intermittent service may be indicated; in the second instance, short-term crisis intervention may be sufficient to restore clients to their previous level of functioning.

10. What Are the Clients' Emotional Reactions to the Problem? When people encounter problems in living, they typically experience emotional reactions to those problems. It is important to explore and assess such reactions for three major reasons. First, people often gain relief from expressing troubling emotions related to their problems. Common reactions to typical problem situations are worry, concern, resentment, hurt, fear, and feeling overwhelmed, helpless, or hopeless. Being able to ventilate such emotions in the presence of an understanding and concerned person is a source of great comfort to many persons. Moreover, releasing pent-up feelings often has the effect of relieving oneself of a heavy burden. In fact, ventilating emotions may have a liberating effect for persons who tend to be out of touch with their emotions and have not acknowledged to themselves or others that they even have troubled feelings.

A second reason for exploring and assessing emotional reactions is that, because emotions strongly influence behavior, the emotional reactions of some people impel them to behave in ways that exacerbate or contribute to difficulties. In some instances, in fact, people create new difficulties as a result of emotionally reactive behavior. In the heat of anger, some persons overreact and physically abuse children and/or spouses. Other individuals may be verbally abusive, behaving in ways that frighten, offend, or alienate family members or other significant people. Powerful emo-

tional reactions may thus be an integral part of the overall problem configuration.

The third major reason for assessing emotional responses is that intense reactions often become primary problems, overshadowing the antecedent problematic situation. Some people develop severe depressive reactions associated with problematic situations. A mother may become depressed over an unwed daughter's pregnancy; a man may react with depression to unemployment or retirement; and culturally dislocated persons may become depressed following relocation, even though they may have fled intolerable conditions in their homeland. Other individuals may react to problematic events with feelings of helplessness or panic that cause virtual paralysis. In such instances, interventions must be addressed to the overwhelming emotional reactions as well as to the problematic situation that triggered them.

The meanings that clients make of antecedent events are particularly important in understanding their emotional reactions and behavior. In one case, parents concluded a daughter was engaging in sexual activity because she was two hours late returning from a date. When she entered the house, they bombarded her with angry accusations, not giving her an opportunity to explain that her date's car had mechanical difficulties. Hurt and embittered by their unfounded accusations, she withheld what actually had happened, causing them to believe their accusations were justified. This incident was a primary antecedent to deterioration in the parent-child relationship.

11. How Have the Clients Attempted to Cope with the Problem, and What Skills Are Required to Resolve It? Further light is shed on clients' difficulties by determining how they have attempted to cope with their problems. The coping methods they employ give valuable clues to their levels of stress and of functioning. Exploration may reveal that a client has marked deficits in coping skills, relying upon rigid patterns that often prove dysfunctional. Some clients employ avoidance patterns through withdrawing or attempting to numb or fortify themselves by using drugs or alcohol. Other clients attempt to cope with interpersonal problems by resorting to aggressive, domineering behavior or by placating or becoming submissive. Still other clients manifest flexible and effective coping patterns but collapse under unusually high levels of stress that would overwhelm even the strongest persons. By contrast, other clients depend heavily upon others to manage problematic situations for them.

Exploring how clients have attempted to cope with problems sometimes reveals that they have struggled effectively with similar problems in the past but are no longer able to do so. In such instances, it is important to explore carefully what has changed. For example, a person may have been able to cope with the demands of one supervisor but not with a new one who is more critical and aloof.

Changes in clients' levels of functioning also occasionally reduce their capacity to cope. Severely depressed clients commonly overestimate the difficulty of their problems and *underestimate* their coping abilities. Some clients are also able to cope effectively in one setting but not in another. Interestingly, some people slay various and sundry dragons at work with dispatch but find themselves unable to cope with the needs and emotions of family members. Some schoolteachers are able to be firm and consistent with challenging pupils but are at a loss as to how to deal effectively with their own children. And finally, some social workers have marvelous ability to listen to and understand their clients only to find they

simply cannot understand the "irrationality" of their own spouses. The point is that by exploring the different circumstances, meaning attributions, and emotional reactions of clients, you will be able to identify subtle differences that account for the varied effectiveness of their coping patterns in different contexts.

Another aspect of assessment is to identify the skills clients must possess to ameliorate their difficulties. Knowledge of needed skills enables you to negotiate appropriate and feasible goals aimed at assisting clients to develop skills not already possessed. To improve parent-child relationships, for example, clients may require the development of listening and negotiating skills. Socially inhibited clients may similarly need to learn skills in approaching others, introducing themselves, and engaging others in conversation. To enhance marital relationships, partners often need to learn communication and conflict management skills. To cope effectively with people who tend to exploit them, still other clients must acquire assertiveness skills. By identifying skills essential to problem resolution, you can formulate appropriate interventions. Fortunately, effective skill development programs have been formulated for these and other skills, which we discuss more extensively in Part 3.

12. What Are the Skills and Strengths of the Clients? An aspect of assessment that is too often overlooked consists of the skills and strengths of clients, as we noted earlier. We have thus included this facet of assessment because of a strong conviction that correction of this imbalance is long overdue. To assist you in perceiving strengths, we have identified in the following list a number of strengths often manifested by clients in initial sessions. We urge you to cultivate your sensitivity to these and other manifestations of these crucial client resources:

1. Facing problems and seeking help, rather than denying or otherwise avoiding confronting them.

2. Risking by sharing problems with the practitioner—a stranger.

3. Persevering in attempting to keep a family together under difficult circumstances.

4. Expressing feelings and views openly rather than being guarded.

5. Exercising resourcefulness and creativity in making the most out of limited resources or managing and surviving upon a meager income.

6. Making sacrifices on behalf of children and others.

7. Seeking to further knowledge, education, and skills.

8. Expressing loving and caring feelings to family members.

9. Asserting one's rights rather than submitting to injustice.

10. Attempting to meet one's debts and obligations despite financial adversity.

11. Seeking to be independent.

12. Seeking to understand the needs and feelings of others.

13. Demonstrating capacity to be introspective and to shift thinking or realign perceptions when presented with new information or alternate views of situations.

14. Owning responsibility for one's own action and showing interest in making changes in *self* rather than focusing extensively on the changes one thinks others should make.

15. Demonstrating capacity for self-control.

16. Demonstrating ability to make individual value judgments.

17. Manifesting emotional capacity to function effectively in stressful situations.

18. Demonstrating ability to abstract and to make connections between causes and effects.

19. Demonstrating ability to form close relationships with others.

20. Demonstrating ability to consider alternative courses of actions and the needs of others when solving problems.

13. What External Resources Are Needed? When clients request services from a social agency, it is essential to determine if the services requested correspond to the functions of the agency and if the agency staff possess the skills required to provide high-quality service. Often when clients apply for services from a social agency or specific practitioner, they have selected that agency or practitioner as a result of knowledge gained from other persons who have utilized the services of the agency or practitioner. In either instance, the service requested may match the services available, and external resources may not be needed.

Many clients, however, have inadequate or erroneous information about an agency's functions or eligibility requirements and/or need services in addition to those provided by an agency, such as medication, rehabilitation services, or special education services. Specific service needs of clients also may be better provided by staff members of other agencies that specialize in certain services (e.g., sex therapy, divorce counseling, and rape crisis counseling), and referral may be indicated to assure that the client receives the highest quality of service. In such instances, the practitioner performs a *broker* or *case manager role.* Performing these roles effectively requires knowledge of community resources or at least knowledge of how to obtain relevant essential information. Fortunately, many large communities have community resource information centers that are of great value to both clients and professionals in locating needed resources. To familiarize you with typical resources available in large communities, we have compiled a list (see Table 8-1), which is intended to be illustrative and not comprehensive.

In certain instances, in addition to the public and private resources listed below, two other major resources should be considered. The first is self-help groups, which have been extremely helpful to some individuals with personal problems. Eschewing professional leadership, members of these groups look to themselves to help each other, and the rapid expansion of such groups in recent years attests to their value. Self-help groups typically provide emotional support and the opportunity to share with and benefit from others who have had to cope with similar problems.

A second major resource, which is often overlooked, consists of natural support systems that may be tapped to counter isolation and difficulties in coping with disruptions caused by transitional stresses. Natural support systems include the family, relatives, friends, neighbors, coworkers, and close associates from school, church, and other social groups.

Some family therapists have developed innovative ways of tapping support systems collectively through an intervention termed *network therapy.* These therapists contend that much of the dysfunctional behavior labeled as mental illness derives from feelings of alienation from one's natural social network, which consists of all human relationships that are significant in a person's life, including natural support systems. Employing network therapy, these practitioners mobilize 40 to 50 significant people who are willing to come together in a period of crisis for one or more members of the network. The goal is to unite their efforts in tightening the social network of relationships for the purpose of offering support, reassurance, and solidarity to troubled members and other members of the social network.

TABLE 8-1 Types of Community Resources

Need	Resources
Income maintenance	Public assistance; Old Age, Survivors, Disability, and Health Insurance (OASDHI); Unemployment Compensation; Workers' Compensation; church welfare programs; food stamps
Housing	Special housing programs for the elderly, other low-income persons and homeless; housing outreach programs; Salvation Army; YMCA, YWCA, migrant housing
Health care	Tax-funded hospitals, local public and private health centers, Shriners hospitals, veteran's hospitals, Medicare, Medicaid, visiting nursing services, convalescent homes, rehabilitation programs
Child services	Day-care centers, child-guidance clinics, child welfare divisions, shelter homes, Children's Service Society, church programs, Head-start program, adoption agencies, school social services, special education and developmentally disabled programs, children's treatment centers, crippled children's services
Vocation guidance and rehabilitation	Job service, public vocational rehabilitation programs, veteran's services, Job Corps, Fountain House and like facilities for mentally disabled persons
Mental health care	Mental health centers, hospitals with psychiatric units, substance abuse centers, private practitioners
Legal services	Legal service societies (United Way), public defender, county attorneys, American Civil Liberties Union
Marital and family therapy	Family service centers (United Way), division of family services (public), ministers, church-affiliated services, private practitioners, mental health centers
Youth services	YMCA, YWCA, public and private recreational programs, local youth service programs, residential treatment programs, youth group homes, juvenile courts, Youth Authority programs
Recreation	Public and private recreation programs and centers, senior citizens centers, arts and handicrafts programs
Transportation	Traveler's Aid Society, local governmental programs, volunteers

Mobilizing social networks is in keeping with the best traditions of social work.

In instances of cultural dislocation, natural support systems may be limited to the family, and practitioners may need to mobilize other potential resources in the community. Assisting Asian refugees poses a challenge, for a cultural reference group may not be available in some communities. The language barrier poses an additional obstacle, and practitioners may need to search for interpreters and other interested parties who can assist these families in locating housing, gaining employment, learning the language, adapting to an alien culture, and developing social support systems.

In still other instances, people's environments may be virtually devoid of natural support systems. Consequently, environmental changes may be necessary to accomplish a better fit between needs and resources, a topic we consider at greater length in the next chapter.

Other Factors in Assessment

Using the 13 questions cited earlier as guidelines in the assessment process elicits comprehensive information that: (1) identifies the participants in the problem system, (2) clarifies how the participants and other factors interact to produce the problematic behavior, (3) defines strengths and limitations of the participants as well as external resources that must be considered in planning interventions, (4) provides indications as to appropriate goals, and (5) points to the interventions that can be employed.

Still other dimensions must be explored and evaluated before an adequate assessment can be completed. These factors include assessing:

1. The individual functioning of clients, including several key intrapersonal subsystems.

2. The motivation of clients to work on specified target problems.

3. Cultural factors embodied in the problem system.

4. Dynamics involved in couple and family systems.

5. Environmental factors that impinge upon the participants in the problem system.

In addition to the preceding factors, which we discuss in the next two chapters, the role of clients in formulating assessments is also critical. Clients' views are a valuable resource in formulating assessments, a resource often ignored, as Prager (1980) has noted:

Clients traditionally have had little if any real input into these professional areas of practice (diagnosis, rehabilitation, and evaluation). . . . it is almost paradoxical that, although mental health clients have spent a good part of their lives learning and implementing skills in relationships and communication, help is still largely defined, planned, and evaluated for them not by them.

(p. 5)

If you involve clients in the assessment process to the fullest extent possible, by inviting their views and responding to them with respect, they are likely to respond similarly to your views. On the other hand, if you attempt to impose your judgments on clients, they are likely to resist either openly or covertly. What we are advocating, then, is an open and mutual process that culminates in a synthesis of your own and your clients' views. The result of such mutuality is likely to be more accurate assessments and greater investment of clients in the assessments as well as in the planning and contracting processes.

9 | Assessing Intrapersonal and Environmental Systems

The Interaction of Multiple Systems in Human Problems

Problems encountered in direct social work practice result from interaction of the intrapersonal, interpersonal, and environmental systems. Rarely are they confined to one of these broad systems, for dysfunction in one system typically contributes to dysfunction in others. Individual dysfunction (e.g., feelings of worthlessness and depression) invariably influence how one relates to other people; interpersonal difficulties (e.g., marital strain) likewise affect individual functioning. Similarly, environmental deficits (e.g., inadequate housing or social isolation) affect individual and interpersonal functioning.

The reciprocal impacts among the three major systems, of course, are not limited to the negative effects of dysfunction and deficits within the systems. Assets and strengths also have reciprocal positive effects. A strong environment may partially compensate for intrapersonal deficits; similarly, strong interpersonal relationships between parents and children may provide positive experiences for the latter that more than compensate for an otherwise impoverished environment.

To adequately assess the many forces that interact to produce problems, it is essential to be well grounded in knowledge about the three major systems that are typically involved in problems. Therefore, we devote this and the next two chapters to assisting you to grasp more fully the complexities of these systems. The present chapter deals with the intrapersonal and environmental systems; the next chapter is focused on interpersonal systems, with particular emphasis on marital and family systems.

The Intrapersonal Systems

In assessing the social functioning of individuals, practitioners often make global judgments, such as "at best this person's level of functioning is marginal." Such a global statement, however, has limited usefulness, for it fails to specify areas in which functioning is marginal. Some individuals, of course, uniformly function at high or low levels, but variability is more often the case. Thorough assessment of the individual considers biophysical, cognitive/perceptual, emotional, behavioral, cultural, and motivational factors. Keep in mind, however, that your written assessment should make reference only to those factors that are salient in understanding the functioning of individuals who are part of the problem system.

Biophysical Functioning

Vital to the functioning of individuals is the biophysical subsystem, which embraces physical characteristics, appearance or presentation, and health factors. These dimensions are critical, for they determine in great measure the client's self-image, others' perceptions of and responses to the client, and the availability of energy to work, recreate, socialize, engage in sex, and cope with life's stresses.

Physical Characteristics and Presentation The physical characteristics and appearance of clients may be either assets or liabilities. In Western society, physical attractiveness is highly valued, and unattractive people are disadvantaged in the realms of social desirability, employment opportunities, and marriageability. Further, the findings of at least one study (Farina, Burns, Austad, Bugglin, & Fischer, 1986) indicate that physical attractiveness facilitates the readjustment of discharged psychiatric patients. It is thus important to be observant of distinguishing physical characteristics that may affect social functioning. Particular attributes that merit attention include body build, posture, facial features, gait, and various physical anomalies that may distort the self-image or pose a social liability.

Aside from physical characteristics, how clients present themselves is also important. Dress and grooming often reveal much about a person's morale, values, and lifestyle. People who present a dilapidated appearance characterized by shabby, inappropriate, or neglected clothes, disheveled hair, poor grooming, and the like may be depressed, have low self-esteem, lack zest for living, or be socially withdrawn. Similarly, clients who walk slowly, manifest stooped posture, talk slowly and without animation, lack spontaneity, and show minimal changes in facial countenance as they talk are likely to be depressed. By contrast, clients who, despite financial difficulties or other untoward circumstances, are neatly dressed and well groomed manifest ongoing efforts to cope successfully and to create a favorable appearance. Still others who are excessively fastidious may tend to be perfectionistic, critical, and, in some instances, self-centered.

Other factors associated with appearance that merit attention include tremors of the hands, facial tics, rigid or constantly shifting posture, and tense muscles of the face, hands, and arms. These physical manifestations usually indicate a high degree of tension or anxiety that warrants exploration. It is normal, of course, for clients to manifest a certain degree of anxiety. In fact, in initial sessions you should make a mental note when clients are relaxed, cool, and even jovial, for such demeanor suggests a client may lack a sufficient degree of anxiety to motivate efforts to change. Another possible meaning is that such a client may tend to relate superficially and may be difficult to engage.

Physical Health Because state of health critically affects virtually all aspects of functioning, practitioners should routinely consider this factor as they explore clients' problems. In addition to causing physical symptoms, ill health can contribute to depression, sexual difficulties, irritability, low level of energy, restlessness, anxiety, inability to concentrate, and a host of other difficulties. It is thus important to determine if clients are under medical care and, if not, when they last had a medical examination. Practitioners should rule out medical sources of difficulties by referring clients for medical examinations when appropriate before attributing problems solely to psychosocial factors. Practitioners have occasionally employed psychotherapy to treat dramatic increases in irritability, sudden losses of emotional control, and other personality changes to discover too late that these changes were caused by brain tumors. To avoid such tragedies, practitioners should be cautious and avoid drawing premature conclusions about the sources of problems when there is even a remote possibility that medical factors may be involved. An excellent book that offers practitioners procedures for screening suspected brain dysfunction and determining whether to refer for further evaluation has been written by Berg, Franzen, and Wedding (1987).

Assessing the health of clients is especially important with special groups known to underutilize medical care. These groups include people who live in poverty, ethnic minority groups, elderly people, immigrants (including refugees), foster children, unwed pregnant adolescents, homeless people, and AIDS victims. Although Medicare and Medicaid have done much to meet the medical needs of the first group (35 million Americans live in poverty, according to a Census Bureau report released in August 1984), substantial gaps still remain, and cost-containment measures taken by the government have widened the gap.

Health care needs of elderly people are among the greatest of the special groups. According to Morrison (1983), "Of people 65 years and older residing outside of institutions, 85 percent reported at least one chronic disease and 50 percent reported some limitations in functional capacity related to chronic health problems" (p. 161). Health problems of aging ethnic minority persons are especially acute because a disproportionate percentage of this group are in the lower socioeconomic strata. A high representation of health problems amenable to early detection and treatment is found among the minority aged, particularly among males. A considerable excess of disease and death due to influenza, pneumonia, and respiratory conditions such as bronchitis, emphysema, and asthma is found among older nonwhite males, whereas nonwhite women show higher mortality rates for diabetes. Health education and preventive measures aimed at early detection and lifestyle modification are needed to reduce illness and death due to these conditions.

Practitioners should be especially concerned about political refugees. Asian refugees in the United States, for example, manifest high rates of tuberculosis, malaria, intestinal parasites, and hepatitis. One expert, in fact, has estimated the percentage of Asian refugees who are carriers of Hepatitis B is from 50 to 100 times greater than in the U.S. population (Wilson, 1984). Compounding their plight is a lack of financial resources to purchase medical care and limited knowledge of Western medical care and of the complex health care provider systems in the United States. Relocation of refugees in localities that have few or no residents from their native lands also creates a sense of isolation, which, combined with the stresses previously cited, often lead to depression. Added to these burdens are difficulties in communicating.

Prenatal care for pregnant adolescents is critically important because of the high risk of adolescent childbearing (e.g., high rate of premature births and handicapped offspring). Pregnant adolescents are notoriously difficult to involve, however, and require special efforts and approaches by practitioners. Research findings reported by Joyce, Diffenbacher, Greene, and Sorakin (1983) indicate that women who delivered babies at a metropolitan hospital *without* prenatal care attributed their failure to receive prenatal care more often to internal factors than to external factors. Internal factors include fear of doctors, depression, denial of pregnancy, and unplanned pregnancy, whereas external factors consisted of inadequate finances, transportation problems, lack of child care, long waiting periods, or difficulties getting appointments. O'Leary, Shore, and Wieder (1984) and Joyce et al. (1983) discuss unique considerations involved in reaching and working with this unique population.

Many homeless people also manifest urgent needs for both medical and dental care and case management services. An excellent reference concerning the health care needs and implications thereof for health care delivery systems is a book edited by Brickner, Scharer, Conanan, Elvy, and Savarese (1985).

People afflicted with AIDS have unique health care needs. Because the disease is terminal and many of its victims are gays, patients have psychosocial needs that go beyond those of people with other illness. Needs for health care and social support are critical, but "Ambivalent community responses to AIDS, especially to its sex and drug-related aspects, has often meant that patients are not afforded the same benefits as others with terminal illnesses" (Moynihan, Christ, & Silver, 1988, p. 380). Difficulties for AIDS victims are even more acute in rural areas, because rural citizens hold more traditional moral values, expect greater conformity to commu-

nity norms, and are less tolerant of diversity. To avoid being stigmatized in rural communities (where people with AIDS report that "... everyone knows everyone, and everyone knows your business" (Rounds, 1988a, p. 258), rural gays maintain a low profile and conceal their sexual orientation. The distance to health care facilities and reluctance of health care professionals to treat AIDS patients in rural communities is another formidable obstacle. Implications for social workers for dealing with such organizational resistance, for assuming organizing roles in both rural and urban areas, and for functioning as case managers in serving the needs of people with AIDS are discussed in Chapter 16.

Attitudes of key family members should also be considered in assessing health problems. In most cultures, the family decides whether or not a member is ill, the meanings of illnesses, and how family members should cope with illness. Moreover, cultural values and lifestyle of a family affect the course of a patient's illness and recovery. The family influences decision making during each phase of a member's illness, beginning with the initial steps involved in seeking medical care, the response to the diagnosis, and the compliance or noncompliance with the treatment recommendations.

Practitioners must also assess how illness of a member affects the functioning of a family. The illness of a member, particularly of a parent, creates imbalance in a family system, often requiring adjustment in role performance by family members. Further, outside resources (e.g., financial aid, homemaking services, or visiting nursing service) may be required to assist families to maintain their equilibrium. Kumabe et al. (1985) have extensively discussed cultural nuances involved in the reciprocal effects of illness and disability and family functioning. We have also devoted a later section in this chapter to cultural factors in illness. An informative casebook that highlights through the case study method the impact of an individual's illness on the family and vice versa has been edited by Doherty and Baird (1987). This book contains studies of 71 cases, a few of which are black and Hispanic families.

Because other systems impact the health of clients, practitioners should also explore the nature of clients' interaction with these systems. Social support systems are particularly important, especially marital and family relationships. Gallo (1982), for example, studied the relationship between the adequacy of social support networks and health of the elderly and reported a high correlation. Research on psychosocial kinship systems also indicates that support networks are critical to sound mental health. Cutler and Madore (1980) report that the support systems of normal people usually contain 20 to 30 people, whereas those of neurotics consist of about one-half that number, and those of psychotics are limited to approximately four or five. Hepworth, Farley, and Griffiths (1988) also emphasize the importance of social support systems in assessing the functioning of potentially suicidal adolescents. We discuss assessment of social support systems later in this chapter.

Use and Abuse of Drugs and Alcohol

Because of the potential for drugs both to enhance and to harm health, it is often important (especially in health care settings) to determine if clients regularly use drugs. Even beneficial drugs can produce side effects that affect the functioning of various biopsychological systems. Drowsiness, for example, is a side effect of many drugs. Changes in sexual functioning may also result from use of certain medications used to treat high blood pressure. A jaundiced appearance, rigid gait, zombie-like countenance, tongue-thrusting, and various involuntary muscle contractions may result from excessive dosages of major tranquilizing drugs used to treat certain forms of psychosis, and medical evaluation of dosage may be needed. Other problems may be associated with the excessive use of minor tranquilizers used to treat anxiety and tension. And these are but a few of the myriad side effects of commonly used drugs. Other health problems may respond favorably to drugs (e.g., premenstrual syndrome, menopausal difficulty, severe depression, attention deficit disorders and hyperactivity in children, and epileptic seizures), and referral to a physician or health care facility may be indicated.

Alcohol abuse is a problem that can severely impair health, disrupt or destroy family life, and create serious community problems. Conservatively estimated to afflict from 9 to 10 million Americans, alcoholism can occur in any culture, of course, but the problem is widespread among Native Americans. Alcoholism is also associated with high incidence of suicide, homicide, and spouse and child abuse, all of which are prominent problems among the Native American population.

Another serious problem associated with alcohol abuse involves adverse effects on offspring produced by alcohol consumption during pregnancy. The effects range from full-blown fetal alcohol syndrome (FAS) to fetal alcohol effects (FAE). At the extreme end of a range of potential effects of alcohol on a fetus, FAS (found in infants of chronic alcoholic mothers who have four to six drinks per day) involves prenatal and postnatal growth retardation, central nervous system involvement, and abnormalities in shape and size of the head and/or facial features (dysmorphology). One of the most serious features of FAS is mental retardation (FAS children in the United States have an average IQ of 65), and the damage is irreversible.

The severity of FAE effects (found in mothers who are social drinkers) varies according to the amount of alcohol consumed, but the risks associated with two drinks daily include miscarriage, prenatal growth retardation, behavioral deficiencies, and various anomalies. With increased consumption, partial effects of FAS may develop. In addition, some newborns manifest withdrawal effects from alcohol such as irritability, tremulousness, alcohol on the breath, transient seizures, and jitteriness. Detailed information about FAS and FAE has been presented in an article by Anderson and Grant (1984), the source of the preceding information.

Anderson and Grant (1984) recommend that during intake interviews practitioners routinely question prospective mothers about their use of alcohol during pregnancy. By taking a history of consumption of beer, wine, and liquor during pregnancy (focusing on frequency, quantity, and variability), practitioners can delineate clients' drinking patterns. Numerous screening tools for alcoholism are also available.

From the initial screening, practitioners can determine if a woman is a problem drinker or is drinking beyond limits safe for fetal welfare. (The limit of safety set by some authors is fewer than two or three drinks daily or fewer than five drinks on any occasion.) If it is determined that a woman drinks beyond the margins of safety, a practitioner should attempt to involve her in a treatment program. Anderson and Grant (1984) have discussed such treatment programs.

Lester (1982) has also delineated the special needs of alcoholic women.

Although many Americans are not yet familiar with FAS, the public as a whole is aware of dangers to health and safety associated with drug abuse. This awareness has resulted from widespread educational programs and from sensational reports by the news media of deaths of celebrities and others caused by drug overdoses as well as news of suicides, homicides, and various types of accidents and addictions associated with drug abuse. Less well known by the public but extremely familiar to social workers are the ravages to individual lives and the disruption and suffering experienced by families of both alcohol and drug abusers.

People abuse many types of drugs. Because immediate care may be essential in instances of acute drug intoxication and because drug abusers often attempt to conceal their use of drugs, it is important that practitioners know the indications of abuse of commonly used drugs. Listed by category in Table 9-1 are the most commonly abused drugs and their indications.

In addition to the indications listed below of abuse of specific drugs, common general indications include the following:

- Changes in attendance at work or school.

- Decrease in normal capabilities (work performance, efficiency, habits, etc.).

- Poor physical appearance, neglect of dress and personal hygiene.

- Use of sunglasses to conceal dilated or constricted pupils and to compensate for eyes' reduced ability to adjust to sunlight.

- Unusual efforts to cover arm and hide needle marks.

Table 9-1 Indications of Abuse of Commonly Used Drugs

Type of Drug	Typical Indications
1. Depressants (downers) including Quaalude, Doriden, and various barbiturates	Intoxicated behavior with no odor of alcohol, staggering or stumbling, falling asleep at work, slurred speech, dilated pupils, difficulty concentrating.
2. Stimulants (amphetamines, including methamphetamine or "speed")	Excessively active, irritable, argumentative, nervous, dilated pupils, long periods without eating or sleeping.
3. Cocaine (also a stimulant)	Energetic, euphoric, fixed and dilated pupils, possible tremors (euphoria quickly replaced by anxiety, irritability and/or depression, sometimes accompanied by hallucinations and paranoid delusions).
4. Narcotics (opium, heroin, morphine, codeine)	Scars on arms or backs of hands from injecting drugs, fixed and constricted pupils, frequent scratching, loss of appetite (but frequently eat sweets). May have sniffles, red, watering eyes and cough until another "fix," lethargic, drowsy, and alternate between dozing and awakening ("nodding").
5. Marijuana (a hallucinogen)	In early stages may be euphoric and appear animated, speaking rapidly and loudly with bursts of laughter; pupils may be dilated and eyes bloodshot; may have distorted perceptions and experience hallucinations; in later stages may be drowsy.
6. Other hallucinogens (LSD, STP, DOM), mescaline, DTM, DET	Behavior and mood vary widely, may sit or recline quietly in trancelike state or appear fearful or even terrified; dilated pupils in some cases; may experience nausea, chills, flushes, irregular breathing, sweating or trembling of hands; may be changes in sense of sight, hearing, touch, smell, and time.

- Association with known drug users.

- Need to steal or engage in prostitution to raise cash to support drug habit.

In assessing the possibility of drug abuse, it is important to elicit information not only from the suspected abuser but also from persons who are familiar with the habits and lifestyle of the individual; drug abusers, including alcoholics, are notorious for minimizing or denying the extent to which they use drugs, and their reports, therefore, are often not reliable.

When exploration reveals a client is a drug abuser (or alcoholic), referral to a drug treatment center (some mental health centers and hospitals have drug abuse units) often is indicated. Staff members of these centers have special skills needed to work effectively with these often difficult clients. Moreover, drug abuse centers often employ group methods that are particularly relevant for work with drug abusers (Alcoholics Anonymous and Narcotics Anonymous are well-established, group-oriented self-help programs recognized for their successes in helping alcoholics and drug abusers respectively).

It is important, of course, to assess problems of drug abuse from a systems perspective. Explorations of family relationships often reveal that drug abusers feel alienated from other family members. Moreover, family members often unwittingly contribute to the problems of both alcoholics and drug abusers. Consequently, many professionals regard problems of drug abuse as manifestations of dysfunction within the family system. Keep in mind that drug abusers affect and are affected by the family system; obviously, the converse is also true.

Mental Disorders

In a number of settings, especially mental health centers and agencies (or private practitioners) that file for third-party insurance payments, practitioners are required to make psychiatric diagnoses for various types of developmental and mental health disorders. To render such diagnoses practitioners must be knowledgeable about and capable of using the Diagnostic and Statistical Manual (DSM III-R) published by the American Psychiatric Association (1987). This manual is updated periodically and DSM IV will be published in the near future. Content related to psychiatric diagnosis, however, is taught in advanced behavior or practice courses and is beyond the scope of this book.

Cognitive/Perceptual Functioning

Assessing how clients perceive their worlds of experience is critically important, for people's perceptions of others, themselves, and events largely determine how they feel and respond to life's experiences in general and to their problematic situations in particular. Perceptions, of course, do not exist separate and apart from meanings that are ascribed to them; hence, we have considered perceptual and cognitive functioning as a single entity. It is the meanings or interpretations of events, rather than the events themselves, that motivate human beings to behave as they do, as we noted in the preceding chapter. Furthermore, every person's world of experience is unique, having been influenced by vastly differing genetic endowments and life experiences. Perceptions of identical events or circumstances thus vary widely according to the complex interaction of belief systems, values, attitudes, state of mind, and self-concepts, all of which in turn are highly idiosyncratic. It follows that to understand and to influence human behavior you must first be knowledgeable about how people think.

People's thought patterns, of course, are influenced by numerous factors, including intellectual functioning, judgment, reality testing, coherence, cognitive flexibility, values, mistaken beliefs, self-concept, and dynamic interaction between cognition, emotions, and behavior. In the following sections, each of these factors is briefly considered.

Intellectual Functioning   Evaluating the intellectual capacity of clients is essential to gearing your verbal expressions to a level that clients can readily comprehend, assessing their difficulties, negotiating goals, and planning tasks that are commensurate with their capacities. In most instances, a rough estimate of level of intellectual functioning is sufficient. Criteria that you may employ include clients' abilities to grasp abstract ideas, to express themselves fluently, and to analyze or think logically. Additional criteria include level of educational achievement and vocabulary employed, although these factors must be considered in relationship to the clients' previous educational opportunities and/or possible learning difficulties. Some adults with average or higher intellectual capacity may be unable to read or write because of learning disabilities or poor instruction.

When clients manifest marked intellectual limitations, it is vital that you employ a vocabulary consisting of easily understood words. In such instances, you should avoid abstract explanations and utilize feedback to ascertain that clients have grasped intended meanings, for to avoid embarrassment, many intellectually impaired clients will pretend to understand when they do not. Greater time and patience are therefore required with these clients. Employing concrete examples of concepts frequently assists such clients to understand complex ideas.

Intellectual capacity, of course, establishes the upper limits of goals that clients can reasonably be expected to accomplish. To encourage clients to pursue goals that exceed their capacities is to assure almost certain failure, which can be devastating when they already are painfully aware of their limitations. This caution is particularly relevant to educational and vocational planning. Failures in these ventures may so discourage clients that they lose confidence in their abilities and simply quit trying—an outcome of near-tragic proportions.

Judgment Some clients (and nonclients, for that matter) who have adequate or even keen intellect encounter severe difficulties in life because of deficiencies in judgment. Clients with poor judgment may experience more difficulties than those with intellectual deficiencies because the former may get themselves into one jam after another. By contrast, some people with intellectual limitations manifest strengths and live stable and productive lives by exercising prudence in making decisions and governing their behavior. Typical manifestations of deficiencies in judgment involve consistently living beyond one's means, entering ventures or get-rich schemes without carefully exploring possible ramifications, quitting jobs impulsively, leaving small children unattended, getting married with little knowledge of the partner, failing to safeguard or maintain personal property, squandering resources, and the like.

Deficiencies in judgment generally come to light as you explore clients' problematic situations and patterns in detail. Often it is apparent that clients act with little forethought, fail to consider probable consequences of their actions, or engage in wishful thinking that things will somehow work out. Other clients manifest repetitive dysfunctional coping patterns that lead predictably to unfavorable outcomes. Failing to profit from past mistakes, these clients appear to be driven by intense impulses that overpower consideration of the consequences of their actions. These impulse-ridden clients may lash out at authority figures or write bad checks, both of which may provide immediate gratification but ultimately lead to loss of jobs, arrest, or other adverse consequences.

Reality Testing This factor is a critical index to a person's mental health. Strong functioning on this dimension involves:

1. Being properly oriented to time, place, and person.

2. Reaching appropriate conclusions about cause and effect relationships.

3. Perceiving external events and discerning the intentions of others with reasonable accuracy.

4. Differentiating one's own thoughts and feelings from those that emanate from others.

Relatively few clients manifest disorientation, but those who do usually are severely mentally disturbed, under the influence of drugs, or suffering from a pathological brain syndrome. Disorientation is usually readily discernable, but when doubt exists, questions about the date, day of the week, current events that are common knowledge, and recent events in the client's life will usually clarify the matter. Clients who are disoriented typically respond inappropriately, sometimes giving bizarre answers. For example, in responding to a question about his daily activities, a recluse reported that he engaged in conversation with his 18 pet dogs.

Deficiencies in formulating cause and effect relationships are relatively common. In explaining reasons for their arrest, delinquents frequently place responsibility outside of themselves by attributing the cause to cops who have it in for them or to a bum rap. One client who stole an automobile externalized actions for his behavior by blaming the owner for leaving the keys in the car. Some clients blame their employers for losing their jobs, even though they habitually missed work for invalid reasons. Still others attribute their difficulties to the fact that fate decreed them to be born losers. It is a welcome strength when clients own responsibility for their actions.

Perceptual patterns that involve distortions of external events are fairly common among clients and may cause severe difficulties in interpersonal relationships—the domain in which perceptual distortions most frequently occur. Mild distortions may be associated with stereotypical perceptions (e.g., "All policemen are cruel and punitive" or "The only interest men have in me is sexual"). Moderate distortions often involve marked misinterpretations of the motives of others and may severely impair interpersonal relationships (e.g., "My boss told me I was doing a good job and that there is an opportunity to be promoted to a job in another department; he wants to get rid of me" or "My wife says she wants to take an evening class, but I know what she *really* wants. She wants to have an affair because she's not satisfied with me"). In instances of extreme distortions, people may manifest delusions that others plan to harm them and on rare occasions take violent actions to protect themselves from their imagined persecutors. Bizarre killings of innocent strangers are sometimes the actions of deranged people attempting to protect themselves from imagined communists, CIA agents, or other feared groups.

Dysfunction in reality testing of psychotic proportions is involved when people project onto others repressed thoughts and impulses that if owned by themselves would obliterate self-esteem and create unbearable anxiety. Self-esteem is thus safeguarded to some degree when, rather than acknowledging thoughts as their own, people "hear" voices (auditory hallucinations) telling them to murder, steal, or commit rape or criticizing them for being utter failures. The cost of such extreme measures to preserve some semblance of self-esteem is the loss of personality integration, for such persons lack the capacity to distinguish between thoughts and beliefs that emanate from themselves and those that originate from external sources. Although dysfunction in reality testing may be rooted in psychological causes such as those just discussed, current theories hold that thought disorder more often results from biochemical and neurological dysfunction, some of which may be linked with genetic factors. Whatever the source, it is vital to recognize such severe cognitive dysfunction, for clients thus affected usually require medication and/or hospitalization.

Coherence Practitioners occasionally encounter clients who manifest major thought disorders characterized by rambling and incoherent speech. Successive thoughts of these persons may be highly fragmented and disconnected from one another, a phenomenon denoted as looseness of association in the thought processes. Thought disorder of this type is a prominent feature of the mental disorder designated as schizophrenia. Severe thought disorder, of course, pervades virtually all aspects of social functioning, often incapacitating a person from performing appropriate social roles. (Incoherence, of course, may also be produced by acute drug intoxication, and practitioners should be careful to rule out this possibility.)

A number of scales are available for assessing mental illness. Schneider and Struening (1983) have developed a behavioral rating scale that is particularly useful for social workers. An advantage of this scale is that it focuses on specific skills required for daily living.

Cognitive Flexibility   Receptiveness to new ideas and the ability to analyze many facets of problematic situations are conducive not only to effective problem solving but to general adaptability as well. Cognitive flexibility is manifested by clients who seek to grow, to understand the part they play in their difficulties, and to understand others; such clients also can ask for assistance without believing it is an admission of weakness or failure. Many people, however, are rigid and unyielding in their beliefs, and their inflexibility poses a major obstacle to progress in the helping process.

A common pattern of cognitive inflexibility is thinking in absolute or black-and-white terms (e.g., a person is good or evil, a success or a failure, responsible or irresponsible—there is no in-between). Clients who think this way are prone to be critical of others who fail to measure up to their stringent expectations. Difficult to live with, many such people appear at social agencies because of marital difficulties or problems in parent-child relations. Improvement often requires helping them to examine the destructive impact of their rigidity, to broaden their perspectives of themselves and others, and to "loosen up" in general.

Negative cognitive sets also include biases and stereotypes that render clients unable to relate to members of certain groups (e.g., authority figures, ethnic groups, and the opposite sex) as individuals. Severely depressed clients evince tunnel vision, viewing themselves as helpless and/or worthless and the future as dismal and hopeless. These clients also selectively attend to their own negative attributes, weaknesses, and failings, leaving no way to feel good about themselves.

Values   An integral part of the cognitive-perceptual subsystem, values strongly influence human behavior, often playing a key role in problems presented by clients. For this reason you should seek to identify clients' values, assess the role they play in their difficulties, and consider ways in which their values can be used to create incentives to modify their problematic behaviors. Further, you have an ethical responsibility to respect the rights of clients to cling to their values and to make choices consistent with them—an obligation that requires awareness of their values.

Many values, of course, are a product of cultural conditioning. Practitioners therefore must have knowledge about the values of clients' cultural reference groups to avoid making errors in assessment. American Indian values, for example, differ sharply from mainstream values on the following: (American Indian values are listed first) (1) harmony with nature versus mastery of nature, (2) orientation to the present versus orientation to the present and future, (3) orientation to "being" activity versus orientation to "doing" activity, and (4) primacy of family and group goals versus primacy of individual goals. In a study comparing 36 practicing American Indian MSW social workers with Anglo-American counterparts, DuBray (1985) found the two groups differed significantly on all these value orientations except (3), despite the fact the American Indian social workers had completed six years of college education. DuBray concluded, therefore, that American Indians prefer traditional value orientations and resist assimilation into the dominant culture. Still, it is important to realize that considerable diversity exists among individuals in any given culture with respect to value preferences.

Value conflicts often lie at the heart of clients' difficulties, as, for example, being torn between a desire for independence on one hand and a desire to be a homemaker on the other. Other clients may be engaged in a tug-of-war between a desire for liberation from an oppressive marital partner and a belief that marriage should be maintained at all costs. Value conflicts may also be central to difficulties between spouses. One partner may strongly value having children, whereas the other partner may reject this value. Conflicts between marital partners over religious values and clashes in beliefs between parents and adolescent children concerning premarital sexual behavior or the importance of education and achievement are also prevalent.

Being aware of clients' values is also prerequisite to employing these values to create incentive for changes in dysfunctional behavior. Clients may express strong commitment to certain values and yet engage in behavior that is in direct opposition to their purported values. When clients are assisted to measure their behavior against the yardstick of values they themselves have identified, they often realize for the first time that their behavior is inconsistent and, more importantly, is self-defeating. An example will clarify this point. First, an adolescent who has vociferously protested that his parents should trust him agrees that being trusted is important to him. The practitioner then clarifies that his persistent lying and deceiving his parents in numerous ways defeats any possibility of his meriting their trust. Only by changing his behavior can he realistically expect them to trust him.

You can determine clients' relevant values by exploring what matters most to them, how they believe spouses should relate to one another, how they think children should be disciplined, and so on. Examples of questions that will clarify clients' values are as follows:

- "You say you believe your parents are old-fashioned about sex; what are your beliefs?"

- "If you could be married to an ideal wife, what would she be like?"

- [*To a couple*]: "What are your beliefs as to how couples should make decisions?"

- "So you feel you're not succeeding in life. To you, what does being successful involve?"

Misconceptions   Clients commonly hold mistaken beliefs about human relationships, sex roles, authority, and countless other facets of life. Increasing emphasis has been accorded to these beliefs, and one prominent school of psychotherapy (cognitive or rational-emotive therapy) posits the tenet that beliefs mediate (i.e., predetermine) both emotions and behavior (Ellis, 1962). Central to the theory of this school of thought is the premise that mistaken beliefs lie at the heart of human maladjustment. In Table 9-2, we have listed a few common misconceptions as well as contrasting functional beliefs.

Because misconceptions lie at the roots of many human problems, it is vital to learn to identify them and to include them in assessments. Goals often involve modifying key misconceptions, the accomplishment of which paves the way to behavioral change.

Table 9-2 Examples of Common
Misconceptions and Functional Beliefs

Misconceptions	Functional Beliefs
It is a disaster if I displease someone, and I must suffer.	I can't be constantly at the mercy of others' reactions to me, or I will be extremely vulnerable to hurt. Pleasing myself is more important than pleasing others.
I am completely at the mercy of circumstances beyond my control and totally powerless.	Although many circumstances *are* beyond my control, there is much I can do to improve my situation.
The world is a dog-eat-dog place. No one really cares about anyone except themselves.	There are all kinds of people in the world, including those who are ruthless and those who are caring. If I seek the latter, I will find them. The world will be a better place if I strive to be a caring person.
All people in authority use their power to exploit and control others.	People in authority vary widely. Some usurp others' rights; others are benevolent. I must reserve judgment, or I will indiscriminately resent all authority figures.
Men's only interest in women is to dominate them and use them for sexual pleasure.	Men are as different from one another as are women. Healthy men and women are interested in sex but not necessarily to use others for selfish pleasure.
To be worthwhile, a person must be thoroughly competent and successful in every endeavor.	Everyone has a range of talents and will do better in some endeavors than in others. No one is perfect, and disappointments are bound to occur from time to time.
It's a terrible blow to lose in competition.	Although it makes me feel good to win, there must be a loser for every winner. There is accomplishment in losing gracefully as well as in winning.
To be worthwhile, one must be the center of attention and admired by everyone.	Self-esteem that depends on constant attention is tenuous. Stable self-esteem comes from within; therefore I must learn to esteem myself.
It is virtuous to sacrifice, suffer, and deprive oneself in promoting the welfare of others.	Although it is desirable to assist others and to be concerned about them, I owe it to myself to seek personal satisfaction also. There is no virtue in unnecessary suffering.

The Self-Concept Convictions, beliefs, and ideas about the self have been generally recognized as one of the most crucial determinants of human behavior. Raimy (1975), who devoted an entire book to the subject (*Misunderstandings of the Self*), has concluded along with many other theorists "that beliefs about the self that are consonant with reality lead to adjusted behavior, whereas inappropriate beliefs lead to maladjusted behavior" (p. 9). It is thus a strength and is conducive to mental health to have high self-esteem and to be realistically aware of one's positive attributes, accomplishments, and potentialities as well as one's limitations and deficiencies. A healthy person can accept limitations as a natural part of human fallibility without being distressed or discouraged. People with high levels of self-esteem, in fact, can laugh at and joke about their limitations and failings.

Many human beings, however, are tormented with feelings of worthlessness, inadequacy, and helplessness. These and other like feelings pervade their functioning in diverse negative ways, including the following:

- Underachieving in life because of imagined deficiencies.

- Passing up opportunities because of fears of failing.

- Avoiding social relationships because of fears of being rejected.

- Permitting oneself to be taken for granted and exploited by others.

- Ingratiating oneself to others.

- Being self-conscious or retiring in social situations to avoid looking stupid.

- Gravitating in social relationships to low-status persons.

- Drinking to excess or taking drugs to fortify oneself because of feelings of inadequacy.

- Devaluing or discrediting one's worthwhile achievements.

- Becoming depressed.

- Failing to defend one's rights.

Extremely low self-esteem also is a primary contributor to mental illness. Certain manifestations of mental illness appear to be dysfunctional efforts to compensate for extremely low self-esteem. Some psychotic patients, for example, delude themselves into believing they are someone else—usually a person of power and status such as Jesus Christ, the Virgin Mary, Napoleon, or some other historical giant. Others project their feeling of worthlessness and hear voices that say, "You're no good" or "You're rotten."

Because clients with poor self-concepts often desperately need help in enhancing their self-esteem, it is vital to assess this dimension of their functioning. Often clients will spontaneously discuss how they view themselves. When they do not, an open-ended response, such as "Tell me how you see yourself," will often elicit rich information. Because many people have not actually given much thought to the matter, they will hesitate or reply, "I'm not sure what you mean; what did you have in mind?" Persistence on your part will usually be rewarded. A further response, such as "Just what comes into your head when you think about the sort of person you are?" is usually all that is needed.

Dynamic Interaction Between Cognition, Emotions, and Behavior   As is apparent in the foregoing discussion, cognitive functioning embraces many critical factors that interact with other variables to influence social functioning. Cognition, for example, plays a powerful role in mediating emotional arousal. Cognitive/perceptual sets, particularly the self-concept, influence both emotions and behavior. Because theoreticians and researchers have increasingly realized the significance of cognitive factors, they have in recent years developed and empirically tested a number of cognitive-behavioral interventions that have widespread application. Accordingly, we have devoted a large portion of Chapter 18 to these interventions.

Emotional Functioning

A vital dimension of human experience, emotions powerfully influence behavior and are of primary concern to social work practitioners. Strong emotions or states of feeling invariably play a central role in the problems of people who seek help. Some persons, for example, are emotionally volatile and engage in violent behavior while in the heat of anger. Others are emotionally unstable, struggling to stay afloat in a turbulent sea of emotion. Some people become emotionally distraught as the result of stress associated with the death of a loved one, divorce, severe disappointment, or another blow to self-esteem. Still others are pulled in different directions by opposing feelings and seek help to resolve their emotional dilemmas. To assist you in assessing emotional functioning, we devote the following sections to vital aspects of this dimension.

Emotional Control People vary widely in the degree of control they exercise over their emotions, ranging from emotional constriction to emotional excesses. Prominent in the former are individuals who are unexpressive, detached, and often withholding in relationships. Out of touch with their emotions, they do not permit themselves to feel joy, hurt, enthusiasm, disappointment, passionate love, elation, and other emotions that invest life with zest, variety, and meaning. Such persons are comfortable analyzing and intellectualizing but retreat from expressing or discussing feelings. They often favorably impress others with their intellectual styles, but sometimes have difficulties maintaining close relationships because their aloofness and emotional detachment thwart fulfilling the needs of others for intimacy and emotional stimulation.

Clients who manifest emotional excesses may have a "short fuse" and react intensely to even mild provocations or overreact to stress with tears, panic, depression, helplessness, and the like. Still others have difficulties in interpersonal relationships because they are excessively grouchy, irritable, glum, or even morose. In considering emotional excesses, cultural factors should be considered, for cultures vary widely in patterns of emotional expressiveness. It is generally accepted, for example, that people of Italian extraction are more emotionally reactive than are Asian and English people, who are known for their emotional reserve. Hispanics also tend to be emotionally reactive as Queralt (1984, p. 118) indicates in his description of Cubans: "Uninhibited

emotionality and a hedonistic tendency that manifests itself through love of comfort, of life, and of pleasure, sensuality, playfulness, lightness, and gaiety are important Cuban traits." Hispanics also vary in emotional expressiveness when they switch from speaking Spanish to English. According to Queralt:

Hispanics generally offer more carefully weighted, rational, and intellectualized messages in English and more emotional messages in Spanish. . . . Hispanics may come across as relatively guarded and businesslike in English, and yet, when switching to Spanish, they frequently become much more open, expansive, informal, jovial, friendly, jocose, explosive, negative, or positive. It is as if two personalities resided in the same person at once.

(p. 119)

In assessing cultural factors, however, it is vital to differentiate individual from cultural factors, for a wide range of emotional expressiveness exists among members of specific cultural groups. Individual patterns thus must be weighed against cultural norms.

Emotional health in any culture, however, involves having control over the emotions to the extent that one is not overwhelmed by them. As implied earlier, emotionally healthy persons also enjoy the freedom of experiencing and expressing emotions appropriately. It is also a strength to be able to bear painful emotions when beset by stress without denying or masking feelings or being incapacitated by them. Further, emotionally healthy persons are able to discern the emotional states of others, empathize, and discuss painful emotions openly without feeling unduly uncomfortable—recognizing, of course, that a certain amount of discomfort is natural. And finally, it is a strength to be able to mutually share deeply personal feelings in intimate relationships.

Range of Emotions Another aspect of emotional functioning involves the ability to experience and to express a wide range of emotions that befit the diversity of situations encountered by human beings. Some people's emotional experiencing is confined to a limited range, which often causes interpersonal dysfunction. A marital partner, for example, may have a "blockage" of tender emotions, causing the partner to feel rejected, insecure, or deprived of deserved affection. Some individuals are unable to feel joy, happiness, elation, or to express much in the way of pleasurable emotions—a dysfunction denoted as *anhedonia*. Still others have been conditioned to block angry feelings, blame themselves, or placate others when friction develops in relationships. Because of the blocking of natural emotions, they often experience extreme tension or physiological symptoms such as asthma, colitis, and headaches when involved in situations that normally would engender anger. And finally, some people, to protect themselves from unbearable emotions, evolved psychic mechanisms early in life that blocked experiencing rejection, loneliness, and hurt. Often such blockage is reflected by a compensatory facade of toughness and indifference, combined with verbal expressions such as "I don't need anyone" and "No one can hurt me."

Emotionally healthy people experience the full gamut of human emotions within normal limits of intensity and duration. It is thus a strength to experience joy, grief, exhilaration, disappointment, pride, discouragement, anger, loneliness, passion, excitement, and all the rest of the full spectrum of emotions. When clients manifest emotional blockages that cause social dysfunction, the practitioner has the task of enabling them to get in touch with the blocked emotions.

Appropriateness of Affect Direct observation of the affect (emotionality) manifested by clients often discloses valuable information about their emotional functioning. Some anxiety or mild apprehension is natural in initial sessions as contrasted to intense apprehension and tension at one extreme or complete relaxation at the other. Spontaneous experiencing and expressing of emotion that befits the content of material being discussed is indicative of healthy emotional functioning. It is thus a strength to be able to laugh, to cry, to express hurt, discouragement, anger, and pleasure when these feelings match the mood of the session. Such spontaneity indicates that clients are in touch with emotions and can express them appropriately.

Inordinate apprehension manifested through muscle tenseness, constant postural shifts, hand wringing, lip biting, and other like behaviors usually indicate a client is fearful, suspicious, or exceptionally uncomfortable in unfamiliar interpersonal situations. Such extreme tenseness may be characteristic of a client's demeanor in other interpersonal situations, a hypothesis that merits consideration in your assessment.

In transcultural work, appropriateness of affect must be considered in light of the impact of cultural differences. As Lum (1982) has indicated, minority persons may feel uncomfortable with nonminorities but mask their emotions as a protective measure. Moreover, in the presence of nonminority practitioners, minority persons may control painful emotions according to culturally prescribed behavior. An Asian-American, for example, may react with politeness, quietness, and friendliness in the face of an overwhelming and threatening situation.

Clients who appear completely relaxed, express themselves freely (if not glibly), and present themselves in a charming fashion often lack appropriate anxiety. Lack of anxiety, in fact, often reflects a denial of a problem and may indicate a lack of motivation to engage in the problem-solving process. Further, charming demeanor may be a reflection of skill in projecting a favorable image when it is advantageous to do so. In some situations, as in sales or promotional work, such charm may be an asset. As viewed by seasoned practitioners who have learned from the painful experience of being led down the primrose path by other "charmers," such behavior often is correctly perceived as a person's camouflage to conceal being self-centered, manipulative, opportunistic, and exploitative in relationships. Such individuals often engender anxiety in those who are victimized by their manipulativeness, but they themselves typically lack anxiety that is prerequisite to wanting to change their own behavior.

Emotional blunting or apathy frequently is indicative of severe mental disorder. It is important to consider this possibility when clients discuss in a detached matter-of-fact manner traumatic life events or conditions, such as murder of one parent by another, deprivation, or physical or sexual abuse. When such emotional blunting appears in tandem with thought disorder, a strong likelihood exists that the client is psychotic and in need of careful psychiatric evaluation.

Inappropriate affect can also be manifested in other forms, such as laughing when discussing a painful event (gallows laughter) or wearing a constant smile irrespective of what is being discussed. Elation or euphoria that is incongruent with one's life situation, combined with constant and rapid shifts from one topic to another (flight of ideas), irritability, expansive ideas, and constant motion also suggest severe dysfunction denoted as manic behavior. Although manic behavior is relatively rare, it is important to recognize manifestations of it, for manic clients urgently need medication and/or hospitalization to safeguard their health or protect them from impulsive and irrational actions, such as squandering resources on foolish investments.

Depression Because depression profoundly affects human functioning and is the most prevalent mental health problem in the United States, practitioners must be able to assess degrees of depression. Moreover, people who are severely depressed may pose suicidal risks, requiring precautionary measures by practitioners.

Mild depression is common and is manifested by feeling states typically described as "feeling down," "having the blahs," or "being in the dumps." Virtually everyone experiences mild depression from time to time, and it is no cause for alarm. Moderate depression, by contrast, produces marked psychic pain (dysphoria) and pervades most aspects of functioning. The depression is usually readily discernible by the observer, and the afflicted person reports feeling depressed. Crying may be frequent, and clients may begin crying uncontrollably and be unable to pinpoint the reasons. Anxiety typically accompanies moderate depression although chronically depressed people may have become numb to the anxiety. Pessimism is common, and sleep disturbances may involve early morning waking and inability to go back to sleep. Consequently, lack of energy is a common complaint.

Severely depressed people manifest constant and profound melancholia. Strangely, crying is not necessarily a paramount feature of severe depression. The emotions are completely blunted by the depression, and the person is entirely void of humor or spontaneity. The facial expression is sad and unchanging, having a mask-like appearance. Movement and speech tend to be slow (denoted as psychomotor retardation) although psychomotor agitation (pacing, fidgeting, and inability to sit still) may also occur. Speech generally is monotonic, drab, and void of animation. The future appears hopeless to severely depressed persons, and they present a picture of mental anguish and utter despair.

Severely depressed persons also typically report a number of physical symptoms. Lack of energy and appetite (sometimes accompanied by weight loss), sleep disturbances, and lack of sexual desire are common symptoms. Cognitive disturbances include feelings of worthlessness that range from feelings of inadequacy to totally unrealistic negative evaluations of one's self. Unrealistic feelings of guilt are also common. Fears of dying or suicidal thoughts also commonly occur. Practitioners should carefully explore the extent of suicidal thoughts. When clients ruminate about suicide, have thoughts of how they might commit suicide, and, in particular, have considered concrete suicidal plans, the risk of suicide may be great. The Hopelessness Scale (Beck, Resnik, & Lettieri, 1974) and the Scale for Suicide Ideation (Beck, Kovacs, & Weissman, 1979) are valuable instruments for assessing suicide potential. When suicide is a distinct possibility, psychiatric evaluation and/or hospitalization should be considered, and antidepressant medication is likely indicated. In fact, psychiatric evaluation is generally advisable in instances of moderate or severe depression. Antidepressant medication often produces dramatic improvements in these instances.

In assessing depression, it is important to identify precipitants that preceded the depressive episode. Commonly an important loss or series of losses have occurred, and clients may need help in working through grief associated with these losses and in developing compensatory sources of need gratification. A careful history including previous depressive episodes and incidence of depression among kin is also important in identifying possible biochemical and congenital factors. Again, psychiatric evaluation may be indicated if biochemical factors are suspected. Depression associated with biochemical factors can often be managed effectively with a carefully controlled medical regimen.

Several psychological scales are available to assess the presence of depression. The General Contentment Scale (Hudson, 1982), developed by a social worker, is easy to administer and score and correlates highly with other widely accepted depression scales, which include the Beck Depression Inventory (Beck, Ward, Mendelson, Mock, & Erbaugh, 1961) and the Zung Self-Rating Depression Scale (Zung, 1965).

Behavior Functioning

In direct practice, change efforts typically are aimed at modifying behavioral patterns that impair the social functioning of clients and others involved in the problem. A child may manifest difficulties in social relationships or not perform adequately in school because of reciprocal dysfunctional behavior on the part of parents, the child, siblings, teachers, or others. Marital partners may be in distress because of dysfunctional behavior on the part of both partners, and the effects of the distress may pervade their functioning as parents, employees, or in other social roles. Adults may also have difficulties in functioning as parents because of dysfunctional behavior of a child (extreme examples of this include autistic and brain-damaged children, who present demanding challenges to the strongest of parents). As you assess behavior, it is important to keep in mind that one person's behavior does not influence another person's behavior in simple linear fashion. Rather the behavior of all participants reciprocally impacts upon and shapes the behavior of others.

Because behavioral change is commonly the target of interventions, you must be skillful in discerning and assessing both dysfunctional and functional patterns of behavior. With respect to direct observation in individual sessions, you will be able to observe certain *social and communication* patterns of clients, as well as some *personal habits and traits.* In conjoint interviews and group sessions, you will be able to observe these types of behavioral patterns and in addition can observe the functioning of clients on the dimensions of *power/control* and *nurturance/support.*

In assessing behavior, it is helpful to think of dysfunction as consisting of *excesses* or *deficiencies* on the part of clients. With respect to the former, interventions are aimed at the goal of diminishing or eliminating behavioral excesses, which include temper outbursts, excessive talking, arguing, overachieving, and consummatory excesses (e.g., overeating, immoderate drinking, and excessive sexual indulgence). With regard to deficiencies, interventions are employed to assist clients to acquire skills and behaviors needed to function more effectively. The behavioral repertoires of clients, for example, may not include skills in expressing feelings directly, engaging in social conversation, listening to others, solving problems, managing finances, planning nutritional meals, being a responsive sexual partner, handling conflict, and others that are essential to effective social functioning.

In addition to identifying dysfunctional behavioral patterns, it is important to be aware of those that are effective and represent strengths. To assist you in assessing both dysfunctional and functional patterns of behavior, we have listed, according to major behavioral categories, numerous patterns of behavior (see Table 9-3). Although the list is extensive, it is by no means comprehensive, nor are the categories all-inclusive. We have, however, included those patterns that most frequently create interpersonal difficulties. As you review the list, you may question whether a few patterns are functional or dysfunctional. This determination, of course, depends on the situational context within which the behavior occurs. Aggressive behavior may serve a self-protective function in a prison environment but may be dysfunctional in family relationships or in most groups. In compiling the list, our frame of reference encompassed typical marital, family, and group contexts.

You will note that the list consists of many adjectives and verbs that are very general and are subject to different interpretations. *In assessing behavior, therefore, it is vital to specify actual dysfunctional behaviors.* For example, rather than assessing a client's behavior as abrasive, a practitioner might specify that the client constantly interrupts his fellow workers, insults them by telling them they are misinformed, and boasts about his own knowledge and achievements. When dysfunctional behavior is thus pinpointed, the changes that must be made become clear.

An adequate assessment of behavior, of course, goes beyond identifying dysfunctional behaviors. You must also determine the antecedents of behaviors—when, where, and how frequently they occur—and specify the consequences of the behaviors as well. Further, you should explore thoughts that precede, accompany, and follow the behavior, as well as the

Table 9-3   Behavioral Patterns

Dimensions of Behavior	Dysfunctional Patterns	Functional Patterns (Strengths)
Power/ control	Autocratic, overbearing, aggressive, ruthless, demanding, domineering, controlling, passive, submissive; excludes others from decision making	Democratic, cooperative, assertive; includes others in decision making, stands up for own rights
Nurturance/ support	Self-centered, critical, rejecting, withholding, demeaning, distant, punitive, fault-finding, self-serving; insensitive to or unconcerned about others	Caring, approving, giving, empathic, encouraging, patient, generous, altruistic, warm, accepting, supportive; interested in others
Responsibility	Undependable, erratic; avoids responsibility, places pleasure before responsibility, externalizes responsibility for problems, neglects maintenance of personal property	Dependable, steady, consistent, reliable; accepts responsibility, follows through, owns part in problems, maintains personal property
Social skills	Abrasive, caustic, irritable, insensitive, aloof, seclusive, sarcastic, querulous, withdrawn, self-conscious, ingratiating; lacks social delicacy	Outgoing, poised, personable, verbally fluent, sociable, witty, courteous, engaging, cooperative, assertive, spontaneous, respectful of others, sensitive to feelings of others; has sense of propriety
Coping patterns	Rigid, impulsive, rebellious; avoids facing problems, uses alcohol or drugs when under stress, becomes panicky, lashes out at others, sulks, uses cold war tactics	Flexible; faces problems, considers and weighs alternatives, anticipates consequences, maintains equilibrium, seeks growth, consults others for suggestions, negotiates and compromises
Personal habits and traits	Disorganized, dilatory, devious, dishonest, compulsive, overly fastidious, impulsive; manifests poor personal hygiene, has consummatory excesses, has irritating mannerisms	Planful, organized, flexible, clean, efficient, patient, self-disciplined, well-groomed, honest, open, sincere, temperate, considerate, even-dispositioned, punctual
Communication	Mumbles, complains excessively, nags, talks excessively, interrupts others, tunes others out, stammers, yells when angry, withholds views, defensive, monotonic, argumentative, taciturn, verbally abusive	Listens attentively, speaks fluently, expresses views, shares feelings, uses feedback, expresses self spontaneously, considers others' viewpoints, speaks audibly and within tolerable limits
Accomplishment/ independence	Unmotivated, aimless, nonproductive, easily discouraged, easily distracted, underachieving; lacks initiative, seldom completes endeavors, workaholic, slave to work	Ambitious, industrious, self-starting, independent, resourceful, persevering, successful in endeavors, seeks to advance or to improve situations
Affectional/sexual	Unaffectionate, reserved, distant, sexually inhibited, promiscuous, lacking sexual desire, engages in deviant sexual behavior	Warm, loving, affectionate, demonstrative, sexually responsive (appropriately)

nature of and intensity of emotions associated with the behavior. We identified these factors in the preceding chapter and earlier in this chapter.

We have also limited the dysfunctional behaviors embodied in the list to *individual* patterns of behavior. The list does not include dysfunctional patterns of *interaction* between two or more persons in marital, family, and group contexts. However, we devote the following chapter to this important topic.

Motivation

The vital importance of motivation to outcomes of the helping process is supported by general agreement among theoreticians and by research findings as well. Simple logic also leads to the conclusion that before persons, couples, families, or groups can solve problems, they must acknowledge such problems and be willing to undertake remedial actions. Without such motivation, helping efforts are doomed to failure; hence, evaluating and enhancing the motivation of clients are integral parts of the assessment process.

Motivation, of course, is a dynamic force that is strongly influenced by ongoing interaction with practitioners, who thus bear the responsibility not only to assess initial motivation but also to enhance motivation that is deficient in strength or direction. By relating facilitatively and determining clients' wants and goals, practitioners often succeed in engendering incentives and engaging clients. Conversely, clients who initially are adequately motivated may lose that motivation if their encounter with a practitioner is negative.

As Reid (1978) has pointed out, motivation consists of two critical aspects. The first aspect is the *direction* of the motivation; that is, toward what goals is the client motivated? Clients are generally motivated to fulfill certain wants or needs. In evaluating the directionality of motivation, the central issue concerns whether or not clients' wants are realistic and achievable. Some clients seek to accomplish goals that exceed their *capacity* (e.g., vocational goals that require aptitude well beyond that possessed by the client). Others manifest wants that require changes beyond the sphere of influence of the client and/or practitioner (e.g., "I want you to persuade my wife to drop her divorce action and to reconcile

with me" or "I want you to get my kids back; they need me and are not happy in that foster home"). In such instances, it is important to tactfully assist clients to recognize the unrealistic nature of their wants and to direct them toward realistic goals that are relevant to their problematic situation (e.g., "Only the judge has the authority to return your children to you, but I'm very willing to assist you in making whatever changes are necessary to meet the conditions he has specified for the return of your children").

The second aspect concerns the *strength* of motivation. Clients often manifest wants but lack the willingness to participate actively in planning and implementing remedial actions. Many clients have misconceptions about the helping role, imputing to the practitioner magical power for solving their difficulties. Others are willing to participate but mistakenly perceive their role as compliantly carrying out the practitioner's directives. Still others manifest strength and independence by correctly perceiving the practitioner as a partner and facilitator. These individuals willingly seek to assume responsibility for mutually exploring their problems and for planning and implementing remedial measures.

Precipitating Events and Motivation By carefully exploring life events that precipitate clients' decisions to seek service, you can often discern both the direction and strength of their initial motivation. When clients voluntarily decide to seek service shortly after critical events and request assistance in modifying behavior or circumstances associated with these events, their motivation is more likely to be adequate in both direction and strength than when their identified problems have existed for many years or when their decision to seek assistance resulted from an ultimatum from a family member or employer. For example, a couple requested marital therapy after an intense conflict that involved both of their parents. After simmering down, they discussed the matter and mutually agreed that the conflict had been extremely painful. They were unable to resolve the situation and decided together to seek professional services to assist them to reach a mutually acceptable solution. They appeared strongly motivated to work toward a realistic goal.

By contrast, another couple sought the services of a marital therapist upon the referral of a lawyer. Before a divorce could be granted they were required by law to see a marital therapist. Their marriage had been stormy for many years, and both partners expressed a desire to extricate themselves from the relationship. Their motivation to utilize marital therapy was deficient both in strength and direction. Further exploration, however, revealed a willingness to explore ways in which they could effect a divorce with minimal psychological damage to themselves and to their children. The practitioner thus succeeded in creating an incentive to work toward this more realistic goal and successfully involved them in the helping process.

Involuntary Clients   As we noted in the last chapter, not all clients acknowledge problems; indeed, in some settings (e.g., child protective services and correctional institutions), the large majority of clients have not acknowledged problems and often are unwilling recipients of services, at least initially. But even in these settings, acknowledgment of a problem is indispensable to successful problem solving. This does not mean that you should write off as lost causes these and other inadequately motivated clients. Social work has

been mandated by society to assist these persons to alter their behavior so that they can function as constructive and contributing members of society. Further, although these clients may lack adequate motivation for change in initial contacts, subsequently they can often be assisted to acknowledge problems and to develop incentives to work toward relevant goals. Skills involved in enhancing motivation are the focal point of Chapter 12.

Cultural Factors

In this and previous chapters, we have discussed many cultural factors in relationship to various aspects of the helping process. In this section, we focus on general cultural factors that are relevant to the process of assessment. Many other cultural factors are discussed in subsequent portions of the book.

Cultural Norms   Knowledge of the norms related to a client's culture of origin is indispensable when the client's cultural background is markedly different from your own. Without such knowledge, you may make serious errors in assessing both individual and interpersonal systems, for cognitive, emotional, behavioral, and interpersonal patterns that are deemed functional in one cultural context may be deemed dysfunctional in another and vice versa. Further, such errors in assessment may lead to selecting interventions that aggravate rather than diminish clients' problems. For example, based on therapeutic work with depressed, lower-class Italian-American women, Weissman, Geanakopolos, and Prusoff (1973) concluded that with this group of women, practitioners should weigh the consequences of encouraging increased assertiveness in marriage, independence from extended family, or more community participation. According to these authors, "Participation in such middle-class modes of social behavior would have been at variance with the norms of their reference group; treatment could be experienced by individuals and family as disruptive rather than helpful" (p. 179). These observations are also germane to work with Mexican-American, Puerto Rican, and Cuban women.

Cultures vary widely in their prescribed patterns of child care, child rearing, adolescent roles, mate selection, marital roles, and care of the aged—to name just a few. In Anglo-American culture, for example, there has been a major trend toward equality of the sexes, resulting in the prevailing view that domineering behavior by husbands is dysfunctional. In fact, such behavior would be regarded as mental cruelty and sufficient grounds for divorce in many states. However, in marriages involving spouses of Hispanic extraction or partners from many Mideastern countries, autocratic behavior by husbands and dependent behavior by wives is the norm.

Patterns of communication between marital partners also vary widely from culture to culture. Among certain American Indian tribes, husbands and wives tend to communicate more with members of their same sex than with each other. Similarly, the extent of communication between parents and children varies substantially from culture to culture.

Differentiating Individual and Culturally Determined Patterns Although knowledge about the client's culture is vital in transcultural work, practitioners must guard against stereotyping clients on the basis of that knowledge. Considerable variation exists among subgroups of identified ethnic groups, and overgeneralizations about members of these groups may obscure rather than clarify the meanings of individual behavior. For example, there are over 400 different tribal groups of Native Americans in the United States, and these groups speak over 250 distinct languages (Edwards, 1983). Comparisons of Plains tribes with Native Americans of the Southwest have revealed sharply contrasting cultural patterns and patterns of individual behavior as well as marked differences in the incidence of certain social problems (May, Hymbaugh, Aase & Samet, 1983). Cubans, Puerto Ricans, and Mexican-American groups also differ widely from one another although they are much more alike than different because of their common Hispanic heritage (Queralt, 1984). Filipinos also embody diverse cultural groups who speak eight major different languages and 75 or more different dialects (Ponce, 1980). Obviously, Asian-Americans also represent many different cultures that share certain characteristics but also differ significantly from one another. In this regard, Gould (1988) negates the myth that Asians and Pacific Islanders are model minorities that take care of their own and should not qualify for the title of disadvantaged. Data reveal that after four years of living in the U.S., almost one-third of Indochinese refugees live below the poverty line and 55 percent of the households still need public assistance. Moreover, these groups manifest problems of wife abuse, physical and mental health problems, and victimization in the forms of violence, vandalism, harassment, and intimidation. Moreover, Chinese and Asian Indians have restricted promotional opportunities as managers despite excellent representation in professional categories.

Within homogeneous cultural groups, wide variations also exist among individuals. Being knowledgeable about the cultural characteristics of a given group is necessary but insufficient for understanding the behavior of individual members of the groups. As with members of the cultural majority, each member of an ethnic minority group is unique. Practitioners, therefore, must consider each ethnic minority client as an individual, for dysfunctional or deviant behavior as viewed from the perspective of the cultural majority may be similarly viewed by members of ethnic minority groups. The task confronting practitioners, therefore, is to differentiate between behavior that is culturally mediated and that which is a product of individual personality. Possession of in-depth knowledge about a given cultural group facilitates making such differentiations, but when in doubt, practitioners are advised to consult with well-informed and cooperative members of the ethnic group in question. Kumabe et al. (1985), for example, have reported an instance involving a neglectful Southeast-Asian refugee mother who appeared to be depressed. After making extended and futile efforts to assist this mother, the practitioner consulted with a fellow refugee of hers and learned that the mother (who spoke little English) was mentally retarded rather than depressed. Further, she had manifested child neglect in her native community before coming to the United States.

Degree of Acculturation In assessing the functioning of ethnic minority clients, it is important to consider the degree to which they have been socialized into the mainstream culture. Ethnic minority clients are actually members of two cultures, and their functioning must be considered in relationship to both their culture of origin and the majority culture. Clients from the same ethnic group may vary widely in the degree of their acculturation, which depends upon a number of factors. Foremost is the number of generations that have passed since the original emigration from the native land. Ordinarily, first-generation minority clients adhere closely to their traditional beliefs, values, and patterns of behavior. By the third generation, however, clients have usually internalized many of the patterns of the dominant culture although they typically maintain many traditional patterns of family relationships.

Even when considering the degree of acculturation of an ethnic minority client, errors can be made if practitioners fail to attend to a client's uniqueness. For example, although *unacculturated* Asian-Americans are generally regarded as emotionally unexpressive and preferring structure and direction by practitioners, Sue and Zane (1987) report that ". . . many . . . seemed quite willing to talk about their emotions and to work well with little structure" (p. 39).

Still, the significance of the different generations to Japanese-Americans is reflected in the fact that this ethnic group specifies by linguistic terms each generation of descendants from the original immigrant group. The terms *Issei, Nisei,* and *Sansei* thus refer to first, second, and third generations respectively. Mass (1976) has discussed characteristics, patterns, and problems of each of these groups. Lott (1976) has presented a similar discussion of different generations of Filipino immigrants.

Other factors also affect the degree of "bicultural" socialization and interactions of ethnic minority clients with mainstream society. One writer (deAnda, 1984, p. 102) identified and discussed six such factors:

1. The degree of commonality between the two cultures with regard to norms, values, beliefs, perceptions, and the like.

2. The availability of cultural translators, mediators, and models.

3. The amount and type (positive or negative) of corrective feedback provided by each culture regarding attempts to produce normative behaviors.

4. The conceptual style and problem-solving approach of the minority individual and their mesh with the prevalent or valued styles of the majority culture.

5. The individual's degree of bilingualism.

6. The degree of dissimilarity in physical appearance from the majority culture, such as skin color, facial features, and so forth.

Culturally sensitive assessment thus carefully considers the degree of biculturalism manifested by a client. Rogler, Malgady, Costantino, and Blumenthal (1987) dramatize this point by reporting how treatment plans with an individual Hispanic client may span the continuum from "most Hispanic" to "most Anglo." Other authors (Kumabe et al., 1985) have reported that varying degrees of acculturation occur among members of the same family and same generation. These authors also discuss and illustrate the complexities involved in acculturation when parents are from different ethnic minority backgrounds, as for example, a Japanese-American married to a Filipino-American. The socialization of children to such parents is tricultural. Such permutations are not uncommon in truly pluralistic societies such as Hawaii, where people often refer to their ethnic heritage as *smorgasbord.* Transcultural work is the rule rather than the exception in such communities, and effective practice requires extensive knowledge of the cultures represented.

Fluency with the English Language Degree of bilingualism is also a major factor that practitioners should consider in as-

sessments involving ethnic minority clients. Clients whose command of English is very limited often have great difficulty in formulating and explaining their problems in a different language. Often an interpreter is needed to bridge the language gap. If an interpreter is not available, it is important to speak in simple terms and to proceed at a slower pace. Clients need ample time to process messages, and practitioners must exercise care in checking out whether clients have grasped the intended meaning of their messages. The converse is also true.

Limited fluency in language can also block ethnic minority clients from access to essential community resources (especially clients isolated from their cultural reference groups). Inability to converse with others and to take advantage of the vast information provided through newspapers, radio, and television not only produces social isolation but also deprives people of information essential to locating and utilizing essential resources. For example, in a research study aimed at identifying factors associated with neglect of children by impoverished mothers, Giovannoni and Billingsley (1970) found that Spanish-speaking mothers were so severely lacking in information that no more than 30 percent of them possessed any knowledge whatsoever about any given community system (p. 201).

Problem-Solving Methods In assessing the functioning of ethnic minority clients and planning interventions, it is important to be aware that members of different cultures define problems in different ways (Green, 1982, pp. 44–47). Behavior that is regarded as normal in one culture may be viewed as deviant in another. For example, as seen from an Asian-American perspective, individualism and aggressive competition (which characterize mainstream society) conflict with traditional Asian respect for authority and filial piety toward parents and ancestors (Ho, 1976, p. 196). Similarly, among Hispanic families the commonly close degree of involvement among family members shows a tendency toward what would be regarded as dysfunctional "enmeshment" (see Chapter 10) among Anglo-American families (Queralt, 1984, p. 117).

Approaches to problem solving also vary among different cultures. Within the mainstream culture, an analytical cognitive style appears to be the most highly valued approach to defining most problems and searching for solutions to them (deAnda, 1984). Certain ethnic minority groups, however, rely on value-laden approaches to coping with problems, thereby exerting pressures on individuals to follow prescriptive courses of action in given problematic situations. Novel and creative solutions are discouraged in such circumstances, for to deviate from culturally prescribed rules may generate overwhelming anxiety and/or guilt for tradition-bound clients.

Variations among cultures are also common with respect to key persons who normally become involved in efforts to solve problems. In most Native American tribal groups, for example, family members actively seek counsel from elderly members of the extended family unit in coping with family problems. The wisdom of the elderly is highly valued, and elderly members of the tribe are accorded much respect (Hull, 1982). When sought for counsel, elderly Native Americans often pass along their wisdom in the form of storytelling, "which does not insult the intelligence or integrity of the listener because one is always free to ignore unacceptable suggestions" (Hull, 1982, p. 343). Asian-Americans similarly look to the extended family for direction in problem-solving situations and value the wisdom of the elderly.

Achieving Credibility   As with all clients, practitioners must achieve credibility with ethnic minority persons to engage them in the helping process. Credibility refers to being perceived as competent, effective, and trustworthy. In part credibility derives from the status a client *ascribes* to a practitioner by reason of education, position, role, age, gender, and other factors emphasized in the client's culture—factors over which a practitioner has little control. Credibility can also be *achieved,* however, through favorable experiences by clients with practitioners who foster respect, confidence, trust, and hope. Sue and Zane (1987) hypothesize that practitioners foster credibility by following three major guidelines:

1. The practitioner must conceptualize the problem in a manner that is consistent with the client's belief systems. Imposing upon clients problem formulations that are antagonistic to clients' belief systems may block achievement of credibility.

2. Expectations of change efforts to be made by clients must be compatible with their cultural values. For example, encouraging an Asian client to express anger directly to a father would require the client to violate a deeply embedded value and would be perceived by the client as destructive and inappropriate.

3. Treatment goals must be consonant with clients' perceptions of desired objectives. When goals reflect the practitioner's agenda rather than the client's, credibility may not be achieved and clients may disengage from the helping process.

Although the above guidelines are applicable to *all* client groups, they are particularly relevant to ethnic minorities.

Prerequisite to adhering to these guidelines, of course, is possessing knowledge about the belief systems and values of a given ethnocultural group.

Cultural Factors in Illness Determining clients' views of causes of illness, physical aberrations, disabling conditions, and mental symptoms is an important task in assessment, for the degree of clients' receptiveness to medical diagnoses and treatment will depend upon the credibility of the same from the client's perspective. In modern Western society, despite the increasing acceptance by professionals of the systems perspective, most people continue to attribute illness to physical causes (i.e., infections, toxins, degenerative processes, heredity, improper nutrition, chemical imbalance, lack of exercise, or other unknown physical factors). People thus tend to be receptive to diagnoses and treatments that match their expectations. Mainstream Americans, for example, are familiar with and accept antibiotics, vitamins, hormones, diverse medications, surgical procedures, radiation therapy, chemotherapy, exercise, and proper rest. By contrast, the majority of mainstream Americans reject acupuncture, herbal therapy, and spiritualistic rituals as legitimate treatments.

Differing from members of the mainstream culture, many ethnic minority clients espouse markedly different beliefs about the causes of ill health or other physical afflictions. Consequently, their expectations regarding diagnoses and treatment may differ sharply from those presented by Western health care professionals. In this regard, Low (1984) has noted: "Numerous cases of ethnic differences in expectations of treatment, behavior and compliance can be traced to cultural distinctions embedded in belief systems and norms of culturally appropriate behavior" (p. 13).

When major discrepancies exist between clients' expectations and physicians' diagnoses and recommendations for treatment, clients tend to covertly reject diagnoses and fail to comply with treatment regimens, often producing confusion and consternation for health care professionals who lack sophistication in understanding the powerful influence of deeply embedded cultural beliefs. Experienced practitioners in health care settings can attest to many instances of clients' noncompliance with medical recommendations based on clashes between Old World and Western medical beliefs concerning causes of illness and physical afflictions. One of many case examples reported by Kumabe et al. (1985) highlights the significance of cultural factors:

Living in Hawaii after migrating from the Philippine Islands five years earlier, the parents of a small child had resisted having surgical repair of their child's cleft lip and palate even though the costs would be paid by insurance. After carefully exploring both the circumstances that preceded the birth of the child and the parents' beliefs regarding the cause of the condition, the social worker learned that the parents attributed the child's condition to punishment from God for their use of withdrawal as a contraceptive measure during sexual intercourse. The father's uncle, who lived with the family, asserted they had interfered with God's will by practicing contraception. The withdrawal method, he claimed, caused deformed babies; because sexual intercourse was never completed, a baby could never be completed either. Fortunately, the practitioner recognized the futility of attempting to dissuade them from their belief and instead referred them for a consultation with a physician of their ethnicity. The Filipino physician readily gained their trust and assisted them to accept that their child's condition was congenital and unrelated to their sexual practices. This consultation paved the way to having the corrective surgery performed and liberated the parents from oppressive guilt.

Cultures that differ sharply from mainstream American culture may attribute illness and other physical afflictions to factors and forces that are discounted or lightly regarded by scientifically oriented Western medical authorities. Hispanic concepts of disease (discussed by Green, 1982), for example, derive from several sources including medieval Spanish traditions brought to the New World by colonizers, the influence of indigenous Indian groups, elements of Anglo traditions made popular through advertising and the mass media, and scientific medical knowledge.

Beliefs of American Indians concerning illness and health parallel Hispanic beliefs in certain respects. Good health requires living in balance with nature, which in turn depends on adhering to a strict set of cosmic laws. The world as viewed by an Indian shaman[1] is made up of both physical and spiritual elements, and every sickness has both a physical and spiritual cause. The philosophy of an Indian shaman, concerning health and sickness, as quoted by Lake (1983), is that:

A healthy person lives by the laws of Nature. An unhealthy person has violated the laws, or he/she can be the recipient of misapplied laws by another's violation through inheritance or witchcraft. Ignorance is no excuse to the Creator's cosmic laws irregardless [sic] of age, sex,

race, nationality, creed, or religion. Healing therefore means the individual must be recreated, reconnected, and/or balanced with Nature; or put back into harmony with the Universal laws and function.

(p. 33)

Lake (1983) lists the cosmic laws as identified by a Yurok Indian shaman, and we recommend this article to those interested in learning more about Indian medical beliefs and practices. It is important for all practitioners, however, to be knowledgeable about the significance of folk healers and shamans in diverse cultures throughout the world. As Canda (1983) points out, shamanism exists on every continent and on the islands in the oceans. Beliefs in supernatural forces, such as witchcraft, evil spirits, curses, and hexes, are widespread among ethnic minority persons, especially those who are poorly educated, from low socioeconomic levels, and closely tied to cultures whose belief systems are rooted in traditional folkways.

Folk healers and shamans are especially important to ethnic minority persons who have recently experienced cultural dislocation. As Delgado (1977) has pointed out, "Supernatural beliefs tend to persist when they offer solutions to significant human problems" (p. 425). Because people who are uprooted are beset with intense stresses as they attempt to adapt to a strange land, they increase their reliance on spiritualism as a means of coping with these stresses. With respect to Puerto Ricans, Delgado reports:

If a Puerto Rican in need of assistance is offered a choice between a medium and a social worker he will probably choose the medium. Social workers lack the prestige given to spiritualists whose roles are sanctioned by the entire society to which they and their clients belong.

(p. 453)

---

[1]A shaman is a sacred specialist who utilizes a technique of ecstatic trance to communicate with spirits and other powerful forces, natural and supernatural. The shaman acquires sacred power from the spiritual realm to heal and to enhance the harmony between the human community and the nonhuman environment (Canda, 1983).

Because of the significance of folk healers and shamans in the lives of many minority persons, practitioners should view these indigenous practitioners as resources. Canda (1983), for example, cites references that report successful informal arrangements between medical professionals and nature healers in the Cook Islands, Nigeria, and Puerto Rico. Kumabe et al. (1985) have also described cases in which social workers have orchestrated the efforts of medical professionals and folk healers in successfully treating ethnic minority clients in Hawaii. Delgado (1977) has presented eight recommendations that can be extremely useful to practitioners in working with clients who believe in the efficacy of spiritualist folk healers.

Cultural Resources   By attending to cultural factors, you may be able to locate or develop indigenous cultural resources that can be tapped to assist clients who are strangers in another culture and who, because of poverty, language barriers, limited experience, and ignorance, do not know what to do or whom to see when confronted with major stress. Other more experienced and sophisticated members of a given cultural group often are willing to assist such clients to find their way through the maze of bureaucratic structures typically involved in communities. Indigenous nonprofessionals have also been employed as staff members to serve as client advocates and to provide direct outreach services to impoverished minority clients (Budner, Chazin, & Young, 1973). Valuable services performed by indigenous nonprofessionals include assuming the role of advocate and interpreter (in both language and policy), assisting people to utilize resources within a given agency, intervening with other social systems to obtain timely responses to needs of clients, providing direct services

(e.g., homemaking, baby-sitting, shopping, and escorting clients to various agencies), discussing problems in times of crisis, and rendering technical assistance (e.g., completing forms, writing letters, and establishing eligibility for services).

Indigenous nonprofessionals have also organized tenant groups among impoverished minority members to obtain essential repairs of facilities and to use legal means of assuring that landlords comply with housing laws. Participating in such groups not only results in improved living conditions but also counters the sense of helplessness and creates cultural reference groups that combat the social isolation commonly experienced by poverty-stricken minority persons. Although in the past few decades problems have been largely associated with Mexican and Puerto Rican immigrants and with Native Americans who have migrated from reservations to urban areas, an influx of Asian and Cuban refugees in the late 1970s and early 1980s has resulted in new populations that are vulnerable to difficulties associated with cultural dislocation.

Knowledge of cultural factors may also assist you in connecting clients with still other valuable resources indigenous to their cultures. Jung (1976) and Homma-True (1976), for example, have described indigenous resources that exist in Chinatowns in two large American cities. Similar resources exist in pockets of ethnic groups located in many other large urban cities.

Extended family members are also an important resource to be considered in work with ethnic minority clients. Filipinos, for example, have a strong sense of loyalty that extends far beyond the nuclear family. Filipinos, therefore, have many people to whom they can look for support and assistance in crisis situations (Ponce, 1980). The same is true of Native

Americans (Lewis and Ho, 1975), Asian-Americans (Homma-True, 1976), blacks (Jones, 1983), Hawaiians (Kumabe et al., 1985), Samoans (Wong, 1983), and Hispanics, although Queralt (1984) indicates, "The value of the extended family for Hispanics has probably been overrated" (p. 117). The extent of availability of extended family support for ethnic minority families, of course, varies according to the number of generations a given family is removed from the original family of immigration.

Attitudes Toward External Help   Behavior of members of certain ethnic minority groups is strongly influenced by their attitudes toward asking for help and by the type of help needed. To Japanese, for example, "The need for mental health services has always been seen as shameful" (Mass, 1976), and people with psychological problems are viewed with disdain as weaklings. Koreans take a similar stance toward mental problems. According to Harvey and Chung (1980), "Koreans find mental illness in a family a source of shame and regard mental illness as a form of deviant and harmful behavior, the causes of which are variously attributable to supernatural forces, such as the displeasure of ancestral spirits, spirit intrusion, somatic-natural conditions, and psychological distresses originating in interpersonal disharmony" (p. 147). Such beliefs share much in common with those of Native Americans, but the approach to treatment differs markedly. Whereas Native Americans turn to indigenous folk healers (e.g., a medicine man), Koreans consider family care as the most logical and effective treatment inasmuch as the cause is believed to be interpersonal disharmony in the family.

In light of attitudes such as those just reported, clients from the ethnic groups cited can be expected to manifest shame and apprehension during an initial interview. Practitioners must be sensitive to the causes of such reactions for two important reasons. First, the client's manifest behavior is likely to be atypical, and assessment of the client's functioning without this knowledge could lead the practitioner to draw erroneous conclusions. Second, such untoward emotional reactions about seeking help can be formidable barriers to establishing trust and rapport. Awareness of clients' feelings, however, enables the practitioner to respond to them with empathy and understanding, which enhances the possibility of working through the feelings.

Negative experiences of certain ethnic minority groups with the dominant culture and particularly with the government also dispose members of these groups to approach helping agencies with skepticism and even hostility. In light of efforts of the federal government first to annihilate Native Americans and then to assimilate them, their distrust of the government is understandable (Hull, 1982). Similarly, skepticism toward Anglo-Americans by blacks, Hispanics, and Asian-Americans is a natural consequence of their histories of being exploited and victimized by overt racism and/or institutionalized racist practices. Behavior of these individuals in transcultural relationships must be assessed accordingly. Moreover, practitioners must be prepared to deal with distrust, fear, and even hostility in transcultural relationships.

Providing Immediate Benefits   In their "critique and reformulation" of ingredients essential to effective cross-cultural work, Sue and Zane (1987) advocate that establishing credibility (which we discussed earlier) and gift giving are indispensable. The term "gift giving" is used symbolically rather than literally and refers to enabling clients to experience a direct benefit from treatment, as soon as possible, preferably in the first session.

These authors use the term "gift" because ". . . gift giving is a ritual that is frequently a part of interpersonal relationships among Asians" (p. 42). Explanations to clients that benefits of the helping process will be forthcoming in the future are insufficient, according to Sue and Zane. Rather, ethnic minority clients, especially Asians, who tend to be skeptical of Western forms of treatment, need demonstration of the direct relationship between activities in the helping process and the alleviation of problems.

What kind of gifts (immediate benefits) can the practitioner provide? One important gift cited is normalization (also denoted as universalization), which refers to "a process by which clients come to realize that their thoughts, feelings, or experiences are common and that many individuals encounter similar difficulties" (p. 42). Use of this supportive technique tends to reduce anxiety associated with the mistaken belief that one's difficulties are strange and different and reflect one's being different and less adequate than others. Other gifts that the practitioner can offer include stress relief procedures, depression relief, clarification of factors producing difficulties, reassurance (when it is reality based), hope, plans for skill training, discussion of promising coping measures, and setting of relevant goals. As with credibility, we believe that "gift giving" is also applicable to nonminority clients, but even more so with minority clients.

In the preceding, we have highlighted major ethnic and cultural factors that are salient to the process of assessment. Space limitations, however, preclude dealing comprehensively with this important topic. Other authors (Devore & Schlesinger, 1981; Green, 1982; Jenkins, 1981; Sue & Moore, 1984; Wright, Saleebey, Watts, & Lecca, 1983) have denoted entire books to ethnocultural factors.

Environmental Systems

The environment was a central concern of pioneers in social work in the late 1800s and early 1900s, but had receded into the background of social work theory by the 1920s, being overshadowed by the impact of evolving theories related to individual functioning, most notable of which was Freudian psychoanalysis. Emphasis on the individual continued to the 1960s and '70s, when it was supplemented by interactional and systems theory (including theories of family therapy). Although theoreticians did not exclude the environment from their formulations, they accorded it minor significance. The emphasis on the person, and to a lesser extent on interpersonal transactions, undoubtedly was a consequence of the fact that theories pertaining to individual and interpersonal functioning were far more developed than theories pertaining to the environment.

A strong resurgence of interest in the environment commenced in the early 1970s. Strongly influenced by ecological theory, systems theory, and by the increased emphasis placed on the environment by prominent ego psychologists, Germain (1973), Meyer (1970), and Siporin (1975) advocated a perspective of social work practice that revolved around systems theory and ecological theory. These theorists incorporated this perspective in their practice textbooks and acceptance of the ecological perspective has steadily expanded.

The ecological perspective does not represent a swing of the pendulum from primary focus on the person to the other extreme of primary focus on the environment. Rather, assessment focuses on the transactions between the two, and problem-solving efforts may be directed to assisting people to adapt to their environments (e.g., training them in interpersonal skills), altering environments to meet the needs of clients more adequately (e.g., enhancing both the attractiveness of a nursing home and the quality of its activities), or a combination of the two (e.g., enhancing the interpersonal skills of a withdrawn, chronically ill person and moving the person to a more stimulating environment).

In assessing clients' environments, attention should be limited to those aspects of the environment that are salient to the problem situation. In some situations, these aspects will be obvious (e.g., crowded housing with unsanitary living conditions or harsh and rejecting parents), but in others they will be more subtle (e.g., lack of encouragement and emotional support from parents). Relevant factors also vary according to the needs of specific clients, which in turn are determined by clients' personalities, states of health, stages of development, interests, aspirations, and other related factors. You should thus tailor your assessments of clients' environments to their varied life situations, weighing clients' unique needs against the availability of essential resources and opportunities within their environments.

Clients' needs, of course, vary widely, but certain environmental resources are universally needed. We have therefore compiled the following list of basic environmental needs, which you can employ in evaluating the adequacy of clients' environments. The list, of course, must be individualized to each client, for needs that are pertinent to one client may not be to another.

1. Adequate social support systems (e.g., family, relatives, friends, neighbors, organized groups).

2. Access to specialized health care services (e.g., physicians, dentists, physical therapists, hospitals, nursing homes).

3. Access to day care services (for working mothers and single-parent families).

4. Access to recreational facilities.

5. Mobility to socialize, utilize resources, and exercise rights as a citizen.

6. Adequate housing that provides ample space, sanitation, privacy, and safety from hazards and pollution (both air and noise).

7. Adequate police and fire protection and a reasonable degree of security.

8. Safe and healthful work conditions.

9. Adequate financial resources to purchase essential resources.

10. Adequate nutritional intake.

11. Predictable living arrangements with caring others (especially for children).

12. Opportunities for education and self-fulfillment.

13. Access to legal resources.

14. Access to religious organizations.

15. Employment opportunities.

Social Support Systems (SSSs)

The first item on the preceding list—adequate social support systems (SSSs)—is increasingly recognized as playing a crucial role in determining the level of social functioning of human beings. Theorists, of course, have long recognized the critical importance of a nurturing environment to healthy development of infants and children. In recent years, however, it has become clear that adults, too, have vital needs that can be met only through a nurturant environment. The literature is replete with articles that accord paramount importance to major deficiencies in SSSs available to people who manifest diverse problems of living. Moreover, articles concerned with strategies for remedying varied problems of clients likewise place heavy emphasis on mobilizing SSSs.

Before considering client groups that are particularly vulnerable to breakdown in social functioning in the absence of adequate SSSs, it is important to clarify the vital needs of people that are met through SSSs. Weiss (1974) has proposed that people in individuals' personal networks (i.e., spouse, family, close kin, friends, and work associates) provide the following:

1. Attachment, provided by close affectional relationships that give a sense of security and sense of belonging.

2. Social integration, provided by memberships in a network of persons that share interests and values.

3. The opportunity to nurture others (usually children), which provides incentive to endure in the face of adversity.

4. Validation of personal worth (which promotes self-esteem), provided by family and colleagues.

5. A sense of reliable alliance, provided primarily by kin.

6. Help and guidance (provided by informal advisors) in resolving difficulties that arise.

The last item may include assistance with child care, financial aid, and other services and resources that close kin typically provide.

Stresses associated with certain problem situations can be so severe that, without consistent and reliable responsiveness from SSSs to the needs specified in the preceding paragraph, afflicted persons may experience serious breakdowns in functioning. Moreover, the severity of stress in certain situations may result precisely from temporary or permanent disruption of major sources of social support. Such stressful situations commonly involve losses through death of loved ones, divorces, children leaving home, job termination, retirement, severance of valued relationships, and so on. In a study comparing depressed people (depression is a common reaction to major losses) who did and did not attempt suicide, for example, Slater and Depue (1981) found that loss of important social support through "exit" events (losses such as those just enumerated) played an important role in initiating suicide attempts. These researchers also concluded that the presence of SSSs tends to buffer the impact of exit events and thereby reduces suicidal risk.

It is thus apparent that, at best, absence of adequate SSSs renders people vulnerable to serious maladaption to external stress and, at worst, is itself a primary source of stress, as with people who are socially isolated or feel alienated from society. By contrast, the presence of adequate SSSs tends to reduce the impact of stressful situations and facilitates successful adaptation. SSSs thus represent a vital resource that practitioners should consider as they assess problems of living. Moreover, social workers increasingly employ interventions that tap the potential of dormant SSSs and mobilize new SSSs in assisting clients to cope with life's stresses.

SSSs are of particular significance with certain client groups who are vulnerable to serious maladaptation because of deficiencies in their social environments. Previously, we cited clients who have sustained losses of important relationships. Another group consists of single parents or parents who receive little companionship and emotional support from their spouses and kin. Because of the heavy demands of child care and limited time and opportunity to participate socially, these parents often are unable to meet their own needs for nurturance. Consequently, such parents feel empty, frustrated, and resentful about ongoing demands for child care, and receive little personal need gratification. Children can thus become objects of their frustrations and resentments, which can lead to child abuse (Salzinger, Kaplan, & Artemyeff, 1983). Parents who received little nurturance as children (particularly if they were abused themselves) are especially predisposed to engage in child abuse (Dougherty, 1983).

Single, elderly people, especially those who have no children or whose children are unresponsive to their needs, are another group for whom SSSs are highly relevant (Sauer & Coward, 1985). Often having restricted financial resources and limited mobility, elderly persons can become socially isolated to the extent that life becomes barren and empty. Depression is common among such persons. Such elderly persons often improve physically and mentally when they move from an austere, isolated environment to one that provides increased activity, improved nutrition, and more frequent social contact (Gallo, 1982). Other elderly persons may have multiple afflictions including chronic illness, infirmity, and impaired vision and hearing. Needs of these persons can be so pervasive that social workers or others can best serve as case managers in coordinating the utilization of essential resources, which may include financial, medical, recreational, transportation, nutritional, nursing, and other services (Steinberg & Carter, 1983).

Chronic psychiatric patients also typically suffer from deficient SSSs. These people lack interpersonal and coping skills essential to maintaining themselves independently in the community, thus requiring practitioners to take an active role in mobilizing multiple resources including SSSs. Practitioners or others can also best serve these clients as case managers (Harris & Bergman, 1987; Rapp & Chamberlain, 1985).

Another group extremely vulnerable to problems associated with deficient SSSs consists of people who experience geographical and/or cultural dislocation. Refugees and immigrants often have acute needs that extend even beyond the need for SSSs, including housing, health care, work training, and language training needs (Mayadas, 1983; Montero & Dieppa, 1982; Timberlake & Cook, 1984). Among refugees are groups with unique needs that must also be considered, including unaccompanied women and children, elderly and disabled persons, and persons who are disabled by acute illnesses.

Other vulnerable client groups who have special needs dependent upon adequate SSSs include pregnant adolescents (O'Leary et al., 1984), teenaged mothers (Barth & Schinke, 1984; deAnda & Becerra, 1984), teen-age parents (Brindis, Barth, & Loomis, 1987), victims of child abuse (Gagliano, 1987), widows and widowers (Lieberman & Videka-Sherman, 1986), families of the mentally ill (Zipple & Spaniol, 1987), terminally ill patients (Arnowitz, Brunswick, & Kaplan, 1983), children of divorced parents (Bonkowski, Bequette, & Boomhower, 1984), developmentally disabled persons (Hill, Rotegard, & Bruininks, 1984), disabled (Kennard & Shilman, 1979; Mackelprang & Hepworth, 1987), transients (Breton, 1984), and persons who have newly moved into communities, particularly rapidly expanding communities (boomtowns). Boomtowns typically have loosely knit social networks, and human service programs tend to lag well behind the needs of citizens. These communities present challenging opportunities to social workers in collaborating to develop natural support networks (Collins & Pancoast, 1976), and to plan service delivery systems that are responsive to the unique needs of each community.

Negative Social Support Systems   To this point we have highlighted the positive aspects of SSSs. The presence of certain types of SSSs, however, may foster and sustain dysfunctional behavior, and practitioners must be alert to this possibility as they assess problem systems. For example, families with overprotective parents thwart the development of autonomy and personal responsibility in their children. Children from such families often fail to develop social skills, problem-solving skills, and the ability to relate in a mature give-and-take manner. Unrealistic expectations of others and excessive dependency are typical manifestations of people reared in such cloistered environments.

Negative social support systems also play a vital role in fostering and maintaining substance abuse. Through an analysis of the social networks of street drug addicts, Fraser and Hawkins (1984) found that these persons are not isolated or lonely but rather report close, sharing, intimate relationships with people whom they like to see. The relationships, however, largely include other drug abusers. Based on their findings, these authors concluded (with respect to *street* drug abuse) that "most drug users are enmeshed in a subculture that rewards hard drug abuse and that endures through residential treatment" (p. 94). Bates (1983) similarly characterizes the social milieu of the Skid Row alcoholic as fostering continued drinking and lacking ingredients essential to competent adult functioning. Fine, Akabas, and Bellinger (1982) believe that problem drinking is also fostered in workplaces that "embody the norms and values of a culture of drinking" (p. 437). Clearly, then, assessment of problems of substance abusers must address the social networks of these clients, and interventions must be directed to replace these networks with cultures of sobriety.

Assessing Reciprocal Interactions Between Individuals and SSSs   In formulating assessments, practitioners must consider the reciprocal interaction between individuals and their SSSs. The responsiveness of SSS members to individuals and families under stress depends in great measure on the nature of previous interactions between these systems. For example, people who have been warm, pleasant, sensitive, and generous in responding to the needs of others are far more likely to receive nurturant social support in times of distress than are people who typically relate to others in an aloof, complaining, aggressive, or withholding manner. Further, people vary widely in their perceptions of the adequacy of social support in times of adversity. Certain people believe they receive inadequate succor from others irrespective of its quality and quantity. A study of neurotics' perceptions of social support received in times of adversity, for example, led Henderson (1982) to conclude that "The crucial property of social relationships, insofar as neurosis is concerned, is not their availability . . . *but how adequate they are perceived to be* when individuals are under adversity" (p. 227). With such individuals, therefore, intrapsychic and personality factors are likely to be strong determinants of how they perceive the adequacy of SSSs. SSSs of clients thus cannot be adequately assessed apart from the clients themselves.

Chronically Ill and Disabled Clients

Some writers and researchers have focused their attention on environmental resources needed by clients who present similar problem situations. Building on Germain's (1977) earlier work, Coulton (1979, 1981), for example, studied the person-environment fit of chronically ill patients suffering from such serious ailments as kidney failure, spinal cord injuries, cancer, diabetes, and arthritis. Based on interviews with these patients, Coulton identified a number of environmental needs (1979, pp. 8–9). Although several of these needs are specific to the population Coulton studied, virtually all of them also appear to be highly relevant to elderly and physically handicapped persons. As you review the list, notice the balanced focus on the person and the environment.

1. Having sufficient opportunities for social relationships.

2. Having sufficient opportunities to express feelings.

3. Having sufficient sources of emotional support.

4. Meeting expectations of self and others.

5. Being able to fulfill responsibilities.

6. Having opportunities to engage in interesting productive activities and achieve goals.

7. Fulfilling the demands of certain situations (e.g., job, social events).

8. Getting information to allow some certainty about the future.

9. Having knowledge about their physical condition, community resources, etc.

10. Knowing where things are, what to expect, how to behave in new settings.

11. Having sufficient financial resources to meet demands and obligations.

12. Having help with physical and self-care needs.

13. Having the means to maintain physical mobility.

In her article, Coulton illustrates each type of need as reflected by actual statements of patients. From these statements,

it was apparent that although the needs cut across all of the patients' environments and were more adequately met in some environments than others, patients varied widely in their degrees of perceived need. Individual patients emphasized certain needs more than others, and their expectations in regard to specific needs also varied considerably. With respect to social relationships, for example, Coulton observed, "it was not the absolute amount of contact . . . but whether the contact seemed to be what they needed" (1979, p. 10). This finding, of course, is consistent with Henderson's (1982) view that *perceived adequacy* of social support is more important than the availability of support. Again, the point is that accurate assessment requires careful individualizing of each client's needs.

Based on her study, Coulton developed a scale that can be employed in assessing the fit between the needs of chronically ill persons and their environments. Studies of such specific client groups make valuable contributions to understanding how environmental planning and modification can enhance the social functioning of these vulnerable client groups.

The importance of environmental factors listed earlier in this section to the social functioning of disabled persons is vividly illustrated by the needs of paraplegics and quadraplegics, whose needs encompass virtually all of those listed. A research study of Mackelprang and Hepworth (1987) of the adjustment of these persons following spinal injury, hospitalization, and rehabilitation efforts indicated that those who attain maximal independence have higher levels of social functioning on several criteria than do those who are dependent upon others for various aspects of daily living. Because paraplegics are paralyzed in their lower limbs and quadraplegics in both upper and lower limbs, achieving maximal independence requires major environmental changes, including housing that provides special access through ramps or lifts, specially equipped kitchens and bathrooms, electric wheelchairs, and environmental control units and devices adapted for other activities of daily living such as eating and grooming. Moreover, opportunities for vocational training, employment, and socialization are essential to the well-being of these persons. Most of those who have the advantage of these special arrangements function amazingly well and report higher levels of satisfaction with their lives than do those who lack these advantages. Needs of these persons and implications for social workers are discussed at length by Mackelprang and Hepworth.

Assessing Homeless Persons

Homelessness is a social problem that has reached alarming proportions in recent years. Estimates of the number of homeless in the United States vary from 250,000 to 300,000 on the lower extreme to 3,000,000 (Connell, 1987). Although homelessness is not a new problem, its scope and the people who make up this population are new. Whereas until the 1970s homeless persons consisted largely of white male chronic alcoholics who lived in the Skid Rows of large cities, homeless people now also consist of unemployed individuals and families who have been evicted from housing, runaway/throwaway youth, women who have left home to avoid domestic violence, and those released from jails and hospitals without adequate financial means (Hagen, 1987a). Substantial proportions of homeless people are now minorities (First, Roth, & Arewa, 1988), women (Hagen, 1987b), and families (Phillips, DeChillo, Kronenfeld, & Middleton-Jeter, 1988). Reasons for homelessness include marked escalation in the cost of housing and a dearth of low-cost housing, the mental health deinstitutionalization movement that returned mental patients from centralized state hospitals to communities (funds intended to provide for these patients were subsequently drastically curtailed), substance abuse, economic recession (in 1982) resulting in a high rate of unemployment, and domestic conflicts.

Because of the heterogeneity of this population, accurate assessment of causes of homelessness and the needs of these people is of paramount importance. Although the need for emergency shelter is shared by all homeless people, other needs may vary widely. For example, the frequency of severe medical and psychiatric illnesses is far greater than for the general population. In addition to common illnesses that afflict the general population, homeless people manifest a much higher incidence of ". . . trauma, infestations such as scabies and lice, problems arising from exposure, nutritional and vitamin deficiencies, and peripheral vascular diseases such as cellulitis and leg ulcers" (Surber et al., 1988, p. 116). Careful assessment and individualization of clients may thus reveal any of the following needs, which were identified in a study by Hagen (1987a) of needs of the homeless in Albany, New York and its environs: food, financial assistance, alcohol treatment, mental health assessment, drug treatment, employment, educational/vocational training, legal assistance, transitional/supportive living, and long-term counseling. Further, because many homeless people (especially the chronically mentally ill, substance abusers, and runaway/throwaway youth) have very limited coping and interpersonal skills, case management services are often needed to ensure that services are actually provided.

Careful assessment of homeless families, which constitute approximately 20 percent of the nation's homeless

(Bassuk, Rubin, & Lauriat, 1986), must also consider the functioning of both parents and children. In a study of single-female-headed homeless families in New York City, Phillips et al. (1988) found that 96 percent of the families experienced failure in the mother's functioning and 51 percent experienced failure in a child's functioning. Further, in addition to having no access to housing other than emergency shelter, these families had experienced other life stresses within the previous year including ". . . serious illness of a close family member (30 percent), death of a close family member (25 percent), pregnancy (33 percent), and separation from a husband or boy friend (31 percent)" (p. 50). The support systems of these families were also woefully inadequate. Clearly these families manifest urgent and multiple needs that must be carefully assessed. (We discuss assessment of family functioning in Chapter 10.)

From the foregoing discussion, it is clear that the problems of homeless people are a prime manifestation of how human problems must be viewed as resulting from transactions between people and their environments. It is also clear how the problems of the homeless have resulted increasingly in the expansion of the case management direct practice role. Responding to the needs of the homeless is a major challenge to communities, to social work, and to allied disciplines. We describe interventions employed with the homeless in Chapter 16.

Instruments for Assessing Environmental Factors

Practitioners and researchers have begun to develop scales for assessing the fit between environmental resources and needs of particular client groups, but the state of the art is still somewhat primitive. Most of the existing scales fail to consider adequacy of resources *as perceived by clients*. One exception is the Interview Schedule for Social Interaction (Henderson, Duncan-Jones, Byrne, & Scott, 1980), which was developed to assess personal networks. This schedule elicits data related not only to availability of social support but also to the adequacy of the support as perceived by the individuals studied.

Social network analysis is a method that holds great promise of advancing knowledge concerning factors in the social environment that influence human behavior. Social network analysis is the study of the web of human interactions that influence behavior. A social network according to Mitchell (1969) is "a special set of linkages among a set of persons with the . . . property that the characteristics of those linkages as a whole may be used to interpret the social behavior of the persons involved" (p. 5). Fraser and Hawkins (1984), you will recall, used social network analysis to study the SSSs of street drug addicts. Emanating from social network theory have been interventions aimed at mobilizing people in social networks to assist clients through periods of extreme stress.

Summary

In the preceding sections, we discussed assessment of physical, cognitive/perceptual, emotional, and behavioral functioning, as well as motivation and cultural and environmental factors. Although we presented each of these factors as discrete entities, we again emphasize that these factors are neither independent nor static. Rather, the various functions and factors interact dynamically over time, and from the initial contact, the practitioner is a part of that dynamic interaction.

Each of the factors is therefore subject to change, and the practitioner's tasks are not only to assess the dynamic interplay of these multiple factors but also to instigate changes that are feasible and consonant with clients' goals.

We also reemphasize that assessment involves synthesizing *relevant* factors into a working hypothesis about the nature of problems and their contributory causes. You thus need not be concerned in every case with assessing all the dimensions identified thus far. Indeed, an assessment should be a concise statement that embodies only pertinent factors.

We also remind you that the scope of this chapter was limited to intrapersonal and environmental dimensions. We purposely excluded marital, family, and group systems, not because they are not important components of people's social environments but because they generally are the *hub* of people's social environments. To work effectively with interpersonal systems, however, requires an extensive body of knowledge about these systems. Therefore, we devote the next two chapters to assessing marital and family systems and growth-oriented groups.

10 ■ Assessing Family Functioning

The Primacy of Family Systems

Of the various systems of concern to social work, the family is of paramount significance, as the family is "the ecological system that nourishes the individual" (Zimmerman, 1980, p. 145).[1] The family further performs essential caretaking functions, as noted by Hartman (1981), who refers to the family as the primary "social service agency in meeting the social, educational, and health care needs" of its constituent members (p. 10). It is also largely within the family that character is formed, vital roles are learned, and children are socialized for responsible participation in the larger society. Further, it is primarily through family interaction that children develop (or fail to develop) vital self-esteem, a sense of belonging, and interpersonal skills.

Because families play key roles in meeting (or failing to meet) the needs of constituent members, practitioners must be skilled in assessing the functioning of families. That task has never been more challenging, for over the past decade there has been a marked growth in both the proportion and diversity of ethnic groups in the United States (Ho, 1987; Mindel, Habenstein, & Wright, 1988). The increasingly culturally pluralistic population in this country challenges practitioners to become culture sensitive to diverse ethnic groups and to extricate themselves from viewing their values and lifestyle as the "standard of reference for all other groups" (Maretzki & McDermott, 1980).

With these challenging tasks in mind, we have written this chapter to assist practitioners to develop skills in family assessment and to adopt a "cultural variant" perspective that will allow them to assess families within their cultural context. In the introductory part of the chapter, we discuss vital dimensions of family functioning and skills relevant to family assessment. In the latter part, we broaden our discussion to consider the cultural context of families, which is a major determinant of family patterns and belief systems.

A Systems Framework for Assessing Family Functioning

In family groups, all members influence and are influenced by every other member, creating a *system* that has properties of its own and that is governed by a set of implicit "rules" specifying roles, power structure,

---

[1]Our definition of *family* is not limited to nuclear families (i.e., once-married couples with children). Recognizing that nuclear families represent only 40 percent of the households in America (Hartman, 1981), our reference to families includes one-parent families, reconstituted families (remarried couples), couples without children, and all other forms of households that consist of members with emotional bonds and mutual obligations who define themselves as families.

forms of communication, and ways of negotiating and solving problems.[2]

Because each family is a unique system, practitioners must develop a systems framework or a perceptual "set" that will enable them to analyze and to understand the behavior of individuals in relation to the ongoing operations of the family group. Therefore, we have devoted this section to vital concepts that will assist you in viewing the family as a system and prepare you for family assessment.

Family Homeostasis

As systems, families develop mechanisms to maintain balance or *homeostasis* in their structure and operations. All families restrict the interactional repertoire of members to a limited range of familiar behaviors and develop mechanisms for restoring equilibrium whenever it is threatened (in much the same way that the thermostat of a heating system governs the temperature of a home). Minuchin (1974) speaks of this tendency of families to maintain preferred patterns as long as possible and to offer resistance to change beyond a certain range of specific behaviors:

Alternative patterns are available within the system. But any deviation that goes beyond the system's threshold of tolerance elicits mechanisms which re-establish the accustomed range. When situations of system disequilibrium arise, it is common for family members to feel that other members are not fulfilling their obligations. Calls for family loyalty and guilt-inducing maneuvers then appear.

(p. 52)

Family Rules

Family homeostasis is maintained to the extent that all members of the family adhere to a limited number of *rules* or im-

plicit agreements that prescribe the rights, duties, and range of appropriate behaviors within the family. Synonymous with such terms as *laws, patterns, regulations,* and *injunctions,* rules are formulas for relationships or guides for conduct and action in the family. Unwritten and covert, rules represent a set of prescriptions for behavior that define relationships and organize the ways in which family members interact. Since rules are implicit (i.e., unwritten laws governing behavior that are often beyond the participants' level of awareness), they must be inferred from observing family interaction and communication. Riskin (1963), in fact, defines family rules as "hypothetical constructs formulated by the observer to account for the observable behavior in the family" (p. 343), whereas Jackson (1965) describes them as metaphors "coined by the observer to cover the redundancy he observes" (p. 589). Examples of covert rules that dictate the behavior of members in relation to vital family issues include: "Father has the final say," "It's okay to talk about sex in front of everyone but Mother," "Don't say what you really feel," and "It is important to respect the personal property and privacy of other family members."

Families do, of course, formulate rules that are openly recognized and explicitly stated, such as "Teenagers are to be in the house by 10 at night," "Children are limited to two hours of TV a day," "There will be no swearing in this house," and "Children don't talk back to parents." In assessing family systems, the practitioner is most interested in implicit rules that guide a family's actions because, to the extent these rules are dysfunctional, they may have insidious effects on the family (e.g., inflicting severe emotional damage on members, limiting the family's ability to accommodate to changing

[2]Although our discussion centers largely on families, the concepts presented are pertinent to couples as well.

circumstances, and restricting choices and opportunities for growth). Because rules are implicit, their damaging impact on the lives of families often goes unrecognized, and members become caught in situations in which their behavior is dictated by forces of which they are unaware. By thus adhering to dysfunctional "rules," family members often perpetuate and reinforce the very problematic behaviors of which they complain.

Although rules govern the processes of families from any cultural origin, they differ drastically from one culture to another. In the Asian culture, for example, major rules governing family processes are similar to the following:

- Do not bring attention to yourself.
- Respect your elders.
- Avoid shaming your family at all costs.
- Bring honor to your family.
- The duty of children is to listen and obey.
- Share what you have with your relatives.
- A wife's duty is to her husband.
- Always defer to authority.

You probably recognize that these rules differ significantly from typical rules of families in Western society, for Western culture stresses competitiveness, assertiveness, and individualism and limits obligations to the nuclear family.

Functional and Dysfunctional Rules
With respect to the preceding discussion, it is vital to recognize that the implicit rules or "norms" found in a family system may be either functional or dysfunctional. Rules that may have destructive consequences for families include the following:

- "Dad can express his needs and wants, but other members of the family can't

express theirs unless they correspond with those of dad."
- "Be careful what you say around mom. She might get upset."
- "Self-control is evidence of strength. Don't let people see your weaknesses by showing affection or anger."
- "Avoid serious discussions of family problems."
- "Don't take responsibility for your own behavior. Always put the blame on someone else."
- "Don't be different from other family members."
- "It is important to win arguments. Losing an argument means losing face."

If rules are functional, however, they enable the family to respond flexibly to environmental stress, to individual needs, and to the needs of the family unit. Functional rules thus contribute to the development of capable, adaptive, and healthy family members. Examples of functional rules include the following:

- "Everyone in this family counts—their ideas and feedback are important."
- "It is acceptable to be different—family members don't always have to agree or to like the same things."
- "It is important to show your positive feelings toward others in the family."
- "It is desirable to talk about any feelings—disappointments, fears, hurts, anger, criticisms, joys, or achievements."
- "It is important to work out disagreements with other family members."
- "It is OK to admit mistakes and to apologize—other family members will understand and will respond with support."

As you observe processes, then, keep in mind that all families have both functional and dysfunctional rules and behavior and that identifying *both* types of rules is critical to making a balanced assessment of family functioning. Remember also that family systems are operated by a relatively small set of rules governing relationships. Understanding families' rules enhances assessment of family systems. Inasmuch as families are rule-governed, many behaviors or communications you observe will likely be stylized or patterned. Be alert to repetitive sequences of behavior in all areas of family life; behaviors that are crucial to the operations of the family will appear over and over. You thus will have many opportunities to observe stylized behavior that is an integral part of the family's functioning.

Violation of Rules When rules are violated and new behaviors are introduced into its system, a family may employ habitual modes of restoring conditions to a previous state of equilibrium, thereby keeping the system "on track." These modes often take the form of negative feedback to members, filled with "shoulds," "oughts," and "don'ts" intended to modify or eliminate behaviors that deviate from the norm. Irregularities in the system may also be counteracted by family members through anger, depression, silence, guilt induction, or other such forms of behavior, as Jackson (1965) indicates:

Thus, if the norm of the family is that there be no disagreement, when trouble begins to brew, we might observe general uneasiness, a sudden tangentialization or change of topic, or even symptomatic behavior on the part of the identified patient, who may act out, talk crazy, or even become physically ill when family members begin to argue. The family is distracted and brought into coalition (frequently against the patient), and the norm holds until next time.

(p. 13)

To grasp the potency of a system in limiting or eliminating proscribed behaviors, note in the following example the pressure exerted by a mother on her daughter to adhere to the rule of "don't disagree with mother." Although daughter resists this pressure at first, mother's greater power prevails, and the daughter's bid to change the rule to "it's all right to disagree" is summarily defeated:

DAUGHTER: I hate living in the city. I want to live in the mountains someday where it snows.

MOTHER: You wouldn't like that at all.

DAUGHTER: I would too like it. I love the snow and the trees and the quietness of the mountains.

MOTHER: *[Voice growing louder; irritation evident.]* Since you have never lived in the mountains, I hardly think you can be an authority on them. You just think you would like it, but you wouldn't. I hate the snow.

DAUGHTER: *[Lapses into silence.]*

In the preceding scenario, the mother's insistence on her own point of view, her refusal to validate her daughter's opinion, and her ultimate put-down that implies the daughter doesn't know what she's talking about serve as effective mechanisms to discourage her daughter's assertive behaviors and to prevent her from achieving a greater degree of autonomy. Habituated behaviors such as these that serve to bring the system back into equilibrium abound within family systems. If the family has a rule that anger may not be expressed in any physically or verbally aggressive manner, family members may stop speaking and ignore an offending member until the latter offers an apology. If the family's rule is that all members should have a sense of humor about negative things that happen to them, a member who fails to see the irony of his situation may be kidded by other family members until he laughs. Further, if the family abides by the rule, "the family comes first and friends and activities second," other family members may make guilt-inducing remarks if a member plans an activity that excludes the family on "family" days (e.g., "Don't you want to be with us on *our* day?").

The preceding examples of rules may remind you of incidents in your own nuclear or extended family in which your behavior was regulated, reinforced, or extinguished by the behaviors of other members of those systems. As you contemplate your own experiences, perhaps you can begin to appreciate more fully the potent influence of the family (the primary reference group of mankind) in shaping and continuing to influence the lives, behaviors, *and* problems of clients, even years after they have physically departed from their families of origin.

Flexibility of Rules   The opportunity to influence rules or to develop new rules varies widely from family to family. Optimally functioning families have rules that permit the system to respond flexibly to change and to evolve new rules compatible with changing needs of family members. Dysfunctional systems, on the other hand, have rigid rules that prevent members from modifying their behavior over time in response to changing circumstances and pressures, thus crystallizing relationships and stereotyping roles.

With respect to flexibility of rules, Becvar and Becvar (1988) introduce the concepts of *morphostasis* and *morphogenesis*. Morphostasis describes a system's tendency toward stability, a state of dynamic equilibrium. Morphogenesis refers to the system-enhancing behavior that allows for growth, creativity, innovation, and change.

A system must be able to find a balance, remaining stable in the context of change and changing in the context of stability, say Becvar and Becvar. In a healthy system, the rules allow for a change when such change is needed to meet individual and family needs. As you assess family systems, then, you must not only identify a family's rules and operations, but also determine the degree of flexibility (or rigidity) of the rules and of the system itself. This may be observed in part by assessing the degree of difficulty a family has in adjusting and maintaining a dynamic state of balance in response to potentially disruptive developments that occur during its life cycle, such as individual maturation, emancipation of adolescents, marriage, birth, aging, and death (Andolfi, 1980). Strains on families often occur when a first child is born, a grandparent comes to live with the family, an adolescent reaches puberty, the last child "leaves the nest," a wife goes to work, or a breadwinner retires. Pressures on families are also caused by ongoing developmental changes of children who press for redefinition of family rules and often pursue interests and values alien to those embraced traditionally by the family. These pressures, write Goldenberg and Goldenberg (1980), cause "disequilibrium within the family system, a sense of loss, and perhaps a feeling of strangeness until new transactional patterns restore family balance" (p. 34). Finally, extreme stress can occur in families from minority cultures whose values, beliefs, and perceptions clash with those of the majority culture.

In addition to assessing the stresses on rules caused by developmental changes and internal events (inner forces), you must also assess the extent to which a family's rules allow the system to respond flexibly to dynamic societal stresses (outer forces), such as those that may occur with the loss of job by a breadwinner, relocation of the family, the occurrence of a natural disaster that affects the family, or the drastic uprooting of the family experienced by political refugees. Ambiguous definitions of role expectations emanating from evolving norms and changing lifestyles in the larger society also cause strains on family systems. Yankelovich (1981) has identified 20 major changes in the norms guiding American life over the past several decades that are transforming the institutions of the workplace and the family. Among the shifting norms that carry the greatest significance for the culture are those relating to sexuality, childbearing, and marriage. In sharp contrast with the past, marriage and parenthood are now rarely viewed as necessary, and people who do not choose these roles are no longer considered social deviants. Further, with the norms affecting whether a wife should work outside the home having reversed themselves within a single generation, more and more women are seeking employment, the male/female division of labor in the family is changing dramatically, and the dual-earner family has become a common phenomenon. Such rapidly changing cultural norms put significant stress on many families.

Responding successfully to inner and outer stressors requires constant transformation of the rules and behaviors of family members to accommodate to necessary changes while maintaining family continuity. Families often seek help because of an accumulation of events that have strained the coping ability of the entire family or of individual members. Studying life-change patterns, Holmes and Rahe (1967) discovered that if individuals encounter too many life changes in too short a period of time, the chances of those persons becoming physically ill,

experiencing accidental injury, or suffering emotional disorders (such as depression) substantially increase. Ironically, even when the changes are for the better—marriage, birth of a child, a better job, a move to a bigger house, a luxurious vacation, or a windfall inheritance—if they are in sufficient degree, they may overwhelm the coping mechanisms of individual members or an entire family system. The concept that the family is a vulnerable system that may break down under accumulated stress is consonant with that of Minuchin (1974), who views many families who enter therapy as "families in transitional situations, suffering from the pains of accommodation to new circumstances" (p. 60). Minuchin, in fact, reserves the label of pathology for those families who "in the face of stress increase the rigidity of their transitional patterns and boundaries and avoid or resist any exploration of alternatives" (p. 60).

It appears that most families have some maladaptive behaviors and rules that do not allow the system to respond readily to dynamic inner and outer forces. In an authoritative study designed to identify the vital characteristics of optimally functioning families, Lewis, Beavers, Gossett, and Phillips (1976) distinguished five levels of family functioning—optimal, adequate, midrange, borderline, and severely disturbed. But rather than families sorting neatly into discrete categories, these researchers pointed out that families fall along a continuum in regard to their functioning, with the most flexible, adaptive, goal-achieving systems at one end and the most inflexible, undifferentiated, and ineffective systems at the other. Elaborating on the implications of this research in a second volume, Beavers (1977) contends that, in terms of relative size of population, moderately dysfunctional families probably comprise the largest group, that is, greater than the family groups at either end of the continuum. The "normal" family in our society thus probably has some maladaptive features, and the "optimally functioning family," as defined by Lewis et al. (1976) is actually an atypical phenomenon.

Content and Process Levels of Interaction

To make adequate family assessments and to identify important rules and behaviors, it is also vital to grasp the concepts of *content* and *process* levels of interaction. Pretend for a moment that the following brief scenario occurs in your office in a family agency as you conduct an initial interview with Mr. and Mrs. Barkley. In response to your inquiry as to the problems they are experiencing, Mr. B. glances at his wife and then indicates that she has been depressed and "sick" for some time, and they have come to the agency seeking help for "her" problem. As you look at Mrs. B., she nods her assent. You are concerned at this moment with what the couple is saying to you (the *content* of the discussion); however, you are also keenly interested in assessing the underlying intent or meaning of messages and in observing the manner in which the spouses are relating or behaving as they talk about their problems. In other words, you are also observant of the *process* that occurs as the couple discusses content. You therefore make mental note of the fact that the husband served as spokesman for his wife (with her tacit approval) and that the problem as defined by both spouses resides with the wife. Both spouses thus disregarded any impact of the problem on the husband, any possible part he might play in reinforcing or exacerbating the wife's depression or other problematic behavior, or any problems the husband might be experiencing. Essentially, with respect to roles, the couple has presented the wife as the "problem person" and the husband as the practitioner's "consultant." Several important interactional behaviors thus occurred at the process level in the opening gambits of the session, revealing information about the manner in which the spouses define their problem and how they relate and pointing to promising avenues for exploration in assessing their problems.

Families' rules are often revealed at the process level—a level often ignored by beginning practitioners as they selectively attend to what clients are "saying." Learning to sharpen one's observational powers to attend to what people are *doing* as they discuss problems is crucial to assessing and intervening effectively in family systems. Otherwise, the practitioner can easily get caught up at the content level and, for example, continue to explore the etiology of Mrs. B.'s "depression" (with the husband as information-giver and Mrs. B. as the passive, identified patient) while ignoring stylized behaviors of the couple that play a vital part in their problems.

Sequences of Interaction

In order to assess family rules adequately, practitioners must also pay attention to *sequences of interaction* that occur between members. All families play out scenarios or a series of transactions in which they manifest redundancies in behavior and communication. Analysis of interactional sequences may reveal functional or dysfunctional coping patterns utilized by members or by the entire family system. In troubled families, however, the scenarios are often destructive, serving to reinforce maladaptive behavior and dysfunctional rules. Observation of these destructive interactional sequences yields rich information concerning communication styles and dysfunctional behavior of individuals and the manner in which all family members reinforce dysfunctional interactions.

The following excerpt from the first minutes of a first session with a family of four—Mr. and Mrs. Andrews and two teenage children—illustrates habituated sequential behaviors that have a negative impact on the system. To put this segment of family process in perspective, it is important to understand that Mrs. Andrews was the person who contacted the family agency, complaining that 17-year-old Christy, an adopted child, was making the family's life miserable by causing family fights and bickering. Mrs. A. further reported that Christy was unresponsive and insensitive to the needs of other family members.

MOTHER: [*To practitioner.*] Christy just won't do what she's told. She doesn't do her share of the work, her room is always a total mess, and she's always criticizing her younger brother. She makes things so unpleasant, too—yelling, swearing, always arguing. [*Glancing at her husband.*] I seem to be the only one in the family who's concerned about her behavior, though. [*Husband averts eyes from wife and shifts his legs away from her.*]

15-YEAR-OLD MARK: [*To practitioner.*] Last Sunday night she even stayed out all night without telling anyone where she was going.

CHRISTY: That's not so. I called mom and told her we had car trouble. It wasn't my fault. [*Angrily.*] You're always on my back.

MARK: You were out drinking with your friends—that's why you didn't come home.

MOTHER: [*To practitioner.*] Christy keeps her own hours and does exactly what she wants to do in the family. She won't listen to me.

CHRISTY: You don't even try to understand me. Nobody in the family does.

MARK: The point of the matter is that you don't care about anyone else in the family.

CHRISTY: What do you know about it? You make me sick.

In the preceding example, the family plays out discordant thematic interaction that, with slight variation, can be observed over and over in the family's transactions.[3] It is as though the family is involved in a screenplay, and once the curtain is raised, all members participate in the scenario according to the family script. It is important to understand that the family script has no beginnings or endings; that is, anyone may initiate the scenario by enacting his or her "lines." The rest of the members almost invariably follow their habituated styles of relating, editing their individual scripts slightly to fit different versions of the scene being acted out by the family. In the scenes, the subjects discussed will vary, but the roles taken by individual members and the dysfunctional styles of communicating and behaving that perpetuate the scenario fluctuate very little.

In the preceding scenario, notice the sequencing of the transactions that took place:

■ Mother complains about Christy and serves as her husband's spokesman, attempting to "shame" him into responding. Responding nonverbally (looking at the floor), Mr. A. declines to participate openly.

---

[3]Although families may engage in destructive sequences of interaction such as the preceding as they first begin to discuss problems, it is vital that practitioners actively intervene early in sessions to prevent these scenarios from being played out and to assist family members to assume more facilitative ways of communicating about their problems.

- Mark joins mother's attack, supporting her position by adding new information that puts Christy in a poor light.

- Christy defends herself against Mark by denying his charges.

- Mark intensifies his attack by bringing in new charges.

- Mother complains further about Christy.

- Christy attacks mother.

- Mark takes the heat off mother by again attacking Christy.

- Christy directs her attack to Mark, who thus succeeded in his efforts to divert Christy's attack on her mother.

In witnessing this and other similar scenarios of the Andrews family, the practitioner may identify patterned behaviors and "rules" governing family interaction that may not be apparent when observing single transactions. For example:

- Mother consistently takes the role of "complainer" or "plaintiff" in her interactions with Christy.

- Father "lets" mother speak for him and avoids the conflict among the other three members by remaining verbally disengaged.

- Mark invariably agrees with his mother on all matters related to Christy and maintains a strong coalition with her by monitoring and reporting on his sister's behaviors. Mother tacitly encourages this coalition by not requesting Mark to stay out of the matter.

- Mother and Christy invariably disagree. Christy is usually engaged in defending herself or counterattacking either Mark or her mother.

- Mark consistently enters the conflict when Christy attacks mother, thus protecting and rescuing mother from Christy's anger.

Sifting out the habituated interactional responses in family processes enables the practitioner to focus interventions strategically on the family's limited number of destructive processes.[4] By analyzing the rules and patterns involved in the interaction, the practitioner has many entry points for intervening in the family processes to bring about systems change. Despite the views of at least two members (Mother and Mark) that Christy is the culprit in the family, it is clear that *all* of the members have contributed to and share responsibility for perpetuating the family's script. Although Mr. Andrews's role is not altogether clear at this point, there are indications that his participation in the family is often nonverbal and indirect. He allows his wife to speak for him and, through his nonintervention, permits the conflict to continue among other family members. Further analysis of Mr. A.'s interactions in the family may reveal a silent coalition between him and his daughter and disclose actions on his part that subtly support Christy in her conflict with his wife. Further exploration might also yield information that the relationship between Mr. and Mrs. A. is conflicted, although they may rarely address their differences openly. One could speculate, in fact, that Mr. A.'s silence spares him the negative "costs" of overt conflict with his wife.

Employing "Circular" Explanations of Behavior

In our previous discussion, we viewed the behavior of the Andrews family from a systems framework, establishing the repetitive nature of interactional behavior and the reciprocal influence of all actors

---

[4]Note that clients may discuss an endless variety of topics or content issues, but their processes contain only a limited number of rules or stylized behaviors.

on the behaviors of other family members. In so doing, we applied a *circular* concept of causality to the Andrews family, demonstrating that each member's behavior becomes a stimulus to all other involved members of the system. This may be contrasted to a *linear* explanation of the causes of behavior in which A event causes B event, B event causes C, and so forth. To illustrate the difference between these two conceptual frameworks for viewing the causality of behavior, we turn once again to the Andrews family. Employing a linear explanation of behavior, one would say: "When mother attacks Christy, she defends herself" or "When Mark attacks Christy, she attacks him back." A circular explanation of behavior would involve the following: "When mother attacks Christy, she defends herself, which angers Mark, who attacks Christy, who then attacks him back, which causes mother to complain further against Christy, who then attacks mother. . . ."

Tomm (1981) underscores that circular and linear concepts of causality reflect contrasting approaches employed by practitioners in assessing and intervening in family processes. He points out, however, that the circular explanation is systemic and preferred by systems-oriented practitioners, not only because it offers a more adequate description of behavior but also because it offers more alternatives for therapeutic intervention. In the preceding example, for instance, a practitioner who operated from a linear orientation would intervene to stop mother from attacking Christy, whereas a practitioner who employed a circular explanation of the causes of behavior would target mother and Christy; mother, Christy, and Mark; or the entire circular pattern for intervention (which would then include father as a silent participant).

Tomm emphasizes that a preference for circularity influences the practitioner's interviewing style in the assessment (and intervention) process:

When conducting a family assessment, it is important to recognize that a process of enquiry exploring *descriptive* characteristics (e.g., "Is mother unhappy?") tends to be linear, whereas an enquiry exploring *differences* (e.g., "Who gets sad the most?") tends to be circular. It is less useful to know whether father is affectionate than to know whether there is a difference in his affection recently compared to before, or whether there is a difference in his affection toward his daughter from that toward his wife. If father is *most* affectionate with his eldest daughter now, he must be *less* affectionate with his wife.

(p. 86)

Utilizing a circular perspective, Tomm notes that there are three types of differences that may be usefully explored in family assessment. These include differences between *individuals* (e.g., "Who gets angry the most?"), differences between *relationships* (e.g., "What is the difference between the way mother treats Christy compared to how she treats Mark?"), and differences between *time periods* (e.g., "How did she treat Christy last year as compared to now?"). By orienting the assessment to solicit information regarding differences, Tomm points out, the practitioner elicits more relevant data and does so more efficiently than would occur by obtaining linear descriptions.

Beginning practitioners tend to employ linear rather than circular perspectives when explaining behavior and to view interactional processes as "action-reaction" cycles, often assigning responsibility or blame for problems to one or more members whose problematic behavior is conspicuous. When not attuned to the repetitive nature of dysfunctional interactions, however, practitioners sharply reduce their ability to help family members, who often need the help of an expert in removing themselves from destructive interactional patterns. When working with families, it is vital that prospective practitioners commit extensive time and effort toward increasing their ability to see the reciprocal nature of behaviors and the interactional patterns involved.

Not unlike beginning practitioners, family members also tend to explain behavior using a linear orientation, often assigning arbitrary beginnings and endings to sequences of interaction in ways that define other members as villains and themselves as victims. Mrs. Andrews and Mark, for instance, viewed themselves as innocent victims of Christy's provocative behavior and defined her as the person who needed to change in the family. "Punctuating" interactional sequences in this manner, according to Sluzki (1975) "constitutes an optical illusion . . . the chicken-egg puzzle is arbitrarily solved by designating one of the participants as the initiator and the other as reactor" (p. 378). To counteract this linear perspective, practitioners must punctuate interactions in ways that define the responsibility of all family members in contributing to and maintaining dysfunctional interactions.

Meaning of Symptoms within a Systems Framework

The circular perspective and the systems framework we are advocating have significance for the manner in which practitioners view *symptoms,* a term that encompasses not only the subjective complaints of individuals but also the beliefs of others (family members, associates, professionals) that something is wrong with the feelings, thinking, or behavior of these persons (Framo, 1970). Departing from the conventional, simplistic view of symptoms as intrapsychic phenomena and as stemming from a disease process within the individ-

ual, in a now classic paper Framo postulates that symptoms are a function of the relationship context in which they are embedded. As Framo explains:

Experience in family therapy has shown that disordered behavior or psychological symptoms, which are frequently etiologically and dynamically obscure from the standpoint of individual psychology, can often be decoded and made intelligible when viewed within the matrix of their intimate social systems. Family transactional findings suggest further the momentous prospect that the intrinsic nature of psychopathology, usually seen as solely the outcome of insolvable intrapsychic conflict, may have to be recast and broadened as a special form of relationship event which occurs between intimately related people.

(p. 271)

Careful observation and analysis of family processes will usually reveal the reciprocal influence of all actors in perpetuating maladaptive or symptomatic behavior. Rubenstein's and Timmins's (1978) description of the relationship patterns established in families with one depressed member serves to illustrate this point:

Whatever the original cause of the severe depression affecting one member of the family, there is always typical, patterned, and repetitive behavior shown by the designated patient. One feature of the repetitive pattern is that there is always a partner to the behavior. The partner may be a spouse, a mother, a sister, an offspring, or the therapist. These partners are the *"caretakers"* of the depressed patient. . . . whatever the cause of the original depression, the partnership insures the perpetuation of the depressed behavior.

(p. 14)

We have discussed the fact that symptoms are *maintained* by the interactional processes of families. In addition, however, they may be *reduced* by changes in these same processes. In instances in which there are "symptom carriers" in the family, then, practitioners must carefully focus their exploration to determine the manner in which the system is reinforcing the maintenance of symptoms and plan their interventions accordingly.

Assessing Problems Employing a Systems Framework

The utilization of a *systems view* of family problems has implications for gathering relevant data in the assessment process. Many clients, even those designated as villains by other family members, see themselves as victims of the actions of significant others or of external forces over which they have no control. Most often they initially enter counseling prepared to "complain" about those who are "causing" their problems, rather than to engage in efforts to change themselves. Because of their selective perception of the "causes" of events, they often do not offer information that assists practitioners to formulate a clear picture of how these problems may be reinforced and exacerbated either by the client or by significant others in the family system. It is important that practitioners have an appropriate conceptual framework and accompanying skills to identify themes within the family's processes and to elicit relevant data about the family system. Otherwise, practitioners may unwittingly adopt clients' definitions of "who has the problem," focus interventions on changing the behavior of these selected persons, and neglect the influence of other significant family members upon the problems in the systems.

It should be noted that although systemic interactional patterns that restrict and mold clients' behavior are woven throughout the fabric of many client problems, practitioners often do not have the opportunity of observing these firsthand. Family members, for instance, may refuse

service or be unavailable because of geographical location. At other times, it may not be expedient to involve key actors who play significant roles in the problems of clients. It is vital to remember when clients describe problems, however, that they often talk extensively about difficulties they are experiencing in relationships with family members or with significant others who are not present. Thus, when you cannot directly observe interactional processes, you have the important task of eliciting highly specific information from clients that will aid you in assessing the interpersonal patterns and rules of the family system. This is best accomplished by carefully exploring a number of *critical incidents* that illustrate problematic behaviors manifested in the family system. In order to identify underlying family patterns, you must elicit descriptive information about the behaviors and communications of all involved actors and establish the sequencing of discrete transactions and events that occurred before, during, and after the identified incident. Inasmuch as clients tend to summarize critical incidents, thereby omitting vital details, it is helpful to explain to them that you are searching for family styles of relating and underscore the importance of carefully identifying each discrete event or transaction that occurred in any critical incident targeted for exploration. We recommend that you request clients to give a verbatim account of an event so that you see what happened as clearly as if you had been present.

Even when clients define their problems as involving some members of a family and not others, it is critical to explore family relationships to the extent that you can identify key interactional patterns and the nature of alignments among various subsystems of the family. In such explorations, it is not uncommon to discover that other persons besides parents (e.g., sibling, stepfather, grandparents) play significant roles in contributing to the problem behaviors of a child brought to an agency. Based on information gained in exploring family affiliative ties and rules, you will often need to "redefine" and expand the problem system to include more actors than originally identified by clients.

In assisting clients to understand the need for an overall assessment of family relationships when they initially believe that only one or two members are involved in problems, it is helpful to explain that the family is a "system" and to stress that the entire family is affected by, and may even exacerbate, problems experienced by one member. Further, you should stress that the causes of problems usually reside largely in interactions that involve various members of the family rather than with individual family members. As underscored by Wile (1978), "family members are as likely to be relieved and grateful as they are to be threatened and resistant when a problem they had attributed to the 'identified patient' is redefined as a general family problem" (p. 16). Wile stresses, however, that this approach holds only to the extent that the practitioner's approach is nonaccusatory and that the practitioner clarifies for the whole family how all involved members are caught in difficult conflicts or dilemmas related to the problematic family situation.

Dimensions of Family Assessment

In explicating integral concepts of a systems framework for viewing family functioning in our earlier discussion, we have set the stage for family assessment. In this section, we present dimensions of assessment that represent guidelines for exploring and organizing the massive data you will gather in working with family systems. These dimensions will also assist you to bring patterned interaction into bold relief and will prepare you to evaluate functional and dysfunctional aspects of family operations—a critical preliminary step to planning interventions to change a family system.

The following list contains the dimensions that we consider at length in the chapter:

1. Outer boundaries of family systems.

2. Internal boundaries and family subsystems.

3. Family power structure.

4. Family decision-making processes.

5. Family affect and range of feelings expressed.

6. Family goals.

7. Family myths and cognitive patterns.

8. Family roles.

9. Communication styles of family members.

10. Family strengths.

11. Family life cycle.

The preceding list contains basic criteria for assessing family functioning. You may wish to refer to Fisher's (1976) extensive review of the literature of family assessment for a more exhaustive compilation of relevant dimensions.

Outer Boundaries of Family Systems

As living systems that are part of still larger systems, families necessarily have diverse transactions with the environment. Families differ widely, however, in the degree to which they are open to transactions with other systems and in the flexibility of their outer boundaries. By *flexibility,* we mean the extent to which outsiders are permitted or invited to enter the family system, members of the family are allowed to invest emotionally and to engage in relationships outside the family, and information and materials are exchanged with the environment. As identified by Kantor and Lehr (1975), there are three prototypical bounding arrangements of families—open, closed, and random. Each of these types involves distinctive styles of relating to the outer environment.

Closed Family Systems Those who hold authority in families perform the bounding functions in such a way that they create discrete family space that exists apart from the larger space of the neighborhood and community. The closed family system thus is characterized by strict regulation that limits transactions with the external environment and restricts incoming and outgoing people, objects, information, and ideas. Locked doors, tight parental control over input from the media, supervised excursions, close scrutiny of strangers, trespass prohibitions, high fences, and unlisted telephones are typical features of closed family systems. The tight boundaries of closed systems serve the function of preserving territoriality, protecting the family from undesired intrusions, safeguarding privacy, and even fostering secretiveness. Authorities in the family maintain tight control of traffic at the family's perimeter, and the bounding function is never relinquished or shared with outsiders or even with family members who have not been assigned the role of performing bounding functions.

Open Family Systems In this type of system, the bounding movements of individual members are regulated by the process of group consensus. Consequently, family boundaries are flexible, extending the territory of the family into the larger community space as well as bringing external culture into the family space. Individuals are permitted the freedom to regulate their own incoming and outgoing traffic to the extent that they do not adversely impact on other family members or violate the family norms. Features of open family systems include having numerous guests in the home, visiting with friends, participating in external activities, belonging to outside groups, participating in community affairs, and permitting free information exchange with minimal censorship of the media. Open bounding within a family fosters beneficial interchange with other members of the community; indeed, guests are not only welcome but are viewed as contributing to the well-being of the family.

Random Family Systems Within this category, family members develop individual bounding patterns in establishing and defending their own and their family's territory. There are no *family* bounding patterns per se, and there may be as many bounding guidelines as there are members in the family; in effect, the random family's bounding pattern is a conglomerate of individual styles. Individual styles collide at times, but there are no fixed patterns, and family members therefore feel no need to modify their styles. Features of family life that are normally confined to a family's space may also occur outside the household. For example, conflicts and affectional expressions may occur in public as well as in the privacy of the home. Random bounding also deemphasizes defending the territorial perimeter of the family, so that limits on entry or exit to the family are not imposed. Indeed, random families tend to extend and broaden prerogatives for entry and exit not only to members but also to guests and strangers.

Knowledge of the three prototypes of family structure discussed in the preceding sections should assist you to identify the bounding patterns of families you encounter in practice. Bear in mind that these three types of family structures are only prototypes and that the actual bounding patterns of families may include aspects of all these types of structures. It is vital, therefore, to assess each family's unique style of transacting with the environment. Remember also that although the bounding pattern of the open system is most conducive to meeting the emotional and social needs of individual members, the strengths as well as the liabilities of bounding patterns must be assessed within the context of each family's unique needs and styles.

In assessing the bounding patterns of families, practitioners must also assess the extent to which relatives or nonrelatives are included in the family's bounding patterns. In Anglo families, for example, practitioners may find grandparents, a live-in boyfriend or girlfriend, or a godparent, who wield considerable influence in the family's affairs. In assessing families from other cultures, practitioners will often find an extended family system that includes many kin who have well-defined obligations and responsibilities to each other. The Puerto Rican (or Hispanic) definition of family, for example, goes way beyond the family of origin, encompassing not only those related by blood and marriage but including those who are tied to it as well through custom (Mizio, 1974). Because of the vital impact of the kinship pattern upon family functioning, we discuss this pattern at length later in the chapter.

Internal Boundaries and Family Subsystems

All families develop networks of coexisting subsystems formed on the basis of gender, interest, generation, or functions that must be performed for the family's survival (Minuchin, 1974).[5] Members of a family may simultaneously belong to a number of subsystems, entering into separate and reciprocal relationships with other members of the nuclear family, depending upon the subsystems they share in common (e.g., husband/wife, mother/daughter, brother-/sister, father/son) or with the extended family (e.g., grandmother/granddaughter, uncle/nephew, mother/son-in-law). Each subsystem can be thought of as a natural coalition between participating members. As Sluzki (1975) states, "intimacy . . . necessarily includes a coalitionary component" (p. 69). Many of the coalitions or alliances that families form are situation-related and temporary in nature. A teenager may be able to enlist her mother's support in asking her father's permission for a special privilege or for new clothing. A grandmother living in a home may voice disagreement with her daughter and son-in-law regarding a particular decision involving one of their children, thus temporarily forming a coalition with the affected child. Such passing alliances are characteristic of temporary subsystems (Goldenberg & Goldenberg, 1980).

Other subsystems, particularly the spouse, parental, and sibling subsystems, are more enduring in nature. According to Minuchin (1974), the formation of stable, well-defined alliances or coalitions between members of these vital subsystems is, in fact, critical to the well-being and health of the family. Unless there is a

---

[5]Information from this section was drawn in part from a discussion by Goldenberg and Goldenberg (1985) of Minuchin's structural approach.

strong and enduring coalition between husband and wife, for instance, conflict reverberates throughout a family, and children are often co-opted into one warring faction or another as parents struggle for power and control. For optimal family functioning, according to Minuchin, the boundaries of these three subsystems must be clear and defined well enough to allow members sufficient differentiation to carry out functions without undue interference but permeable enough to allow contact and exchange of resources between members of the subsystem and others. Minuchin, in fact, points out that the clarity of the subsystem boundaries is of far more significance in determining family functioning than the composition of the family's subsystem. According to Minuchin, a parental subsystem that includes a grandmother or a parental child may function quite adequately, for instance, if the lines of responsibility are clearly defined.

The relative integrity of the boundaries of the spouse, parental, and sibling subsystems is determined by related rules of the family. A mother clearly defines the boundary of a parental subsystem, for instance, in telling her oldest child not to interfere when she is talking to a younger child about assigned chores that the child has left undone. The message, or "rule," then, is that children are not allowed to assume parenting roles with other children in the family. The mother, however, may delegate responsibility for parenting to her oldest child when she leaves the home. Nevertheless, the "rules" regarding who does the parenting and under what circumstances clearly delineate the boundaries of the parental and sibling subsystems.

The clarity of boundaries within a family is a useful parameter for evaluating family functioning. Minuchin (1974) conceives of all families as falling somewhere along a continuum of extremes in boundary functioning, the opposite poles of which are disengagement (diffuse boundaries) and enmeshment (inappropriately rigid boundaries). Family closeness in an enmeshed family system is defined as everyone thinking and feeling alike. Membership in such families requires a major sacrifice of autonomy, thereby discouraging members from exploration, independent action, and problem solving. Members of disengaged families, on the other hand, tolerate a wide range of individual variations by members but are apt to lack feelings of family solidarity, loyalty, and a sense of belonging. Members of such families find it difficult to give or to get support from other family members. Family organization in such systems is unstable and chaotic, with leadership often shifting moment to moment. In disengaged families, only high-level stresses upon one family member appreciably affect other members or activate the family's supportive systems. These systems, in fact, tend not to respond when a response is appropriate (parents may not worry when their adolescent child stays out all night). At the enmeshed end of the continuum, one member's behavior immediately affects others, reverberating throughout the family system. Members tend to respond to any variations from the accustomed with excessive speed and intensity, with parents becoming very angry, for instance, if a child does not eat everything on his plate.

Enmeshment and disengagement as processes are not necessarily dysfunctional. According to Minuchin, every family experiences some enmeshment or disengagement in its subsystems as a family goes through developmental phases. During a family's early developmental years, mother and young children may represent an enmeshed subsystem, with father in a peripheral position. Adolescents gradually disengage from the parental-child subsystems as they get ready to leave home. But continued operations by a family at either extreme of the continuum may signal the presence of maladaptive patterns and rules that hinder the growth needs of members. Many relatively dysfunctional and highly intractable coalitions between members occur in families who adopt enmeshed styles of relating. Mother and child in a highly enmeshed subsystem may form a coalition against father. In another instance, a mother may relinquish many of her parenting functions to become a member of a sibling subsystem as manifested by a mother's descriptive message—"I treat my daughter just like my sister." A "parental" child may join an executive subsystem, forming a destructive coalition with the parents against other children in the family. Or a woman may "parent" both her grown daughter and the daughter's children, thus interfering with her own offspring's parental functioning. An entire family may also shun one member whose behavior deviates from the family's prescribed norms.

In disengaged families, by contrast, coalitions may be formed between some members, but these alliances are apt to be fragile and transitory, based on immediate gratification of the needs of family members who abandon the alliance once their needs are temporarily satisfied or the coalition no longer serves their purposes. In disengaged families, it is the relative *lack* of opportunity to form stable alliances that is detrimental to the growth needs of individuals. The resulting "disconnectedness" of this transactional family style leaves members isolated and alienated from each other and unable to utilize family resources or emotional supplies.

In addition to considering the processes of enmeshment and disengagement, you should also be aware that many distressed families "choose" a scapegoat, who is identified by other members as the person responsible for the system's ills. This person, whom the family often refers to the practitioner for help, in a sense sacrifices his/her own growth for the unity of the group by becoming the target of family frustrations and providing a basis for solidarity among other members. It is important to understand when encountering and working with this phenomenon that scapegoating is perpetuated by *all* group members, including the scapegoated person, who usually participates fully with other members of the family in the behaviors necessary to maintain both the status quo and the myth that one person is responsible for the family's problems. Children, as powerless members of the family, are particularly susceptible to this role, often carrying it into adulthood. Many theorists stress the importance of the role of the scapegoated child in allowing marital partners to divert the focus from their own conflicted relationship by focusing instead on the troublesome child.

Alignments between particular family members and outsiders may also cause acute family stress. Grandparents living outside the home may take the side of children in family disputes and provide a refuge for them, which may interfere with parents and children working out their difficulties. A 15-year-old girl may begin to keep company with an older man and, despite her parents' objections, may continue to see him surreptitiously. Ignoring his wife's protestations, a husband may also keep late hours and spend an inordinate amount of time with a "best friend," going to bars, playing poker, and the like. Further, either spouse may begin an affair with another person while continuing in the marital relationship.

Even practitioners may form inappropriate alliances with clients that interfere with family members working together on their problems. The authors are aware of one instance in which a woman had had 30 years of intermittent therapy with several practitioners. Although many of her problems were marriage-related, her husband had been seen only twice by these practitioners, each time to consult with them about his wife's problems rather than to participate in any change process. Although this example is extreme, clients are often seen individually for therapy when their problems either emanate from or are exacerbated by marital or family relationships.

Family Power Structure

Closely related to the process of forming subsystems and negotiating coalitions in a family are the vicissitudes of power relationships in the system. Power can be thought of as the capacity of one member to induce change in the behavior of another family member. The more "need fulfilling" resources one person has in a family in relation to other members, the more power that person wields in the family. Needs include requirements for economic support, social rank, love, affection, and approval while resources include the ability to provide these need-fulfilling elements to another person.

All families develop a power structure that defines the relative influence that each member has upon other members of the system and who will participate in what way in decision making. It is through this power structure that systems are able to maintain the behavior of individuals within acceptable limits and to provide leadership to assure that maintenance functions of the family will be carried out, thus maximizing the possibility of survival of the group.

Distribution and Balance of Power   Families are often viewed as having single monolithic power structures—either the husband or the wife makes all the decisions, or both participate equally. In actuality, multiple power structures exist in families. Wives may be more influential in some decisions and husbands in others, depending on expertise or jurisdictional "agreements" among spouses. Since both partners share in the family's decision-making process (although possibly to an unequal extent), it is important to determine who may be the most influential in which decisions and how the balance of power is distributed in the family.

To the extent that children are able to influence decisions made by the husband and wife executive subsystem or to assume "decider" roles themselves, they also play a part in the family's power structure. Minuchin (1974) has observed that some families develop a "parental child" who cares for siblings in the absence of parents. If the child has been delegated appropriate authority, the family system may function smoothly and the child may develop responsibility and capability beyond his or her years. If parents abdicate their responsibilities or do not explicitly delegate authority, however, the child may be forced to assume control and decision-making functions beyond his/her developmental capacity, producing stresses that often result in adolescent rebellion and mishandling of younger siblings.

Culture plays a powerful role in defining the allocation of power in families. Consider, for example, Zborowski's and Herzog's (1952, p. 138) description of a Jewish woman: "She was a perfect Jewish woman, clear, patient, hardworking, and silent, submissive to God and to her husband, devoted to her children . . . her own well-being was unimportant." Many cultures are male oriented and clearly define the female's role as subordinate to that of the male, stripping her of any power. Because of many complex factors, including industrialization, the higher level of education of women and their entrance into the work force, and the equal rights movement, families in Western society are moving toward more egalitarian definitions of male-female roles; however, many families continue to suffer stress because of the difficulty in resolving discrepancies between traditional and new egalitarian definitions of male-female roles. As immigrant families enter the United States, they too face resolution of the same issues, a subject we discuss later in the chapter.

Stuart (1980) uses a "power-gram" to assess the power imbalances in a marriage and to ascertain the various decision-making areas in which individual spouses have authority to make decisions or share vested power. In determining how power is apportioned in the marriage, Stuart provides spouses with a list of areas in which couples commonly make decisions (p. 266). It includes the following items:

1. Where couple lives.
2. What job husband takes.
3. How many hours husband works.
4. Whether wife works.
5. What job wife takes.
6. How many hours wife works.
7. Number of children in the family.
8. When to praise or punish children.
9. How much time to spend with children.
10. When to have social contacts with inlaws and relatives.

11. When to have sex.
12. How to have sex.
13. How to spend money.
14. How and when to pursue personal interests.
15. Whether to attend church and, if so, which church to attend.

Individual spouses are then asked to rate each of the preceding according to who *usually* has the responsibility for making decisions in each area, using the following scale:

1. Almost always husband.
2. Husband, after consulting wife.
3. Both share equally.
4. Wife, after consulting husband.
5. Almost always wife.

Once ratings have been obtained, individual spouses are once again asked to rate the decision-making areas according to *desired* authority ratings; that is, the extent to which each *would like* authority to make decisions to be distributed among the partners. Finally, couples are asked to negotiate a desired balance of power in areas identified as being of primary importance to them in the relationship. Thus, both partners are able to indicate their view of the present and desired balance of power and, with the partner, to negotiate new decision-making rules.

Shifts in Power   In assessing family systems, it is also critical to understand that the power base of a family may shift with inner and outer stressors bringing upon the system pressures to which the family must accommodate. For instance, the contribution of an independent income increases the wife's power in a family; further, the higher the wife's education relative to her husband's education, the greater her power. Thus, as many more women enter the occupational world or seek higher levels of education as a result of current changing social conditions, dynamic changes are occurring in the balance of power in families. The power base in a family may also shift as a result of other factors. The influence or authority of a power figure may diminish if that person does not provide effective leadership in times of crisis. On the other hand, if the power figure successfully handles a crisis, that person's authority in a family may perceptibly increase.

With immigrant families, shifts in power can occur when the male cannot secure employment in the new country. For example, in Puerto Rican families, the sense of being a *macho completo* (complete male) goes hand in hand with being a provider or protector of his family. When the male cannot find work and his wife, who can more easily secure employment, takes a job as a domestic or perhaps a sewing machine operator, the role reversal causes tremendous strains on the family, realigning the power base of the family and often causing the wife to have contempt for the husband she can no longer view as "macho" (Mizio, 1974).

Families encounter many stressful situations (e.g., loss of a job, reduced coping capacity caused by mental illness, debilitation resulting from an accident, or a wife's entering the work force) that may challenge the balance of power and cause realignments in the power base of the family. In fact, the emotional impact of these stressors and the tumultuous upheaval caused as family members struggle for power and control in a transitional situation may play a key role in a family's difficulties. In assessing family systems, therefore, you must not only determine how power has been distributed in the family but also whether changing conditions of the family are "threatening" the established power base. You must also assess the extent to which the family's "rules" allow the system to reallocate power flexibly and to adjust roles to meet the demands of the family's changing circumstances. Finally, you must assess how husband and wife view the relative vestment of power in the family, for even if power is unequally distributed, both may be well satisfied with the arrangement. Under such circumstances, unless power dynamics play a significant role in family problems, it is not appropriate to seek to make adjustments in this area.

Covertly Held Power   It is important to keep in mind that power in a family may be held at a covert as well as an overt level. For instance, one partner may be formally acknowledged as the power figure in the family, a position usually accorded to the person in the family (traditionally the husband) who has more economic resources, social status, or skills in managing enterprises and thus more power over family decisions. However, power can be usurped from this power figure or from the husband-wife executive subsystem through various covert coalitions that may be formed in the family. A strong alliance between a child and a grandmother, for instance, may substantially weaken the power base of the parents. Similarly, in a male-dominated patriarchial family, a power bloc made up of mother and daughter may undermine the authority of the father.

Although almost all cultures appear on the surface to be male dominated, practitioners should avoid making premature decisions concerning which member or members of the family hold the power. At a covert level, women often maintain a central and powerful role in the family, despite subservient role definitions. Speaking of Mexican-American families, for example, Falicov (1982) observes that while there is outward compliance with the cultural ideal of male dominance and female submission, this is often "a social fiction." Observers often fail to notice a culturally acceptable but less obvious norm—that of *hembrismo* or *marianismo,* "the undercover power and family centrality of the self-sacrificing mother" (p. 139).

The covert power that women hold in some cultures despite their subservient status has been referred to as a paradox by some authors. Speaking of Italian women, Rotunno and McGoldrick (1982, p. 347) observe that, "Although men are the central authority figures ... and women are considered the servers of men ... the mother ... plays a very powerful role, especially in her son's affections (as his wife will hardly fail to notice)." The same type of paradox in the Jewish culture has also been observed by Herz and Rosen (1982, p. 374):

Wives were often referred to contemptuously and viewed as inferior to their husbands. On the other hand, they were extremely powerful in the primary role that they played in the home. In actual daily living they took the lead and made basic decisions about the destiny of their families. This is, of course, a paradox: women are powerful, while at the same time compelled to deny that they are.

Persons also exercise covert power in a family through use of emotional or physical symptoms. Haley's (1963) description of the interpersonal dynamics involved in a classic case of handwashing compulsion illustrates how power in a relationship may accrue to a person manifesting symptomatology and how symptoms, as interpersonal events, may be used to define and control relationships. In Haley's case, a woman sought therapy because she felt compelled to wash her hands and to take showers numerous times a day. Exploring the problem with the woman and her husband (a couple who had recently emigrated from Germany to the United States), the practitioner found that they were engaged in a bitter struggle over this compulsion. The husband, tyrannical about all details of the couple's life, constantly demanded his own way and insisted that his wife respond obediently to him at all times. Trying to gain control over his wife's symptomatic behavior, the husband constantly forbade her to wash her hands, followed her around to make sure that she was not washing them, and timed her showers and rationed her soap. Although unable to openly oppose her husband on any issue—except the handwashing—the wife defeated her husband's maneuvers by pointing out that she had no control over her compulsion. Further, through this symptom, she was able to avoid responding to other requests he made of her. For example, the husband liked the kitchen clean and the dishes done promptly, but his wife could not do the dishes because, once she placed her hands in the dishwater, she was compelled to go on washing them. Further, although her husband insisted on a spotlessly clean house, she could not clean the house because she was busy washing her hands.

Through her handwashing compulsion, the wife gained the upper hand in her relationship with her husband, and as Haley points out, although the husband insisted on being master of his house, "He was dethroned by the simple washing of a pair of hands" (p. 14).

Children as well as adults may gain control in a family through extreme symptomatology. Such children receive at least momentary gratification through the attention they receive for their fits, withdrawal periods, runaways, psychotic episodes, and so on. Also, as persons who carry the labels "sick," "bad," or "different," these children require special consideration. Further, the role of deviant often exempts them from responsibilities and relieves them from the necessity of coping with reality beyond the limits that the family sets for them.

It should be noted that although a person with symptomatic behavior may have considerable leverage and power in a family, all members of the family tacitly support the perpetuation of symptoms through their own behavioral contributions to family patterns that have developed. Vogel and Bell (1960) astutely observe the role of parents in supporting the dysfunctional behavior of their children:

In all instances, while the parents explicitly criticized the child and at times even punished him, they supported in some way, usually implicitly, the persistence of the very behavior which they criticized. This permission took various forms: failure to follow through on threats, delayed punishment, indifference to and acceptance of the symptom, unusual interest in the child's symptom, or considerable secondary gratification offered the child because of this symptom.

(p. 390)

Assessing Power A number of factors, then, must be addressed in assessing the power base and the manner in which power is distributed in the family, including who holds the "balance of power"; who, if anyone, is the formally designated leader; to what extent power is covertly held by members who have aligned to form a power bloc; and to what extent covert power accrues to individual members who are manifesting extreme symptomatology in the family. The role of a family's culture in determining the distribution of power, of course, must also be considered.

Keep in mind that family struggles over power issues and the resulting destructive coalitions that are formed are manifested in families' processes. Observation of family interaction often reveals "an affect-laden process in which coalitions are being proposed, accepted, modified, locked, tested, qualified, broken, rejected, and betrayed in a constant flowing process" (Sluzki, 1975, p. 69) as warring factions compete for power and for definition of the relationship (i.e., who has control over whom). Key information about these processes may be gleaned by keeping the following questions in mind when viewing family operations:

1. Who does what and who comments on it?

2. Who speaks for whom?

3. Who speaks first?

4. Who speaks at the same time as someone else?

5. Who interrupts whom?

6. Who agrees with whom?

7. Who does the most speaking?

8. Who decides who decides?

9. Whose ideas are usually adopted when the family engages in decision making?

10. Who seems to hold the ultimate authority for making decisions, regardless of who originated the ideas the family is considering?

Bear in mind that all families must address power issues and allocate power in some manner—it is the *functionality* of the power structure in meeting individual psychological needs and promoting the health of the system that must be determined in assessing this dimension of family functioning. Assessment questions that address the functionality of the power structure include:

1. Is the family's power structure stable, allowing the system to carry out its maintenance functions in an orderly manner,

or does the power base shift as members compete for power?

2. Does the power base reside within the executive subsystem or within covert coalitions in the family?

3. Are members of the family content with the relative distribution of power?

Family Decision-Making Processes

Closely tied to issues of power is the family's style of decision making. Families range in extremes from leaderless groups in which no one has enough power to determine and direct activities or to organize decision-making processes to families in which virtually absolute power to make decisions is rigidly held by one member. Although effective deliberation and decision making are critical in determining the well-being of the system and its responsivity to individual family members, most families do not consciously select a modus operandi for making family decisions. Rather, the family's style of decision making usually evolves in the formative stages of development of the system, often patterned after decision-making approaches modeled by parents in the families of origin of the marital partners. Further, the persisting conflicts experienced by troubled families can often be traced largely to the inability of marital partners over the years to resolve, at a covert level, incompatible expectations (emanating from role models they have experienced) regarding the distribution of power and the manner in which decisions should be made in the family. As children are added to the system, they too may be pulled into the conflict as neither parent is fully successful in wrestling power from the other.

In order to assess the functionality of decision-making processes found in fami-

lies, it is important to understand vital ingredients that are inherent in effective problem solving with family systems:

1. Effective decision making requires open feedback and self-expression among members. Classifying all interpersonal systems as either *closed* or *open,* Satir (1967) contrasts these two modes in relation to the relative autonomy of individual members and their freedom to express themselves within these systems. Members of closed systems are expected to have the same opinions, feelings, and desires and, thus, must be very cautious about what they say. Open and congruent self-expression is viewed as deviant or "crazy" by other members of the system, and differences are treated as dangerous, requiring members to close themselves off from others in order to remain in the system. On the other hand, an open system permits its members to converse freely and relate to each other without fear of negative judgment. Differences are viewed as natural and welcomed by all. Further, members use such mechanisms as compromise, agreeing to disagree, or taking turns to negotiate and resolve differences. In the open system, members can say what they think and feel without fear of destroying themselves or others in the system. In systems that do not allow feedback regarding feelings, preferences, and opinions, members are stifled, pressured to ignore their own needs and wishes and to conform, without complaint, to maladaptive processes in the system. Without open feedback and self-expression, decision-making processes are not responsive to needs of individual members that emerge as the system goes through transitional developmental phases that demand adaptation to inner and outer stresses and crises.

2. Effective decision making requires a philosophical or attitudinal set on the part of each family member that all members

of the system "count," that is, that each member's needs will be taken into consideration in decision making that will affect that member.

Satir (1967) has identified four exhaustive solutions to what she calls the "self-other" dilemma in relationships that apply to decision-making processes in families:

a. In the first position, the person *discounts the wants of self* ("I count myself out"). Operating from this position, people handle differences by submitting, agreeing, placating, apologizing, or in other ways discounting their own needs (regardless of how they really feel) when negotiating with others.

b. In the second position, a person *discounts the wants of the "other"* ("I count you out"). In this position, persons may behave by finding fault, blaming, and disagreeing with others, thus leaving no room for negotiating differences.

c. In the third position, the person *discounts the wants of both* ("Let's count us both out"). Operating from this position, persons may exclude both themselves and others by being irrelevant, changing the subject, leaving the situation, or behaving in other ways that make it impossible to negotiate differences openly with others.

d. In the fourth position, a person *takes into account the wants of other parties involved* ("I count myself in but try to make room for others"). In this position, a person openly and clearly negotiates differences with others and permits or invites others to do the same.

Satir describes the fourth position as the only "growth-producing" solution to negotiation of differences between self and others. This alternative allows individual members to flourish while remaining a part of the system—and vitalizes and energizes the system itself. By contrast, the other three positions may promote individual survival at the expense of others in the family and cause conflict, intrigue, and resentment in the system that divert energies from productive tasks and block the family's developmental progress.

These positions can be viewed as interpersonal patterns or styles of individual family members that are consistently expressed in the family. In decision making (as well as other interpersonal events), individual family members and the family as a unit may "count in" some members and "count out" others. Before a family may become an optimally nurturing environment for individual growth, all members must be "counted in" in the sense that their needs are considered when important decisions affecting them are made in the family. Members of the family are likely to contribute productively when they know that every member "counts" and that needs, rather than power, are at issue in the decision-making process. In traditional patriarchal families, the issue of the wife's feeling "counted in" in the decision-making process (even if both spouses agree that the husband should have the final say) is of obvious importance. Further, although children should have considerably less power than parents in a family and often should not be vested with decision-making authority in problem-solving processes, they should have the opportunity to express themselves or to give feedback in relation to decisions that affect them. Examples of such decisions include activities in which the family engages, responsibilities assigned them in the home, and personal leisure time activities in which they engage.

3. Effective decision making requires members of a family system to think in terms of *needs* rather than solutions. Members of families are often conditioned by life experiences to see problem

solutions in terms of dichotomies—"either we do things your way or mine; one of us has to lose"—a narrow approach to problem solving that centers on competing solutions, preventing negotiation and compromise. "Do what I want, think what I think, feel what I feel"—in other words, "Do things my way"—is often the position taken by individual family members as they attempt to coerce or coax others to adopt their solutions to life's problems. Operating from the principle that love and total agreement go together, they, in effect, take the position, "If you love me, you will do what I want. If you don't, you are bad" (Satir, 1967). Taking a trivial example of a couple attempting to negotiate differences when A wants to go out for a hamburger and B wants to go out for a chicken dinner, Satir describes (p. 14) how persons with dysfunctional communication styles disagree:

a. We find them vacillating and postponing: "Let's decide later what to eat."

b. We find them trying to coerce: "We are going to eat hamburgers!"

c. We find them trying to delude each other: "They are both food, so let's eat hamburger."

d. We find them trying to undermine each other: "You don't really like chicken" or "You must be crazy to like chicken."

e. Always we find them accusing and evaluating morally: "You are bad and selfish for not wanting to eat hamburger. You never do what I want. You have mean intentions toward me."

A couple with functional styles of disagreeing, on the other hand, would be more likely to solve their problems by taking turns, by finding an alternative that pleases them both, or by going their separate ways—one to eat chicken, the other to eat hamburger.

In focusing immediately on "win-lose" solutions when there is a problem, family members prevent any creative and conflict-free negotiations that emanate from and meet the needs of all involved. Needs include basic conditions (e.g., to be trusted, to be considered) that must be addressed in order to arrive at a satisfactory solution. In the preceding example, for instance, a basic need of the couple may be to spend the evening together, and a viable solution must necessarily take this need into consideration.

4. Effective decision making requires the ability of family members to generate alternatives, which is closely parallel to group brainstorming in which members generate options, no matter how far-fetched, without criticism or censorship. Individuals manifest this skill when they:

draw from a repertoire of ideas that are not merely variations on a single theme but rather different categories of solutions to a given problem. The issue is whether the individual thinks in terms of options: "I could do this, or that, or I could even do that . . ." or, in contrast, characteristically forecloses without considering alternative routes.

(Spivack, Platt, & Shure, 1976, p. 5)

In the assessment process, then, your task is to determine to what extent families identify alternatives in contrast to quarreling over competing solutions.

5. Effective decision making requires ability on the part of family members *to weigh* alternatives. Decisions may be made in families after information gathering, input by members, and deliberation; or decisions may be made impulsively without gathering or weighing relevant information or without considering the needs of family members in relation to possible solutions.

6. Effective decision making also requires that the family organize to carry

out decisions through assignments to individual members. Planning to implement
a decision is just as important as making
the decision initially. Some systems are so
disorganized and chaotic that members
have great difficulty either in making a
decision or implementing it. In other systems, members lack motivation to carry
out decisions because their input was not
elicited or considered in the decision-
making process. Thus, even when decisions have been made in the system, the
process may break down at the point of
implementation. Ascertaining the extent
to which families can implement as well
as make decisions is a key task in assessing family functioning.

7. Effective decision making also requires the system to allow for negotiation
and adjustment of earlier decisions based
on new information and emerging individual and family needs. Some systems, of
course, are much more responsive and
flexible in relation to this item than others.

In assessing the family's decision-
making style, then, you should elicit information and view the processes you observe in relation to the preceding criteria.
Keep in mind that you are looking for
functional as well as dysfunctional patterns in each of these areas. Keep in
mind, too, that the decision-making skills
we have described encourage optimum
family functioning as it is perceived in
Western culture. These decision-making
skills are usually lacking in troubled families and are often underdeveloped even
in well-functioning families in Western
culture. Such skills are also often lacking
in families from different ethnic backgrounds, for many cultural groups have no
frame of reference for "joint decision
making" and, in fact, espouse cultural
values prescribing behavior that is in direct contradiction to the methods of decision making we discuss here and in Chap-

ter 15. Including family members in
decision making and assuring that the
needs of all are satisfied is a Western
culture ideal advocated by helping professionals and social scientists. Although we
espouse the need for families to learn
skills in decision making, practitioners
must assess whether introducing these
skills to family members will facilitate
family functioning or cause family disruption by disturbing patterns that are deeply
engrained and culturally sanctioned.

Family Affect and Range of Feelings Expressed

In their authoritative research on characteristics of distressed and optimally functioning families, Lewis et al. (1976) stress
that feelings expressed in a family are
intimately related to the structure of the
system. In systems that have rigid, inflexible boundaries, unclear structure, and
the lack of differentiation of members,
the prevailing mood may be one of despair, hopelessness, depression, anxiety,
hostility, guilt, cynicism, or apathy. Commenting on this phenomenon in a later
volume, Beavers (1977) speculates on the
reason for the negative affective climate
that permeates such severely dysfunctional families:

I believe *expectations,* that is, the results one
expects from human encounters, are central
to these observations. Severely dysfunctional
family members believe that encounters inevitably produce a destructive result, that human
interaction is necessarily oppositional. To appreciate this expectancy is to understand the
result of disturbed communication patterns:
the prevention of genuine encounter. It also
explains the pervasive, unpleasant feeling
tone, since the choice is either to avoid conflict
and to be alone or to engage in encounters that
threaten the self, relationships, and the family
system.

(p. 50)

By contrast, Beavers points out that optimally functioning families have a permeating atmosphere of optimism, empathy, warmth and affect, goodwill, and positive emotional tone, based on the expectation that human encounters produce satisfaction and that responsiveness to others and clear expressions of feelings will be rewarded.

Although observation of the system as a whole will reveal a "family character" in regard to mood or tone, expressions of individual affect may vary within the range tolerated by the family system. Further, individuals from different families develop diverse styles in relation to the range and intensity of feelings expressed. Some individuals, for example, seem emotionally numb or almost void of feelings, experiencing great difficulty "getting in touch with" any inner emotions. Other persons may readily express one particular kind of feeling, such as anger or feelings of despair or guilt, but not be able to reveal tender and vulnerable feelings, such as love, care, hurt, or pain. Still other persons are able to experience and express a wide range of feelings with little difficulty. While some individuals are placid and slow to register emotions, others are mercurial, responding intensively to the slightest stress or turn of events. Finally, while some persons are "incurable optimists," others are intractably depressed or pessimistic or experience extreme mood swings between optimism and despair.

The extent to which family members are able to express caring and love for each other is a vital dimension of assessment. Clients vary dramatically in their ability to "own" or to express verbally their tender feelings of caring to other family members. For instance, in response to a question of whether she ever told her daughter that she loved her, one client declared emphatically, "I could never do that!" Manifesting caring through touch or other nonverbal manifestations is also very difficult for some clients. Many parents, for instance, rarely touch or hug their children once they are old enough to dress, feed, and care for themselves. Since members of family systems vary in their ability to tolerate and express verbal and nonverbal affection and in their preferred modes of expressing tender feelings, you will need to weigh a family's style in relation to the following questions to gauge the amount of change that may be necessary or feasible:

1. To what extent are care and affection expressed verbally and nonverbally and by whom?

2. To what extent are caring behaviors perceived and/or appreciated by intended recipients?

3. To what extent are individual members dissatisfied with low levels of caring messages from others in the family?

4. To what extent do individual members of the family feel they would like to increase caring messages to others or to be the recipients of such messages?

5. How flexible are individual members and the system as a whole in making adjustments in this area? What are the tolerable limits?

In summary, we recommend that you assess the functionality of the family's affective styles, both at the individual and systems level, in meeting the basic nurturing needs of family members. Keep in mind, however, that you must assess the affectional patterns of ethnic minority families in the context of the family's culture, for the culture will dictate to a large extent whether and in what ways family members show affection to each other. In Polish families, for example, "mutual respect rather than displays of affection is the most noticeable external trait in the husband-wife relationships" (Mondykowski, 1982, p. 398).

Family Goals

The family is a social organization in which members typically cooperate and coordinate their efforts in order to achieve certain goals. According to Briar (1964), family goals spring from two primary sources. First, families usually adopt and have in common goals established by society; that is, socializing of children, transferring major cultural patterns essential to the maintenance of society, and meeting certain personal needs of family members. A second source of goals instrumental in shaping family structure is individual goals that marital partners bring with them into the family.

Goals that families espouse may be openly recognized and articulated by the family or they may be covert and even beyond the family's awareness. "We want to put the kids all through college" or "We want to retire by the time Ted's 45 years old" are examples of explicit goals held by a family. Covert or unrecognized goals that may have a profound influence on a family system might be, "We have to be at the top of the social ladder" or "We have to present the picture of being an ideal family." Briar points out that goals often are not explicit, and that when families are in crisis, the system's goals and their ordering often become more apparent, for at these times families may be forced to choose between competing goals and values. Briar observes, for example, that a wide variety of responses would be observed if one were to study a number of families confronted with a sudden and drastic reduction in income:

One family, for example, will give first priority to the expenditure of its limited financial resources to maintaining a very adequate diet for the children and will sacrifice other things in order to do so. Another family will sacrifice other things, even food, in order to make sure that the children are exceptionally well dressed. Still another family may sacrifice everything else to maintain payments on an expensive car. Such differences, which at first seem erratic and even irrational, often are comprehensible when the prior goals and aspirations of the family are understood.

(p. 250)

In most families, members vary in regard to the goals each considers important and the value each attaches to common goals. As in any organization, a family functions best when there is a high degree of consensus concerning family goals and provision within the system to negotiate and to take into consideration the unique needs, aims, and wishes of individuals. Briar, in fact, observes that, "The degree of consensus which develops among family members regarding the ranking of family goals can be a crucial factor in the family's ability to cope appropriately with crises" (p. 248). Because goals often are not explicit, however, differences among family members in relation to major goals and expectations may not be worked through, creating dissension and disappointment within the group. Further, because of pressures from the most powerful or influential members of the group, the family may give lip service to particular goals, although several or the majority of the members may not agree in principle with them. These families then become particularly vulnerable to breakdown under stress.

Many interactional patterns in families evolve in part to achieve goals. Briar, in fact, observes that if practitioners examine the family's interactions without considering the goals of the system, they may miss the meaning of patterns they identify. To illustrate this and other points that we have discussed throughout this section, consider the following case example of a covertly held goal around which family energies are extensively organized:

In the White family, an overriding goal of the family was to "keep the house clean," a goal set and maintained by Mrs. White, who felt constant inner pressure to keep her house tidy in order to avoid criticism from her own mother and other relatives. Often depressed, Mrs. White spent much of her time in her room and participated only infrequently in the housecleaning; however, she kept constant pressure on her younger daughters, ages 14 and 16, to keep the house clean and orderly. To her two older girls, attending school and holding down part-time jobs, however, she gave permission to participate only minimally in housecleaning chores because "they're tired when they come home and need time to relax and study." Seeing the older girls often excused from housecleaning (even when they left messes), the two younger girls were extremely resentful and often complained bitterly to their father about the situation. Further, they attacked the older girls with accusations such as "You don't act like you're members of the family" or "You don't care about anybody around here." Assuming the role of their absent mother, they monitored the older sisters, pointing out the messes they had created and ordering them to clean them up, which the older girls always refused to do. Feeling mistreated and misunderstood, the older daughters defended themselves and counterattacked by name-calling and threatening. Trying to maintain peace, Mr. White consistently served as a mediator between the warring factions and often picked up or cleaned the house to avoid the inevitable disputes that would arise when chores were assigned to his daughters. Whenever his wife intermittently emerged from her room, Mr. White also felt compelled to serve as mediator between her and the daughters because she usually found something out of order and would angrily blame one of the younger daughters for "not doing her job."

In our illustration, all of the White family adhered to the mother's goal of keeping the house clean. Because the younger girls experienced much more pressure than the older girls, however, more of their energies were invested in carrying out or in persuading other members of the family to implement this goal. The unequal distribution of pressure in the family had shaped the alliances that were in place at the time this family initially sought therapy. Only as the practitioner carefully explored and clarified the family goal and rules associated with it were family members able to recognize the extent to which their behaviors revolved around this goal.

In summary, then, we offer the following questions to assist you in assessing family goals:

1. To what extent do clear goals guide the family's organization?

2. To what extent are members aware of the overriding goals of the family?

3. To what extent is there shared consensus among members regarding major goals and the priorities assigned to these goals?

4. To what extent is family conflict caused by the lack of consensus regarding primary goals of individual family members?

5. How functional are commonly held goals in meeting the needs of individual members and promoting the well-being of the group as a whole?

6. To what extent are the manifest dysfunctional interactional patterns related to covert goals espoused by the family?

In making assessments, also remember that it is important to identify strengths of families in relation to the preceding questions. For example, to the extent that goals are clear, that consensus exists regarding major goals, and that goals serve the needs of the individual members and of the group, families manifest key strengths on this dimension of family functioning.

As a word of caution, practitioners must view the family's goals in the family's cultural context and avoid the hazard of assessing the goals against those deemed desirable in Western culture. For example, Montiel (1973, p. 25) cites biased descriptions of "deficiencies" of Mexican-American families found in literature that is culture- and class-bound: "Parents indulge male children, which limits their desire to achieve; do not encourage independence; teach their children lax habits; do not stress education; are oriented to the present; speak only Spanish; and think too much about their own misfortunes." To avoid such biased evaluations, then, it is important not to view a family as deficient because it does not espouse mainstream American goals. Rather, it is important to determine the goals of such families and to assess them in the context of their cultural reference groups.

Family Myths and Cognitive Patterns

Earlier in this chapter, we discussed family rules and emphasized how they pervade all aspects of family life. Rules have both a behavioral and a cognitive component; that is, the behaviors manifested by family members flow from and are inextricably related to *shared cognitive perceptions* or *myths* about each other, the family unit, and the world at large. These shared perceptions may be congruent with the views of neutral outside observers or may be distortions of reality, that is, "ill-founded, self-deceptive, well-systematized beliefs" uncritically held by members (Goldenberg & Goldenberg, 1980, p. 65). Such distortions are often

part of the beliefs or myths subscribed to by the family that help shape, maintain, and justify interactional patterns and relationships, as the following case excerpt illustrates.

Over the past four years, 10-year-old Jeffrey Richards has been in constant difficulty with his teachers at school because of open defiance of classroom rules, argumentative behavior, and physical skirmishes with other children. As a result of these problems, Mr. and Mrs. Richards have changed Jeffrey's enrollment from one school to another several times during the past three years. Sharing the cognitive set that "the world is out to get us," Mr. and Mrs. R. view teachers and principals alike as punitive and vindictive and their son as "misunderstood." Given this perceptual set, they regard each school contact as a battleground in which they must argue, protest their rights, and defend their son. Continually bombastic, they alienate school personnel, pushing them to take extreme stands on issues that might otherwise be mutually negotiated if the parents were amenable. Further, the parents' constant negative and angry comments at home regarding Jeffrey's teachers and his school reinforce and foster their son's negative classroom behavior.

In the preceding example, the dysfunctional behaviors and cognitive processes of the Richards family are mutually reinforcing. The myths determine the behavior, which predictably elicits negative responses from school personnel. In turn, the family's negative encounters with the school reinforce and confirm their perceptions of the world as dangerous and their view that authoritarian figures cannot be trusted and are out to get them.

Other myths may also prevail in family systems, shaping the behavior and interactions among family members or with outsiders, including the following:

■ "Things are permanent and unchange-able in our family. No matter what we do, we are powerless to change our circumstances. We are victims of fate."

■ "Mother doesn't care about the kids; Dad does."

■ "Problems in the family will take care of themselves."

■ "It's a sign of weakness to apologize."

■ "Whenever anything goes wrong in the family, it is important to determine who is at fault."

■ "It's important to get even with people who hurt you."

■ "People (or a certain category of people) are no good."

Among the most destructive myths are persistent beliefs that single out one member as being different or deviant from the group, causing untold damage in human development. Assigned labels such as *sick, bad, crazy,* or *lazy,* a family member often becomes the scapegoat who is sacrificed in the interest of group unity, a phenomenon we discussed earlier in the chapter. Goldenberg and Goldenberg (1980) comment on this particularly harmful form of mythology, indicating that by labeling a member as deviant, the family:

is making a statement that the other family members are all well! This myth, once it becomes operational, may stay on (sometimes passed on from generation to generation) as an integral part of the family's transactions, a buffer against sudden change, the basis for explaining all interactions involving that labeled person. Because of its usefulness as a homeostatic mechanism, the myth is resistant to change. Despite efforts by the family to seek help for the "sick" person, they are likely to resist change and fight to maintain the status quo. To abandon the myth is to open up the issue of their own disturbances or dysfunction as a family.   (p. 69)

In many families (even relatively healthy ones!), members may carry permanent labels, such as "black sheep of the family," "intellectual one," "baby of the family," "strict parent," "family pet," "clown," "good child," or "dumb." These labels stereotype roles of family members, causing other members to relate to them on the basis of a presumed single characteristic and to overlook a wide range of attributes, attitudes, and feelings. With only a narrow range of behavioral options open to them, the growth of these members may be stifled. It should be noted that even positive labels (e.g., talented, handsome, bright) may separate and estrange a member of the family from others, for other members may resent the inordinate amount of attention, praise, and recognition accorded to the labeled member, whom they perceive as the favored one or pet of the family.

The processes of dysfunctional families are often replete with numerous myths. Wynne, Ryckoff, Day, and Hirsch (1958) speak of the concept of *pseudomutuality,* which refers to efforts of distressed families to maintain the appearance of having open, mutual, "give-and-take" relationships when, in fact, this is not the case. Through the pervasive myth that there is a close fit between their behavior and those of others in the family, members are forced into formal roles, sacrificing individuality in favor of uniformity and primary allegiance to the group. Any divergence from rigid family rules in the form of opinion, behavior, or attitude is forbidden, lest it lead to a disruption of the system or shake the illusion of family unity. This rigidly structured system is held together by yet another myth, a catastrophic expectation that open divergence from assigned roles will lead to personal and family disaster. Through myths calling for family unity, members of the family become so locked into fixed roles that it is almost impossible to escape. Wynne et al. contrast the phenomenon of pseudomutuality, thought to be characteristic of family organizations in which schizophrenia develops, to that of *mutuality,* a state of affairs in which each family member forms a separate and unique identity while respecting and valuing the uniqueness of others in the family. Differences and conflicts in such families are negotiated through open group process and decision making, rather than obscured or whitewashed.

Note that culture determines many of the cognitive patterns held by families. Cuban immigrants, for example, show a significantly greater fatalistic orientation than Anglo-Americans, frequently using linguistic expressions that allude to destiny, life, luck, God's will, and "what was written" (Queralt, 1984, p. 118). Just as Cubans have a fatalistic orientation, each cultural group has characteristics that influence members' view of their world. Noninterference as a way of being, a value characteristically held by American Indians and Alaska Native families, alters their perception of the world (Attneave, 1982). Deference to authority, a cultural value espoused by Asians, also influences the cognitive patterns developed by members of that culture.

Family Roles

Each person in a family carries a multiplicity of roles that are integrated into the family's structure and represent certain expected, permitted, and forbidden behaviors (Jackson, 1965). Although family roles may be assigned on the basis of legal or chronological status, traditionally many roles have been delegated to family members on the basis of gender. Thought to be more aggressive than women, males have been viewed as more suited for *instrumental* roles, such as earning money

or making decisions. Women, by contrast, have been thought to be more nurturant, cooperative, emotional, and tender and suited for *expressive* activities, such as providing nurturance, caring for children, expressing affection, and the like (D'Andrade, 1974). However, forces associated with the sexual revolution that has taken place during the past decade are changing and equalizing the roles and status of the sexes, freeing both men and women to assume roles once thought to be biologically determined and to be the territorial prerogative of one sex or the other.

In many marriages, the pervasive movement to equalize sexual roles has called into question traditional perceptions of marital roles, particularly in families in which previously unemployed wives have entered the work force. Consequently, many couples have had to change their living styles drastically. Couples have coped with these profound changes in various ways, some clinging tenaciously to traditional roles despite significant changes in their life situations and the world around them. Other marital partners have welcomed role changes and have made marked accommodations and changes in role definitions. Still other partners have experienced major disruptions in their relationships, culminating in severe conflicts and even divorce.

In accurately assessing the extent to which role performance and definitions are factors in problems of families, you must consider many factors including those associated with the sex-role revolution. To assist you in considering these various factors, we provide the following list of questions that bear on role assessment in families:

1. To what extent are role assignments in the family made on the basis of sexual status rather than factors such as abilities, interests, and available time of individual members to perform various roles?

Assigned by gender, marital roles may be inequitable in relation to the available time spouses have to perform them. Further, marital problems are often caused by one or both partners operating from a marital "contract" made years ago specifying "traditional" roles that are no longer functional in light of changing family circumstances. "You said you'd never go to work!" or "You said I'd never have to work!" are common indictments made by marital partners when the wife either wants or is forced to seek employment.

2. How clearly defined are roles in the family? Role strain may occur between marital partners when roles are ambiguous or too global, fostering dissension as a result of differing perceptions of expected role performance. Further, as we pointed out earlier, role boundaries between children and parents may be blurred. In extreme cases, such roles may even be reversed. Boszormenyi-Nagy and Spark (1973) refer to this process as *parentification* of children, a situation in which children are forced to take care of childlike parents and/or younger siblings at the sacrifice of their own childhood.

3. How satisfied are marital partners with their prescribed roles, and to what extent is each willing to consider adjustments when dissatisfaction is a key factor in family problems? Further, how flexible is the entire family system in readjusting roles in response to everyday pressures and changing circumstances? Role dysfunction may occur as members are pressed into rigidly defined roles that drastically restrict their range of behaviors. Rigidly defined roles place family members in a bind, for they must either accommodate, sacrificing their individuality in the process, or rebel, losing favor and alienating themselves from other family members. Rigid role prescriptions offer families little opportunity to adjust flexibly to outer pressures. Further, ill-defined roles make it difficult for systems to adjust adequately to changing circumstances or to mobilize under crisis situations.

4. How adequately do spouses perform in their designated roles as marital partner and parent?

5. To what extent do one or both marital partners receive messages from significant others outside the family (parents, other relatives, friends) regarding what their role definitions "ought to be"? What effect does this input have on the system?

6. To what extent are pressures and stresses caused in the family by *role overload,* a state of affairs caused when marital partners play too many roles at home and at work for the time and energy they have available?

As you consider the preceding guidelines in assessing the functioning of a family, you will probably note a number of family strengths. Marital partners may have clearly defined their roles, for example, and be functioning quite adequately as parents. Or if partners are dissatisfied with their roles, they may recognize the need to make adjustments during marital therapy and readily try to accommodate to the other partner. Our point is that in the assessment process it is important to recognize and accredit the many strengths that couples and families may manifest with respect to role functioning—strengths that may otherwise be obscured by their presenting difficulties.

As you assess the processes of any family, you must necessarily take into consideration the role of culture in determining the definition of roles and the distribution of labor in the family, for each culture has different expectations or norms concerning male-female roles. Wong (1983, p. 28), for instance, describes female and male roles in Samoa:

In Samoa, men are dominant in rank and women are subordinate such that women "stay put" on their home grounds and men move about. . . . The women are assigned work which is considered light (matweaving) and men perform work which is heavy (preparing the umu). Women's tasks are usually focused around the household compound or village center (housekeeping and sanitation), whereas the activities of men are away from the household compound and village center (hunting and plantation work).

Because each culture has its own definition of male-female roles, practitioners must determine these roles for ethnic minority families, assess their "goodness of fit" with the needs of family members, and determine to what extent families are amenable to change culturally determined roles that adversely affect family functioning.

Communication Styles of Family Members

One theme that cuts across many cultural groups is that of patterns discouraging the open expression of feelings. Although Western culture espouses the value that openness and honesty are the best policies, the reality is that most people have considerable difficulty in asserting themselves or in confronting others, particularly in ways that are facilitative rather than destructive. Because of strongly embedded norms, people in many other cultures are much less open than even those in Western society. In Asian culture, for example, free participation and exchange of opinions contradict Asian values of humility and modesty (Ho, 1987). In Hawaiian culture, "it is totally unacceptable to resolve conflicts openly and through confrontation" (Young, 1980, p. 14). The Irish, too, have communication patterns that differ from the Western ideal as McGoldrick (1982b, p. 315) observes:

The Irish often fear being pinned down and may use their language and manner to avoid it. The affinity of the Irish for verbal innuendo, ambiguity, and metaphor have led the English to coin the phrase "talking Irish" to describe the Irish style of both communicating and not communicating at the same time.

Problems experienced by some families, then, may partially arise because of cultural prohibitions against openness, and in some instances, practitioners can assist clients to understand their cultural norms and make decisions as to whether they are willing to change communication patterns and styles that impact negatively on relationships. In other instances, practitioners may need to work more subtly to bring about enough openness in the system to promote the growth of family members. Falicov (1982, p. 148) describes such an indirect approach in working with Mexican-Americans:

When feelings are subtly elicited by the therapist, Mexican Americans respond much more openly than when they are asked to describe and explain their feelings and reactions. An experiential communication approach with emphasis on "telling it like it is" or "baring one's soul" or interpretations about nonverbal behavior will be threatening insofar as it challenges inhibitions about personal disclosure and supports symmetrical interactions.

Whether or not family communication patterns are culturally influenced or determined, they may be faulty, causing significant problems and pain for family members. Practitioners thus must be prepared to assess the impact of a family's communication styles upon the problems of members. To do so, they must be aware of the complexities of communication and prepared to assess the functionality of members' communication styles across a number of dimensions, as illustrated in the following discussion.

Congruence and Clarity of Communication Family members convey messages through verbal and nonverbal channels and qualify those messages through other verbal and nonverbal messages. A task of practitioners, therefore, is to assess the *congruency* of communications, that is, whether there is correspondence between the various verbal and nonverbal elements of messages. According to Satir (1967) and other communication theorists, messages may be qualified at any one of three communication levels:

1. *Verbal level*—When people explain the intent of their messages, they are speaking at a metacommunication level. For example:

- "I was trying to see if you agreed with me."

- "I thought you were feeling bad, and I was trying to comfort you."

Contradictory communications occur when two or more oppositional messages are sent in sequence via the same verbal channel:

- "I love you. . . . I hate you."

- "You should follow my advice. . . . You need to make your own decisions."

2. *Nonverbal level*—People qualify their communications through many nonverbal modes, including gesture, facial expressions, tone of voice, posture, intensity of eye contact, and the like. Nonverbal messages may:

a. Reinforce verbal messages.

- A mother smiles at her child and says, "I love you."

- A husband says to his wife that he is pleased that she has found a new job, and his countenance conveys his genuine pleasure.

b. Contradict or modify verbal expressions.

- A lover says, "Come closer, darling, let's make love," and then stiffens.

- With a bored look on his face, a friend says, "Of course I'm interested in what you've been doing lately."

c. Contradict or modify nonverbal expressions.

- A person behaves seductively but pulls back when the other makes affectional overtures.

- A visitor puts on his coat to leave and then lingers in the doorway.

3. *Contextual level*—The situation in which communication occurs also reinforces or disqualifies the verbal and nonverbal expressions of a speaker. For example, a mother leans over to her misbehaving child during church services and threatens, "If you don't stop that, I'm going to spank you *right now!*" The context or situation in which she sent the message, then, inherently disqualifies her verbal expression.

Functional communicators identify discrepancies between levels of communication and seek clarification when a person's words and expressions are disparate. They also are receptive to feedback and clarify their own communications when they have sent incongruent messages. Vital to assessment, then, is the task of ascertaining the extent to which there is congruence or correlation between the *verbal, nonverbal,* and *contextual* levels of messages on the part of individuals in a family system. The more distressed the system and the more symptomatic the behavior, the more likelihood that surface messages are contradicted by other communications that leave family members bewildered, angry, hurt, and in binds from which they see no way of extricating themselves.

In addition to considering the congruence of communications, it is important to assess the *clarity* of messages. Laing (1965) uses the term *mystification* to describe how some families befuddle or mask communications and obscure the nature and source of disagreements and conflicts in their relationships. Mystification of communications can be accomplished by myriad kinds of maneuvers, including disqualifying another person's experience ("You must be crazy if you think that"), addressing responses to no one in particular when the intent of the speaker is to relay a message to a certain person, employing evasive responses that effectively obscure knowledge of the speaker, or utilizing sarcastic responses that have multiple meanings and are hard to decipher (Lewis et al., 1976). A more exhaustive listing of response categories that represent obstacles to communication and may serve to cloud communications is provided and delineated in the following section.

Barriers to Communication   In Chapter 7, we identified a number of barriers to communication that, when utilized by practitioners, block client communication and impede therapeutic progress. Likewise, clients often repetitively respond with these and other similarly destructive responses in their communications with others, preventing meaningful exchanges and creating conflict and tension in relationships. In the following list, we include categorical responses that obstruct open communication and prevent genuine encounters in relationships:

1. Prematurely shifting the subject or avoiding topics.

2. Overgeneralizing.

3. Asking excessive questions.

4. Sympathizing, excusing, or giving false reassurance.

5. "Mind reading," diagnosing, interpreting.

6. Dwelling on negative historical events in a relationship.

7. Underresponding.

8. Failing to express opinions.

9. Verbally dominating interaction.

10. Speaking in a categorical, "black-and-white," "I'm-right-you're-wrong" manner.

11. Agreeing or disagreeing excessively.

12. Giving advice frequently.

13. Negatively evaluating, blaming, name-calling, or criticizing.

14. Directing, ordering, threatening, admonishing.

15. Using caustic humor, excessive kidding, or teasing.

Assessment of problematic communication of couples and families must also include behaviors on a nonverbal level including, for instance, glaring, turning away from a family member, turning red in the face, fidgeting, shifting posture, pointing a finger, raising the voice, looking with menacing expressions or with expressions of disgust or disdain. As we emphasized in the previous section, the practitioner also needs to be aware of discrepancies between verbal and nonverbal levels of communication.

All families have communication barriers within their conversational repertoires. Members of some families, however, monitor their own communications and adjust their manner of responding when they have had a negative impact on another person. Indeed, such families have "rules" that prevent many kinds of negative communications, for example, "We do not yell or call people names in our family," or "It is important to listen attentively when someone is talking to you." Other families have destructive entrenched styles of communication that pervade many of their exchanges, and members manifest little awareness of their aversive styles. Further, members of these families tend to assume little responsibility for the negative impact of their communications upon others and resist giving up destructive modes of communication in favor of others that are more facilitative. As you observe the communication styles of families, then, it is important to assess: (1) the presence of patterned negative communication, (2) the pervasiveness of such negative patterns, and (3) the relative ability of individual members of the system to modify habituated communication styles.

In addition to assessing the preceding factors, it is also vital to ascertain the various combinations of styles that occur repetitively as individual members of the system relate and react. For instance, in a marital relationship, one partner may frequently dominate, criticize, or accuse the other, whereas the other may defend, apologize, placate, or agree, as illustrated in the following exchange between two marital partners (Larsen, 1982):

WIFE: You never spend time with Jody [*their child*]. It's more important to you to play with your CB radio and talk to people you don't even know.

HUSBAND: I do spend time with her [*gives example*]. You just don't ever notice.

WIFE: I do notice. You spend precious little time with her. You can hardly wait to get back to your radio.

HUSBAND: Last Saturday I spent several hours with her. [*Begins to elaborate on how he spent the time.*]

In the preceding exchange, the wife consistently attacks the husband, who just as consistently defends his position, thus manifesting a "fault-defend" pattern of marital communication (Thomas, 1977). Such patterns that involve exchanges of different types of behavior have been designated as complementary patterns. In such instances, the conflictual issues or content discussed changes, but the stylized categories of communication of each partner and the manner in which they orchestrate their scenario remains unchanged. Further, repetitions of the same type of partner-to-partner interchanges will be manifested across many other areas of the couple's interaction.

The thematic configurations that occur in marital communication are limited in number and vary from couple to couple. For instance, rather than the "fault-defend" pattern just illustrated, spouses may engage in reciprocal or symmetrical patterns in which each attacks, blames, and continually finds fault with one another, i.e., a "fault-fault" pattern. Another marital pair may "collude" by talking only about superficial matters or matters extraneous to the relationship, thereby consistently avoiding disagreements or openly sharing feelings or complaints.

Assessing the communications of entire families is much more complex than assessing couple communication because of the greater number of relationships involved. Each person in the family has stylized ways of communicating that interface in patterned ways with the thematic communications of other family members. For example, a father may continually serve as a spokesperson or "mind reader" for others in the family (e.g., "You don't really feel that way" or "Randy, you're not hungry; you just like to eat"). Stylized reactions of family members to the father's patterned behavior may range from objections to the mind-reading activity ("That's *not* how I feel!") to nonverbal withdrawal (e.g., turning away from the father, slumping in chair), or tacit approval ("We always see eye to eye").

Receiver Skills A third critical dimension of communication is the degree of receptivity or openness of family members to the inner thoughts and feelings of other members in the system. Receptivity is manifested by the use of certain "receiving skills," which we will discuss shortly. Before considering these, however, it should be stressed that, in severely disturbed families, members rarely validate through attentive, supportive, or encouraging responses the unique perceptions and responses of others. Rather, the reactions of members are often in the form of ridicule, negative evaluation or depreciation of character, or other critical or disparaging remarks that consistently punish or invalidate the expression of personal thoughts and feelings of members. In such families, members also engage frequently in "dual monologues"; that is, they communicate simultaneously without acknowledging the responses of others. In healthy families, by contrast, members invite, welcome, and acknowledge the views and perceptions of each other. Members also feel free to express agreement or disagreement openly, knowing that even though so doing may sometimes spark conflict or argument, their rights to varying perceptions of events are protected within the system.

When comparing processes of optimally functioning families with those of troubled families, it becomes evident that the former possess several categories of verbal and nonverbal responses that are noticeably absent in the latter. Included in these responses are messages that convey understanding, demonstrate respect for the uniqueness of the sender's experience, and invite further expression and exploration. Facilitative responses that convey such understanding and acceptance are as follows:

1. Physical attending (i.e., direct eye contact, receptive body posture, attentive facial expressions).

2. "Listening" or paraphrasing responses by family members that restate in fresh words the essence of a speaker's message (e.g., "You seem to be saying that . . . ," or "I sense you're feeling . . .").

3. Responses by receivers of messages that elicit clarification of messages (e.g., "I'm not sure what you meant. Will you tell me again?" "Am I right in assuming you meant . . . ?").

4. Brief responses that prompt further elaboration by the speaker (e.g., "Oh," "I see," "Tell me more.").

In assessing communication styles of families, you must gauge the extent to which individual members (and the group at large) utilize the facilitative categories of communication identified in the preceding list. Many distressed families almost entirely lack these response categories in their communication repertoires. Fortunately, educative interventions can be employed to assist members to develop these communication skills.

Sender Skills A fourth critical dimension of communication is the extent to which members of families can share their inner thoughts and feelings with others in the system. Lewis et al. (1976) refer to this quality as "I-ness," that is, "the ability of individual family members to express themselves clearly as feeling, thinking, acting, valuable, and separate individuals and to take responsibility for thoughts, feelings, and actions" (p. 57). Operationalized, "I-ness" involves messages in the first person (commonly referred to as "I" messages) that openly and congruently reveal either pleasant or unpleasant feelings, thoughts, or reactions experienced by the speaker—"I (feel,

think, want) _____ because_____ ."
Healthy families allow members to be
candid, open, and congruent. Feelings are
shared freely, and people can apologize
and admit mistakes. By contrast, in disturbed families, communications are
characteristically indirect, vague, and
guarded, and individuals fail to take responsibility for feelings, thoughts, or their
own participation in events. Rather, members of these families are likely to use
"you" messages that obscure or deny responsibility for the speaker's feelings or
attribute responsibility for the feelings to
others (e.g., "You've got me so rattled, I
forgot"). Such messages are often replete
with injunctions (shoulds and oughts) concerning another's behavior or negatively
evaluate the receiver of the message (e.g.,
"You're really lazy, Jenny" or "You
shouldn't feel that way.").

Responses That Acknowledge Strength and Achievement and Accredit Growth

Critical to the development of high self-
esteem in individual family members are
messages from others that consistently
validate a person's worth and potential.
Such responses are rare in most troubled
family systems. Rather, the communication repertoires of such families are characterized by constant negative messages
that put down, evaluate, blame, attack,
criticize, or otherwise humiliate or invalidate the experiences of the members of
these systems. Children's self-esteem is
particularly vulnerable to such destructive communication processes. Unless
children frequently receive positive messages from others outside of the family
that disconfirm the negative and destructive messages, they gradually internalize
the deficient view of self portrayed by
parents and siblings. Further, as a result
of incessant repetitions of destructive
messages, children may develop negative

behaviors that match the predictions contained in the parents' messages (e.g.,
"You're just like your father; you'll never
succeed at anything."). Finally, children
often become conditioned to the extent
that they ignore or discount all positive
messages that are incongruent with their
negative views of self, thereby perpetuating the defective and flawed self-image
mirrored by others. These negative views
of self and the tendency of children to
"deflect positives" and to "play out" in
life the negative and ominous predictions
of significant others become an inherent
part of their adult character traits.

By contrast, members of healthy family
systems put more emphasis upon positive
attributes of members and what they can
become rather than on deficiencies and
dire predictions. Members of such systems, for example, view mistakes not as
failures, but as opportunities for growth.
When family members consistently respond with messages that validate the
inherent worth and unique achievements
of others in the system, the self-esteem of
participants continues to grow, and the
strong concept of self that a child develops in such a nourishing environment
becomes relatively impervious to the
storms of adult life.

Healthy families have many ways of validating the worth of members, including
warm physical expressions (touching, hug-
ging, tousling hair, and the like), direct verbal expressions of caring (e.g., "I love
you"), verbal and nonverbal attentiveness
to messages from others, and attention by
members to activities in which others in the
family are engaged (e.g., father notices his
young son playing with a baseball and begins teaching him to throw and catch the
ball). To a certain extent, most healthy families are also able to accredit the strengths,
growth, and positive actions of the members of the system, although the capacity of

even these families to observe and to give positive feedback on these vital areas is usually somewhat underdeveloped.

Family Strengths

All families, even those that function marginally, have a range of individual and group strengths that you should identify during the assessment process. However, because of the deeply entrenched focus on pathology in the helping professions, practitioners sometimes must revise their perceptional "sets" in order to discern undergirding strengths of the family that are not evident at first glance. Highlighting what *is* going right and what *is* working in troubled families is difficult because members of these families usually dwell upon problems and troubles. Thus, in assessments that involve families or couples, observing and accrediting the strengths inherent in the system requires deliberate and disciplined effort on your part.

In assessment, you also need to pay particular attention to the strengths of families from various cultural groups. Many of these groups have suffered historic discrimination or, as political refugees, have suffered extreme losses, including the loss of identity that accompanies loss of homeland, reference and support groups, and social and vocational roles that come with being political refugees. Often demoralized by discrimination, crippled by family disruption, and handicapped by difficulties with language, lack of education or job skills, and lack of resources or knowledge of how to obtain them, many minority families often feel powerless to cope with overwhelming circumstances. Yet these families have many strengths, and it is vital that practitioners identify these strengths and use them in the treatment process to empower families to accomplish desired changes. Speaking of black

families, Weaver (1982, p. 103) aptly captures the challenge practitioners face in accrediting and utilizing strengths to promote the well-being of troubled families from all cultures:

It is crucial to begin with the strengths of the family system; families move on strengths, not weaknesses. There is inherent strength in the design of every family and the social worker must help families use their own strengths in making choices and decisions that will enable them to achieve their own goals.

A study of the cultural backgrounds of families may reveal some of the strengths commonly found in members of their culture, including, for example, the commitment of many cultures to take care of their extended kin. The Hawaiians' generous hospitality, the American Indians' attitude of working in harmony with natural forces, the Jewish commitment to learning and achievement, and the German work ethic (manifested in respect for thoroughness, solid craftsmanship, and attention to detail) all represent significant strengths indigenous to each cultural group.

You should be able to identify many strengths of families and couples by observing their processes carefully. Examples of vital strengths include being willing to talk about problems or to accept help, demonstrating commitment to tackle painful issues, expressing caring feelings for family members, attempting to observe and discover the system's processes, or manifesting willingness to make adjustments or changes that will benefit the family.

The Family Life Cycle

The last criterion for assessing families involves the developmental stages through which families as a whole must pass. Based on the seminal work of Duvall (1977) and other theorists, Carter and McGoldrick (1988) offer a conceptual framework of the life cycle of the middle-class American family. This model, involving the entire three- or four-generational system as it moves through time, includes both predictable development events (e.g., birth, marriage, retirement), and those unpredictable events that may disrupt the life cycle process (e.g., untimely death, birth of a handicapped child, divorce, chronic illness, war, etc.).

Carter and McGoldrick identify six stages of family development, all of which address nodal events related to the comings and goings of family members over time. These stages include "the unattached young adult," "the new couple," "the family with young children," "the family with adolescents," "the family which is launching children," and "the family in later life." To master these stages, families must successfully complete certain tasks. The "unattached young adult," for example, must differentiate from the family of origin and become a "self" before joining with another to form a new family system. The "new couple" and the families of origin must renegotiate their relationships with each other. The "family with young children" must find the delicate balance between over- and under-parenting. In all the stages, problems are most likely to appear when there is an interruption or dislocation in the unfolding family life cycle, signaling that the family is "stuck" and having difficulty moving through the transition to its next phase.

Variations, of course, will occur in the family life cycle among cultures. Every culture marks off stages of living, each with its appropriate expectations, defining what it means to be a man or woman, to be young, to grow up and leave home, to get married and have children, and to grow old and die.

A Format for Employing Dimensions of Family Assessment

In the previous sections, we discussed in depth a number of pertinent criteria for assessing the behavior of couples and families at individual and systems levels. In employing these dimensions to formulate assessments and plan interventions, we recommend you utilize the following format:

1. Identify the dimensions that are most relevant to your clients. Although the dimensions apply to the processes of all couples and families, some may not be pertinent when viewed in the perspective of the presenting complaint and the nature of the help requested by the family. For example, a family may seek help because of stress caused by the advanced senility of an aged relative living in the home. Initial exploration may reveal no major deficits in functioning (e.g., ineffective style of decision making) that are contributing to the family's problem. Thus, the practitioner would narrow the assessment to an exploration of factors that contribute to the specific problem identified by the family.

2. Utilize the dimensions to guide your exploration of family behavior. After the first session, review the dimensions and develop relevant questions to further your exploration in subsequent sessions.

3. Utilize the dimensions as guidelines for compressing raw data into themes and patterns. Determine the family's or couple's rules or habitual ways of relating in relation to *each* relevant dimension. For example, ask yourself what the family's rules are in relation to decision making, communicating, and the other dimensions. Refer to appropriate discussions in the book for guidelines that will help you pinpoint specific rules.

4. Based on the dimensions, develop a written profile of functional and dysfunctional behaviors of *individual* members of the system. For example, with respect to the dimension of communication, a family member may often paraphrase messages of others and personalize statements (functional behaviors). The same family member may be prone to interrupt and to talk excessively, thus monopolizing the session at times (dysfunctional behaviors). Developing a profile of these two types of behavior for each family member will serve as a conceptual framework not only for assessing behaviors but for planning interventions as well.

5. Employ the dimensions to assess relevant behaviors of the *entire family,* developing a profile of salient functional and dysfunctional behaviors that are manifested by the system itself. Again utilizing the dimension of communication, functional behaviors of a family may include occasional listening responses and responses that acknowledge the contributions of others (e.g., "You did a good job"). In contrast, dysfunctional responses manifested by the same family may include labeling of members (e.g., "You're dumb") and frequent expressions of anger toward others.

Assessing Families in Their Cultures

As we have stressed throughout the chapter, practitioners must acquaint themselves with the cultures of families, for family behavior makes sense "only in the larger cultural context in which it is embedded" (McGoldrick, 1982a, p. 4). In a broader sense, however, practitioners face an even more challenging task of becoming open to cultural variability and the relativity of their own values. This means that practitioners must step outside their own belief systems and "no longer be 'triggered' by ethnic characteristics they may have regarded negatively nor be caught in an ethnocentric view that their group values are more 'right' or 'true' than others" (McGoldrick, 1982a, p. 25). Toward these ends we have committed the remainder of this chapter.

To this point, we have identified various dimensions of family assessment and have emphasized the need for practitioners to address two basic questions in relation to these dimensions:

1. What are the individual and family patterns in each of these areas?

2. To what extent are these patterns responsive to the needs of members and of the family as a whole?

The answer to the second question is critical in determining the direction of treatment with many families. When practitioners discern functional patterns, they seek to expand members' awareness of the family's strengths by highlighting these patterns. When practitioners discern dysfunctional patterns, however, they bring these patterns to the attention of family members to assist them to make decisions concerning whether to change them. Practitioners, of course, will find both functional and dysfunctional behavior in all families, irrespective of culture.

Practitioners must view the concepts of functional and dysfunctional within the context of the normative behavior of a family's culture, for what is dysfunctional in one culture may not be in another. Gwyn and Kilpatrick (1981) and Weaver (1982), for example, stress that the black culture is a distinct culture, and nonblack practitioners can often mistake black behavior patterns and lifestyle for dysfunction.[6] With respect to Latino families, Bernal and Florez-Ortiz (1982) also caution practitioners to be clear about the use of such terms as "enmeshment," "fusion," and "undifferentiated ego mass," for "the healthy interdependence of Latino families may appear as pathological fusion to the non-Latino observer" (p. 363). Numerous other authors offer similar cautions against practitioners imposing their own cultural biases on the ethnic families they serve. When such occurs, practitioners may intervene in ways that actually disrupt family functioning. Red Horse, Lewis, Feit, and Decker (1978), for instance, report several case examples of practitioners making grave errors in intervening with American Indian families. Not understanding the culture of these families, practitioners can punish Indian families for acting normally and can cause "irreparable alienation between family and human service professionals" (p. 68).

Ironically, even when practitioners understand the culture of various ethnic groups, the danger exists of stereotyping minority people. It is thus imperative that practitioners realize that members of minority groups may differ considerably from descriptions of typical behavior of such groups. Queralt (1984), for example, dispels the myth that there is a "typical Hispanic." Although Spanish-speaking people share some aspects of Hispanic heritage, similar language, and variations of a Catholic ideology, they nonetheless belong to diverse cultures and nationalities and vary in many other respects. Queralt also emphasizes that the norma-

tive values of a minority group are not necessarily professed by each and every member of that group. It would be difficult, for example, to find Cubans who showed absolute conformity with traditional Cuban-Hispanic values. Further, as Queralt points out, the values of cultural groups are not fixed but are always evolving and may be impacted by the degree of acculturation to mainstream society. The implications of Queralt's observations are critical to practitioners, for each family system is unique, and practitioners must be able to individualize each family within its cultural context.

As practitioners assess the processes of families from various cultural groups, they must also be cognizant of the extent to which a family has become acculturated into the mainstream culture, as we discussed in Chapter 8. All ethnic minority groups in the United States who have migrated or come as refugees face issues related to acculturation. The problems Asian refugees face in acculturating to mainstream society are extreme and plainly visible to practitioners. However, as McGoldrick (1982a) observes, even families who have migrated several generations ago continue to experience the complex stresses of migration, "having been forced to abandon much of their ethnic heritage . . . and thus hav(ing) lost a part of their identity." Such stresses "may be 'buried' or forgotten, but they continue . . . to influence the family's outlook" (p. 12).

In assessing the functioning of families of immigrants, practitioners must gain information concerning the family's migration and look for the continuing stresses on the family of accommodating to two (and sometimes more) cultures. McGoldrick (1982a) observes that the reasons immigrants left their countries—political persecution, poverty, wish for adventure, or the like—as well as whether they came alone to the new

---

[6]That nonblack practitioners often mistakenly view black cultural differences as dysfunction is understandable when viewed in light of Jones's (1983, p. 419) observation that "the black family is often viewed strictly as an impoverished version of the American white family, characterized by disorganization and a 'tangle of pathologies.' "

culture or with others have a significant impact on their adjustment.

Family disruption is a frequent theme in immigrant and refugee groups. The amount of disruption to Asian, Cuban, or other refugee families who have been uprooted from their homelands and have suffered losses in all aspects of their lives is particularly extreme. Queralt (1984, p. 119), for instance, describes the family disruption typically experienced by Cuban families:

Separations and lack of news from spouses, parents or children who were unable to leave Cuba or who did not choose to do so often cause grief, anger, anxiety, or guilt. Intergenerational conflicts are common as youngsters become acculturated more rapidly than their elders. Other family problems are related to the dramatic shifts in roles experienced by Cuban women . . . (who) must now work outside the home in order to provide needed income while continuing to bear the burden of housekeeping and child rearing.

Immigrants experience family disruption as factors such as migration, the mass media, and the new-found independence of working women call traditional values into question (Ghali, 1982). The migratory experience often causes family disruption also because migration-related tasks, such as finding work, preparing food, clothing, shelter, and learning a new language, often preempt the completion of family development tasks (Bernal & Florez-Ortiz, 1982).

Practitioners also need to assess the family's relative effectiveness in coping with its situation and rejuvenating its "connectedness" or roots with its cultural reference group. Timberlake and Cook (1984), for example, describe the coping efforts of Vietnamese refugees to rebuild their lives:

Family units react to the life crisis of uprooting and separation by seeking to mend or to re-

constitute their traditional structures as rapidly as possible. . . . families split apart during evacuation and resettlement work hard at rebuilding a social network by incorporating distant relatives, friends, and even strangers who are also refugees. (Indeed, the phenomenon of having literally been in the same boat seems to generate strong mutual support among refugees.) As more members are incorporated into the family unit. . . . the Vietnamese extended family (is) gradually restored.

(p. 110)

Practitioners must also assess a family's need for basic resources, such as food, health care, housing, financial aid, or job training, and their ability to secure such resources. Assisting families to meet their "survival" needs must often take precedence, in fact, over interventions to change family dynamics or to teach marital or parenting skills. Such interventions are simply not relevant to families who are in dire need of basic sustenance.

Finally, practitioners must assess the extent to which relatives, family, and friends are able to provide the family with needed support. In so doing, practitioners must be cognizant of the extended family pattern, which appears consistently in many cultural groups in the United States and is characterized by the inclusion of a complex kinship network of blood and nonrelated persons. Examples of cultural groups that have strong, well-developed extended family patterns include Hispanics, Asians, blacks, Hawaiian and other South Pacific groups, American and Alaskan Indians, Irish, and Italians. Wide variability exists, however, in these patterns. The extended network of a black family, for example, differs dramatically from that of Irish, Italians, or Mexican-Americans. American Indian family networks also assume a structure radically different from other extended family units in Western society.

11 ■ Assessing Group Processes

Assessment: A Vital Process for Group Practitioners

To competently serve as therapeutic agents, group leaders basically have a twofold task: (1) to accurately *assess* individual and group dynamics and (2) to *intervene* effectively to modify processes central to the growth of both individuals and the group. Accurate assessment of group processes must precede and undergird effective interventions. Leaders who fail to carry out thorough and ongoing assessments are prone to initiate interventions indiscriminately and overlook strategies that could enhance individual and group functioning. In such cases, interventions may be inappropriate, unproductive, or even destructive.

This chapter provides a framework that will enable leaders to assess group processes effectively and, ultimately, to sharpen their interventions to enhance the functioning of individuals and groups.

A Systems Framework for Assessing Groups

Like families, groups are social systems characterized by lawfulness and regularity. The operations within all social systems share an important principle, namely, that persons who comprise a given system

gradually limit their behaviors to a relatively narrow range of patterned responses as they interact with others within that system. Groups thus evolve implicit rules or norms that govern behaviors, shape patterns, and regulate internal operations. Employing a systems framework in assessing the processes of groups, leaders attend to the reciprocal patterned interactions of members, infer rules that govern those interactions, and weigh the functionality of the rules and patterns.

Knowledge that group processes can be conceptualized and organized into response patterns enables leaders to make systematic, ongoing, and relevant assessments. This knowledge can be comforting to inexperienced group leaders, who often feel they are floundering in group sessions. Some beginning group leaders, in fact, are greatly relieved and gain considerable confidence as they realize it is possible to "make sense" out of group process.

As leaders observe groups to discern patterned behaviors, they must concurrently attend to behavior manifested by individuals and by the group itself. Observing processes at both levels is difficult, however, and leaders sometimes become discouraged when they realize they attended more to individual dynamics than to group dynamics (or the converse), causing their formulations of either individual and/or group patterns to be vague or incomplete. We thus discuss strategies for accurately assessing both individual and group patterns in the remainder of the chapter.

Assessing Patterned Behaviors of Individuals

Some of the patterned behaviors group members manifest are *functional,* that is, enhance the well-being of individual members and the quality of relationships. Other patterned behaviors are dysfunctional in that they erode the self-esteem of members and are destructive to relationships. Many members of growth groups, in fact, join such groups because certain of their patterned dysfunctional behaviors produce distress in interpersonal relationships for themselves and others. Often, of course, these members are not aware of the patterned nature of their behavior nor of the fact that some of these entrenched behaviors cause interpersonal problems. Rather, group members often regard other persons as the source of their difficulties.

A major role of leaders in growth groups, then, is to aid members to become aware of their patterned behavioral responses, to determine the impact of these responses on themselves and others, and to choose whether to change such responses. To carry out this role, leaders must formulate a profile of the recurring responses of each member.

Understanding Content and Process

To formulate accurate assessments of individual behavioral responses, you must apply the concepts of *content* and *process,* which we discussed in the preceding chapter. To refresh your memory, content refers to verbal statements and related topics that members discuss, whereas process involves the ways members relate or behave as they interact in the group and discuss content. To expand your understanding of the concept of group process, consider for a moment the following description of a member's behavior in two initial group sessions:

In the first group meeting, John moved his chair close to the leader's. Several times when the leader made statements, John expressed agreement. In the second group meeting, John again sat next to the leader and used the pronoun "we" several times, referring to opinions he thought were jointly held by himself and the leader. Later, John tried to initiate a conversation with the leader concerning what he regarded as negative behavior of another group member in front of that member and the rest of the group.

This example describes *how* John is behaving and communicating rather than *what* he is saying, and thus it deals with process rather than content.

It is at the process level that leaders discover many of the patterned behavioral responses of individuals. The preceding example reveals John's possible patterned or thematic behaviors. For example, we might infer that John is jockeying to establish an exclusive relationship with the leader and bidding for an informal position of co-leader in the group. Viewed alone, none of the discrete behaviors in the preceding excerpt provides sufficient information to justify drawing a conclusion as to a possible response pattern. Viewed collectively, however, the repetitive responses warrant inferring that a pattern does, in fact, exist.

Identifying Roles of Group Members

In identifying patterned responses of individuals, leaders also need to attend to various roles members assume in the group. Members, for example, may assume *leadership* roles that are formal (explicitly sanctioned by the group) or informal (emerge as a result of group needs). Further, a group may have several leaders who serve different functions or who head rival subgroups.

Some members may assume *task-related* roles that facilitate the group's efforts to define problems, to implement problem-solving strategies, and to carry out tasks. These members may propose goals or actions, suggest procedures, request pertinent facts, clarify issues, or offer an alternative or conclusion for the group to consider. Other members may adopt *maintenance* roles that are oriented to altering, maintaining, and strengthening the group's functioning. Members who take on such roles may offer compromises, encourage and support the contributions of others, or suggest group standards. Still other members may assume *self-serving* roles by seeking to meet their own needs at the expense of the group. Such members attack the group or its values, stubbornly resist the group's wishes, continually disagree with or interrupt others, assert authority or superiority, display lack of involvement, pursue extraneous subjects, or find various ways to call attention to themselves.

Members may also carry labels assigned by other members, such as "clown," "uncommitted," "lazy," "dumb," "silent one," "rebel," "overreactor," or "good mother." Such labeling stereotypes members, making it difficult for them to relinquish the set of expected behaviors or to change their way of relating to the group. Hartford (1971, p. 218) elaborates:

For instance, the person who has become the clown may not be able to make a serious and substantial contribution to the group because, regardless of what he says, everyone laughs. If one person has established a high status as the initiator, others may not be able to initiate for fear of threatening his position. If one has established himself in a dependency role in a pair or subgroup, he may not be able to function freely until he gets cues from his subgroup partner.

One or more members may also be assigned the role of scapegoat, bearing the burden of responsibility for the group's problems and the brunt of consistent negative responses from other members. Such individuals may attract the scapegoating role because they are socially awkward and repeatedly make social blunders in futile attempts to elicit positive responses from others (Balgopal & Vassil, 1983; Klein, 1970). Or they may foster the role because they fail to recognize nonverbal cues that facilitate interaction in the group and thus behave without regard to the subtle nuances that govern the behavior of other members (Balgopal & Vassil, 1983; Beck, 1974). Individuals may also unknowingly perpetuate the scapegoating role they have assumed in their nuclear families. Although group scapegoats manifest repetitive dysfunctional behaviors that attract the hostility of the group, the presence of the scapegoating role signals a group phenomenon (and pattern), the maintenance of which requires the tacit cooperation of all members.

Individuals may also assume the role of an isolate, the characteristics of which Hartford (1971) described:

The social isolate is the person who is present but generally ignored by the others. He does not seem to reach out to others or he reaches out but is rejected. His lack of affiliation with others in the group may be due to lack of capacity on his part to get along with others, or he may differ in values, beliefs, and lifestyle from others enough to be deviant. He is not generally the scapegoat for if he were, he would be getting attention, however negative. The true isolate is ignored, his contributions go unnoticed, his opinions are not asked for.

(p. 208)

It is important to identify roles that members assume because such roles profoundly affect the group's capacity to respond to the individual needs of members and its ability to fulfill therapeutic objectives. Further, identifying roles is vital because members tend to play out in growth groups the same roles that they assume in other social contexts and need to understand the impact of dysfunctional roles on themselves and others. Some members, of course, assume roles that strengthen relationships and are conducive to group functioning. By highlighting these positive behaviors, leaders enhance members' self-esteem and also place the spotlight on behaviors other members may emulate.

Developing Profiles of Individual Behavior

In assessment, group leaders need to develop accurate behavioral profiles of each individual. To carry out this function, leaders record functional and dysfunctional responses of members manifested in initial sessions. The following lists of such typical behaviors should aid in this task.

Functional Behaviors

1. Expresses caring for group members or significant others.

2. Manifests organizational or leadership ability.

3. Expresses self clearly.

4. Cooperates with and supports others.

5. Assists in maintaining focus and helping the group accomplish its purposes.

6. Expresses feelings openly and congruently.

7. Accurately perceives what others say (beyond surface meanings) and conveys understanding to them.

8. Responds openly and positively to constructive feedback.

9. Works within guidelines established by the group.

10. "Owns" responsibility for behavior.

11. Risks and works to change self.

12. Counts in others by considering their opinions, including them in decision making, or valuing their differences.

13. Participates in discussions and assists others to join in.

14. Gives positive feedback to others concerning their strengths and growth.

15. Accredits own strengths and growth.

16. Expresses humor facilitatively.

Dysfunctional Behaviors

1. Interrupts, speaks for others, rejects others' ideas.

2. Placates, patronizes.

3. Belittles, criticizes, or expresses sarcasm.

4. Argues, blames, attacks, engages in name-calling.

5. Verbally dominates group "air time."

6. Gives advice prematurely.

7. Expresses disgust and disapproval nonverbally.

8. Talks too much, too loudly, or whispers.

9. Withdraws, assumes role of spectator, ignores, shows disinterest.

10. Talks about tangential topics or sidetracks in other ways.

11. Manifests distractive physical movements.

12. Is physically aggressive or "horses" around.

13. Clowns, mimics, or makes fun of others.

Table 11-1   Examples of Behavioral Profiles of Group Members

Name	Descriptive Attributes	Functional Behavior	Dysfunctional Behavior
June	35 years old Legal secretary 8-year-old son Divorced five years	Gave positive feedback several times Expressed feelings clearly Outgoing and spontaneous; adds energy to group	Ruminated several times about the past Sometimes interrupted others and dominated discussion
Raye	29 years old Homemaker Three children	Articulate Sharp at summarizing feelings of group Expressed ambivalence about attending group	Seemed to have self-doubt concerning validity of own opinions
Janet	34 years old Clerical supervisor Divorced one year	Initiated group discussion of several topics	Was dogmatic and unyielding about several of her opinions Became angry several times during session; appears to have short fuse
Pam	35 years old Truck driver Six children Divorced three years	Joined in discussions Accredited self for several strengths	Responses indicate she labels and puts down her children Twice challenged the comments of others
Dixie	30 years old Homemaker Two children Divorce in progress	Stated she came to group despite considerable apprehension Artist; exhibits paintings	Very quiet in session Acts intimidated by group Sat in chair slightly outside circle
Rachael	30 years old Unmarried	Readily shared problems Responsive to others Able to describe feelings Articulate	Seemed to pull the group toward feeling sorry for her through constant story-telling
Karen	31 years old Homemaker Three children Divorced one year	Seemed eager to work on problems Talked about self introspectively	Several times appeared to appease others rather than expressing how she really felt about issues
Elaine	45 years old Cafeteria worker Two teenagers Divorce in progress	Listened attentively to others Nodded approvingly when others spoke	Did not speak up in group

14. Aligns with others to form destructive subgroups.

15. Intellectualizes or diagnoses (e.g., "I know what's wrong with you").

16. Avoids focusing on self or withholds feelings and concerns pertinent to personal problems.

Table 11-1 is a record of a women's support group that illustrates how leaders can develop accurate behavioral profiles of each member by keeping track of the functional and dysfunctional behaviors manifested by members in initial sessions.

The profile of group members' behaviors in Table 11-1 identifies specific responses manifested by individuals in the group but does not necessarily identify their *patterned* or *stylized* behaviors. Recording specific responses of individuals at each session, however, aids in identifying recurring behaviors and roles members are assuming. With regard to roles, for example, a glance at the preceding profiles suggests that Dixie is vulnerable to becoming an isolate in the group.

Identifying Growth of Individuals

Because growth occurs in subtle and diverse forms, a major role of leaders is to document (and to assist the group to document) the incremental growth of each member. To sharpen your ability to observe growth of individuals, we suggest that you develop a record-keeping format that provides a column for notations concerning the growth members make from one session to the next or across several sessions. Without such a recording system, it is easy to overlook significant changes and thus miss vital opportunities to substantiate the direct relationship between their efforts to change and the positive results they attain.

The Impact of Culture

Assessment of individual functioning, of course, must be tempered by the individual's cultural background. Tsui and Schultz (1988) stress that "the group norms comprising the so-called therapeutic milieu are actually Caucasian group norms that, in themselves, resist intrusion and disruption from minority cultures" (p. 137). Thus, the behavior of a minority group member might be significantly negatively influenced by a group comprised largely of Caucasians, all sharing common values, who try to assimilate the minority member into what they see as the therapeutic milieu.

Gaining Information from Other Sources

In addition to direct observation, information concerning the behavioral styles of members can be obtained from many other sources. In the formation phase of the group, for example, leaders can elicit pertinent data in preliminary interviews with the prospective member or from family members, agency records, or practitioners who have referred members to the group. Within the group, leaders may also glean substantial data concerning patterned behavior of members by carefully attuning to and exploring members' descriptions of their problems and interactions with others.

Assessing Cognitive Patterns of Individuals

Just as group members develop patterned ways of behaving, they develop patterned cognitions, that is, typical or habituated ways of perceiving and thinking about themselves, other persons, and the world around them. Such patterned cognitions, discussed in depth in Chapter 18, are manifested in the form of silent mental speech or internal dialogue that individuals utilize to make meaning of life events. To use an analogy, it is as though various types of events in a person's life trigger a tape recording in his/her mind that automatically repeats the same messages over and over, coloring the person's perceptions of events and determining his or her reality. Examples of negative internal dialogue that tend to create problems for group members include repeated messages such as "I'm a failure," "I'll never be able to succeed," and "Other people are better than I am."

Patterned cognitions and behavior are inextricably related and reciprocally reinforce each other. The following example of a group member's problem illustrates the marriage between cognitions and behavior and the insidious effect that negative cognitions may have on a client's life:

Jean, a 25-year-old dental assistant, entered an adult support group because of problems at work that were jeopardizing her position. As

Table 11-2   Examples of Cognitive Themes of Group Members

Name	Functional Cognitions	Dysfunctional Cognitions
June	It's OK to risk talking about feelings. Other people will usually treat those feelings with respect and be responsive. I can do things to make myself feel better. I can get help from this group.	I've been hurt by the past. I don't think I'll ever get over it. I will always blame myself for what happened. I can't stop myself from talking so much. I always do that when I get anxious.
Raye	I care about other people. I want to help them. I'm willing to risk by staying in this group because I know I need help.	Other people's opinions are more important than mine. If I express my opinion, other people may disagree with me and/or think I'm not very bright. People in this group may not like me.
Janet	I have personal strengths. There are some good things about me. I'm a survivor. I can take care of myself.	My ideas, beliefs, positions are right; those of other people are wrong. I have to be right (or others won't respect me). You can't trust other people; they will hurt you if they can. The less you disclose about yourself, the better.

Jean reported her problems to the group, the following situation unfolded: Jean was experiencing severe negative reactions toward her employer, Dr. A. An attractive young dentist, Dr. A was the "darling" of the large dental organization for which Jean worked. Watching Dr. A, who was single, pursue other young women in the office, Jean concluded that he was disinterested and "bored" with her and that she was doing an inadequate job. As Jean worked daily with Dr. A, she made repeated statements to herself such as "He doesn't like me," "He'd rather have someone else as an assistant," and "There's something wrong with me." Jean worked at hiding her growing resentment toward Dr. A but ultimately could not contain her feelings. Defensive and easily riled because of what she constantly said to herself, Jean repeatedly snapped at Dr. A in front of patients. Angered and confused by Jean's irritable behavior, Dr. A began to grow annoyed himself and to relate to Jean more and more coolly. Jean interpreted Dr. A's behavior as evidence that she was correct in her conclusion that he did not like her and that she was inadequate not only as an assistant but as a person as well.

Because patterned behavioral and cognitive responses are inextricably interwoven and perpetuate each other, leaders must be able to intervene in groups to modify dysfunctional cognitions. Preliminary to intervening, however, leaders must fine-tune their perceptual focus to identify the thematic cognitions that are manifested in members' verbal statements. The following statements, for example, reveal conclusions members have drawn about themselves and others:

- Husband (*about wife's behavior*): She doesn't allow me to smoke in the house. (My wife is in charge of me.)

- I can't tell people how I feel. (If I do, they'll reject me or I will hurt them.)

- Member of alcoholics group: If I can't trust my wife, how can I stop drinking? (My fate rests in the hands of someone else.)

In the same manner that group leaders observe and record functional and dysfunctional behavioral responses of members, they can record the cognitive themes or patterns of members. Returning to the example of the women's support group cited earlier, note the cognitive responses of several members recorded by the leader in the same session, as illustrated in Table 11-2.

Leaders can help group members to identify cognitive patterns during problem exploration by asking questions such as, "When that happened, what did you say to yourself?" "What conclusions do you draw about others under those circumstances?" or "What kind of self-talk did you use to make yourself depressed when that happened?" Leaders can also teach groups to recognize manifestations of patterned cognitions. As the group grasps the significance of internal dialogue and attends to cognitive patterns manifested by members, leaders should accredit the group's growth by giving members descriptive feedback concerning their accomplishments.

Assessing Group Processes

As a group develops, it may not evolve patterned responses that support its therapeutic objectives. A group, for example, may split into several self-serving factions or subgroups that compete for control. Or members may develop a habit of socializing rather than focusing on legitimate group tasks. Some members may also repeatedly scapegoat other vulnerable members, harassing those members and blaming them for various group ills. In these and myriad other ways, groups may develop redundant behaviors that undermine the ability of members to aid each other in alleviating problems.

A primary role of group leaders is to observe evolving group behavior and to assess whether emerging patterns of behavior undermine or support the therapeutic purposes of the group. Once leaders have made such a determination, they then intervene to nurture functional group behaviors and to assist the group to modify behaviors destructive to individuals or to the group.

In order to view group behaviors in perspective, leaders must be able to assess these behaviors in the context of stages of group development. Successful groups progress at different tempos through natural stages, ultimately achieving full maturity, or the group's "working stage." These stages are described in the next section.

Stages of Group Development

Various models of group development provide practitioners frameworks for organizing a large body of observations and group properties and identifying thematic group behaviors. All the models identify progressive steps in group development, although they may organize these steps into four, five, or even six stages. For our purposes, we utilize a model developed by Garland, Jones, and Kolodny (1965), which delineates the following five stages:

1. Preaffiliation.
2. Power and control.
3. Intimacy.
4. Differentiation.
5. Separation.

We also refer you to Anderson (1979), Garland et al. (1965), Griffiths (1976), Hartford (1971), and Johnson (1974), sources from which we have drawn information in filling in the Garland, Jones, and Kolodny model.

Stage 1. Preaffiliation—Approach and Avoidance Behavior

The frame of reference used by Garland et al. to describe the group's initial stage is that of *approach-avoidance* behavior of members, whose tentativeness toward involvement in the group is reflected in their vacillating willingness to assume responsibility, to interact with others, and to support program activities and events. Hesitancy to participate is also manifested by tentative verbalization, and silence is common as members operate as separate individuals and are preoccupied with their own problems and feelings of uneasiness and apprehension that emanate from their first encounter with the group. Often fearful and suspicious, members tend to be apprehensive regarding the responses of others to their expressions, fearing possible domination, aggression, isolation, rejection, and hostility. Thus, behavior is wary, sometimes even provocative, as members assess possible social threats and attempt to discern the kinds of behaviors the group wants and expects. Members also tend to identify each other by status and roles and engage in social rituals, stereotyped introductions, and detailed intellectual discussions. They are uncertain as to how the group will benefit them, and their understanding of the group's purpose is fuzzy. At times, members employ testing operations to "size up" other members, to test the group's limits, to find out how competent the leader is, and to determine to what extent the leader will safeguard the rights of members and protect them from feared hurt and humiliation. Members also move tentatively toward the group at times as they seek to define common ground with other members, search for viable roles, and seek approval, acceptance, and respect. Much of the initial communication in the group is also directed toward the leader, and some members may openly demand that the practitioner assume a "take charge" approach by forcefully making decisions regarding group issues and structure and by issuing prompt directives to control the behavior of members.

Stage 2. Power and Control— A Time of Transition

The first stage merges imperceptibly into the second as members, having determined that the group experience is potentially safe and rewarding and worth preliminary emotional investment, shift their concerns to matters related to autonomy, power, and control. The frame of reference for this stage is that of *transition* in that members must endure the ambiguity and turmoil of change from a nonintimate to an intimate system of relationships while they try to establish a frame of reference whereby the new situation becomes understandable and predictable. Moving from a struggle of whether they "belong" in the group, members now become preoccupied with how they "rank" in relation to other members. Turning to others like themselves for support and protection, members evolve subgroups and a hierarchy of statuses, or social pecking order. Gradually, the processes of the group become stylized as various factions emerge and relationships solidify. Conflicts between opposing subgroups often occur in this stage, and members may team together in expressing anger toward the leader, other authority figures, or outsiders. Disenchantment with the group may show itself in hostilities, anger, striking out, withdrawal, or in confusion about the group's purposes. Verbal abuse, attacks, and rejection of lower status members may also occur, and isolated members of the group who do not have the protection of a subgroup may discontinue coming to sessions. Attrition in membership may also take place as individuals find outside pursuits more attractive than the conflicted group experience; depleted membership, indeed, may put the group's very survival in jeopardy.

Stage 3. Intimacy—Developing a Familial Frame of Reference

Having clarified and resolved many of the issues related to personal autonomy, initiative, and power, the group moves from the "preintimate" power and control stage to that of intimacy. As the group enters this stage, conflicts fade, personal involvement between members intensifies, and there is growing recognition of the significance of the group experience. Members also experience an increase in morale and "we-ness," a deepening commitment to the group's purpose, and heightened motivation to carry out plans and tasks that support the group's objectives. Mutual trust also increases as members begin to acknowledge each other's uniqueness, spontaneously disclose feelings and problems, and seek the opinion of the group. In order to achieve desired intimacy, however, members may suppress negative feelings that could produce conflict between themselves and others. In contrast to earlier sessions, members express genuine concern for absent members and may reach out to invite them to return to the group.

During this period of development, a group "character" also emerges as the group evolves culture, style, and a set of values. Clear norms are established, based on personal interests, affection, and other positive forces. Roles also take on form, as members find ways of contributing to the group, and leadership patterns become firmly settled. The frame of reference for members is a familial one as members liken their experience to that of their own nuclear families, occasionally referring to other members as siblings or to the leader as the "mother" or "father" of the group.

Stage 4. Differentiation— Developing Group Identity and an Internal Frame of Reference

The fourth stage is marked by tight group cohesion and harmony as members come to terms with intimacy and make choices to draw closer to others in the group. In this stage, group-centered operations are achieved, and a dynamic balance between individual and group needs evolves. Members, who participate in different and complementary ways, experience greater freedom of personal expression and come to feel genuinely accepted and valued as their feelings and ideas are validated by others in the group. Gradually, the group becomes a mutual-aid system in which members spontaneously give emotional supplies in proportion to the needs of each individual.

In experiencing newfound freedom and intimacy, members begin to perceive the group experience as unique, and as the group creates its own mores and structure, in a sense it becomes its own frame of reference. Customs and traditional ways of operating emerge, and the group may adopt a "club" name or insignia that accurately reflects the group's purpose. The group's energy is now channeled into carrying out purposes and tasks that are clearly understood and accepted. New roles, more flexible and functional than before, are developed to support the group's activity, and organizational structures (e.g., officers, dues, attendance expectations, rules) may evolve. Status hierarchies also tend to be less rigid, and members may assume leadership roles spontaneously as the need for particular expertise or abilities arises.

By the time the group reaches the differentiation stage, members have accumulated experience in "working through problems" and have gained skill in analyzing their own feelings and those of others in communicating their needs and positions effectively, in offering support to others, and in grasping the complex interrelationships that have developed in the group. Having become self-conscious about their own operations, groups bring conflict out into the open and identify obstacles that impede their progress. All decisions are ultimately the unanimous reflection of the group and are rigidly respected. Disagreements are not suppressed or overridden by premature group action, but rather the group carefully considers the position of any dissenters and attempts to resolve differences and to achieve consensus among members. New entrants serve as catalysts and may express their amazement at the insight shared by older members, who in turn become increasingly convinced of the value of the group. Members may now publicize their group meetings among peers, whereas previously membership in the group may have been linked with secret feelings of shame. Secure in their roles and relationships in the group, members may become interested in meeting with other groups or in bringing in outside culture.

Stage 5. Separation—a Time of Breaking Away

During this phase, members begin to separate, loosening the intense bonds often established with other members and with the leader, and to search for new resources and ties to satisfy needs. Group members are likely to experience a broad range of feelings about leaving the group and may manifest strikingly different behaviors in reaction to separation. Rather than identifying the various feelings and reactions of group members that may occur during the separation phase, however, we have reserved our treatment of this topic for Chapter 21, where we also discuss strategies the practitioner may implement in managing termination.

In summary, it is important to view dimensions of assessment such as decision making, roles, power structure, and communication in relation to the group's evolutionary development. The more advanced the group, the more functional are the behaviors of individual members in each of these areas. Likewise, the more functional the behavior of individual members, the more quickly the group moves through its various stages. The practitioner's role is thus to accelerate the group's development by helping members to assume functional behaviors consonant with each of the dimensions identified.

Importance of Understanding Group Development

Understanding stages of group development assists leaders to anticipate the thematic behaviors characteristic of each stage and to recognize the significance of behaviors as they occur in the group. Without this knowledge, leaders are prone to make errors, such as expecting group members to begin in-depth explorations in initial sessions or mistakenly concluding they have failed in their role when groups manifest the turmoil and discord typical of the power and control stage.

Leaders who lack knowledge of stages of group development may also ignore, rather than encourage, fleeting positive behaviors that herald the group's approaching a more mature stage of development. A vital role of leaders, in fact, is to aid groups in accelerating their progress by fostering functional behavior early in the group's life. Practitioners must thus be able to identify functional and dysfunctional group behaviors that emerge in early sessions and intervene to assist members to adopt behaviors that enhance the group's objectives. Practitioners, for example, may assist groups to "stay on task," to "count in" all members in decision making, to foster free expression of feelings, and to adopt many other behaviors that are hallmarks of a seasoned and fully developed group. Without a clear understanding of patterned behaviors of a mature group, practitioners cannot fulfill this role.

Identifying Patterned Group Behavior

To heighten your awareness of functional and dysfunctional patterned behaviors that may occur in groups, we provide contrasting examples of such behavior in Table 11-3.

The functional behaviors in the table are characteristic of a mature therapeutic group. However, note that facilitative group behaviors may emerge in the initial stages of development (i.e., preaffiliation, and power and control stages). These behaviors are usually fleeting, for the group must accomplish a number of developmental tasks, such as building trust and defining common interests and goals, before attaining the supportive and productive behaviors of the group's working stages (i.e., intimacy and differentiation stages). Brief or short-lived positive behaviors manifested early on in

groups include behaviors such as the following:

- The group "faces up to" a problem and makes a necessary modification or adjustment.

- The group responds positively the first time a member takes a risk by revealing a personal problem.

- Members of the group are supportive toward other members or manifest investment in the group.

- The group moves in a positive direction without the leader's guidance or intervention.

- The group works harmoniously for a period of time.

- Members effectively make a decision together.

- Members adhere to a specific group guideline, such as maintaining focus on work to be accomplished.

- Members give positive feedback to another member or observe positive ways the group has worked together.

- The group responsibly confronts a member who is dominating interaction or interfering in some way with the group's accomplishing its task.

- Members pitch in to clean up after a group session.

The preceding list of positive behaviors, of course, is by no means exhaustive. Once practitioners fine-tune their observational skills to register positive group behavior, they will catch glimpses of many newly developing behaviors that enhance a group's functioning. Practitioners can then intervene to facilitate the group's adoption of such functional behaviors. Their challenge, of course, is to focus on these fleeting behaviors before the moment is lost by authentically disclosing

Table 11-3 Examples of Group Behavior

Dysfunctional Group Behavior	Functional Group Behavior
Members talk on a superficial level and are cautious about revealing their feelings and opinions.	Members openly communicate personal feelings and attitudes and anticipate that other members will be helpful.
Members are readily critical and evaluative of each other; they rarely acknowledge or listen to contributions from others.	Members listen carefully to each other and give all ideas a hearing.
Dominant members count out other members in decision making; members make decisions prematurely without identifying or weighing possible alternatives.	Decisions are reached through group consensus after considering everyone's views and feelings.
	Members make efforts to incorporate the views of dissenters rather than to dominate or override these views.
Members focus heavily on negatives and rarely accredit positive behaviors of others.	Members recognize and give feedback regarding the strengths and growth of other members.
Members are critical of differences in others, viewing them as a threat.	Members recognize the uniqueness of each individual and encourage participation in different and complementary ways.
Members compete for the chance to speak, often interrupting each other.	Members take turns speaking.
Members do not personalize their messages but instead use indirect forms of communication to express their feelings and positions.	Members use "I" messages to speak for themselves, readily owning their own feelings and positions on matters.
Members speak for others.	Members encourage others to speak for themselves.
Members display disruptive behavior incompatible with group guidelines.	Members adhere to guidelines for behavior established in initial sessions.
Members resist talking about the here and now or addressing personal or group problems. Resistance may include distractive maneuvers such as fingering objects, whispering, and throwing spitballs.	The group is concerned about its own operations and addresses obstacles that prevent members from fully participating or the group from achieving its objectives.
Members show unwillingness to accept responsibility for themselves or the success of the group and tend to blame the leader when things are not going well.	Members assume responsibility for the group's functioning and success. The group manifests commitment by staying on task, assuming group assignments, or working out problems that impair group functioning.
Members dwell on past exploits and experiences and talk about issues extraneous to group purpose. Members also focus on others rather than themselves.	Members concentrate on the present and what they can do to change themselves.
Members show little awareness of the needs and feelings of others; emotional investment in others is limited.	Members are sensitive to the needs and feelings of others and readily give emotional support. Members also express their caring for others.

positive feelings and by documenting in behavioral terms the positive movement they have observed (Larsen, 1980).

The group may also manifest transitory negative behaviors in initial sessions. These dysfunctional behaviors may signal evolving group patterns that are not firmly "set" in the group's interactional repertoire. Counterproductive behaviors that may evolve into patterns include any of the examples of dysfunctional behavior listed in Table 11-3.

Just as we have suggested that you employ a record-keeping system for recording the functional and dysfunctional responses of individual members, we also recommend using the same type of system for recording the functional and dysfunctional behaviors of the group itself, adding a column to record the growth or changes that you note in the group's behavior.

Identifying Group Alliances

As members of new groups find other members with compatible attitudes, interests, and responses, they develop patterns of affiliation and relationship with these members. As Hartford (1971) points out, subgroup formations that evolve include pairs, triads, and foursomes. Foursomes generally divide into two pairs but sometimes shift to three and one. Groups as large as five may operate as a total unit, but generally these groups begin to develop subdivisions influencing "who addresses whom, who sits together, who comes and leaves together, and even who may meet or talk together outside of the group" (Hartford, 1971, p. 204).

Subgroupings that invariably develop do not necessarily impair group functioning. Group members, in fact, often derive strength and support from subgroups that enhance their participation and investment in the larger group. Further, it is through the process of establishing subgroups, or natural coalitions, that group members (like family members) achieve true intimacy. Problems arise in groups, however, when members develop exclusive subgroups that disallow intimate relationships with other group members or inhibit members from supporting the goals of the larger group. Competing factions can often impede or destroy a group.

To work effectively with groups, leaders must be skilled in identifying subdivisions and assessing their impact on a group. To recognize these subdivisions, leaders may wish to construct a sociogram of group alignments. Credited to Moreno and Jennings (Jennings, 1950), a sociogram graphically depicts patterned affiliations and relationships between group members by using symbols for people and interactions. Hartford (1971, p. 196) illustrates a sociogram that captures the attractions and repulsions among group members:

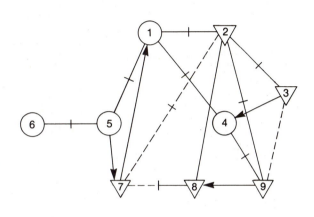

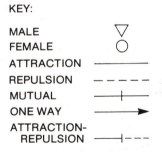

KEY:

MALE	▽
FEMALE	○
ATTRACTION	——————
REPULSION	— — — — —
MUTUAL	——+——
ONE WAY	————▶
ATTRACTION-REPULSION	——+— —

Source: Margaret Hartford, *Groups in Social Work* (New York: Columbia University Press, 1971), p. 196. By permission of Columbia University Press.

Sociograms are representations of alliances in a group at a given point, since alliances do shift and change, particularly in early stages of group development. Charting the transitory bondings that occur early in group life can be invaluable to leaders in deciding where and when to intervene to modify, enhance, or stabilize relationships between members.

We suggest you construct a sociogram of members' interactions after every session until you are confident that group relationships have stabilized in positive ways that support the group's therapeutic objectives. Be creative with your sociograms. You may wish to use different colors to show attractions, repulsions, or strength of relationships or to place members closer together or farther apart to convey emotional closeness or distance. Avoid trying to capture in a single sociogram the exact nature of relationships each member has with every other one in the group, as the drawing will become overly complicated. Rather, depict only the major subgroupings in the group and identify the relationships in which major attractions or repulsions are occurring.

Identifying Power and Decision-Making Styles

Groups as well as families develop ways of distributing power among members. To assure their needs are not discounted, some members may make bids for power and discount other members. Others tend to discount themselves and permit more aggressive members to dominate the group. Still others value power and actively pursue it as an end in itself. Involved in power struggles, groups may initially fail to make decisions on an "I count-you count" basis. Further, subgroups may try to eliminate opposing factions from the group or align themselves with other members or subgroups to increase their power. Groups, in fact, are sometimes torn apart and meet their demise because unresolved power issues prevent the group from meeting the needs of some members.

Power struggles that arise in groups are often caused by members aggressively competing over solutions to a problem. Interested members or factions may vigorously advocate opposing solutions that they are not willing to relinquish. Given these conditions, some members will win, and some will lose because ultimately only one of the competing factions can prevail.

Similar to assessing families, when assessing groups practitioners need to identify the current capacity of members to share power and resources equally among themselves and to implement problem-solving steps that assure "win-win" solutions (see Chapter 15). Increased ability of the group to "count in" all members must necessarily occur for the group to advance through stages of development into maturity. Zastrow (1987), in fact, points out that "when power is relatively balanced, members are generally more cooperative, believing they can influence the efforts of others" (p. 60). Members are also more committed to implementing decisions if they think they have had a fair say in making those decisions. Leaders can thus accelerate the group's progress through the various stages by assuming a facilitative role in teaching and modeling facilitative decision making and assisting members to adopt explicit guidelines for making decisions in initial sessions.

Group Norms and Values

Of central importance to group assessment are *group norms,* a term that refers to implicit expectations and beliefs shared by members concerning how they or others should behave under given circumstances. Norms are regulatory mechanisms that give groups a measure of stability and predictability by providing members with information concerning what they can expect from each other.

Norms may define *specific* behaviors of individuals that are appropriate or permissible or define the *range* of behaviors that are acceptable in the group. Group norms are thus similar to the family "rules" discussed in the previous chapter.

Just as families have processes for dealing with rule violations, groups also develop sanctions to reduce behaviors that are considered deviant and to return the system to its prior equilibrium (Lieberman, 1980). For example, an implicit group norm may be that the opinions of the informal leader are not to be challenged by other group members. If a new group member treads on this norm by questioning the opinion of the informal leader, other members may side with the informal leader against the "upstart," pressuring him or her to back away.

People often learn about the norms of particular groups by observing situations in which norms have been violated. Speaking of group members, Toseland and Rivas (1984, p. 67) note that, as members watch the behavior of others, "soon it becomes clear that sanctions and social disapproval result from certain behavior and that praise and social approval result from other behaviors." Once members realize that sanctions are applied to certain behaviors, they usually attempt to adapt their behavior to avoid disapproval or punishment. Sanctions are powerful regulators of behavior, as Lieberman (1980, p. 501) has observed: "Ordinarily, sanctions do not need to be exerted frequently or vigorously; rather, the anticipation of sanctions is often as effective in controlling deviant behavior as is actual application."

The extent to which members adhere to norms often varies. Some norms are flexible, and the psychological "costs" to members of violation are low or nonexistent. In other instances, the group's investment in norms is significant, and group reaction is severe when members violate such norms. The relative status of members, that is, the evaluation or ranking of each member's position in the group relative to the others, also determines the extent to which members adhere to norms, as Toseland and Rivas (1984, pp. 68–69) observe:

Low-status members are the least likely to conform to group norms since they have little to lose by deviating. This is less likely if they have hopes of gaining a higher status. Medium-status group members tend to conform to group norms so that they can retain their status and perhaps gain a higher status. High-status members perform many valued services for the group and generally conform to valued group norms when they are establishing their position. However, because of their position, high-status members have more freedom to deviate from accepted norms.

Norms may or may not support the therapeutic objectives of a growth group and should be viewed as to whether they are beneficial or detrimental to the well-being of members and the overall treatment objectives of the group. Examples of norms that may be functional and dysfunctional are presented in Table 11-4.

All groups develop norms, and once certain norms are adopted, they influence the group's response to situations and determine the extent to which the group offers its members therapeutic experiences. A major leader's role, therefore, is to identify evolving group norms and influence them in ways that create a positive ambience for change. Discerning them is often difficult, however, inasmuch as such norms are subtly imbedded in the group process and can be inferred only from the behavior occurring in the group. Leaders may be able to identify norms by asking themselves key questions such as the following:

Table 11-4 Examples of Group Norms

Functional	Dysfunctional
Risk by spontaneously revealing personal content about yourself.	Keep the discussion centered on superficial topics; avoid risking or self-disclosing.
Treat the leader with respect and seriously consider the leader's input.	Play the game, "Let's get the leader." Harass, criticize, or complain about the leader whenever the opportunity arises.
Focus on working out personal problems.	Spend time complaining about problems and don't commit the energy necessary to work them out.
Allow members equal opportunity to participate in group discussions or to become the focus of the group.	Let aggressive members dominate the group.
Talk about any subject pertinent to your problem.	Don't talk about emotionally charged or delicate subjects.
Communicate directly to other group members.	Direct comments to the leader.
Talk about obstacles that get in the way of achieving the group's tasks.	Ignore obstacles and avoid talking about group problems.

1. What subjects can and cannot be talked about in the group?

2. What kinds of emotional expressions are allowed in the group?

3. What is the group's pattern with regard to working on problems or staying on task?

4. Do group members consider it their own responsibility or the leader's to make the group's experience a successful one?

5. What is the group's stance toward the leader?

6. What is the group's attitude toward feedback?

7. How does the group view the contributions of individual members? What kind of labels and roles is the group assigning to them?

Asking such questions also enables leaders to increase their observations of redundant or patterned behavior of members. This is a vital point, for patterned behaviors are always undergirded by supporting norms. Another strategy for identifying norms is to explain the concept of norms to group members and to ask them to identify the guiding "rules" that influence their behavior in the group. This strategy enables members to bring to a conscious level the group norms that are developing and to make choices concerning norms that will increase therapeutic possibilities.

In addition to norms, every growth group will create a set of values held in common by all or most of the group's members that include ideas, beliefs, ideologies, or theories about the truth, right or wrong, good or bad, and beautiful or ugly or inappropriate (Hartford, 1971). Examples of such values include the following:

This is a "good" group and worth our commitment and investment of time. (Or, this is a "dumb" group. We're not going to get anything out of it.)

It is "bad" to betray confidences to outsiders.

People who belong to different groups (e.g., authorities, persons of a different race, religion, status) are "bad" or inferior.

It is undesirable to show feelings in the group. It is fun to try to outwit authority figures (particularly applicable to groups of juvenile or adult offenders).

Just as the group's "choice" of norms significantly affects its capacity to offer a therapeutic milieu, so does the group's "choice" of values. Similar to norms, values can be categorized as functional or dysfunctional when viewed in light of the group's therapeutic objectives. Values that encourage work on personal problems or self-disclosure, acceptance of others, and a positive attitude toward the group, for example, are functional to the group's development. By contrast, values that discourage self-disclosure, create barriers in relationships or negative attitudes toward the group, or prevent members from working on problems are obviously dysfunctional.

12 ■ Enhancing Motivation with Involuntary and Ambivalent Clients

Challenges Involved in Working with Involuntary Clients

Before engaging effectively in the problem-solving process, clients must first acknowledge having a problem and be willing to work toward resolving it. Some people contact professionals, however, to appease irate spouses or parents and merely go through the motions of utilizing service. Services are imposed upon others who are involuntarily confined to correctional or mental health institutions (captive clients). As a condition of probation or parole, services are mandated for some people, whereas others are involuntary recipients of services because of investigations required by law in response to complaints about child neglect and/or abuse. The problems of such clients have been termed *attributed problems* by Reid (1978), because *others* attribute problems to them; they themselves do not necessarily acknowledge problems. Reid further maintains that until people acknowledge problems and agree to work on them they are *respondents* rather than clients, a view also held by Alcabes and Jones (1985), who refer to such people as *applicants*.

Because involuntary clients may totally lack motivation to change and even voluntary clients often manifest weak motiva-

tion, practitioners must possess skills for enhancing clients' motivation. Research findings of Gomez et al. (1985) document the importance of skills in developing motivation and overcoming the resistance of involuntary clients. In their study of the outcomes of casework with Chicano clients in a mental health setting, they found that these skills were positively associated ($r = .39$) with client satisfaction. Our objective in this chapter is to assist you in developing relevant skills. By employing these skills, you will improve your batting average in engaging inadequately motivated clients—which is all you can realistically expect, for such clients are a difficult challenge to even highly skilled practitioners.

Applying Concepts from Social Psychology

The fact that involuntary clients are coerced to enter relationships with professionals or do so under duress has prompted Cingolani (1984) to propose that social workers adopt a *social conflict approach* to work with these clients rather than a *therapeutic approach*. According to the social conflict perspective, work with involuntary clients is in reality "a political process—one that involves socially sanctioned use of power or influence in a context of conflicting interests between the client and some part of his or her environment" (p. 442). Using this approach, practitioners choose to enact a role of enforcer, negotiator, mediator, or advocate and coach, as contrasted to the traditional therapeutic role.

Another social work theorist (Rooney, 1988) advocates that *reactance theory,* formulated by Brehm and Brehm (1981), provides relevant concepts for work with involuntary clients. Rooney has adapted these concepts to direct social work practice and has presented guidelines for their use. Although both social conflict theory and reactance theory fill a void in theoretical constructs related to involuntary clients, before discussing the application of some of these concepts we would like to clarify that we believe they can be integrated with, rather than used in place of a *therapeutic approach.* The basis of our position should become clear in the following discussion.

Based on reactance theory, Rooney[1] posits that when people are coerced into seeing a social worker they experience the coercion as a threat to a valued freedom and react negatively with hostility, overt resistance, or passive-aggressive behavior.[2] The challenge of the practitioner is to minimize or reduce the reactance by responding in ways that lessen the client's perceived threat to freedom. Put another way, the practitioner seeks to create cognitive dissonance for the client by responding in unexpected ways that reduce threat. The practitioner thus:

1. Emphasizes choices that *are* available.

2. Contracts in ways aimed at restoring freedom.

3. Fosters maintenance of *some* current behaviors to minimize clients' fears of losses.

4. Focuses on limited and specific changes rather than on global and sweeping changes that would be threatening and unacceptable.

5. Maximizes self-determination within parameters determined by the situation.

By responding in these unexpected ways, practitioners convey the impression of desiring to be an ally rather than an adversary. The practitioner is interested in helping the client to make the best of a difficult and vexing situation without neglecting professional responsibilities as a representative of society.

Initial Contacts

Principles of reactance theory are particularly relevant during the initial stages of work with involuntary clients, for reactance is strongest at this time. Further, it is during this stage that roles are clarified and problems are explored. How practitioners manage the negative reactions of clients and the realities of the situation that must be negotiated largely determine whether a workable (though possibly strained) alliance or an adversarial relationship will evolve. Tasks in preparing for the initial contact, according to Rooney, are threefold.

1. *Identify nonnegotiable requirements.* With clients who are involuntary for legal reasons, nonnegotiable requirements stipulated by the law and by legal authorities (usually a judge, probation or parole

---

[1]We wish to acknowledge that much of our discussion of the application of reactance theory is based on Rooney's earlier cited article.

[2]Passive-aggressive behavior in this instance refers to covert and subtle ways of undermining or resisting the practitioner's efforts (e.g., forgetting appointments, being sullen, silent, tardy, uncooperative, and so forth).

officer, or child welfare official) must be made explicit. (Although practitioners seek to form a working relationship with clients, they represent an agency given authority and responsibility by society to maximize compliance by clients with stipulated requirements.) Once nonnegotiable requirements have been determined, areas wherein choices can be exercised can also be identified.

2. *Determine negotiable requirements and areas of choice.* This task involves assisting clients to distinguish nonnegotiable requirements from those that are negotiable. For example, although clients may be required to have periodic meetings with the practitioner or another professional, they may be allowed to determine where and when the meetings will be held. The client who is mandated to undergo psychological testing may also be given options in selecting from a number of acceptable psychologists. When self-determinism and freedom are thus maximized in these and other ways, reactance by clients tends to be reduced.

3. *Monitor own feelings.* Because personal feelings can color perceptions of what is and what is not negotiable, it is vital that practitioners monitor their feelings regarding an alleged offense by a client. As we have previously noted, practitioners are human and may have strong emotions about certain offenses. Monitoring personal reactions can avert letting feelings contaminate perceptions. Otherwise practitioners may set overly stringent requirements and unwittingly foster negative reactance by clients.

Structure of Initial Interviews

During the initial session, after an appropriate introduction and brief warm-up period, the first task is to *explain the cause of the interview and the requirements.* Al-

though most involuntary clients have some awareness as to why they are being seen, it is advisable to review the matter, for clients are entitled to an explanation. This explanation should include:

1. *The practitioner's understanding about factors that resulted in the mandated referral.* For example, "I've been notified by the court that a condition of your probation is that you receive psychotherapy," or "I'm from Children's Protective Services and have been assigned to investigate a complaint of child neglect."

2. *The practitioner's role and relationship to the legal referral source.* For example, "The court makes referrals to our agency because we specialize in therapy with people involved in sexual activities between adults and children," or "It's my responsibility to investigate reports of child neglect."

3. *Nonnegotiable requirements.* For example, "The judge has ordered us to work with you weekly for a minimum of three months," or "The court requires a report on each complaint within _____" (specify period of time).

4. *Procedures mandated by the referral source.* For example, "The judge requires me to make an initial report and a progress report after 10 weeks," or "After I have determined the facts and submitted a report, the court will decide whether to dismiss the complaint or to take further action."

5. *Negotiable requirements and choices available to the client.* For example, "You have some choices about the days we meet and whether we meet once weekly for an hour or twice for one-half hour. I want you to decide what fits best for you," or "If I caught you at a bad time I can drop back a little later. Would that be more convenient?"

After making the above explanations, the practitioner can expect a negative reaction from most clients. The next activity, therefore, is to resolve hostility or defensiveness, skills we discuss after a brief detour.

To this point we have discussed the initial contact with clients who are legally mandated to see practitioners. Other clients are not legally compelled to see a practitioner, but do so with great reluctance because of social coercion (threats) by a spouse, employer, or parent. In such instances they have "chosen" to seek help not because they desire it, but to placate the other party and thereby avoid the threatened consequences. During the early portion of interviews with these clients, it is inappropriate to follow the preceding guidelines. Rather, clients will explain their views as to why they have come. As they do so, they typically manifest hostility and defensiveness because of the coercion others have exerted upon them. After their explanation, then, the task is to resolve their negative reactions to their perceived loss of freedom.

Resolving Negativism and Hostility

The desired outcome of initial sessions with involuntary and socially coerced clients is to engender the desire to alter some aspect of their life situations. But before attempting to generate incentives, it is essential to neutralize clients' negative feelings associated with having to see a practitioner. Until these negative feelings are resolved, it is futile to attempt to create incentive for change.

Involuntary clients typically and understandably resent being forced to participate in interviews or group sessions. Although their resentments are generally toward those who participated in the events leading to the mandatory referral—a spouse, parents, neighbors, or law enforcement personnel—you become the displaced object of the resentment when you encounter the client for the first time. Bear in mind that the client's open hostility or sullenness is merely directed toward you as a symbol of the client's frustration and not to you as a person. Otherwise, you may respond defensively or counterattack, thereby increasing and reinforcing hostility rather than mitigating it.

Negativism and resentment may also emanate from clients' perceptions that they are being mistakenly blamed for difficulties that preceded the referral. Having to see a professional thus is a blow to the self-esteem of persons who see the sources of difficulties as residing outside of themselves. A husband may resent being forced to see a practitioner by a wife who complains that he is unloving, critical, and distant when his view is that his wife has for years excluded him from family activities and has rebuffed his affectional gestures. Similarly, adolescents resent being identified as the problem bearer and being coerced to see a professional for truanting and ungovernable behavior when they perceive their parents as causing the problems by being demanding, unreasonable, and punitive. Residents of youth correctional institutions or mental institutions likewise initially resent having to attend interviews with a staff member or to participate in group sessions when they don't believe they belong in the institution.

Still other clients, particularly children and adolescents (who typically lack knowledge about the role of professionals), fear that practitioners will control or punish them in some ill-defined way. Consequently, they are usually apprehensive when they enter an initial session, expecting the practitioner to be stern, punitive, and authoritarian. Wary of the practitioner, they fear they will have to surrender part of their autonomy or freedom. Consequently, they often present themselves in a sullen manner, disclosing as little as possible.

Common to all of the preceding reactions is a negative mind-set toward practitioners, who represent a threat and are perceived by clients as enemies. The most effective strategy to penetrate defensiveness and negativism and to establish a relationship beachhead is to respond in ways that are antithetical to a client's expectations. We recommend that you start where the client is by utilizing empathic responding to elicit the client's negative feelings until the negativism subsides. As clients give vent to negative emotions and practitioners respond with understanding rather than with criticism and defensiveness, emotional catharsis and defusing of the emotions occur. Equally important, the client's negative mind-set gradually yields to a more realistic appraisal of the practitioner. Having drained off the resentment and experienced the practitioner as a sensitive, accepting, and understanding person, clients tend to lower their guards, often welcoming the opportunity to discuss their life situations with someone who appears interested and concerned and who seeks neither to blame nor to exert pressure.

The outcome implied in the preceding description represents the ideal, of course, and involuntary clients have a penchant for not conforming to the ideal. Irrespective of your skills, some clients will not engage in the helping process. But if you follow the outlined strategy, many will mellow considerably and will reach the point of being receptive to exploring their difficulties. It has been our experience, however, that beginning practitioners prematurely assume that negativism has been resolved and launch an exploration that immediately sinks under the weight of continued opposition. In the following excerpt, illustrating application of the skills with a husband whose wife demanded he see a marital therapist (under threat of filing for divorce), notice how the therapist stays with the client's feelings until it is apparent the client is ready to explore the relationship.

PRACTITIONER: Let's start by your telling me why you've come.

CLIENT: [*Bristling.*] First, I want you to know I'm not here because I want to be. My wife told me if I didn't make an appointment to see someone, she was going to give me my walking papers.

PRACTITIONER: So you're here under pressure. You must resent having to come against your will.

CLIENT: [*Emphatically.*] You're damned right. Wouldn't you?

PRACTITIONER: Well, I can understand how you'd be pretty burned about it.

CLIENT: She blames me every time we get into an argument. I know I'm not perfect, but she's not either.

PRACTITIONER: So you resent having all the blame dumped on you. Right?

CLIENT: You bet! She's no jewel, but she acts like she is. And I'm always made out to be the villain.

PRACTITIONER: But you don't see it that way. It seems unfair to you.

CLIENT: That's putting it mildly. Grossly unfair—that's how it seems to me. If anyone should be here, it's her.

PRACTITIONER: It really infuriates you to have to be here instead of her.

CLIENT: That's for sure. But what choice do I have? It's come here or else.

PRACTITIONER: So you really feel trapped. You come here, or she calls it quits.

CLIENT: Yeah, and that's no choice really. You don't call it quits after 24 years. Hell, she's the center of my life. She has her faults, but we've had our good times.

PRACTITIONER: And the prospect of losing her is a grim one to face.

CLIENT: Yeah! But I'm not going to wallow in the mud to please her either. Maybe I've got some problems, but I've got my good points, too.

PRACTITIONER: Everyone has some problems.

CLIENT: That's just it. I'm no worse than anyone else, and she has as many problems as I do. Why should I be the one to have to come?

PRACTITIONER: I can understand your resentment. Would you feel differently if she came too?

CLIENT: Well, I still wouldn't like it, but it would be more fair.

PRACTITIONER: It's painful to have to ask for help under the best of circumstances.

CLIENT: Yeah! But I know things have been rocky in our relationship since our last kid left home. Gloria gets depressed and seems on edge a lot of the time. I guess I'm uptight, too.

PRACTITIONER: So, you've both felt under a lot of stress.

CLIENT: [*Nods his head in agreement.*] Yeah, it's been pretty rough.

The client's anger has dissipated somewhat and he seems ready to explore the problem. (The practitioner proceeds to explore the situation further and subsequently introduces the possibility of working with both partners.)

Notice in the preceding excerpt that in addition to empathizing with the client's feelings, the practitioner did not challenge the client's perceptions and beliefs but rather accepted them as potentially valid (as contrasted to attempting to persuade the client to acknowledge his problems). Notice also that when the client declared, "Maybe I've got some problems," the practitioner wisely did not misinterpret this message as indicating the client was acknowledging problems and was ready to explore them. Rather, the practitioner responded with understanding and respect, deferring exploration until it was apparent the client's negativism had melted.

In protective service settings, the task of resolving negativism is even more challenging. Because clients sometimes have no advance warning about the practitioner's visit, they have no opportunity to compose themselves and to put their situation into perspective. In addition to experiencing immediate resentment toward whoever made the complaint, they are often overwhelmed with the threat represented by the practitioner's authority and the fear of the possibility of losing custody of their children.

For practitioners, the challenge is further compounded by having to make visits knowing that they are likely to be viewed as unwelcome intruders and even as enemies. Moreover, practitioners are confronted with the formidable task of using authority in an assertive but benevolent manner, which requires assuming multiple roles of advocate for the children, the parents, the agency, and the community. Although the task is not impossible, clients understandably initially tend to view the roles as mutually exclusive. By being empathically responsive and conveying understanding, however, practitioners often succeed in being perceived by clients as an ally rather than an enemy, as illustrated in the following excerpt from an initial home visit:

PRACTITIONER: Hello, are you Mrs. Thomas?

CLIENT: Yes, I am.

PRACTITIONER: I'm Mrs. Grant from the child welfare division of the social services department. I'd like to talk with you if I may.

CLIENT: [*Appears stunned.*] Child welfare? Why do you want to talk with me?

PRACTITIONER: Mrs. Thomas, our agency is charged by law with the responsibility of safeguarding the health and well-being of children. Whenever we receive a report that children are being neglected or mistreated, we're obligated to investigate the report. We received. . .

CLIENT: [*Interrupting angrily.*] You mean someone turned me in? Who'd do such a rotten thing? Whoever it was—it just isn't true. I take care of my kids. What terrible thing am I supposed to have done? [*Voice trembles, near tears.*]

PRACTITIONER: I can understand this is a shock to you. But please understand, I'm not accusing you of anything. I just need to explore the situation with you. Could I come in?

CLIENT: Of course. [*They enter and take seats.*] My house is in kind of a mess right now. Please tell me, what am I supposed to have done?

PRACTITIONER: The report was that you've been leaving your children unattended for several hours at night and that they've been going to the neighbors asking for food.

CLIENT: So that's it! [*Irately.*] I'll bet it's those damn neighbors who turned me in. It'd be just like them.

PRACTITIONER: I can understand you'd feel upset. I know this is distressing to you.

CLIENT: [*Nods in agreement—close to tears.*] My neighbors are so smug. They don't know what it's been like since my husband ran out on me. They don't have to worry about where the next meals are coming from.

PRACTITIONER: It's been pretty rough, I gather.

CLIENT: I'll say it has. What I get from welfare—it's just not enough. My husband left me with a lot of bills. My welfare check doesn't begin to cover the bills and the expense of four little kids.

PRACTITIONER: So that's been a constant worry. I can understand you've been pretty worried.

CLIENT: And now *this* on top of everything else. You wonder what's the use of even trying.

PRACTITIONER: This has been a real blow, I know. You're feeling rather discouraged right now.

CLIENT: [*Nods head affirmatively.*] I've been feeling so down lately. Just the four kids and the four walls. I've felt like I've been going stir crazy.

PRACTITIONER: [*Nods head to convey understanding.*] Please go on. I'd like to understand more of what it's been like for you.

CLIENT: I guess I got to feeling desperate. Like I had to get out. But I haven't had any money to hire a baby-sitter. I thought maybe the kids would be OK if I left for a little while. An old girlfriend got me a date, and we double-dated a couple of times last week. But I didn't think anything like this would happen. [*Trembling.*] You're not going to take my kids away, are you?

PRACTITIONER: We only remove children from their parents as a last resort, Mrs. Thomas. My function is to assist you so that you *can* give the children the care they need. [*She appears somewhat relieved.*] That means, of course, that you can't leave your children without care at night, but I'd be happy to think with you about other ways you could relieve some of the pressures you've been under.

CLIENT: I never knew what a struggle was until Neal ran off with another woman. [*Her defensiveness has virtually disappeared, and she continues to report information about stresses in her life.*]

Notice in the preceding excerpt that the practitioner began the contact by explaining the purpose of the visit and attempting to clarify her role as a child protective services worker. Before she could complete the explanation, however, Mrs. T. reacted with strong emotion, as often happens. Wisely, the practitioner responded by empathizing with Mrs. T.'s feelings and clarifying that she was not accusing Mrs. T. but needed to explore the situation. After being asked about the complaint and again experiencing a negative reaction to her explanation, the practitioner again responded with empathy and understanding, which tended to reduce Mrs. T.'s reactance. As the practitioner continued to respond empathically, Mrs. T.'s negative feelings gradually subsided and she began to relate information that gave the practitioner perspective of the events that preceded the complaint. By further eliciting and reflecting feelings and conveying understanding and acceptance of her frustrations and needs, the dialogue evolved to the point where it was timely for the practitioner to make an overture aimed at forming an alliance that could be used later in the interview to negotiate relevant goals and a contract (i.e., "I'd be happy to think with you about other ways you could relieve some of the pressures you've been under"). Notice also that in her last message, the practitioner defines her protective role but places it in a problem-solving context.

Not all protective service visits culminate with favorable outcomes, as veteran protective service workers will attest. In some instances, clients refuse to engage in a discussion and may even threaten violence if the practitioner does not leave immediately. (If violence appears imminent, the latter is well advised to retreat hastily.) If clients make no threat but refuse to talk with practitioners and ask them to leave, the latter can use confron-

tation facilitatively, employing the leverage of authority,[3] as illustrated in the following excerpt and discussed in the next section.

CLIENT: Look, I don't have to take any crap from you. You're on my property, and I want you off!

PRACTITIONER: You're right, you don't have to talk with me. But you have a right to know something before I leave. If you refuse to talk with me, you're making it worse for yourself. The police will likely be asked to come with a warrant, and you won't have any choice then. It would be better for you if that didn't happen, but it's up to you.

CLIENT: [*Disgustedly and with irritation.*] Well, that's not much of a choice, is it? You've got me between a rock and a hard place.

PRACTITIONER: Please understand, I don't like having to put you in this situation. But it's my job, and I have to make a report to the court.

CLIENT: OK! OK! I hear you. I don't like it, but I hear you. Come on in.

Using Confrontation Facilitatively

As is apparent from the preceding excerpts, work with involuntary clients is not for the weak-hearted or thin-skinned. Practitioners in settings that are affiliated with legal and judicial systems have authority and a responsibility to exercise that authority in ways that are consistent with the purposes of those systems.

---

[3]For a discussion of the use of authority with mandated clients see Hutchinson, E. D. (1987). Use of authority in direct social work practice with mandated clients. *Social Service Review, 61,* 581–598.

Notice in the preceding excerpt that the practitioner did not flaunt her authority but used confrontation facilitatively by respecting the client's right not to cooperate while pointing out the adverse consequences of refusing to do so. The practitioner thus maximized self-determination, but emphasized the nonnegotiable requirement that someone must investigate the complaint. Given the difficulty and strain of the situation, the practitioner wisely conveyed a desire to assist the client to avoid an even more aversive situation. Using leverage and authority firmly but facilitatively thus tends to reduce reactance without compromising professional responsibility.

After using confrontation to clarify nonnegotiable requirements, the practitioner can then respond empathically to the client's negative feelings, as we discussed in the preceding section. Combining these techniques often reduces negative reactance and makes it possible to explain the practitioner's role and mandated procedures, as happened in the preceding excerpt.

Negotiating Workable Contracts

Achieving a workable contract with involuntary and socially coerced clients is a challenge because these clients typically lack initial motivation to engage in the helping process. The objective, of course, is to assist them gradually to identify goals based on acknowledged problems and a desire to change. When this has been achieved a person becomes a "legitimate" client and a "therapeutic" approach can be implemented. Until that happens, the practitioner will have to settle for negotiating a workable agreement that falls short of a "therapeutic contract." In the following we discuss strategies of negotiating workable agreements.

Agreeable Reframed Mandate

As Rooney (1988) points out, involuntary and socially coerced clients often express their own views of problems or situations that resulted in the mandated referral. Typically their views diverge from the views of the legal authority or person(s) who mandated the referral. The strategy in such instances is to search for common ground that bridges the differing views. Reframing the definition of the problem in such a way that adequately addresses the concerns of the client as well as the referral source reduces reactance and makes a workable agreement possible.

This strategy was illustrated in the first excerpt presented in this chapter involving the husband whose wife threatened to "call it quits" if he didn't seek professional help. The client could not accept that he was the sole cause of the problem, but through skillful handling did acknowledge that the relationship was "rocky" and that he was "uptight." He was receptive to entering *marital* therapy rather than individual therapy if his wife would participate. Another example would be reframing the problem of a rebellious adolescent referred by the parents as a *family* problem that requires participation of other family members.

Negotiating a Problem Search

Another strategy involves taking a neutral position regarding the existence or nature of problems and negotiating a period of problem search with the client. This strategy reduces reactance by demonstrating respect for clients' views and avoiding engendering opposition that occurs when a practitioner insists on a given perspective of the problem.

It is important to introduce this strategy in a nonthreatening manner. For example: "I can see you don't agree with _____ that you have a problem. In all honesty I don't know you well enough to render a judgment one way or the other. I'm wondering if you would consider our talking for two or three sessions to explore your life situation further. If we explore your situation further it will become clearer to us what, if anything, is going wrong." The advantage to this strategy is that practitioners buy time to establish rapport with clients and assist clients to explore their situations more thoroughly and realistically.

Bargaining with the Client

Rooney (1988) refers to this strategy as "Let's make a deal" (p. 138). The leverage derives from the fact that a client may have private concerns exclusive from the problem that precipitated the referral. For example, a patient in a mental institution may reject the view that he has problems with sexual impulses, but may express concerns over being inhibited in social situations. The practitioner may agree to focus on the latter if the patient will agree to explore the former. The possibilities of such bargaining are virtually limitless. The potency of this strategy derives from being able to offer a payoff to a client (create an incentive). Skillful practitioners are alert to potential payoffs that can be tapped in the service of enhancing motivation, as we discuss later.

Getting the Mandate off Your Back

With some involuntary clients, none of the preceding strategies is viable and the only recourse left to the practitioner is to appeal to clients' desire to be free of the restraints imposed by the mandating referral source. We discuss and illustrate this strategy later in the section "Creating Incentives."

Exploiting Self-Defeating Consequences

With clients who deny problems and adamantly oppose efforts to involve them, practitioners can minimize reactance by not attempting to dissuade them from their views or not selling them on the need for help. Rather, the practitioner can adopt a neutral stance but exploit the leverage represented in the self-defeating consequences of inaction. For example, by failing to abide by mandated requirements probationers can be sure of being incarcerated; a youth in a correctional facility can prolong his confinement by denying problem behaviors obvious to others; and the recalcitrant spouse can face the inevitability of divorce by resisting taking constructive action. The leverage of this strategy is compelling. Further, reactance is minimized because the impetus for change comes not from the practitioner but from the undeniable realities of the consequences that will ensue.

Rooney discusses the application of reactance theory to work with involuntary clients at length in his recent book (Rooney, in press).

Resolving Ambivalence

In addition to involuntary clients, others also experience strong ambivalence about engaging fully in the helping process. (Most clients experience some ambivalence.) In some instances, the negative aspect of the ambivalence tends to abate when they have a positive experience with the practitioner in the initial session. Other clients hold back, thereby reducing opportunities for positive interaction. In such instances, you must recognize their ambivalence and assist them to resolve it before an effective working relationship can evolve. Ambivalence may emanate from numerous sources, including the following:

1. Skepticism about practitioners based on previous experience.

2. Reluctance to expose one's private life.

3. Misgivings based on misconceptions of the helping process.

4. Fears of discovering something terrible about oneself.

5. Apprehension that the practitioner might be critical, condemning, or controlling.

6. Uncertainties about wanting to change.

7. Reluctance to spend money for something intangible.

8. Cultural or racial differences between client and practitioner.

If you fail to recognize manifestations of ambivalence, you leave clients to struggle with it alone, and clients often resolve such struggles by not returning after initial sessions. Other ambivalent clients who have been involved in sessions with spouses, family members, or group members may return for additional sessions because of their affiliations with the other members but may participate in a half-hearted fashion. The success of these units in accomplishing their goals, however, depends on full participation of all members, which underscores further the need to recognize and resolve ambivalence.

Manifestations of ambivalence may be obvious, such as expressing skepticism, misgivings, or fear. When clients openly express their ambivalence, you have the opportunity to explore and allay their misgivings and to obviate misconceptions by answering questions and clarifying the nature of the helping process and of your respective roles. In such instances, ambivalence often yields to open and frank discussion, and clients subsequently engage in the exploratory process.

Although less obvious, other manifestations of ambivalence are usually detected by perceptive practitioners. These manifestations include focusing on "safe" topics, asking an inordinate number of questions about counseling or therapy, volunteering little information and letting others take the lead in conjoint or group sessions, sitting apart from other participants, appearing bored, whispering to other group members, and making disparaging remarks in group sessions. When you encounter manifestations of ambivalence in *individual* sessions, it is generally advisable to encourage clients to express their feelings about coming for help, employing an authentic response such as: "I'm sensing that you have some mixed feelings about seeing me. I wonder if you could share your feelings in that regard." Although initially hesitant in expressing untoward attitudes and fears, ambivalent clients will generally appreciate your perceiving their conflicted feelings. Moreover, they may welcome the opportunity to talk through the negative aspects of their ambivalence. Bear in mind that the positive aspect of their ambivalence motivated them to seek help, and it may be a powerful force for constructive change if liberated from the countervailing negative force. As noted earlier, when clients rationally analyze negative attitudes and fears, they are often able to resolve them and then to engage actively in the helping process.

The following excerpt illustrates this process with a client whose ambivalence stemmed from a misconception about the helping process:

PRACTITIONER: You discussed your problem very openly at first, but you seem to be uncomfortable now—as though something is troubling you. I wonder what you're experiencing at this moment.

CLIENT: Oh, I don't know. I guess I'm thinking maybe it was a mistake to come.

PRACTITIONER: How do you mean?

CLIENT: [*Pause.*] I guess I'm feeling that in the final analysis, I'm the one who has to face my problems and do something about them. It's something I have to do alone. Neither you nor anyone else can do it for me.

PRACTITIONER: In a way, you're right, and it takes some strength on your part to recognize that ultimately you're the one who has to cope with your problems. On the other hand, you may be able to cope with them more effectively by thinking them through with another person. Sometimes we're so close to our problems we can't be sure what's causing them, and that makes it difficult to know how to solve them. As I see it, my role would be to assist you in seeing your problems more clearly so that together we could plan effective ways of coping with them. Of course, you'd be the one to choose the best course of action and then to apply it.

CLIENT: What you're saying makes sense. [*Pause.*] Still I somehow feel I shouldn't need help from someone else.

PRACTITIONER: Like you should just be able to do it alone? It must have been really tough for you deciding to come.

CLIENT: I struggled with it for a couple of weeks. Finally I decided, "Well, what have you got to lose?"

PRACTITIONER: I'm pleased you made that decision. But your struggle's not over, I gather. You know, when it comes right down to it, it takes a lot of strength and courage to ask for help. Some people go through life needlessly enduring painful situations because they're too proud to ask for help. I have trouble seeing that as strength. If anything, it's a weakness to let pride get in the way of taking a step that could make life better. I may be biased, but that's how I see it.

CLIENT: I hadn't thought of it that way, but I can't argue with you. I'm glad you said that because I'm feeling better about being here. I guess it has been a blow to my pride. But I can see it might really help me.

Ambivalence also commonly occurs on the part of one or more family or group members in initial group sessions. A useful technique of "smoking out" ambivalence in a group context is to ask family or group members early in the first session to rate their feelings about participating in the group on a scale from 1 to 10 (where 1 represents "I'd rather be almost anywhere else, and I could care less about being involved" and 10 represents "I'm delighted and eager to begin"). After members report their self-ratings, you can invite them to share their related feelings and concerns with the group. It is important, of course, to respect their right not to disclose feelings and to accept negative feelings that are expressed.

Clients who rate themselves at the middle or lower end of the scale have significant reservations about participating in the helping process. It is important to explore these reservations by asking them to explain the reason for their particular ratings, encouraging their expanded verbalization by utilizing empathic responding and other verbal following skills.

When one client has finished expressing misgivings, the practitioner can suggest that others in the group may also have reservations and invite responses from others. Realizing that others also have mixed feelings tends to reduce anxiety and establishes a common ground.

The technique of having members "quantify" their feelings is also invaluable in situations in which marital partners or family or group members convey through verbal messages or nonverbal behavior (e.g., sitting apart from the group or looking disgusted or bored) their opposition to coming to the session. In whatever manner it is conveyed, this information sets the individual apart from the rest of the group as the "uncommitted" one. In marital or family therapy, in fact, others often label this member as the *identified patient*. Having all family members rate their feelings on the 1-to-10 scale, however, underscores that *every* member is experiencing ambivalence about participating in the helping process. By encouraging other members to express their reservations and fears, the practitioner shifts the focus from the identified patient and momentarily establishes that person as "one of the group" rather than as a deviant. This intervention facilitates accomplishing the important task of "delabeling" a member who is being scapegoated by the family.

In assessing the motivation of each member, it is important to determine who initiated the request for help, how the decision was ultimately made, and, in the case of children, what they were told about why they were coming. Some parents may tell children that they are going for a ride or that they are going to see a counselor because they have been bad or are causing troubles. Even when parents accurately explain the reason for seeing a practitioner, children tend to be unclear about what family practitioners actually

do and often fear the worst. Parents may also unrealistically expect the practitioner to magically "cure" the child while they watch. Thus, it is vital to explore participants' expectations and to explain carefully the role of the practitioner and clients. Clarifying roles and correcting misconceptions about the helping process enables clients to assess realistically their own motivation for pursuing help. Further, empathically focusing on the anger or resentment of some family members about being "forced" to come to the session reduces negativism, enabling clients to consider more rationally whether they might benefit from counseling.

A vital task near the end of a session is to assist *all* members to weigh the advantages and disadvantages of committing themselves to work on problems and to make a conscious choice about whether to return for future sessions. A simple way of determining whether ambivalent or negative feelings have been mollified is to ask members to rate their feelings again toward the end of a group session. If members' feelings remain unchanged, the family therapist or group leader may wish to talk with pertinent members individually to resolve feelings that pose a barrier to engaging in the group process.

Creating Incentives

When you have successfully resolved the negativism of clients, the next major task is to attempt to create an incentive for change. Your challenge in creating an incentive is to identify an area of discomfort in a client's life that might be eased or obviated through the helping process. Motivation for change thus is enhanced when clients receive a payoff (want) that justifies their subjecting themselves to an alien and threatening venture. Captive clients in institutional settings may lack incentives to change personal behavior, yet want to have increased privileges or to be released from the institution. The parents of neglected and/or abused children generally want to retain or regain custody of their children. Persons on probation or parole want the mandate off their backs. Spouses want to save their marriages and reduce their conflicts. Wants such as those enumerated provide a point of entry into the helping process and a basis for negotiating a contract, as illustrated in the excerpt below from an initial interview with an adolescent in a correctional center.

In the following excerpt, notice how the practitioner employs empathic responses to convey understanding of David's feelings, particularly in response to the latter's natural desire to want to gain release from the institution. By accepting the client's goal as valid, the practitioner conveys his desire to be David's ally, which disarms and engages him. It is important to recognize that in so doing the practitioner is not being deceptive, but relates openly and honestly in establishing a basis for negotiating a legitimate goal and developing a mutually acceptable contract. Although David demonstrates no motivation to modify his behavior, his keen incentive "to get out of this joint" is used as a springboard to create incentives for other changes that could lead to his ultimate release. Although the strategy illustrated applies to a correctional setting, the principle can be applied to many situations.

PRACTITIONER: Hi, David, I'm Mr. Pack, your new social worker. I thought I'd like to get acquainted with you today.

CLIENT: You mean I've got another social worker? What happened to Hinds—did he quit?

PRACTITIONER: Not exactly. He was ill for a week, and then he was transferred suddenly because of a cutback in state funds. It happened so quickly that he didn't get a chance to talk with you before he left. He asked me to explain to you how badly he felt.

CLIENT: It don't really matter. I'd only seen him a couple of times.

PRACTITIONER: Well, it mattered to him. He really did feel bad, and I can understand having a new social worker after seeing him just a few times could be upsetting to you.

CLIENT: Naw, no big deal, man. Social workers don't help you anyway.

PRACTITIONER: Sounds like your experience with them hasn't been the best. Anyway, David, I'd like to hear how things have been going and talk to you about how I might be helpful.

CLIENT: I'll tell you how you can be helpful. You can get me out of this joint.

PRACTITIONER: [*Laughs.*] I'd guess that'd be a help, all right. Actually, I might be able to help you to get out if you're serious.

CLIENT: No kiddin'? You mean you can get me out?

PRACTITIONER: Well, not right this moment. No one can do that. What I mean is that I can help you to plan what you have to accomplish to get released.

CLIENT: Oh, sure. I knew you were jiving me.

PRACTITIONER: No, I wasn't jiving you at all. I'm dead serious about wanting to help you get out. I know it's no picnic being here.

CLIENT: You better believe it ain't no picnic, man. What you going to do to get me out?

PRACTITIONER: Well, it's not just what *I'd* do. We'd have to do it together. And it would take some thinking and doing on both of our parts.

CLIENT: I don't know what you're talking about, but I know one thing for sure. I want out of here.

PRACTITIONER: If you want out badly enough, we could begin to talk about what changes you'd need to make, and I could help you plan how you could make those changes. It would take some time and some hard work on your part, but I'm willing to pitch in with you if you'd be willing to do your part. It wouldn't be easy. What do you think?

CLIENT: I can't see I've got much choice. I ain't got nothin' to lose, I guess. But I ain't making no promises.

PRACTITIONER: I'm not asking you to. But I am asking you to give it your best shot. Otherwise, you won't accomplish much.

Cultivating Hope

Although many clients acknowledge problems and manifest incentives to change, their motivation may be severely dampened by skepticism about their capacity to change. These clients typically have experienced failure and have low self-esteem and, as a consequence, "after a realistic goal has been agreed upon, find it difficult to feel that the goal is realistic" (Smaldino, 1975, p. 329). Often their motivation fluctuates widely. Impelled by a spark of hope, they make an appointment, but as they reach the point of formulating goals, their motivation often ebbs, pulled by the tides of past failures and fears of future reoccurrences.

Because hope is an indispensable component of motivation, one must often assume responsibility for fostering this precious ingredient. This means that you yourself must believe that clients can take constructive action, that the present and future can be improved, and that you can strengthen the clients' coping capacities and assist them to achieve their potentials more fully. This means that you too need a sense of self-efficacy in your role as change agent. Similarly, the most effective means of encouraging clients is by enhancing their sense of self-efficacy in performing their role in the helping process. By accrediting strengths manifested in the initial session that can assist clients in tackling problems, you may engender the courage they need to continue in the helping process. Acknowledging problems and seeking help is the first step of that process and one that requires a certain measure of strength. Cooperating in exploring problems and risking by sharing personal feelings and experiences also are evidences of strengths that facilitate successful problem solving.

In conveying encouragement, it is important not to do so indiscriminately, for clients discern false reassurance and tend to respond to it not only with increased uncertainties about their own capacities to change but with doubts about practitioners' credibility as well. Realistic encouragement must be based on a belief that the factors producing the problematic situation are subject to change. Moreover, the client must have the capacity and the motivation to implement essential remedial actions. Because these factors are critical, we recommend that encouragement be couched in a way that clarifies the client's responsibility in producing a favorable outcome, as illustrated in the following:

"As I consider your problem, I feel hopeful that you can work it out. Whether you succeed or not, of course, depends most on your willingness to work hard at accomplishing the goals that we develop and to endure the discomfort involved in making changes. Others have worked out similar problems in the past, and I see no reason why you can't."

Highlighting Strengths

Both you and your clients will tend to see a realistic basis for hope if you highlight clients' strengths and successful outcomes of their previous coping efforts. This requires you to be attuned to evidence of their strengths and previous successes. Without your assistance, many clients will overlook their strengths and successes because their life experiences (particularly the lack of encouragement from significant others) have conditioned them to be selectively aware of only their weaknesses, shortcomings, and failures. The following are examples of positive messages that you can give in sessions to highlight strengths and to inculcate hope. Notice that in giving feedback, the practitioner authentically shares feelings and concretely describes the events that document clients' strengths and resources:

[*To a couple*]: "I've been impressed with something I want to call to your attention. Although it's been embarrassing to you, you have been very open and honest with each other and with me. [*Refers to specific situations.*] That willingness to risk will help a great deal as we tackle your problems."

[*To a family*]: "We've spent most of our time today talking about some very touchy problems. As we have, I noticed several times that family members made a real effort to try to understand the feelings of others. [*Gives examples.*] I also noticed that you joked together even when there was strain. I was also pleased with how willing all of you were to assume individual tasks to accomplish outside of our session. With this kind of family commitment, we should be able to accomplish a lot."

Facilitating Positive Interaction

Another avenue for creating hope is to enable clients to have successful experiences in communicating and relating with each other. If you have intervened successfully to assist clients to supplant dysfunctional interactions with more facilitative ways of relating (e.g., checking out perceptions of messages, listening attentively to others, and sharing underlying feelings of love, concern, or hurt), you can point to these behaviors as indicators that positive changes are possible. Further, you can convey to clients that they can exercise control over their own behaviors and, if they are willing to make the effort, they can improve many aspects of their relationship. Such responses tend to counteract initial feelings of powerlessness that many clients experience and to generate hope and motivation to work on problems.

Modifying Cognitive Sets

Still another way of inculcating hope with clients who believe they are powerless to improve their situations is to focus on negative cognitive sets that underlie their sense of powerlessness. Some clients impute their difficulties to forces beyond their control (e.g., "Others just see me as someone they can use") or believe that improvement cannot occur unless other persons or circumstances change (e.g., "There's no way our marriage can improve as long as my husband locks all of his feelings inside himself"). To engender motivation and hope in such instances, you must counter clients' feelings of powerlessness by assisting them to recognize that change on their parts can indeed improve their situations.

To alter negative cognitive sets such as those just cited, it is essential to:

1. Reframe the problem so that clients can see that change is possible.

2. Convey a genuine belief in clients' ability to improve a situation they previously construed as unchangeable.

The skill of *reframing* (Watzlawick, Weakland, & Fisch, 1974) or redefining problems requires the ability to place clients' difficulties in a fresh perspective that suggests constructive actions clients can take to resolve impasses. In seeking to reframe a problem, the crucial questions that can guide you to a fresh perspective are, "How does the client contribute to the problematic behavior of others?" or "What changes in the client's behavior would likely effect positive changes on the part of others?" In the preceding situations, the practitioner could gradually assist clients to reframe problems as follows:

1. I think of myself as having so little to offer that I permit myself to be taken for granted and used by others. If I learn to respect myself more, I can set limits with others and expect more from them in return for my favors. Others will respect me more if I respect myself.

2. I can help my partner share his feelings by creating a climate conducive to his doing so. If I do not criticize and pressure him, he may open up more. I can ask him how I can make it easier for him to express his feelings and can indicate my willingness to change my own behavior accordingly.

In assisting clients to reframe their problems, finesse is required. Head-on confrontations produce defensiveness and project an image of the practitioner as one who arbitrarily attempts to impose his or her views on others. To assist the client in the first situation to reframe the problem as suggested, it would be vital to explore carefully the client's self-perception. By eliciting feelings of doubt and low self-esteem and connecting them with the client's self-effacing interpersonal behaviors, the practitioner enables the client to gradually achieve realization that his/her own emotions and behaviors foster the exploitative behavior of others. This realization also empowers the client to make changes.

In the second situation, the practitioner would also guide the client to recognize the part she plays in her husband's emotional secrecy. It would be crucial to elicit minute details of the partners' interactions, focusing on the wife's behaviors, so that she could become aware that her responses may discourage her husband from behaving in ways she purportedly desires. In her frustration, for example, she may put down his efforts to express himself by interrupting, disagreeing, or criticizing him for being verbally incompetent. If this client were seen conjointly with her husband, the practitioner might also request that she express her desires for increased emotional expression to him and ask him how she can make it easier for him to express himself. With sensitive guidance by the practitioner, the husband may risk expressing himself, which in itself is a beginning. More importantly, however, he may identify behavior on her part that blocks his communication.

The second guideline, to express a genuine belief in the client's ability to improve the problematic situation, is relatively straightforward and easy to implement if you are successful in implementing the first guideline. Nevertheless, expressing a genuine belief in the client's ability to take remedial action often expands hope.

If you neglect to impart hope to clients who have an established cognitive pattern of expecting to fail, you may unwittingly set into motion a self-fulfilling prophecy that may doom the helping process to failure. Posited by the eminent sociologist Robert Merton (1967), the concept of self-fulfilling prophecy is an extension of W. F. Thomas' theorem that, "If men define situations as real, they are real in their consequences." Thus, if clients define themselves as impotent in coping with their problematic situations, they are likely to cope in an impotent manner. To counter and/or avoid negative self-fulfilling prophecies of the client and possibly of yourself, we recommend you adopt the stance of *maintaining an expectancy of therapeutic success,* a stance that is empirically supported (Morgan, 1961).

To counter the erosive effects of negative expectancies, you can emphasize with clients that their *attitudes* toward accomplishing their goals are at least as important as their *abilities.* If they expect to fail, they will probably exert at best a half-hearted effort, which is unlikely to produce the desired effects. It is thus important in initial sessions that you assist clients to become aware that they are dwelling on negative and self-defeating patterns, which set them up for failure. These dysfunctional cognitive sets often involve distorted self-perceptions and low esteem. Examples of such negative sets are as follows:

- "Why should I succeed in this? I've failed in everything else I've tried to accomplish."

- "Our family's just different. Everyone does their own thing, and no one seems to care about each other. It's always been that way, and I can't see how coming here's going to make any difference."

Obviously, such negative cognitive sets not only deflate motivation but pervade many, if not most, aspects of clients' lives. In assisting clients to become aware of their self-defeating cognitive patterns, you can create opportunities for clients to choose whether to make these negative cognitions the focus of initial change efforts. We discuss at length the process of changing negative cognitions in Chapter 18.

13 ■ Negotiating Goals and Formulating a Contract

The Rationale for Contracts

After exploring problems sufficiently and reaching agreement as to the nature of the problems and the systems involved, the practitioner and client(s) are ready to formulate a contract. Contracting is the natural culmination of the first major phase and the introduction of the change-oriented (goal attainment) phase—the heart of the helping process. Contracts specify goals to be accomplished and the means of accomplishing them, clarify the roles of the participants, and establish the conditions under which assistance is provided. An initial contract thus is an agreement that guides practitioners and clients in their joint efforts to achieve specified objectives.

Research findings attest to the value of social work contracts. Commenting on the significance of these findings, Rhodes (1977) observed that "ambiguities about the contract and its unsystematic application as a principle of practice may account for a consistently high percentage of unplanned client withdrawal" (p. 125). Additional evidence of the importance of the contract has been provided by Wood (1978), who reviewed numerous outcome studies of direct practice and reported that in a substantial number reporting negative outcomes, explicit contracts were not employed by practitioners. However, studies that reported positive outcomes typically utilized contracts.

To use contracts to maximal advantage, you must be aware of their component parts and be skillful in systematically negotiating them. The purpose of this chapter is therefore to assist you to gain knowledge and skill in utilizing contracts effectively. In the first portion, we discuss the process of negotiating goals. The remainder of the chapter is committed to other components of the contract and to the actual process of mutually formulating a contract.

Goals

The importance of formulating goals has been emphasized in social work literature for many years. Analyses of outcome research studies, however, have disclosed deficiencies in defining goals on the part of practitioners that may have contributed significantly to poor outcomes. Reid (1970) concluded that practitioners were overly general in specifying goals, leading to "unrealistic aspirations and to repeated shifts in direction" (p. 145). Wood (1978) drew similar conclusions, cautioning that setting vague or unreasonably high goals "is to subject clients to a cruel and destructive experience in disappointment, frustration, and erosion of their confidence in their own capacities" (p. 453). Wood also found many instances in which goals were set in advance without consulting clients. In such instances, poor outcome could well have resulted from the fact that the clients and practitioners were working toward different ends. If practitioners' goals failed to match clients' goals, it is reasonable to assume that the latter would have experienced frustration, confusion, and discouragement.

The Purpose of Goals

Goals specify what clients wish to accomplish. Inherent in goals are desired changes in clients' life situations that correspond to wants and needs identified when problems were explored and assessed. Goals thus are inextricably connected with and flow directly from the assessment process. Indeed, as you explore clients' wants and needs, you are engaging in preliminary goal selection work.

Goals serve the following valuable functions in the helping process:

1. Assure that practitioners and clients are in agreement about objectives to be achieved.

2. Provide direction and continuity to the helping process and prevent needless wandering.

3. Facilitate the development and selection of appropriate strategies and interventions.

4. Assist practitioners and clients to monitor their progress.

5. Serve as outcome criteria in evaluating the effectiveness of specific interventions and of the helping process.

Utilizing goals to perform the preceding functions requires knowledge of the types of goals, criteria for selecting them, and knowledge of and skill in negotiating goals, each of which we consider in the following sections.

Types of Goals

Goals may be categorized in a broad sense as *discrete*, on one hand, and *ongoing* or continuous, on the other. Discrete goals consist of one-time actions or changes that resolve or ameliorate problems. Examples include obtaining a needed resource (e.g., public assistance or medical care), making a major decision (e.g., deciding whether to keep an unborn infant or place it for adoption), or making a change in one's environment (e.g., changing living arrangements). Ongoing goals, by contrast, involve actions that are continuous and repetitive, and progress toward such goals is therefore incremental. Examples of ongoing goals include managing conflict effectively, expressing feelings openly, asserting one's rights, setting limits with children, controlling anger, and participating in group discussions.

Another factor that determines the types of goals is the systems or subsystems targeted for change. With individual clients, the targets of change typically involve intrapersonal subsystems as well as the client's interaction with the social and physical environment. Goals with individual clients commonly involve changes in both overt and covert behaviors. Common examples include changes in *cognitive functioning* (e.g., reducing the incidence of self-depreciating thoughts), changes in *emotional functioning* (e.g., reducing the frequency and intensity of depressive feelings), or *behavioral changes* (e.g., reducing or eliminating consumption of alcohol). Goals may also include changes in interpersonal behavior (e.g., asking women for a date or engaging others in conversation).

When the target system is a couple, family, or group, goals typically embody changes on the part of all relevant participants in the system. In these larger systems, goals may be held in common by members of the system (shared goals) or may involve agreed-upon exchanges of different behavior (reciprocal goals). Examples of *shared* goals include marital partners agreeing to listen to one another without interrupting or to adopt a certain strategy of decision making. Family members and group members may agree to pursue a shared goal of supplanting critical, demeaning messages to others with positive, emotionally supportive messages. The distinguishing feature of shared goals is that all members are committed to change their behaviors in essentially the same way.

With *reciprocal* goals, members of a system seek to solve interactional problems by exchanging different behaviors. For example, a couple may seek help because they communicate infrequently and are becoming increasingly emotionally distant. The wife may complain that her husband seldom talks with her, and he may counter that he gradually stopped talking with her because she seldom listened and instead criticized him and ridiculed his points of view. After exploring their problem, the couple may agree to a shared goal of increasing their verbal exchanges and further agree to reciprocal individual subgoals that include attentive listening by the wife and increased verbal sharing by the husband. Reciprocal goals thus tend to be quid pro quo in nature; that is, each person agrees to modify personal behavior contingent upon corresponding changes by the other.

Guidelines for Selecting and Defining Goals

Because goals serve several vital functions (listed earlier), it is important to select and define them with care. The following guidelines will assist you in advancing your proficiency in formulating goals.

Goals Must Relate to the Desired End Results Sought by Clients To be adequately motivated, clients must believe that accomplishing selected goals will enhance their life situations by resolving or mitigating their problems. Clients are thus likely to pursue only those goals in which they are emotionally invested; therefore, practitioners who define goals unilaterally or attempt to impose goals on clients are unlikely to enlist their cooperation. In fact, clients are likely to respond by resisting or by terminating prematurely. In negotiating goals, you should have no hidden agendas and should accord the client the final authority in selecting appropriate goals. This does not mean that you should assume a passive role in negotiating goals. To the contrary, clients will look to you for guidance in selecting goals, and you have a responsibility to share your expertise in this regard. We discuss your role in negotiating goals in a later section.

Goals Should Be Defined in Explicit and Measurable Terms To provide direction in the helping process, goals must specifically define the desired end results so that all participants are clear about changes to be accomplished within the problem system. In other words, each actor should be able to specify what she or he will be doing differently or what environmental factors will be changed. Goals should thus be defined in specific rather than general terms. The logic of this principle is analogous to the logic involved in planning to travel from one point to another. To achieve a given destination, a traveler pinpoints the destination and then plans an appropriate itinerary. Although all pathways lead to Rome, as the old saying goes, one is unlikely to reach Rome by specifying one's destination as the Northern Hemisphere or Europe. Yet some goals defined by practitioners have been equally nebulous (e.g., "to improve the Youngs' marital relationship," or "to increase the solidarity of the Williams family"). Small wonder that "drift" (Reid, 1970) or wandering in the helping process sometimes occurs and that a substantial number of clients report being unclear about what a practitioner has been seeking to assist them to accomplish.

Appropriately stated, goals specify both overt and covert changes to be accomplished and should be measurable. Overt behavioral changes (e.g., "Jimmy will complete his homework each evening before watching television") can be observed by others, making precise measurement possible. Covert changes (e.g., curtailing derogatory thoughts about one's self) are also measurable, but only by the client. Measures of covert behavior thus are more subject to error as a result of inconsistent self-monitoring, the effects of self-monitoring on the target behavior, and other factors.

The lists presented in Table 13-1 will further assist you in discriminating between global and explicit goals. Included in the lists are goals that involve both overt and covert behaviors. Notice that explicit goals refer to specific behaviors or environmental changes that suggest the nature of corresponding remedial interventions.

It should be apparent by now that goals can be expressed at various levels of abstraction. Since clients tend to define goals generally, you will need to assist them in defining goals with increased specificity. The specific goals listed in the table, in fact, may be thought of as subgoals of the global goals listed in the left column. By moving to specific subgoals, you thus partialize or dissect global goals into behaviorally defined component parts. These latter components then become the targets of systematic efforts addressed to change.

Another aspect of defining a goal explicitly involves *specifying essential behavioral changes of all persons in the target system with respect to shared or reciprocal goals.* Observing this guideline assures that all participants are clear about the part they play in accomplishing the overarching goal that relates to the broader system. For example, if a global or *ultimate* goal in family therapy is to reduce conflict and to achieve closer and more harmonious family relationships, family members must be clear about their individual goals in relationship to the larger system. The same principle applies in marital therapy and other small groups.

A final aspect of defining goals explicitly is to specify the degree or extent of change desired by clients. With goals that involve ongoing behavior, growth is potentially infinite, and it is desirable, therefore, to determine the extent of change sought by the client. The advantage of specifying desired levels of change is that practitioners and clients mutually agree to the ends sought by the latter. For example, clients who seek to enhance their social skills and to expand their social participation commonly aspire to varying levels of goal accomplishment. One client may be satisfied with being able to engage

Table 13-1   Global and Specific Goal Statements

Global	Specific
1. Gain increased control over emotions	1. Reduce frequency and intensity of anger outbursts by discerning cues that elicit anger, using internal dialogue that quells anger, and employing relaxation procedures that counter anger
2. Improve social relations	2. Approach others and initiate and maintain conversation by employing listening skills and furthering responses
3. Enhance social environment	3. Obtain living arrangements in a center for elderly persons that provides social activities
4. Enhance self-esteem	4. Arrest habitual negative self-statements by engaging in self-dialogue about their destructive consequences; align performance expectations with realistic criteria; attend to strengths and positive qualities; silently express self-approval when merited
5. Improve quality of parenting	5. Demonstrate competence and responsibility in assuring continuous child care, planning and preparing nutritious meals, and maintaining adequate sanitary and hygienic conditions
6. Increase social participation in a group context	6. Resolve fears of "looking stupid," initiate discussion of personal views, ask questions, participate in group exploring and problem-solving activities
7. Improve marital communication	7. Express needs and wants to each other, listen without interrupting and check out meaning attributions, increase frequency of positive messages, avoid competitive interactions, reduce critical and blaming messages
8. Relate more comfortably with opposite sex	8. Explore and resolve fears of rejection, introduce self and initiate conversations, ask for date, engage in appropriate activities

minimally in occasional conversations limited to co-workers and relatives, whereas another may aspire to engage openly and actively in a broad array of social situations. Marital partners who seek to reduce the frequency and intensity of conflict likewise differ in their definitions of acceptable levels of goal attainment. Some couples seek total elimination of intense conflicts that involve yelling, name-calling, and other like behaviors. Other couples seek only to reduce the frequency of aversive interactions.

Goals Must Be Feasible Selecting unachievable goals sets clients up for failure

that may produce discouragement, disillusionment, and a sense of defeat. Therefore, it is vital to consider both the capacity of clients for accomplishing goals and possible environmental constraints that militate against goal accomplishment. In most instances, clients possess the capacity to accomplish goals they set for themselves, and it is desirable to affirm the validity of their goals and to express belief in their capacity to attain them. Occasionally, you will encounter clients who are grandiose or who deny personal limitations that are obvious to others. In these instances, you can perform a valuable service by sensitively and tactfully assisting them to lower their aim to the upper range of what is realistically achievable.

With respect to environmental constraints, it is important to weigh opportunities, the receptiveness and capacity of significant others to change along desired lines, economic and employment conditions, group and community attitudes, and other related factors. The following examples illustrate the importance of considering environmental opportunities. A client may wish to move from a convalescent facility to the residence of relatives, but the latter may be unwilling or unable to provide the accommodations and care needed. An intellectually capable person with severe speech impairment associated with cerebral palsy may aspire to become a professional counselor, but employment opportunities for such a person may be virtually nonexistent.

Goals Should Be Commensurate with the Knowledge and Skill of the Practitioner You should agree to joining clients in working toward only those goals for which you have requisite knowledge and skill. Certain problems and goals require high levels of expertise that you may not yet have attained, and it is your responsibility to clients, the profession, and yourself not to undertake interventions for which you lack competence. Certain problems, for example, require competence in family therapy, sex therapy, behavior modification, and specialized knowledge of emotional disorders and treatment techniques.

If you are receiving supervision from a person who possesses the requisite competence, it is ethical to contract for goals beyond your competence, for you have access to the guidance needed to enable you to render the essential service. Otherwise, you are ethically bound to undertake only goals commensurate with your competence and to refer clients who re-

quire service beyond your competence to other qualified professionals. The question could be raised, of course, as to what course of action one should follow if qualified professionals are not available, as often occurs in rural areas. Under these circumstances, the choice may be between no service or less than optimal service. In our judgment, practitioners are justified in extending service in such cases under two provisions. First, practitioners are obligated to explain their limitations with regard to the goals in question, enabling the client to decide on an informed basis whether to proceed or not. Second, the practitioner should be confident that undertaking the goals does not place clients or others at risk. With severely depressed clients, for example, the risk of suicide may preclude undertaking treatment without medical consultation and without arranging precautionary measures with significant others. A similar risk may exist when clients have a history of violent behavior that poses a threat to others. Consultation and hospitalization should be considered before undertaking treatment in such instances.

Whenever Possible, Goals Should Be Stated in Positive Terms That Emphasize Growth Defining goals in ways that stress growth highlights beneficial changes or gains that will accrue in the lives of clients as a result of attaining goals. In formulating goal statements, stipulating negative behaviors that must be eliminated tends to draw attention to what clients must give up. Even though clients ordinarily welcome relinquishing dysfunctional behavior (e.g., tearing themselves down, fighting, and eating or drinking to excess), they may feel a sense of impending loss, for even though such behaviors produce stress and problems, clients are accustomed to living with

Table 13-2 Negative and Positive Goal Statements

Negative	Positive
1. To reduce the frequency of criticism among family members	To increase the family members' awareness of each other's strengths and to increase the frequency of positive messages
2. To eliminate pouting and cold wars between marital partners	To deal with disagreements openly, promptly, and constructively
3. To eliminate subgroupings and nonparticipatory behavior by group members	To unite efforts of group members in working collectively and to draw each member into participation
4. To eliminate or reduce the frequency of drinking binges	To achieve ever-increasing periods of sobriety, taking one day at a time
5. To eliminate yelling at the children and resorting to physical punishment	To consistently apply new ways of influencing and disciplining children, such as utilizing "time out" procedures, increasing positive feedback, and employing a problem-solving approach with them

them. Psychologically defining goals in terms of gains rather than losses tends to enhance motivation and to mitigate opposition to change. Examples of contrasting negative and positive goal statements are included in Table 13-2.

Avoid Agreeing to Goals about Which You Have Major Reservations Instances sometimes occur in which it is neither ethical nor wise to enter into agreements to pursue certain goals. Clients may request your assistance in pursuing goals that are incompatible with one of your major values. Values, of course, are highly individual, but many practitioners have serious reservations about working with clients whose life philosophies, moral values, or sexual practices diverge markedly from their own. Because of deeply held religious or moral beliefs, some practitioners cannot work effectively with people who are considering abortions, seeking help in enhancing homosexual relationships, or planning to relinquish custody of children to pursue personal interests. If clients pose goals about which you have strong reservations, it is generally wise to refer them to another professional person who is com-

fortable in working toward such goals. It is important to explain your reason for making the referral, being careful to safeguard the client's self-esteem. For example: "I'm sorry I can't join you in working toward that goal. You and I have different values, and mine would get in the way of giving you the help you're seeking. I'm not faulting you for being different from me. We're all different, and that's how it should be. I do want to help you obtain the service you need, however, and if it's agreeable with you, we can explore that together."

Occasionally, you may also have reservations about clients' goals that appear to be potentially harmful to the physical or mental well-being of themselves or others. An adult may have a goal of using devious means to regain custody of children in foster placement. A pregnant adolescent may seek to enlist your assistance in planning to entrap an unwary male into marrying her. In these and similar situations, you would be justified in declining to assist clients in their planned ventures. In such instances candidly but tactfully explain the basis of your misgiving, expressing your willingness to consider other goals.

Goals Must Be Consistent with the Functions of the Agency Explorations of problems and clients' wants sometimes disclose desired changes that are incompatible with the functions of the agency. For example, after exploring a couple's problems in a family service agency, it may be apparent that the couple's primary need relates to vocational counseling, a service not provided by the agency. Similarly, in hospital settings, clients often manifest problems that require services beyond the scope of the hospital's function, such as marital therapy, mental health services, or financial assistance. In such instances, it is appropriate to assist the client to secure the needed services through referral to another agency.

The Process of Mutually Selecting and Defining Goals

Having considered the rationale of employing goals and delineating criteria for selecting and defining them, we are now ready to consider the actual process of negotiating goals. This process consists of several activities that may be implemented in the following sequence, adapting the sequence to the circumstances of each case.

1. Determine clients' readiness to negotiate goals.

2. Explain the purpose of selecting and defining goals.

3. Elicit goals from clients, suggest other potential goals, and then mutually select those that are appropriate.

4. Define the goals explicitly, and specify the extent of change desired by clients.

5. Determine the feasibility of targeted goals, and discuss potential benefits and risks associated with them.

6. Assist clients to make a choice about committing themselves to specific goals.

7. Rank goals according to clients' priorities.

To clarify how to implement these steps, we will briefly discuss each one in the following sections.

Determine Clients' Readiness When you believe you have explored clients' problems sufficiently, it is appropriate to determine if your clients concur with your opinion and are ready to negotiate goals.[1] A message similar to the following may be used to assess clients' readiness: "You've provided a good description of your problems and situation, and I feel I have a pretty good grasp of them. I wonder if you feel ready to talk about some specific goals at this point or if you feel we need to discuss some additional information first." If the client conveys readiness, you can advance to the next step.

With respect to cultural factors regarding timing in setting goals, the findings of a study (Taussig, 1987) comparing Anglo and Mexican-Americans revealed no differences between the groups in response to reactions to early goal setting. Both groups reacted positively.

Explain the Purpose of Goals Explaining the purposes of goals increases clients' receptivity to the process and fosters their participation. It has been our experience that clients respond positively to such explanations, readily grasping and appreciating the significance of goals in the problem-solving process. Usually a brief explanation is all that is needed. Your explanation, of course, should be consistent with the functions of goals

---

[1]The time required for an adequate exploration varies but usually ranges from 45 minutes to 90 minutes. Initial *conjoint* interviews typically require about 30 minutes more than individual interviews.

listed early in this chapter and should emphasize the importance of clients' participation and ultimate authority in selecting goals. An example of such an explanation follows:

"We've been exploring your problems at some length, and you've indicated a number of things you'd like to be different in your life (or marriage or family). I'd like to think with you now about some specific goals you'd like to accomplish. Selecting goals assures that we're all trying to accomplish the same results. They also provide a sense of direction and serve as guideposts to make sure we stay on track. With goals, we can also evaluate your progress and determine how successful we've been in our work together. It's important that the goals represent the changes that are most important to you. I have some ideas about goals, which I'll share with you. Actually they'll likely be much the same as yours. When we have taken a look at all of them, we'll sort out the goals you regard as most important."

If clients appear confused or manifest misgivings about proceeding further, you will need to explore their feelings and perhaps clarify further the function of goals. If clients respond positively, you are ready to advance to the next step.

Mutually Select Appropriate Goals   The process of selecting goals begins by asking clients to identify goals they would like to achieve. An effective way of assisting them is to employ messages similar to the following:

- "If we succeed in our work together, how will you think and behave differently?"

- "If your family could be the way you would like it to be, what would you as family members be doing differently?"

- "It's been very evident in our session so far that both of you want to improve your marriage. I'd like to hear from each of you as to specific improvements you'd like to achieve."

Notice that each message requests clients to identify specific changes desired, which paves the way to the next step. If clients have difficulty identifying goals, you can prompt them by making reference to problems and wants identified during the exploratory process and suggest they consider changes related to those problems and wants. The following is an example of such a prompting message: "As you talked about your difficulties with your daughter, you mentioned you were sick of the constant bickering between the two of you. I wonder if you might like to work toward making changes in your relationship with her?"

With little encouragement, most clients will identify key goals. We recommend that as they define goals you write them down, explaining that because goals are extremely important, you are keeping a record of them.

As clients verbalize goals, you may need to interject comments that seek clarification or to suggest rewording a goal to clarify its meaning or enhance its specificity. It is important, however, not to take liberties with clients' goals but to gain their approval of rewordings. It has been our experience that if you offer suggestions tentatively and respectfully, clients welcome them.

Clients often identify most or all of the goals that must be accomplished to obviate their problems. Frequently, however, because of your external vantage point, goals will occur to you that clients have overlooked or omitted. Consequently, you have a responsibility to introduce these goals for clients' consideration. In introducing such goals, it is important to offer them as suggestions and to explain your reason for offering them, referring to related information revealed earlier in the session.

Define the Goals Explicitly   After mutually selecting goals, you are ready to refine them by defining them explicitly and determining the extent of change desired by the client. If you were successful in the previous step, this task may require little or no further attention. If the goals were expressed in somewhat general terms, however, you will need to increase their specificity. Examples of messages you can employ to enhance the specificity of goals were presented in the preceding section. You may need to supplement these messages with suggestions of your own as to pertinent behavioral changes that would operationalize general goals.

With respect to determining the desired extent of changes, you can employ messages similar to the following:

- "You say you want to improve your housekeeping. What standards do you want to achieve?"

- [*To marital partners*]: "You've identified the goal of expressing more affection for one another. How much affection will be sufficient for you?"

- [*To family members*]: "Your goal of wanting to do more things together as a family appears to be well worth pursuing. What is the extent of family-centered activities you would like to achieve?"

Determine the Feasibility of Goals and Discuss Their Potential Benefits and Risks   Before settling upon goals, it is important to ascertain their feasibility and to assess the benefits and risks associated with them. To assist clients to evaluate the feasibility of questionable goals, you can employ responses similar to the following:

- "What obstacles do you foresee that might block you from achieving this goal?"

- "That sounds like an almost superhuman goal. I'm wondering how realistic it is."

- "Your goal is certainly an ambitious one. I can sense how you'd like to accomplish it, but I'd hate to see you struggle for a goal that may be out of reach. Let's think about what you'd have to do to accomplish your goal."

Discussing benefits that will derive from attaining goals tends to enhance clients' commitment to exerting vigorous efforts to achieve them. A response similar to the following assists in identifying such benefits:

- "What benefits do you expect to reap by achieving this goal?"

- [*To marital partners*]: "How will your marriage be enhanced by achieving this goal?"

- [*To family members*]: "In what ways will your family life improve by successfully accomplishing this goal?"

You also have an obligation to assure that clients weigh possible risks associated with attaining goals. Enhanced functioning sometimes entails growth pains and negative as well as positive consequences. Examples of the former include losing a job by being assertive with an unjust employer, being rejected when making social overtures, experiencing increased pressure and family conflict by going to work, and suffering from anxiety and discomfort by exposing painful emotions to family and group members.

Clients have a right to be aware of potential risks, and you may be vulnerable to lawsuits if you neglect your obligation in this regard. Because clients may lack awareness of certain risks, you may need to draw their attention to them. Clients may also be aware of risks you have overlooked, and it is therefore important to inquire as to risks they may anticipate.

Assist Clients to Make a Choice about Committing Themselves to Specific Goals

After discussing the benefits and risks of pursuing specific goals, the next step is to weigh these potential consequences and to reach a decision about making a commitment to strive to attain the goals in question. In most instances, benefits are likely to outweigh risks, and clients will manifest adequate readiness to contract to work toward the goals. A simple but effective means we have employed to assess clients' readiness is to ask them to rate this factor on a scale from 1 to 10, where 1 represents "extremely uncertain and not at all ready" and 10 represents "optimistic, eager to start, and totally committed." Most clients report their readiness in the range of 6–8, which usually indicates sufficient willingness to proceed with the contracting process. When clients rate their readiness at 5 or lower, they usually are unready to proceed.

Occasionally, clients manifest marked ambivalence, indicating the need to explore their reservations further. Should this occur, we recommend that you accept their misgivings and avoid attempting to convince them about the desirability of proceeding further. It is important, of course, to determine if their misgivings are realistic or are based on irrational fears (e.g., a parent may be hesitant to pursue a goal of setting consistent limits for a child because of fears of losing the child's love, or a sexually inhibited woman may fear that if she lets herself experience sensual feelings she will lose control of herself and become a slave to sexual impulses). When you encounter irrational fears you should assist the client to realize that the fears may be an important dynamic in the problem and that it would be unfortunate to decide against working to accomplish a worthwhile goal on the basis of unrealistic fears. Rather, the client may choose to pursue the goal of resolving the fears before undertaking related goals. Negotiating such an intermediate goal reduces the threat of the primary goal and enhances the readiness of the client to enter a working contract.

When clients manifest continued ambivalence, it is appropriate to suggest that they may desire additional time to ponder a decision. We recommend that you express your willingness to think with them further about the matter inasmuch as discussing feelings and concerns with another person often serves to clarify issues and to resolve feelings. Again, we emphasize the importance of not exerting pressure upon clients to continue. It has been our experience that clients who reluctantly submit to pressure often fail to return for scheduled sessions. Clients thus tend to exercise their right to self-determination when practitioners unwittingly fail to respect this right fully.

Rank Goals According to Clients' Priorities

After clients have settled upon goals and have committed themselves to working toward them, the final step in goal negotiation is to assign priorities to the goals. (Usually clients select from two to five goals.) The purpose of this step is to assure that beginning joint-change efforts are directed to the goal that is most important to clients. This step further assures maximal responsibility and participation in the process by clients, thereby enhancing their motivation to work on goal attainment. As a lead-in to the ranking process, we recommend a message similar to the following: "Now that you've settled upon these goals, it's important to rank them according to priority. I suggest you start with the goal most important to you; then you can rank the others as you see fit. We'll get to all of them in time but we want to be sure to start with the most important one."

When the target system involves more than one person, different members may accord different priorities to goals. Further, members may have individual goals as well as shared or reciprocal goals. If the target system is a couple, a group, or a family it is desirable to have goals that pertain both to individuals and to the larger system. With larger systems, it is desirable to have lists of goals for both individuals and the systems and to rank the goals for each person and the system. In ranking goals for a system, you may need to assist members to negotiate rankings where differences exist.

Baseline Measurement

To evaluate the effectiveness of interventions and of clients' progress toward achieving goals, some practitioners obtain measures of the incidence of problematic behaviors before implementing change-oriented interventions. For example, if a goal were to increase the frequency of positive messages, clients would be instructed to keep a daily tally of the number of such messages they convey for a period of one week. The daily average thus would serve as a baseline against which progress could be measured. Similar baselines can be determined for behaviors that involve eliminating temper tantrums, overeating, speaking up in social situations, expressing troubling feelings, listening to one's children, and a myriad of other possible target behaviors. Such measures quantify problem behaviors and make it possible to ascertain both weekly progress and ultimate outcomes of change efforts. In addition, clients are enabled to discern small incremental changes that might otherwise escape detection, which often sustains and enhances their motivation. A further advantage of obtaining baseline measures is that if interventions are not achieving measurable results, the practitioner can negotiate with clients to implement other interventions.

Baseline measures are not feasible with discrete goals, for evaluating the efficacy of helping efforts in such instances is a clear-cut matter; either clients accomplish a goal or they do not. Because progress toward *ongoing* goals is incremental and is not subject to fixed limits, employing baseline measures is an effective way of avoiding subjective judgments about degrees of progress.

Baseline measurements are obtained before change-oriented interventions are implemented. You may obtain these measurements either by having clients make retrospective estimates of the incidence of behaviors targeted for change or by obtaining data before the following session. Although less accurate, the former method often is employed because change-oriented efforts need not be deferred pending the gathering of baseline data. This is a key advantage, for acute problems often demand immediate attention and delaying intervention for even one week may not be justifiable. On the other hand, delaying interventions for one week while gathering baseline data often does not create undue difficulty, and the resultant data are likely to be far more reliable than mere estimates.

When determining the baseline of target behavior by retrospective estimates, it is common practice to ask the client to estimate the incidence of the behavior across a specified time interval, which may range from a few minutes to one day depending upon the usual frequency of the target behaviors. Time intervals selected for frequent behaviors, such as nervous mannerisms, should be relatively short (e.g., 15-minute intervals). For relatively infrequent behaviors, such as temper tantrums, intervals may consist of several hours.

When baseline measures are taken of current overt behaviors, repeated frequency counts across specified time intervals are typically employed. The time intervals selected should be those during which the highest incidence of behavioral excesses occur or times in which positive behaviors are desired.

Frequency counts may be made by clients, by observers, or by practitioners themselves (when the target behavior occurs in conjoint or group sessions). Because it is convenient, practitioners often have clients record personal behaviors that occur outside the therapeutic sessions. Baselines obtained through self-monitoring, however, are not true measurements of behavior under "no treatment" conditions, for self-monitoring itself often produces therapeutic effects (Gingerich, 1979). For example, monitoring the rate of a desired behavior may influence a client to increase the frequency of that behavior. Similarly, measuring the rate of negative behavior may influence a client to reduce its frequency. These effects of self-monitoring on the behavior being monitored are termed *reactive effects.* Viewed by a researcher, reactive effects are a source of contamination that confound the effects of interventions being tested. From a clinician's viewpoint, however, self-monitoring may

be employed to advantage *as an intervention* precisely because reactive effects tend to increase or decrease certain target behaviors. In fact, Paquin (1981) has written about using self-monitoring for this purpose in marital and family therapy. Although desired changes may result from self-monitoring of either positive or negative behaviors, selecting positive behaviors is preferable because doing so focuses on growth related to positively defined goals.

Self-administering scales are also useful for obtaining baseline data. Many psychological scales are available but the Clinical Measurement Package or CMP developed by Hudson (1982), a social worker, is especially useful. This package includes nine different scales that practitioners can employ to obtain baseline data on depression; self-esteem; marital, family, and sexual adjustments; parents' attitudes toward children and children's attitude toward parents; and peer relations. Each scale can be self-administered and scored quickly and easily, and a manual provides explicit and helpful instructions for interpreting scores as well as information regarding the reliability and validity of the scales. We urge all direct practitioners to become familiar with and to employ this excellent resource.

Baseline data can also be obtained for *covert* behaviors, such as troubling thoughts or feelings (e.g., irrational fears, depressed states, or self-depreciating thoughts). Clients may make frequency counts of targeted thoughts or rate degrees of emotional states. Where goals involve altering feelings, such as anger, depression, loneliness, and anxiety, it is desirable to construct self-anchoring scales (Bloom, 1975) that denote various levels of an internal state. To do this, employ a five- or seven-point scale that represents varying levels of internal states ranging from absence of the troubling feeling or thought on one end to maximal intensity on the other. To "anchor" such scales, ask clients to imagine themselves experiencing the extreme degrees of the given internal state and to describe what they experience. You can then use the descriptions to define at least the extremes and the midpoint of the scale. Developing scales in this manner quantifies internal states uniquely for each client. In constructing self-anchoring scales, it is important to avoid mixing different types of internal states, for even though emotions such as "happy" and "sad" appear to belong on the same continuum, they are qualitatively different, and mixing them will result in confusion. Figure 13-1 depicts a seven-point anchored scale.

Clients can employ self-anchoring scales to record the extent of troubling internal states across specified time intervals (e.g., three times daily for seven days) in a manner similar to that of making frequency counts of overt behaviors. In both instances, clients keep tallies on the target behaviors. A minimum of 10 separate measures is generally necessary to discern patternings of data, but urgent needs for intervention sometimes require practitioners to settle for less.

After obtaining these separate measures, the next step is to transfer the data to a graph on which the horizontal axis denotes time intervals and the vertical axis denotes frequency or extent of behav-iors. Simple to construct, such a graph makes it possible to evaluate the progress of clients and the efficacy of interventions. Figure 13-2 is an example of such a graph, which depicts the incidence of anxiety before and during the implementation of change-oriented interventions. Note that the baseline period was seven days and the time interval selected for self-monitoring was one day. Interventions were employed over a period of four weeks. From the graph, it is apparent that the client experienced some ups and downs (as usually occurs), but marked progress was achieved.

Comparing data gathered during a baseline period with data recorded during the change-oriented period (and preferably follow-up data as well) is not only valuable in evaluating progress with individual clients but in testing the efficacy of specific interventions. Research designs conducted in this fashion are designated as single-subject designs. When used for research purposes, stringent guidelines should be followed, and doing so may conflict with delivering services in an optimal fashion (Gambrill & Barth, 1980; Thomas, 1978). Further, rigorous research employing single-subject design requires knowledge beyond the scope of this book. For those interested in studying single-subject research, Bloom and Fischer (1982), Jayaratne and Levy (1979), and Tripodi and Epstein (1980) have written informative texts.

Figure 13-1 A Sample of a Self-Anchoring Scale for Anxiety

1	2	3	4	5	6	7
Least anxious (calm, relaxed, serene)		Moderately (tense, uptight, but still functioning with effort)			Most (muscles taut, can't concentrate or sit still, could climb the wall)	

Formulating a Contract

When you have completed the process of negotiating goals with clients, you are ready to formulate a *contract*. Writers generally agree that a contract should include the following elements:

1. Goals to be accomplished (ranked by priority).

2. Roles of the participants.

3. Interventions or techniques to be employed.

4. Time frame and frequency and length of sessions.

5. Means of monitoring progress.

6. Stipulations for renegotiating the contract.

7. Housekeeping items, such as beginning date, provisions for canceling or changing scheduled sessions, and financial arrangements.

Although it is the final discrete activity of the first phase of the helping process, contracting continues throughout the entire course of the helping venture. Goals are fluid and should be expanded or modified as situations change and new information comes to light. Time limits, types of intervention employed, frequency of sessions, and participants in the helping process may be altered according to the changing circumstances of each case. It is for these reasons that item 6, providing stipulations for renegotiating contracts, is included in the list of essential elements of a contract. Ongoing explicit understandings between practitioners and clients are vital. Keeping the contract updated also conveys continuing respect for the client and enhances ongoing motivation and cooperation. The initial contract thus is only preliminary and must be tailored to fit the changing circumstances of each case.

Practitioners formulate contracts with varying degrees of formality. Some use *written contracts* that specify each of the items listed and provide space for entering details. The clients and practitioner sign the contract, giving it much the same

Figure 13-2   Sample of Graph Recording Extent of Anxiety during Baseline and Intervention Periods

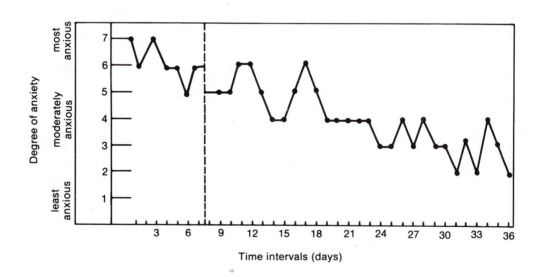

form as a legal contract. The rationale for using a written contract is that it emphasizes the commitments both clients and practitioners make and minimizes the possibility of misunderstandings. The document, of course, is not legally binding, and this should be clarified verbally or stipulated in the written contract. Otherwise clients may believe they are justified in filing suit for malpractice if they do not achieve the goals of the contract.

Other practitioners, including the authors, prefer *verbal contracts,* which include all of the same provisions but without the sterility and finality of a legal contract. (We do recommend that you record in your notes the goals and their priority rankings, which makes them available for review and emphasizes the seriousness of goal setting.) Our preference is based on the more personal and spontaneous interchange involved in reaching an informal contract. Research comparing the efficacy of written versus verbal contracts with respect to process and outcome measures disclosed no superiority of one method of contracting over the other (Klier, Fein, & Genero, 1984).

We now consider elements 2 through 7 in greater depth. Item 1 (goals) was considered earlier in this chapter.

Roles of the Participants

An important but often neglected aspect of contracting is to clarify the roles of client and practitioner as well as the nature of the problem-solving process. Unsophisticated clients, especially those from lower socioeconomic levels, often have little understanding of the helping process and may have expectations that are discrepant from those of the practitioner, which may impair the helping process. Based on a research study that focused on the expectations of clients and

therapists, Aronson and Overall (1966) attributed the higher rate of discontinuance from therapy of lower-class clients (as compared to middle-class clients) to unacknowledged discrepancies in expectations. Mayer and Timms (1969) also found from research interviews with dissatisfied lower-class clients that a major source of dissatisfaction was clashes of perspectives or expectations between clients and social workers. These researchers found that many clients were almost totally unaware that the social worker's approach to problem solving differed fundamentally from their own. Many of the clients studied did not clearly convey their expectations to the social workers, underscoring the necessity to explore carefully this aspect of clients' requests for assistance.

In another study, Rhodes (1977) focused on the contracts of 15 pairs of practitioners and patients in a Veteran's Administration outpatient medical and psychiatric facility. Based on an analysis of patients' and practitioners' perceptions of their roles, she found substantially different perceptions in several instances and concluded that practitioners failed to define clients' roles adequately. She also reported that practitioners did not develop full mutuality in the contracting process; rather, the therapist's activities overshadowed those of patients.

Other researchers have demonstrated the value of attending carefully to client's expectations and to role clarification. In a pilot study involving 26 clients, Perlman (1968) found that she and two other social workers were able to lower the drop-out rate of clients during the intake process by concentrating on eliciting clients' conceptions and expectations of the helping process and by clarifying discrepancies between expectations and what realistically could be offered. Efforts thus were directed specifically to discrepant role expectations. The results indicated a reduction in the drop-out rate. Equally important, Perlman found that the rate of return could be predicted more accurately when it was determined whether or not clarity of expectation and mutual agreement were achieved in the interviews. The potency of using a "role induction interview" to increase the continuance of clients beyond the initial interview has been demonstrated by Hoehn-Saric, Frank, Imber, Nash, Stone, and Battle (1964). Clients prepared by role induction continued therapy at a higher rate and fared better in treatment than control clients who received no special preparation. Similar findings have been reported by Zwick and Atkinson (1985), who used a videotape for "pretherapy orientation."

Apparently the early research findings cited above have borne fruit, for at least one study (Klier et al., 1984) involving family therapy revealed that clients were clear about mutual role expectations and goals and that discrepancies between the perceptions of practitioners and clients regarding roles and goals were minimal. The following guidelines will assist you to achieve similar positive results in role clarification.

1. *Determine the clients' expectations.* The varied expectations that clients bring to initial sessions include lectures, magical solutions, advice-giving, changing other family members, and so on. In the previously cited study conducted by Perlman, only 6 of the 26 clients had realistic expectations of what the practitioner might do with or for them. With minority clients, especially those who are largely unacculturated, sensitively exploring expectations and modifying one's role when indicated are critical, as we discussed in Chapter 6.

Clients sometimes convey their expectations without prompting from a practitioner. For example, after reciting the difficulties created by her son, a mother declared, "We were hoping you could talk with him and help him understand how much he is hurting us." Notice that the mother's "hope" involved a *request* for specific action by the practitioner. When clients thus express their expectations spontaneously, you have the opportunity to deal with those that are unrealistic. Frequently, however, clients do not openly express their expectations, and you will need to elicit them. Effectively determining what clients would like the practitioner to do requires appropriate timing. It is important not to probe expectations until you have established rapport, because the client's request often turns out to be a most intimate revelation. Seeking disclosure too soon thus may put clients on the defensive (Lazare, Eisenthal, & Wasserman, 1975). According to the authors cited, it is also important not to elicit the request at the end of the session, for so doing "deprives the clinician of the opportunity to negotiate or work with the request" (p. 554). The practitioner thus should seek to weave exploration of clients' expectations into the natural flow of the session sometime after clients have had ample opportunity to report their difficulties and to discern the sensitive understanding and goodwill of the practitioner.

If clients have not spontaneously revealed their requests and timing appears appropriate, you can elicit their requests by asking a question similar to one of the following:

- "How do you *hope* (or *wish*) I (or the agency) can assist (or help) you?"

- "As you thought about coming, what were your ideas as to the nature of help you wanted?"

Lazare et al. (1975) report they have been most successful in eliciting requests by using the words *wish* or *hope.* They recommend *not* asking "What do you want?" or "What do you expect?" as clients are likely to perceive these questions as confrontations. These authors also comment that eliciting requests often requires persistence, persuasion, and compassion because clients take a certain amount of risk in disclosing specific requests. If prodding is required, these authors recommend (p. 554) responses similar to the following:

- "You must have had some idea when you decided to come."

- "It is important for me to know what your wishes are even if I may not be able to fulfill them."

2. *Briefly explain the nature of the helping process, and define your relationship as partners seeking a solution to their difficulties.* Clients commonly hope that practitioners will give them advice that they can implement and thereby quickly remedy their problematic situations. They will relinquish these unrealistic expectations with a minimum of disappointment and discouragement in favor of a more realistic understanding if you clarify how you can actually be of help and why it would be futile to approach their problems in the manner they expected. It is very important to convey your intent to help clients find the best possible solution and to clarify that offering advice prematurely would likely be a disservice to them. In the absence of such an explanation, clients may erroneously conclude you are unwilling to meet their expectations because of a lack of concern for them. In this regard, Mayer and Timms (1969) found that clients who were dissatisfied with service for interpersonal problems reasoned that the counselor's failure to give concrete advice stemmed from a lack of interest and desire to help. Taking

the time to explore expectations and to clarify how you can help thus prevents clients from drawing unwarranted negative conclusions that may result in discontinuance.

At this point, it is important to clarify that we are not arguing against the value of advice. Research indicates that clients not only desire advice but often benefit from it (Davis, 1975; Reid & Shapiro, 1969). Our point is that to be effective, advice must be based on adequate knowledge of the dynamics of a problem and of the participants in it. Such a grasp is unlikely to be achieved in an initial session. Clients usually readily comprehend the reasons why offering advice would likely be ineffectual if you offer an explanation *and clarify further how you can help.* We have emphasized the latter point because clarifying how you *can* help engenders hope. You can assist clients to modify unrealistic expectations and clarify your respective roles through a message similar to the following:

"I can sense the urgency you feel in wanting to solve your problems. I wish I could give advice that would lead to solving them. You've probably already had plenty of advice, because most people offer advice freely. It's been my experience, though, that advice is cheap and that what works for one person (couple or family) may not work at all for another. At this point, offering advice would be like playing God because I don't have enough information yet to know what's best for you.

"As I see it, our task is to work together in considering a number of possible options so that you can decide what solution fits best for you and your situation. In the long run, that's what will work best for you. But it takes some time and a lot of thought."

Notice that the preceding role clarification embodies the following essential elements referred to earlier: (1) acknowledging and empathizing with the client's unrealistic expectation and sense of urgency, (2) expressing helpful intent, (3) explaining why the client's unrealistic expectation cannot be fulfilled, and (4) clarifying the helping process and defining a working partnership that places responsibility on the client for actively participating and ultimately making choices as to courses of action to be taken in solving problems.

When clients seek help for marital problems, they commonly view the partner as the source of difficulties and have the unrealistic expectation that the marital therapist will influence the partner to shape up. Because this expectation is so pervasive, we often elicit partners' expectations early in the initial session (individual or conjoint) and clarify the helping role, thereby setting the stage for more productive use of the exploration to follow. Clarifying the process early in the session tends to diminish mutual blaming and competing. Moreover, partners are less likely to respond defensively when the practitioner refuses to be drawn into the "blame game" and focuses instead on assisting each person to become aware of his or her part in the difficulties. The following excerpt of an actual session typifies our approach to role clarification with marital partners:

PRACTITIONER: How much understanding do you have about how marital therapy works?

HUSBAND: Not very much, really. We just know we need help because we're fighting all the time. [*Wife nods in agreement.*]

PRACTITIONER: Perhaps it would be helpful if I took just a few minutes to explain how I work with couples. Would that be agreeable with you?

HUSBAND AND WIFE: [*Both nod affirmatively.*] Yes, we'd like that.

PRACTITIONER: OK, then, I'll explain it as best I can and give you a chance to ask any questions. It's important that all three of us have the same understanding about what we're going to be doing. [*Couple nod in understanding.*] As I see it, my role is to help each of you to understand yourself and your partner better. Marital problems usually are caused by the fact that the needs of one or both partners aren't being met adequately. Lots of factors can block the meeting of important needs, and when they do, problems in relationships develop. My job is to help each of you to understand your partner's needs better and to be more aware of your own needs so that you can express them clearly to your partner. Accomplishing that means you have to communicate in such a way that you really understand each other better. So another part of my job is to help you to communicate more effectively.

WIFE: Good! We need that. Our communication is really bad. We can't seem to talk without getting into a fight.

PRACTITIONER: Well, we'll need to work on that. Part of my job will be to help you see what's going wrong in your communication and to help you get back on track by learning new ways of communicating. In some ways, that means I'll function much as a teacher at times.

HUSBAND: That's OK. If it will help, I'm willing to learn.

PRACTITIONER: That willingness will be a real asset. Another thing that's important to understand is that I can't help by getting involved in assigning blame to one of you or the other. It's been my experience that most marital partners believe the other person is causing the difficulties, and many of their struggles involve blaming each other. Usually it isn't one or the other who's at fault. Both partners contribute to the difficulties, and my task is to assist each of you to see the part you play in them. It's important you understand that. Otherwise, you might think I'm siding with your partner when I focus on your part. I won't be taking sides, but if it feels to you like I am, please let me know. Otherwise, you're likely to resent me, and I won't even be aware of it. To work effectively together we'll have to be open with each other. I'll be open with you, but I have to expect the same of you. [*Pause.*]

WIFE: That makes sense. I'll do my best. [*Partner agrees.*]

PRACTITIONER: I'll want to talk with you more later about how you can get the most out of marital therapy, but I think I've given you a pretty good overview. Any questions before we begin to explore your problems?

HUSBAND: Not really. You've painted a pretty clear picture.

WIFE: I'm glad we're going to talk about needs. A lot of my unhappiness has to do with needs of mine that aren't being met.

Further clarification of the roles of the participants will occur later in the session as the participants negotiate goals and formulate a contract.

Implied in the above excerpt is another aspect of the client's role—*to be open in sharing feelings, thoughts, and events.* By explaining the rationale for openness and by expressing your intent to communicate openly, you enhance clients' receptiveness to this factor. The following illustrates one way of explaining this aspect of the client's role:

"For you to benefit to the fullest, you will need to be as open as possible with me. That means not holding back troubling feelings, thoughts, or events that are important. I can understand you and your difficulties only if you're open and honest with me. Only you know what you think and feel; I can know only as you share with me. Sometimes it's painful to share certain thoughts and feelings, but often those are the very feelings that trouble us the most. If you do hold back, you'll need to remind yourself you may be letting yourself down. If you're finding it difficult to share certain things, let me know. Discussing what's happening inside you— why it's difficult—may make it easier to discuss those painful things.

"I'll be open and honest with you, too. If you have any questions or would like to know more about me, please ask. I'll be frank with you. I may not answer every question, but I'll explain why if I don't."

To enhance clients' participation in the helping process, it is also important to emphasize that they can accelerate their progress by working on their difficulties between appointments. Some clients mistakenly believe that change will result largely from what occurs in sessions. In actuality, the content of sessions is far less significant than how clients apply information gained. The following excerpt illustrates clarifying this aspect of a client's responsibility:

"We'll want to progress toward your goals as rapidly as possible. One way you can hasten your progress is by working hard between our sessions. That means carrying out tasks you've agreed to, applying what we talk about in your daily life, and making mental notes or actually writing down thoughts, feelings, and events that relate to your problems so we can consider them in your next session. Actually, what you do between sessions is more important in accomplishing your goals than the session itself. We'll be together only a brief time each week. The rest of the week you have opportunities to apply what we talk about and plan together.''

Still another aspect of the client's role involves *keeping appointments*. This factor is obvious, but discussing it emphasizes clients' responsibilities and prepares them to cope constructively with obstacles that may cause them to fail or to cancel appointments. The following is an example of a message that clarifies this aspect of the client's role:

"As we work together, it will be most important for you to keep your appointments. Unforeseen things such as illness happen occasionally, of course, and we can change appointments when this happens. At times, however, you may find yourself feeling discouraged or doubting if coming here really helps. It's also possible you may feel upset over something I've said or done and find yourself not wanting to see me. I won't knowingly say or do anything to offend you, but you may have some troubling feelings toward me anyway. The important thing is that you not miss your appointment, because when you're discouraged or upset we need to talk about it. I know that may not be easy, but it will help you to work out your troubled feelings. If you miss your appointment, you may find it even harder to return.''

A final factor relates to the fact that difficulties are inherent in the process of making change. Clarifying this reality further prepares clients for the inevitable resistance they will experience. By anticipating these difficulties, clients are enabled to conceive of resistances as natural obstacles that must be surmounted, rather than yielding to them or feeling defeated. An explanation similar to the following clarifies the vicissitudes of the change process:

"We've talked about goals you want to achieve. Accomplishing them won't be easy. Making changes is seldom accomplished without a difficult and sometimes painful struggle. People usually have ups and downs as they seek to make changes. If you understand this, you won't become unduly discouraged and feel like throwing in the towel. I don't mean to paint a grim picture. In fact, I feel very hopeful about the prospects of your attaining your goals. At the same time, it won't be easy, and I don't want to mislead you. The important thing is that you share your feelings so that we can keep on top of them.''

Over the years, numerous clients have reported retrospectively that they appreciated explanations similar to the preceding. When the going became rough and they began to waver in pursuing their goals, they recalled that such discouragement was natural and, rather than discontinuing, mustered the determination to persevere.

In addition to clarifying the client's role, it is vital to clarify your own role. Again, it is desirable to stress you will be a partner in helping clients to understand their difficulties more fully. Because you have an outside vantage point, you may be able to assist them to see their difficulties in a new perspective and to consider solutions they may have overlooked. We recommend that you clarify further that although you will be an active partner in considering possible remedial actions, the final decisions rest with them. You will help them to weigh alternatives, but your desire is to see them develop their strengths and to exercise their capacities for independent action to the fullest possible extent. It is also important to emphasize that one of your functions is to assist them to focus on strengths and the incremental growth they achieve. Stress that although you will actively assume this function in the initial stage of the helping process, you will be encouraging them to learn to recognize and accredit their own strengths and growth independently.

Another aspect of the helping role that you should clarify for clients is that you will assist them in anticipating obstacles they will encounter in striving to attain their goals and will help them formulate strategies to surmount these obstacles. Clarifying this facet of your role further reinforces the reality that change is difficult but you will be with and behind them in offering support and direction.

Interventions or Techniques to Be Employed

This aspect of the contract involves specifying interventions and techniques that will be implemented to accomplish goals. During initial contracting it is often possible to specify interventions only on a somewhat global level, such as individual, conjoint, or family sessions or a mixture of them. You can, however, specify you will be logically discussing problematic situations and considering alternate remedial courses of action, which is common to virtually all problem-solving efforts. Although somewhat global, this type of activity is one of the major "treatment typologies" described by Hollis (1972), who designates it as "reflective discussion of the person-situation configuration" (pp. 109–138).

In some instances, depending upon your assessment, you can discuss interventions with greater specificity. You may thus specify such interventions as relaxation training; identifying and eliminating irrational thoughts, beliefs, and fears (cognitive restructuring); role-playing and behavioral rehearsal; self-management techniques; and developing skills (e.g., communication, assertiveness, problem solving, and conflict resolution). In other instances, you may consider employing these and other interventions or techniques later as your assessment changes. *Irrespective of when you consider implementing interventions, it is vital to discuss them with clients,* to present a brief overview of the intervention, to elicit clients' reactions, and to gain their consent. Bear in mind that contracting is an ongoing activity.

Temporal Conditions

Another integral aspect of the contract involves the duration of the helping process and the frequency and length of sessions. With respect to duration, there are basically two patterns—time-limited service (also known as planned short-term service) and open-ended service. The former pattern involves a specified maximum number of sessions (usually within a limited time frame), whereas the latter pattern does not specify time limits. Both patterns have existed in social work for many decades. The open-ended pattern is historically tied to the diagnostic school of casework, which developed from roots in Freudian psychoanalytic theory. Time limits were introduced by Otto Rank, a contemporary of Freud, and were adopted by the functional school of social work, which emerged in the 1930s.

More recently, time limits were incorporated as a major component of the task-centered system of social work, a model of practice that emerged in 1972 (Reid & Epstein, 1972). This model, which has gained wide acceptance, was developed as a result of compelling research evidence. One of the important studies that provided this evidence had been conducted by Reid himself with a colleague (Reid & Shyne, 1969). This study was designed to compare the efficacy of time-limited casework with open-ended casework, and the results indicated that clients who received service under the former method achieved results that equaled (and sometimes exceeded) those achieved under the latter pattern. Moreover, the results were as durable, as measured six months following termination of service. This and other studies supporting the comparative efficacy of time-limited interventions have been reviewed by Reid and Epstein (1972) in social work and by Orlinsky and Howard (1978), Butcher and Koss (1978), and Luborsky et al. (1975) in clinical psychology. Those reviewers uniformly concluded that the balance of evidence indicates time-limited interventions are equally effective as open-ended interventions.

The use of time limits is supported by grounds other than the research cited above. From a strictly logical standpoint, it can be persuasively argued that most humans tend to intensify their efforts to accomplish a given task when a deadline exists, as, for example, last-minute cramming that students do before an examination. Time-limited service thus employs time as a dynamic to counter the human tendency to procrastinate.

Still another argument supportive of time limits is that even in planned *long-term* treatment, most of the gains are achieved early in treatment (i.e., by the fifth or sixth session). Moreover, irrespective of the intended length, most treatments turn out to be relatively brief as indicated by the findings of several studies, some of them national in scope. The National Center for Health Statistics, for example, reported in 1966 an average of fewer than five contacts for the almost 1 million psychiatric patients seen during that year. Even more impressive is the fact that if only those patients who actually began treatment are considered, the median duration of treatment is between five and six sessions (Garfield, 1971).

The advantages of time-limited interventions have far-reaching implications for practitioners, including the following:

1. Time-limited service is cost-effective. Results equal to those of open-ended service can be achieved at much less cost.

2. More clients can be served under time-limited patterns. The problem of waiting lists can be reduced appreciably when agencies adopt time-limited services as the primary pattern of service delivery (as many have).

3. Time limits foster optimism of clients when practitioners express confidence that improvement is possible in a short time.

4. Time-limited service facilitates the process of termination by introducing it during the preliminary contracting phase. By knowing the duration of service in advance, the client has opportunity to work through reactions to terminating.

5. Time limits sharply demarcate the problem-solving process into the beginning, middle, and ending phases.

In addition to the above implications, two others warrant discussion. First, by adopting time-limited intervention as the primary mode of service delivery, an agency can accommodate more clients over a span of time, which enhances the likelihood of being able to provide service when it is needed most. This is a crucial advantage, for research indicates that delays in providing service impact negatively on results. Based on a review of three research studies that uniformly reported negative correlations between delays of actual beginnings of service following intake and attained outcomes, Orlinsky and Howard (1978) concluded: "The message to the therapist appears to be that [patients] should be seen as promptly as possible" (p. 312).

The second additional implication concerns the matter of employing time-limited service with disadvantaged clients, who represent the major population served by social workers. Based on research findings Lorion (1978) and Reid (1978) have concluded that lower-class clients better utilize and prefer structured and time-limited interventions. Indeed, both the earlier research that provided the impetus for developing the task-centered system and later research that undergirds subsequent refinements of the system have been conducted largely with lower-class clients.

The task-centered system has broad applicability to client populations. Indeed, adaptations have been tested for most settings in which social workers practice (Reid, 1987). Further, the approach has been adapted to and tested with groups (Larsen & Mitchell, 1980; Fortune, 1985a; and Garvin, 1985) as well as with families (Fortune, 1985b; Reid, 1985).

Are time limits effective with ethnic minority groups? Based on a previously cited outcome study of mental health services provided to Chicano clients, Gomez et al. (1985) concluded, ". . . the short-term casework services provided had a positive effect on the problems of Chicano clients and . . . clients were highly satisfied with the services" (p. 482). One must be cautious about generalizing to other populations, but there is no reason to believe results would be different with other ethno-cultural groups.

Time limits, of course, are not appropriate for all client populations. For clients whose goals involve or whose problems are related to deeply ingrained personality dysfunction, long-term therapy may be essential. Time limits with institutionalized mentally ill patients or chronically mentally ill outpatients for whom practitioners have ongoing responsibility are impractical, except when circumscribed problems of living are defined as goals. Similarly, time limits with assigned clients who are legally confined to correctional institutions or who are on probation or parole for extended periods of time are also inappropriate. Even in these instances, however, time limits may be used selectively to assist clients to achieve circumscribed goals.

The lengths of time limits vary across different theories or models of social work, counseling, and psychotherapy. Because of the extensive use of and substantial research with the task-centered system, a social work model, we recommend following the time limits commonly employed under this system. Most task-centered contracts specify from 6 to 12 sessions over a time span from two to four months (Reid, 1987). Given this flexibility, you can negotiate with the client for the specific number of sessions. Both clients' preferences and your best estimate of the number of sessions required should be considered. The advantage of determining clients' preferences, of course, is that mutuality in contracting is enhanced and clients are more likely to react positively to time limits when they have participated in selecting them.

Another aspect of time structuring pertains to the frequency of sessions. Orlinsky and Howard (1978) reviewed research studies that focus on this factor and found that the studies varied considerably in design and quality, making it difficult to draw definitive conclusions. Their overall impression, however, was that relatively intense schedules (i.e., once or twice weekly) produce the most favorable results. They offered no empirical support for *very* intensive schedules (e.g., everyday sessions). In social work, weekly sessions are the norm, and there appears no reason to modify this practice. But two sessions per week may be justified in cases that require intensive support and monitoring, although the cost factor must be carefully considered. Provision can also be made in contracts for spacing sessions further apart during the terminal phase of the helping process.

To enhance mutuality in contracting, it is generally desirable to elicit clients' preferences related to the frequency of sessions. Occasionally, clients may request more frequent sessions than appear justified, and you will need to express your recommendations. It has been our experience that most clients look to the practitioner for recommendations and readily agree to them. Although it is desirable to gain input from clients, you should make the ultimate decision.

A final time factor concerns the length of each session. Again, research offers no solid guidelines as to superior arrangements. A 50-minute session for individuals is the prevailing norm, but more time (usually one and one-half to two hours) is frequently allotted to intake sessions and to regular family and group sessions. Because some children and adolescents have difficulty tolerating 50-minute sessions, shorter but more frequent sessions are a common variation.

Means of Monitoring Progress

Stipulating in the contract how progress will be monitored serves the vital function of fostering an action-oriented mind-set that is conducive to change. Maintaining an expectancy of change enhances motivation and actualizes a positive self-fulfilling prophecy, as we noted in Chapter 12.

Means of evaluating progress vary according to the nature of the problem and the type of baseline data obtained during the assessment phase. If the initial measurement devices consisted of frequency counts, self-anchoring scales, or other scales, the same types of measurement should be employed to monitor progress. Comparisons of baseline data with data obtained periodically during the helping process indicate increments of progress that otherwise might not be discerned.

If baseline data are not available, a crude method of attempting to quantify progress is to ask clients to rate their progress on a scale of 1 to 10 where 1 represents no progress and 10 denotes complete achievement of a given goal. Comparing their ratings from one time to the next gives a rough estimate of clients' progress.

Another method of assessing progress is to depict it graphically on a chart. Calibrated drawings of thermometers with a scale from 1 to 10 can be employed for each goal, and clients can color in the thermometers to reflect their progress. This method is particularly appealing to children, who derive satisfaction in coloring in the units as they achieve progress. The dramatic effect is further enhanced when accompanied by recognition from the practitioner and family members.

The frequency of monitoring sessions should be negotiated. We find that clients often ask us for recommendations and that spending a few minutes every other session to evaluate progress works out well. Some clients may prefer to take a few minutes each session, whereas others may prefer to discuss progress less frequently. We recommend that you be flexible but not allow more than three sessions between discussions of progress.

Less frequent monitoring dilutes the benefits achieved by highlighting growth and by maintaining focus on desired changes.

Stipulations for Renegotiating the Contract

Because contracting continues during the entire helping process, it is important to clarify for clients that conditions in the contract are subject to renegotiation at any time. Circumstances change, new facts emerge, assessment evolves, progress occurs (we hope), and resistances surface—these and other changing factors require that the contract be constantly updated to maintain its relevance and fit. We therefore recommend that you explain that any participant in the helping process (including you) may request modifications in the contract at any time. Such an explanation further highlights the expectancy of change and enhances full mutuality in the helping process.

Housekeeping Items

The final element involved in formulating a contract includes establishing a beginning date, clarifying provisions for canceling or changing scheduled sessions, and firming financial arrangements (when fees are required). With respect to changes in appointments, it is important to stress that clients are responsible for time that has been set aside for them. Should legitimate circumstances warrant changing or canceling an appointment, they should generally provide advance notice of *at least* 24 hours so that the time can be rescheduled for others. Ordinarily, it is desirable (and indeed often essential) to charge clients for appointments they fail to keep, inasmuch as the time was allocated for them. Explicitly discussing these matters emphasizes the importance

of attending sessions, tends to avoid misunderstandings, and reduces the frequency of changes, cancellations, and failed appointments.

Discussing financial arrangements is painful for many students, who often are not comfortable in requiring others to pay for their services. This discomfort is understandable in light of the fact that students generally are inexperienced and unsure of the value of their services. Still, many agencies have policies that require payment for services, and the majority of clients expect to pay for them. Moreover, students receive supervision that enhances the quality of their services, and many provide services of high quality.

Students should bear in mind that part of competency is being able to handle financial arrangements effectively, which requires discussing them openly and without apology. Recognizing that clients *expect* to discuss fees may assist you in dealing with this matter more comfortably. Your responsibility, of course, does not end after negotiating the contract. If clients fail to pay fees according to the contract, you should explore the matter with them promptly. Procrastinating only makes it more difficult. Moreover, failure to pay fees may result from negative feelings toward the practitioner, financial strains, or irresponsibility in meeting obligations, any of which merits immediate attention.

Contracting and Formulating Goals in Growth-Oriented Groups

All of the preceding content concerning goals and contracting also applies to growth-oriented groups. In addition, however, you must be knowledegable about essential considerations that pertain specifically to such groups. We have thus devoted the final portion of this chapter to these considerations. Although many of the concepts presented apply to activity groups, to task groups, and to other types of groups, the following content relates specifically to therapeutic groups wherein members are seeking to make behavioral changes.

Establishing Group Purpose

Clarifying the overall purpose(s) of a group is vital, for the group's objective(s) influences all the processes that follow. Further, as Levine (1967) underscores: "Clarity about the purpose for which the group is formed provides a framework for observation, assessment, and action [and] provides a base for the group members to develop a bond and a means for attaining their common goals" (p. 2). Thus, clearly delineating the basic purpose of a group provides the base upon which specific goals and objectives may be constructed. General group purposes may include overarching goals such as the following:

1. To provide through a forum for discussion and education an opportunity whereby divorced women with small children who live in a rural area may explore and seek solutions to common problems, such as a sense of alienation, scarcity of resources, and lack of opportunities for adult companionship.

2. To provide an opportunity for members to learn assertiveness skills and to practice applying them in real-life situations.

3. To establish a governing council for nursing home residents through which they may participate in decision making that affects them and the quality of life in the home.

4. To assist incarcerated adolescents to adhere to written contracts that specify behavioral changes upon which release is contingent, including improvements in school performance, behavior toward peers and staff, and the like.

The overall purpose of a planned group should be established by the practitioner in consultation with agency administrators prior to forming the group. Goals subsequently negotiated by the group should reflect the perspectives of the agency, the client(s), and the practitioner.

The Agency and Practitioner's Perspective

Because of the agency's key role in determining and/or influencing purpose, practitioners must assure that agency objectives are reflected in the group's overall purpose. However, the agency and practitioner may not always share a common perspective regarding desired goals for a new group. Differences in the views of the agency and practitioner may occur, for instance, because of the latter's personal or professional orientation or because of preferences of either the agency or the practitioner for particular theories, ideologies, or techniques not espoused by the other. (A practitioner in a correctional setting may espouse a rehabilitative approach, but the institution may be oriented to punishment and security; or an agency may have a practice of not using time limits, whereas a practitioner may prefer to use time limits.)

In the preformation period, then, practitioners must be clear about their own objectives for a proposed group and must engage in dialogue with administrators and staff for the purpose of eliciting their views concerning group purpose. In cases where agency and practitioners' goals differ, practitioners must address such disparities with administrators and bargain for a general group purpose that is agreeable to both parties.

The Client's Perspective

At the point of entry to a group, the clients' goals may differ considerably from either those of the agency or the practitioner. Schopler and Galinsky (1974) emphasize that the client's goals may be influenced by many internal or external forces:

> The expectations held by significant others (e.g., husband, mother, teacher) for the client may . . . influence the client's perspectives of his problem and his motivation to do something about it. His capabilities provide resources and define limits for work on his problems and his contributions to the group. Further, as he enters the group, each client has some idea, however vague, of what the worker, agency, and group will be like . . . based on personal experiences from school, work, and friendship groups and from reports of others. Thus various factors determine what goals the client sees as relevant and what goals he thinks are attainable. (p. 128)

The practitioner must then carefully explore clients' expectations of the group and help them to develop individual and collective goals that are realistically achievable. The practitioner must further work to bring harmony between individual, group, and agency purposes. Other perspectives, however, must not supersede clients' goals, as clients are the consumers of the service offered. The need to highlight and preserve clients' goals is reflected in the findings of Levinson (1973). Analyzing 61 group work articles, Levinson identified several common patterns concerning the consequences of agreement or disagreement of purpose between the practitioner and group members. When the purposes of practitioners and members were in accord or when the purposes of the two diverged but the practitioner went along with the group's purpose, groups tended to operate optimally. However, when the practitioner advocated purposes that were rejected by members, groups prematurely dissolved.

Establishing Specific Individual and Group Goals

After having established an overall purpose for the group and convened the group, the practitioner engages members in formulating specific goals at both individual and group levels. Individual goals embody the hopes, expectations, and objectives of members as they enter the group. Group goals, on the other hand, "are the emergent product of the interaction of all participants together, the organizer and the members, as they express their ideas and feelings about the reasons for the existence of the group and its anticipated outcomes. Group goals include, therefore, rationale, expectations and objectives toward which the group puts its collective efforts" (Hartford, 1971, p. 139).

The following list contains examples of specific goals that may be formulated at either individual or group levels:

1. To expand awareness of one's own behavior (or the group's processes).

2. To identify one's own self-defeating behaviors and to replace these with more functional behaviors.

3. To develop problem-solving skills that enhance decision making in both individual and group contexts and to apply them to specific problems.

4. To discern strengths and incremental growth in one's self and in others and to give and receive positive feedback in relation to the same.

5. To relate to others with increased genuineness.

6. To become more liberated from external imperatives, that is, "shoulds," "oughts," and "musts."

7. To learn how to make direct requests for what one wants.

8. To learn how to hear accurately the messages of others and to convey one's understanding of these messages to others.

9. To grow in self-acceptance and to explore hidden potentials and creativity.

10. To increase one's capacity to care for others and to manifest that caring.

11. To learn to express thoughts, feelings, needs, and ideas to others.

12. To develop trust in one's own judgment.

Conducting a Preliminary Interview

Before convening a group, practitioners often meet individually with potential group members for the purpose of establishing personal relationships, exploring relevant concerns, and formulating initial contracts with those motivated to join the group. Conducting individual interviews is essential to composing a group carefully, which entails selecting members according to predetermined criteria and including those who have specific behavioral or personality attributes thought to be beneficial for the purposes of the group. Further, when composing a group of weakly motivated clients (e.g., delinquents, court-referred parents, or felons), having an individual interview is a vital first step in assisting potential members to identify relevant problems and to enhance their motivation to work on them.

Pregroup meetings with potential members assist practitioners to gain essential information that may be of substantial value in selecting and directing interventions to those members in early sessions. (Because of the time limitations in regular group sessions, such vital information may not otherwise emerge for several weeks.) Further, conducting preliminary interviews enables practitioners to enter initial group sessions with a previously established relationship with each member, a distinct advantage given the fact that leaders must attend to multifarious communication processes at both individual and group levels. In addition, previous knowledge about individual members facilitates grasping the meaning of the behavior of those members in the group, thus enabling practitioners to focus more fully on group processes and the task of assisting members to develop relationships with each other. Establishing rapport with the leader prior to initial sessions also enables members to feel more at ease and to open up more readily in the first meeting.

Objectives that practitioners may wish to accomplish in preliminary interviews include the following:

1. Orienting potential members to proposed goals and purposes of the group, its content and structure, the philosophy and style of the leader in managing group processes, and the respective roles of the leader and group members. As you

discuss each of these aspects of the group, you should elicit the client's reactions and suggestions that would enable the group to better serve the client's needs. You should also discuss time, place of meetings, length of sessions, and the like. In addition, you may wish to emphasize commonalities that the client may share with other persons interested in joining the group, such as problems, interests, concerns, or objectives.

2. Eliciting the client's view of prior group experiences, including the nature of the client's relationship with the leader and other members, the client's style of relating in the previous group, the goals that the client accomplished, and the personal growth that was achieved. You may need to explore negative feelings more fully if it appears these may impair participation in the proposed group.

3. Eliciting, exploring, and clarifying clients' problems, and identifying those that are appropriate for the proposed group. In some instances, either because clients are reluctant to participate in the group or because their problems appear to be more appropriately handled through other treatment modalities or community agencies, you may need to refer them to other resources. With respect to treatment approaches, Garvin (1981) emphasizes that "the client's choice of individual, group, or family services should be an informed one based on information regarding different forms of interpersonal helping and what they are like" and suggests employing media aids such as films, tapes, or even comic books to portray what happens in the agency's groups (p. 75). Garvin also emphasizes that some clients' problems are better addressed within a family than a group context. To determine which modality is mutually preferable, Garvin identifies the following three criteria (p. 74):

a. Is the problem maintained by processes operating in the family as a system? (See Chapter 10.)

b. How will the family respond to changes the individual may choose to make, and will these responses support or retard such changes?

c. Does the individual wish to involve the family, and is the family amenable to such involvement?

4. Exploring the client's hopes, aspirations, and expectations regarding the proposed group (e.g., "What would you like to be different in your life as a result of your attending this group?").

5. Identifying specific goals that the client wishes to accomplish, discussing whether these goals can be attained through the proposed group, and determining the client's views as to whether the group is an appropriate vehicle for resolving personal problems. It is critical, of course, to respect a client's right *not* to participate in a group. Garvin, Reid, and Epstein (1976) emphasize the need to put "high priority on the client's autonomy, particularly his right to freedom from imposed or deceptive treatment." These authors recommend employing a specific contract that protects each client from "help for a condition he may not wish to change or from treatment for an unacknowledged problem" (pp. 242–243). Thus, if the client manifests a lack of motivation to attend the group or to work on problems, you should engage the client in carefully assessing whether participating in the group would be beneficial.

6. Identifying and exploring potential obstacles that might prevent clients from participating in or receiving desired benefits from the group, including reservations they may have about attending the group. Other obstacles may include

shyness or nonassertiveness in group situations, opposition from significant others about entering the group, a heavy schedule that would likely preclude attending all group meetings, or problems in finding baby-sitters. After exploring obstacles, it is appropriate to assist clients in generating possible alternatives that might obviate these obstacles. In some cases, obstacles may preclude clients from group participation.

7. Mutually developing a profile of the client's attributes and determining any that the client might like to enhance through work in the group.

A Rationale for Group Guidelines

Developing consensus concerning guidelines for behavior (e.g., staying on task) among group members is a vital aspect of contracting in the initial phase. Although in the literature group guidelines are sometimes termed *group rules,* we recommend using the former term because the latter suggests regulations imposed upon a group rather than guidelines voluntarily developed by members to guide the group's processes and actions. In formulating guidelines with the group, the practitioner takes the first step in shaping the group's evolving processes to create a "working group" capable of achieving specific objectives. Attempts to formulate guidelines often fail to achieve this intended effect for three major reasons.

First, a practitioner may establish parameters *for* the group, merely informing members of behavioral expectations to which they are expected to adhere. In so doing, the practitioner may unintentionally convey the message, "This is my group, and this is how I expect you to behave in it," which may negate later actions by the practitioner to encourage members to assume responsibility for the group. Without consensus among members concerning desirable group guidelines, power struggles and disagreements also may ensue among members as to the appropriateness of certain behaviors. Further, members may not feel bound by what they consider the "leader's rules" and may, in fact, deliberately test them, creating a counterproductive scenario. Members may thus cast the practitioner in the role of "authoritarian parent" and assume the role of "errant children."

Second, the practitioner may discuss group guidelines only superficially and neglect either to identify or to obtain commitment to guidelines. Such neglect by a group leader is very unfortunate, for the extent to which members delineate specific and functional parameters greatly influences the extent to which they will modify their behavior in future sessions to conform to adopted guidelines or to achieve stated group objectives.

Third, even when the group adopts viable guidelines for behavior within the group, the practitioner may erroneously assume that members will subsequently conform to these guidelines. To the contrary, there is often little relationship between contracted behaviors and actual behaviors. Establishing group guidelines merely sets guideposts against which members may measure their current behavior. Practitioners must consistently intervene to assist members to adhere to guidelines and to consider discrepancies between contracted and actual behaviors before negotiated behaviors actually become normative.

Formulating Group Guidelines

Because formulating guidelines is a critical process that substantially influences the success of a group, we offer the following suggestions to assist you.

1. Introduce the group to the concept of *decision by consensus* (explained later in this section), and solicit agreement concerning adoption of this modus operandi for making decisions *prior* to formulating group guidelines.

2. Ask group members to share their vision of the kind of group they would like to have by responding to the following statement: "I would like this group to be a place where I could. . . ." Reach for responses from all members, and once this has been achieved, summarize the collective thinking of the group. Offer your own views of supportive group structure that assists members to work on individual problems or to achieve group objectives.

3. Ask members to identify guidelines for behavior in the group that will assist them to achieve the kind of group structure and atmosphere they desire. You may wish to brainstorm possible guidelines at this point, adding your suggestions. Then, through group consensus, choose those that seem most appropriate. If there are nonnegotiable agency rules (e.g., adolescents often are not allowed to smoke in correctional settings), you should present the rules, explain their rationale, and encourage discussion of them.

There are many guidelines that you and a group could establish. Guidelines that we have found helpful in promoting supportive group processes and a relaxed, open, and "low-risk" atmosphere include the following:

- Personalizing statements by using "I" messages, for example, "I (think) (feel) (want). . . ."

- Keeping group discussion focused on the present rather than the past.

- Giving members an option to "pass" if they are not emotionally ready to address certain problems or issues.

- Keeping confidences in the group.

- Focusing extensively on strengths and incremental growth of members.

- Maintaining group focus on the work to be accomplished.

- Extending "emotional courtesies," such as attentive listening, checking out perceptions, and speaking in turn.

- Focusing on obstacles in the group process that prevent the group from working on tasks or accomplishing group goals.

Depending on the setting and purpose of your group, you may need to develop additional guidelines that pertain to other group behaviors or activities. The following sections contain guidelines adopted by many groups that have proven conducive to achieving individual and group objectives.

Group Format Many therapeutic groups die on the vine through attrition of members who become dissatisfied because their own goals are not met and/or because of low group productivity. Other groups, suffering from the same maladies, struggle through to the end without ever achieving the purposes for which they were formed. Many of the ills of such groups can be attributed to two major flaws in group structure:

1. Global and amorphous goals that have no clear or logical connection to problems under consideration.

2. A loosely conceptualized group format that lacks guidelines to enable members or leaders to organize their time and energy effectively.

Pursuing ill-defined objectives within a structure that provides few guidelines for efficient use of time can defeat the best-intentioned leader or group. Developing a group structure during the initial phase that embodies the following activities, however, assists leaders and members to focus their energies on therapeutic objectives actively and efficiently.

1. Define group and individual goals in behavioral terms and rank them according to priority.

2. Develop an overall plan that organizes the work to be done within the number of sessions allocated by the group to achieve its goals.

3. Specify behavioral tasks to be accomplished outside the group each week that will assist individuals to make desired changes.

4. Achieve agreement among members concerning weekly format and agenda, i.e., how time will be allocated each week to achieve goals. For instance, a group might allocate its weekly two hours to the following format:

15 min.	1½ hours	15 min.
Reviewing and monitoring tasks.	Focusing on relevant content and formulating tasks.	Evaluating group sessions.

Avoid imposing structure upon a group; rather, assist the group to evolve a format that will facilitate achieving the group's proposed objectives. The structure adopted by your group should also be flexible enough to accommodate to group processes and to the needs of members. To assure its continued functionality, review the format periodically throughout the life of the group.

We are not recommending that your group adopt all of the preceding suggestions, but we stress the need for a clearly conceptualized format that provides the means for evaluating the ongoing process of group members. Our position is based on a conviction that, regardless of the therapeutic modality utilized, clients have a right to receive help within a format that provides for accountability in the form of continuing and concrete feedback concerning their progress. Although we recognize that some group purposes are not compatible with the preceding guidelines, we contend that many groups are so loosely structured that it is difficult to pinpoint concrete individual changes achieved as a result of the group experience. In our opinion, it is not justifiable to allocate resources and time of both practitioners *and* members to such groups.

Group Decision Making   Effective deliberation and decision making are critical in determining the productivity and success of a group. To achieve its objectives, every group ultimately develops methods of making decisions. Left to their own devices, however, groups may evolve counterproductive decision-making processes. Some groups, for example, permit the power for making decisions to be vested in a few members, "counting in" some members and "counting out" others. This modus operandi perpetuates conflict and intrigue in the group, causing unrest and resentments that divert energies from productive tasks and block developmental progress.

Members of newly formed groups have varying styles of making decisions and do not know *how* to make decisions effectively *as a group.* As a result, most therapeutic groups learn problem solving through extended trial-and-error processes, gradually gaining from their mistakes (we hope). Most groups, however, can quickly learn to adopt a model of *decision by consensus,* given effective leadership in educating the group. Further, equipping groups with an effective decision-making model in the early stages of development can expedite group process and assist groups in more readily achieving an advanced level of group functioning. Our decision-by-consensus method can be taught early in the first group session according to the following sequence:

1. Explaining that groups need a decision-making method that gives each person equal vote and "counts everyone in."

2. Gaining group acceptance of this method of making decisions.

3. Explaining steps for effective decision making (these steps are discussed in Chapter 15).

4. Identifying the leader's function in assisting the group to make decisions that meet the needs of all members.

5. Using the decision-by-consensus approach in setting up the initial contract and focusing explicitly on the process to enhance group awareness of the use of this approach.

Help-Giving/Help-Seeking Roles Groups formed to assist individuals with personal problems benefit from clarification of what might be termed *help-giving* and *help-seeking* roles. Although the two terms are self-explanatory, you may wish to assist the group to operationalize these roles by considering behaviors embodied in them. The help-seeking role, for example, incorporates such behaviors as making direct requests for help, authentically sharing one's feelings, being open to feedback and demonstrating willingness to test new approaches to problems. The help-giving role involves such behaviors as listening attentively, refraining from criticism, clarifying perceptions, summarizing, maintaining focus on the problem, and pinpointing strengths and incremen-

tal growth. A critical aspect of the help-giving role you should clarify for group members is the necessity of exploring personal problems of fellow members carefully before attempting to solve them. Otherwise, groups tend to move quickly to giving advice and offering evaluative suggestions about what a member "ought" or "ought not" to do. You can further help the group to adopt these two roles by highlighting instances in which members have performed in either of these helping roles, accrediting them accordingly.

Visitors A group convened for therapeutic purposes should develop explicit guidelines specifying whether and under what conditions visitors may attend group meetings. If the group has an open format, allowing frequent changes in membership, the presence of a visitor will have little impact. However, in closed groups (i.e., ones that do not usually add members once the group has convened), visitors can have a devastating effect on group processes, causing members to refrain from sharing feelings and problems openly and creating resentments toward the member (or practitioner) who invited the visitor and thereby violated the integrity of the group. Anticipating with members the possible impact of visitors upon the group and establishing procedures and conditions under which visitors may attend sessions can avert group turmoil as well as embarrassment for individual members.

New Members Procedures for adding and orienting new members may also need to be established. In some cases, the group leader may reserve the prerogative of selecting members. In other instances, the leader may permit the group to choose new members, with the understanding that choices should be based on certain criteria and that the group should achieve consensus regarding potential members. In either case, procedures for adding new members and the importance of the group's role in orienting them should be clarified.

Individual Contacts with the Practitioner   Whether you encourage or discourage individual contacts with members outside the group depends on the purpose of the group and the anticipated consequences or benefits of such contacts. In some cases, individual contacts serve to promote group objectives. For example, in a correctional setting, planned meetings with an adolescent between sessions provide opportunities to focus on the youth's dysfunctional behaviors in the group and to develop an individual contract with the youth to modify them. In the case of marital therapy groups, however, individual contacts initiated by one spouse may be a bid for an alliance with the practitioner against the other partner or may be perceived as such by the other spouse. If you have questions regarding the advisability of having individual contacts outside the group, you should thoroughly discuss these questions with members and mutually develop guidelines pertaining to this matter.

Cleanup   Making group decisions regarding cleanup before having to contend with a messy room is an effective strategy that encourages members to assume responsibility for themselves and for the group. Resentments fester and subgroupings destructive to group cohesiveness tend to form when some members consistently stay to help with cleanup and others do not.

Use of Recorder   You should always gain the group's permission before recording a group session. Further, before asking for a decision you should provide information concerning the manner in which the recording is to be utilized outside the session. Reservations regarding recording the session should be thoroughly aired, and the group's wishes should be respected.

Use of Profanity   Although some practitioners believe that group members should be allowed to use whatever language they choose in expressing themselves, profanity may be offensive to some members, and the group may wish to develop guidelines concerning this matter.

Attendance   Discussing the problems that irregular attendance can pose for a group before the fact and soliciting commitment from members to attend regularly can do much to solidify group attendance in future group sessions. Further, late arrivals and early departures by group members can be minimized if the group develops relevant guidelines in advance. Allowances on an individual basis are needed, of course, to accommodate the schedules of members in special instances with the understanding that these situations should be rare. To expedite adherence to a group contract regarding a time frame, you should start and end meetings promptly and extend meetings only after the group has made the decision to do so. Although you may sometimes feel the press of unfinished business at the end of a meeting, holding group members beyond the scheduled time without their consent violates the group contract and may create resentment.

Eating, Drinking, Smoking   Opinions vary among group leaders concerning these activities in groups. Some groups and leaders believe these activities distract from group process; others regard them as relaxing and actually beneficial to group operation. You may wish to elicit views from members concerning these activities and develop guidelines with the group that meet member needs and facilitate group progress.

Programming At times, group formats include activities or exercises. Unfortunately, however, such programming does not always *directly* relate to the group's purpose; further, the activities or exercises in which the group participates may not be discussed by members for the purpose of learning from the experience or relating it to behavioral changes members wish to achieve. Thus, when programming is utilized, practitioners need to discuss with members the manner in which such activities can be best utilized to meet specified objectives and to plan with them ways of evaluating and generalizing the group's experience.

Remember that guidelines are helpful only to the extent that they expedite the development of the group and should be reviewed periodically to assess their functionality in relationship to the group's stage of development. Outdated guidelines, of course, should be discarded or reformulated. Further, when a group's behavior is incompatible with group guidelines, it may be advisable to describe what is happening in the group (or request that members do so) and, after thoroughly reviewing the situation, ask the group to consider whether the guideline in question is still viable. If used judiciously, this strategy not only helps the group to reassess guidelines but also places responsibility for monitoring adherence to guidelines with the group, where it belongs. Leaders who unwittingly assume the role of "enforcer" place themselves in an untenable position, for group members tend to struggle against what they perceive as authoritarian control on the leader's part.

Part 3

The Change-Oriented Phase

After formulating a contract, the participants enter phase two of the problem-solving process—the goal attainment or change-oriented phase. In this phase, practitioners and clients mutually plan and implement strategies to accomplish the goals selected. Implementing these strategies involves employing interventions and techniques specified in the contract and contracting to use others as changing circumstances dictate. Before considering these factors further, however, a preview of Part 3 of the book is in order.

A Preview of Part 3

The present chapter considers planning general strategies for attaining goals, implementing these strategies by partializing goals, formulating and implementing tasks, and maintaining continuity within and between sessions. In subsequent chapters of Part 3, we briefly explicate a number of widely used interventions, many of them empirically grounded, that can be employed within these general strategies. We also identify others that we cannot delineate because of limited space but will list references so that you can study them independently. Given the large number of treatment models in the helping professions and an even larger number of specific interventions, it is not possible to include all of them in a single volume.

Chapter 15 is devoted to widely used interactions employed to increase clients' vital coping skills in independent problem solving, interpersonal relationships, and assertiveness. Chapter 16 focuses on environmental interventions and social planning. In Chapter 17 we delineate interventions employed to enhance interaction of families and groups. Chapter 18 is devoted to interventions that have broad application to physical, cognitive, emotional, and behavioral functioning. These include muscle relaxation training, cognitive restructuring, self-instruction, and stress inoculation training.

Techniques employed to expand self-awareness and to pave the way to change (additive empathy, interpretation, and confrontation) are considered in Chapter 19. Part 3 concludes with Chapter 20, which is concerned with ways of changing organizations and managing resistances to change of individuals, families, and groups.

14 ■ Planning and Implementing Change-Oriented Strategies

Planning Goal-Attainment Strategies

As we emphasized in Chapter 13, it is vital to include clients in planning strategies to accomplish goals. Besides safeguarding clients' rights to self-determination, including clients in selecting interventions enhances the likelihood of their cooperation. Clients who do not understand an intervention and its relevance to their problems and goals are unlikely to be invested in the change effort and may cooperate in a halfhearted fashion or not at all. To achieve cooperative participation, *interventions must make sense to the client.*

Involving clients in planning strategies, of course, does not mean discussing strategies in detail or even identifying all strategies that will be employed. Clients are generally satisfied with a brief explanation of rationale for and descriptions of strategies.

Effective interventive strategies must flow from the assessment of the problem and must be the most relevant and promising means of achieving the goals posited in the contract. This point may seem elementary, but such is not the case. A review of social work outcome studies by Wood (1978) revealed that unsuccessful research studies failed to explain the relationship their interventions bore to problems, goals, and contracts. To avoid mismatches between interventions on one hand and problems and goals on the other, it is important that interventions be relevant to the target system or subsystems and to clients' specific problems. For example, if a client's depression appears to be caused by social isolation associated with an impoverished physical and social environment, employing an intervention aimed at enhancing the client's self-awareness (i.e., an insight-oriented therapy) is inappropriate and doomed to fail. Similarly, planning separate sessions for marital partners when their marital problems appear to be produced largely by dysfunctional communication and interaction makes little sense unless there are compelling reasons for not seeing the partners conjointly. And finally, implementing an intervention aimed solely at assisting a child-abusing parent to gain emotional control when that parent's loss of control appears to be triggered by overwhelming stresses associated with inadequate finances, poor housing, responsibilities for many children, lack of support systems, and severe marital conflict is tantamount to prescribing an aspirin for severe bacterial infection.

374

The importance of careful planning in direct practice has been emphasized by Rosen, Proctor, and Livne (1985). For a discussion of components that practitioners should consider in planning treatment strategies, you will find this article useful.

Matching Interventions to Target Systems

To achieve effective outcomes, interventions must be directed to the systems implicated in problems and must be appropriate for those systems. To accomplish this is no small task, for one must be knowledgeable about the broad array of interventions and techniques and skillful in selecting and employing them. Many of these interventions are appropriate only for individual problems, some are appropriate for modifying dysfunctional interactions in families and groups, and still others relate to modifying the environment. It is important, therefore, to select and employ interventions that match systems targeted for change. Mismatches tend to lead to negative outcomes, often in the form of premature terminations by clients. In a study of conjoint marital therapy, for example, Ehrenkranz (1967) found that although the social workers correctly saw couples conjointly for marital problems, they failed to use several important techniques and procedures specified in the literature as basic to modifying dysfunctional interaction. For example, workers made little use of on-the-spot clarification of marital interaction, a technique fundamental to conjoint marital therapy. Ehrenkranz attributed the inappropriate use of techniques by these workers to their failure to perceive the difference in the conditions that apply to conjoint interviews as compared to individual interviews. Thus, it is vital not only to direct interventions to appropriate target systems but also to employ techniques that match these systems.

Matching Interventions to Developmental Phases

Because clients vary in levels of achieved maturity, it is vital to match interventions to their developmental phases. Young children typically lack the capacity to think abstractly, so play therapy, structured group activities (with leaders employing behavior modification techniques), mutual story telling directed at enhancing coping skills and teaching moral principles (Gardner, 1971), skill development groups, and parent-management training are commonly employed. When parent-child interactional difficulties appear to underlie rebelliousness, truanting, substance abuse, antisocial behavior, and other related problems, family therapy may be the treatment of choice. Parent training groups are also increasingly employed to assist parents to enhance their skills in communication, setting limits, negotiation, and problem solving.

In some instances severe family problems associated with children and adolescents require interventions involving environmental changes. Residential treatment, inpatient psychiatric treatment, confinement in correctional facilities, and other such programs may be required. Severe problems of child neglect/abuse may necessitate temporary or permanent removal of a child to a safe environment.

We will not attempt to discuss interventions appropriate for all developmental phases. It is sufficient to reemphasize that you should carefully consider the developmental stages of individuals and families in planning interventions.

Matching Interventions to Stressful Transitions

As we indicated in Chapter 8, clients' problems are often associated with overwhelming stresses precipitated by major life transitions. Crisis intervention and the task-centered system, which we discuss in this chapter, are models that have general application to transition problems. In recent years support groups have also been used extensively to cope with transition problems. These groups include divorce groups, rape crisis groups, groups for parents whose children have died, groups for farm families in crisis (Van Hook, 1987), groups for wives who learn their husbands are gay or bisexual (Auerback & Moser, 1987), and groups for widows and widowers (Lieberman & Videka-Sherman, 1986), to mention just a few. Schwartz (1975) has written an informative article reviewing the use of such groups for assisting with problems of transition.

Matching Interventions to Ethnocultural Groups

As we have stressed in previous chapters, accurate assessment of the problems of ethnic minority persons requires knowledge of both their culture and their degree of acculturation. The same is true when planning interventions. Long-term insight-oriented interventions, for example, are ineffective for the majority of Hispanic clients (Rogler et al., 1987), whereas short-term interventions are effective (Gomez et al., 1985). Folk stories *(los cuentos)* have been used effectively in work with Hispanic children (Rogler et al., 1987).

A useful guideline to planning interventions with ethnic minority persons (and other clients, for that matter) is to solicit their views as to what needs to be done to remedy their difficulties. Their suggestions will be in harmony with their beliefs and values. Moreover, their views about essential changes are often on target; they lack only the "know-how" required to accomplish the changes. Deficiencies in the latter are often associated with limited knowledge about available resources and about the complexities of our service delivery systems. Determining clients' views enables the practitioner to suggest interventions that clients will perceive as relevant and to couch the rationale for selecting them in terms that make sense to clients. Including clients in the planning of interventive strategies enhances their cooperation, as we noted previously.

Another important factor to consider in planning interventions with ethnic minority clients is the importance in some cultures of family ties and the extended family. Citing the fact that in Mexican-American culture the family is the primary source of identity and of support in times of crisis, Rothman, Gant, and Hnat (1985) recommend that family therapy, including the extended family or *familia,* should be considered regularly. These authors recommend that ". . . with the agreement of the client, members of the family should be used as resources, as advocates, and in other supportive ways" (p. 202). Further, because of the patriarchal family structure and the esteemed position of elders, they recommend involving extended family elders in treatment, according them due respect.

A General Strategy for Attaining Goals

In this chapter, we delineate an approach to attaining goals that is both systematic and efficient. The approach is based on advances in methods that have resulted from the advent of short-term interventions over the past 30 years and particularly the task-centered system, which has evolved over the past 18 years. Prior to the 1960s, open-ended, long-term interventions (for intrapersonal and interpersonal problems) were the prevailing norm in social work practice and in allied disciplines. Practice theories posited the belief that attempts to produce change are always opposed by countervailing forces, including unconscious resistances, inertia, fear of the unknown, and vicissitudes in the helping relationships. Resistance to change was viewed as a powerful force that required an extended time to resolve.

In the 1960s, authors began to challenge the prevailing views of resistance and advocated that the lengthy time often required for successful treatment could result from defective treatment methods. Masserman (1965) took the position that resistance may be a healthy response to poor treatment technique. Wolberg (1965) specifically criticized the practice in long-term therapy of "permitting the patient to wallow in resistance until he somehow muddles through," noting that "Where time is of no object the therapist can settle back comfortably and let the patient pick his way through the lush jungles of his psyche" (p. 235). Wolberg further faulted long-term therapists for their passivity and their failure to provide direction.

Recognizing that the sources of resistance included defects in the helping process was a theoretical milestone, for it opened the door to major changes in the process that held promise of accelerating the rate of clients' progress. Short-term therapies subsequently evolved rapidly, achieving in the 1960s a strong momentum that has continued to the present. Numerous research studies also disclosed with unanticipated consistency that brief therapies were as effective as long-term therapies and, in some instances, more effective.

Early short-term therapies, however, were not systematic and provided few guidelines to practitioners (with the exception of time limits) as to how they should provide direction to the helping process. Wolberg (1965) acknowledged this dilemma when he lamented that, "The most pressing problem that confronts us today in short-term therapy is that we do not possess an adequate methodology. We apply the same tactics that we find useful in prolonged treatment" (p. 128). The development of the task-centered system, a method characterized by highly specified tactics of intervention, was a tailor-made solution to this problem. This system, from which we have drawn heavily in the present chapter, has the key advantage of providing a framework that accommodates interventions and techniques from many practice models.

The task-centered system has been adapted to virtually all the settings in which social workers practice and its efficacy has been empirically established with many different client populations (Reid, 1987), as we noted in Chapter 13. Nevertheless, we are not recommending wholesale adoption of the system. Indeed, time limits, which are central to the system, are not feasible for certain types of clients and problematic situations, as we noted earlier. However, many of the tactics of the system can be employed to increase the efficiency of other types of interventions. Progress can often be accelerated in open-ended interventions, for example, by maintaining sharp focus and continuity—another key aspect of the system. In fact, *the major components of task accomplishment—namely, preparation, implementation, and follow-up—undergird all the more specific change-oriented interventions.*

Partializing Goals

The first task in developing strategies to attain goals is to reduce them to manageable parts. These parts consist of discrete actions to be undertaken by the client and, in some instances, by the practitioner. The actions may be covert as well as overt. Cognitive "actions" may include dismissing irrational fears of being ridiculed when one expresses a view or reminding oneself that it is not a disaster to make ordinary mistakes inasmuch as all humans occasionally make mistakes.

Partializing goals is not a new technique in social work practice; indeed, partialization has long been a basic tenet of practice theory (Perlman, 1957, pp. 147–149). Yet, in reviewing seven outcome studies of intensive services rendered to welfare recipients by public agency workers, Wood (1978, p. 443) noted that social workers in *successful* projects were apparently more skillful in partializing problems and goals than were workers in unsuccessful projects. It thus appears that partialization is underutilized by at least some practitioners.

Even goals formulated with a high level of specificity often are complex and involve multiple actions that must be completed in proper sequence. Because of this complexity, many clients feel overwhelmed and are unable to break their ultimate goals into constituent parts that are less intimidating. As they dissect them into bite-sized portions, guided by practitioners, they become emboldened to undertake discrete corrective actions (tasks), which lead to goal accomplishment.

Partializing thus involves operationalizing goals by dissecting them into subgoals and tasks that specify explicit actions prerequisite to goal accomplishment. To illustrate this process, we consider three varied goals and identify subgoals associated with them.

1. The ultimate goal of a single mother is to regain custody of children removed from her custody because of neglect. As the practitioner and the mother explore conditions that must be met to regain custody, they partialize the goal into the following subgoals:
   a. Improve conditions in the home by developing and following a housekeeping schedule developed in collaboration with the practitioner.
   b. Institute acceptable hygienic and nutritional standards (enlist services of a public health nurse to provide instruction and temporary supervision).
   c. Improve parenting effectiveness by participating in a parenting class and in a parents' group.
   d. Explore and develop support systems that will make child care available, thereby freeing time to socialize in the evenings.

2. The ultimate goal of a couple is to reduce the incidence and severity of marital conflict. The goal is partialized into the following subgoals:
   a. To reduce criticism and put-downs that provoke defensiveness and recriminations.
   b. To avoid venting anger on one another; to explain that one is angry but not express raw anger; to identify and express feelings underlying anger, such as hurt or disappointment, or feeling discounted.
   c. To identify sources of anger and to learn and apply effective conflict resolution skills.
   d. To work together in identifying problems and employing problem-solving strategies.

e. To increase positive, supportive messages (compliments, approval, affection, and appreciation).

3. The goal is to improve sanitation in an apartment house by bringing pressure to bear on a recalcitrant landlord to fulfill his obligations. Subgoals include the following:

a. Talk with other tenants and mobilize an action group.

b. Plan meetings of the tenants to enlist leaders and develop strategies.

c. Explore legal resources and obtain legal counsel.

d. Present a formal grievance to the landlord and express intention of resorting to legal means to force him, if necessary, to make needed improvements.

e. File a complaint with the health department and initiate court action, if necessary.

From the above examples, it is apparent that subgoals may involve actions on the part of the client, the practitioner, or both. In the first illustration, for example, the practitioner may assume responsibility for enlisting the services of a public health nurse. In the third example, the practitioner may explore possible legal resources, subsequently involving the client or representatives of the tenants' group in talking with legal counsel.

Partializing Group Goals

The same processes also pertain to a family or a therapeutic group. In such cases, the entire group may engage in formulating relevant subgoals to accomplish an identified group objective. For example, to achieve a group goal of preparing for discharge from a psychiatric hospital, a group of adult men and women may decide on the following courses of action:

- Visit the halfway house to which they will be discharged, and discuss facets of the program, such as daily schedule, living arrangements, rules concerning behavior, and the format of the biweekly group therapy sessions.

- Investigate leisure time community resources, such as theaters, restaurants, and facilities for recreation.

- Invite several discharged patients who are successfully living in the community to share their experiences with the group.

- Plan several activities in the community, such as shopping or going out to dinner, and discuss the reactions of group members upon return to the hospital.

After partializing goals into subgoals, the next step is to order the subgoals so that they flow from one to another in a natural sequence, as was done in the preceding example of the goal of improving sanitation. Subgoals sometimes tend to be disconnected, however, and do not fall into logical sequence, as is true in the preceding illustration of the goal of assisting a mother to regain custody of her child. In such instances, you must determine which subgoal is of most immediate concern to the client and focus your beginning change efforts on that subgoal. However, you should note one caution: it is important to settle upon a subgoal that poses excellent chances for successful accomplishment by the client. Success with one subgoal engenders confidence and courage to tackle another; failure produces discouragement and undermines confidence in the helping process.

Formulating Tasks

After contracting to begin work on a subgoal, the next step is to develop the means for implementing it. This involves mutually planning tasks or actions clients must accomplish to attain a given subgoal. Tasks may consist of either behavioral or cognitive actions that require effort (and often discomfort) on the client's part. The following lists illustrate both behavioral and cognitive tasks.

Behavioral tasks:

a. To phone for information about a rehabilitation program.

b. To convey feelings of hurt to a significant person.

c. To study each day for a specified length of time.

d. To follow a schedule for completing household tasks.

e. To give positive feedback to a family member at least three times daily.

Cognitive tasks:

a. To meditate for 30 minutes daily.

b. To engage in cognitive rehearsal involving talking to an employer.

c. To keep a daily tally of self-demeaning thoughts over three one-hour intervals.

d. To recognize manifestations of anger arousal before they mount out of control.

e. To spend 15 minutes in the morning anticipating difficulties that may develop at work and mentally rehearse coping responses.

Essential tasks are sometimes readily apparent. Further, clients themselves sometimes propose tasks, and if such tasks are realistic, it makes good sense to endorse them because clients are likely to be committed to tasks they themselves identify. In many instances, however, tasks are less readily apparent, and it becomes necessary to explore alternate ways of accomplishing a subgoal. The challenge is to select a promising alternative that optimally fits a particular client.

An effective way of identifying alternatives is to brainstorm with clients. Brainstorming involves the creative process of mutually focusing efforts on generating a broad range of possible options from which clients can choose. (We discuss brainstorming at greater length in the next chapter.) Although useful in any context, brainstorming is particularly fruitful in yielding alternatives in work with groups or families. If clients overlook options, it is important to suggest additional ones to assure a broad range of alternatives. We have found that practitioners often need to assume the initiative, as many clients fail to generate alternatives. Keep in mind that if clients were able to formulate detailed and effective remedial courses of action, they likely would not have needed assistance in the first place. Clients generally are receptive to suggested tasks, and research indicates little difference in the rate with which they accomplish tasks suggested by practitioners as compared to those they propose themselves (Reid, 1978, p. 251).

It is important that you be sensitive to clients' reactions to tasks that you propose, for further research (Reid, 1978) indicates that "the degree of the client's apparent commitment or expressed willingness to work on the task was positively related to task progress" (p. 250). Although clients may be just as committed to tasks you introduce as to their own, if you attempt to "assign" tasks, thereby failing to enlist their commitment, it is unlikely they will expend their best efforts in implementing tasks, if indeed they undertake such tasks at all. The same principle applies in working with groups or families. Persons in these systems may be quick to come up with tasks they think other individual members should assume.

Thus, it is important for the group leader to protect individual members' right to choose—without pressure—which tasks they will undertake and, indeed, whether they will undertake any tasks. A common mistake of beginning practitioners is to conclude erroneously that clients are resistant to change when, in fact, they are resistant to having tasks imposed upon them. Such resistance often manifests an assertion of individuality—a healthy assertion in our opinion.

To demonstrate how tasks flow from subgoals, we return to one of the examples we cited earlier. Don and Jean identified a general or ultimate goal of reducing their marital conflict by communicating more effectively. By exploring the specific ways they would communicate differently if they accomplished their goal, the practitioner assisted them to break the goal down into several subgoals, one of which was, "We will express ourselves without antagonizing each other." Further exploration of how they antagonized each other revealed that in discussing various topics, Jean often felt her husband demeaned her by invalidating her opinion, which "gets my hackles up." Don agreed her complaint was legitimate and expressed a desire to avoid putting her on the defensive. He explained, however, that he had been very unhappy at work where he was deriving little satisfaction and sense of accomplishment. Jean acknowledged his difficulties, complaining that, "He often comes home from work looking very glum, which tends to cast a dark cloud over the family." He agreed this was true, adding he didn't feel very important to anyone. He explained further that, "I need strokes, and if she would give me some strokes I would have a brighter attitude and be less inclined to put her down." Jean said if this would help she

would be happy to give him some strokes, which wouldn't be difficult because of his many good qualities.

The practitioner observed that each was giving the other valuable information that if acted upon could assist them in achieving their subgoal of expressing themselves without antagonizing each other. After exploring their feelings and ascertaining that both were receptive to making changes in line with the discussion, the practitioner and the clients formulated the following reciprocal tasks:

1. When Jean expresses her opinions, Don will listen attentively without criticizing or belittling her. He will also endeavor to be more positive when he comes home after work.

2. Jean will be more attentive and supportive of Don, expressing affection and greater interest and concern over his frustrations at work.

Both Jean and Don agreed to keep daily tallies of the number of times they performed the actions inherent in their respective tasks, willingly committing themselves to increase the frequency of these actions to at least twice daily during the first week.

To illustrate further, let us consider another subgoal—to talk with other tenants and mobilize an action group—taken from a preceding example. This subgoal already embodies an action strategy but can be partialized still further by developing plans for contacting specific tenants, including setting a time frame for accomplishing the tasks and preparing the presentation to be made to other tenants. Specified at this level, both the practitioner and clients are clear about the task to be accomplished before the next session (assuming the clients manifest commitment to the task).

Notice that the preceding tasks have been formulated in terms of positive behaviors that clients are to perform rather than behaviors from which they are to refrain. Positively framed tasks that specify undertaking desired behaviors highlight growth and gains that clients will achieve. By contrast, tasks that specify eliminating negative behaviors focus exclusively on what clients are to give up. Clients tend to be more enthusiastic about tasks oriented to growth and achievement, and accomplishing such tasks often motivates them to undertake even further changes.

Certain situations present opportunities for combining tasks that involve decreasing the frequency of dysfunctional behaviors and increasing the frequency of related functional behaviors. A parent, for example, may agree to implement tasks that involve decreasing nagging and increasing expressions of approval when a child performs assigned duties. Similarly, a client may agree to dismiss negative thoughts about a spouse and to increase the frequency of thoughts about the spouse's positive attributes. Still another example may involve reducing time spent brooding over disappointments and increasing time spent in recreational activities with friends.

The process of partializing goals into subgoals and ultimately into tasks occupies a substantial portion of the time in the early portion of the change-oriented phase. Much time is also spent in preparing to accomplish one or more tasks before the next scheduled session. We clarify the rationale for this in later sections of this chapter.

Although it is often appropriate to identify more than one task, it is important to identify and carefully plan implementation of at *least* one before concluding a session. In fact, many clients ask for "homework assignments." Mutually iden-

tifying tasks and planning implementation of them in each session sharpen the focus on change and facilitate progress by maintaining action-oriented involvement of clients between sessions. Without such actions, sessions become primarily verbal, and little or no change may occur between them. The ongoing focus upon task accomplishment, by contrast, concentrates, intensifies, and accelerates the helping process.

Planning Task Accomplishment

After settling upon one or more tasks, the next step is to assist clients in preparing to implement each task. Skillfully executed, this process augments clients' motivation for undertaking tasks and substantially enhances the probability of successful outcomes. A systematic approach termed the *task implementation sequence* (TIS) has been described by Reid (1975), who reported research findings to the effect that clients were more successful in accomplishing tasks when TIS was employed than when it was not.

The TIS involves a sequence of discrete steps that encompass major ingredients generally associated with successful change efforts. Although Reid recommends that the TIS be applied systematically, he also cautions practitioners to be sufficiently flexible to permit adaptation to the circumstances of each case. Reid's caution, of course, also applies to modifying the TIS to fit a group format. The TIS thus embodies the following steps:

1. Enhance clients' commitment to carry out a specific task.

2. Plan the details of carrying out the task.

3. Analyze and resolve obstacles that may be encountered.

4. Have clients rehearse or practice the behaviors involved in carrying out the task.

5. Summarize the plan of task implementation, and convey both encouragement and an expectation that the client will carry out the task.

Before considering each of the above steps, it is important to recognize that the accomplishment of a task often poses a formidable challenge to clients. It would be simplistic to assume that merely agreeing to carry out a task assures that the client has the knowledge, courage, interpersonal skill, and emotional readiness to implement a task successfully. Clients who possess these ingredients are unlikely to need the assistance of the practitioner in the first place. Moreover, if a client is ill-prepared to undertake a task, the probable outcome will be failure either to attempt the task or to complete it successfully. Either outcome is likely to cause the client to feel discouraged and to experience lowered self-esteem and subsequent difficulty in facing the practitioner. Resistance can thus be engendered, which might be manifested by not keeping the next appointment or diverting attention from the pertinent task.

Having clarified the challenges inherent in tasks, let us consider each step in more detail.

1. Enhancing Commitment to Carry Out a Task Directly aimed at enhancing motivation to carry out a task, this step involves clarifying the relevance of tasks to clients' goals and identifying benefits that will result from carrying out tasks. The rationale of this step is that to follow through with tasks, clients must perceive gains that outweigh potential costs (including anxiety and fear) associated with risking new behavior. Because change is difficult, involving apprehension, discomfort, and uncertainty, this step is especially critical when clients' motivation to carry out a given task is questionable.

In many instances, the potential gains of carrying out a task are obvious, and it would be pointless to dwell on this step. The potential gains of applying for a job interview or securing essential information about eligibility for financial assistance are self-evident. The benefits of other tasks, however, are less apparent, and a discussion of them may be essential for the client to grasp the relationship between the task and the goals. Benefits of following a medical regimen may not be clear if a client's physician has not explained the need for the regimen and the consequences of not following it. Similarly, the benefits of keeping a daily log on self-defeating thoughts may be unclear to a client who does not see the connection between this task and an ultimate goal of overcoming depression.

It is preferable to begin implementing step one by asking clients to identify benefits they will gain by successfully accomplishing a task. Clients are usually able to identify obvious benefits but may overlook others that are less apparent. Consequently, you may need to bring the latter to their awareness.

To illustrate this process, we consider an actual case situation involving a male client in his early 20s who was distressed over the fact that when he took his girlfriend on a date they frequently encountered some of her friends, and she often left him standing for lengthy intervals while she conversed with them in a foreign language that he neither spoke nor understood. After exploring his reactions of feeling left out, less important to her than her friends, and frank irritation over her insensitivity to his feelings, he agreed to work on the task of directly but tactfully expressing his feelings to her.

When asked what benefits he would gain by carrying out the task, he replied that he would feel better about dealing with her rather than just feeling irritated and left out. The practitioner agreed, adding he would also feel stronger and experience more self-respect for facing the problem rather than avoiding it. Furthermore, his girlfriend would also likely respect him more, and they would gain experience in dealing with relationship problems. Last, he would be taking an important step toward accomplishing one of his ultimate goals—to resolve his mixed feelings toward his girlfriend.

Just as it is important to identify benefits, it is also essential to consider possible risks of carrying out tasks. (Recall our making this same point in the last chapter with respect to the process of selecting goals.) Again, we recommend you ask clients to identify risks and then add others that occur to you. In the case situation discussed in the foregoing paragraph, the client expressed concern that his girlfriend might take offense and construe his expressing his feelings as an attempt to control her. He described her as independent and somewhat domineering. Further discussion, however, led him to conclude this was not a real risk because he needed to learn to stand up to her in any event. Otherwise, he might be inviting being dominated, and that was unacceptable to him. He definitely wished to carry out the task even though it might introduce some strain in the relationship.

In work with growth groups, practitioners can use group process to good advantage in assisting individual members to weigh the benefits and risks of individual goals. In using group process, it is important to elicit expressions from other group members. Preferably, this should take place after a member considering a potential change has had an opportunity individually to contemplate the relative benefits and risks in assuming a task. As "outside consultants" who often share many of the same situations and dilemmas as the person contemplating the task, other members often make a penetrating analysis of the costs and rewards involved.

In enhancing motivation to change ingrained behaviors, it is sometimes essential to create immediate incentives by planning tangible rewards for carrying out planned actions. One client had a long-established pattern of going on eating binges, during which she would consume large quantities of food, to her later chagrin. She initially viewed herself as helpless to control her impulses to gorge herself, attributing her difficulties to "lack of willpower." Careful assessment had led the practitioner to disagree with her explanation, inputing her problem instead to (1) mistaken and demeaning beliefs about herself and (2) the habituated use of eating as a substitute for gratification she was not gaining through more appropriate modes of behavior.

To enable her to experience success in exercising self-control, the practitioner suggested that she identify something she wanted badly and earn the privilege of acquiring it by modifying her eating habits during the week. (Her previous longest time of maintaining control of her eating was four days.) With a smile, she responded that she had wanted to purchase a pair of leather boots for several months but had not done so because it seemed extravagant. She and the practitioner then negotiated an agreement whereby she could reward herself by buying the boots if she ate only at mealtimes and consumed average portions of food over the week's time. She could also have one small snack each day but only by making a conscious choice to do so and then eating it while sitting at the dining room table. On the other hand, if she indulged in a binge, she would forfeit the right to purchase the boots for at least four months. She appeared excited about the challenge and agreed to share it with her husband, whose knowledge of it would create additional incentive. (He had earlier encouraged her to buy the boots.) If she successfully implemented her task, she was to reward herself further by expressing silent approval and to remind herself she had consciously made decisions to exercise self-control. Further, she was to think of herself as capable of increasing self-control week by week.

In her session one week later, the client's success was mirrored in her countenance as she greeted the practitioner. With obvious pride, she described how she had constantly reminded herself she could exercise self-control, and her success over the week's time gave substance to her thoughts. She described how pleased her husband was with her success and how they had planned to celebrate by going together to purchase the boots. The initial success was the first of a series of similar successes that led to increased self-confidence and to eventual mastery of her excessive eating.

Rewarding oneself (self-reinforcement) to enhance the incentives for completing a task is particularly relevant when changes sought involve yielding pleasures of consummatory excesses and carrying out essential activities that may be perceived as aversive, e.g., studying, cleaning the house, mowing the lawn, doing the dishes, or planning and preparing regular meals. Possible rewards should be considered in light of each client's uniqueness, but the following are typical examples: going to a special movie or artistic production; allocating time to engage in special activities, such as reading a novel, going swimming, or going bowling; visiting or shopping with a special friend; or purchasing an inexpensive but significant article of clothing or tool. Because clients' preferences differ, the challenge is to assist them in identifying rewards that represent true incentives to them.

Rewards can also be utilized to create incentives for children to complete tasks, such as completing homework assignments, showing caring behaviors to siblings, picking up after themselves, or doing household chores. In addition to negotiating tasks with children, practitioners often establish complementary tasks with parents or other significant persons for the purpose of assisting children in carrying out their tasks or modifying dysfunctional behavioral patterns that involve *both* children and parents. When rewards are used to create incentives for children, it is important during the early stages of change to provide rewards immediately after children perform desired behaviors. It is also important to reward small changes; otherwise, children may become discouraged and give up, believing they cannot meet the standards expected by parents. Naive parents and practitioners mistakenly assume that elaborate long-range rewards (e.g., get a bicycle in June) will motivate children to make changes. In actuality, even for older children, smaller rewards given soon after the behavior are far more effective as motivators.

In setting up tasks with accompanying rewards for children and parents (or significant others, such as teachers), the following guidelines are helpful:

a. Frame tasks so that what children and parents are to do and when they are to do it are explicitly defined. For example, with an eight-year-old child who frequently argues and complains when parents make requests of him, a task can be formulated so that the child will carry out the requested actions immediately. The task also specifies what the parent is to do in a given circumstance (e.g., make the request in a calm and cheerful manner).

And finally, the task specifies the time frame and conditions under which the task is to be performed (e.g., every two hours, twice daily, each Wednesday, for the next four days).

b. Designate points that children can earn for performing specified target behaviors, and establish a method of keeping track of the points (e.g., each time the child responds appropriately to requests, the parent will enter a mark on a chart constructed conjointly by the parents and children).

c. Establish a reward for earning a specified number of points for specified periods of time (e.g., if the child earns five points by 8 o'clock each night, he or she will have a choice of playing a short game or having a parent read a story). Whenever possible, it is important to offer "relationship" rewards, as contrasted to ones that are monetary or material. Relationship rewards involve time spent in an attractive activity with a parent or other significant person. It is also important to invite children to choose the type of reward they wish to earn, since they will choose rewards that have maximal value as incentives.

d. Give a bonus for consistent achievements of tasks over an extended period of time (e.g., if the child achieves a quota of five points each day for seven consecutive days, he or she and the involved parent will celebrate by going out for a hamburger and drink).

e. Teach parents or others to give consistent positive feedback regarding the child's progress, and negotiate tasks related to expressing encouragement and approval as the child engages in task-related efforts.

Tasks buoyed by creative rewards can do much to reduce parent-child tensions, motivating both adults and children to focus on developing positive behaviors. One parent, who was consistently embarrassed in restaurants by the disruptive behavior of her five children, readily consented to a task of monitoring her children's positive behaviors during the meal. Also giving her children the task of reporting to her their *positive* actions, the mother gave them credit by recording one point for each positive action. At the end of the meal, each child had earned enough points (at the rate of a penny a point) to redeem them for an afterdinner treat (something they usually received anyway). Although the mother spent more time recording points than eating, she was ecstatic about the successful outcome of the activity and particularly about the sharp increase in caring behaviors manifested by her children toward each other and toward her during the evening, which, incidentally, generalized to other situations throughout the week. She also reported experiencing more positive feelings toward her children.

2. Plan the Details of Carrying Out the Task This step is vital in assisting clients to prepare themselves for all the actions inherent in a task. Most tasks consist of a series of actions or subtasks to be carried out sequentially, including both cognitive and behavioral subtasks. For example, before carrying out an overt action, such as asking a boss for a raise, requesting repairs from a landlord, or submitting to a painful medical examination, clients often benefit by preparing themselves psychologically. This may involve reviewing potential benefits, dismissing needless fears by reminding themselves of reality factors, mustering courage by accrediting themselves for past successes, recalling the encouragement of the practitioner, and praying for strength if they are religiously inclined. By planning such cognitive strategies, clients are better able to cope with the inevitable ambivalence and trepidation associated with implementing new actions.

Planning overt actions involves considering details of actual required behaviors. For example, in the first case cited under step 1, the client would need to consider when he would talk with his girlfriend, how he would introduce the topic, express his feelings, and cope with possible reactions on her part. The more detailed the plans, the greater the likelihood of success. Moreover, by discussing discrete actions, you increase opportunities to elicit cues to misgivings, fears, or behavioral deficiencies that must be remedied if clients are to complete tasks successfully.

Task planning may also involve overt actions by the practitioner that must be coordinated with the client's actions. For example, an unemployed and unskilled young adult may be interested in obtaining vocational guidance. A task may be to take tests that assess aptitudes and interests. Task planning may involve telephone calls by the practitioner to locate an appropriate resource and to convey information to the client, as well as subsequent actions by the client to arrange to take the tests and have the results interpreted. Subsequent tasks may involve exploring and arranging appropriate vocational training, locating financial resources, and the like. In group contexts, a group or family member might also informally assist a designated person in planning and carrying out actions outside the group.

In many instances, a critical aspect of task formulation is to specify carefully the conditions under which the task will be carried out. For example, a sixth-grade boy who constantly disturbs his peers and irritates his teacher through boisterous talk and teasing behavior may accept a task of listening attentively when the teacher is speaking during the one-hour arithmetic class and raise his hand three times to answer questions during that time. He is to carry out this task each day

for the next five days. A grandmother who is living with her son and daughter-in-law and whose specialty is monitoring and critically reporting to the parents all of their children's negative behaviors may be asked during a family therapy session to assume a task of reporting *positive* behaviors directly to the children and to the parents. This grandmother may agree to work on this task extensively during the upcoming weekend, a time when all of the children are at home. It has been our experience that if the time for implementing tasks is left indefinite, clients (and practitioners) tend to procrastinate until it is too late to implement requisite actions effectively. Although we have not subjected our impression to empirical testing, we are convinced that clients implement tasks at a higher rate when specific times are stipulated than when they are left indefinite. In determining a time frame, it is also important to elicit feedback from clients regarding the amount of time they feel is needed to accomplish a specific objective rather than to set a time frame arbitrarily.

In selecting and planning tasks pertaining to *ongoing* goals, you should observe an additional caution. Because progress on such goals is incremental, it is vital to begin with relatively simple tasks that are within the clients' capacity to achieve. The chances of clients undertaking more difficult tasks later are much enhanced if they achieve success on initial tasks. Conversely, if they experience failure on initial tasks, their confidence and courage may decline, and they may be reluctant to undertake additional ones. It is thus preferable to have the first task be too easy than too difficult.

3. Analyze and Resolve Obstacles Based on a recognition of the inevitability of forces that counter the client's thrust for change, this step is aimed at countering these forces.[1] Implementing it involves anticipating, analyzing, and obviating obstacles that may be encountered as the client seeks to accomplish a task. Employed effectively, this step is a powerful technique for enhancing task accomplishment and for accelerating change.

With commonplace tasks, obstacles are generally minor and can often be readily identified by asking clients what difficulties, if any, they expect to encounter. Included in such tasks are those requiring simple actions, such as telephoning a community agency that the client and the practitioner have just discovered, which holds promise of providing needed assistance. A caveat should be observed, however—what is a simple action for most people may be difficult for a few. Making a telephone call was an overwhelming task for one client. Mildly brain damaged and overprotected by his parents for all his 19 years, the client had depended on them to make telephone calls for him because he feared he would "foul up and sound stupid." In such instances, fears may pose formidable barriers to accomplishing a task and may require careful exploration and working through before they are overcome.

When tasks are complex, obstacles likewise tend to be complex and difficult to identify and resolve. Tasks that involve changes in patterns of interpersonal relationships tend to be multifaceted, encompassing subsidiary but prerequisite intrapersonal tasks as well as a mastery of certain interpersonal skills. Successfully resisting unwanted sexual advances, for example, may involve overcoming powerful fears that refusal to submit will result

in utter rejection. The irrational belief that one has nothing to offer other than sex must be supplanted by a belief about one's self that is aligned with reality. The client must also master new behaviors that tactfully but firmly set limits with predatory males.

Clients vary widely in their capacity to anticipate obstacles. Consequently, it is vital to elicit from them (and from members when in a group context) possible obstacles to achieving their planned course of action. Observations regarding obstacles may also be made by the practitioner. In introducing the possibility of relevant obstacles, it is vital to safeguard the client's self-esteem by explaining that obstacles are common to many people. An example of an obstacle that had to be identified involved a withdrawn, late adolescent client whose goal was to mingle socially with others. She was embarrassed and hesitant to reveal that she was afraid of accepting an invitation to visit a peer in her neighborhood because her legs might become rubbery and she might vomit on the neighbor's rug. Similarly, a musically talented male client who wished to play the organ for others was afraid to display his talents because others might perceive him as a weirdo or homosexual.

As these examples imply, psychological barriers to accomplishing tasks are often encountered regardless of the nature of the target problem. Overlooking such barriers may in some instances cause needless difficulties in the accomplishment of tasks and, in others, result in outright failure. Applying for a job, submitting to a medical examination, talking to a schoolteacher, expressing tender feelings—these and a host of other seemingly everyday tasks are charged with strong emotionality for some people and may be threatening.

---

[1]Much of the information in this section is taken from D. H. Hepworth (1979), "Early removal of resistance in task-centered casework." *Social Work, 24,* 4, 317–323 (the publisher's permission is gratefully acknowledged).

Prerequisite to the successful accomplishment of a task, therefore, may be a subsidiary task of neutralizing untoward emotions. This can often be accomplished in a brief time by eliciting and clarifying the apprehension, rationally analyzing it, and modeling and rehearsing the behavior required to implement the task successfully. In other instances, more extensive efforts are required. Whatever time and effort are invested are likely to be rewarded by achieving a higher rate of success in accomplishing tasks. An economy of time is also effected, since failures in implementing tasks further extend the time required for successfully implementing them.

Other cues and techniques may also facilitate identifying obstacles. In discussing plans for implementing a task, you should be alert to nonverbal cues that indicate apprehension on the client's part about undertaking the task. Such cues include looking away from you, speaking diffidently and unenthusiastically about the task, changing the topic, fidgeting atypically, and tightening facial and body muscles. If you detect such reactions, you should further explore the presence of undisclosed barriers or work further on resolving obstacles already identified.

Vital to successful task implementation is the client's readiness to tackle the mutually negotiated task. Such readiness, however, should not be confused with feeling comfortable; it is neither realistic nor desirable to expect the client to feel altogether comfortable with the task. A certain amount of tension and anxiety is to be expected and may positively motivate the client to risk the new behavior embodied in the task. Inordinate anxiety, by contrast, may be a major deterrent to undertaking the task or may impair the client's effectiveness upon attempting it. Obviously, when clients report that they

did not carry out a task, you should consider the possibility that the task was premature and that unresolved barriers remain. Another possibility is that the client was inadequately committed to the task, an important factor to be discussed later.

A simple yet effective way to gauge readiness for undertaking tasks is to ask clients to rate their readiness on a scale from 1 to 10, with 1 representing total unreadiness and 10 complete readiness. It is important to explain first that a certain amount of apprehension is natural and should not deter the client from trying out new behaviors; indeed, relative freedom from apprehension is not achieved before implementing the task but is rather a by-product of successful implementation. This explanation is important because many clients are overly hesitant to risk themselves and needlessly postpone taking actions.

When clients rate their readiness at 7 or higher, you can assume a sufficient degree of readiness and suggest that they appear prepared to undertake the task. Also provide support by expressing restrained confidence that the client can successfully implement the task and by conveying an expectation that the planned actions will be carried out. Exploring the reasons why clients rate themselves at 7 rather than 10 on the readiness scale will often give you vital information concerning potential obstacles to change, including reservations they may have about completing the task.

After identifying barriers to change, you must next assist the client in overcoming them. Barriers encountered most frequently include *deficiencies in social skills* and *misconceptions and irrational fears* associated with performing tasks. The former is a formidable barrier that must be overcome, for one may lack the skill and experience to know how to carry out a task. In such instances, clients commonly fear bungling a task and appearing ridiculous as a result. Undertaking the task thus is perceived as placing one's self-esteem in jeopardy.

Modeling and behavioral rehearsal in sessions may assist clients to gain the courage and skills necessary to carry out interpersonal tasks. In some instances, however, more intensive interventions may be required, such as personal effectiveness training and assertiveness training.

The second major type of barrier to task accomplishment involves misconceptions and irrational fears that embrace misunderstandings of the self, stereotypic perceptions of others, and intense apprehensions based on grossly distorted and dreaded consequences of actions. Cognitive theorists present a compelling case to the effect that the quality and intensity of emotions experienced in a given situation are largely determined by the perceptions and attributions of meaning associated with that situation. Inordinate fear and apprehension are thus cues that something is amiss in the client's patterns of thought. Your task is to elicit the problematic emotions, to identify their cognitive sources, and to assist clients in aligning their thoughts and feelings with reality. Removing this barrier usually enables clients to move several points higher on the readiness scale.

Resolving misconceptions, perceptual distortions, and irrational fears was once believed to require a lengthy expedition into the unconscious to discover the genesis of such inhibiting forces. In recent years, however, new techniques (see Chapter 18) have been used successfully in eliminating fears and misconceptions rapidly without shifting the focus to the remote past.

4. Have Clients Rehearse or Practice Behaviors Involved in Carrying Out Tasks   Certain tasks involve skills clients lack or behaviors with which they have had little or no experience. Step 4 is thus aimed at assisting clients to gain experience and mastery in performing behaviors essential to task accomplishment. Successful experience, even in simulated situations, fosters belief in having the ability to carry out a task effectively. Having an expectancy of success is vital, for as Bandura (1977) has indicated, "The strength of people's convictions in their own effectiveness is likely to affect whether they will even try to cope with given situations" (p. 193). Bandura builds a strong case, documented by research evidence, to the effect that the degree of positive expectation that clients have in their ability to perform tasks effectively determines how much effort they will expend in attempting tasks and how long they will persist in the face of obstacles or aversive circumstances. It follows that a major goal of the helping process is to enhance clients' sense of self-efficacy with respect to the tasks they select.

Research evidence cited by Bandura (1977, p. 195) indicates that, once established, self-efficacy and skills tend to be transferred by clients to other situations that they previously avoided. According to Bandura, people receive information about self-efficacy from four sources: (1) performance accomplishments, (2) vicarious experience, (3) verbal persuasion, and (4) emotional arousal. Of these four sources, performance accomplishment is especially influential because it is based on personal mastery experience.

Major methods of increasing self-efficacy through performance accomplishment include assisting clients to master essential behaviors through modeling, behavior rehearsal, and guided practice, all of which we discuss at length later in this chapter. An example of performance accomplishment would be assisting family members to master certain communication skills during actual sessions.

Vicarious experiences gained by observing others demonstrate target behaviors or perform threatening activities without adverse consequences can also generate expectations in clients that they too can master the target behaviors. Efficacy expectations based on observing the practitioner or others model desired behaviors, however, are likely to be weaker and more vulnerable to change than expectations based on performance accomplishment. Information about one's capabilities based on assumptions that one can perform comparably to a model are hardly as persuasive as direct evidence of personal accomplishment.

Although verbal persuasion is widely employed to enhance self-efficacy (because it can be easily implemented), it too is weaker than performance accomplishment because it is not grounded in authentic experience. Attempting to reassure or convince clients that they can perform new behaviors, therefore, has definite limitations as an enduring source of personal self-efficacy. Nevertheless, it can and does contribute to successful performance when accompanied by measures that equip clients for effective action. Verbal persuasion contributes by raising *outcome expectations* rather than enhancing self-efficacy per se.

The fourth source of information about self-efficacy, emotional arousal, is based on the fact that the perceived level of emotional arousal affects how people perform. Clients who are extremely anxious or fearful about performing a new behavior are unlikely to have much confidence

they can perform the behavior competently. Many interventions are therefore directed to reducing anxiety or fear or to influencing clients *to believe* they are not fearful or anxious. Evidence cited by Bandura indicates that to be effective, reductions in emotional arousal must be genuine and not based on deceptive feedback aimed at assuring clients they are not anxious when they are anxious. Emotional arousal obviously is an undependable source of self-efficacy because it too is not related to actual evidence of capability. Perceived self-competence tends to reduce emotional arousal rather than the converse.

Having defined the sources of information about self-efficacy, we return to the topic of behavioral rehearsal. As employed in actual sessions, behavioral rehearsal assists clients to practice new coping patterns under the tutelage of the practitioner. Indications for using behavioral rehearsal include situations that clients feel inadequately prepared to confront. When clients manifest strong uneasiness or appear overwhelmed by the prospects of carrying out a given task, behavioral rehearsal is an effective way of developing requisite skills and reducing the threat posed by the action. Such tasks usually involve interacting with significant other people with whom strain already exists or is expected to develop as a result of the planned actions. Typical examples include asserting one's rights to an authority figure; expressing feelings of hurt or rejection to one's spouse; or making a social overture to a member of the other sex.

Role-playing is the most common mode of behavioral rehearsal. Before engaging clients in rehearsal of desired behaviors, however, practitioners can use role-playing to have clients demonstrate their initial levels of skills, thus enabling practitioners to model skills that build on clients' extant skills. Practitioners frequently model behavior that clients are expected to perform before actually having them rehearse the behavior. Used particularly when the requisite behavior is unfamiliar to the client, modeling has been amply documented as an effective means of enabling clients vicariously to learn new modes of coping behavior, as we noted earlier.

In employing modeling, ask the client to play the role of the *other* person involved in the real-life difficulty and, in doing so, to simulate as accurately as possible the anticipated behavior to be encountered in the actual situation. The role-playing thus enables you to model appropriate responses to behavior that has previously overwhelmed the client. After the role-playing, it is productive to discuss what happened, focusing on the client's reactions and on questions and concerns as well. It is also beneficial to explain your rationale for particular responses and to share difficulties you may have experienced. It has been our experience that in assuming the role of clients, we often gain new insights and fuller appreciation of the difficulties they encounter.

If your coping in the modeling situation falls short of being effective, it is appropriate and even helpful to acknowledge the difficulties you experienced and to consider mutually other possible coping responses. Indeed, it is desirable to model imperfect *coping efforts* rather than *mastery,* for research indicates that clients benefit more from observing a "coping model" (Kazdin, 1979: Meichenbaum, 1977). A coping model, according to Cormier and Cormier (1979), "shows some fear or anxiety, makes errors in performance and shows some degree of struggle or coping while performing the behavior or activity" (p. 263). These authors suggest that clients identify more easily with and are less threatened by a coping model than one who performs flawlessly or perfectly.

Modeling need not be limited to overt behaviors, for clients may also benefit from modeling of covert coping with cognitive barriers to task accomplishment. Covert modeling involves expressing aloud thoughts and feelings associated with manifest difficulties and demonstrating appropriate ways of coping with related problematic thoughts and feelings. As with modeling of overt behavior, covert modeling should demonstrate coping rather than mastery. Meichenbaum (1977) has written extensively about and provided numerous examples of covert modeling.

After completing a modeling exercise, the next step is to reverse the roles so that the client rehearses the actual target behavior and you assume the role of the other significant person. In so doing, it is important that you attempt to approximate the anticipated behavior of the other person, including tone of voice, facial expressions, gestures, choice of words, and provocative behavior as modeled earlier by the client. The responses of the client to your simulated behavior provide an opportunity for corrective suggestions and for identifying need for additional practice, as well as for reinforcement and encouragement. Moreover, clients' readiness to tackle situations in real life can best be assessed by observing their behavior in rehearsal. Most important, clients' confidence to carry out tasks is enhanced by practice. You can further enhance clients' self-efficacy by expressing confidence in their ability to carry out the planned task successfully, providing your support and encouragement are genuine.

As clients mobilize the strength and courage gained through behavioral rehearsal and face problems head-on rather than avoid them, their previous greatly feared consequences dwindle into realistic perspective. Clients have affirmed the effectiveness of modeling and behavioral rehearsal numerous times for the authors by reporting that their practice during sessions was the single most important factor in assisting them to accomplish their tasks. Behavioral rehearsal, incidentally, need not be confined to sessions. It is often productive to encourage clients to continue rehearsing target behaviors outside the interviews by pretending to engage in real-life encounters.

Modeling and behavioral rehearsal need not be confined to relationships between practitioners and individual clients. Often, a client in a group or family session may be able to provide effective and realistic coping modeling for another group member. Indeed, a rule of thumb in conducting group role-playing sessions is to tap group resources for coping models whenever possible, which enhances the help-giving role of group members.

Closely related to behavioral rehearsal, *guided practice* is another form of performance accomplishment, which differs from behavioral rehearsal in that it consists of in vivo rather than simulated behavior. Using guided practice as a mode of intervention, you assist clients to gain mastery of target behaviors by coaching them as they actually attempt to perform the target behaviors. For example, in conjoint marital sessions, you may assist clients to master skills in solving problems or resolving conflicts by instructing them as they deal with actual problems or conflict situations. Guided practice is particularly relevant to family and group contexts. Skills in brainstorming, active listening, assertiveness, and control of anger—to name just a few—can be effectively learned through guided practice in groups.

Guided practice is an especially potent method of inducing change. The practitioner can observe live behavior and provide immediate corrective feedback as well as encouragement and approval. Observing behavior directly is especially valuable in marital and family sessions, for opportunities exist to intervene immediately when dysfunctional behavior occurs. Such on-the-spot interventions enable you to clarify what is going wrong, to explain more effective ways of coping, and to coach clients in employing more competent behavior.

5. *Summarize the Plan of Task Implementation* This final step involves reviewing the various actions clients are to carry out in accomplishing a task. Implementing this step, which is done in the concluding segment of an individual or group session, enables clients to emerge from the session with a clear understanding of what they are to do and in what sequence. To enable clients to gain maximum benefit from this step, we recommend that you ask them to review details of their plan for implementing the task, including strategies for coping with obstacles that may be encountered. By eliciting clients' descriptions of their plans, you can assess whether certain aspects of the plan need to be further clarified. To counter procrastination, it is advantageous to specify the time frame for implementing the plan.

After summarizing the plan of task implementation, it is appropriate to terminate the session. An effective way of closing the session is to express approval of clients' plans and expectations that they implement them. Because results cannot be accurately predicted, however, it is desirable to convey restrained optimism. We recommend you also express interest in hearing about their experience at the beginning of the next session.

Maintaining Focus and Continuity

The strength of the task-centered system lies in its focus on change through task accomplishment and its systematic format that promotes continuity of change efforts. Individual sessions are sharply focused, and continuity is maintained from one session to the next. Each session begins with a review of clients' experiences in implementing tasks that were agreed upon during the previous session. There are two major objectives and benefits of discussing clients' experiences in implementing tasks. First, both clients and practitioners can identify ways in which clients can further improve their effectiveness in performing newly developed behaviors. This discussion may further enhance clients' comfort in coping with problematic situations and suggest additional activities in the session to refine their skills. A second benefit is that the practitioner can explore clients' perceptions of their impact on others and their feelings as they implemented the tasks. This discussion provides an opportunity to identify additional work to be done and prepares the ground for mutually planning future tasks.

Still another benefit of reviewing task implementation is that you can reinforce clients for carrying out planned tasks. When clients report successes, it is appropriate to express your delight, to accredit their strength and progress, and briefly to share in savoring their successes. Your own way of conveying your positive feelings is best, but the following is a typical message:

[*Smiling with pleasure*]: "I'm delighted with how well you did. As I listened to you describe how you talked with your teacher, I was impressed with how clearly you expressed your feelings. Your teacher must have been impressed too, because you shared a part of yourself she hasn't seen before."

In reviewing task accomplishments, it is critical to elicit details as to actions or behaviors that assisted clients in achieving a task. Even when tasks have been only partially completed, it is important to focus on results clients achieved as a consequence of their efforts. In so doing, it is important to connect clients' efforts with the results that they attained, underscoring that in accomplishing specified tasks, they demonstrated ability to shape their own lives. Establishing that clients have more control than they had previously realized is a powerful force for countering feelings of helplessness, hopelessness, and depression that many clients experience.

Although they may report improvements in problem situations discussed in previous sessions, some clients attribute the reasons for these changes to circumstances beyond themselves. Through careful exploration, practitioners often are able to establish that changes occurred (at least in part) through clients' efforts. Establishing such cause-effect relationships is critical to successful outcomes, for clients are thereby enabled to view themselves as actors who have the potential to solve their problems and to enhance their life situations.

After completing a review of task implementation, you mutually plan additional tasks that enable clients to progress closer to their focal goals. In addition to following the steps previously delineated for defining tasks, it is important in working toward accomplishment of *ongoing goals* to plan tasks that involve incremental changes and build on one another. Planning tasks that are graded in difficulty enhances chances of successful accomplishment and tends to increase clients' motivation to exert greater efforts in the change process.

To illustrate gradual progression in developing tasks, we consider an extremely self-conscious, socially inhibited client in his early 20s, who negotiated a goal of being able to socialize with his fellow workers in the shipping department of a large wholesale supply firm. He rarely engaged in discussions with co-workers, his conversations being limited to job-related topics. To accomplish his goal, the following tasks were mutually negotiated and accomplished sequentially as listed:

1. Smile at workers and look them in the eyes upon arriving at work.

2. Verbally greet co-workers each morning and when leaving work say "see you tomorrow." (Expect startled reactions from co-workers.)

3. Greet co-workers and ask "How are you doing, (person's name)?"

4. Ask if he can join co-workers at lunch.

5. Listen to co-workers at lunch and "shut off" thoughts about possible negative impressions they may have of him.

6. Make at *least* one comment or ask one question at lunch.

7. Make at least three comments at lunch.

8. Make overtures to initiate conversation at other times by picking up on topics discussed at lunch.

9. Share at least one personal view or experience during luncheon discussion.

10. Ask a co-worker to join him for a cold drink at break time.

Extensive planning, including modeling, behavioral rehearsal, and discussion of problematic feelings, was involved in preparing to execute each of the preceding tasks. As the client successfully accomplished the tasks, he decided to risk himself in social relationships away from work and formulated a new goal of asking a female out on a date. To accomplish this goal, progressive tasks building on those previously listed were negotiated.

In actual practice, progress is rarely as smooth as implied above. Not infrequently clients fail to carry out tasks or to achieve the desired results when they do. Occasionally, unforeseen circumstances, such as illness, crowded schedules, and unavailability of others involved in tasks preclude task accomplishment between sessions, necessitating carrying them over to the next week.

Clients may also fail to carry out tasks because of weak commitment to them, emergence of more pressing problems, negative reactions to the practitioner or to the group, or inadequate preparation. In any event, it is vital to explore the reasons carefully, attempting to resolve factors that have blocked implementation if both you and the clients agree the task remains valid. If you determine the task is not valid, it is important to shift your focus to more relevant tasks, as we discuss later. The importance of commitment to the task has been documented by Reid (1977), who cited this factor as "the only consistent statistically significant predictor of task progress" (p. 69).

A lack of commitment is not to be confused with a lack of readiness. In the former, the willingness to change is absent; in the latter, clients possess the willingness but are blocked from acting by other barriers. One frequent cause of a lack of commitment to undertake interpersonal tasks is a covert unwillingness to own one's part of a problem. A spouse or parent may pay lip service to carrying out a specific task but subsequently report feeble excuses for not doing so. Inwardly, unwilling clients often blame others for their difficulties and passively wait for others to initiate corrective actions. In such instances, it is important to explore further the interactions between clients and other actors and to clarify which part of the difficulty is owned by each. Confrontation may also be used to help clients recognize their responsibility for maintaining the undesired status quo by waiting for others to change. If clients exhibit a continued unwillingness to work on tasks, it is appropriate to question their willingness to change.

A lack of commitment to carry out specific tasks is also frequently associated with a general lack of motivation. In these instances, it is the worker's challenge and responsibility to engage such clients by creating an incentive for change, as we discussed in Chapter 12. Persistent failure to carry out tasks, however, belies expressed intentions; inaction certainly speaks louder than words, and in such instances, the advisability of continuing should be carefully weighed.

In some instances, what appears at first blush to be clients' lack of commitment to tasks may in actuality be a reflection of other more pressing concerns. Clients with multiple problems and limited coping skills may be beset between sessions with difficulties that supersede the focal problem. Such situations require judicious handling, for the practitioner and clients are faced with a difficult decision. On one hand, it is important to be flexible and to shift focus when emerging problems demand immediate attention. On the other hand, some clients are constantly besieged with "crises," and shifting from one to another amounts to little more than a Band-Aid approach.

Although you should be flexible in shifting focus, you must avoid letting crises dictate change efforts. Some clients who live from crisis to crisis benefit in the long run by seeing individual tasks through to completion, taking brief detours only to "apply Band-Aids" as needed. By successfully completing individual tasks, they gain increments of positive coping strengths they can apply to other crises.

Clients may not implement tasks in other situations because of overriding problems they have not as yet revealed. Some clients disclose only relatively minor difficulties during initial interviews and defer revealing more burdensome problems until they feel more comfortable in sharing them. Tasks agreed upon initially thus may not be valid in that they do not relate to the clients' paramount concerns. When this occurs, it is proper to shift the focus to more burdensome difficulties and to formulate new goals and tasks accordingly. It is important, however, to be satisfied that you are shifting focus for valid reasons and not reinforcing a pattern of avoidance.

A variety of other reasons may be responsible for task failure. In marital therapy, individual spouses often renege on their commitments to carry out tasks because each does not trust the other partner to carry out his or her part of the bargain. Further, during the week, one or both partners may gather "evidence" that the other spouse is uncommitted to the agreed-upon task, thus justifying his or her own noncompletion of it. Adequate preparation for an initial task in marital therapy thus entails exploration of the trust issue and establishment of a contract that each partner will strictly monitor his/her own task regardless of whether the other person does or does not.

When a client's problems involve the family system, it is important to include relevant members of the family in the sessions. Practitioners often defeat their client's objectives (and their own) by limiting their contacts to the individual client when the behaviors of other persons in a system impinge greatly on identified problems. Although at times families will accommodate an individual member who steadfastly achieves and maintains changes in the system, in many instances families defeat the individual's change efforts. Some families are so disorganized or insensitive to individual change efforts that they discourage any positive efforts of individual family members to modify behavior. Further, other families have dysfunctional interactional patterns that are so pervasive and intractable that it is extremely difficult for members to make needed behavioral changes without great cost unless adjustments are made in the entire system. In such situations, it is vital to involve all family members in sessions to assess individual needs as well as family dynamics and to include them in goal and task planning.

A factor that practitioners must consider in assisting groups to assume tasks is the group's stage of development. Group members have difficulty accomplishing significant change-oriented tasks in the first two stages of group development. In these stages, members tentatively test out the practitioner, other group members, and the group itself, at the same time attempting to find their own positions. Thus, they sometimes have little psychic energy or commitment to accomplish individual or group tasks. For this reason, tasks should be kept simple, and accomplishing them should not require an inordinate amount of investment by members. For instance, asking a newly formed group of delinquent adolescents in a correctional facility to make changes in their behavior toward staff or peers before they are "emotionally committed" to the pur-

poses of the group is doomed to failure. On the other hand, asking members to assume small tasks during the week so that the group might participate in an attractive activity may appeal to them.

Negative reactions to the practitioner may also block task accomplishment. Such reactions often result when the practitioner assigns tasks unilaterally. Wise (1977) explains that assigning tasks in such a manner tends to activate negative feelings in clients akin to those experienced in childhood toward a parent when unpleasant chores were assigned. To avoid balkiness or negativism, Wise recommends (as we do also) that you take care not to impose assignments on clients.

Another factor that may block task accomplishment is failure on the practitioner's part to follow up on task implementation. If practitioners neglect to review the client's experience in implementing a task, the client (or practitioner) may shift the focus to other topics before actually seeing previous efforts through to completion. Such shifts disrupt the continuity of change efforts and foster "drift," which dilutes and prolongs the helping process. For this reason, it is vital to review progress in implementing tasks, preferably at or close to the beginning of each session.

A final factor sometimes involved in failures either to attempt or to implement tasks successfully involves inadequate preparation. A practitioner may overestimate the coping skills of clients or may not devote sufficient time and effort to the task implementation sequence, leaving clients ill-prepared to cope with tasks' demands. Actually, it is preferable for clients not to attempt tasks rather than to attempt them and fail because they are not adequately prepared. In the former instance, blows to self-esteem are usually minimal, and additional efforts can be made to prepare a client more adequately. Failure, by contrast, may damage self-esteem and undermine confidence in the helping process.

Even when preparation has been adequate, successful outcomes of task efforts are not assured. Unanticipated reactions of others, ineffectual task performance, panic reactions, inappropriate task selection based on inaccurate assessment and adverse circumstances may block goal attainment. To avoid or minimize undue discouragement by clients when results are negative, it is helpful to interpret such results not as failures but as indications of the need for additional information and task planning. Negative results, in fact, sometimes serve a constructive purpose in further elucidating dynamics of problems, thereby enabling clients and practitioners to sharpen their assessment, goals, and tasks.

Evaluating Progress

A final mode of maintaining focus and continuity is to evaluate progress toward goal attainment regularly. Monitoring progress serves the following objectives:

1. By eliciting clients' views of their progress or by comparing latest rates of target behavior with the baseline, you maintain focus on goals and enhance continuity of change efforts.

2. Clients gain perspective not only in determining where they stand in relationship to ultimate goals but also to their pretreatment level of functioning. Discerning incremental progress toward goals tends to sustain motivation and to enhance confidence in the helping process and in the practitioner.

3. Eliciting clients' feelings and views regarding progress enables practitioners to detect and to work through feelings of

disappointment and discouragement that may impede future progress and lead to premature discontinuance.

4. Practitioners can evaluate the efficacy of their interventions and change strategies. If a given approach fails to yield positive results within a reasonable time, more of the same is unlikely to produce different results. In this regard, we recommend you apply the maxim, "If what you're doing isn't working, try something different."

5. Indications of marked progress toward goal attainment alert practitioners to possible readiness by clients to shift the focus to another goal or to consider planning for termination if all goals have been substantially achieved.

Evaluation of progress should be conducted periodically in accordance with the agreement negotiated in the contracting process. Progress should be monitored every two to three sessions at a minimum. Methods of assessing progress should also be those negotiated in the contract.

Crisis Intervention (CI)

Crisis intervention (CI) is another widely employed general interventive strategy or modality. This modality shares much in common with task-centered casework: (1) is time limited, (2) focuses on problems of living rather than psychopathology, (3) is oriented to the here and now, (4) involves a high level of activity by the practitioner, (5) employs tasks as a primary tactic of change efforts, and (6) is an eclectic framework that can accommodate various practice theories and interventions. Because crisis intervention addresses urgent crisis situations precipitated by stressful events, maturational crises, and acute transitional situations, its potential use is somewhat more limited than that of task-centered casework.

Tenets of Crisis Intervention Theory

Basic to CI theory is the concept that when people are beset by a crisis, a potential exists for them to cope in ways that are either adaptive or maladaptive. According to CI theorists, most crisis situations are limited to a period of four to eight weeks, during which time people manage to achieve a degree of equilibrium, which may be equivalent to, lower than, or higher than the precrisis level of functioning. Life crises can thus be viewed as presenting potential threats that can permanently impair people's level of functioning or as painful challenges that embody opportunities for growth in personal strength and coping capacity. CI theory emphasizes the importance of intervening immediately to assist clients who are overwhelmed by crises. Timely intervention is critical not only to prevent deterioration in functioning but also to reach people when their defenses are low and their receptiveness to therapeutic interventions are greatest, as occurs during acute periods of crises.

Most CI theorists accept Caplan's (1964) definition of a crisis as an upset in a steady state (state of equilibrium) that poses an obstacle, usually important to the fulfillment of important life goals or to vital need satisfaction, and that the individual (or family) cannot overcome through usual methods of problem solving. A crisis thus is stressful and disruptive and can adversely affect biological, psychological, and social functioning and can produce disturbed emotions, impair motor functioning, and negatively impact

ongoing behavior. Crisis situations have a subjective element, for people's perceptions and coping capacities vary widely. What is severely stressful and overwhelming for one person or family may be stressful but manageable for others. Nevertheless, although crisis situations or events (denoted as *hazardous events)* are diverse, most people would agree that natural disasters, death of a loved one, disabling or life-threatening illness or injury, cultural dislocation, rape, out-of-wedlock pregnancy, and other like events usually pose a crisis to those involved.

Hazardous events can be experienced as a threat, challenge, or loss (Rapoport, 1970). A threat (e.g., possibility of losing a job, spouse, home, or valued status) may involve anticipated loss of an individual's sense of integrity or autonomy. A threat thus involves high anxiety and apprehension about a possible future dreaded event. A challenge involves anxiety over the possibility of failure in the immediate future, as for example, not performing adequately on a new job or failing an examination crucial to one's future. Challenge, of course, also involves motivation to succeed and hope of success. Loss, by contrast, involves an acute sense of deprivation resulting from an event that has already occurred, such as a death, divorce, or move from one's homeland. Loss, therefore, produces depressed affect associated with the grieving process.

CI theory posits that people's reactions to crises typically involve going through different stages. Theorists differ as to whether three or four stages are involved, and they also label the stages somewhat differently. The differences are relatively minor, however, and our description involves a synthesis of stages identified by various authors. The first stage involves an initial rise in tension accompanied by shock and perhaps even denial of the crisis-provoking event. To reduce the tension, persons resort to their usual emergency problem-solving skills, and when these fail to alleviate the tension, heightened tension ensues. At this point, the person or family enters the second stage, which is characterized by tension so severe that the person feels confused, overwhelmed, helpless, angry, or perhaps acutely depressed. The length of this phase varies according to the nature of the hazardous event, the strengths and coping capacities of the person, and the degree of responsiveness from social support systems.

As people move from stage 2 to stage 3, they resort to different coping tactics, the outcome of which depends upon whether these tactics are adaptive or maladaptive. If the tactics are maladaptive, tension may continue to escalate and the person may suffer a mental breakdown or, in extreme instances, attempt suicide. If the efforts are adaptive, the person regains equilibrium and perhaps achieves a higher level of functioning.

According to CI theory, crisis periods are time limited and people achieve a degree of equilibrium for better or for worse during this time. Consequently, immediate intervention aimed at restoring clients to their precrisis level of functioning or better is crucial. Departures from the traditional weekly 50-minute sessions are common, and some clients may even be seen daily during acute periods of crisis.

Time limits (generally six to eight weeks) are employed in CI, although some clients require even shorter periods of time. Practitioners assume an active role and deliberately employ their authority and expertise to inspire the hope and confidence so badly needed by clients. The temporal focus of CI is on the here and now, and goals are limited to alleviating distress and enabling clients to re-

gain equilibrium. No attempt is made to deal either with precrisis personality dysfunction or intrapsychic conflict, although even minor changes effected through CI may provide the impetus for enhanced personal and interpersonal functioning as well as improved transactions with social support systems.

The heart of CI involves delineating tasks that clients must perform to achieve a new state of equilibrium. Although practitioners are active and directive in defining tasks, clients should be encouraged to participate to the extent of their capability, for their active participation fosters autonomy. Obviously, clients' abilities to participate actively are limited during periods of severe emotional distress but increase as the distress subsides.

After completion of the essential tasks, CI moves into the final major activity, which consists of *anticipatory guidance.* This activity, which has preventive implications, involves assisting clients to anticipate future crisis situations and to plan coping strategies that prepare them to face future stresses without becoming immobilized.

Having reviewed the essential concepts of CI, we now turn to procedures for implementing the modality.

The Initial Phase of Crisis Intervention

During the initial phase of CI, the practitioner's objectives are (1) to relieve the client's emotional distress, (2) to complete an assessment, and (3) to plan the strategy of intervention, focusing on relevant tasks the client must perform. The following sections briefly focus on each of these processes.

Relieving Emotional Distress Drawing out clients' emotions and responding empathically to them often assist clients to unburden themselves of painful and sometimes overwhelming emotions. Practitioners can also provide needed emotional support as they encourage clients to ventilate pent-up emotions by reassuring them that their emotions are a natural reaction to an extremely distressing situation.

When clients in an acute crisis are immobilized by tension and anxiety, deep breathing and progressive muscle relaxation procedures (see Chapter 18) can be helpful in alleviating tension and in assisting clients to gain composure (Lechnyr, 1980a). Practitioners should also consider the need for antianxiety or antidepressant medications in extreme instances, which necessitates referral to a physician.

Use of social support systems may also reduce emotional distress for some clients. Friends and loved ones may provide comfort and compassion that clients sorely need to buffer the devastating impact of certain crises. Clients' church affiliations can also be a source of great emotional support. Local church leaders can often provide solace and guidance and rally the support of church members. Moreover, support groups for diverse crises are available in many communities. Practitioners may need to develop such resources in others.

Assessment Because of the short time involved in CI, practitioners concurrently assess and alleviate clients' emotional distress. Objectives of the assessment involve determining the nature of the crisis situation, its significance to and impact on the client(s), factors or events that precipitated the crisis, adaptive capacities of the client, and resources that can be tapped to alleviate the crisis situation. These factors are crucial to formulating tasks that must subsequently be accomplished.

The nature of a crisis, of course, provides valuable clues as to the sources of clients' distress. Losses, for example, leave people bereft of vital sources of emotional supplies and typically produce grieving reactions. The meanings people attach to losses of close kin vary considerably, however, leading to differing emotional reactions. A client who has been extremely dependent on a spouse may react to the spouse's death not only with grief but also with feelings of helplessness and hopelessness concerning ability to manage independently. A client whose relationship to a deceased spouse or parent was ambivalent and conflictual may react to the death with feelings of guilt, hostility, or even relief.

Practitioners, therefore, must determine the unique meaning of crisis situations to each client. Determining the meaning and significance of precipitating events can be highly therapeutic to clients. Through exploring precipitating events and other factors that bear on clients' reactions, practitioners enable clients to view their situation in a new perspective, which can foster hope. Many clients, in fact, improve dramatically as they gain expanded understanding of the complex forces involved in their crisis situations and their reactions to them.

Assessing clients' capacities for adaptive coping involves not only determining their current level of functioning but also their precrisis level. Obviously, to restore clients to their previous level of functioning, one must first ascertain that level. Knowledge of adaptive capacity is also essential to formulating relevant tasks and selecting appropriate interventive techniques. Practitioners, therefore, must rapidly assess individuals' and families' precrisis functioning.

Cultural factors are also vital in assessing clients' reactions to crisis situations. Situations deemed as crises vary widely from one culture to another, as do the reactions to them. Divorce or unwed pregnancy, for example, require considerable adaptation in most cultures but may pose an extreme crisis to first generation Asian-Americans because of the social ostracism, loss of face, and shame involved for persons in Asian cultures. The extremity of the stress involved in such situations has led to suicide in some instances.

It is important to note, as Lukton (1982) and others have stressed, that use of CI need not be limited to people who ordinarily are psychologically intact. Target groups for CI have been extended to include marginally functioning people with chronic problems. Moreover, even acutely psychotic people can be helped. A psychotic break, in fact, may be viewed as a way of responding to a crisis state and as an opportunity for developing more effective coping mechanisms and interpersonal skills (Lukton, 1982, p. 277). (With clients whose precrisis level of functioning was marginal, referrals to other resources for additional help following the crisis period may be indicated.) Crisis teams have also been employed in the public sector (e.g., in hospital emergency rooms, youth service centers, and mental health centers) to provide immediate assistance aimed at stabilizing people and their families and preventing relapses of psychiatric patients.

Another aspect of assessment in CI is to determine clients' social support systems, for "interventions that enhance the natural helping network can be enormously helpful in crisis intervention" (Lukton, 1982, p. 280). Practitioners can enhance natural helping networks by mobilizing family, friends, neighbors, the clergy, or cultural reference groups. Another valuable resource is self-help groups, which consist of people with similar problems. Members of self-help groups provide mutual support and assistance to each other in solving problems.

Contracting and Planning   Contracting in CI involves basically the same elements as those described in Chapter 13. The overall goal, to restore equilibrium, is applicable to all cases, but subgoals and tasks vary according to the nature of the crisis situation and the unique characteristics of each person and/or family. Similar crisis situations, of course, involve similar tasks that must be accomplished, and the literature contains many articles that identify tasks relevant to specific crisis situations such as rape (Holmes, 1981), out-of-wedlock pregnancy (Chesler and Davis, 1980), and cultural dislocation (Golan and Gruschka, 1971). Lukton (1982) has cautioned, however, that in addressing the same types of crisis situations, different writers often identify different tasks. Moreover, the sequence of accomplishing tasks may vary from client to client. Practitioners, therefore, can benefit from available knowledge in determining and negotiating essential tasks but must consider the individuality of each client situation.

In negotiating time limits, it is important to involve clients (thereby increasing their autonomy) by soliciting their views as to how long they believe they will need to "get back on an even keel." Many will suggest just a few weeks, which is the time ordinarily required. Some clients will suggest only two to three weeks and will, in fact, require no more. When clients are reluctant to commit themselves, practitioners can suggest that from four to eight weeks are usually sufficient and ask the client to select a limit, recognizing that fewer sessions may prove ample.

Problems of Transition   An exception to the use of the usual time limits involves clients in certain states of transition, such as adapting to the death of a spouse or child, single-parent status following divorce, retirement, and a new country and culture. Golan (1980, 1981), Lukton

(1982), and others argue persuasively that traditional CI is not appropriate for such transition states that require "identity transformation and role change that continues long after the acute phase of disorganization is overcome" (Golan, 1981, p. 264). With respect to loss of a child, research cited by Videka-Sherman (1987) indicates that "... grief after a child dies lasts a very long time and may actually intensify over the first 1–2 years following the child's death. Social workers must be very careful not to impose unrealistic expectations that acute grief will end in 6 months or even in 1 or 2 years" (p. 109). Weiss and Parkes (1983) report similar findings regarding the time required for spouses to adapt following the death of a mate. In such instances, principles of CI are relevant to the acute phase of disorganization, but extended service is required for clients to adapt to new roles and to develop new sources of emotional supplies. The phases of crisis resolution thus are far longer for this group than earlier believed.

Task Implementation

In facilitating clients' accomplishments of tasks deemed essential to mastery of crisis situations, practitioners should observe the guidelines to task implementation delineated earlier in this chapter. Practitioners assume an active and directive role and give advice to a greater extent than when using other approaches. Still, it is important to foster client autonomy by involving clients in planning for task implementation and by encouraging and reinforcing independent actions whenever feasible.

Space limitations preclude our giving examples of tasks appropriate for specific types of crisis situations. Numerous examples are provided, however, in books and articles that discuss particular types of crisis situations.

Anticipatory Guidance

During the concluding phase of CI (after the crisis has subsided), practitioners engage in anticipatory guidance, an activity of major preventive significance. This activity is a strong feature of CI, and we urge practitioners to include it in the terminal phase of any practice model. Anticipatory guidance involves assisting clients to anticipate future crises that might develop and to plan effective coping strategies (based on knowledge gained during the preceding period of problem solving) they can employ to avoid being overwhelmed in the future. Relevant strategies might include analyzing sources of distress, recalling and accrediting successful efforts in coping with past crisis situations, anticipating needs, identifying and utilizing support systems and other potential resources, and formulating and implementing essential tasks. It is important, however, not to convey an expectation that clients should be able to manage all problem situations independently in the future. Indeed, during the process of termination, practitioners should express continuing interest, reassure clients that the door is open should they need future help, and explain that the practitioner will be contacting them soon to check on their continued progress.

Of necessity, the preceding discussion of CI has been brief. For more extensive expositions of CI, we recommend books by Aguilera and Messick (1982), Golan (1978), and Puryear (1979). For a critique of CI, we recommend Lukton's (1982) article.

15 | Enhancing Clients' Problem Solving, Social Skills, and Assertiveness

Humans constantly encounter situations, events, and problems that require coping responses. Effective coping with the diverse demands of daily living requires skills in making decisions, communicating, solving problems, resolving conflicts, and a host of other skills, collectively referred to as social competence. Increasing evidence from research studies suggests that possession of social competence is essential to sound mental health and behavioral adjustment. Ineffective coping in problematic situations, in fact, can lead to emotional and behavioral disorders that severely impact social functioning and may require professional treatment.

Clients seek professional help when their coping efforts have failed to remedy problematic situations. Varying widely in their coping capacities, some clients possess meager skills and others have rich coping repertoires that have been temporarily overwhelmed by virtually insuperable stresses. It is the former group, however, that most frequently comes to the attention of social workers.

Over the past 15–20 years human service practitioners and researchers have increasingly devoted attention to ways of increasing clients' coping capacities by assessing and remedying deficiencies in social competence. Skills training programs have been developed for many skills. However, three areas of skills training that have broad application have received the most attention in the literature. These skills, to which this chapter is devoted, are problem solving, interpersonal skills, and assertiveness. Chapter 17 is also devoted to interactional skills and Chapter 18 deals with vital coping skills associated with the biophysical and cognitive systems.

Problem-Solving Skills

Teaching clients problem-solving skills can equip them to cope more effectively with the myriad difficulties they will encounter in the future. A major advantage of learning problem solving is that the principles can be readily transferred from one situation to another.

At this point, some clarification is in order. We have previously made repeated reference to the problem-solving process, and you may well be confused as to why clients need additional assistance in learning to apply problem-solving strategies. After all, clients and practitioners engage in problem solving, so isn't it logical to assume they learn the process? The answer is that most clients probably do learn something about the problem-solving process, but what they usually learn is likely to be incomplete, uneven, and poorly conceptualized. In fact, although practitioners engage in problem-solving efforts with clients, many have difficulty delineating precisely the elements of independent problem solving. This does not mean practitioners are not effective in assisting clients to solve problems. Rather, our point is that utilizing problem solving to assist clients in coping with discrete problems and teaching them the principles in preparation for coping independently with future problems are different processes, though they share much in common. We propose that practitioners engage in both processes, thereby seeking not only to remedy immediate problems but also to enhance clients' future coping capacities.

Our proposal is not new. About 19 years ago, behaviorally oriented psychologists (D'Zurilla & Goldfried, 1971) advocated that practitioners assist clients to enhance their problem-solving skills. These authors maintained that much of what was viewed as abnormal or disturbed behavior could be viewed as resulting from ineffective behavior that fails to solve life's challenging problems and leads to undesired effects such as anxiety and depression. Support for their view came from the research of Spivack, Platt, and Shure (1976), who reported two major findings. First, deviant or abnormal people manifested inferior skills in problem solving compared to "normal" people. The former group (1) generated fewer possible solutions to hypothetical problem situations than the latter, (2) suggested solutions that often were antisocial, and (3) had very inaccurate expectations about probable consequences of alternate solutions. Other researchers

similarly found deficiencies in problem-solving skills among conflicted marriages as compared to nonconflicted marriages (Vincent, Weiss, & Birchler, 1976). Subsequent studies have extended the findings to conduct-disordered adolescents (Tisdelle & St. Lawrence, 1988), antisocial children (Kazdin, et al., 1987), depressed children (Weisz, et al., 1987), Vietnam veterans with posttraumatic stress disorder (Nezu & Carnevale, 1987), suicidal psychiatric patients (Schotte & Clum, 1987), alcoholics (Jacob, et al., 1981), and schizophrenics (Kelly & Lamparski, 1985).

The second major finding of Spivack, et al. (1976), was that promising results were obtained in several projects in which "deviant" subjects received systematic training in problem solving. Of particular relevance have been similar results indicating that instruction in and practice of problem-solving skills assist antisocial children (Kazdin, et al., 1987), nondelinquent early adolescents (LeCroy & Rose, 1986), predelinquent youth (Kifer, et al., 1974) and delinquent adolescents (Tisdelle & St. Lawrence, 1988) to deal with conflictual situations more effectively. Other findings indicate that training in problem solving also assists families to function more harmoniously (Blechman, 1974; Blechman, et al., 1976).

Still another study (Nezu, 1985) found that self-appraised effective problem solvers reported less depression, less anxiety, a greater sense of internal control, fewer problems, and less distress than those who appraised themselves as ineffective problem solvers. Research findings thus strongly document the importance of skills in problem solving.

By mastering a systematic approach to making decisions and solving problems, clients gain the following benefits:

405

1. Learn a process that promotes collaboration, cohesiveness, and mutual respect among family or group members.

2. Prevent interpersonal conflicts produced by dysfunctional modes of reaching decisions or solving problems.

3. Reduce tension, anxiety, and depression by solving stress-producing problems effectively.

4. Generate a wider range of options for coping, thereby enhancing chances of selecting maximally effective decisions or solutions.

5. Enhance the likelihood that family and group members will commit themselves to implementing options that are selected.

6. Increase confidence, self-efficacy, and self-esteem by acquiring a mode of problem solving that can be employed in future problematic situations.

7. Prevent children from developing dysfunctional coping patterns by including them in effective problem-solving efforts and by teaching and guiding them in employing such efforts.

Embedded in the preceding benefits and central to the rationale for independent problem solving is the preventive function of this intervention. Clients gradually achieve mastery of skills that they can transfer to the real world. Their dependence on practitioners gradually decreases, and their self-reliance increases.

Before delineating problem-solving strategies and methods of assisting clients to learn them, we wish to clarify that theory related to making decisions and solving problems is not limited to the helping professions. Because of the importance of decision making in business management, governmental policy formulation, public administration, and other phases of life, numerous articles and entire books have been devoted to this topic.

Irrespective of their fields, all authors agree that effective problem solving involves a systematic approach consisting of several discrete phases. Although their definitions of these phases vary somewhat, all authors' views of the basic elements involved in problem solving are similar. The strategy we delineate is a synthesis of our own ideas with those of several authors, most notable of whom are Janis and Mann (1977), Gordon (1970), and Jacobson and Margolin (1979). We have adapted this strategy particularly for interpersonal situations typically encountered in families and groups.

Preparing Clients to Learn Problem-Solving Skills

Before delineating the steps involved in problem solving, we first discuss conditions prerequisite to introducing this intervention. Preparing clients is critical, for unless they are receptive (1) to learning the process and (2) to engaging in collaborative efforts with the practitioner and with each other, employing this intervention is likely to be futile. Early in the helping process, clients often meet neither of these conditions, and practitioners therefore face the challenges of enlisting their willingness to engage in the process and of fostering a collaborative set (Jacobson & Margolin, 1979, pp. 134–141).

Several strategies can be employed to influence clients to adopt a collaborative set, including the following:

1. Lay groundwork during the initial contracting process.

2. Demonstrate the need to learn problem solving by focusing on the destructive impact of dysfunctional interaction.

3. Intervene to increase positive and collaborative interactions.

4. Accredit collaborative efforts and highlight the connections between these efforts and positive outcomes.

5. Define problems as belonging to a system rather than to any one person.

In the following sections, we consider the preceding strategies in greater detail.

Lay Groundwork during the Initial Contracting Process

We consider the learning of problem-solving skills a vital component of most contracts established by the practitioner with couples, families, or groups. As you may recall, in Chapter 11 we encouraged practitioners to develop a contract with new groups to the effect that all members will be "counted in" in decision making and also stressed the need for practitioners to teach decision-making steps to groups in initial sessions. In Chapter 10 we also emphasized that many families have both dysfunctional interactional patterns and ineffective styles of decision making that discount the needs of some or *all* members—which perpetuates resentment, unrest, and conflict. Thus, opportunities to negotiate the goal of learning to apply effective problem-solving methods often occur when clients are seen in conjoint sessions. For example, we have worked with many couples and families with presenting problems similar to the following:

- "Our ideas about childrearing are totally different, which creates constant friction between us and confuses our children."

- "We bicker constantly in our family about who should do the dishes, vacuum the rugs, and cut the grass. We just can't seem to work together on anything."

Common to each of the preceding presenting complaints is failure of the participants to work collaboratively in solving problems related to carrying out vital functions within a family. By reflecting these complaints in terms of wants, you focus on the necessity for collaborative problem solving and thus pave the way to negotiating a goal of learning mutual problem solving, as illustrated in the following responses to the above presenting problems:

- "You seem to be saying you're working at cross purposes in rearing your children, which causes divisiveness between you and is hard on your children. I gather you're feeling a need to resolve your differences and *to learn to work together as partners.*"

- [*To family member*]: "Sounds like the constant bickering creates a strain and leads nowhere. I'm sensing that learning ways of *working together as a family* in planning to get things done could improve things in your family."

Clients generally respond affirmatively to such messages, indicating some degree of receptivity to learning collaborative problem solving. The practitioner can then suggest that later in the session they may want to consider a goal of learning a problem-solving process that has proven effective in resolving difficulties similar to their own. Subsequently, during the contracting process, clients themselves may select as goals learning to make decisions or to cope with marital or family difficulties without excessive conflict. If clients do not identify such goals, you may make reference to the difficulties they described earlier and again suggest that seeking to develop effective problem-solving strategies may be an effective way of remedying identified problems and of averting similar problems in the future.

Demonstrate the Need to Learn the Problem-Solving Process

This strategy can be employed in tandem with the preceding strategy or can be introduced later at an expedient time. Implementing the strategy in the former instance involves providing an expanded explanation of the benefits of learning to collaborate in problem solving. In the latter instance, after observing clients engage in competitive, unproductive interaction that produces strain and bad feelings, the practitioner capitalizes on their obvious frustration by emphasizing the destructive impact of the interaction, drawing attention to how each participant contributes to the dysfunctional behavior, and presenting a case for learning effective problem-solving strategies. Executed well, such a timely intervention often motivates clients to welcome modifying their contract to include a goal of learning problem-solving strategies. The following illustrates application of this intervention strategy in the third interview with Rose and Gary Wilson, a couple who sought help with difficulties involving intense conflicts in many aspects of their marriage. The practitioner intervenes following a heated interchange between the partners involving Rose's criticism of Gary's handling of their eight-year-old son, Danny

PRACTITIONER: You're both pretty angry with each other right now, and if you continue along the same lines, you're likely to get even angrier. Let's stop a moment and consider what's happening between you.

GARY: You're damn right I'm mad. She always thinks she has the answers. It's like my opinion couldn't possibly be worth anything.

ROSE: That's not true, and you know it. It's just that you expect too much of Danny.

GARY: [*Shakes head in disgust.*] What's the use? I can't get through to her.

PRACTITIONER: Wait a minute! I know that you both have some strong feelings right now and it is hard to disengage, but it is very important that we look at what's going wrong. Are you willing to do that now? [*They agree.*] Both of you have your ideas about what you need to do with Danny—right? [*Each nods.*] What's happening is that each of you believes you're right and you're trying to convince the other. Then each of you gets uptight because the other doesn't listen and puts your ideas down. So you end up arguing. Am I right? [*They concede this happens.*] You get into a battle of "Who's right," and both of you only lose when you get caught up in that. You get mad at each other, and your communication breaks down just as it did a few moments ago.

ROSE: Well, I think you've described it pretty well. But what do we do about it?

PRACTITIONER: [*Smiling.*] I thought you'd never ask. All kidding aside, what I'd like to suggest is that the two of you consider working toward a goal of learning a method of solving problems that avoids getting into hassles. It involves working together, seeking to understand each other's views, and searching together for solutions that are acceptable to both of you, rather than struggling over who's right. The advantage of learning this method is that you learn to work *with* rather than against each other.

GARY: That'd be different for a change.

PRACTITIONER: Then I take it it has some appeal to you. [*Both nod in agreement.*] Do you feel it might be a goal you'd like to tackle, then?

ROSE: I'm game. I think it might really help us. What we're doing now isn't working —that's for sure. How about you, Gary?

GARY: Let's do it.

Obtaining a commitment to work collaboratively is an important step in achieving a climate conducive to the change process, but it would be naive to assume that commitment alone is sufficient. Persistent effort is required to break established patterns of interaction. The same applies to formed groups, for members bring with them patterns of communication they habitually employ in other contexts. Furthermore, people can employ only those skills they already possess. Therefore, for some clients, learning to solve problems collaboratively may entail learning a new set of skills. Consequently, the next two strategies are essential in assisting contentious members of systems to achieve a collaborative set.

Intervening to Produce Collaborative Interactions

Tactics involved in this strategy are twofold. First, the practitioner actively intervenes to arrest negative, competitive, and other destructive patterns of interaction. Interrupting such dysfunctional interaction, the practitioner translates or redefines negative, blaming messages into expressions of needs or wants or requests for change. The second tactic involves inducing collaborative interaction by teaching clients to express their needs, to listen attentively, to personalize their feelings, and to give positive feedback. The potency of collaborative interaction derives from the fact that enabling clients to engage in such interactions assists them to *learn* new modes of behavior and to *experience* the benefits of them. Experiencing the benefits of collaborating enables clients to gain a measure of success and satisfaction from this different mode of relating, which in turn encourages additional efforts to collaborate with other members of the system and with the practitioner. Implementation of the preceding techniques is illustrated in the following excerpt involving parents and an adolescent daughter:

DAUGHTER: [*To parents.*] You're on my back all the time. Why don't you get off my case for a change? [*Attacking, blaming message.*]

FATHER: We wouldn't be on your case if you'd get in at night when you're supposed to. [*Counterattacking message.*]

DAUGHTER: Well, if you'd quit bugging me, maybe I'd feel more like getting in. Besides, you expect me to be home before any of the other kids, and it isn't fair. [*More of same.*]

MOTHER: I don't think 11 o'clock is unreasonable. [*Defensive response.*]

PRACTITIONER: I'd like to stop and see if we can understand better just what's troubling everyone here. Each of you has some needs that aren't being met, and let's begin by seeing if we can identify what those needs are. I'd like each of you just to listen and try to understand the other person's needs. You may not agree with each other, but I would like to ask you to hold your disagreement for a while. Just try to understand. Let's begin with you, Betty. From what you were saying, I sensed you're wanting more room to move around. You'd like more freedom, am I right?

Notice the destructive interaction among the family members characterized by verbal attacks, blaming messages, defensiveness, and counterattacks. The practitioner intervenes and begins to translate the blaming messages into needs. The practitioner further requests the participants to listen to and to attempt to understand each other's needs. We now pick up the interaction where we left off.

DAUGHTER: Yeah! That's right. I get tired of being nagged all the time.

PRACTITIONER: OK. But let's stay with what you want. Would you tell your parents specifically what positive changes you'd like? Tell them what you'd like them *to do,* not what you feel they're doing wrong. OK? [*Maintaining focus on her want; suggesting she request positive change.*]

DAUGHTER: I'll try. Well, I'd like you to give me more freedom. I feel you're trying to control me, and I'm able to run my own life. You act like you don't trust me.

PRACTITIONER: [*To parents.*] So she's telling you she wants more freedom and wants to be treated as an adult. Was that the message you got? [*Still focusing on her wants; checking out meaning attribution with parents.*]

FATHER: Yeah, but—

PRACTITIONER: I would appreciate it if we could save the "but" for later. Right now I think it's important to work on understanding your needs. [*To parents.*] Let's turn to your needs now. What positive changes would each of you like to see happen?

In this last response, the practitioner assertively intervened to avert sidetracking that would likely follow father's "but." The practitioner maintains focus on the participants' needs, shifting to the parents' needs. Now return to the interaction.

MOTHER: I'd like Betty to get in earlier. I worry when she stays out late.

PRACTITIONER: That tells me you have some fears. Can you tell Betty what those fears are?

MOTHER: Betty, I know you're basically a good kid. But I do worry. Even the best of kids can get into trouble when they spend too much time together late at night.

PRACTITIONER: [*To Betty.*] Betty, I hope you're hearing what your mother is telling you.

She's expressing a concern for you—not distrust or wanting to control you. [*To mother.*] Why all the concern? Please tell Betty. I'll tell you in a minute why I ask.

In the last response, notice how the practitioner facilitates understanding and positive interaction by clarifying that mother's fears emanate from positive concern, not from distrust or a desire to control Betty. In the last question, the practitioner seeks to elicit further positive feelings, as reflected in the continuation of the interaction.

MOTHER: Well, Betty, it's because we—well—you're our only daughter. We love you. We don't want anything bad to happen.

PRACTITIONER: I'll tell you now why I asked. I sensed you were concerned because Betty's so important to you. But I'm not sure that message had gotten through to Betty. [*To Betty.*] What you've thought is that your parents have wanted to control you. Do you hear that underneath all of their negative messages is love and concern for you? [*Clarifying further the parents' positive concerns and facilitating positive feedback.*]

DAUGHTER: I do right now. But that isn't what I've been hearing lately. No way!

PRACTITIONER: But you hear it now. How does that make you feel right now? Can you tell your parents? [*Maintaining focus on positive feedback.*]

DAUGHTER: Good. Real good. Like maybe they're not so bad after all.

PRACTITIONER: Well, maybe you're beginning to understand each other a little better. [*To father.*] We didn't hear from you, dad. Could you let us know your needs or wants? [*Drawing father into discussion of needs and wants.*]

FATHER: My wife expressed them pretty well. Not much I could add.

PRACTITIONER: Nevertheless, I'd like Betty to hear it from you. Could you tell Betty your feelings?

Notice in the preceding excerpts that the practitioner identified the needs of each participant, an important step in problem solving discussed at length later in the chapter. Further, the practitioner actively intervened each time the participants began to revert to negative messages. By being attuned to the concerns and underlying love inherent in the mother's statement, the practitioner rechanneled the interaction in positive directions. The practitioner thus elicited feelings of caring, and what began as typical dysfunctional interaction was converted into an embryonic form of collaborative communication. This strategy incidentally provides participants with an initial "success" experience in communicating in a positive manner about problems, which has the usual effect of engendering a spark of hope among family members that, indeed, they may be able to work out their conflicted relationships with each other. The practitioner would need to continue to maintain control of the session by intervening actively, thereby gradually creating a climate conducive to subsequent collaborative problem solving. We cannot emphasize too strongly your responsibility as a practitioner in converting negative interaction to positive interaction. Except for making an initial assessment, no constructive purpose is served by passively permitting clients to engage in destructive patterns of communication, whether the target system be a couple, family, or group.

Accredit Collaborative Efforts

This strategy is employed to reinforce spontaneous collaborative behavior on the part of clients and to enhance their awareness of consequent beneficial effects by highlighting connections between positive behavioral changes and its beneficial effects. Although collaborative behavior tends to be self-reinforcing because it produces positive results, expressing recognition and approval of collaborative efforts further reinforces such behavior. Moreover, assisting clients to discern the association between their collaborative behavior and its favorable results further enables them to make choices to interact collaboratively, as illustrated in the following:

PRACTITIONER: [*To group.*] I'd like to point out something that just happened that pleased me a great deal. You'll recall in our first session you agreed as members to assist one another to understand each other's problems better and to work cooperatively in searching for solutions. I know we struggled in our last session with interruptions and with members trying to talk at the same time. Well, what pleases me is that during these past minutes as Julie shared her problems we really began to work as a group. Everyone listened, no one interrupted, and several of you supported Julie in her struggle to express herself. As a result, Julie appeared to open up and shared more with us. I was really impressed with how you pitched in as a group. Julie, I'd like to hear how it felt to you.

JULIE: Well, it was hard at first, but like you said, it got easier. I really felt everyone was behind me. It felt great.

Define Problems As Belonging to the System

When a client reveals a problem, significant others tend to see the problem as residing solely with that person and to disclaim any part in it. From the standpoint of systems theory, however, problems of one member are problems of the system, and other members share responsibility for working out solutions. Moreover, solutions are far more likely to be efficacious if contributions of all members to the problem are considered and if all participate in planning corrective measures. In formed groups, the situation is somewhat different, for members have not contributed to the preexisting problems of others. In becoming part of the new system, however, each makes a commitment to assist other members, and each member shares responsibility for contributing to the effective functioning of the group. Further, as groups evolve, all participants contribute in some manner to dysfunctional group processes.

The following are typical examples of how participants mutually contribute to problematic situations:

1. Mrs. Adams complains her husband spends little time with her. He agrees but explains he spends increasing time away from home because she nags and badgers him constantly.

2. Mr. Sharp expresses a desire for his wife to make sexual overtures. She explains she has desires to do so but when she has made overtures in the past he has rebuffed her. To avoid the resultant hurt, she decided not to take the risk.

3. Parents of 15-year-old Alan complain he seldom talks to them about his daily activities. He agrees but explains when he has shared in the past his parents criticize him or give him lectures.

It is apparent in the preceding examples that all of the participants play a part in the problems. Your task is to assist all parties to own up to their respective parts and to agree to make behavioral changes accordingly. This is no small task, for

people tend to be more aware of and to focus more on the distressing behaviors of others than on their own; hence, their tendency is to define solutions in terms of changes *others* need to make. However, by intervening and guiding clients to interact collaboratively, you assist them not only to reveal their respective perceptions of problematic situations but also to listen attentively to other's views. You can further enhance their receptivity to owning their respective parts by explaining that successful change results from each person working to change his/her own behavior, not from trying to change others.

Perhaps the most effective strategy of assisting people to define problems as mutually owned is to appeal to their self-interest. If they can see a payoff for themselves, they will be inclined to participate in seeking a solution. For example, if a husband is helped to consider how his wife's depression or unhappiness impacts negatively on him, dampening his interaction with her and reducing his own satisfaction and happiness, he is likely to be receptive in helping her to overcome her depression. Through this involvement, he may also be helped to see how he has contributed to her depression. Similarly, if you assist family members to recognize that improved functioning of one person enhances relationships and solidarity within the system, they will be more likely to accept responsibility for participating actively in problem solving.

By defining problems as mutually owned and clarifying the part each participant plays in maintaining them, you enhance the likelihood that participants will be willing to initiate positive behavioral changes. Manifest willingness on the part of one person tends to foster reciprocal willingness by others. None loses face because none is defined as the sole cause of the problems. Moreover, impasses tend to dissolve as each person becomes aware that others care enough to acknowledge their parts and to commit themselves to making changes. Vicious cycles begin to be supplanted by collaboration, compromise, and mutual reinforcement for these same behaviors.

Introducing the Problem-Solving Process

After clients have begun to engage in collaborative interactions, have demonstrated beginning awareness of behaviors entailed in such interactions, and have contracted to learn the problem-solving process, it is appropriate to introduce them to the process and then to guide them in applying it to some of their problems. Before defining the formal process, however, it is vital to explain conditions prerequisite to using it effectively. Carefully explaining these conditions and the rationale behind them further enhances receptivity and prepares clients to implement the process successfully.

Introducing clients to the process begins by clarifying its nature with an explanation similar to the following:

"Let's begin by clarifying what the problem-solving process is all about. Basically, it's an approach that will enable you to collaborate in solving problems or in reaching decisions effectively. It involves a number of steps that will assist you to define problems accurately and to generate several possible solutions so that you can select the best possible one. The best option is the one that meets your needs best, so another step involves

helping you to identify and understand each other's needs. There are also guidelines that will assist you to work together and to avoid needless and unproductive hassles."

It is also critical to clarify that the process is *effective* and that clients can succeed in applying it but only if they commit themselves to following the steps and guidelines. However strong their good intentions, they will tend to revert to habitual patterns of interaction, and if they permit this to happen, they will likely end up arguing, blaming, or playing "who wins." For this reason, it is vital to differentiate problem solving from other interactions. Clients must understand that when they agree to engage in problem solving they commit themselves to follow the structured pattern of interaction. In sessions, the practitioner will guide them in adhering to these steps and guidelines. Outside the sessions, they must exercise strict discipline to avoid falling into habitual patterns of interaction.

Emphasizing the effectiveness of problem solving is critical for two reasons. First, the success of any intervention is partially a function of clients' confidence in its efficacy. Conveying belief in the efficacy of an intervention tends to engender confidence and to enhance the likelihood of clients exerting their best efforts in carrying out their part. The second reason is that stressing the efficacy of an intervention places primary responsibility for the outcome on clients. This is appropriate, of course, only when an intervention is known to be efficacious and when the practitioner is expert in implementing it. Given these conditions, placing primary responsibility on clients for the outcome counters the tendency of some clients to absolve themselves from responsibility of claiming an intervention doesn't work, when they have made only a halfhearted effort.

Managing Interaction during Problem Solving

Before teaching the actual steps of the problem-solving process, it is important to be prepared to manage clients' interaction and to guide them so that they adhere to the steps and thereby achieve successful results. Toward this end, the practitioner should assist clients to observe the following guidelines:

1. Be specific in relating problems.

2. Focus on the present problem rather than on past difficulties.

3. Focus on only one problem at a time.

4. Listen attentively to others who are sharing problems.

5. Share problems in a positive and constructive manner.

In the following sections, we delineate each of these guidelines.

Guideline 1. Be Specific in Relating Problems

To define a problem accurately, it is essential to express it so that others can determine the specific nature of one's concerns or needs. Further, specifying problems with precision avoids the confusion and misunderstanding that may result from expressing them in vague and general terms. You can utilize the skill of seeking concreteness to elicit specific details of clients' problems. Keep in mind that when clients express problems glo-

bally, you will need to press for details and clarify the importance of pinpointing difficulties.

Guideline 2. Focus on the Present Problem Rather Than Past Difficulties

As you help clients to define problems, it is important to maintain focus on the present. Needless and fruitless arguments over circumstances and details tend to ensue when clients dredge up numerous examples of problematic behavior from the past. Details of recent difficulties do help in pinpointing problematic behavior at times, but more than a few examples amount to overkill. We therefore recommend that you develop a contract with clients specifying the need to focus on present problems and that you intervene to refocus the process when clients begin to employ lengthy recitations of past events as verbal ammunition against others.

Guideline 3. Focus on Only One Problem at a Time

Clients often have a tendency to bring up a problem and then rapidly shift to another, which diffuses their effort and impairs the helping process. Shifts in focus (known as sidetracking) may result from deliberate diversionary tactics or occur because some people have difficulty staying on one topic for any length of time.

When clients sidetrack, it is important to intervene and bring them back to the original problem. It is also important to assist them to discern sidetracking by labeling it and clarifying how it blocks problem-solving efforts. You can further assist clients to cope independently by intervening when sidetracking occurs, asking them to identify what they are doing. They will usually correctly identify their shift in focus. An effective method of assisting clients to reduce sidetracking is to negotiate tasks with them to monitor their interaction between sessions, attempting to avoid sidetracking, gently drawing attention of others to the fact they are sidetracking, and refocusing on the original topic.

Guideline 4. Listen Attentively to Others Who Are Sharing Problems

Implementing this guideline means that others must suspend judgment about the validity of a person's concerns and feelings and hold in check the natural tendency to express contrary views or to advise the person as to what she or he should do to resolve the problem. To ascertain that one fully understands what the other person is saying, it is important to check out perceptions by giving feedback. Summarizing what one has heard is an effective means of providing feedback that enables the person who has shared the problem to determine if others have accurately understood the intended message.

This guideline is critical, for how others respond to the sharing of a problem determines whether a positive and collaborative climate will evolve or whether defensiveness will ensue. Although providing feedback may seem artificial and mechanical, it is a powerful way of enhancing collaborative communication.

You can facilitate clients' implementation of this guideline by instructing those who are to be recipients of a problem-sharing message to listen carefully and attempt to understand the sender's message and feelings. Ask clients to attempt to shut off their own thoughts and to put themselves in the shoes of other persons so that they can be fully attuned to those

such persons. After they have received the message, ask them to check out with the sender what they have heard; be prepared to intervene should the recipient of the message respond negatively. Coach them in using feedback until both sender and receiver agree upon the intended meaning of the message.

Guideline 5. Share Problems in a Positive and Constructive Manner

The way in which a person presents a problem sets a tone that tends to elicit either concern and collaboration or defensiveness and resistance from other participants. In presenting a problem or concern that involves the behavior of another participant, it is important to express the concern without blaming or attacking the other person. Expressing problems in the form of accusations, such as "You're insensitive to my feelings," "You never notice how hard I work," or "You've been staying out too late," tends to engender defensiveness or countercriticism, undermining the process almost before it starts. It is thus important that the person presenting the problem begin by expressing positive intent and by owning personal feelings rather than focusing on what another person is doing wrong. An effective way of introducing concerns is to send a positive, caring message before bringing up a concern. For example, contrast the following two messages and consider the likely impact upon a recipient:

[*To husband*]: "Jim, you're a good provider and a hard worker. I want you to know I appreciate that. But lately I've been alone an awful lot, and I've been feeling depressed. I need more time with you."

"Jim, you're a workaholic, and I'm getting fed up with it. You think more of your work than you do of me. You leave me alone so much I'm getting stir crazy."

Clients usually require help in expressing problems without blaming or attacking. When they express their problem or concerns in a negative manner, it is important to intervene immediately to avert destructive interaction. Explaining how blaming messages cause others to bristle or asking recipients of blaming messages to express their reactions assists clients to differentiate between positive messages that involve ownership of feelings and negative, accusatory messages. After making this clarification, coach the client in couching the concern or problem in a positive manner. During the course of subsequent interactions, you will likely need to intervene many times, for the pull of habituated patterns of communication is strong and clients revert to these patterns frequently.

In sharing problems, some clients also need help in learning to avoid making overgeneralized or absolute types of statements, such as "You *never* clean up after yourself," or "I *always* have to remind you to do your chores." Overgeneralizations have a virulent effect on communication not only because they are accusatory but also because they are generally inaccurate. Recipients of such messages typically counterattack, seeking to disprove the validity of the accusation. Arguments then ensue and disputes tend to escalate.

When clients send overgeneralized messages, immediate interventions are indicated. We recommend you stop the interaction, label the message as an overgeneralization (defining what that means), and clarify the destructive impact of such messages. You can then request the sender of the message to send an accurate and positively phrased message, coaching the person as needed.

Steps for Problem Solving

In the following sections, we delineate the steps of the problem-solving process and present techniques in assisting clients to master each step. To assist clients in grasping and applying this process, we recommend that you provide them with a reference sheet that lists the steps.

Before discussing the process with clients, explain that implementing the process does not *assure* that resultant decisions and solutions will always produce desired results, for outcomes cannot always be predicted with accuracy. Employing the process avoids discord, however, and substantially enhances the chances of achieving favorable outcomes. Realistically, this is all that can be expected, for outcomes are usually determined by the interplay of many factors, some of which cannot be anticipated. Because the future is uncertain and all human beings are subject to error, even the best executives sometimes make decisions that lead to poor outcomes.

The steps of the problem-solving process are as follows:

1. Acknowledge the problem.

2. Analyze the problem and identify the needs of participants.

3. Employ brainstorming to generate possible solutions.

4. Evaluate each option, considering the needs of participants.

5. Implement the option selected.

6. Evaluate the outcome of problem-solving efforts.

We consider each of these steps in the following sections.

Step 1. Acknowledge the Problem

The rationale for this step is self-evident. Because of the human tendency to procrastinate, people often do not face problems until they become so severe that they can be ignored no longer. Furthermore, because facing problems often produces discomfort, some people attempt to rationalize their problems away or to ignore them in the hope they will disappear. While it is true that some problems do clear up without planned corrective action, more often they worsen and expand, sometimes leaving in their wake irreparable damage, great expense, and mental anguish.

Explain this step to clients in a straightforward fashion, emphasizing that in their early stages problems usually are manageable. But if ignored, problems may escalate severely, leading to disastrous outcomes.

Step 2. Analyze the Problem and Identify Needs of Participants

This step is crucial, for participants in a problem situation often are prone to jump prematurely to considering solutions before they have accurately analyzed the problem. Consequently, their solutions may be misdirected, resulting in wasted time and energy and causing discouragement and frustration. Moreover, clients' ensuing interaction may be adversarial, centering around whose proposed solution should be adopted. In fact, clients often *start* their "problem solving" with arguments over incompatible solutions rather than first assessing needs and then developing creative solutions that meet the needs of all concerned.

As you assist clients to analyze problems, it is important *not* to dwell on their problem at length or to engage in deep psychological probing aimed at discovering root causes of difficulties. The objective is not to search for causes, for doing so often leads to unproductive speculation. Rather, the purpose in analyzing problems is to discover factors that produce clients' difficulties and to identify the needs of participants that must be met in order to solve the problem to the satisfaction of all persons involved. To define problems accurately, clients must learn to adhere to the following guidelines:

1. Pinpoint problematic behaviors and explicitly express feelings related to them (e.g., "When you go to a bar after work, I resent it and feel unimportant to you").

2. Analyze who owns what part of the problems.

3. Specify needs of the participants germane to the problematic situation.

Earlier we discussed the first two guidelines at length and need not elaborate further on them. The third guideline, however, merits elaboration. Specifying the *needs* of participants in problem situations is critical for two reasons. First, to be acceptable, any solution must satisfactorily meet the needs of all participants. Therefore, it is logical to identify the needs in advance so that clients can employ them as criteria for assessing possible solutions. Second, by sharing personal needs, clients are far more likely to gain receptive listening from other participants than by complaining about what others are doing. Identifying needs in problem solving further enhances collaboration because mutually seeking to determine and to understand each other's needs fosters mutual caring and respect. Equally important, identifying needs paves the way for arriving at a solution that best meets the needs of all concerned—the hallmark of effective problem solving.

The following are examples of messages that identify needs of clients:

- "I don't like your going to the bar with your buddies several nights in a row. I feel unimportant to you when you spend so little time with me. I'd like to share more evenings with you."

- "It humiliates me when you get on my case in front of my friends. I would like to feel I can bring my friends home without fear of being embarrassed."

Notice that in the preceding messages the sender specifies the problematic behavior, the situational context, the emotional reaction to the behavior, and the unmet needs or wants. In addition, the senders own their own feelings, avoid accusatory comments, and focus on the immediate present.

Identifying needs of participants requires careful structuring of processes and active intervention, particularly in family sessions, for clients are quick to move from needs to accusations and criticisms of others. To avert defensive responses, it is often necessary to help clients reframe negative messages by modeling "I" messages for them and coaching them to alter parts of their subsequent messages so that they accurately identify and own their feelings and express their needs. Further, it is often necessary to guide recipients of "problem" messages to assume an "understanding" stance by using feedback to ascertain if they have grasped the intended meaning of the initial message.

To structure processes in a manner that assists clients to identify and to value the needs of each other, we recommend you implement the following sequence of actions:

1. Explain that the most effective solution to a problem is the one that best meets the needs of everyone concerned.

2. Clarify that the needs of every person are important and that no one will be counted out in the problem-solving process. All persons will be asked in turn to identify their needs, and others will be asked to listen attentively and to seek to understand, seeking clarification as needed.

3. Ask for a volunteer to write down needs as they are identified. If no one volunteers, you may request that a person serve as a recorder or do it yourself.

4. Ask each person in succession to identify his or her personal needs, encouraging open discussion and requesting clarification when expressed needs are vague or confusing. Begin with the person who initially identified a problem. Assure that needs are recorded, and have the recorder check with participants to ascertain that their needs are accurately worded and that none is omitted.

Before participants identify their needs, it is important to ask them not to challenge the needs identified by other participants or to debate whose needs are of highest priority when potential conflicts are apparent. Stress that identifying needs should be limited to just that. Further, clarify that assigning priorities and resolving conflicts come later in the problem-solving process. It is also vital to intervene to stop criticism or arguments, should either occur during discussion of needs.

Although identifying needs is important in problem solving with couples, families, and groups, we have chosen a family system to illustrate this process. The Taylor family has had frequent family squabbles about use of the family automobile. The practitioner sees this as an opportunity to assist the family in learning problem-solving skills, and the parents and their two teenage children, Bert and Renee, both of whom drive, are receptive to learning this process.

The parents define the problem as heated arguments among family members over who will use their automobile on frequent occasions. They indicate the children make excessive requests for the car, creating difficulties for them in meeting their obligations. The children mildly protest that they need a car for special activities. The practitioner intervenes, explaining that all the family members have needs and that the objective is to seek a solution that best meets all their needs. Mr. Taylor nods with understanding and assures Bert and Renee that their needs are important and that they will work together to develop a solution to their liking. The practitioner then explains the importance of recording the needs, and Renee volunteers to serve as recorder. In the ensuing discussion, the following needs are identified:

BERT: Transportation for dates and for going to athletic events held at other schools.

RENEE: Transportation to sorority meetings and to go to a drive-in movie or to engage in other recreation with friends.

MRS. T.: Transportation to the hairdresser's once a week and to the grocery store; also needs to visit her widowed mother several times a week and take her on errands.

MR. T.: Transportation for bowling on Tuesdays and for usual dinner date on Friday night with Mrs. T.; also needs the car to drive to work.

Having identified their needs, the Taylors are ready to advance to step 3. We will rejoin them in step 4.

Step 3. Use Brainstorming to Generate a Range of Possible Alternatives

To enhance the likelihood of reaching sound decisions, participants need to consider a number of possible alternatives. Otherwise, they may limit their deliberations to one or two obvious options and overlook others that are more promising. A strategy that produces a wide range of possibilities is to engage in *brainstorming,* which consists of freewheeling discussion aimed at generating many possible solutions. Therefore, request all participants to stretch their thinking in identifying several creative solutions. If participants are hesitant or unable to suggest many alternatives, it is appropriate for you to offer additional possible solutions. The goal of effective decision making is to arrive at the best possible solution, not one that is merely satisfactory.

To maximize the productivity of brainstorming, it is essential that participants foster a climate of openness and receptivity to each other's ideas. Therefore, you should request that all participants refrain from criticizing or ridiculing suggestions, however impractical or absurd they may seem. Otherwise, participants will be hesitant to share their ideas for fear they will be rejected as stupid or silly. This step encourages the family or group norm that everyone is important and that criticism is detrimental to the system's process.

The brainstorming, then, should be open, spontaneous, and freewheeling. Encourage participants to contribute their ideas and give them positive feedback when they do so. The goal is to promote enthusiastic participation without evaluating any of the proposed solutions. To facilitate the subsequent process of evaluation, it is desirable to ask the recorder to list each proposed solution on a sheet of paper or on a chalkboard, leaving room on one side to enter ratings, as we illustrate later.

Step 4. Evaluate Each Alternative and Select the Most Promising One

This step is the heart of the decision-making process. If participants satisfactorily complete the preliminary steps, they enter step 4 with a cooperative frame of mind, ready to measure solutions generated in the preceding step against the needs of each participant. The objective of step 4 is to carefully weight the pros and cons of each solution and to select the one that best meets the needs of all participants. Evaluating solutions in this manner avoids needless and unproductive hassles and power struggles and employs the decision-by-consensus principle. Because the problem-solving method thus averts power struggles, it has been termed a *no-lose* method. The final solution has maximal fit for all participants, and each person, in effect, "wins."

To implement this step, guide the participants in evaluating each proposed solution generated. Ask the recorder to read each proposed alternative, and guide the participants in turn to rate the solution as to whether or not it meets their needs. Ratings can be assigned by using a plus to indicate an acceptable solution, a minus for an unacceptable solution, and a neutral rating (zero) for a solution that meets needs only marginally. An alternative method of rating is to ask participants to assign ratings based on a scale from 1 to 10, where 1 represents "totally fails to meet my needs" and 10 represents "completely meets my needs." Either of these methods enables participants to discern solutions that best meet the needs of all participants.

To illustrate this process, we return to the hypothetical case of the Taylor family, listing each alternative generated by the family and rating it according to whether or not it meets the needs of family members, as shown in the following illustration:

Possible Solutions	Ratings			
	Father	Mother	Bert	Renee
1. Buy a second car	−	−	+	+
2. Reduce social and recreational activities that require driving	0	−	−	−
3. Reduce need for car by walking and catching bus when feasible	+	+	+	+
4. Attempt to form car pools for various events	+	+	+	+
5. Double-date more frequently, reducing the times a family car is required	+	+	+	+
6. Meet as a family at the beginning of each month and week to determine members' needs for car and to plan schedule according to priorities negotiated by family	+	+	+	+

Having the family inspect the ratings of alternate solutions reveals that proposals 1 and 2 fail to meet the needs of most family members; after discussion, therefore, the family members eliminate these alternatives from further consideration. Proposals 3, 4, 5, and 6, however, appear to be promising alternatives, inasmuch as all family members rate them as pluses. The family members conclude these solutions are not in conflict with one another and may be combined to resolve the problem adequately.

As they consider solution number 3, Mr. T. indicates he could catch the bus to work instead of driving, except on Wednesdays when he needs the car. Mrs. T. volunteers to curtail driving to the grocery store by planning needs for the week and limiting her shopping to weekly visits. She also believes she could reduce trips to her mother's apartment by combining shopping trips with social visits and compensate by phoning her mother more frequently.

With respect to proposed solution number 4, Mr. T. expresses his intention to suggest to other members of his bowling team that they form a car pool for bowling nights. Renee and Bert follow suit by volunteering to explore car pools to attend sorority meetings and athletic events. Bert also agrees to comply with solution number 5 by double dating more often. All agree that proposal number 6 would prevent arguing and result in decisions fair to all family members.

Pleased with the results of their deliberations, the Taylors believe they will be able to meet the transportational needs of each family member. Equally important, they emerge from the problem solving with mutual respect and high family morale.

Choosing an alternative often does not proceed as smoothly as it did for the Taylors, and the stakes are sometimes much higher. Furthermore, two or more alternatives may receive an equal number of plus ratings, and the participants may be forced to choose only one of them. When this occurs, you will need to assist the participants to analyze further the acceptable alternatives. This is best done by having participants identify the pros and cons of each option and assign weights according to the relative importance of each factor. To enhance this process, have the recorder list the pros and cons so that comparisons can be made readily and objectively.

In weighing pros and cons, it is critical to guide participants in considering the likely consequences of each acceptable alternative, keeping in mind the following: "Is a certain decision likely to produce lasting beneficial results by getting to the core of a problem, or is it merely relieving pressure temporarily and postponing an inevitable and painful course of action that will be even more difficult later?" "How is a decision likely to affect relationships among the participants?" "Has sufficient information been gained to assess the probable effects of a given solution?" "Are personal biases producing favoritism for one alternative over another?" You can play an active and vital role by encouraging participants to share their ideas and by supplementing their discussion by pointing out consequences they may have overlooked. Your role in this regard is vital, for clients learn from your modeling. Modeling related to considering consequences of decisions is particularly beneficial, as many clients tend to be impulsive and fail to anticipate probable consequences of their actions.

After participants have weighed the pros and cons of acceptable solutions, ask them to rerate these proposed solutions, employing the scale from 1 to 10 described earlier. (Because all the remaining solutions are acceptable, the "plus-minus" scale is no longer applicable.) On the basis of the new ratings, guide the members in selecting the solution that they have given the highest overall ratings.

Step 5. Implement the Option Selected

After the participants have selected an option, explain that the next step is to implement it with enthusiasm and confidence. After all, they have done their best to reach a sound decision, and they will enhance the chances of achieving a successful outcome by wholeheartedly applying themselves to implementing it. It is important to emphasize this point because some people tend to dwell on uncertainties and to delay actions because of lingering doubts. Others carry out solutions in a halfhearted manner, which sabotages the chances of successfully solving the problem. Many well-conceived solutions fail not because they are defective but because of defective execution, which may result from hesitation, doubt, and fears of bungling.

Step 6. Evaluate the Outcome

Effective problem solving does not end after participants have implemented an alternative. Because of human fallibility and life's vicissitudes, even carefully chosen and well-executed solutions sometimes fail to achieve desired results. Consequently, it is vital that participants systematically monitor the effects of their chosen course of action. Keeping records based on careful and consistent observations assists them to make thorough and objective evaluations and thus determine early on if their solution is working as planned.

To assist clients to evaluate outcomes of solutions, it is important to explain the value of monitoring and to guide participants in developing a mutually acceptable strategy of monitoring. Appropriate strategies may involve keeping daily logs that record the incidence of desired behaviors or, in the case of the Taylor family, maintaining records to determine if the incidence of family squabbles over the car have decreased. Similarly, parents who have implemented a strategy to reduce the frequency of a child's temper tantrums can evaluate the effectiveness of their strategy by recording daily over several weeks the frequency of the tantrums.

A less rigorous method of monitoring is to hold regularly scheduled meetings in which participants share their views as to how solutions are working. Groups, for example, may agree to review over a course of several weeks whether strategies developed by members to keep the group on task are indeed proving effective. Scheduled meetings of couples and families also have the advantage of promoting sustained collaborative efforts by participants.

When a solution has not produced positive results over a reasonable trial period, participants can safely conclude their solution is ineffective. This need not cause alarm, as they likely have not assessed the problem accurately. Further efforts may identify a more efficacious solution. To assist participants to develop a more effective solution, have them return to step 2 and repeat the process. It is possible their first solution failed because their problem formulation was inaccurate. When participants are confident of their problem formulation, however, ask them to return to step 3 and carefully review other alternate solutions or generate additional ones. Assisting them to follow the guidelines and steps presented earlier will expedite their devising an effective and timely solution to their problem.

Expediting the Development of Clients' Problem-Solving Skills

Although couples and families may select the development of problem-solving skills as a goal in initial sessions (with the practitioner's help), the practitioner may not actually *teach* members these skills until a later date. With respect to groups, an important aspect of the practitioner's role in an initial session is to assist the group to agree to use a decision-by-consensus method for solving problems and to teach steps for decision making to members. The problem-solving method can be taught to groups, families, or couples using a structured learning experience to facilitate the learning of the steps. Actual practice of the steps, however, should occur in an informal manner that provides for maximum interaction among members. An ultimate goal of the practitioner, in fact, is to help clients learn to apply problem-solving steps spontaneously in their relationships with others.

It is to be expected that clients will struggle in adhering to the steps and guidelines at first. Even in couple, family, and group sessions you will need to intervene actively when participants get off track or begin to engage in dysfunctional interactions. By intervening and clarifying the destructive nature of their interaction, you can guide clients to achieve positive outcomes. Gradually, you can give them increasing responsibility for getting back on track by asking family or group members to identify what is going wrong and by challenging them to take corrective action. You can also anticipate with them how they will encounter similar obstacles outside of sessions and participate with them in planning corrective strategies.

When evaluating clients' efforts to employ problem solving, keep in mind that the hard-won ability to make decisions collaboratively with others is a reflection of substantial growth in a number of areas. Clients may falter in their first tentative efforts to apply the problem-solving process because implementation of a decision-by-consensus approach requires

extensive adjustments in the individual styles of many members. For example, many families must alter crystallized dysfunctional patterns in order for members to count each other in and to acknowledge and address the needs of members through problem solving. It is also difficult for a newly formed group to orchestrate a problem-solving process that effectively meets the needs of all concerned when members are strangers with no previous experience in mutual problem solving. The ability of formed groups to solve problems consistently in a facilitative manner, in fact, is a sure sign that such groups have achieved the working stage of development.

The following statements illustrate the practitioner's role in facilitating development of problem-solving skills early in initial or group sessions:

1. "As we make this decision, let's consider members' needs first and then develop a number of possible solutions before we decide on a course of action."

2. "The experience we just had is an example of decision by consensus. What did you observe as we went through this process?"

3. "I'm really pleased with the way the group attacked this problem; everyone's needs were considered. We chose our solution from several alternatives, and everyone seems satisfied with the decision."

Thus, by intervening to guide groups through problem solving (message number 1), assisting them to discuss their efforts to make decisions collaboratively (message number 2), and accrediting their increments of growth and success (message number 3), you can assist members to assume increasing responsibility for self-directed problem solving.

Applying Problem Solving with Individuals

Although our preceding discussion and examples of problem solving related to couples, families, and groups, the steps are equally applicable to work with individuals. Individuals function within an interpersonal context and need to learn skills that apply to that broader arena of life. In enabling individual clients to solve problems, you must also guide them through essentially the same steps as outlined in this chapter. *It is vitally important to teach them the process of problem solving while guiding them through it.*

The step concerned with generating numerous alternatives is particularly vital in working with individual clients. Clients can learn to engage in individual brainstorming, thereby expanding their range of options and avoiding impulsive actions. With clients who tend to act impetuously, learning to generate alternatives, to assess their pros and cons, and to weigh possible consequences of actions may significantly enhance their social functioning by equipping them with new and more effective coping patterns.

Facilitating Transfer of Problem-Solving Skills

Enabling clients to apply problem-solving processes in the real world is a challenging task. Because the process embodies a number of discrete concepts and skills and requires both commitment and self-discipline, mastering it requires persistent and determined effort. The benefits more than justify the efforts, and it is important to emphasize to clients the benefits that will gradually accrue if they persevere until they achieve mastery.

As you guide clients through the steps, they gain rudimentary skills in applying the process. These "in-session" activities are merely a means to an end. The ultimate proof of the pudding lies in whether clients succeed in applying the process outside the session. It is vital, therefore, that you employ strategies that enhance the transfer of skills gained in guided practice to the arena of daily life.

You can assist clients to expand and to transfer their problem-solving facility by negotiating with them tasks of applying the process to problems that emerge between sessions. Suggest to clients that they agree to assist each other to adhere to the steps and guidelines by gently drawing deviations to the attention of each other and facilitatively suggesting they get back on course. By applying the process independently, they will gain additional practice and will experience rough spots that can be explored and ironed out in their next session. As they disclose new problems, you can assist them to develop their skills further by asking them to employ problem solving in developing solutions during the session. Applying the process under your tutelage provides additional opportunity for them to refine their skills and to discover their soft spots. As you observe them effectively following the steps and guidelines, you can accredit their progress, thereby enhancing their confidence and reinforcing their efforts.

You will further enhance transfer of the skills to the real world by intervening less frequently and giving less direction as clients demonstrate increasing mastery of the process. By giving them increasing responsibility to monitor their own behavior and to make their own "interventions" when their efforts go awry, you are preparing them for successful independent problem solving. You will, of course, need to continue making timely interventions and to coach them until they are better able to stand on their own feet. But always bear in mind that you achieve ultimate success with clients when they are able to function effectively without your services

Social Skills Training (SST)

Training in social skills has expanded over the past two decades; the literature contains a plethora of articles describing SST programs and reporting evaluations of them. SST programs have been employed to teach a wide variety of skills. Moreover, such training has been used for both primary prevention and remediation of deficiencies. In this section we explain the rationale of SST for prevention and remediation, identify target groups, enumerate various skills, and describe a format that can be employed for teaching various skills.

Rationale for and Uses of SST

Beginning with Rapoport (1961) almost 30 years ago, prominent social workers have increasingly promoted the development of primary preventive programs in social work. The rationale for preventive programs is that efforts to prevent social dysfunction by equipping people with coping skills reduces the possibilities of later maladjustment, unhappiness, failure to develop potentials, and loss of productivity. Moreover, preventive programs cost only a fraction of the cost of remedial programs such as mental health treatment, foster care, substance abuse treatment programs, public assistance, and correctional institutions, to name just a few.

Research studies too numerous to mention also document the importance of adequate socialization during childhood and adolescence to adequate adjustment. Children who are deprived of adequate socialization fail to learn certain vital social skills and are at risk to experience a variety of personal and interpersonal difficulties. For example, a recent study (Weisz, et al., 1987) revealed that perceived personal incompetence by children is linked with depression in childhood. Other research studies (summarized in LeCroy, 1983) have documented the importance of skills in forming peer relationships to the healthy socialization of children. As a consequence of these findings, practitioners have developed preventive skill training programs (LeCroy & Rose, 1986), including one that uses a game format (LeCroy, 1987).

Preventive SST has been employed in middle schools by LeCroy (1983) to teach three primary skills: making requests of others; resisting peer pressure, which is prerequisite for "saying no to drugs"; and maintaining friendships. Jason and Burrows (1983) SST have developed a program for assisting high school seniors to cope with the transition associated with completing high school. Schinke, Blythe, and Gilchrist (1981) have used SST for teaching pregnancy prevention skills to young people in a school setting. Skills in managing provocative situations and controlling anger have been included in a program developed by Kolko, Dorsett and Milan (1981) for adolescent patients in a psychiatric hospital.

The rationale for SST in remediation programs is similar to that just discussed. Social dysfunction is commonly associated with deficiencies in social skills essential to achieving self-esteem, forming satisfying interpersonal relationships, and performing various social roles effectively.

Deficiencies in social skills contribute to difficulties involving loneliness and depression, marital dysfunction, parent-child problems, family breakdown, employment problems, various mental health problems, and other difficulties. As a consequence SST programs are often included in services offered by university counseling centers, family service agencies, mental health programs (both inpatient and outpatient), substance abuse treatment centers, adolescent residential and correctional programs, and in many other settings.

Skills selected for remedial SST are diverse and vary according to the setting and the target problems of clients typically served. Among the more common skills are various parenting skills, assertiveness, listening to others and sending clear messages, personalizing feelings, making requests, initiating and maintaining conversation, making friends, managing anger, and solving problems. With clients who have far-ranging deficiencies, skills may include personal grooming, using public transportation, ordering meals, making telephone calls, and initiating conversation, to name just a few.

Assessing Skill Deficiencies

The first step in employing SST is to determine the skills targeted for training. When deficiencies are readily apparent this is a simple task. Adolescents who are easily provoked to anger and discharge anger in violent and destructive ways, for example, lack skills in coping with provocation and controlling anger. Socially inhibited people commonly lack skills in making social overtures, maintaining conversation, and asserting themselves. Certain clients, will themselves identify deficiencies and request assistance in learning certain social behaviors, for example, accepting compliments or overcoming extreme sensitivity to criticism.

With other clients, however, as with those who have multiple deficiencies or those whose deficiencies are more subtle, assessment is more complex. Parent-child difficulties, for example, may involve parental deficiencies in providing encouragement and approval, expressing expectations, setting limits, managing demands or tantrums, being firm and consistent, being flexible, or listening to children without lecturing or being critical. Schizophrenic clients may manifest multiple deficiencies that require extensive SST. To identify specific deficiencies of schizophrenics, Curran, et al. (1985) recommend administering a scale that covers major areas of psychosocial functioning and identifies stressors to which patients have not adapted adequately. Various other instruments have also been developed by behaviorally oriented marital and family therapists to assess skills and deficiencies of partners in performing various marital roles. These and related instruments are described in the *Handbook of Measurements for Marriage and Family Therapy* (Fredman & Sherman, 1987).

Identifying Components of Social Skills

After selecting a social skill for training, the next step is to break down the skill into its discrete components or subskills. This process is essentially the same as that of dissecting tasks into behavioral units, as discussed in Chapter 14. As with dissecting tasks, the analysis should consider cognitive and emotional components as well as specific behaviors, for fears and uncertainties often must be mastered before clients can effectively perform requisite actions. We discussed this process at length in Chapter 14 and illustrate it later in this chapter in the section on assertiveness training.

Format for Training

SST can be conducted in sessions with individuals or in a group context. We have chosen to focus on group context; however, you can follow essentially the same format in sessions with individuals because the principles and steps are virtually identical. When using a group, it is important, of course, to prepare members for the group, as we discussed in the latter part of Chapter 13. Once the group has been constituted, the following steps are typically followed.

1. Discuss the Rationale and Describe the Skill

This first step is critical to successfully engaging members in learning a selected skill. Participants must believe that developing the skill will benefit them. To enhance the relevance for participants we recommend you briefly introduce the skill, alluding in general to situations in which it is applicable, and then elicit from participants specific relevant social situations that have posed difficulties for them and have led to adverse outcomes because of ineffectual coping. For example, if the selected skill is assertively resisting peer pressure you might use a message similar to the following:

"Learning to say 'No!' with firmness and not giving in to pressure from other kids can help you avoid doing things you don't really want to do and things that can get you into trouble. Probably a number of you can recall times you gave in to pressure and later regretted it. I know I can (*gives an example*). How about the rest of you? Could you share times when you wished you had been able to say 'No'?"

As participants share experiences, commend them for risking with the group. After a number of participants have

shared experiences, you can further attempt to enhance their motivation by asking if they can think of several benefits of learning the skill. Initiate the discussion by listing an advantage on a chalkboard (e.g., don't get started on drugs and have higher self-respect). Compliment persons who identify advantages and list the advantages on the chalkboard, elaborating on advantages when clarification is needed.

2. Identify the Components of the Skill

Explain that the skill involves a number of different components. Then list each component on the chalkboard, explaining its significance to successfully employing the skill. It is helpful as you do so to involve participants by asking if they have had difficulties with the component being discussed (e.g., the cognitive/emotional component —hearing the reactions of peers if one refuses to participate in a certain problematic activity). Explain that the group will discuss and practice each component.

3. Model the Skill

Recall from an earlier chapter that vicarious learning is the second most potent source of self-efficacy. To tap this source, you can model the component of the skill (using *coping* modeling rather than mastery) or ask if a member of the group will volunteer to model the skill. After the modeling a critique or discussion by participants regarding their observations is often fruitful in highlighting aspects of the target component that contribute to effective and ineffective performance.

4. Role-Play Use of Each Component

Explain that the most effective way of learning a skill is to practice until one feels confident in applying the skill.

Therefore, participants will take turns practicing each component and will give feedback to each other to assist in further developing the skill. Ask for a volunteer to begin role-playing and set the stage by prescribing roles they are to play. (You will need to prepare for this step by identifying problematic situations typical of those that participants commonly encounter. You can also enlist the aid of participants in identifying relevant situations.) It is desirable to begin with less difficult situations and as participants demonstrate the ability to apply the skills, more challenging situations can be role-played. Before beginning the role-playing, ask participants to observe carefully so that they can provide feedback to each other.

5. Evaluate the Role-Play

After each episode of role-playing invite participants to provide feedback. To foster a climate that is conducive to openness, encourage participants to give positive feedback initially. You may wish to initiate the process or add feedback about positive aspects of the participant's role-play that may have been overlooked.

For maximum benefit, feedback should be addressed to both verbal and nonverbal behaviors. For example, a participant may employ appropriate words but may speak hesitantly with a subdued tone of voice or may avoid eye-to-eye contact with the other protagonist. When such nonassertive behaviors are evident, it is beneficial to have the participant engage in further practice, seeking to modify the behaviors in question. Again, positive feedback should be given for even slight improvements and participants should be requested to evaluate their own performance, focusing on both positive and negative aspects, and to share feelings experienced during the role-play. Discussion of feelings that inhibit performance can be valuable in identifying common barriers to implementing the skill effectively.

6. Combine the Components in Role-Play

After participants have role-played and demonstrated adequate mastery of the various components, have them take turns role-playing the skill itself. Continue to have members give feedback to each other and continue practicing until they manifest self-efficacy with respect to the skill. A simple way of assessing the self-efficacy of participants is to have them rate their readiness to perform the skill in real-life situations on a scale from 1 to 10, where 1 represents a total lack of confidence and 10 represents complete confidence. Ratings of 7 or higher generally indicate adequate mastery.

7. Apply the Skill in Real-Life Situations

This step entails applying the skill in actual social situations, the ultimate test of the skill training efforts. Preparing participants adequately for this crucial step begins with eliciting situations that are likely to occur during the forthcoming week and obtaining the commitment of participants to apply the newly gained skills in these situations. Reviewing components of the skill and practicing application of them further prepares participants. Anticipating difficulties that will likely arise and preparing to surmount them through rehearsing appropriate thoughts and behaviors produces maximal preparation and self-efficacy.

Subsequent debriefing sessions provide opportunities to discuss and analyze the experiences of participants in applying the skill. The practitioner should encourage participants to accredit successes, enthusiastically drawing attention to specific behaviors and cognitions that resulted in successful outcomes. Such focusing draws the attention of participants to their mastery of components targeted for learning and further enhances their self-efficacy.

Not all participants report successes, of course, and even those who achieve successful outcomes may report aspects of their performance that were flawed. Debriefing sessions thus provide opportunities for additional practice in enhancing and refining skills. Step 7 thus may be extended for several weeks, depending upon the needs of participants and the feasibility of doing so.

Game Formats for Learning Skills

Another format for assisting people to learn problem solving and social skills is the use of games specifically developed for those purposes. Use of a game format has a number of advantages, including the following cited by Rabin, et al. (1985):

1. Many participants are receptive to this approach because games are expected to be fun.

2. Experimentation with new forms of behavior is natural in the context of a game.

3. Games with easily understood rules exert powerful control over the behavior of players.

4. Well-designed rules promote learning at participants' own pace with a minimum of failures.

5. Skill-training games foster adaptive interdependence of players and minimize the need for a third party.

Because the game format is a recent innovation, empirical support for this approach is scanty. Nevertheless, the rationale for the format appears sound and preliminary findings are promising. Rabin, et al. (1985) describe the Marriage Contract Game, which was designed to teach marital partners the skills of successful problem solving and of warm and open communication. Outcome findings of the use of the game with four distressed couples who had requested treatment for a child and were averse to marital therapy indicated these couples learned to solve problems and to communicate positive feelings along the dimensions targeted by the game. Other improvements were also noted.

The game format appears particularly promising for work with children because of the high appeal of games to children. LeCroy (1987) has reported that the use of a board game designed to teach social skills that are components of social competence produced results that were equivalent to but not superior to results achieved using a standard social skills group. The game format had been designed partly as a response to difficulties encountered by social workers in involving children in formal skills groups. According to the group leaders who employed the game, children responded positively to the game and group attractiveness and cohesion increased.

Based on the limited experimentation described in the preceding, it appears that expanded use of and testing of the game format is warranted. This format offers a new approach to teaching skills to children and adults who might otherwise be resistant to participating in formal skills development programs.

Assertiveness Training

Deficiencies in assertiveness pervade many aspects of interpersonal difficulties, and assertiveness training (AT) as a clinical intervention has been applied in diverse settings to almost every major diagnostic classification or behavioral disorder. Particularly relevant for both battered wives and their abusive husbands, AT achieved popularity with the publication in 1970 of *Your Perfect Right: A Guide to Assertive Behavior* (Alberti & Emmons, 1970, 1974) and has since become a widespread movement in the United States.

The construct of assertiveness has been defined in various ways. Our definition, which synthesizes some of these definitions and adds our own interpretation, is that assertiveness embodies specific components of behavior that enable individuals to express their opinions, feelings, wants, and preferences in a manner that respects the rights and feelings of others even when such expressions risk aversive consequences such as criticism, disapproval, or punishment. This definition is sufficiently broad to encompass many situations and behaviors. Assertiveness, in fact, is not a unitary construct, as revealed by Bucell (1979), who empirically studied behaviors embodied in various assertiveness inventories. Bucell identified the following relatively distinct types of assertive behaviors or response classes: (1) refuse requests, (2) express unpopular opinions, (3) admit personal shortcomings, (4) accept compliments, (5) express positive feelings, (6) make requests for changes in behavior, and (7) initiate and maintain conversations.

The first step in AT, therefore, is to identify the response class in which training is needed. After doing so you can prepare the client(s) for training following the guidelines and steps delineated earlier in the section on skills training. Training can be implemented either with individuals or in a group context. As with training in other social skills, modeling, behavioral rehearsal, and guided practice are crucial aspects of AT. To avoid redundancy we will not delineate steps involved in AT but refer you to a chapter by Schroeder and Black (1985) that describes in detail AT aimed at teaching conversational behavior.

Cultural Factors

Before discussing assertiveness further, we emphasize that assertiveness training is not appropriate for clients whose culturally prescribed roles prohibit assertive behavior. Asian-American cultures, for example, prescribe deference to authority. Similarly, women from traditional Hispanic, Latino, and Asian cultural backgrounds are expected to be submissive to their husbands. Assertiveness training could compound rather than resolve difficulties for such clients. Nevertheless, minority clients need to learn to assert their legal rights to resources to which they are entitled. Practitioners, therefore, often must assume an advocacy role in assisting them to gain assertiveness in dealing with bureaucratic structures.

Differentiating Assertiveness from Other Response Styles

In preparing clients for AT, it is important to differentiate assertiveness from the response styles of *aggressiveness* and *nonassertiveness*. We have previously defined assertiveness but add that the basic message relayed by persons who are relating assertively is that they "count" and that their ideas, perceptions, and opinions are important. By contrast, nonassertiveness involves the violation of one's own rights "by failing to express honest feelings, thoughts, and beliefs and consequently permitting others to violate oneself, or expressing one's thoughts and feelings in such an apologetic, diffident, self-effacing manner that others can easily disregard them" (Lange & Jakubowski, 1976, p. 9). Persons who relate nonassertively attempt to appease others and to avoid conflict, conveying through their behavior that their needs, wants, and opinions are not important and that others are superior to them.

The third response style, *aggression,* as defined by Lange and Jakubowski (1976), involves "directly standing up for personal rights and expressing thoughts, feelings, and beliefs in a way which . . . violates the rights of the other person" (p. 10). Persons who relate aggressively seek to dominate others, ignoring their needs, wants, and feelings.

The idea of relating assertively has had immense popular appeal to the lay public. Many people have problems with nonassertiveness or timidity, frequently permitting themselves to be pushed aside or discounted by others. Unable to express themselves effectively in a wide variety of situations, such persons often feel unappreciated, taken for granted, and exploited by others. Many other persons, who relate aggressively, often suffer the loss of significant relationships because others weary of their abrasive, debasing response styles. As a result, such persons unwittingly deprive themselves of opportunities to receive essential warmth, support, and affection. Still other persons vacillate between aggressive and nonassertive or passive behavior, failing to develop an effective and comfortable style of relating to others.

Clients often seek (or are coerced to seek) professional assistance because of problems that can be traced to habitual styles of relating aggressively or passively. Experienced over long periods of time, such difficulties may cause or contribute to low self-esteem, depression, or marked anxiety in interpersonal situations.

Congruence between Verbal and Nonverbal Behavior

Nonverbal components of messages may either strengthen and complement an assertive statement or contradict it. Persons who wring their hands, look at the floor, or stammer, for instance, do not appear assertive no matter how assertive the verbal content of their message. Practitioners must thus observe clients' nonverbal behaviors to determine whether these behaviors convey assertiveness, aggressiveness, or nonassertiveness. Common nonverbal behaviors associated with assertive relating and the other two response styles include the following:

Assertiveness	Aggressiveness	Nonassertiveness
Relaxed posture	Glares	Evasive or fleeting eye contact
Direct eye contact	Tightened fists	
	Clenched jaws	Nervous gestures
Firm and moderate tone of voice	Pursed lips	Flushed face
	Rigid body posture	Soft, whiny, or pleading voice
Fluent speech pattern	Sarcastic or belittling tone of voice	
Appropriately varied facial expressions		Hesitant speech
	Loud speech	Nervous laughter or throat clearing
Moderately expressive gestures	Finger pointing	
		Clammy hands

In assisting clients to develop nonverbal behaviors that are compatible with assertive relating, you may wish to refer to Serber (1977), who delineates procedures for shaping this vital dimension of communication.

Cognitive/Perceptual Obstacles to Assertiveness

Developing assertiveness is not easy for practitioners or clients. Clients often experience extreme tension and paralyzing emotions that block them from asserting themselves despite strong desires to do so. These powerful emotions are generally a product of deeply embedded mistaken beliefs, of which clients usually have limited or vague awareness. Consequently, practitioners need to assist clients to expand their awareness of these irrational beliefs and to replace them with realistic conceptions.

Common misconceptions that inhibit assertiveness include: (1) distorted beliefs that one's obligations to others far outweigh one's own wants or rights, (2) extreme concern with pleasing or impressing others favorably, and (3) grossly distorted fears about the consequences of asserting oneself with others. With respect to distorted beliefs, many clients were conditioned as children to believe that it is bad or selfish to accord equal significance to personal wants and needs as compared to responding to the needs or wants (and sometimes demands) of others. To feel they are "good" persons (or, rather, not *bad* persons), such individuals develop keen sensitivity to the wants of others, sometimes going to extremes to please them, often at great expense to themselves. Saying no (and sometimes even thinking it) automatically triggers feelings of guilt and badness. Sadly, these individuals are so governed by the wants and expectations of others that they are often out of touch with their own needs and wants.

The second and third types of misconceptions are inextricably linked with the first. Having an inordinate need to please or impress others derives from the mistaken belief that one's worth as a person is directly proportional to the extent that one gains the approval of others. Generally rooted in early life experiences in which parental love and approval were not expressed generously and were contingent upon pleasing the parents, such beliefs link self-esteem exclusively to the reactions of others. Self-esteem, under such circumstances, is tenuous at best, and it is overwhelming to such persons to risk incurring the displeasure of others. The tacit motto of these persons is, "I am of value only as I win approval from others." The irony in this motto is that persons who seek excessively to please others tend to attain the opposite effect, for others often take them for granted and devalue them. Such persons need to adopt instead the realistic belief that people tend to value those who value themselves and are assertive.

The third type of misconception involves fearing disastrous consequences if one asserts one's rights, wants, or feelings. Some people, who were severely punished as children for not conforming to parental demands, experience vague fears of being physically or verbally abused if they assert themselves. Others have conscious fears of being rejected or literally abandoned (as they feared in childhood) if they assert themselves. These feared reactions are of catastrophic proportions, and it is understandable that these people are extremely threatened by the prospects of asserting themselves.

Assisting clients to surmount the obstacles described in the preceding involves an approach that blends muscle relaxation training (to reduce tension), cognitive restructuring, self-instruction (to identify and master the irrational fears), and behavioral rehearsal (guided practice) to acquire the verbal and nonverbal skills involved in assertive behavior. We discuss these interventions at length in Chapter 18.

16 Modifying Environments, Developing Resources, and Planning

Effects of Mismatches between Clients' Needs and Environmental Resources

We turn our attention in this chapter to interventions employed to enhance the social and physical environments of people. Increasingly it is recognized that earlier efforts of social workers in assisting clients to adapt to their environments were often misdirected and that dysfunction of clients may reflect a need to adapt environments to clients' needs. For example, practitioners who treated clients in institutional settings (e.g., mental hospitals and youth correctional centers) came to realize that it was futile to return clients to the very environments that spawned their dysfunctional behavior. Unless the dysfunctional factors in such environments were remedied, clients rapidly reverted to the same or worse problems than they originally manifested. Consequently, practitioners have devoted increasing attention to client groups that are particularly vulnerable to problems associated with inadequate environmental resources. This concern is reflected by a burgeoning literature related to concerns about and ways of improving clients' environments through innovative direct service, advocacy, and the promotion and development of social policies and programs addressed to populations at risk.

Vulnerable Client Groups and Types of Interventions

Mismatches between clients and their environments result from two major types of circumstances: (1) substantial deficiencies in resources normally needed by people at various developmental stages and (2) *unusual* needs of people that result from developmental difficulties (e.g., mental retardation, autism, cerebral palsy, learning disabilities, congenital deformities, and cystic fibrosis), disabilities caused by illness or injury, mental disorders, degenerative disorders, severe stress, cultural dislocation, and environmental disasters.

Vulnerable populations of the first type include infants, children, and adolescents who are neglected and/or abused and who otherwise receive inadequate parenting; children and adults who live in impoverished environments; people who are denied resources and opportunities because of race, ethnicity, age, sex, or other factors; adults whose spouses lack the capacity to impart warmth, affection, and respect; and people who lack essential support systems. Vulnerable populations of the second type include children and adults who are afflicted with incapacitating illnesses or suffer from various forms of physical and mental disability; elderly clients who are unable to care for themselves; refugees; and people who have lost their homes and possessions as a result of natural calamities.

Many different forms of intervention can be used to improve the environments of such vulnerable groups. Although these interventions are diverse, they incorporate a limited number of general strategies, which we have classified as follows:

1. Enhancing intrafamilial relationships.

2. Supplementing resources in the home environment.

3. Developing and enhancing support systems.

4. Moving clients to different environments.

5. Using case management.

6. Enhancing interactions between organizations and institutions.

7. Improving institutional environments.

8. Empowering clients.

9. Developing new resources.

10. Employing advocacy and social action.

11. Planning and organizing.

In the following sections, we discuss these strategies and the vulnerable populations to which they apply. Limited space precludes discussing specific interventions in detail, but we have included selected references that explicate them in greater depth.

Before proceeding further, we wish to emphasize that environmental interventions are generally implemented in concert with other interventions. Because problems are multidimensional and involve reciprocal interaction among multiple systems and subsystems, interventions

aimed exclusively at the environment may ignore dysfunction in individuals, thereby addressing only part of a problem. Children who are neglected or abused by parents often manifest psychological damage that requires attention aside from efforts to improve the social environment afforded by parents. Moreover, children's behavior impinges on parents and may play a major role in precipitating physical or sexual abuse. Another way of thinking about it is that every actor may be viewed as a central figure or as a part of the environment of other actors, depending upon one's vantage point.

Still another important factor in implementing environmental interventions is that clients' reactions to proposed environmental changes must be considered as an integral part of such interventions. Clients often experience intense emotional reactions to environmental change, and neglect of these reactions may produce frustration and failure for practitioners as they attempt to implement what would appear as appropriate and beneficial interventions. Clients may openly or passively resist the practitioner's efforts. Furthermore, clients may appear to go along with interventions but subsequently respond with depression associated with losses of familiar surroundings, significant relationships, or a sense of independence. It is thus critical to elicit clients' feelings and to respond sensitively to them. Given these considerations, we now focus on the categories of environmental interventions.

Enhancing Intrafamilial Relationships

Within families, the members constitute the primary resource for meeting vital human needs, such as nurturance, guidance, protection, nutrition, health care, affection, and companionship. Often parents and spouses and other care providers lack the capacity to provide emotional resources needed by other family members. Family members may also interact in destructive ways that impair the ability of members to respond to each other's emotional needs. For example, by constantly criticizing one's spouse, a marital partner fails to provide essential approval and encouragement to that spouse, who may respond by withholding affection and acts of consideration. Neither partner is likely to fulfill the needs of the other until changes are made in the marital system. Interventions aimed at enhancing family relationships in such instances are discussed in Chapter 17.

When parents abuse, neglect, or otherwise fail to provide adequate care and guidance to their children, practitioners often employ multiple interventions to enhance family functioning. Prominent among these interventions are various forms of home-based care, which have been summarized by Kaduchin and Martin (1988, pp. 83–142). Home-based care is typically aimed at strengthening parental functioning to prevent placement of children in foster homes or institutional settings. Contemporary home-based care is still in its infancy, but efforts are being made to identify factors that are critical to the success of these multidimensional programs (Bribitzer & Verdick, 1988; Reid, Kagan, & Schlosberg, 1988). Other interventions include using parent aides (Miller et al., 1984) and homemakers (Kaduchin & Martin, 1988, pp. 143–172); working directly with children (Lamb, 1986); employing group work with parents (Kruger et al., 1979); using Parents Anonymous self-help groups (Moore, 1983); blending social services and social support (Miller & Whittaker, 1988); and employing parent education programs (Barozzi & Engel, 1985).

Two types of family structure that are especially vulnerable to dysfunction are one-parent families and stepfamilies. The single parent is often beset by financial difficulties and by stresses related to having to fulfill multiple roles that are normally distributed between two parents. Moreover, the single parent has personal and social needs that compete with performing these multiple roles. Garfinkel and McLanahan (1986) have published an informative book concerned with single mothers and their children. Greif (1985) has written a book based on surveys of single fathers concerning their experiences extending from the divorce process through different stages of single parenting. Bowen (1987) has also written concerning problems of single fathers.

Stepfamilies also are at risk because of possible stresses associated with the absence of a history of emotional bonding among stepmembers, divided loyalties of children, unclear expectations of family members, possible differences in lifestyles between previous families, questions of turf, and conflicts in role definitions. Visher and Visher (1988) have written an authoritative book that defines therapeutic strategies in work with stepfamilies. Dahl, Cowgill, and Asmundsson (1987) have reported findings based on interviews with remarried families. These authors report the first year for remarried families typically is difficult and that it takes from three to five years before these families achieve cohesiveness and a sense of belonging.

Supplementing Resources in the Home Environment

By augmenting resources in deficient home environments, it is often possible to meet clients' needs adequately, sparing them and other family members the trauma and possible psychological damage that ensues as a result of separation and/or admission to institutions. Visiting nurses and Meals on Wheels, which delivers hot meals to homebound persons, may make it possible for elderly and/or disabled persons to live independently. Moreover, disabled persons who earlier would have had to reside with others or in institutions are now able to live independently as a result of instruction in self-care, new devices that enable them to perform housekeeping functions, independent living centers, and volunteers who assist them to dress and perform other daily tasks (Mackelprang & Hepworth, 1987; Milofsky, 1980).

The large proportion of elderly persons in the United States who cannot live alone and care for themselves are cared for by relatives (Kulys & Tobin, 1980), contrary to a pervasive myth that Americans neglect their elderly and shirk responsibility by placing failing parents in nursing homes. Ordinarily, care provided by relatives is superior to that provided in institutions, as the latter tends to promote feelings of dependence, passivity, and inactivity in residents. Based on experiments in providing care at home for the elderly, Pelham and Clark (1985) have written a book that contains recommendations aimed at enhancing home care for elderly persons.

Homemaker Service

Homemaker service is a valuable resource when a family has no parent who can adequately perform crucial aspects of the traditional homemaker's role. Homemaker service may involve shopping, cleaning, preparing balanced meals, budgeting, doing the laundry, and teaching these same skills to clients. Homemakers also model effective interpersonal and child management skills, thereby enabling clients to learn the same. Equally important, they offer "on-the-spot availability," permitting them gradually to build trust and provide a "corrective emotional experience" for clients, thereby fostering positive change (Stempler & Stempler, 1981). The authors just cited define the partnership between social workers and homemakers in serving families and provide an excellent example of teamwork in assisting an unstable minority family referred to protective service because of child neglect. For a comprehensive discussion on the varied uses of homemaker services, we recommend a chapter by Kaduchin and Martin (1988, pp. 143–172).

Household Items

Some family units, including single-person households, lack basic resources essential to health and effective home management. Refugees, for example, sometimes struggle to live without adequate cooking utensils, warm clothing, beds, blankets, and even food. However, even long-term residents who struggle on meager incomes have needs for acquiring essential goods or replacing worn-out and often dangerous appliances.

Social workers are in a strategic position to identify items that people living in impoverished conditions urgently need. Beyond identifying such needs, practitioners have a responsibility to initiate remedial actions, which may include drawing the needs of people to the attention of appropriate agencies or engaging in direct efforts to supply the needs of clients. Practitioners may contact church, civic, or private service organizations that provide concrete goods for people in need; request special funds from public assistance agencies; or assist clients in purchasing essential items through various thrift stores that cater to low-income people. In other instances, practitioners may need to organize programs to assist groups of people with extensive needs.

Day Care

A valuable resource that not only enriches the environments of children but serves a preventive function as well, day-care programs provide opportunities for preschool children to develop skills in observing, communicating, and interacting with others. Varied day-care activities also assist children to increase their physical strength and coordination and to develop a positive self-concept. Day-care programs are particularly valuable to working mothers but can be of value to all families by providing learning experiences for children during a period when they learn rapidly, as well as creative and healthy experiences in separation for both parents and children. Moreover, day-care programs provide opportunities to identify troubled families and to provide services that can strengthen family functioning (Friedman & Friedman, 1982). For an excellent discussion of uses of day-care services, relevant policies and issues, and a comprehensive list of references, we recommend a chapter by Kaduchin and Martin (1988, pp. 173–217).

Developing and Enhancing Support Systems

As we discussed in Chapters 8 and 9, many people's problems are caused in large measure by the absence of social support systems. In recent years, social workers have increasingly employed interventions that tap natural and formal support networks and develop new ones that can provide vitally needed resources.

Natural Support Systems

Relatives, friends, neighbors, church organizations, clubs, family physicians, and the like comprise natural support systems. People who have roots in a community generally have established helping networks that respond supportively in times of adversity. Refugees and immigrants, however, may totally lack support systems, with the exception of the immediate family. Native Americans and Eskimos who move from reservations or the bush to urban centers may be equally or more isolated, as the gap between their cultures and urban American life may be even greater than it is for immigrants. However, even local people may have weak kinship ties, lack close friends, and have no linkages with neighbors or other potential support groups. Still other clients are homebound and lack access to many of the support systems that would otherwise be available. American newcomers to boomtowns also lack natural support systems, although they may be able to develop them more readily because they do not have to cross cultural barriers or learn a new language.

Knowledge and skills related to mobilizing natural helping networks have increased greatly in recent years. For example, Garbarino, Stocking, and associates (1980) and Ballew (1985) have provided practical guidelines on how to mobilize relatives, neighbors, and friends into support systems to assist practitioners in detecting, preventing, and treating cases of child abuse and neglect. Such support systems are not only valuable but virtually essential because practitioners can spend only limited time with clients, whereas members of support systems can often be available at short notice when crises develop and can perform ongoing monitoring that is impossible for professional people.

Research has also disclosed that neglectful mothers often feel lonely and isolated even though they may reside in neighborhoods regarded as normal in supportiveness (Polansky, Ammons, & Gaudin, 1985). Recognizing this problem, Lovell and Hawkins (1988) developed and evaluated a group intervention to prepare these mothers to expand their personal social networks. The intervention led to increased involvement with professionals but had little effect in expanding other social supports. Based on these findings, the authors recommended that such mothers receive training in social skills aimed at equipping them to meet others, to engage in social conversation and other related social skills.

Other researchers (Miller & Whittaker, 1988) have developed "blended" programs to increase social support for families at risk of maltreating their children. Another effective support program consists of parent cooperatives that have mutual exchanges of baby-sitting services. Such arrangements provide welcome respite for parents otherwise confined by constant responsibilities of caring for children.

Still another natural support system that practitioners can tap in the neighborhoods of many clients is the church. Parishes and congregations are natural ecological structures and as such may offer many resources needed by clients such as a reference group, spiritual stimulation, social activities, recreational programs, home visiting, short-term homemaking when clients are ill, and concrete services for elderly and homebound persons. Joseph and Conrad (1980) have defined the potential resources often available in "parish neighborhood communities," and these resources often are particularly relevant to the needs of immigrant families.

Tapping natural social support networks has proven to be of great value in therapeutic work with varied target groups, including mental health clients (Biegel & Naparstek, 1982; Gottlieb, 1985). Social support systems are especially needed by schizophrenic clients, whose social networks typically are limited to five to six persons, a mere fraction of the numbers in the networks of mentally healthy persons (Crotty & Kulys, 1985). Other client groups for whom mobilizing of social supports has been effective include the homeless (Hutchinson, Searight, & Stretch, 1986), and the elderly (Sauer & Coward, 1985), to name just a few.

In rural settings, where social services tend to be scant, practitioners must become thoroughly familiar with care-giving persons who are a part of communities' natural helping networks. Such indigenous helping persons include welfare workers, grocers, barbers, insurance agents, ministers, civic leaders, schoolteachers, health department nurses, county officials, and the like. By consulting with the welfare worker or leaders of local service clubs, practitioners can also identify other indigenous care-givers whom rural residents turn to because of their reputations for being helpful to people in times of crisis. Conklin (1980) has discussed the use of indigenous care-givers in rural communities. The effectiveness of natural helpers in rural areas has been documented by Patterson et al. (1988). Cohen and Adler (1986) have discussed the role of social network interventions with an inner-city population, and Mitchell (1986) has reported how volunteers can be used to enhance informal social networks.

Although several books have discussed the principles and techniques of *network therapy* (Froland et al., 1981; Whittaker, Garbarino, and associates, 1983; Gottlieb, 1981; and Rueveni, 1979), systematic exploration of the use of social network concepts is still in its infancy. As McIntyre (1986, p. 421) has reminded us, "Current use of network ideas . . . is often more akin to metaphor and analogy than to precise meaning and careful testing of concepts, methods, and measures." McIntyre identifies trends, strengths, and gaps in knowledge about social networks, as well as problems and directions for future work. Schilling, Schinke, and Weatherly (1988) also caution that social workers may be overestimating the potential of support networks and that it is unrealistic to suggest that the problems of homeless adults, runaway youths, and mentally ill persons in our communities, who generally lack social supports, can be remedied by simply tapping the reservoirs of natural social supports, which, in fact, do not exist. Schilling (1987) acknowledges the essential nature of social support systems but warns that adverse consequences may result from inappropriate implementation of support-enhancing interventions. To assist practitioners to use such interventions discriminately, Auslander and Litwin (1987) have developed an analytic paradigm that aids in assessing the appropriateness and efficacy of a given intervention.

Self-Help Groups

Falling between the natural helping systems of families and neighbors and the formal helping systems of social agencies, self-help groups have organizational structures similar to those of fraternal organizations or civic groups. Self-help groups consist of people who share common conditions, experiences, or problematic situations (e.g., obesity, alcoholism, child abuse, minority status, history of mental disorders, being parents of developmentally disabled children, or being single parents) and mutually seek to assist each other to enhance their coping capacities related to their common factors. The help these groups provide is available without charge and is based on the experiences of members rather than professional expertise. Largely self-governing and self-regulating, self-help groups generally have effective communication networks among members that, in addition to regular group meetings, provide opportunities for both telephone and face-to-face contacts. Certain self-help groups that assist members to gain control of problematic behaviors (e.g., Alcoholics Anonymous and Parents Anonymous) encourage members to contact each other when stresses threaten to overpower their controls. Knowing that caring others are available is a source of great support to members, especially early in their involvement with the group (before growth has occurred). Other sources of support from self-help groups include the following:

1. Having a reference group wherein one shares common problems or concerns with others and is accepted by them.

2. Gaining hope based on the knowledge that other members have experienced similar difficulties and are coping (or have coped) successfully with them.

3. Confronting problems and accepting responsibility for them as a result of confrontations by other members.

4. Putting their problems in perspective and applying knowledge and skill derived from the experiences shared by others.

As is apparent from this list, self-help groups can be extremely valuable to members, as attested by countless testimonials of members of groups such as

Alcoholics Anonymous. Research has indicated that a service model for child-abusing parents that includes lay or parent-aide counseling (Cohn, 1979) and Parents Anonymous (Holmes, 1978; Moore, 1983) is somewhat more effective *and* less costly than other alternatives. A similar research study (Galanter, 1988) of psychiatric patients revealed a decline in both symptoms and need for psychiatric treatment after patients joined Recovery Inc., a self-help organization for former mental patients. Lieberman and Videka-Sherman (1986) have reported on a study that documents the positive effects of a self-help group for widows and widowers. The vigor of the self-help movement prompted Vattano (1972) to refer to it as the "power-to-the-people movement."

Other self-help organizations include the National Alliance for the Mentally Ill, which has state chapters for mentally ill persons and their families (see Zipple & Spaniol, 1987); Parents Without Partners (for single parents—see Harris, 1966); Narcotics Anonymous, Compassionate Friends (for bereaved parents); the Naim Conference (for widows); Mended Hearts (for people who have had heart surgery); and Weight Watchers (for people with weight problems—see Stuart, 1977). This list does not include many other local self-help groups that consist of parents of retarded children, compulsive gamblers, disabled persons, and various self-improvement groups.

Because of the significance and value of self-help groups, social workers must be knowledgeable about them and competent in relating to them. For example, in functioning as a broker or case manager social workers need to be knowledgeable about self-help organizations in their community and skillful in making referrals when appropriate. Practitioners also need to be familiar with how self-help groups function so that they can work in

synergy rather than in competition with these programs. A book by Remine, Rice, and Ross (1984) is particularly helpful in this regard.

Still another challenge to social workers is to serve effectively as consultants to self-help groups without diminishing their independent functioning. The primary benefit of self-help groups is that they tap the strengths of group members, fostering independence and self-esteem in the process. Nevertheless, these groups can often fulfill this function even more effectively with periodic input from professional consultants. Coplon and Strull (1983); Mallory (1984); Toseland and Hacker (1982); and Vattano (1984) have described how social workers can interface effectively with self-help groups.

Practitioners can also serve as organizers where resources are sparse and appropriate self-help groups do not exist. By working with clients who demonstrate leadership potential, a practitioner may stimulate them, assisting them as needed, to contact a national or regional self-help organization for the purpose of establishing a local chapter. If a national organization does not exist, the practitioner may serve as a catalyst and consultant in organizing a local group, which necessitates working with selected lay leaders in recruiting members, developing objectives and bylaws (if needed), arranging facilities, planning refreshments, and developing an organizational meeting. During the fledgling stage of the group, the practitioner should maintain a low profile but continue to nurture the group to the extent necessary in achieving its potential for autonomous functioning.

Using Volunteers

Volunteers have long been a resource to social workers for enhancing the environments of clients. Indeed, social work as a profession sprouted from seeds planted by early volunteers—a fact that was acknowledged in a policy statement on volunteers and social service systems made by the delegate assembly of the National Association of Social Workers in 1977 (*NASW News,* 1977). Volunteers are persons who render services to social service agencies and clients without remuneration. The importance of tapping the resources afforded by volunteers greatly expanded in the 1980s as a result of drastic cutbacks in governmental funding of social services. An example is the increased utilization of volunteers to expand the social support networks of clients (Mitchell, 1986).

Volunteers perform a broad spectrum of activities, thereby extending the services delivered by social work agencies. Big Brothers (Royfe, 1960), for example, is a national organization of adult male volunteers who provide one-to-one relationships with male children who do not have fathers in the home. Panzer, Wiesner, and Dickson (1978) have described a similar local program instituted for developmentally disabled children. College students have served as volunteers in providing ongoing relationships with emotionally disturbed children deemed likely to benefit from such relationships (Witkin, 1973). Resourceful social workers have also enlisted high school and college students to tutor children who are doing poorly in school and whose parents lack either the inclination or competence to assist them. Other practitioners have enlisted older neighbors to assist such children and to provide nurturance that is deficient in these children's homes. Such as arrangement not only enriches the lives of children but also meets a need of retired persons to remain contributing members of society.

Volunteers can also perform other significant services, such as preventing child abuse and neglect (Rosenstein, 1978),

serving as mentors to abusing parents (Withey, Anderson, & Lauderdale, 1980), transporting clients to and from hospitals, reading to the blind and to children who require long-term hospitalization, entertaining and visiting with nursing-home patients, and providing companionship to the depressed elderly (Frankle & Gordon, 1983) and to dying patients. Still other volunteers have aided minorities and other disadvantaged persons in securing needed services and concrete resources by serving as interpreters, expediters, and advocates.

Volunteers have also been employed successfully in enhancing the physical environments of clients. Practitioners have worked through churches, youth organizations, service clubs, labor unions, and schools and universities to recruit volunteers to improve homes and yards—one of many potential activities that volunteers can perform to enhance the environments of clients.

Implementing volunteer programs is no simple matter. Indeed, Feinstein and Cavanaugh (1976) maintain that "the dearth of relevant uses of volunteer skills is due not to the volunteers themselves but to the professionals, who, for the most part, are not equipped or willing to deal with them" (p. 14). A crucial task practitioners face in using volunteers is to provide opportunities that are satisfying and growth producing. In addition to this task, implementing volunteer programs requires skills in recruiting, screening, training, placing, supervising, and maintaining positive collaborative relationships between professional staff and volunteers.

Haeuser and Schwartz (1980) maintain that a good volunteer program requires the leadership of a professional volunteer administrator, who should be expert both in clinical service and in management. Schwartz (1984) has compiled numerous essays that deal with the topic of interaction between volunteers and social agencies. Hunt and Paschall (1984) give many guidelines concerned with implementation of volunteer groups employed to improve mental health services. Many of the guidelines are also applicable to other settings.

Formal Support Systems

Numerous types of social agencies and community resources have evolved in response to needs of clients for environmental supports. The Salvation Army, for example, provides food and shelter for short periods of time, and organizations such as the YWCA and senior citizens' centers provide opportunities for social interaction, recreation, and education in crafts and hobbies. The Red Cross provides shelter, food, and medical services to victims of natural disasters, fires, and accidents that affect substantial numbers of people. In addition, various types of hospitals, convalescent homes, residential treatment centers, and correctional institutions provide resources for people who require intensive care or special types of environments. Other formal programs, such as rape crisis centers, have evolved to meet needs of people for specialized forms of support as a result of crises or trauma.

Social agencies can also provide support systems composed of groups of clients who have special needs as a result of shared conditions, problems, or developmental crises that have produced marked stress and/or drastically diminished their support systems (e.g., death, divorce, retirement). Practitioners thus form groups of clients who share these factors in common. These groups thus serve a function of mutual support similar to self-help groups. Growth groups differ from self-help groups in that members are selected and a professional serves as a group leader. Growth groups also differ from self-help groups in that the former may be open-ended or closed-ended, whereas the latter are generally open-ended (closed-ended groups consist of a limited number of selected persons and new members are not admitted to the group—unless by group consensus—after the group is formed).

Growth groups may include many different client populations. Different types of parents' groups are employed to enhance parental functioning in general, to assist abusing parents (Dougherty, 1983; Kruger et al., 1979), and to support and assist parents to cope more effectively with emotionally disturbed children (Rubin, 1978) and autistic children (Samit, Nash, & Meyers, 1980). Single parents (and stepparents) can receive support and assistance in parenting through growth groups. Growth groups are also employed to assist marital partners to strengthen their marriages (Occhetti & Occhetti, 1981) and to enable children to cope more effectively with alcoholic parents (Hawley & Brown, 1981).

Clients who have experienced severe losses or whose environments have been disrupted by stresses associated with major transitions often experience crises that without intervention can produce deterioration. Growth groups often provide timely emotional support and foster effective coping by members. Group interventions thus have been employed successfully with widows (Toth & Toth, 1980), bereaved parents (Soricelli & Utech, 1985), people who are retiring, persons going through divorce (Bonkowski & Wanner-Westly, 1979; Shelton & Nix, 1979; Taylor, 1980), and pregnant teenagers (Barth & Schinke, 1984). Others for whom groups have been employed include families of homocide victims

(Miller, Moore, & Lexius, 1985), adult female victims of childhood sexual abuse (Deighton & McPeek, 1985), elderly clients (Milinsky, 1987), female victims of child maltreatment (Gagliano, 1987), wives who have learned their husbands are gay or bisexual (Auerback & Moser, 1987), and adult male victims of childhood sexual abuse (Bruckner & Johnson, 1987).

Still other vulnerable groups that can benefit through group interventions are the severely ill, physically disabled, handicapped, and developmentally disabled (Carasquillo et al., 1981). Practitioners have effectively used group interventions to assist patients with serious heart problems, cancer patients and their families (Arnowitz et al., 1983; Johnson & Stark, 1980), disabled and handicapped clients (Bender & Wiley, 1982; Lister & Lazar, 1974), and handicapped children (Castle, 1980). And finally, group intervention has been a support system and source of growth for mentally ill clients (Ely, 1985; Walker & McLeod, 1982).

Moving Clients to a Different Environment

This strategy is by far the most drastic one because it involves moving people from familiar environments to ones that range from less familiar to altogether different. Because uprooting people from their usual environments, however undesirable they may be, generally produces trauma in varying degrees, this strategy is employed as a last resort when other less drastic strategies are impracticable or have failed to remedy an intolerable environmental situation. This strategy is thus appropriate only when vital resources are not available or cannot be developed sufficiently early in a given environment to safeguard the safety, health, and well-being of vulnerable clients.

Circumstances that justify employing this strategy include the following:

1. Physical abuse or neglect of children or adolescents.

2. Sexual abuse of children.

3. Physical abuse of women.

4. Abuse of elderly parents.

5. Children who are ungovernable.

6. Clients with unusual needs that demand special care.

7. Loss of housing because of eviction or natural disaster.

Note that the first four situations listed involve removal of clients from existing environments because their health, safety, and/or physical and psychological development are in jeopardy. In the case of children, protective service practitioners carry a grave responsibility in safeguarding the health and safety—indeed the lives—of children at risk. When complaints are received or referrals are made (often by physicians or schoolteachers), these practitioners must carefully assess whether children should remain at home while efforts are made to strengthen the functioning of parents or whether the degree of risk warrants the immediate removal of a child to a temporary shelter home or to a foster home.

When abuse or neglect is flagrant and parents manifest marked deficiencies in providing essential care, the decision to remove children may be clear-cut. In other instances, the decision may be difficult, because deciding what course of action is in the best interest of children is a complex matter. Children have a powerful need for a sense of rootedness, which develops when they live in a predictable, permanent environment where they are accepted and loved. Transplanting them to foster homes is traumatic, and repeated changes from one foster home to another create insecurity, mistrust of others, hostility, and low self-esteem. Because of evidence that severe psychological damage may ensue when children are shifted from one foster home to another, there has been a marked emphasis in recent years on *permanency planning;* that is, planning for children whose social environments have been disrupted so as to provide opportunities that enable them to gain a sense of permanence or belonging to a group of people who are committed to each other. Having a sense of permanence enables children to develop enduring human attachments. Such attachments occur, however, only if certain crucial ingredients exist in the relationships between children and parents (or surrogate parents). These ingredients include continuity (ongoing predictive availability of parents to respond to children's needs), stability (absence of major disruption or stress in the parent-child relationship), and mutuality of interaction that reinforces the importance of child to parent and vice versa (Hess, 1982). Permanence is also vital because it provides a framework within which children gradually absorb a value system and develop a sense of identity. A comprehensive discussion of the concepts and methods of permanency planning is presented in a book by Maluccio, Fein, and Olmstead (1986). Seltzer and Bloksberg (1987) have also discussed permanency planning and its effects on foster children.

Because of the importance of a sense of permanence to children, child welfare workers strive, whenever feasible, to retain children in their homes by working with parents and family systems to reduce stresses upon parents, to modify dysfunc-tional behavior of children, to enhance family relationships, and to assist parents to cope with stress without violence. Compher (1983) has described a continuum of services practitioners can provide to families to prevent the necessity of child placement. When it is necessary to move children to other environments, child welfare workers should work with the child and family to reunite them as soon as feasible. Research (Pike et al., 1977; Stein & Gambrill, 1977), in fact, has indicated that a substantial percentage of children can be returned to their parents following intensive social work interventions. To enhance family functioning to the extent that abused children can remain or return to their homes generally requires multiple interventions and a multidisciplinary approach that, in addition to social workers, may include physicians, judges, public health nurses, police, clergy, mental health professionals, school personnel, and early childhood educators.

Because of the many disciplines and services essential to successful interventions, practitioners should assume the role of case manager in linking children and their families to relevant service providers. The importance of actively fulfilling this role is emphasized by disquieting findings reported by Turner (1984) to the effect that children who were successfully reunited with their parents following foster care received extensive community services, whereas children who had to be removed again from their parents' care following reunification received much less service. The findings of another study of child placement (Rapp, 1982) also suggest that child care practitioners need to consider and utilize community resources more fully in serving the needs of children and their families.

Despite the trend toward keeping children in their homes, it is often essential to remove children at least temporarily to protect them from continued abuse and/ or neglect. Child welfare workers are responsible for acting in the best interest of children and must take decisive action when recurrent abuse appears to be a danger. Accordingly, protective service workers must often place children in shelter homes or foster homes. How do practitioners assess the likelihood of recurrent abuse? According to federally funded research based on 11 separate child abuse and neglect projects:

The single best predictor of reincidence appeared to be the severity of the case at intake. In other words, clients with a previous history of abuse or neglect, clients who had severely abused or neglected their children immediately prior to treatment regardless of their previous history, and clients whose households contained a wide range of stress factors that apparently triggered the maltreatment were more likely again to abuse or neglect their children severely while in treatment.

(Cohn, 1979, p. 515)

The responsibility of protective services workers to assess the possibility of recurrence and to monitor cases closely is further underscored by the finding from the same study that "Of 1,724 parents studied, 30 percent were reported to have severely abused or neglected their children while in treatment" (p. 514). Clearly, practitioners must guard against being overly zealous about not removing children temporarily from their homes.

Acknowledging the "enormous benefit" of the current emphasis of not separating children from their families, Wilkes (1980) cautions that "the attack on unwarranted separation of children from their families has, however, had some destructive effects on the handling of warranted separations" (p. 27). Wilkes cites several destructive effects, which revolve around the danger that practitioners may lose their objectivity and fail to

remove children who would benefit from being separated from their parents. Although experts agree that separation of children from parents should be only temporary when parents manifest motivation, commitment, and capacity to improve their functioning as parents, some parents' commitment is only intellectual, and other parents are likely to remain unfit.

When natural parents fail to respond adequately to consistent efforts to assist them or lack the capacity to be competent parents, child welfare workers should work toward arranging other permanency planning outcomes. According to the Adoption Assistance and Child Welfare Act of 1980 (P.L. 96–272), other options in order of preference are adoption, guardianship, and long-term foster care. Analysis of outcomes of child welfare services under permanency planning, however, indicates that these services have achieved only moderate success. In their review of research on the results of each kind of placement, Barth and Berry (1987) found that reunification of children with birth families "fails most often to be free from abuse and to yield developmental well-being" (p. 82). An implication of this disquieting finding is that services to reunified families should be more intensive and longer in duration, extending for as long as two to three years.

The findings on outcomes of older-child adoptions provide a pleasant contrast to those of family reunification, causing Barth and Berry to conclude that this option appears to be a highly favorable form of placement. Little is known about outcomes involving the guardianship option, but findings regarding long-term foster care are more favorable than had been anticipated. Research evidence indicates that this option does not preclude lifelong attachments. Many children in foster care maintain contact with their siblings and more than one-half relocate and live with one of their birth parents following foster-care placement.

Irrespective of the placement option employed, adults who function as parents need not only support services but formal training in parenting skills. Based on a review of parent training programs employed in child welfare, Berry (1988) concluded that actual training often was not provided and that disruption in placements could likely be reduced by affording such badly needed training to natural parents, adoptive parents, and foster care parents.

Still other options are available when children must be removed from their homes. One such option is family-centered group care (Finkelstein, 1980). This intervention involves placing a child in a substitute familylike environment but maintaining the focus on the problem family, with the goal of permanently discharging the child as rapidly as possible. Treatment is aimed at enhancing family functioning by opening communication in the family system. Parents visit the residential center at least twice weekly, learning how to communicate more productively and how to gain control of their youngster.

Recognizing that permanency planning options are sometimes impractical for older youths in foster care, child welfare practitioners have increasingly employed still another option—preparing youth for independent living. Trends and needs in programming for independent living have been discussed by Cook (1988) and an entire issue[1] of *Child Welfare* has been devoted to vital topics relevant to this option.

Sexual abuse of children (incest) also often warrants temporary removal of children and/or abusing parents from the home while essential changes in the functioning of the family are undertaken. Numerous articles concerned with sexual abuse have been published.[2] Anderson and Shafer (1979) have described an interdisciplinary approach to intervening in cases of child sexual abuse that involves using the authority of the court to separate the abused child from the parent (often by placing the parent in jail). During the period of separation, the parents and child are treated separately. Family reunification occurs in planned phases, and family therapy is employed as the primary mode of intervention. As with physical abuse, close monitoring is essential in these cases to protect children from recurrences of sexual abuse.

Abuse and neglect are by no means limited to children. During the past decade, social service practitioners have "discovered" that physical and sexual abuse of adolescents also occurs. Concerned about this group, social workers have attempted to develop programs responsive to their needs. Whereas with children the ultimate goal of intervention generally is to return them to an improved familial environment, with adolescents the goal is often to assist them to make a stable adjustment outside the home. According to Garbarino (1980), "Many social service practitioners believe that mistreated adolescents may be better off in the short run, and even in the long run, if these youths have a safe and developmentally enhancing alternative to strife-torn homes" (p. 123). (Garbarino and others [1986] have written an informative book

---

[1] *Child Welfare*, LXVII, November/December, 1988.

[2] An entire issue of *Social Casework* (68, Feb. 1987) has been devoted to child sexual abuse. Conte has also written a concise overview of child sexual abuse: Conte, J.R. (1987) Child sexual abuse. *Encyclopedia of Social Work*, Vol. I. Silver Spring, Maryland: National Association of Social Workers, 255–260.

aimed at assisting practitioners to understand families at risk for maltreating adolescents.) When it is not feasible to reduce family strife to tolerable limits and to increase family support to adolescents, "runaway" houses and group homes can be used as a substitute environment. To help abused youth, Garbarino also recommends that networks of services be established, including youth hot lines, self-help groups, volunteers, schools, and youth-serving agencies.

Battered Wives

Changes to new environments may also be required when adults are abused. As with abuse of adolescents, society has largely ignored wife-beating until recent years. Increasingly, however, communities are developing programs for battered women that include temporary shelter, legal services, financial aids, and personal counseling, as well as assertiveness training. Roberts (1981) has written a useful book based on surveys of crisis services, including shelters, for battered women and their children.

Although sheltering wives from serious injury or worse is a vital measure in crisis situations, effective treatment of wife battering must be multidimensional. Battered wives need to engage in long-term planning that considers the viability of their marriages, available resources, and living arrangements after they leave the shelters. Moreover, they need to explore their patterns of interaction, possible low expectations of marriage, and possible psychological problems. Roberts (1984) has edited a book that delineates intervention strategies and treatment programs for battered wives and their families. Walker (1984) has also detailed the complexities of the battering syndrome.

The problem of battered wives must be viewed from a systems perspective to be fully comprehended. Dynamics that impel the male batterer must be understood and modified. Male batterers often lack confidence and are unassertive, resorting to violence when their tenuous self-esteem is threatened. Interventions aimed at strengthening control of anger, such as we detail in Chapter 18, are helpful, especially when implemented in the context of the marital relationship (i.e., including both partners in the treatment program). Treatment programs for husbands and wives have been delineated by Edleson (1984), Neidig and Friedman (1984), and Sonkin, Martin, and Walker (1985).

It is also important to consider battering in a societal context, for as Davis (1987) has clarified, society has historically tended to foster the sexist view that men have a right to dominate their wives and to resort to violent means if necessary to ensure that right. To some extent, this unrealistic and unjust belief may be embedded in the psyches of both sexes, thereby contributing to the phenomenon of wife battering.

Abuse of the Elderly

The picture is much less bright for elderly persons who are abused by noninstitutional care-givers, usually their adult children. Awareness of the citizenry about abuse of the elderly is limited, and pertinent laws, policies, and programs have not yet evolved. When faced with a choice of leaving their children's home, nearly the only option available to elderly parents who are unable to care for themselves fully is institutional care—a grim and unacceptable prospect to many such persons. However, one promising alternative, still in its infancy and unavailable in the majority of communities, is foster care for elderly persons. Social workers can play a major role in implementing adult foster care by recruiting and training foster parents, by matching elderly persons to foster homes, and, after placing them, by maintaining continued interest in elderly persons and their problems (Sherman & Newman, 1979). Such programs, of course, are feasible only when governmental policies support them.

Social workers, of course, should expand their knowledge about abuse of the elderly and advocate policies that protect the safety and dignity of this vulnerable group. Excellent references on this topic include a review of the literature by Giordano and Giordano (1984), an article on issues for the practitioner (Bookin & Dunkle, 1985), and a book by Quinn and Tomita (1986).

Changes to Therapeutic Environments

Practitioners also find it necessary to move clients from one environment to another when clients manifest emotional disturbances that warrant intensive professional care or behavior disorders that require a controlled environment. Residential group homes, staffed by professionals, often are employed with groups of children and adolescents. The goal of such programs is to return children to their homes whenever possible, and toward this end, certain programs involve parents as *treatment partners* (Krona, 1980). Programs vary according to the type of youth and the degree of interest and involvement on the part of parents. When parents manifest little motivation or competence for providing suitable environments for their children, group homes have been used successfully as alternatives to institutions. Gordon (1978) has described one such program where the professionals and residents govern the facility by "participatory democracy"—

that is, they and the teenagers jointly run the house (p. 362). Mutual respect is cultivated by the staff, and the residents gradually turn to the staff and to each other for emotional support much as children turn to parents and siblings in healthy, functioning, intact homes. The residents thus gradually gain a feeling of permanency in this environment. Still another type of residential treatment center for severely disturbed adolescents that employs modeling and cognitive-behavioral strategies within a family-style environment has been described by Rosen, Peterson, and Walsh (1980). Whittaker (1979) has also written an authoritative book concerned with residential care for disturbed youth.

For adolescents who pose a threat to the safety of others, secure facilities are essential. The current trend is to place delinquent adolescents in alternate community youth centers rather than in large state institutions, as was the practice until recent years. The community centers ideally should provide educational, recreational, and social opportunities as well as therapeutic group experiences that enable residents to engage in problem solving, skill development, and other growth experiences. In addition, programs at such centers should embody work with families aimed at enhancing functioning to the extent that youth can be discharged to their homes whenever feasible. A major advantage of community youth centers is that they are generally located within reasonably short distances from the families of youths, making it possible to maintain close contact.

Special environments are often required for severely emotionally disturbed adults. Many general hospitals and community mental health centers have psychiatric wards, making it possible for patients to receive treatment within their communities. The thrust of such programs is to return patients to their homes as rapidly as possible and to avoid the trauma and stigma of placing them in large state institutions geographically isolated from society. Some patients require care for longer periods than community facilities can provide, necessitating hospitalization in larger state institutions. Even in the latter facilities, however, the orientation is to return patients to their local communities as rapidly as possible.

Environments in state mental institutions have been improved markedly over the past few decades. Efforts are made to provide privacy for patients; and programs offer opportunities to work, to socialize, to engage in recreation, and to participate in skill-development activities, group therapy, and patient councils that are involved in governance of such institutions. Efforts are also made to involve relatives of patients in the treatment program so that patients can be released to an enhanced family environment whenever possible. However, some families of chronic mental patients lack the resources or commitment to provide care for them, requiring that other environmental arrangements be made. Sheltered environments, such as halfway houses, often are employed to assist patients in returning to their communities. Nursing homes also are employed for patients who cannot live independently with their families. A relatively new and attractive resource for chronic mental patients is adult foster care similar to that previously described for elderly patients (Miller, 1977).

Still another situation that warrants arranging for people to move to different environments involves geographical isolation that precludes people from relating meaningfully to others. Such a circumstance is conducive to becoming depressed, for interaction with significant others is a powerful human need. Asimos (1979) reports how members of a group of suicidal persons assisted a widow who lived in an austere and isolated environment to move to accommodations that afforded opportunities for meeting and interacting with people. Her depression not only lifted, but she remarried within a few months! Wetzel and Redmond (1980) have also reported the significance of environmental factors in contributing to depression.

Physical factors sometimes dictate a change in environment. Clients with respiratory disorders may be at risk in environments that are high in air pollution. Other environments may pose problems in sanitation, have inadequate heating or cooling facilities, or pose hazards to the health and safety of children and other vulnerable persons. Some families may be crowded into apartments that lack privacy and adequate sleeping arrangements. It is sometimes possible to remedy certain adverse circumstances by exerting pressure on landlords or governmental officials, but even at best, some situations remain grossly deficient in resources. In such instances, changes in environment may be the only viable alternative.

Using Case Management

The role of case manager, more than any other direct practice role, entails work at the interface between clients and their environments. The role has rapidly evolved to a central one in direct practice in response to the rapid expansion of vulnerable client groups who otherwise would not receive essential resources and services because they lack the physical mobility, mental ability, knowledge of resources, experience, maturity, verbal skills, or assertiveness required to avail themselves of needed resources. Referring to one such vulnerable group, deinstitutionalized chronic psychiatric patients, both McCreath (1984) and Ely (1985) have documented that it is common to find such patients with vital needs that are unmet because appropriate agencies are not providing the services or because clients have not made their needs known. The consequences are suffering and increased vulnerability of clients to deterioration in functioning. The same can and does occur with other vulnerable groups, which we discuss later.

Vulnerable groups in need of case management typically require extensive services and resources, including those provided by systems of health care, mental health, rehabilitation, education, child protection, housing, employment, and other related systems. Because of the pervasive needs of these clients, it is vital that one of the service providers, typically a social worker, be designated as case manager. Such an arrangement affixes responsibility for planning and orchestrating the delivery of services in a systematic and timely manner. Moreover, designating a case manager empowers one person to arrange meetings with or otherwise communicate with other agencies to identify additional needed services, to avoid duplication of services, to develop unified strategies for dealing with difficult and/or manipulative clients, and to avoid working at cross purposes.

Social workers are uniquely qualified to serve as case managers by reason of their knowledge of community resources, their skills in communication and advocacy, and the purposes and objectives of the profession as defined in Chapter 1. To refresh your memory, the central objec-

tives include (1) helping people to obtain resources, (2) facilitating interactions between individuals and others in their environment, and (3) making organizations responsive to people. Serving as case manager thus is consonant with the spirit of social work, and practitioners should willingly assume if not actively seek this role.

In carrying out the case management function, practitioners actually perform their roles somewhat differently according to the type of setting and role definitions within specific agencies. In some community mental health settings, practitioners may function as therapists and as case managers to the same clients (Johnson & Rubin, 1983; Lamb, 1982). By contrast, as members of a hospital interdisciplinary team that plans discharge of psychiatric patients, practitioners may supervise paraprofessionals who actually carry out the role of case managers (Altman, 1982). Interestingly, a nationwide survey (Bernstein, 1981) of case managers in 15 community-support projects revealed that 60 percent of the case managers were trained therapists. Still another survey of directors of mental health centers in Georgia disclosed that 75 percent of the directors expected case managers to perform therapy (Bagarozzi & Kurtz, 1983).

To work effectively in linking clients with resources, case managers maintain close contact with other service providers, negotiating, coordinating services, and ensuring that essential linkages are in place and that services are delivered in a timely manner. To perform these functions a case manager must have extensive knowledge of community resources, rights of clients, and policies and procedures of various agencies and must be skillful in mediation and advocacy.

In addition to conversing extensively with service providers, case managers who perform dual functions must be skillful in direct work with clients. This requires skills in assessing clients' needs and strengths and in enabling clients to control their lives to the fullest extent possible. Based on the assessment, the case manager and the client negotiate specific and reasonable goals that can be achieved within a short period of time. As in other forms of direct practice, the case manager engages clients in mutually delineating tasks essential to goal attainment and reaches explicit agreements about who will do what and when they will do it. To orchestrate tasks related to utilizing resources outside the agency, the case manager must also engage all involved parties in planning task accomplishment. This explanation of the case manager's functions is necessarily limited. For a more detailed explanation we recommend publications by Roberts-De Gennaro (1987) and Weil, Karls, and associates (1985).

Although the needs of vulnerable groups served by case managers are generally pervasive, they vary from one group to another and even within broad client groups. (Recall, for example, from Chapter 9 that homeless people are a heterogenous population with widely varying needs.) Space limitations preclude discussing the needs of each group, but in the following we identify vulnerable groups and relevant references: foster children and multideficit families at risk for child maltreatment and/or neglect (Ballew, 1985; Compher, 1983; Turner, 1984), chronically mentally ill and disabled (McCreath, 1984; Miller, 1983; Rapp & Chamberlain, 1985), physically disabled (Akabas, Fine, & Yasser, 1982), chronically ill (Harris & Bergman, 1987), frail elderly (Fauri & Bradford, 1986), homeless (Brickner et al., 1985; Bean, Stefl, & Howe, 1987; Phillips et al., 1988), and teenage parents (Brindis, Barth, & Loomis, 1987).

Enhancing Interactions between Organizations and Institutions

Effectively meeting clients' needs often requires concurrent efforts of several organizations and disciplines, and close collaboration is essential. Joint planning, clear definitions of roles, and ongoing dialogue among the principals are required to avoid confusion, monitor progress, and maintain adequate working relationships. These processes are facilitated by case management, as previously noted.

Effective interaction among organizations is also often needed to enhance aspects of the environment of a single client or family or of a group of clients that share a common condition. In the first instance, a practitioner may enhance a child's school environment by assuming a *mediating* role between the home and school. The practitioner may assist the parents to work in closer collaboration with the teacher in enhancing the child's functioning in the school. In the second instance, a practitioner may join with other health care professionals in raising the standards for nursing homes (Coulton, 1981), residential centers, or day-care centers. Practitioners may also work with public officials to enhance transportation for the elderly, recreation and education for the developmentally disabled, and so on. Marburg (1983) has reported on successful efforts in establishing effective treatment networks to meet the mental health needs of Native Americans.

Still another area that requires effective interaction among organizations involves assisting clients in making major transitions from one environment to another. For example, when clients are discharged from mental or correctional institutions to the community or to their families, provisions for continued service and support are essential. Otherwise, the client and/or the family or institution may be unprepared or unable to cope with the stress of the adjustments required, and the transition may result in early and traumatic failure for all parties. Ongoing liaison, joint discharge planning, and case management facilitate such transitions.

Improving Institutional Environments

We have previously referred to a few measures that have been taken to enhance the quality of life in state mental institutions, residential treatment centers, and group homes for youth. In this section, we briefly consider ways of enhancing three major facets of institutional environments—namely, staff, program, and physical facilities.

Staff, of course, are the heart of an institution's environment. When staff are dedicated, caring, responsive to residents' or patients' needs, and congenial with each other, the institutional environment tends to be warm and conducive to growth and well-being on the part of all concerned. By contrast, when staff are impersonal, cool, and abrasive and interact with residents no more than is necessary, an institution's atmosphere tends to be sterile, cold, and conducive to withdrawal, deterioration, and low morale. Selecting staff who are warm, accepting, and genuinely interested in helping others is the first step in developing a supportive institutional environment. Such persons play a key role in fostering trust and risking from clients.

The program of an institution is also crucial. Stimulating, constructive, and growth-promoting programs tend to enhance the functioning of clients, whereas custodial care that fosters idleness produces the opposite effects. The introduction in the 1950s of socioenvironmental programs in mental institutions contributed to the dramatic results in eliminating wards populated by regressed patients, most of whom were regarded as hopeless.

An important factor in institutional programming involves the extent to which residents can exercise choice and control in their daily living. When people have little control over what happens to them, they tend to become helpless, hopeless, and depressed. To enhance choice and control, progressive institutions foster democratic participation in governance of the institution to the extent that such is feasible. Mental hospitals and correctional institutions thus often have ward or unit councils through which residents have input into decision-making processes. Even some nursing homes have resident councils that foster choice. Mercer and Kane (1979), in fact, have reported a study indicating that nursing home patients in an experimental group who were given choices in caring for a plant and participating in a resident council made improvements beyond a control group in reduction of hopelessness, increased physical activity, and psychosocial functioning.

Other aspects of institutional programs should involve education for youth, intellectual stimulation for adults, training opportunities for prisoners, social skill development programs for residents with deficiencies, and opportunities for social interaction. Art, music, and dance therapies have also been described by numerous authors as methods of fostering expression and creativity in institutions. Kelen (1980) described a study involving an environmental intervention with nursing home patients that involved teaching them to write and appreciate poetry. Patients selected to participate in the experimental intervention manifested increased levels of well-being and self-expression over those who did not.

Other programs employed to enrich activities within nursing homes include having volunteers visit with lonely patients and provide entertainment. Cooley, Ostendorf, and Bickerton (1979) have described an innovative program for Native Americans in nursing homes that involves bringing in leaders, youth, and publications from the reservation monthly to overcome the isolation of these patients and to provide linkages to their native culture. According to these authors, this program has greatly enriched the lives of these people.

The last major factor involved in enhancing institutional environments involves physical facilities and the use of space. Accommodations that foster social interaction and yet permit privacy are highly desirable. For ambulatory residents, a leisure room with television and various games fosters social interaction and constructive activity. Likewise, facilities that permit vigorous physical activity are essential in correctional institutions.

In nursing homes and hospitals, it is desirable to locate patients close to a window so that they can view the outside world. When patients share rooms, they should be permitted to choose roommates with whom they are compatible. Few things can be more demoralizing than occupying limited space with people who wear on one's nerves. In matching patients in both hospitals and nursing homes, it is also important to respect the rights of nonsmokers. Obviously, many other factors come into play in matching roommates, and perfect matches are seldom achieved. Still, practitioners should be sensitive to patients' needs and should be patients' advocates with administra-

tive staff when mismatches adversely affect their well-being.

Empowering Clients

Certain clients, including vulnerable groups whom case managers serve, are unable to avail themselves of essential environmental resources because of a sense of powerlessness. Just as case managers seek to empower their clients by assisting them to exercise control over their lives to the fullest extent possible, other practitioners should attempt to empower clients who manifest powerlessness for other varied reasons. By empowering we mean enabling clients to gain the capacity to interact with the environment in ways that enhance their need gratification, well-being, and satisfaction. To gain a sense of power, of course, requires that essential resources be available in the environment. Moreover, a sense of power is closely linked to a favorable self-image, strong self-esteem, self-confidence, and high morale. These attributes, however, are reciprocally influenced by the quality of the environment. Nutritive environments that produce strong goodness of fit between people's needs and corresponding resources foster these positive attributes. Conversely, poor goodness of fit caused by major environmental deficiencies tends to foster powerlessness, helplessness, low self-esteem, and depression.

Groups of people who often manifest powerlessness in coping with the environment include the poor and oppressed; immigrants and refugees; minority groups; persons with addictions; groups who are stigmatized and discriminated against or otherwise denied full access to societal resources; and the vulnerable groups previously identified who require case management, a major method of empowerment. Assisting these and other clients who manifest powerlessness to develop their latent powers and to exert these powers to obtain needed resources is the goal of empowerment.

Strategies of empowerment involve teaching clients about the dynamics of power and about the resource systems germane to their needs. Other strategies include assisting clients, families, and groups to discover and employ their strengths, to supplant negative and distorted self-perceptions with more realistic ones (see Chapter 18), to expect more for themselves, to learn about and to assert their rights, to develop essential social skills, to create alliances, to build coalitions, to overcome organizational barriers (see Chapter 20), and to engage in political action (Pinderhughes, 1983, p. 334). Practitioners often join clients in action-oriented strategies, thereby modeling skills that clients vicariously learn. Still other interventions that empower clients are using self-help groups, forming support groups, and using case management. In the following we illustrate some of these strategies as employed with two groups of clients urgently in need of empowerment.

Empowering People with AIDS

People with AIDS experience stigmatization in our society to the extent of being shamed, shunned, and denied access to resources and emotional support when they critically need such resources. Further, "AIDS has become associated with horrifying negative pictures of incapacitation, abandonment, rejection, hatred, physical and mental deterioration, and deformity" (Haney, 1988, p. 251). These perceptions have a forceful impact on people with AIDS and disempower them by disconnecting them from loved ones and obliterating previous sources of self-

esteem and satisfaction such as work activities, social interaction, physical appearance, recreational activities, plans for the future, hopes, and dreams. In addition to suffering these severe losses people with AIDS tend to experience isolation, alienation, and aloneness, sometimes going into hiding and avoiding medical treatment.

Patrick Haney (1988), who died of AIDS early in 1988, left behind a legacy of guidelines for empowering people with AIDS. The following discussion is based on his article, which was published just a few months after his death.

An important step in empowering people with AIDS (and others who feel powerless) is to modify the mindset of being a victim. Perceiving oneself as a victim fosters passivity and a sense of helplessness. As one anonymous person with AIDS confided to Haney (1988):

> Not buying into the victim mindset is keeping me alive. . . . At this time in my illness I am not helpless and I am anything but passive in dealing with it. I can look around and I see incredibly courageous men who inspire me with their strength. These men continue to defy the odds and say no to AIDS. They give me hope. They give me strength.
>
> (p. 252)

To assist people with AIDS to avoid or to relinquish the victim mindset, practitioners themselves must eschew the belief that people with AIDS are victims. Rather, they are people with AIDS who have the capacity to continue to find meaning and satisfactions in their lives.

Another way of empowering people with AIDS is to focus more on opportunities for making the most of a bad situation and to focus less on the fatalistic aspects of the disease. This does not mean denying the very real and tragic aspects of having AIDS. It is a reality, however, that the life expectancy of people with AIDS has increased substantially over the past few years. Further, it is empowering to focus on making the most of living and not dwelling on dying. In this regard Haney's account of his personal experience is informative and helpful:

Some of the positive consequences I have experienced . . . include learning to accept my limitations, learning to cope by getting in touch with my strengths, experiencing a clarity of purpose; learning to live one day at a time; learning to focus on the good in my life here and now; and the incredibly moving experience of having complete support and love from my family, friends, lover, people I hardly know, and sometimes even complete strangers.

(p. 252)

The importance of emotional support for people with AIDS cannot be overestimated. If the person with AIDS lacks family and friends who are supportive, social workers must assist them to find people who can provide that support and must, themselves, be caring and supportive. Social workers can also participate in developing support groups, which Haney describes as "incredibly potent." He attributed his overcoming his preoccupation with a "death is inevitable" mindset to participation in such a group:

I overrode my fears and I'm thankful I did. I met two other persons with AIDS who had been living with their illness for almost three years. These two men were joking, laughing and having a good time. Here were two men with a supposedly fatal disease acting as if nothing were wrong. They were acting like a couple of well people, which really eroded the negative mindset I had. It was the beginning of my learning to cope. . . . I found a place where I belonged.

(p. 252)

We cannot do justice to Haney's suggestions in this short space and recommend

that you read his brief article. It is significant to note that he found meaning and purpose in his shortened life by founding an AIDS information and referral service and by establishing a support network entitled the Persons With AIDS Coalition. Other formal support networks that employ volunteers have been developed in large cities that have substantial numbers of people with AIDS. Strategies that sustain and support workers and volunteers have been discussed by Lopez and Getzel (1987), who also provide valuable information about the disease, its impact upon people, and issues and challenges faced by professional workers and volunteers.

Empowering people with AIDS also requires work with communities aimed at mobilizing various groups, educating community residents, developing service networks, and coordinating services. Case managers can perform a valuable role in ensuring continuity of care for people with AIDS. Rounds (1988a) has discussed implications of developing resources for people with AIDS in rural communities. Honey (1988) has written a similar article that addresses critical issues related to meeting the needs of people with AIDS who live in the inner city of large urban centers.

Empowering Immigrants and Refugees

As immigrants and refugees are transplanted into an alien society, they may experience a sense of powerlessness, generally after the initial excitement wanes and the realization sets in that hopes and dreams may be unattainable. Many factors contribute to the sense of powerlessness, including "language barriers; unfamiliarity with American customs, rules, and norms; subtle discrimination and prejudice against minorities in society; and most important the loss of social support networks, status, roots, and the 'connectedness' that are found in the native environment'' (Hirayama & Cetingok, 1988, p. 42). Moreover, normative interpersonal behaviors from their native culture, such as obedience, acceptance, loyalty, deference to authority, and cooperation, may not serve them well in a culture that prizes assertion, persuasion, candor, and confrontation.

Initial efforts to empower immigrants and refugees typically involve assisting these people to meet basic needs for the necessities of life. One can hardly have a sense of power if one lacks adequate shelter, clothing, food, health care, and money to pay for ongoing necessities. Social workers thus initially provide concrete assistance in locating housing, clothing, bedding, jobs, and temporary income until families can provide for themselves.

Empowering immigrants and refugees also requires teaching them about the majority culture, including facts about housing, transportation, shopping, gaining employment, and banking. Empowering also requires teaching them about societal institutions and resources including health care, education, community services, communication media, pertinent laws, government, political processes, and the like. Another aspect of empowerment entails learning about rights and developing skills in communicating with employers, health care providers, grocers, teachers, neighbors, and so forth. Still another vital aspect involves assisting these people to build social networks of friends, both within and outside of their ethnic reference groups. In this regard, members of pertinent ethnic groups who have earlier successfully adapted to American culture often are excellent resources in assisting immigrants and refugees "to learn the ropes" (Cameron & Talavera, 1976). When such persons are not available, other public-spirited persons (older people are an excellent resource) can often be recruited to befriend, teach, and advocate for refugees and immigrants. Social workers can also empower these people by assisting them and/or joining them in alliances and coalitions aimed at breaking down organizational barriers to the provision of needed resources.

Other ways of empowering Asian immigrants and their families have been discussed by Hirayama and Cetingok (1988). Solomon (1976) has written about ways of empowering black people in oppressed communities.

Developing New Resources

In the preceding sections, we have identified numerous resources and interventions that practitioners employ to enrich the environments of clients. However, it is important to keep in mind that these resources have evolved only gradually through the efforts of dedicated people who have recognized the needs of fellow human beings and have exercised leadership in organizing other concerned people to bring needed resources to fruition. Many of these resources are not available in a large number of communities, especially smaller ones. In fact, rural areas, emerging communities, and boomtowns usually have a dearth of resources. Moreover, as physical environments change, technology advances, and political and social circumstances relentlessly change, social workers are constantly confronted with the need to organize new resources in response to existing and evolving needs of people. For example, during the past decade homelessness, violence in the home, increasing numbers of people with AIDS, domestic hunger (Brown, 1988), and crises caused by farmers losing their farms have emerged as major social problems.

Organizing efforts to develop new resources are indicated when it is apparent that significant numbers of people within given ecological boundaries (e.g., neighborhood, community, institutions, ward of a hospital, or parish) have important needs for which matching resources are not available. For example, in rapidly expanding communities, women may be confined and lack social and recreational opportunities (Gaylord, 1979); youth may not have access to recreational facilities or programs; adult males may lack opportunity for recreation other than going to bars; and single parents may lack access to day-care programs—to name just a few needs. As a result of these deficiencies, the following social problems typically occur in boomtowns: the incidence of depression among women is high; delinquency skyrockets; rape occurs with alarming frequency; alcoholism and prostitution are rampant; and child abuse and family breakdown occur at high levels.

To prevent or at least to reduce the incidence of such problems, practitioners face the challenge of developing support systems for women, establishing recreational programs for people of all ages, developing indigenous networks to prevent and monitor child abuse, establishing rape crisis programs, developing adult education programs, developing neighborhood support networks, and so on. Practitioners must work closely with existing social service agencies, enlist indigenous leaders in the community, organize task groups that consist of vulnerable persons and advocates, work with elected public officials and private industry, and establish lobbies to influence state legislators when laws or public funds are needed.

The need to organize people and to mobilize resources is by no means limited to rapidly expanding communities. Re-

sources for certain vulnerable groups may be woefully inadequate even in large urban communities. It is in large urban areas, in fact, where social workers and clients have been most involved in mobilizing innovative and vitally needed resources. The problem of developing resources for the homeless in our urban communities, for example, is a challenge of the first magnitude, as we discuss later.

Practitioners play an enabling role in organizing activities, working *with* rather than *for* clients. This is an important point for the following reasons:

1. The chance of achieving successful results is far greater when clients participate actively in formulating and implementing plans. Because they directly experience the impact of deficient resources, clients can provide valuable information and can often present their plight to responsible authorities in dramatic and forceful ways. Furthermore, there is strength in numbers. City officials are more likely to be impressed at public meetings when a large number of well-organized people appear to present their case than when only a few social workers and a handful of clients appear.

2. Clients are more likely to use, publicize, value, protect, and enhance resources when they have participated in planning and developing them.

3. Resources are more likely to have optimal fit for consumers when consumers have participated in developing them.

4. Clients gain a sense of power when they realize they participate in improving their circumstances. By asserting their needs, they counter the devastating sense of powerlessness that pervades many of the disadvantaged people in our society. They learn that they *do* count and *do* possess power to shape their destiny (O'Connell, 1978).

5. By joining others in working toward a common goal, people gain a sense of unity and belonging. An action group becomes a support network that has intrinsic value to members apart from its express purpose.

As implied in the preceding list, the challenge of developing new resources often entails advocacy and social action, topics we discuss later.

Resources for the Homeless

Of the vulnerable groups, homeless persons perhaps have the greatest needs, although the homeless are a heterogeneous group, as we noted in Chapter 4. Common to all the homeless, however, are needs for shelter and food. In addition, certain homeless people need health care, mental health treatment, medications, jobs, employment counseling, rehabilitation services, and social support.

Resources needed vary according to causes of homelessness, which vary substantially from one community to another. Interestingly, data for 13 cities compiled by the U.S. Conference of Mayors indicated that about two-thirds of the homeless in those cities were minority persons, of whom almost 52 percent were blacks (First, Roth, & Arewa, 1988). Analysis of the data compiled led to the conclusion that homelessness among minority persons was associated with joblessness, the lack of marketable skills for many minority youth, and expensive or nonexistent low-income housing. Providing shelter, food, and other necessities for this group is vital, but a long-range solution requires social planning efforts at federal, state, and local levels. Beginning efforts have been made but the problem has not been adequately addressed at higher levels of government. Clearly, policy decisions must address root causes of the problem and must consider issues related to social justice and equality. In this regard data from interviews with homeless persons in Ohio indicate these people "... want to and can be employed if given access to the job market. Social policy efforts should target the employment of these individuals and individuals who are marginally employed and at risk of becoming homeless" (First et al., 1988, p. 123).

Low incomes and insufficient low-cost housing cause homelessness for whites as well as people of color. The federal housing voucher program (which provides supplementary income earmarked for housing) has assisted over 115,000 families in our nation to afford more adequate housing (Office of Policy Development, 1988). An excellent example of social planning, this program is a major step in the right direction, but the large numbers of people who remain homeless indicate the need for additional programs that address the problem of joblessness and marginal employment opportunities.

People who are chronically mentally ill or who are substance abusers also comprise a major group of the homeless. In addition to food and shelter, many of these persons urgently need health care, mental health services, medications, and sometimes psychiatric evaluations and short-term hospitalization. Some of these people, however, are fiercely independent, distrustful, and wary of becoming involved in health care and mental health systems. Community-sponsored shelter programs, subsidized by funding from mental health programs, often employ staff who are skillful in engaging such persons through informal interaction and by using case management skills to connect these people with resources relevant to their needs. Fortunately, some community leaders, in concert with professionals and committed lay people, have been successful in establishing effective walk-in shelter programs for homeless persons. Staff of these facilities often gradually gain the confidence of these clients and become major sources of social support. Some facilities have also enlisted homeless persons in groups that function as support systems and serve therapeutic and skill-development functions as well (Breton, 1984; Ely, 1985). The ultimate goals of working with chronically mentally ill homeless people are to locate them in permanent housing, to connect them with mental health programs, and to meet their needs for health care, rehabilitation, and social support.

Emergency shelters have also served single-parent homeless families, the majority of whom manifested failures in crucial aspects of family functioning. In addition to providing for the usual concrete needs of these families for shelter, food, and physical safety (some women had been physically abused), social workers provide treatment that integrates crisis intervention, problem-solving, task-centered services, and life-space interviewing. Space limitations preclude elaborating upon this approach, which has been described by Phillips et al. (1988). Overall, evaluation of the results indicated that the majority of the families made significant progress in achieving goals that had been formulated.

Employing Advocacy and Social Action

We define advocacy as the process of working with and/or on behalf of clients (1) to obtain services or resources for clients that would not otherwise be provided,

(2) to modify extant policies, procedures, or practices that adversely impact clients, or (3) to promote new legislation or policies that will result in the provision of needed resources or services.

Advocacy has long been deemed an obligation of social workers. The obligation was reaffirmed by a report of the professional organization's Ad Hoc Committee on Advocacy (*Social Work,* 1969) and again in 1979 by the profession's new code of ethics, which clearly articulates in Article VI the ethical responsibility of social workers to serve as advocates for clients:

> The social worker should act to ensure that all persons have access to resources, services, and opportunities which they require.
>
> (Item 2)

> The social worker should advocate changes in policy and legislation to improve social conditions and to promote social justice.
>
> (Item 6)

Situations that practitioners encounter, however, can present ethical dilemmas as to what type of advocacy actions are most appropriate. We refer you to an article by Gilbert and Specht (1976) for a discussion of these conflicts.

Case and Class Advocacy

Advocacy embodies two separate yet related facets, the first of which involves working with and on behalf of individual clients or families to assure that they receive benefits and services to which they are entitled and that the services are rendered in ways that safeguard their dignity. Because this aspect of advocacy is on behalf of an individual or family, it is denoted as *case advocacy,* corresponding closely to one dictionary definition of an advocate as "one who pleads the cause of another."

The second aspect of advocacy involves acting to effect changes in policy, practice, or laws that affect all persons in a specific class or group—hence this type is denoted as *class advocacy.* Class advocacy is much broader in scope and, in essence, is a form of *social action.* Although the two types of advocacy are different, they are also highly interrelated. As Holmes (1981) points out, one may serve as a case advocate for a client who has been denied a particular service or benefit because of a dysfunctional policy, but if the advocacy action results in gaining that benefit, a precedent may be set that leads to a change in policy affecting all others in the same position as the client. "In other words, class advocacy may be viewed as an extension of case advocacy" (Holmes, 1981, pp. 33–34).

Indications for Advocacy

Advocacy may be appropriately employed in numerous situations, including the following:

1. When an agency or staff person refuses to deliver all services or benefits to which a client is entitled.

2. When services are delivered in a dehumanizing manner (e.g., when rape victims are humiliated).

3. When clients are discriminated against because of race, religion, creed, or other factors.

4. When gaps in services and benefits cause hardship or contribute to dysfunction.

5. When governmental or agency policies adversely affect people in need of resources and benefits.

6. When clients are unable to act effectively on their own behalf.

7. When numerous people have common needs for which resources are not available.

8. When clients have unusual needs for immediate services or benefits because of a crisis situation (e.g., migrants who are seriously ill or have acute financial needs).

9. When clients are denied civil or legal rights.

10. When procedures or facilities of organizations adversely affect clients.

Targets of advocacy may be individuals, agencies or organizations, public officials, courts, legislatures, and divisions of government. Tactics thus must vary considerably according to the target system. Sosin and Caulum (1983) have developed a useful typology of advocacy that assists practitioners in planning appropriate advocacy actions. By determining whether the advocacy situation exists in the context of an alliance, a neutral context, or an adversarial context, practitioners can determine what is to be advocated, what level (individual, administrative, or policy) of advocacy is appropriate, and what strategy should be adopted. Space limitations preclude elaboration of this typology, and we therefore recommend you read this informative article.

Albert (1983) has analyzed the process of advocacy in relationship to rule making by governmental administrative agencies. Viewing the process from a legal framework, this author presents helpful guidelines and identifies opportunities and techniques for intervening into the rule making or regulatory process. Nulman (1983) and Pinderhughes (1983) have written informative articles that discuss empowerment and advocacy for families. Pearlman and Edwards (1982) have discussed ways in which practitioners can organize *client advocacy groups* for the purpose of effecting improvements in neighborhood environments. Rose and Black (1985) have written a book concerned with an advocacy/empowerment approach that seeks to restore a sense of human dignity and personal responsibility to mental patients after their return to the community following hospitalization. Dane (1985) has also discussed the use of professional and lay advocacy aimed at enhancing the education of handicapped children. Several of the preceding authors stress that the *sense of empowerment* clients gain through organized advocacy actions may be more significant than the changes themselves.

Self-Determination and Advocacy

In considering advocacy interventions, practitioners must bear in mind that they should strictly observe the client's right to self-determination. If clients do not wish to assert their rights, practitioners are ethically bound to respect their wishes. If clients wish to pursue action, practitioners must be sure they are addressing the client's interests as the client defines them (Kutchins & Kutchins, 1978). Further, practitioners should go no further in advocacy activities than the client wishes to go. Practitioners also have a responsibility to discuss with clients possible negative aspects of advocacy activities. For example, because advocacy may involve adversarial interaction with pertinent target systems, the client risks generating antagonism or ill will with others that may be disadvantageous in the future. Implementing advocacy actions also typically involves a certain amount of strain and tension; moreover, a positive outcome cannot be assured. However, in discussing possible adverse consequences, it is important not to be unduly discouraging and

to assist the client to weigh pros and cons, leaving the final decision to the client.

Still another caution is that before undertaking advocacy actions, practitioners must be certain that the client's situation justifies assertive action. It is important to be certain that the client's account of being denied resources, discriminated against, or treated shabbily is based on fact and does not involve distortions or omissions. For example, a client who claims to have been denied medical care may not have followed a physician's recommendations. Similarly, a client's complaint of being discriminated against by having to wait a long time in an agency before being seen may be a result of understaffing produced by limited funds rather than discrimination. Other clients who complain about not being treated with dignity may be primary contributors to their difficulties as a result of obnoxious and provocative behavior. Our point is that it is prudent to assess situations carefully, thereby avoiding drawing premature and erroneous conclusions that may lead to undesired and embarrassing consequences.

Techniques of Advocacy and Social Action

There are many techniques of advocacy and social action, and deciding which techniques to employ is a highly individualized matter that depends on the nature of the problem; the wishes of the client, family, or group; the nature of the system targeted for advocacy actions; the personality and individual style of the practitioner; the political climate; and the extent to which the practitioner's agency will support different interventions. In a given situation, a practitioner may employ several interventions but a rule of thumb is to employ no more than are necessary and to cause no more disruption than is required to achieve a given objective. Although militancy may be required in some instances, it should be employed with discretion, for the price of accomplishing certain gains through militant action may be more than offset by the ill will and possible negative image generated.

The following techniques include those employed most often in advocacy and social action.[3]

1. Conferring with Other Agencies

When problems involve denial of resources or dehumanizing treatment by another agency, case conferences may be held with appropriate staff persons or with administrators to present the grievance. It is advantageous to have the client accompany you; otherwise, you are presenting information that is actually hearsay. And clients often gain strength from learning to deal head-on with such situations. Generally, it is prudent to present the client's case in a firm but dignified manner. If the other parties appear indifferent or otherwise manifest unwillingness to take appropriate remedial measures, it may be necessary to serve notice of intention to pursue the grievance further by contacting higher authorities or initiating other more vigorous measures.

2. Appeals to Review Boards

Most agencies and governmental bodies have procedures of appeal for clients who believe they have been unjustly denied services or benefits. Often successful appeals result in changes in procedures and policies.

3. Initiating Legal Action

When clients' rights are violated and the preceding in-

terventions fail to achieve redress, filing a legal suit may be an appropriate alternative. However, clients often lack the resources to hire a private lawyer, and it may be necessary to engage a United Way legal service agency or legal services provided through public funds. Clients, of course, must be willing to testify in court.

4. Forming Interagency Committees

When individual agencies are unsuccessful in effecting essential changes, several agencies may combine their efforts in attacking common problems. Committees may be formed that plan collective action directed at modifying the practices of a problem agency or organization or at filling a gap in community services.

5. Providing Expert Testimony

Social workers may exert a powerful force in influencing the development of public policies or developing resources by speaking forcefully about clients' problems and needs in the political and public arenas.

6. Gathering Information through Studies and Surveys

The impact of testifying in public is much enhanced when social workers can provide concrete data to support their positions. Conducting studies and surveys and reviewing the literature thus arm the social worker with information that can be employed in responding to the penetrating and hostile questions sometimes raised in public hearings and in direct contacts with public officials and legislators, as we discuss later.

7. Educating Relevant Segments of the Community

Often the strongest enemy to developing progressive policies and programs is ignorance of decision makers about the issues. To educate the public in general and decision makers in particular, all forms of media should be considered,

---

[3]The authors wish to acknowledge that much of the discussion related to techniques is based on: Arnold Panitch, Advocacy in practice. *Social Work*, 1974, *19*, 326–332.

including press campaigns; telephone contacts; local television programs concerned with public issues; panel discussions at local, state, and national conventions; exhibits; and speeches at meetings of influential civic organizations.

8. Contacting Public Officials and Legislators

This can be a powerful way of promoting needed policies and programs. Social workers may contact legislators and public officials directly or may appear at committee meetings to present information that legislators need to make informed judgments. To be effective in these endeavors, social workers must be knowledgeable about how special interest groups influence legislators. Smith (1979) has written an informative article explicating six "generalizations" involved in influencing legislators. We briefly mention just two of these generalizations and strongly urge you to read her entire article.

One generalization is that "Knowledge of legislators' role concepts (or orientations) is crucial in determining their behavior toward interest groups, which is usually congruent with their role concepts" (p. 235). Legislators' behavior can be understood by knowing whether they tend to assume the role of facilitator, resister, or neutral. The facilitator generally is receptive to information from special interest groups and is knowledgeable about their existence. This type of legislator represents the most fertile ground for special interest groups.

The second generalization is that "The provision of technical and political information is a significant influence to which legislators respond in the political process" (p. 235). The need for and value of being equipped with relevant knowledge has been affirmed by studies of legislatures in four states. Significantly, "The most important factor governing the influ-

ence of a group and one that outweighed others, was the ability of a group to provide lawmakers with both technical and political information" (p. 235). Obviously, social workers who aspire to influence legislators must first do their homework.

9. Forming Agency Coalitions

This technique involves forming an ad hoc group of agencies that are committed to a specific objective. The advantages of this intervention are twofold. First, decision makers tend to be more influenced when numerous agencies present a united front; second, a given agency is less vulnerable to attack when it is but one of many different organizations joined in a common effort. As Panitch (1974) points out, however, there may be a problem in joining a coalition in that "the issue at hand may become too generalized to meet the wishes of member organizations" (p. 331).

10. Organizing Client Groups

This intervention involves forming action groups for social change that consist of consumers who have a mutual problem. The social agency initiates formation of the group, stimulates it to take action, and serves a consultative role in assisting it to obtain information, gain access to selected people, and act in concert with other community groups. Organizing client groups is especially appropriate for minority groups, who often feel impotent from a political standpoint. Lum (1982) has reported a vignette illustrating the successful work of a practitioner in organizing blacks to advocate for rights that had been violated in a public housing project.

11. Developing Petitions

This activity is used to call attention of decision makers to an issue and to exert pressure for accountability on a public official by expressing the voice of a constituency.

12. Making Persistent Demands This technique involves going beyond the usual appeal process by bombarding officials with continuous letters and telephone calls. Although this intervention stays within the law, it approximates the use of harassment as a pressure tactic.

As is apparent, the foregoing interventions include both case advocacy and social action. Effective social action, according to Grinnell and Kyte (1974, p. 482), requires a rational, planned approach that consists of the following steps:

1. Define the problem.

2. Systematically diagnose the people, structure, or system to be changed.

3. Assess both the driving forces that may promote change and the resistance forces that may conceivably retard it.

4. Identify specific goals.

5. Carefully match mechanisms or strategies of social action with the goal desired.

6. Make a feasible schedule for implementing the plan of action.

7. Incorporate in the plan a feedback process for evaluating the changes that the action stimulates.

In addition to these steps, certain ingredients are required for effective social action. Not all individual practitioners possess these ingredients, but O'Connell (1978, p. 199) maintains that effective social action *agencies* possess the following characteristics:

1. A *cause* worth getting excited about.

2. *Genuine* concern for that cause.

3. An ability to keep the cause in *focus*.

4. Acceptance of *activism* as the way to make things change with no apologies for being activists.

5. *Tenacity*—it is interesting to note that John Gardner, a leader of the Common Cause organization, concluded: "The first requirement for effective citizen action is stamina."

6. Successful advocates really *understand* how their government and service systems are organized *and* changed. Blind emotion may work a few times, but a successful, sustained effort requires know-how.

7. To make a difference in any major cause there is a need for people in real *numbers*. Politicians have learned to look behind angry shouts to see if there are voters behind all that noise. It helps to have power people, and the best combination is to have both the numbers and the power people, but if a choice has to be made, take numbers.

8. The effective social action agency must be *independent*—free to tackle anybody *or* cooperate with anybody.

Organizing clients and planning social action embody numerous skills that are beyond the scope of this book. A helpful resource that deals with methods of effecting social change in the political arena is a book by Haynes and Mickelson (1986).

Social Planning/Community Organization

A macro approach to enhancing environments and improving social conditions, the practice method of social planning/community organization (SP/CO) goes beyond typical direct practice activities in that the focal units with which practitioners engage are larger systems such as neighborhoods, citizens groups, representatives of organizations, agency executives, and governmental leaders. The joint efforts of the participants are typically directed to solving social problems ranging in scope from those of various resident groups on one end of the continuum to international problems on the other end. Policies and programs of national scope that have emerged over the past 25 years as a result of intensive planning aimed at social problems include the Community Health Act (1963), the Economic Opportunity Act (1964), the Model Cities Program (1967), the Housing and Community Development Act (1974), the Jobs Training Partnership Act (1983), and the Title XX amendments to the Social Security Act (1974), to name just a few. Current problems upon which planners are or should be focusing include homelessness, child and spouse abuse, substance abuse, adolescent pregnancy and child bearing, adolescent runaways, poverty of single-parent families, high rates of unemployment of minorities, and problems of the disabled and chronically mentally ill.

Although practitioners with expertise in SP/CO typically perform planning roles in urban centers and even larger systems, direct practitioners may need to engage in SP/CO activities in rural areas, where experts in planning usually are not available. In rural areas practitioners may join with community leaders in planning to remedy problems associated with lack of transportation for residents with health care needs, needs for child care, problems of child neglect and/or maltreatment, needs for recreational programs, isolation of the elderly, and other such problems. It is important, therefore, for all practitioners to have at least rudimentary knowledge of the principles and skills involved in SP/CO.

As with direct practice, the problem-solving process is central to practice involving SP/CO. However, the problem-solving process at the macro level differs widely from that at the micro level, and social workers in SP/CO "... seem to have more in common with professionals in other fields who are engaged in the same type of efforts, such as trade unionists, politicians, and city and regional planners" (Gilbert & Specht, 1987, p. 610). Before implementing the problem-solving process, planner-organizers must identify and recruit people who will provide funding and other support to undertake a SP/CO effort, identify a problem to which the planning or organizing efforts will be directed, or agree to work on a problem that has previously been identified. The next step is to select goals and to develop a plan that brings together and mobilizes those who have been recruited, organizational and political support, funding sources, and community support essential to attainment of the goals. Implementing these activities requires some of the same skills employed in direct practice, for example, interviewing skills and the ability to facilitate group development by applying knowledge of interpersonal relationships and group dynamics. Other skills required include those embodied in policy analysis and program evaluation, research methods, management of data, and sociopolitical processes.

Problem Identification and Analysis

Different theorists conceptualize the problem-solving process in SP/CO in different ways, each theorist defining different numbers of stages that vary according to the levels of elaboration of relevant tasks. For our purposes, we use the general four-phase process identified by Gilbert and Specht (1987, p. 613), which consists of (1) identification and analysis of a problem, (2) development of a plan of action, (3) implementation of the plan, and (4) evaluation of its outcome. At this level of abstraction the process is similar to that of the problem-solving process of direct practice.

The first task in identifying and analyzing the problem is to assess the state of the target system (e.g., neighborhood, community, county, or state). Although conceptual approaches to problem analysis vary, common elements in the frameworks of prominent experts include ". . . the need to identify which social values are threatened by the situation, to carry out a detailed analysis of who is affected and the scale of the problem, and to delineate the etiology of the problem" (Moroney, 1987, p. 598). Further, the analysis also addresses the political environment, assessing the readiness of the target system to deal with the problem and to allocate resources to remedy or mitigate the problem.

Identifying the causes of the problem is central to problem analysis. Although founded in the scientific method, this process varies according to the theoretical premises and values of the problem analysts, as attested to by the varying explanations offered as to the causes of poverty, crime, adolescent pregnancy, and other social problems. Approaches to identifying causes of problems often begin by compiling data regarding the incidence and distribution of the social problems in terms of age, sex, race, income levels, severity, duration, and so on. After the data is analyzed, inferences are made concerning causes of the problem.

Another useful method employed in problem analysis entails applying techniques that produce information used to predict demands for services and fiscal resources needed. These techniques, which include social surveys, estimates of future populations and compositions of the same, as well as trend and probability analyses, are beyond the scope of this book.

Another aspect of problem analysis, which follows the steps described in the preceding paragraphs, is needs assessment. The task involved in needs assess-

ment is to estimate from the focal system the numbers of people at risk and in need of remedial measures. Defining needs, however, is an elusive task because need is a complex concept that can be stated in four different ways: (1) normative need, (2) perceived need, (3) expressed need, and (4) relative need. (See Moroney [1987] for elaboration on these different aspects of needs.) Needs can be assessed by utilizing professional judgment and social surveys (normative needs), by holding public forums (perceived needs), determining the number and profile of people who seek a service (expressed needs), and assessing relative need by measuring ". . . differences in levels of services in different geographical areas, weighting each area's statistics to account for differences in population and social pathology" (Moroney, 1987, p. 599). Because each approach deals with a different aspect of need, comprehensive needs assessments employ all four different approaches.

Developing a Plan of Action

After identifying and analyzing a problem, the next phase of SP/CO entails developing a plan of action. Ideally, the concept of rationality is embedded in the process of developing a plan of action. Adhering to this concept, planners objectively use information they have gained to describe, to understand, and to make predictions about phenomena in question. Economic rationality requires determining the single or "best" remedy for the focal problem. Ideally, selecting a remedy thus entails identifying all reasonable strategies, assessing the likely consequences of each strategy, and evaluating each set of consequences. Evaluating the cost-effectiveness of each alternative is also part of the process. This task involves determining which alternative will generate the most favorable ratio between valued input and valued output, or in other words, seeking to achieve maximal return for the least investment.

In fact, planning and organizing based exclusively on the concept of rationality are generally impractical, and decisions about alternatives typically must consider complex factors that include political realities in the focal system, limited funding, and the possible impact of special interest groups. Because of the magnitude of these and other realities, "The technical aspects of designing the 'best' programmatic solutions are deemphasized in favor of sociopolitical behavior that seeks the agreement of relevant interest groups. From this perspective, interactional tasks such as bargaining, exchange, compromise, and building consensus emerge as the predominant features of the problem-solving process" (Gilbert & Specht, 1987, pp. 614–615). Less than ideal, this approach has been called "incremental decision making" because it seeks to improve upon the shortcomings of present policies rather than to select superior courses of action that are likely to be rejected. In this regard, findings of one research study (Gilbert & Specht, 1979) revealed that *mobilization of strong political support* correlated highest with positive outcomes of Title XX allocations of resources for the aged. So much for the idealism of rational planning!

Implementation of the Plans

After plans have been accepted, support mobilized, and funding allocated, implementation of the program selected commences. This involves performing internal administrative tasks including selecting, training, and supervising staff; providing for intraorganizational communication and quality control; and establishing policies and procedures that serve the interests of both consumers and staff. Other tasks entail managing external relations with other service organizations, funding sources, consumer groups, governmental entities, employee unions, and so forth. Maintaining positive relationships with these various entities is crucial, for their support is indispensable if a new program is to flourish. Managing external relations thus is a primary activity required of planners and organizers.

Evaluation of Outcome

Evaluation seeks to assess the extent to which programs are successful and to identify ways of improving them. Program evaluation thus involves ongoing systematic monitoring of the program's impact, which requires development and implementation of techniques of data management. Systematic analysis of data enables planners to determine if the program is functioning effectively and accomplishing the goals for which it was planned. Evaluation also enables planners to determine which strategies are most effective under which conditions and with which populations.

Program evaluation requires expertise in research design, techniques of measurement, and statistical analysis. Techniques involved in these processes, however, are sophisticated and beyond the scope of this book. Knowledge requisite to implementing these processes is commonly embodied in research courses that deal with program evaluation.

Because of limited space, the foregoing discussion of SP/CO is sketchy at best. For more extensive overviews, we refer you to chapters by Gilbert and Specht (1987) and Moroney (1987), the sources of much of the preceding information. These chapters also include extensive references to relevant articles and textbooks that discuss SP/CO in depth.

17 ▌Enhancing Interpersonal Relationships

Therapeutic Implications of Clients' Interactional Patterns

Because many human needs can be met only through interactions with significant others, the quality of those countless interactions strongly determines the nature of emotional involvement and the degree of satisfaction or stress that people experience in daily living. Habitual destructive reactions by parents (e.g., rejecting, critical, or demeaning messages) tend to warp the attitudes of children toward themselves and others and to produce dysfunctional patterns of behavior. Either the lack of positive interactions or the presence of repetitive destructive interactions between children and adolescents and their peers can also impair social and emotional development. Interactional difficulties between adults (e.g., constant marital conflict) or lack of close relationships also contribute to marital breakdown, violence among family members, social isolation, and various forms of mental dysfunction. It is thus crucial that practitioners be competent in assisting clients to replace destructive interactional patterns with more facilitative ways of relating to each other.

We devote this chapter to interventions and techniques you can employ to enhance the interactions between clients and significant others. Mastering the content of this chapter and practicing relevant skills will advance your competence in the following:

1. Engaging couples and families in the helping process and orchestrating initial sessions.

2. Assisting marital partners and members of families or growth groups to enhance their interaction by increasing positive feedback.

3. Modifying dysfunctional patterns of interaction.

4. Modifying misconceptions and distorted perceptions that impair interaction.

5. Modifying dysfunctional family alignments.

Interventions and techniques that are discussed in this chapter may be adapted to work with couples, families, and groups.

Initial Contacts with Couples and Families

To enhance the functioning of marital and family systems, practitioners must be skilled in engaging members of these systems and in focusing on the systems per se. Because clients generally do not think from a systems perspective, it is essential to manage initial contacts in ways that are conducive to working with couples and families, rather than with individual members. In this section, then, we describe ways of handling initial contacts that lay the groundwork for implementing the systems-oriented interventions that we later focus on in this chapter.

The Initial Telephone Contact

If the family has previously been screened for a family approach by an agency intake worker, all that the practitioner may need to do in the initial contact is to work out details related to the appointment.[1] If there has been no previous contact with the caller, the practitioner may need to accomplish several other vital objectives, one of which is to determine whether intervening at a family level is appropriate. Practitioners can generally utilize a family approach whenever a caller complains of difficulties that involve immediate family members or other persons living under the same roof, such as a relative, friend, or live-in partner. When problems involve persons less intimately involved with the caller (e.g., employer, parents who live elsewhere), the practitioner usually makes an initial appointment to see the caller only.

Other critical objectives of the initial telephone contact include reaching an agreement as to who will be attending the first session and establishing rapport with the client who initiated the call. Striking a balance between conveying empathy for the client and establishing expectations regarding the initial contact is sometimes

difficult, but as demonstrated shortly, skills delineated in earlier chapters aid in this task.

The initial contact should be kept short and focused on relevant objectives to avoid becoming entangled in the caller's personal problems. To this end you may wish to utilize the following guidelines:

1. Ask the client to describe the problem *briefly,* and empathically respond to the client's messages—a strategy that not only helps establish rapport but also yields important information. Also elicit information that will help you determine who else is involved in the problem. When you believe you have established beginning rapport and have heard the presenting complaint, summarize the client's view of the problem and relevant feelings and emphasize the client's needs or wants.

2. If your exploration reveals that family involvement is appropriate, introduce the client to the "family approach," using a message such as the following:

"In helping people with the kinds of problems you've described, the most effective approach is having other family members come for sessions also. It has been my experience that when one person hurts, other members also usually experience stress and discomfort. Members of the family affect and influence each others' problems. Equally important, changes in one member require changes and adjustments in other family members as well. People accomplish the kinds of changes you're wanting more rapidly when all family members work together than when being seen individually. For this reason, it will be important that other members of the family be involved in the helping process."

3. Specify which family members you want to see in the initial session. Practitioners who espouse a family systems orientation differ in their views as to

---

[1]Because of the complexity of family issues and processes, practitioners usually meet with families for sessions of an hour and a half.

whether the entire family should be included in the initial session, with some strongly advocating involving *all* members from the beginning. Because inexperienced practitioners commonly encounter difficulties managing initial contacts with entire families (which requires advanced skills), we recommend a less ambitious approach. When a caller complains of problems involving a spouse or live-in partner, ask that person to bring the partner to the initial session. (It is *critical* to try to involve both partners, since resolution of such relationship problems usually requires adjustments by both parties.)

If a parent identifies a child-related problem, request that both parents or the single parent attend the first session *without* the child (or children) unless the parent strongly objects or there are unusual contraindications (e.g., a child threatening suicide). We also recommend that you include in this session any other adult who serves a parental function in the home (e.g., boyfriend or grandmother). *When you make this request, however, it is vital to convey your plans to involve other members of the family within a week or two.* In specifying which members you wish to see in the initial session, take the stance of *assuming* that everyone is willing to be involved (e.g., "Would Tuesday at 7 P.M. be suitable for you and your husband?"). Also avoid asking questions that open up the issue of whether others *will* be involved (e.g., "Will your husband come for counseling?").

4. Explore and resolve negative reactions of clients to involving others. Some clients comply with requests to bring specific family members to the initial session, but others offer excuses such as, "My husband has to work," "She won't come," or "He's not the one with the problem." These messages often reflect the caller's reluctance to include other members as well as reluctance of others to attend sessions.[2] In fact, the family member who initiates contact with the agency or practitioner may have a vested interest in *excluding* other family members. Keep in mind that clients often engage in what is called the *absent member maneuver* (Sugarman, 1981). By excluding important family members, they avoid painful issues but ironically also undermine the therapy process.

Despite the advantages of seeing both partners, the parents, or other specified family members together, you must respond sensitively to a caller's reactions to your requests. Otherwise, your initial contact may be your last. When clients openly state they do not want to involve other family members, it is important to explore their reasons thoroughly. You should stress during the exploration that other family members can play an important role in helping to find a solution to the problem. If clients do not subsequently modify their position, however, you should "begin where they are" by arranging to see whom they are willing to bring. As Garfield (1981) indicates: *"One wishes for therapists the wisdom to know when family participation is a necessity, the courage to press for it when it is, and the humility to take what they get"* (p. 9).

When clients maintain other family members are *unwilling* to attend sessions, ask their permission to contact those persons directly. If you gain permission (as will usually happen), you may wish to utilize an approach similar to that recommended by Kaslow (1981) for contacting "reluctant" fathers:

---

[2]A reference that deals comprehensively with the topic of engaging resistant family members is A. Gurman (Ed.), *Questions and answers in the practice of family therapy.* New York: Brunner/Mazel, 1981.

Mr. X, this is Dr. K. As you may know, your wife has contacted me for an appointment to discuss her concerns about your son, Jerry. She tells me you are quite busy, but *I am sure you are also interested in your son's well-being* (school work, health, or whatever the presenting problem appears to be), and I wanted you to know *how important your participation is.* As a matter of fact, I will not be able to be of much assistance without your input and collaboration.

(pp. 27–28)

After conveying such a message, you should explore the client's reactions. Although you may wish to reiterate your views that the client's participation in *at least* the first session is very important, you should respect a decision of the client not to participate and exert no further pressure. Exerting pressure tends to alienate the client and may destroy future opportunities for involving others. With skillful handling of their contacts with families, practitioners are sometimes able to dissipate strong resistance, thereby making it possible to involve key family members later in the helping process.

Managing Initial Contacts with Parents

Earlier we recommended that beginning practitioners meet with only the parents in initial sessions and include children in subsequent sessions. This strategy gives practitioners more time to become acquainted with the problems of the family and, on the basis of known information, to plan strategies with their instructors or supervisors for engaging other members and anticipating problems that may occur later. Having an initial session with parents also provides the opportunity to establish rapport with them, enhancing the potential to influence the parents in later sessions involving children. Practitioners

also have an opportunity to assess whether modifications by the parents are needed *before* they meet with children. Some parents, for example, manifest such ingrained and severely dysfunctional styles of relating to their children that initial attempts to see the entire family would be disastrous. Further, having an initial session with parents enables practitioners to clarify the systemic nature of problems and to emphasize the need for parents to concentrate on changing their own behaviors.

When meeting with parents in initial sessions, practitioners can begin to delabel children who are identified as problem bearers. They may also clarify that although the parents may believe that one child is responsible for the family's difficulties, entering the family session in this frame of mind will cause the identified patient to feel defensive and to resist becoming involved in the helping process. Practitioners can further emphasize that even though one person may cause significant strain in the family, all family members are usually involved in the problem and need to make some changes. Practitioners can thus inform the parents that they will be working in the family session "to take some heat off" one member of the family and to engage all members in a discussion of changes they would like to make to alleviate *family* problems. Practitioners may need to reassure the parents that they will also be helping the child to change, but they should stress that change is less difficult if the child does not believe that other family members expect him or her to make changes expressly to accommodate them. (A similar strategy is appropriate when the designated problem bearer is an adult.)

Interviewing parents in an initial session also makes it possible to plan how best to bring an identified child into the helping process. Rather than seeing a child individually, for example, a practitioner may wish to interview all the children together or to see the "problem child" with a sibling near his or her age. Seeing the identified patient with others imparts the message that the practitioner views the problem as residing in the system rather than in a problem bearer.

By interviewing parents first, practitioners can also help them to plan how to explain to their children why they are seeking professional help and can coach them in preparing a child. The parents' explanation should clarify that the *family* is having problems (not that the family is having problems *with the child*). The parents should also give children a general explanation of what to expect when the children meet with a practitioner and should listen carefully to reservations they may have about coming to the sessions.

Practitioners can also coach parents to behave constructively when children attend sessions. For example, a practitioner may suggest that parents try to create a climate conducive to open communication by withholding blaming messages, focusing on positive behaviors of their children, and listening attentively to them. Further, the practitioner can ask each parent to refrain from using dysfunctional communication identified in the initial session. Coaching parents to relate in positive ways to their children in initial sessions is critically important, for a key role of practitioners is to foster positive interactions among family members.

If parents do bring the "problem-bearing" child to an initial session, a practitioner should interview the child first, giving the child a chance to "tell his story" without the practitioner having been biased (as the child perceives it) by information provided by the parents. After interviewing the child, the practitioner should then interview the parents, reserving the latter part of the session for seeing all participants. At this time, the practitioner may wish to emphasize the systemic nature of the family problem, assist members to share individual goals with each other, and formulate family goals.

Orchestrating the Initial Family Session

The initial session with couples and families is crucial. Clients' experiences during this session determine in large measure whether they will engage in the helping process and contract to work toward specified goals or whether they will decide against proceeding further. Moreover, clients perceive the initial session as a prototype of the helping process. To lay a solid foundation for future work with families, it is important that practitioners accomplish a number of objectives. We briefly discuss each of these objectives in this section but first list them for use as a guide in both planning for and evaluating initial sessions:

1. Establish a personal relationship with individual members and an alliance with the family as a group.

2. Clarify expectations and explore reservations about the helping process.

3. Clarify roles and the nature of the helping process.

4. Elicit the family's perception of the problem(s).

5. Identify needs and wants of family members.

6. Define the problem as a family problem and begin to delabel any identified patients.

7. Begin highlighting individual and family strengths.

8. Begin drawing repetitive dysfunctional communications to the attention of family members and discuss whether they wish to change these patterns.

9. Begin assisting members to relate to one another in more positive ways.

10. Communicate hope that the family can change.

11. Establish individual and family goals.

12. Gauge motivation of family members to return for future sessions and negotiate a contract.

13. Negotiate tasks to be accomplished during the week.

14. End the session by summarizing problems discussed, goals formulated, and progress achieved.

You will note these objectives are essentially the same as those identified in earlier chapters of the book. In the following sections, however, we explain how to accomplish these objectives specifically in work with families and couples. The following discussion will also assist you in consolidating knowledge and skills that have been presented earlier.

1. *Establish a personal relationship with individual members and an alliance with the family as a group.* In working with families (or groups), practitioners have a twofold task of establishing personal relationships with each individual while developing a "connectedness" with the family as a unit. To cultivate relationships with family members, practitioners can employ several techniques. The technique of *socializing* involves the use of social chitchat and is used briefly by practitioners at the beginning of the session to reduce tension.

Practitioners can also employ joining or coupling techniques (Minuchin, 1974) to expedite their entrance into the family system. One way practitioners "join" the family is to respect family rules (for example, allowing a husband to be spokesperson for the family), even though they may intervene later to change such rules. Practitioners also convey their acceptance of the family by highlighting strengths or offering support to threatened members. Another way of joining the family involves mimicking the family's affect and style. If the family is jovial and expansive, for example, the practitioner may use expansive body movements or animated speech. The practitioner also mimics the family's language and idioms and consciously makes statements that establish similarities or parallels between him/herself and clients (e.g., "Oh, I had a dog almost like that"). Minuchin has described how he sometimes uses a proverbial aunt to establish alliances with various family members. This aunt always has interests and attributes similar to those of various family members (e.g., "I had an aunt who always used to wear the shade of blue you have on today. She must have had a dozen dresses that color").

A third technique, *facilitating,* involves the use of empathic responses to establish emotional linkages with individual members. Empathic responding can be particularly useful in developing relationships with reserved family members. For instance, when members do not respond spontaneously to new topics of discussion, a practitioner can solicit a response (e.g., "Jan, I don't think you've said what you experienced when you learned you were coming here. Could you tell me how you felt?"). The practitioner can then respond empathically to what that member says or does. The practitioner thus reaches for the responses of reticent or less assertive clients and "stays" with such clients briefly to encourage them to open up but does not press them. After repeatedly experiencing empathic responses from practitioners that reflect their verbal and nonverbal messages, such clients often begin to participate more actively.

In addition to the preceding strategy, practitioners should also endeavor to distribute time and attention somewhat equally among members, to highlight individual strengths, and to intervene when one member speaks for another or when one member is the target of blaming or put-down messages (techniques for which are discussed later in the chapter). Through such interventions, practitioners demonstrate positive regard for individuals and the value they place on the unique contributions of each.

Practitioners also develop rapport with members by addressing observations and questions to the *family,* as illustrated in the following messages:

- "How do people in this family let each other know they care about each other?"

- "What is it like to be a member of this family?"

- "From what you've said, it appears that *all* of you would like others in the family to listen more carefully when you speak."

Such responses not only facilitate developing a "connectedness" to family members at a group level but also serve to heighten their awareness that their family often functions as a unit, and that as members of this unit, they have common aspirations, goals, and (at times) shared emotions.

2. *Clarify expectations and explore reservations about the helping process.* Family members have varying and often distorted perceptions of the helping process

and may also have misgivings about participating in sessions. To identify obstacles to full participation in these areas (which is prerequisite to establishing a viable contract), it is helpful to elicit the responses of all family members to questions such as the following:

- "What were your feelings about coming today?"

- "On a scale of 1 to 10, in which '1' represents 'I didn't want to come at all' and '10' represents 'I could hardly wait to get here,' how would you rate yourself?"

- "What do you *hope* might happen in our meetings together?"

- "What are your fears about what *might* happen?"

As you elicit reservations, fears, and even hopes from individual family members, you can broaden the focus to the family by asking, "I'm wondering if others share the same feelings as. . . ." As members acknowledge similar feelings, they often begin to realize that despite feeling some degree of alienation from others in the family, they share certain common concerns—a realization that tends to draw members toward each other.

Exploring reservations about participating in the helping process often diminishes negative feelings or enables clients to lay them aside. If certain clients continue to manifest strong opposition to participating, you can address their reluctance by asking them one or both of the following questions and exploring their subsequent responses:

1. "What (if anything) would make you feel better about participating?"

2. "Given how you feel, are you willing to stay for the rest of the session and decide at the conclusion as to whether you will return?"

Manifesting willingness to negotiate the terms under which clients participate and acknowledging their right to make a choice often reduces negativism to the point they will agree to continue for the remainder of the interview and, at times, to return for further sessions. Bauman (1981) also identifies other strategies of engaging a resistant member:

These can include a request for the resistant adolescent or adult to attend sessions, while being under no obligation to participate. The paradoxical technique of telling the resistant member not to talk, to read a book, or just be present in the session, places no direct pressure on the person to contribute. It may take as long as eight sessions, but eventually fears can be allayed, leading to full participation. I have noted that silent members are closely attuned to the process, and when a sensitive area is broached, they often forget their defensive stance and join in the process.

(p. 19)

3. *Clarify roles and the nature of the helping process.* In exploring misgivings and reservations, practitioners must often explain the nature of the helping process and also clarify both their own and clients' roles. When an explanation is not necessary early in the session, however, practitioners often defer it until they engage clients in negotiating a contract, an activity that takes place in the closing minutes of the meeting.

4. *Elicit the family's perception of the problems.* In initiating discussion of problems, practitioners ask questions such as "Why did you decide to seek help?" "What kind of changes do you want to achieve?" or "How could things be better in the family?" Barker (1981) discusses the practitioner's role in structuring initial discussion of the family's problems:

It is usually best to ask the parent [these questions] first, then the children. If both parents are present, the therapist should ask

them both and leave it to them to decide who will answer; the process by which they decide who is to speak is often itself of interest to the therapist. By the end of [the problem] stage the therapist should have sought everyone's opinion on each of the problems that have been mentioned and should have enquired how they have tried to solve each one. It is very important to be clear what methods the family has already tried in attempting to overcome their difficulties.

(p. 54)

5. *Identify needs and wants of family members.* As practitioners engage the family in a discussion of problems, they listen for needs that are inherent in their messages and can inform clients that they are doing just that, as illustrated in the following explanation:

"You're here because some of your wants or needs are not being met in the family. As we discuss the family's problems, therefore, I'm going to ask you to help me identify those needs and wants. In turn, we will consider them as we formulate goals and plan our change efforts."

Even early in the session, the practitioner "reaches" for needs of participants through empathic responses, as illustrated in the following excerpt from a family session:

JED: [*16 years old, to parents*] You don't ever let me do anything with my friends. [*Feels angry, resentful, cheated, stifled; wants more autonomy and freedom.*]

PRACTITIONER: It sounds to me, Jed, as though you feel boxed in and controlled by your parents—that you'd like more freedom to move around and more trust from them. Am I hearing your needs correctly?

Other family members, perhaps uneasy about where the discussion may lead, may interrupt such messages or in some way discount them. For example, Jed's father (Mr. B.) might respond:

"We're just not about to let you run around wherever you want, particularly with that friend who's been coming to the house lately. You'd just get in more trouble."

The practitioner, however, can prevent family members from sidetracking from an exploration of needs by using the technique of temporarily "putting clients on hold." This technique involves blending an empathic response that addresses the participant's feelings with a focusing response that structures the interaction to achieve the immediate objective of the practitioner. To illustrate:

"I hear your concern about your son—you don't want him to just run loose. I also know *you* have some important needs that I'd like to discuss in a minute. But first, I'd like to ask you to identify Jed's needs. What do you hear him saying he needs or wants?"

As just illustrated, the practitioner works to enable members to *acknowledge* each other's needs.

In initial discussions of needs, the practitioner also corrects misperceptions often held by some members that a discussion of the needs of one person means that the practitioner will support that person's position. In the following message, for example, the practitioner allays Mr. B.'s fear that the practitioner may support his son's bid for freedom at his own expense:

"Identifying needs precedes problem solving. When we get to the point of considering solutions, we'll identify options that might help you and Jed with problems you've pinpointed and select ones that meet *both* your needs."

In exploring needs, it is important to identify needs of participants within the context of various family relationships (e.g., husband/wife, mother/daughter). In our illustration below, which we pick up at the point where the practitioner returns to the father's needs, notice that he works to establish *common* needs of father and son:

PRACTITIONER: You probably noticed that I kept the discussion focused on Jed's needs. I did so because it is critical for me to understand what each of you wants. I'd like you to help me to identify *your* needs now. You were saying, "I can't go along with Jed's just running around. That worries me."[3] What needs do you have?

MR. B.: I guess I need to know where he's going—after all, I'm responsible for him. And I need to know he's not getting in trouble when he's gone. There's been too much of that.

PRACTITIONER: Jed, could you hear what your father said?

JED: He said he needs to know where I am and what I'm doing.

PRACTITIONER: Good. I'm pleased that you could hear his needs so readily. I'm going to try filling in your dad's message. I think he's also saying, "I need those things because I care very much about my son."[4] Is that accurate, Mr.B.? [*Father nods.*]

PRACTITIONER: I'd like you to tell that directly to Jed.

MR. B.: I do care. [*Hesitates.*] I've felt shut out of your life for a long time, though.

PRACTITIONER: Tell Jed more about what you're experiencing.

MR. B.: We don't talk anymore, Jed. I miss those close times we used to have when we went hunting and fishing together. It's almost like I've lost a son.

---

[3]Notice that the practitioner picked up from where he had left off with the father by utilizing an empathic response that reflected the father's feelings.

[4]In this instance, the practitioner employs an additive empathic response to reach for the positive feelings inherent in the client's message, a potent technique for highlighting caring feelings of participants and for facilitating more positive interaction.

PRACTITIONER: It's like there is a big gulf that separates you from Jed now. You seem to be saying, "I miss him terribly." I think we're getting to a vital need you have—to feel closer to Jed. [*To Jed.*] I'd like you to tell your father what you're experiencing right now.

JED: I didn't know you felt that way. I haven't ever heard you talk like that before.

PRACTITIONER: See if you can tell your dad how you *feel*.

JED: I feel bad. But I can't talk to him. All he does is bad-mouth my friends. He's always critical of what I'm doing.

PRACTITIONER: Try to talk directly to your dad rather than to me, and tell him what you need from him.[5]

JED: I'd like to be able to talk to you without always ending up in an argument over my friends.

PRACTITIONER: I think that both you and your dad share a common need there. [*Looks at Mr. B., who nods.*] What about being closer to your dad—do you want that?

JED: Yeah, I miss the good times we used to have, too.

By identifying and highlighting common needs, the practitioner employs a potent intervention that enables participants to focus on their similarities rather than their differences and to formulate goals they can mutually achieve to improve their relationship.

6. *Define the problem as a family problem and delabel identified patients.* Earlier in the chapter, we modeled the type of message you can use in clarifying the systemic nature of problems. Continue to maintain that stance throughout the family session, emphasizing that every member's perspective is important; that family members can do much to support the change efforts of other family members; that all members will need to make adjustments to alleviate stress upon the family; and that the family can do much to increase the quality of relationships and the support that each member receives from others.

Despite efforts to influence members to define problems as belonging to the family, you will often encounter a persistent tendency of some members to blame others for problems. Your consequent task is twofold: first, you must monitor your own performance to ensure that you do not collude with some family members in labeling others as problem bearers and as the persons responsible for the family's ills. It is thus essential to espouse the circular orientation to causality of behavior explicated in Chapter 10 and to remember that it is simplistic to account for events in family systems on the basis of actions and reactions; rather, family members *reciprocally* influence each other in ways that perpetuate patterns of interaction. A useful rule of thumb when you become aware that you are viewing one or more members as responsible for family problems is to consciously pull back from the immediate interaction in order to gain perspective on how other family members may be contributing to the behavior of the person(s) in question.

Your second task is to *delabel* identified patients and engage members in assuming appropriate ownership for the part they play in the family's problems. One vital strategy for accomplishing these objectives is to explore relationships *between* family members in lieu of focusing on the behavior of individual members. For example, you may center on a dyad (brother/brother), then move to a triad

---

[5]The practitioner persists to get Jed to talk to his father by repeating his instructions. Clients often need extensive coaching in learning to talk directly to significant others about sensitive topics, a subject we discuss more fully later in the chapter.

(father/son/son), and finally explore interrelationships involving all four family members (mother/father/son/son). It is also vital to plan interventions to change the relationships among these various subsystems, a subject upon which we elaborate later in the chapter.

Another key strategy for delabeling identified patients is to focus initially on the role of blamers (or plaintiffs) in the difficulties about which they complain. This strategy counteracts the tendency of these family members to attribute blame to others and highlights the fact that they, too, are contributing to the problem. To illustrate this strategy, consider the example of a mother who complains about her son's behavior. Rather than turning to the son, the practitioner utilizes such questions as the following to focus on the mother's participation in the problematic situation:

- "You've said that your son refuses to talk to you about his problems. When you want him to talk to you, how do you approach him?"

- "When he says he doesn't want to talk to you, how do you respond? What do you experience at such moments?"

After first posing questions to the mother, the practitioner can then divide responses between mother and son and determine the son's participation in the identified problem by asking questions such as the following:

- "How does your mother approach you when she wants to know how you feel?"

- "What is your reaction to her approach?"

- "What might she do differently that would make you feel more like talking to her?"

This line of inquiry emphasizes the reciprocal nature of the problem. Further,

the last question enables the practitioner to set the stage for identifying positive behaviors each participant would like from the other. If both are receptive, the practitioner can help them formulate a reciprocal task that each can work on during the week to improve their relationship.

Another way in which practitioners can maintain focus on a plaintiff is to ask that person to change a complaint to a request, as illustrated in the following transaction:

WIFE: [*To husband.*] I can't ever seem to talk to you because you always have your head buried in a newspaper or are watching TV.

PRACTITIONER: Carol, I'd like you to tell your husband what you'd like him to do differently.

This strategy helps to divert focus from an identified patient. In addition, such interventions influence plaintiffs to consider behavior they *would like* and provide valuable information to others concerning desired changes.

Another strategy that practitioners can employ when parents complain about their children is to focus on the way the *parents* work together in coping with problems presented by the child. Such an exploration often reveals disagreements between parents as to how they manage (or should manage) the child, ways in which they may be working at cross-purposes, dysfunctional communication patterns that block them from effectively discussing the problem, ways in which they may use the child as a pawn in their relationship, and the like. If either parent raises questions about the exploration (e.g., "I don't see how talking about our relationship relates to our child's problem"), the practitioner should fully explore the parent's view and elicit concerns the other parent may have. At the conclusion of the exploration, however, the practitioner should emphasize the importance of the parents' being able to communicate and work together in assisting their son with his problems. Before proceeding to other subjects, it is also important to develop a minicontract with parents that specifies that they are willing to examine their own relationship and to consider making beneficial changes.

Another promising strategy for shifting focus from the identified problem bearer and assisting other family members to assume responsibility for making changes themselves is to ask them, "What would you like to change in *your* way of relating that might encourage your child (or another person) to change . . . ?" Another version of this message is the following:

"I know that you would like _____ to make some changes, but you must also have some thoughts about changes you might wish to make that would help you cope more effectively with _____. Could you identify changes of this kind you'd consider making?"

In helping family members to take responsibility for personal changes (rather than waiting for others to change), it is critical to emphasize that members cannot change each other and that each individual can alleviate problems only by concentrating on changing his or her *own* behavior.

7. *Begin highlighting individual and family strengths.* In work with families, practitioners highlight strengths at *two* levels—the strengths of *individual* members and of the *family* itself. At the individual level, the practitioner observes the strengths and resources of members, drawing them to the attention of the family (e.g., "I really like your sense of humor. I think it might keep us from becoming too serious about ourselves in our sessions."). At the family level, the practitioner re-

ports the strengths she or he observes in the way members operate as a group (e.g., "In your family, I sense that even though there are problems, you can count on one another. You seem to have a strong sense of loyalty to each other"). Because of the importance of focusing on strengths, we discuss this topic at length later in the chapter.

8. *Begin drawing repetitive dysfunctional communications to the attention of family members and discuss whether they wish to change these patterns.* If dysfunctional communications occur during the initial session (as they frequently do), practitioners often intervene to *counteract* their influence without focusing on the dysfunctional communication per se. For example, a practitioner can translate a blaming message into a neutral one by empathically reflecting the feelings and wants of the sender of the message. Or, when one client speaks for another, the practitioner can intervene to elicit the personal views of the latter. As the session proceeds, the practitioner begins to draw dysfunctional communications to the family's attention through responses such as the following:

- "I observed [*describes behavior and situation*] occurring between family members. Did you see the situation in the same way?"

- "Did you notice what went wrong as you talked about . . . ?"

Questions such as these help clients to become aware of dysfunctional patterned communications. However, the practitioner also needs to stimulate participants to analyze their behaviors further and to consider whether they wish to modify such communications. This can be accomplished by asking clients questions similar to the following:

- "How would you like to relate instead?"
- "How would behaving differently change your relationship?"
- "Given the problem the behavior creates in the relationship, how important is it to you to change the behavior?"

Utilizing this line of exploration in initial and subsequent sessions, you can assist family members to define for themselves the relative functionality of behavior and to make choices as to whether they wish to change it. If they choose to modify their behavior, you can negotiate relevant goals that will guide their efforts (and yours) in the helping process.

9. *Begin helping members to relate to each other in more positive ways.* We discuss strategies for accomplishing this objective later in the chapter.

10. *Communicate hope that the family can change.* Although we discussed this topic at length in Chapter 12, we remind you that you can engender significant hope in a family by assisting individual members to see how *they* can make changes that will reduce pressures. When family members mistakenly believe that the only hope for alleviating their problems involves changes by others (who choose *not* to change), they feel powerless and helpless—and thus defeated.

11. *Establish individual and family goals.* Chapter 13 deals extensively with this subject. Remember, however, to formulate goals based on your earlier exploration of wants and needs. Goals that flow from this exploration should include individual goals, goals for the entire family, and goals that pertain to subsystems (e.g., "Father and Jed, you indicated you wanted to explore ways of getting closer to each other").

12. *Gauge interest of family members in returning for future sessions and negotiate a contract.* Because family members do not always reveal their feelings openly, never assume that all members want to return for another session (even if you were successful in engaging members and sparking their interest in working on problems). You can employ the scale described earlier to assess the difference between the attitudes of participants at the beginning and end of the session. Also ask about reservations that participants may still have about engaging in the helping process, and after exploration, if reluctant members decide to return for another session, indicate that you will continue in future sessions to discuss their feelings about continuing. It is important to stress that it may take a number of sessions before *any* family member decides to participate fully or to commit to making changes. If family members are sufficiently motivated to return for another session, specify the time of the next session, who will be involved, and negotiate other elements of a contract as delineated in Chapter 13.

If a member is not willing to meet with the family, contract to see that person individually for one or more sessions if possible. During your meeting(s) endeavor to establish a relationship that provides a positive emotional experience, and use the time to explore and resolve obstacles to participating in family sessions. Paralleling this work, help other family members to identify and modify dysfunctional processes that may discourage the participation of the absent member, and generally prepare them for the return of that person.

13. *Negotiate tasks to be accomplished during the week.* Although we discussed tasks at length in Chapter 14, we reemphasize that tasks should directly relate to

goals identified by individual members or by the family itself.

14. *End the session by summarizing the problems discussed and goals, tasks, and progress achieved.* Wrapping up the session by summarizing major topics, goals, and tasks highlights what was accomplished in the session, tends to engender hope, and increases the momentum of change efforts.

Involving Family Members in Subsequent Sessions

In working with families, practitioners do not always need to see *all* family members or other parties who contribute to family problems. It is generally counterproductive to include children under age seven in family sessions once you have completed your assessment. The determination of *whom* to include and *when* to include them in subsequent sessions flows from the assessment process and the goals the family has formulated. Later, for instance, we discuss how practitioners can plan sessions based on goals that have been established with members to modify or strengthen various family relationships. Practitioners can also include various family members (and nonmembers) as problems arise when it appears that participation of these persons is critical to resolving the family's difficulties.

Enhancing Interaction by Increasing Positive Feedback

Positive feedback from significant others (i.e., expressions of caring, approval, encouragement, affection, appreciation, and other forms of positive attention) is a vital source of nourishment for self-esteem, high morale, emotional security, confidence, and feeling valued by others. Consistent and frequent positive feedback is essential to children and adults alike. Moreover, destructive patterns of interaction often derive from deficiencies in positive feedback in families. In this section, then, we delineate techniques for assisting clients to increase positive feedback, thereby fostering interpersonal climates conducive to harmonious relationships and well-being of individuals.

To enable clients to increase positive feedback, practitioners must be skilled in:

1. Engaging clients in assessing the extent to which they give and receive positive feedback.

2. Educating clients as to the vital role of positive feedback.

3. Teaching clients to express their needs for positive feedback.

4. Teaching clients to discern the needs of others for positive feedback.

5. Cultivating positive perceptual sets.

6. Enabling clients to give and receive positive feedback.

7. Assisting clients to increase levels of positive feedback.

In the following sections we focus on each of these skills.

Engaging Clients in Assessing the Extent to Which They Give and Receive Positive Feedback

Relationships often flounder because participants fail to meet each other's needs for positive feedback. You can directly explore this dimension of communication by asking clients how often and in what manner they convey positive feedback to significant others. Questions you might ask in marital or family sessions to achieve this end include the following:

- "How do you send messages that let family members [or your spouse] know that you care about them?"

- "How frequently do you send such messages?"

- "How often do you give feedback to others concerning their positive actions?"

In instances of severe marital or family breakdown, clients commonly acknowledge they send positive messages infrequently or not at all. In some instances, they may actually experience only weak positive feelings, but usually they experience more than they express.

Besides exploring how spouses or family members convey positive feedback, you can also explore their desires to receive increased feedback from each other. Questions that elicit such desires include:

- "When was the last time you received positive feedback from other family members concerning some action or behavior on your part?"

- "Would you like to receive more positive feedback from others in the family? What kind of feedback?"

- "Are you satisfied with the number of caring messages you receive from other members of the family? What changes would you like?"

Discussing how clients send positive messages or to what extent they desire increased positive feedback often opens up channels for positive communication that have been dammed by repetitive arguments, criticisms, blaming messages, and putdowns.

Educating Clients as to the Vital Role of Positive Feedback

As clients communicate about their needs to receive positive feedback, they begin to appreciate the significance of this dimension in interpersonal relationships. You can expand their awareness of the significance of positive feedback and enhance their motivation to increase the same by further explaining why this dimension is crucial. The logic behind increasing positive feedback is straightforward, and clients generally grasp it readily because it rings true in terms of their own needs and experiences.

Explanations vary according to whether the unit of concern involves parent-child, marital, family, or other interpersonal relationships. The following axioms may apply to one or more of these units, and you can include in an explanation those that seem appropriate.

1. All people need positive feedback to maintain high morale.

2. To exert their best efforts, people, especially children, need encouragement and approval.

3. Unsolicited expressions of love and approval are far more powerful and reassuring than solicited expressions.

4. Satisfaction and happiness in marital and family life are strongly determined by the degree of positive feedback members give each other.

5. Encouragement and approval are much stronger motivators than criticism and disapproval.

6. People never outgrow the need for love, approval, and encouragement.

7. Feeling taken for granted is a threat to the stability of marriages.

8. Love and respect among family members are indispensable to harmonious and happy family life.

9. People need positive feedback every day; occasional feedback is insufficient to sustain self-esteem.

10. Individuals, couples, and families fail to achieve their potentials if they do not strive to grow in their capacity to provide and receive positive feedback.

Teaching Clients to Express Their Needs for Positive Feedback

Teaching clients to express their needs involves assisting them to send personalized messages in which they own their feelings and wants. The following are examples of messages that explicitly express needs for positive feedback:

- [*Marital Partner*]: I've been troubled lately because I haven't felt very important to you. You've been working such long hours, and we haven't had any time together for the last week. I need to know that you still love me.

- [*Adolescent*]: I've felt really discouraged since I showed you my report card yesterday. I really worked hard this term, and when you saw my grades, the only thing you seemed to note was the one B. It didn't seem to matter that the rest were A's. Sometimes I wonder if I can please you at all. I need to know that you're pleased with how I'm doing.

In earlier chapters we discussed how to assist clients to personalize messages. We also illustrated how, through on-the-spot interventions, you can coach clients to formulate authentic messages that clearly express their feelings and needs. Reviewing that discussion will assist you in helping clients to express their needs for positive feedback, as will reading the case illustration below.

RUTH: [*To husband.*] I work really hard at keeping the house clean, but you never seem to notice it. All you notice is what I haven't done—like yesterday when you chewed me out for not cleaning the fingerprints off the bathroom door.

CARL: Well, let's face it, you hadn't done it, and you admitted it.

PRACTITIONER: Carl, Ruth was expressing an important need, and I don't want that need to get lost in an argument. Ruth, think for a moment about what you said. What is the need you were referring to?

RUTH: [*Pause.*] Do you mean his not noticing what I do?

PRACTITIONER: In a way, yes. What I'm meaning is your need for messages that give you credit for what you do and let you know you're appreciated. Is that what you need?

RUTH: Yes, I do need that. I get so discouraged at times. Like I never really please Carl.

PRACTITIONER: [*To Carl.*] She's sharing something that's very important. You both need to feel valued by each other, and that requires getting positive feedback for who you are and what you do. Without positive feedback, partners begin to feel discouraged and insecure, and relationships suffer. [*To both partners.*] To make sure you're aware of each other's needs for positive feedback, both of you need to send clear messages about *your* needs and to be sensitive to your *partner's* needs. Ruth, I'd like you to start over and express your need to Carl. This time, however, be sure you own your need and send an "I" message. [*Practitioner had previously instructed couple about personalizing messages.*] I'll help you if you'd like.

RUTH: I hope I don't blow it. [*Very deliberately.*] Carl, I need to know you're pleased with me. It seems I can't please you [*voice quivers*]—no matter how hard I try. [*Tears.*]

PRACTITIONER: I know that was hard for you, Ruth, but I was impressed with your message. Your feelings and need came through clearly. [*To Carl.*] What are you feeling now about what Ruth just said?

CARL: I'm feeling like a heel, I guess. I didn't know she felt as strongly as she does.

PRACTITIONER: Can you tell Ruth that?

CARL: This isn't easy. Ruth, I'm sorry. I know I've been overly critical at times. You are a good housekeeper, and I want you to know that I'll try to be less critical.

PRACTITIONER: [*To both.*] I'm very pleased with how you just communicated. You've been getting down to some really important needs and feelings. I'd like to point out something else that's also important to getting your needs on the table. That has to do with tuning in to the needs of your partner for positive feedback. That means each of you has to learn to listen for needs that lie behind words, complaints, accusations, and tears. Ask yourself, "What is my partner needing?" By listening for needs, you can prevent a lot of hassles and meet each other's needs more effectively.

Teaching Clients to Discern Others' Needs for Positive Feedback

Enhancing clients' sensitivity to the needs of others for positive feedback involves assisting them to listen attentively. Because others often do not express needs openly and clearly, clients' efforts must extend beyond just listening. They must also learn to "tune in" to needs that are

veiled behind complaints, questions, and actions of others. Because it is difficult for clients to attune to the needs inherent in the messages of others, it is important that you take full advantage of "teachable moments" to help them to learn this skill, as presented in the preceding excerpt.

Notice that the practitioner focuses sharply on Ruth's needs and plays a facilitative role in prompting her to express her need directly to Carl. The practitioner likewise uses the opportunity to advantage by having Carl provide feedback to Ruth, thus performing a vital role in *facilitating positive interaction between the partners.* This is a crucial point, for by serving as catalysts, practitioners enable clients to learn by *actually engaging in positive interaction,* a much more effective mode of learning than merely having clients talk about what they need to do. Notice also that the practitioner addresses the need for learning skills to *both* members. By not singling out one member, the practitioner avoids appearing to side with one or the other partner. The practitioner could further stress the needs of both participants for positive feedback by centering the exploration on Carl to identify how often and in what ways he receives positive feedback from his wife and then negotiating a mutual task with partners to increase such feedback during the coming week.

Cultivating Positive Perceptual Sets

Before clients can provide positive feedback, they must first be aware of the strengths, positive attributes, and actions of others. Some clients, of course, have perceptual sets that are attuned to the positive attributes and behaviors of others, but others habitually perceive weaknesses and flaws in the personalities and actions of others. As systems, families and groups may also constantly focus on what others are *not* doing or on what they *should* be doing, thereby excluding acknowledgment of positive coping behaviors and efforts. The practitioner, then, has the responsibility of bringing negative perceptual sets to the attention of families and groups and helping them learn to focus on positive behaviors. Strategies for accomplishing these tasks are delineated in the following subsections.

Sensitizing Members of Families and Groups to Positives Practitioners can set the stage for helping families and groups to develop positive perceptual sets by negotiating an explicit contract specifying that, in addition to focusing on self-defeating behaviors and other obstacles that prevent members from achieving their goals, a group will accord equal weight to accrediting strengths and incremental growth of members. The practitioner then actively intervenes in the early stages of the helping process to highlight strengths and growth and to help families and groups to incorporate "attention to positives" as part of their normative behavior. The practitioner's subsequent role in this regard is exemplified by the following intervention at the beginning of a third session with a family:

"It's likely that if I asked you what went wrong this week, you could probably easily identify a number of incidents. For the next few minutes, though, I'm going to ask you to tell me some of the things that went *right*. This may be hard to do, but I'm going to help you stay with my question because it's important for you as a family to learn to focus on the positive behaviors of members and to identify positive changes that occur."

Practitioners may wish to ask the family (or couple) this question each week until members themselves spontaneously report incidents that involve positive behaviors of other members, thus indicating the family has internalized the value of focusing on positives.

Reviewing Progress and Accrediting Incremental Growth Practitioners may also increase a family's or group's sensitivity to positives by engaging members in briefly reviewing at each session's end the work that has been accomplished, including incremental growth achieved by individuals or by a family or group. Increments of growth are often manifested very subtly in the helping process, and practitioners must therefore make a concerted effort to focus the attention of clients on these positive indicators of progress, as illustrated in the excerpt below from an actual session with a couple. In this session, which involves a husband (an ex-convict) who lacks perceptiveness of his own and others' feelings, the couple discusses an incident that followed the husband's spending $400 to have his motorcycle repaired. Because of the expense, his wife did not share his enthusiasm over having the motorcycle in running order.

WIFE: I think you were disappointed because I didn't say more about your getting your motorcycle fixed.
HUSBAND: I was! It hurt me because you weren't happy that I got it fixed and that now you can go riding with me.
PRACTITIONER: [*To husband.*] Did you notice anything different about the way you just expressed yourself?
HUSBAND: What, that I'm saying "hurt" and all that shit?
WIFE: That's incredible!
PRACTITIONER: That's a big breakthrough, Rick. I don't believe I've ever heard you spontaneously express your feelings.

HUSBAND: I'm just being an old softy. I'm just "washing out." You might as well just run a hose in here and wash me out of the place.

PRACTITIONER: Not so! Rather than being a softy, you're becoming much more aware of your feelings and are learning to express them. I was also pleased that you observed so quickly the change you had made. Your wife also noticed. Did you hear her say, "That's incredible?"

In this excerpt, the practitioner enables the husband to observe his own growth and also accredits the wife's astuteness in noting the subtle changes her husband manifested. Intellectually more capable than her husband, the wife learned in earlier sessions to give her husband positive feedback (and to express feelings). It was striking that the husband (whose ability to think abstractly appeared severely limited) slowly gained skills over a period of five months due in large part to the practitioner's (1) persistent efforts to model and explain skills, (2) heavy focus on his strengths and resources, and (3) concerted effort to acknowledge *any* signs of incremental growth.

To highlight incremental growth, practitioners may also wish to ask members to contrast their current functioning with their functioning at an earlier time, as illustrated in the following message:

[*To family*]: This is your fourth session. Let's see if you can identify any changes you've made in the way you communicate by contrasting how you related today with the way you related in the first session. I have some observations about that, but first I would like to hear yours.

Emphasizing the Need for Balanced Positive and Negative Feedback

As practitioners observe that group members are tentatively moving into their first authentic encounters, they should intervene in negative interactions to draw the group's attention to providing balanced feedback. Practitioners thus remind members of the provision in the contract for focusing on positives as well as negatives, as illustrated in the excerpt below from a second group session with adult members.

GARY: [*To Wayne, in irritated voice.*] When you keep machine-gunning me with questions like that, I feel like I'm being interrogated.

WAYNE: I didn't know I was coming across like that. Frankly, I just wanted to get to know you better.

PRACTITIONER: [*To Wayne.*] You said in the first session that you'd like to use the group as a way of getting feedback about how you come across to other people. I'm wondering if this might be a time for this. Are you game?[6]

WAYNE: Yeah. I don't know what's coming, but I really think I do need to know more about how other people perceive me. I was really surprised at what Gary said.

PRACTITIONER: [*To Wayne.*] Good. I can understand you may have reservations, but I'm also pleased that you're willing to take a risk this early in the group. [*To group.*] Since this is the group's first experience with giving feedback to members, I'd like to remind you of our contract not only to help members

---

[6]Note that the practitioner *asked* the member if he wanted feedback from others in the group. By extending this courtesy, the practitioner defines the member as being in control of the situation and underscores his right to make a choice concerning whether he becomes the focus of the group. In so doing, the practitioner models behavior that may become normative and often alleviates the fears of members that they will become the target of overriding and unsolicited negative feedback from the group. The practitioner may facilitate the group's "asking permission" before highlighting individual members by discussing this procedure with members and inquiring as to whether they would like to incorporate the procedure into the group's contract.

identify problems but also to share positive observations you may have. I'm not asking you to "pull punches" with Wayne. I don't think, in fact, he would want that. I am asking you to give him feedback across a number of different behaviors. As you do so, I'd also like you to try to personalize your statements. I'll help you with this.

The group's first experience in giving feedback to members is crucial in setting the tone for all that follows. By intervening to guide the group's first tentative efforts to drop facades and to engage at an intimate level, the practitioner enables the group to have a successful experience and to incorporate "attention to positives" as a part of its character. As members gain confidence that a group will attend to positives as well as problematic behaviors, they often increase their level of participation and take initiative in soliciting feedback from the group.

The principle of giving balanced feedback also applies to families. Practitioners must often similarly intervene when families are focused exclusively on negatives and assist members to put the behaviors of individual members into perspective.

Employing Tasks to Enhance Perceptual Sets Practitioners can also assist clients to develop positive perceptual sets by negotiating tasks that clients can implement between sessions. For example, they can further expand spouses' awareness of the frequency with which they provide positive feedback by negotiating the task of having them keep a daily tally of the number of positive messages they send their partners over a period of one week.[7] Clients (and practitioners) thus not only

gain a clear picture of their performance on this dimension but also develop a baseline against which they can later assess their progress in increasing positive feedback. Monitoring also provides advantages because, without explicitly planning to do so, clients often begin to increase the frequency of the desired behavior.

Another task that assists spouses to view their partners more positively is to have them compile lists of their partners' positive qualities. Practitioners may ask partners to begin by writing down at least 10 positive qualities and, without discussing their lists, bring them to the following session. In the session, the practitioner asks the spouses to read their lists to each other. This activity is beneficial in affording practice to spouses both in giving and in receiving positive feedback.

After having clients read their lists to each other, practitioners may ask them to discuss their reactions to hearing the positive feedback. Generally, clients report positive reactions, which provides an opportunity to reemphasize the beneficial consequences of positive feedback. Practitioners can further negotiate tasks of having the spouses review their lists daily, with the objective of expanding them on an ongoing basis. A related task is to ask spouses to focus not only on their partners' positive attributes but on those of others as well, especially when they find themselves thinking negative thoughts about others. By systematically focusing on the positive attributes of others, clients can gradually achieve more positive perceptual sets.

Enabling Clients to Give and to Receive Positive Feedback

To assist clients in learning to convey positive feedback, practitioners can teach them to personalize messages and guide them in practicing giving positive feedback to others. Practitioners should ask

---

[7]A small mechanical hand counter is useful for keeping daily tallies.

clients to base their practice messages on recent situations during which they experienced positive feelings but did not share them with others. Timely use of this educative intervention assists clients to conceptualize the elements of positive messages and to develop skill in authentically sharing their positive experiencing.

Practitioners may also need to assist some clients to learn how to *accept* as well as to give positive feedback. By deflecting positive feedback, in fact, these clients discredit information that could significantly increase their self-esteem. In the following example, the practitioner intervenes to help one group member acknowledge and accept positive feedback.

KIM: [*To Pat.*] I know you get discouraged sometimes, but I admire the fact that you can manage four children by yourself and still work. I don't think that I could ever manage that in a million years.

PAT: I don't always manage it. Actually, I don't do near enough for my children.

PRACTITIONER: I hear you saying, Pat, that you feel inadequate as a mother—and I'll ask you in a moment whether you'd like to return to those feelings—but right now would you reflect on what you just did?

PAT: I guess I didn't acknowledge Kim's compliment. I didn't feel I deserved it.

PRACTITIONER: I wonder if others of you have experienced the same feelings when someone has given you a compliment.

The last response broadens the focus to include the experiences of other group members, which should lead into a discussion of the difficulties individuals sometimes encounter in accepting positive feedback.

The practitioner may wish to help Pat or the entire group to identify negative

cognitive patterns that underlie discomfort in receiving positive messages (e.g., "I have to do things perfectly" or "Nothing I do can be very good"). The practitioner may also ask members to decide whether they would like to use the group experience to enhance their responsiveness to positive feedback.

Assisting Clients to Increase Levels of Positive Feedback

After completing the activities previously delineated, clients are ready to work on the ultimate task of increasing their rates of positive feedback. Practitioners can assist them by negotiating tasks that specify providing positive feedback at higher levels. Clients, of course, must consent to such tasks and determine the rate of positive feedback they seek to achieve. We recommend that practitioners have clients review their baseline obtained earlier and encourage them to set a daily rate that "stretches" their usual level but not to an unrealistic extent. For example, a husband whose mean baseline daily rate in giving positive feedback to his wife is 0.8 might select a beginning level of giving positive feedback twice daily. The client could then gradually increase the number of daily responses until reaching a self-selected optimal rate of five times daily.

As some clients implement the task of increasing positive feedback, they may inappropriately employ insincere positive expressions. Practitioners should caution against this, as such expressions have a hollow ring and create discomfort for both sender and receiver. Practitioners can stress, however, that as clients practice attuning to positives, they will gradually gain a natural facility for perceiving actions or qualities that warrant positive feedback.

In planning with clients to implement this task, it is important to adhere to the task-implementation sequence. In part, this involves anticipating obstacles, two of which are by far the most common. First, clients who have been inhibited in expressing feelings report discomfort with expressing caring messages, explaining, "It just doesn't come naturally to me." Practitioners should respond empathically to clients' discomfort but explain that engaging in new behaviors is bound to be uncomfortable and that if clients will risk themselves and endure the discomfort, they will gradually gain facility and comfort in expressing positive feedback.

The second common obstacle is that others may not respond favorably to clients' increased level of positive feedback and, instead, may question their sincerity. Because some clients have given virtually no positive feedback previously, the skepticism of others is understandable. Practitioners can assist clients to deal with others' skepticism by modeling and having clients rehearse appropriate coping behavior (including asserting the sincerity of their efforts) and by emphasizing the necessity of persisting in their efforts despite obstacles.

As with all tasks, it is vital to review clients' experiences in succeeding sessions. Clients may have experienced difficulties that warrant exploration, may continue to struggle with awkwardness or discomfort, or may report highly favorable reactions from others. Reviewing outcomes is vitally important, for practitioners can then give encouragement and positive feedback to clients, enable them to savor their successes, and, if warranted, point to the need for additional effort.

As clients implement tasks of increasing their rates of positive feedback, they will need to continue keeping tallies of instances in which they give such responses. Through monitoring, they not only maintain an ongoing record of their progress but also reinforce themselves each time they record a tally. Of course, the ultimate reinforcement derives from improved interactions with others. By giving positive feedback to others clients increase the likelihood of receiving the same in return.

Tasks for Couples One of many tasks you can employ to increase positive interactions between marital partners involves a strategy developed by Stuart (1980) aimed at increasing mutual demonstrations of caring behaviors by partners. By asking each partner, "Exactly what would you like your partner to do as a means of showing that he or she cares for you?" you assist each partner to identify desired actions that become a resource to the other. As each partner identifies caring behaviors, the other writes them down. You then ask each partner to assume the task of carrying out a specified number of caring behaviors identified by the other, using his or her respective list of positive actions as a resource. Another basic aspect of this activity involves each partner's expressing positive feedback in the form of appreciation when the other partner performs one of the actions from the list.

Tasks and Activities for Families and Groups A task that cultivates positive feedback among family members involves the activity or game of "Guess Who?" In this game, family members sit in a circle and a parent presents each member with a slip of paper and a pencil. A parent then instructs members of the family to write down something they like about the person sitting on the member's right. (Family members who are unable to write may ask another member to write for them.) The slips are then folded, put into a hat, and mixed up. In succession, each family member draws a slip from the hat, reads it aloud, and members guess which person matches the written description. Family members then shift positions in the circle and repeat the procedure until they have had the opportunity to write about every other family member. This game assists you to center the attention of family members on the positive attributes of others. It further provides feedback to each member about strengths and attributes as perceived by other family members.

An exercise that promotes positive feedback among family and group members (which is appropriate in groups only after members have become well acquainted) involves asking the family or group to "spotlight" each member in turn. Other members then give positive feedback about the strengths of the person in the spotlight. If it is necessary to prime the group, you may initiate positive feedback regarding strengths or growth of a member each time the spotlight shifts.

Tasks for Parents Preliminary to negotiating tasks with parents to increase positive feedback to their children, you can request that parents list functional and dysfunctional behaviors of each child. You then ask parents to choose the three dysfunctional behaviors they would most like to change. The next step is to negotiate a task that involves parents giving positive feedback at opportune times during the week when the specified behavior is *not* occurring (e.g., when the child is *not* fighting with a sibling). Further instruct the parents to give positive feedback when children manifest behaviors the parents would like them to assume *in place of the*

targeted behaviors (e.g., when the child *has* told the truth or *did* follow through on an assigned task). Parents are understandably handicapped in using this strategy if children's usual behaviors do not include the behaviors that are desired. For instance, children may never pick up their clothes or do their homework until specifically asked or only after continual nagging. In such instances, you will first need to motivate children by establishing an agreement that they may earn certain rewards in exchange for specified behavior.

Because parental attention to children's behavior is a potent force for modifying or reinforcing behavior, it is vital that you work intensively with parents so that they master the skill of positive feedback and learn to reward their children's positive behaviors systematically. We thus ask parents to reinforce the positive behaviors of children that they earlier identified, incrementally increasing the number of positive responses over a period of time. For example, a child may sometimes relate to siblings in a caring way, display a keen sense of humor that lifts family spirits, or take responsibility seriously. Parents, unfortunately, often take such behaviors for granted. But children need to know what they are *already* doing that pleases parents. If parents want their children to assume particular behaviors, they must give them positive feedback when those behaviors occur. Note the reinforcing property of the following parental messages:

- "I want you to know how much I enjoy your sense of humor. Sometimes you absolutely crack me up! It really lightens my day."

- "I really like it when you come up and hug me like that. It was such a pleasant surprise, and I could really feel your love coming through. I want you to know that I really love you!"

- "When I asked you if you had pushed your little brother down just a minute ago, you said 'Yes.' I appreciated your telling me the truth. I know it was hard for you to do that, knowing that I was angry when I asked. Being honest is very important to me, and I'm glad that you made the choice to tell the truth."

Used consistently by parents, messages such as these have a significant effect in shaping a child's personality and cultivating desired attributes. We cannot overemphasize the importance of taking a *preventive* approach with families by teaching members to emotionally nourish and support each other. Families that implement this approach raise the self-esteem of all members.

Strategies to Modify Dysfunctional Interaction

Interactional difficulties that clients commonly present include repetitive heated arguments, struggles over power and authority, conflict over issues related to dependence and independence, dissension in making decisions, friction associated with discrepant role perceptions and/or fulfillments, and other forms of defective communication. As we noted in Chapter 11, interpersonal conflicts tend to be redundant; that is, in relations with others, individuals repeat over and over again various types of dysfunctional interaction that predictably lead to the same negative consequences. To assist clients to evolve more functional patterns of communication and interaction, you must be expert in employing appropriate interventions and techniques. In this section, we delineate guidelines and techniques that you can employ in modifying dysfunctional interaction as you work with marital partners, families, groups, and other types of relationships. Note that teaching communication skills to clients is a vital aspect of modifying dysfunctional communications.

Metacommunication

To modify dysfunctional communication, participants must discuss such communication, analyzing their behaviors and emotional reactions as well as the impact of the interaction on their relationship. Such discussions are termed *metacommunication,* for they involve *communication about communication.* When practitioners discuss with clients communication that has just occurred, they too are engaging in metacommunication. Indeed, much of marital, family, and group therapy involves metacommunication. Likewise, when practitioners discuss relational reactions that occur in the context of the helping relationship, they are metacommunicating, for they are clarifying the meanings of messages and actions. Still other examples of metacommunication are messages that clarify intentions (e.g., "I'm only kidding" or "I want to talk with you because I feel bad about the strain between us") or messages that "check out" or seek clarification of others' messages that are vague or ambiguous (e.g., "I'm not sure what you mean by that" or "Let me see if I understood what you were saying").

Skills in metacommunication play a vital role in effective communication, for persons who metacommunicate often avoid needless misunderstandings (by checking out the meanings of messages) and provide feedback that enables others to make choices about modifying ways of communicating that are offensive or abrasive. Moreover, people who metacommunicate well thrash out conflicts with a minimum of antagonism and disruption in their relationships. A major role of practitioners, therefore, is to assist clients to learn to metacommunicate effectively.

Although skills in assisting people to metacommunicate are important with all client systems, they are especially critical in working with families that manifest dysfunctional patterns of communication, including frequent use of disconfirming, incongruent, and double-bind messages. Metacommunication involving these extreme forms of dysfunctional communication is indispensable to obviating their pernicious effects on family members. Families that extensively employ these forms of communication often metacommunicate little, if at all, which means that vulnerable family members are entrapped in processes that produce low self-esteem, blur personal identity, warp perceptions of the world, and foster disordered thinking. It is thus crucial to intervene into these dysfunctional processes and to teach family members to metacommunicate effectively. The following excerpt illustrates use of metacommunication to enhance communication between Anne, age 14, and her mother Mrs. T., who acts as a spokesperson for Anne and sends disconfirming messages.

PRACTITIONER: Anne, could you tell me how you've been doing in your gym class? I know you were having a rough time in gym.

MRS. T.: It's been *really* rough for her, having to change clothes and shower in front of all the other girls. She feels like she's in a goldfish bowl. I mean—I know what it's like because I went through it when I was in junior high. [*Anne lowers her head and looks at the floor.*]

PRACTITIONER: Excuse me, Mrs. T., but you were speaking for Anne. Anne, I'd like to hear from you what it's been like. [*Intervening to counter Mrs. T.'s acting as Anne's spokesperson.*]

ANNE: [*Looking up slightly.*] Well, it's been going a little better, I think. The gym teacher hasn't been after me. In fact she was pretty friendly this last week. And I . . . [*Mrs. T. interrupts.*]

MRS. T.: But it *hasn't* been going better, Anne. [*Disconfirming Anne as a separate person.*] When you shower, you just feel everyone's eyes are glued on you.

PRACTITIONER: [*To mother.*] I'd like to hear from Anne herself about how she feels about showering. [*To Anne.*] I know your mother's view, but I don't know what your experience has been.

ANNE: Actually, it hasn't been like my mother said. It was bad until the past couple of weeks, but I've made friends with a couple of girls, and we shower together. It isn't nearly as bad now.

MRS. T.: But you were saying . . . [*Practitioner interrupts to avert another disconfirming message.*]

PRACTITIONER: Anne, when your mother spoke for you the first time, you looked at the floor as if you were distressed. I wonder if you could tell your mother how you feel when she speaks for you. [*Encouraging metacommunication.*]

ANNE: I don't mind, sometimes. But, Mother, you don't always know how I feel. You get your feelings mixed up with mine, and it confuses me. I want to speak for myself.

MRS. T.: But, darling, I was just trying to help. I know how hard it's been for you. I mean—you understand that, don't you?

ANNE: I guess so, but I wish you wouldn't do it so much.

PRACTITIONER: [*To mother.*] I know you're trying to help, Mrs. T. But what do you hear Anne telling you? [*Using meta-communication to check out Mrs. T.'s perception.*]

MRS. T.: That she doesn't want me to say how she feels?

PRACTITIONER: Yes. I think Anne's saying that she's needing to be her own person. Is that right, Anne? [*Using meta-communication to check out meaning attribution.*]

ANNE: Yes, I want to grow up. I don't want to be a little girl anymore. [*Mrs. T. squirms.*]

PRACTITIONER: [*To both.*] What we've been talking about is very important in improving your communication as well as helping Anne to grow up. [*To Mrs. T.*] Though you're meaning to help, your assumptions about Anne's feelings are sometimes inaccurate. If you want to understand Anne, you'll need to ask how she feels rather than assume you know. [*To Anne.*] If you want to help your mother understand, you'll need to remind her not to speak for you when she does. And you'll also need to tell her your real feelings rather than just keeping them inside. I was very impressed with how you did that with your mother just now. I know that was difficult for you.

Notice in the preceding excerpt that the practitioner assertively intervened to prevent the interaction from following its usual destructive course. By not permitting Mrs. T. to act as Anne's spokesperson, by involving the participants in metacommunicating about the impact on Anne of Mrs. T.'s behavior, and by defining how both can modify their dysfunctional pattern of communication, the practitioner initiated corrective processes. Of course, many such interventions over a period of time are required to produce enduring changes.

Modifying Dysfunctional Family Rules

Dysfunctional family rules can also severely impair the functioning of family members. Because family rules are covert, it follows that changes can occur only by bringing them into the open. The practitioner thus assists family members through metacommunication to acknowledge and consider the impact of rules on family interaction. Openly discussing rules suggests options for replacing them with other processes that better serve the needs of all family members. Practitioners prepare families to consider rules by introducing them to the concept, as illustrated in the following message:

"As we begin work on problems the family is experiencing, we need to know more about how your family operates. Every family has some rules or understandings about how members are to behave. Sometimes these rules are easy to spot. 'Each person is to clear his own plate when leaving the table' is a rule that all members of a family might be expected to follow. This is an *apparent* rule because every member of the family could easily tell me what is expected of them at the end of the meal. But the family's behavior is also governed by other rules that are less easy to identify because they are *hidden*. Even though members follow these rules, they are often unaware that they exist. In the next few minutes, I'm going to ask you some questions that will help you to understand these two kinds of rules better and to identify some of the ones that operate in your family."

The practitioner can then ask the family to list some apparent rules and coach the family, if needed, by asking questions such as "What are your rules about bedtime?" (or watching television or getting the work done around the house). Once family members have identified some of their common and readily apparent rules the practitioner can then lead them into a discussion of implicit rules by asking them to identify guidelines they follow with regard to any of the dimensions of assessment listed in Chapter 10. For example, the practitioner might ask family members to identify family rules about showing anger or positive feelings or to explore facets of decision making or power (e.g., "Whom do the kids go to in the family when they want something?"). Rather than engaging the family in a lengthy exploration, practitioners should use the discussion to illustrate the presence of hidden rules that significantly influence their behavior. In the discussion, practitioners should stress that certain rules may undermine opportunities for members to achieve their maximum potential and, in fact, may be destructive to the growth and well-being of both individuals and the family itself.

After explaining the concept of rules to the family, practitioners can utilize this concept in assisting members to identify their patterned ways of interacting. Consider the practitioner's role in this regard in the following excerpt from a third session with Mr. and Mrs. Johnson and their three daughters:

MARTHA: [*Age 14.*] You took my blouse again—right out of my closet—and you didn't ask. That really gripes me.

CYNTHIA: [*Age 15.*] Well, you borrowed my brush last week, and you still have it.

FATHER: You girls need to learn to ask to borrow each other's belongings.

PRACTITIONER: Stop for a minute and take a look at what's happening. Martha, what did you notice *you* were doing?

MARTHA: She made me really mad.

PRACTITIONER: This is going to take some effort from you because you're still mad, but see if you can stay with me. What were *you* doing?

MARTHA: I told Cynthia I was mad at her.

PRACTITIONER: Good! [*To Cynthia.*] Then what did you do?

CYNTHIA: I told Martha she didn't have any right to complain because she wasn't returning things either.

PRACTITIONER: The two of you then were engaged in what we've earlier referred to as blaming messages—do you see it the same way? [*Girls nod. To father.*] I wonder if you observed what you did when your daughters were involved in their argument?[8]

FATHER: I was trying to get them to stop arguing and blaming each other—like usual.

PRACTITIONER: We may have the makings of a hidden family rule. Let's explore a little more to find out for sure. [*To family.*] While I'm asking a few questions, let's see if you can figure out what the rule is. [*To 13-year-old Jennifer.*] You weren't involved in this argument. Do you argue with anyone in the family?

JENNIFER: [*Laughs.*] My mother and my sisters.

PRACTITIONER: When you get in an argument with your mother, what happens?

JENNIFER: If my dad is there, he tries to stop it. Sometimes he tells my mother to go upstairs, and he'll talk to me.

PRACTITIONER: [*To mother.*] When your husband does that, what do you do?

MOTHER: Sometimes I let him handle the problem with Jennifer or one of the other girls. But when he gets involved like that, it makes me so furious that sometimes he and I end up in a fight ourselves.

PRACTITIONER: We need to do a lot more work to understand what happens in

---

[8]Notice that the practitioner employed the technique of asking family members to report on their own behavior. This technique assists clients to reflect upon their own (rather than others') contributions to dysfunctional interactions.

such situations, but for the moment, let's see, father, if you can put your finger on the rule.

FATHER: I guess I'm always trying to stop everyone from fighting and arguing in the family.

PRACTITIONER: It does appear that you are the family's mediator. I would think that would be a very difficult role to play.

FATHER: Well, there are no rewards for it, I can tell you that!

PRACTITIONER: There's more to the rule. Who lets father be the mediator?

MARTHA: We do.

PRACTITIONER: That's right. It isn't father's rule; it's the family's rule. It takes the rest of the family to argue and father to break up the fights.

There are many avenues that could be explored in this scenario, but the practitioner chose to narrow the focus by assisting the family to identify one of its major rules. After further exploring specific patterned interactions of the family, the practitioner can introduce questions such as the following that will help the family to weigh whether or not they wish to continue relating under the old rule.

To father:

- "How effective are you in actually stopping family members from fighting?"

- "What are your worst fears about what might occur in the family if you didn't play that role?"

- "Would you like to free yourself from the role of being the family mediator?"

To other family members:

- "Do you want father to continue to be the third party in your arguments?"

- "What are the risks to your relationship if he discontinues playing the role of mediator?"

- "Do you want to work out your own disputes?"

Questions such as these focus on the participation of *all* members in the patterned interaction and assist the practitioner and members to determine the *function* of the behavior in the system. To assist the family to modify their rule, the practitioner will need to teach family members new skills for resolving disagreements. The practitioner will also need to coach the father in declining the role of mediator and to coach others in requesting that he let them manage their own conflicts.

On-the-Spot Interventions

A form of metacommunication, on-the-spot interventions are a potent way of modifying dysfunctional patterns of interaction by intervening immediately when such communication occurs between spouses, family members, or members of formed groups. On-the-spot interventions are appropriate when clients send fuzzy or abrasive messages; when receivers distort meanings of or fail to respond appropriately to important messages; when actors imply but do not explicitly express wants, needs, or feelings; and when destructive interaction occurs. In implementing on-the-spot interventions, practitioners focus on the destructive impact of the preceding communication (labeling the type of communication so that clients themselves can subsequently identify their dysfunctional behavior) and facilitatively teach and guide participants to implement more effective ways of communication.

This technique is illustrated in the next excerpt, which depicts a practitioner intervening into a "blind-alley" argument, one that cannot be resolved because neither party can be proved right or wrong.

HUSBAND: I distinctly remember telling you to buy some deodorant when you went to the store.

WIFE: You may have thought you did, but you didn't. I'd have remembered if you said anything about it.

HUSBAND: But you *didn't* remember. I told you for sure, and you're copping out.

WIFE: [*With obvious irritation.*] Like hell you did! You're the one who forgot to tell me, and I don't appreciate your telling me I copped out.

PRACTITIONER: Let's stop for a moment and consider what's happening between you. Each of you has a different recollection of what happened, and there's no way of determining who's right or wrong. You were involved in what I call a blind-alley argument because you can't resolve it. You just end up arguing over who's right and feeling resentful because you're convinced the other is wrong. This doesn't help you solve your problem but only creates distance in your relationship. Let's go back and start over, and I'll show you a more effective way of dealing with the situation.

After labeling the dysfunctional interaction and guiding clients to communicate constructively, practitioners often subsequently intervene into related dysfunctional interactions but challenge clients themselves to identify their dysfunctional behavior and to modify it accordingly. For example, a practitioner may interrupt interaction, exclaiming, "Wait a minute! Think about what you're doing just now and where it's going to lead you if you continue." If clients fail to discern the nature of their behavior, the practitioner can again label the dysfunctional process and review with them more effective processes. In modifying dysfunctional patterns, the intermediate objective is for clients to arrest their dysfunctional behav-

ior by recognizing it, metacommunicating about it, and substituting newly gained communication skills. The ultimate goal, of course, is for them to *eliminate* the dysfunctional processes through concentrated efforts between sessions.

Guidelines for Making On-the-Spot Interventions

1. Focus on Process Rather Than Content As we noted in Chapter 11, you can be infinitely more helpful to clients in enhancing interaction by focusing on interaction processes rather than on the content of conflicts. Conflicts typically are manifested over content issues, but *how clients interact* in dealing with the focal point of a conflict is far more important than the focal point itself. As we illustrated in the preceding excerpt, the issue of who is right in a given dispute is usually trivial when compared to the destructive effects of dysfunctional processes such as belittling, dominating, name-calling, threatening, arguing bitterly, or resorting to violence.

You should usually ignore topics of disputes, focusing instead on assisting clients to learn to listen attentively and respectfully, to employ effective decision making, to own feelings, to examine their own parts in problems, to increase positive feedback and reduce negative feedback, to compromise, to disengage from competitive interaction, and to implement effective conflict-resolution tactics. Clients, of course, will confront countless potentially conflictive situations but will manage them without damaging their relationships if they master effective patterns of communication that preserve mutual respect and self-esteem. Indeed, well-adjusted families differ from poorly adjusted families not in the sheer number of conflictive events but in the fact that the former manage conflict effectively, whereas the latter do not.

2. Give Feedback That Is Descriptive and Neutral Rather Than General and/or Evaluative

As you intervene, it is important to present feedback in a neutral manner that does not fault clients and that enables them to pinpoint specific behavior that produces difficulties. Feedback that evaluates their behavior produces defensiveness; general feedback fails to focus on behavior that needs to be changed. To illustrate, consider a situation in which a marital partner glares at his spouse and says: "I've had it with going to your parents' house. You spend all the time visiting with your mother and treat me like excess baggage. You can go by yourself in the future." A general and evaluative message would be: "Garth, that message was an example of poor communication. Try again to send a better one." Contrast the preceding message with the following one, which is neutral and behaviorally specific: "Garth, I noticed that when you just spoke to Barbara, you glared at her and sent 'you' messages that focused on what you thought she was doing wrong. I watched Barbara as you spoke and noticed that she frowned and seemed to bristle. I'd like you to get some feedback from Barbara about how your message affected her. Barbara, would you share with Garth what you experienced as he talked?"

In the last message, the practitioner implies the client's message was dysfunctional but avoids making an evaluative judgment, as the practitioner did in the first example. Moreover, by describing specific behavior and eliciting feedback about its impact, the practitioner enhances the possibility that the client will be receptive to examining his behavior

and to modifying it. Note that this message also highlights the interaction of *both* participants, as specified in the following guideline.

3. Balance Interventions to Divide Responsibility

Because more than one client is involved in conjoint or group sessions, practitioners must avoid singling out one person as being the sole cause of interpersonal difficulties. Otherwise, that person may feel the practitioner and others are taking sides and placing the blame on him or her. By focusing on all relevant actors, the practitioner distributes responsibility, models fairness, and avoids alienating one person. Moreover, although one person may contribute more to problems than others, all members of a system generally contribute to difficulties in some degree. The following excerpt illustrates balancing an intervention in a marital therapy session:

WIFE: It makes me furious that you always come home late. It ruins dinner, and the kids keep asking why you're not home. What burns me most is that you don't even bother to call. What does it take to get you to call? I've been pleading with you now for two years.

HUSBAND: I have to work late at times, and I can't help it. You know that. If you'd just relax and take things more in stride, life would be more pleasant.

PRACTITIONER: Both of you seem to have some feelings and needs that are legitimate, but for some reason you seem to be stuck and unable to work things out. [*To wife.*] You resent his being late and wish he'd call so you could plan accordingly and not be hassled by the kids. [*To husband.*] You have to work late and resent being hassled over that. I'd like to explore what both of you can do to make things better for each other.

In group sessions, similar situations often occur, as illustrated in the following:

HAL: Mack, you really tick me off. You're always finding fault with everyone. Don't you ever find anything good to say about someone?

MACK: Look who's blowing off. Mr. Goody-two-shoes. Why don't you come down from your cloud and get a look at the real world?

PRACTITIONER: [*Addressing each in turn.*] Hal, it sounds like you're annoyed because you think Mack continually tears down others in the group. Mack, I gather you were irritated—and maybe even a little hurt—by Hal's comments. Sounds as though you think maybe he doesn't see things accurately either.

In both of the preceding excerpts, the practitioner responds empathically to the feelings of the participants, thus validating the feelings of each. In so doing, the practitioner remains neutral rather than siding with or against either of the participants. The empathic responses also soften the impact of the participant's attacking message. The practitioner can also guide Hal and Mack in working out their problem by focusing on both participants and facilitating positive interaction between them:

PRACTITIONER: I'm going to ask the two of you to try to work this out together. Hal, will you tell Mack once again how you feel, but this time personalize your message? Mack, when he's finished, will you try to paraphrase what he said? Then I'd like you to tell Hal your feelings while he listens. I know it will be hard for both of you to listen to the other because you're both angry, but I'm going to ask you, as well as the rest

of the group, to try to *understand* more about what is happening between the two of you.

When dysfunctional interactions such as the preceding occur in groups, practitioners may need to address interventions to three or four persons or even the entire group.

4. Balance Interventions to Distribute Time and Focus Equitably As diverse interactions occur among family and group members, practitioners must make choices about intervening in processes so that all members have opportunities to focus on their concerns. Ordinarily, group contracts specify that members should have equal opportunities to use the resources of the group, and therefore, practitioners and members share responsibility for implementing the contract. When intervening in such situations, remember that although it appears that some members of a group or family are monopolizing the interaction, exploration of the situation usually reveals that less aggressive members are contributing to the problem through their own inactivity. Thus, practitioners must address the responsibility *all* participants have in maintaining the status quo, highlighting *inaction* as well as *action* in their interventions.

5. Direct Messages from Participants to Each Other Because spouses and family members need to learn to communicate effectively with each other, practitioners must facilitate effective communication between them rather than acting as an intermediary. Clients often complain or express feelings to a practitioner that concern a spouse or other family members, and it is easy in such instances to fall into the pattern of communicating with individual members rather than directing them to talk to each other. But clients do not gain essential skill in communicating with each other by talking through the practitioner. Therefore, practitioners should often redirect messages to the parties whom they concern, which is accomplished by utilizing a message such as, "Would you tell your partner, please?"

Sometimes practitioners err by asking members to express directly to others messages that are hostile, blaming, or critical. Such messages may exacerbate an already strained situation and lead to arguing or fighting among participants. Before redirecting messages, then, you must consider the likely consequences of the ensuing interaction. When redirecting messages, actively intervene to facilitate positive interaction by coaching clients to own feelings, to translate complaints to expressions of needs or requests for change, to metacommunicate by clarifying positive intentions, and to avoid harsh tones of voice or hostile facial expressions.

In some instances, when clients begin to talk but do not face one another or maintain eye contact, you may need to interrupt and direct them to face one another and to look each other in the eye, as illustrated in the following message:

"Please stop for just a moment. You were talking to the floor [or wall, or me], not to _____. Will you please start again, but this time talk directly to _____."

Assisting Clients to Disengage from Conflict

One of the most common (and destructive) types of dysfunctional interaction involves arguments that quickly escalate, producing anger and resentment between participants. Intense competitiveness of-

ten is involved, and neither person is willing to let the other be one-up by winning the argument. The content issues involved are secondary to the fact that on a process level each participant is struggling to avoid being one-down, which would mean losing face or yielding power to the other.

To assist clients to avoid competitive struggles, you can use metacommunication about the dysfunctional process, emphasizing that *all* participants lose competitive arguments because of the negative feelings and emotional estrangement that ensue. It is also vital to stress that far more important than winning an argument is safeguarding mutual respect.

Having provided the rationale, you next introduce them to the concept of disengaging from conflicts, which simply means that participants arrest escalating arguments by declining to argue further. A graceful way that spouses or family members can disengage is by making a comment similar to the following: "Listen, it doesn't really matter who's right. If we argue, we just get mad at each other, and I don't want that to happen."

You can further assist couples to arrest arguing between sessions by teaching them to employ code words that signal the need to disengage. We recommend that you challenge partners to develop their own code words, an activity that most clients enjoy. Our clients have developed code words such as "truce," "draw," "peace," and "time out."

Although the process of disengagement is easy to learn, it is not simple for many clients to apply because of their virtually reflexive pattern of responding competitively. You will thus need to intervene frequently at first, gradually transferring responsibility to them for recognizing and disengaging from competitive struggles.

Negotiating tasks of applying disengagement in their interaction between sessions is essential in transferring use of this process to their daily lives.

Modifying Dysfunctional Complementary Interaction

The converse of competitive interaction is characterized by submissiveness or passivity on the part of one partner in the face of dominance by the other. Over time, this *complementary* type of relationship often proves dysfunctional to one or both partners. The submissive partner may grow to resent the domineering one and may engage in passive resistance or openly challenge the spouse. Moreover, the domineering partner may weary of assuming the dominant role and/or devalue the spouse, perceiving the passivity as weakness. In either event, destructive interaction may ensue, culminating in their seeking marital therapy.

In modifying dysfunctional complementary relationships, it is vital to work with both partners so that you can assist each in adapting to changes that bring the relationship more into balance (assuming the partners have chosen that goal). The submissive partner will need assistance in becoming more assertive and the dominant partner will need assistance in learning to share power and to encourage and reinforce assertiveness by the spouse. By relating to the partners as a system, you avoid the pitfall of severely disrupting the relationship by assisting one partner to make changes that are threatening or unacceptable to the other.

Negotiating Agreements for Reciprocal Changes

During the course of marital and family therapy, a client will sometimes spontane-ously propose to make a specific change in behavior if another person will agree to make a reciprocal change. Such conditional proposals reflect the fact that people unconsciously attempt to maintain balance in relationships, a phenomenon described by Lederer and Jackson (1968) as *the quid pro quo.* For example, a marital partner may agree to be more affectionate if the spouse will agree to be less sexually demanding. Or parents may agree to permit their children to watch a favorite television program if the children complete their homework by a specified time. The reason clients are more receptive to making changes when other parties agree to make reciprocal changes are twofold. First, people are more prone to give when they know they are getting something in return. Second, when all involved parties agree to make changes, no single person loses face by appearing to be the sole cause of an interactional problem.

Contracting for reciprocal changes can be a powerful way of inducing change. A particular advantage of reciprocal contracting is that it counters the tendency of many clients to wait for others to initiate changes. Another advantage is that in working on reciprocal tasks, clients are *mutually* involved in a change venture. This mutual involvement may spark collaboration in other dimensions of relationships, an important gain for couples whose interactions have been largely competitive rather than collaborative.

Clients are unlikely to implement reciprocal contracts if they have not moved beyond competitive bickering and blaming each other for their problems. We thus recommend deferring use of this technique (unless clients spontaneously begin to negotiate) until you have assisted them to listen to each other attentively and to express their needs and wants. It is also essential that they demonstrate a commitment to wanting to improve their relationship. This latter condition is especially crucial, for as Jacobson (1978) has pointed out, if clients view their own or others' changes as emanating primarily from meeting stipulations of an agreement, rather than from caring and commitment to the relationship, they are likely to devalue the changes. Therefore, we strongly recommend you have clients explicitly clarify that caring for the other person is the primary factor motivating willingness to make changes (when such appears to be the case). A practitioner's efforts in this regard are illustrated in the following excerpt:

PRACTITIONER: [*To husband.*] Could you tell your partner your reasons for agreeing to the change we've discussed?

HUSBAND: I think she must know that.

PRACTITIONER: [*To husband.*] Would you check that out with her?

HUSBAND: [*To wife.*] You know, don't you?

WIFE: I think I do, but I'd like to hear it from you.

HUSBAND: The only reason is because— dammit, you're the most important person in the world to me. [*Choking up.*] I know I haven't shown it, but it's true.

WIFE: I appreciate that. It's nice to hear.

Practitioners can employ reciprocal contracts to enhance interaction in diverse problematic situations, as illustrated in the following:

- Husband agrees to visit wife's parents if wife agrees to talk with her mother about not taking over discipline of the children.

- Parents agree to increase allowance if child agrees to save a certain amount of it.

- Wife agrees to have meals on time if husband agrees to stop reading newspaper when called to dinner.

- Husband agrees to express feelings more if wife agrees to listen without interrupting or disagreeing.

In employing reciprocal contracting, it is wise to place maximal responsibility on clients for making proposals. By so doing, you enhance the investment of clients in proposed changes. Moreover, clients often generate innovative and constructive proposals that might not occur to a practitioner. To engage clients in making proposals, you can use a message such as: "It's clear both of you are unhappy with the situation. I'd be interested in hearing each of you make proposals as to what you could do to make it better." With some encouragement, most clients make proposals, but you may need to prompt them by suggesting possible reciprocal actions. As you mutually consider proposals, it is important to guard against encouraging clients to undertake overly ambitious actions. Clients (and naive practitioners as well) are prone to want to effect major changes immediately, which is commendable but unrealistic. Bear in mind that people change by increments and that encouraging them to attempt overly difficult tasks sets them up for failure and disappointment. Moreover, failure in implementing tasks tends to cause clients to lose confidence in the helping process. It is vital, therefore, to encourage modest tasks that are commensurate with clients' capacities and motivation. By successfully accomplishing small reciprocal changes, clients experience the benefits of both giving and getting, which enhances their motivation to attempt additional reciprocal tasks.

Another caution you should observe in negotiating reciprocal contracts is that clients should avoid undertaking *multiple* changes at the same time. Multiple tasks dilute efforts and reduce chances for successful accomplishment. Single changes, by contrast, foster concentrated efforts and enhance the likelihood of successful results.

As clients discuss proposals, you should attend carefully to nonverbal messages that suggest misgivings, apprehension, or opposition to carrying out the contract. Clients are sometimes hesitant to express their opposition and may agree to a contract to which they are not actually committed and have no intention of fulfilling. Empathic responsiveness to such nonverbal cues, however, may encourage them to disclose misgivings. By exploring the nature and source of misgivings, you may be able to assist clients to resolve them. If they prove unreceptive to the proposed changes, you can encourage them to identify changes they *are* willing to make. Our point is that it is critical to avoid contracts and tasks that clients are unlikely to accomplish successfully.

After eliciting or offering one or more feasible proposals for a reciprocal contract and determining that clients are willing to carry out the contract, you assist them to reach an explicit agreement. This agreement specifies tasks clients are to implement before the next session. It is important to plan with clients for implementing the task by following the steps of the task-implementation sequence, delineated in Chapter 14. As you plan with clients for task implementation, it is also vital to stress that each person must exercise *good faith* in carrying out his or her part of the contract, as illustrated in the following message:

"I am pleased that you have both agreed to make the changes we've discussed because the changes can make things better for both of you. To carry out

these changes successfully, however, each of you will need to carry out your part irrespective of whether the other does. If you wait for your partner to carry out his or her part first, you may both be waiting for the other to make the first move by the time of our next session. Remember, failure by the other person to keep the contract should be no excuse for you to do likewise. If your partner doesn't keep the agreement, you can take satisfaction in knowing you did your part."

Emphasizing the individual responsibility of all participants in the helping process to fulfill their respective commitments, as in the preceding message, counters the tendency of clients to justify their inaction in subsequent sessions by asserting, "He (or she) didn't carry out his part. I knew he wouldn't, so I didn't do my part."

During the next session, it is vital to follow up on clients' experience in implementing their agreement. If results have been favorable, discussion of their reactions often results in further expressions of positive feedback between participants and leads to discussion of other ways of achieving further positive interaction. If one or more clients have not fulfilled their agreement, you can explore their interactions of the previous week, focusing on obstacles that prevented them from doing so.

Modifying Misconceptions and Distorted Perceptions

Clients' cognitions often embody erroneous beliefs that produce dissatisfaction in marital and family relationships, engender resentments toward others, and contribute to dysfunctional interaction. Three common examples of mistaken beliefs manifested in marriages, families, and groups are:

1. It's important to get even with people who hurt you or take advantage of you.

2. All people in authority (especially police) exploit their authority to the detriment of others.

3. We must conceal the fact that we have conflict in our family; otherwise, people will think badly of us.

Unrealistic expectations of others and myths are two other forms of misconceptions that contribute to interactional problems. As with rules, myths and unrealistic expectations often are not readily apparent, and practitioners must sometimes infer them by exploring clients' expectations of each other, of marriage, and of family relationships. Myths are also similar to rules in that they govern family operations by shaping beliefs, expectations of spouses, family members, and other relatives. Lederer and Jackson (1968), Glick and Kessler (1974), and Goldenberg and Goldenberg (1985) have identified numerous myths and unrealistic expectations that can profoundly influence interactions in marital and family relationships. Common examples of such myths include the following:

1. Family members should meet all their emotional needs within their family.

2. Spouses should know without being told their partners' needs, feelings, and wants.

3. If partners are well matched and love one another, a successful marriage will evolve with no effort.

To eliminate misconceptions and dispel myths, draw them to the awareness of clients, gently assist them to accept the error in the misconceptions, and focus on how they affect marital, family, and group interactions. Because misconceptions and myths commonly protect clients from having to face certain unpleasant realities and to make changes that are perceived as threatening, clients often do not relinquish them without a struggle. To facilitate their making essential changes, you must recognize that making changes entails resolving fears and risking the consequences of learning and implementing new behavior. Responding empathically to these fears and providing emotional support to clients as they struggle with their ambivalence toward change often supply the impetus that clients need to change their patterns of interaction.

To illustrate this process, we consider a family in which an adolescent, age 17, manifests extreme tension and anxiety. During family sessions, it has become apparent that the parents have exerted intense pressure on him to perform well academically and have made it clear they expect him to become a doctor. It has also been apparent that they mistakenly believe the myth that by trying hard enough anyone can become anything he wants. In an effort to reduce the pressure on the son by dispelling the myth and modifying the parents' expectation, the practitioner arranges to meet separately with the parents. The following excerpt is taken from that session.

PRACTITIONER: I've been very concerned that Gary has been making an almost superhuman effort to do well in chemistry and physics but still is floundering in these subjects. I get the impression he believes he has to become a doctor at any price and that one reason he's so uptight is that he realizes he isn't cutting it despite his efforts. It's terribly important to him to meet your expectations, and he's falling short even though he drives himself.

FATHER: I know he's working hard, but it'll come. He can become a doctor if he really wants to. I could have been a doctor if I had applied myself, but I didn't. I goofed off too much. I don't want Gary to make that mistake.

PRACTITIONER: I can sense your concern for Gary. Still, I've gained the impression that both of you convey to your children the belief that they can become anything they want and that Gary is blaming himself because he's not making it, irrespective of how hard he tries.

MOTHER: Don't you think anyone can succeed in anything if they try hard enough?

PRACTITIONER: That belief doesn't square with what we know about differences between people. People have different aptitudes and talents. For example, I couldn't be a dentist, jeweler, surgeon, or pianist or handle many other types of work that require finger dexterity. I couldn't be an engineer or draftsman because I have difficulties in visualizing spatial relationships. Everyone has certain aptitudes and certain limitations. What's important in career planning is discovering what our aptitudes are and making choices that match them. I'll bet both of you can identify talents and limitations you have.

Notice that in seeking to dispel the family myth, the practitioner focused on the destructive impact of the myth on Gary. Notice also that the practitioner authentically disclosed his own limitations. This tactic switched the focus from the abstract to the concrete and provided strong evidence of the error of their belief. The practitioner then further attempted to invalidate the myth by asking them to apply it to themselves.

Practitioners also frequently encounter clients who have distorted perceptions of one another that contribute to dysfunctional interactions. As you will recall from Chapter 10, labeling others is a common form of such perceptual distortions. The effect of labeling is tantamount to that of wearing blinders, for labels obscure perceptions of others' strengths, limitations, feelings, beliefs, interests, goals, attitudes, hopes, and the like. Instead, one's perceptions are limited to attributes and behaviors that are inherent in the label.

When practitioners observe the process of labeling (e.g., "You're lazy," "stupid," "frigid," "rigid," or "undependable"), it is important to intervene, highlighting the negative impact of labeling on the person being labeled (labeling produces defensiveness and resentment) and the fact that labeling limits awareness of the other person, produces friction, and stifles the development of closeness. In focusing on the destructive impact of labeling, the practitioner must be careful to label the process and not the client who has labeled another person. Moreover, it is important to respond empathically to the frustrations the client experiences with the "labeled" person, as illustrated in the following example.

WIFE: [*To husband.*] I came home so excited about the teacher's report of Jamie's progress. So I tell you, and what do I get? Zip, that's what. You're just a wet blanket!

PRACTITIONER: Just a moment. Let's look at what's happening. [*To wife.*] You're saying you were, and still are, disappointed with Rex's response. I can sense your frustration. But by labeling him as a wet blanket, you're putting him on the defensive, and you're going to get sidetracked. Let's see if we can stay with both of your feelings and understand what both of you are experiencing right now.

After delabeling the other person, the practitioner assists the clients to explore feelings and cognitions and to make specific requests for change.

Modifying Dysfunctional Family Alignments

As we emphasized in Chapter 10, all families develop patterns of affiliation between members that either enhance or impair opportunities for individual growth or the family's ability to carry out operations vital to its survival. Interventions to modify alignments are generally indicated:

1. When bonds are weak between spouses or other family members or when one family member is alienated from others.

2. When there are enmeshed alliances between members that block them from developing appropriate bonds with other members (or outsiders).

3. When two members of a family attempt to cope with dissatisfaction or conflict in their relationship by forming a coalition with a third family member. This phenomenon, referred to as *triangulation,* most frequently involves marital partners who use a child as a pawn in their struggles.

4. When family members are "disengaged" or alienated from one another,

tending to go their own ways with little reliance on each other for emotional support.

5. When members of the family have formed alliances with persons outside the immediate family (e.g., friends and relatives) that interfere with their performing appropriate family roles or providing appropriate emotional support to other family members.

In intervening to modify alignments, the practitioner may endeavor to achieve any of the following:[9]

- To *dissemble* an alliance, which involves breaking it down. For example, a practitioner may assist a single parent to disengage from a destructive relationship with a boyfriend.

- To *develop* alliances, which involves cultivating new alliances or strengthening relationships that are underdeveloped. A practitioner can thus assist a new stepfather and stepson to explore ways they can develop a relationship or can work with siblings who have been estranged to strengthen their emotional bonds.

- To *reinforce* an alliance, which involves acting to maintain the alliance or to amplify its scope and/or strength. For instance, a practitioner may enable parents to increase their ability to operate as an effective executive subsystem.

- To *loosen* an alliance, which involves helping members who have heretofore been enmeshed to reinvest some of their emotional energy in others.

Before practitioners intervene to modify family alignments, they should involve

---

[9]Several of the items delineated were adapted from a chapter by Aponte and Van Deusen (1981), which discusses structural family therapy.

the family in determining whether and in what ways such changes should take place. The practitioner's first task in this respect is to assist family members to observe the nature of their alignments. This may be accomplished by asking questions that stimulate family members to consider their alignments:

- "If you had a difficult problem and needed help, whom would you seek out in the family?"

- "Sometimes members of a family feel closer to some members than to others and may pair up or group together. Which members of your family, if any, group together?"

- "In most families, members argue to some extent. With whom do you argue? With whom do other members argue?"

The practitioner can also bring alignments and coalitions to the family's attention as they are manifested in the session. For example:

- [*To wife.*]: It seems that you're the hub of the family. Most of the conversation seems to be directed through you, while you [*husband*] seem to be an observer or onlooker to the family's discussions.

As family members become aware of their alignments, the practitioner must assist them to consider whether they wish to become closer to others and to identify obstacles that could prevent that from happening.

Another avenue for enabling family members to observe their alliances and to make decisions concerning possible changes involves asking them to make a drawing on a sheet of paper showing family relationships. Members are instructed to use rectangles in their drawing to represent each person in the family.

Rectangles can be of any size and located any place on the paper. Practitioners coach family members to position the rectangles in ways that depict relative closeness and distance among family members. After family members have completed their drawings, the practitioner asks them to draw their family relationships as they would *like* them to be on the other side of the paper. In a subsequent discussion, the practitioner first asks members in turn to share their drawings of existing family relationships and then assists the family to formulate conclusions concerning the nature of alignments and the emotional closeness and distance that members experience in their relationships with others (e.g., "It appears, then, that father and Jeff feel quite close to each other, but that you, Mike, don't feel as close to your father as Jeff does"). The practitioner then asks members to explain their second drawings that show how they would like family relationships to be. During the discussion, the practitioner highlights the desires of members to increase their closeness to others and assists them to formulate goals that reflect changes they would like to make.

Yet another strategy for assisting members to analyze their family structure is to involve them in family sculpting (Constantine, 1978; Jefferson, 1978; Papp, 1976). This technique, which involves having members arrange themselves spatially in a tableau to create a physical representation of the family's relationships, starkly reveals the family's alliances. Since family sculpting is a potent technique for helping families to discern dysfunctional family alignments and to recognize the need to realign their relationships, we suggest that you become adept at using this strategy.

Practitioners' actions to engage the family in discussions related to their family structures often stimulate family members to begin changing the nature of their alignments. Practitioners can also assist members to modify various alignments by employing one or more of the following interventions:

Strengthening Marital Coalitions and Marking Generational Boundaries

In optimally functioning families, strong marital coalitions exist, and generational boundaries are clearly demarcated so that parents neither triangulate children nor permit them to intrude into the marital or parental systems. In working with families that manifest weak marital coalitions, therefore, practitioners face the challenge of assisting spouses to strengthen their relationships and to present a united front in their interactions with their children. Otherwise, children learn to relate primarily to the most permissive parent and turn to that parent with requests for privileges, emotional support, and affection. Some such children become adept at playing one parent against the other, which fosters marital divisiveness and produces strain between children and the "excluded" parent. The hazards for the development of such an inimical family climate are especially great in remarried families with older children because loyalties and emotional bonding between parents and stepchildren often are lacking. The difficult challenge that confronts such families is to develop unity and cohesiveness when two families have joined together.

Strategies for strengthening marital coalitions include the following:[10]

1. Interspersing conjoint meetings involving only the marital partners with meetings of the total family and with the children of a subunit. Meeting with only the parents enables practitioners to clarify the need for a united front and to develop relevant tasks aimed at strengthening the marital coalition. Such meetings also enhance the visibility of generational boundaries.

2. Negotiating tasks with spouses to engage in some conjoint activities outside the home that exclude children. Parents are to plan activities independent of their children and to implement them, leaving a note informing the children only that they will be gone for a specified time. Upon returning, they are to offer no more than a brief matter-of-fact explanation, and in no event are they to respond defensively. Repeated implementation of such conjoint activities establishes generational boundaries and conveys a clear message to children that parents are united and committed to safeguarding their private domain.

3. Negotiating agreements between parents that they will present a united front in parent-child transactions requiring decision making and/or disciplinary actions. Practitioners assist parents to agree that they will remove themselves from the presence of children to decide upon an appropriate course of action. Parents further agree that when a child approaches only one parent, that parent defers a decision until she or he can discuss the matter with the other and reach a joint decision (exceptions must be made, of course, when an immediate decision is essential). Parents further agree that neither will intervene when the other is disciplining a child, unless it is to support the parent.

4. Negotiating agreements that parents will not intercede into their children's

---

[10]We wish to acknowledge that these strategies are based in part on techniques described by H. C. Masson and P. O'Byrne, *Applying Family Therapy* (New York: Pergamon Press, 1984).

squabbles (except when a child's safety is in jeopardy). Parents should be instructed to leave the room when squabbles develop (or insist that children leave the room) and to explain that they expect their children to resolve their own disputes independently. By refusing to be drawn into children's squabbles, parents further clarify generational boundaries and avoid having to take sides in children's conflicts.

5. Negotiating agreements between parents that they will not permit children to assume a parental role with siblings (e.g., an older child deciding what television programs siblings will watch or forcing a younger child to complete a chore). By clarifying that the parents will make such decisions and have the final word, parents further define generational boundaries and avoid role diffusion.

Utilizing Space

Practitioners may employ space as a tool to facilitate communication and to strengthen and weaken emotional bonds by directing certain family members to sit next to each other (when seeking to strengthen bonds) or placing family members between certain others (when seeking to weaken attachments). Moreover, by having a person who often takes a plaintiff's role sit next to, rather than across from, a person whom she or he usually complains about or attacks, the practitioner takes the latter "out of the line of fire," thereby disrupting the usual pattern of interaction.

Arranging Sessions for Various Groupings of Family Members

Based on a determination (in consultation with the family) as to which alignments need to be modified, the practitioner may wish to arrange sessions with individuals so as to enhance opportunities of members to make designated changes. If a mother and son are involved in an enmeshed relationship that excludes the father, the practitioner can arrange to see the father and son alone for several sessions to plan ways of developing a closer relationship. During this time, the practitioner continues to meet conjointly with the spouses for the purpose of assisting them to strengthen their marital relationship. *When practitioners endeavor to loosen bonds between clients, they should simultaneously work to strengthen other bonds or to develop other alliances so that clients are not left with unmet emotional needs.*

Formulating Tasks That Strengthen Relationships or Encourage Rearrangements in Alignments

Practitioners can modify various alignments by asking various groupings of family members to assume relevant tasks. For example, when bonds are strong between a father and one son and weak between the father and another son, it is important to preserve the strong bonding in the first relationship while strengthening the bonding in the second. The practitioner may thus formulate a task with the father to spend a specified amount of time daily with *each* son and plan activities involving both sons at least once a week. In another situation, a practitioner may seek to modify a parent-child coalition that is maintained by the mother's encouraging the child to tattle on another child who is excluded from the coalition. To dismantle the coalition, the practitioner can ask the favored child to assume a task of reporting to the mother the *positive* behaviors of the other child during the week. In turn, the practitioner can negotiate with the mother the task of refraining from accepting negative feedback (e.g., "I don't need to know about that. Thank you anyway") and rewarding the favored child for conveying positive information about the other.

Intervening in Families and Groups: A Cultural Perspective

Utilizing an Ecological Approach with Families

Although this chapter has focused on modifying dysfunctional processes of families and groups, it is imperative that practitioners utilize an ecological approach that places equal emphasis on meeting minority families' immediate survival needs (employment, day care, housing). Sager, Brayboy, and Waxenburg (1970, p. 122) observe that the threat to survival leaves families "no time to luxuriate with purely psychic rumination. The actual threat to life is the number one priority. . . . Families that face external threat as well as internal psychic danger tend to see their problems largely in terms of environmental perils and obstacles." Practitioners thus must focus on family-environmental interaction, which includes intervening to address problems of housing, public assistance, and unresponsive social institutions and working with the extended family or other key people to reduce dysfunctional interaction and to increase support to a family. Pinderhughes (1982, p. 91), in fact, warns that failure of practitioners to focus on family-environmental interaction "may lead to a distorted understanding of family functioning and to interventions that may be pathogenic."

Engaging the Family

Describing work with Latino families, Bernal and Flores-Ortiz (1982) offer suggestions that are applicable in engaging most minority families. These authors suggest that practitioners welcome clients in their native language and have objects and symbols of the family's culture in their offices and waiting rooms. They also stress the importance of working through the father, who holds the position of power in most families. Addressing the father first and asking his permission to speak to other family members shows respect for culturally prescribed roles and hierarchy and conveys to the family that these roles and rules are not being challenged at the outset of therapy. The authors also caution that a family may view practitioners as they do medical doctors, ascribing to them power and authority and expecting them to give directives and advice and to provide a "cure" for the problem. Practitioners must thus be active, serving as advocate, friend, and advice-giver in order to assure the family's continuance in therapy.

Techniques of coupling or joining discussed earlier are particularly crucial in involving minority families. Engaging in sufficient warm-up periods, answering clients' questions warmly and directly, and showing a keen interest in the family's cultural background are but a few of the techniques practitioners can use to develop rapport. Home visits are invaluable to practitioners in assessing a family's functioning in its natural environment, enabling them to convey interest in the family by inquiring about portraits, cultural objects, and other items of interest. Attendance at events such as a wedding or family outing, of course, serves the same purpose.

The Practitioner's Role as a Culture Broker

As families struggle with the disparity between old and new values, practitioners may take on the role of "culture broker" by suggesting ways of incorporating and choosing between such values. In so doing, practitioners need to consider three acculturation issues identified by Spiegel (1982, pp. 44–45):

(1) the value patterns characteristic of the family's culture of origin; (2) where the family is in the acculturation process—that is, what values have been or are being changed at the time of intervention; and (3) the family's understanding or misunderstanding of mainstream American values.

The practitioner's role as culture broker may also extend to helping families to choose the roles and rules they may wish to incorporate in their family structure to meet the needs of individuals and of the family itself. Practitioners can assist families to understand the relativity of their own values, that they have choices about the values, rules, and roles they adopt, and that there are costs and benefits to the choices they make.

Avoiding Confrontive Techniques

With many ethnic families, confrontation techniques appear doomed to failure. In working with Asian-Americans, for example, Ho (1976) observes that confrontive approaches need to be supplanted with a directive approach that emphasizes humanistic attitudes and concrete service. The author also observes that to be effective group work approaches must be modified for most Asian-Americans for the following reasons:

For treatment groups to produce therapeutic results, members are expected to confront

each other openly from time to time. Such aggressive behavior, however, is looked upon as rude by Asian-Americans, who are taught to respect and not to openly challenge others' views. Free participation and exchange of opinions in a group also contradict Asian values of humility and modesty. . . . Group interaction requiring members to compete with each other will further alienate Asian-Americans, who do not wish to be singled out as winners or as losers, both of whom are considered deviants from the Asian cultural norm.

(p. 199)

Ho points out that Asian-American group members usually welcome participation in groups that offer

the opportunity to share problems and help each other with them. The concept of mutual aid and reciprocity is so humanistic and so fundamental to Asian culture that group members operating in this fashion are no longer conscious of the cultural inhibitions and defenses previously prohibiting social work intervention with their problems.

(p. 199)

The author also recommends that practitioners be assertive and structured in early stages of group interaction to allay anxiety and ambiguity that threaten Asian-American clients.

Removing Cultural Barriers in Groups

Groups composed of members from different ethnic groups pose particular challenges to practitioners, who, in addition to bridging the gap between themselves and group members, must also assist members to relate to each other. Doing this is no small task, for members of any ethnic group are susceptible to having prejudices against other such groups. One technique that appears particularly promising in eliminating prejudices and breaking down barriers involves eliciting folktales and folklore from group members. Greenbaum and Holmes (1983) suggest using the technique as a means of developing rapport and gaining information about a family's culture. However, this technique can also be utilized in groups because it offers rich insights into cultural differences and provides "recurring themes which reflect a people's perception of their world, hopes, dreams, values, beliefs, customs, frustrations, humor and problems as well as a means of solving them" (p. 417). Other techniques used to remove cultural barriers involve asking members to explain their own customs and values concerning such subjects as open expression of feelings of love and affection, male-female roles, family support systems, or childrearing practices.

18 Relaxation Training, Cognitive Restructuring, and Stress Inoculation

Interventions for Modifying Intrapersonal Systems

In this chapter, we narrow our focus to interventions that are applicable to specific aspects of individual functioning. Recall from Chapter 8 that clients' problems may be associated with biophysical, cognitive, emotional, and behavioral dysfunction. In this chapter, we delineate interventions that address these dimensions either directly or indirectly.

The first intervention, muscle relaxation training, involves working directly with the biophysical dimensions of problems. This intervention is valuable in assisting people to cope with powerful emotions and tension states that can impair individual functioning. The second intervention, cognitive restructuring, embodies techniques that practitioners employ in assisting clients to eliminate thoughts, beliefs, and images that foster problematic emotions and behavior. Self-instruction, a component of cognitive restructuring, is also a useful tool that clients can learn to employ in accomplishing tasks and performing various roles more effectively.

Stress inoculation training, the third intervention, entails integration of relaxation training, cognitive restructuring, and both overt and covert behavioral rehearsal. Mastery of this intervention, as well as those previously identified, thus equips practitioners with multidimensional skills that are applicable in enhancing clients' biophysical, cognitive, emotional, and behavioral functioning. Because clients' problems rarely are confined to only one dimension of functioning, practitioners may employ all of the interventions delineated in this chapter, together with other interventions, in work with any given client.

Muscle Relaxation Training

Although muscle relaxation as a means of coping with tension was first described by a physiologist (Jacobson, 1929) 60 years ago, the helping professions were slow to adopt this procedure as a means of assisting people to cope with problems of living. Almost 30 years later, Wolpe (1958) described muscle relaxation training as the first phase of a behavioral therapy procedure (systematic desensitization) he developed to desensitize people to various types of phobias (irrational fears). It has only been in the past 15 years, however, that muscle relaxation has come into its own as a discrete therapeutic procedure. To the best of our knowledge, Vattano (1978) was the first social work author to describe muscle relaxation procedures and to recommend this intervention for management of stress.

Uses of Muscle Relaxation

Numerous studies have reported that muscle relaxation has been used successfully to assist clients with problems related to high blood pressure, insomnia, asthma, tension and migraine headaches, anxiety, epileptic seizures, and compulsive behavior.

Moreover, Reynolds & Coats (1986) found that relaxation training was effective in treating moderately depressed adolescents, and Deffenbacher et al. (1987) have reported that relaxation training, used with cognitive procedures and social skills training, is effective in reducing clients' levels of anger. Muscle relaxation training also occupies a central role in the Lamaze (1958) method of childbirth. Lechnyr (1980a) describes the use of deep muscle relaxation in tandem with hypnosis as an adjunct to psychotherapy involving clients in states of emotional crisis. Goldfried (1977) has also reported the use of muscle relaxation as a procedure for coping with anxiety-producing situations (e.g., taking an examination or giving a speech). Practitioners thus may employ muscle relaxation training to particular advantage with clients who:

1. Are chronically tense and anxious.

2. Are acutely anxious as a result of a crisis situation.

3. Are anxious and fearful about various anticipated events or situations.

4. Have tension headaches, migraines, tightness of the chest, breathing difficul-

ties, and other psychophysiological reactions *when medical causes have been ruled out.*

5. Suffer with insomnia.

6. Have difficulty controlling anger.

7. Are moderately depressed.

Major advantages of relaxation training include the fact that it is a simple procedure that clients can readily learn and can practice at home, which enables them to master the procedure in a few weeks' time. Another advantage is that clients can employ abbreviated forms of muscle relaxation in diverse stressful situations, thereby reducing tension and enhancing coping efforts. Muscle relaxation also shares much in common with meditation and is a major component of other interventions, including biofeedback (Lechnyr, 1980b), stress inoculation (Meichenbaum, 1977), and systematic desensitization (Wolpe, 1958). The combination of muscle relaxation training and cognitive restructuring is especially potent in reducing or neutralizing anxiety associated with feared situations and in assisting persons who engage in violence (especially in child and spouse abuse) to gain control of their anger (Edleson, 1984; Neidig & Friedman, 1984; Saunders, 1984).

Cautions

Although muscle relaxation training can be employed in diverse situations, it is important to employ this procedure with discrimination, for there are limitations and contraindications associated with this modality. For example, although muscle relaxation training is useful in assisting people to regain emotional control following a crisis, it should not be employed as a substitute for coping with situations that have created or contributed to the crisis. If a crisis is precipitated by sudden loss of a job, family disruption, loss of housing, unplanned pregnancy, or other stress, to achieve *enduring* benefit, you must implement other interventions that address the sources of the crises. When clients are distraught, panicky, or otherwise overwhelmed by intense emotionality, however, muscle relaxation serves as a useful adjunct in assisting them to regain equilibrium, thereby enabling them to begin exploring their problems.

Another caution relates to clients with motor disorders (e.g., cerebral palsy) or muscular or skeletal disorders. These clients should not engage in muscle relaxation exercises without clearance from a physician.

Implementing Muscle Relaxation Training

While instructing clients in muscle relaxation, it is important to observe the guidelines spelled out in the following sections.

Explaining the Rationale of the Procedure and Gaining Consent   To gain maximal cooperation of clients, practitioners should explain the purpose of muscle relaxation and obtain their consent. It has been our experience that clients readily and willingly agree to participate in the procedure, for they typically are highly motivated to gain alleviation from the discomfort produced by excessive tension, anxiety, or fear. In explaining the rationale, we recommend you include the following factors:

1. The causes and adverse effects of excessive tension.

2. The beneficial effects of muscle relaxation.

3. The diverse uses of muscle relaxation.

4. The need to develop a "muscle sense"; that is, to recognize the presence of excessive tension.

5. The need to practice to gain mastery of the procedure.

The following is an example of an explanation of the rationale of the procedure:

Life can be pretty hectic, causing people to become tense at times. When this happens, they often tighten their muscles, sometimes without even being aware of it.

Sometimes, when people become tense or uptight, they experience pain in various muscles. Prolonged tension can produce muscle spasms, headache, and even gastrointestinal difficulties caused by involuntary contractions of the smooth muscles in the stomach and the intestines.

When people are chronically tense, they may experience other physical reactions such as elevation in blood pressure and heart rate, headaches, and nervous stomach. Excessive muscle tension also burns up energy rapidly and can produce fatigue. Muscle tension can also interfere with sleep. Fortunately, by learning to relax the skeletal muscles, you can counter all of these negative effects. Some individuals who have practiced and gained skill in muscle relaxation have reported improvements in blood pressure, heart rate, sleeping, or reductions in headaches and other symptoms produced by tension. Muscle relaxation can also be used to cope more effectively with anger and with situations that ordinarily cause tension.

Muscle relaxation first involves developing awareness of the sensation of tension in your muscles. The procedure heightens awareness of the sensations of tension in various muscle groups, and you'll become keenly aware of the difference between tension and relaxation. You're also going to learn how to instruct your muscles to relax so that when you're aware of tension you can consciously reduce it.

I'm going to instruct you in a procedure that you can practice in your home. By practicing each day, you'll become more and more skillful so that you won't need to relax all of the muscle groups separately. Some people, in fact, learn to relax in a matter of a few seconds but only after much practice. I'll tell you more about how to practice later.

Clarifying Conditions Conducive to Relaxation Optimal conditions for relaxation training include a comfortable and quiet environment. Further, furniture that permits relaxed posture should be employed, such as a reclining chair or padded chaise lounge. When instructing a group, padded floor mats or blankets may be used if appropriate furniture is not available.

Clients should wear loose-fitting clothing that permits freedom of movement. We recommend that you explain to clients that tight-fitting clothing restricts movements and produces discomfort that may be distracting. It is also desirable to suggest that clients make these same arrangements for comfort when they practice relaxation training at home. As they gain facility in relaxing their muscles, the environment becomes less important. Indeed, the ultimate goal is for them to learn to relax in stress-producing situations.

Guidelines for Instructing Clients To assist you in instructing clients in muscle relaxation, we offer the following guidelines, which involve a synthesis of procedures developed by Jacobson (1929), Bernstein and Borkovec (1973), and ourselves. We recommend that you study these guidelines until you have memorized them and that you practice instructing friends, relatives, or student colleagues in muscle relaxation before applying the procedures with individual clients or groups.

1. Allow sufficient time to apply the procedure. Preliminary discussion, implementation of the procedure, and subsequent discussion and planning usually consume the largest part of a 50-minute session.

2. Explain that when you ask clients to tighten a group of muscles, you do not mean for them to tense the muscles as hard as they can. Tightening muscles to the extreme can strain a muscle; tightening them to the point of uncomfortable tension is sufficient.

3. Explain that to enhance muscle relaxation, clients should breathe deeply, exhaling all the air, and think the word *relax* when you instruct them to relax. (Deep breathing facilitates relaxation as does thinking the word *relax*.). Ask them to practice with you. Model taking three or four deep breaths and exhaling completely. Ask them to do the same, concentrating on the word *relax*. Explain that you will remind them of this procedure with the first two muscle groups, but thereafter you want them to continue this breathing procedure without further reminders.

4. Explain that as clients relax their muscles they may experience warm, heavy, or tingling sensations. They should not be alarmed because these sensations are merely indications that they are succeeding in achieving relaxation.

5. Explain that you will be practicing muscle relaxation along with them. Practicing in concert with clients enhances timing in giving instruction and models appropriate behaviors. Moreover, clients are less likely to feel awkward and self-conscious if you participate with them in applying the procedure.

6. Speak with a relaxing and soothing tone of voice but avoid being dramatic. When you use the word *relax,* express it slowly and softly in a manner that fosters relaxation.

Instructing Clients in Applying the Procedure After you have explained the rationale of muscle relaxation, provided the explanation of the procedure as detailed in the preceding guidelines, and obtained clients' consent, you are ready to instruct them in applying the procedure.

Instructing clients in muscle relaxation involves five discrete activities (Bernstein & Borkovec, 1973) that occur in the following sequence:

1. Draw the client's attention to the appropriate muscle group.

2. Instruct the client to tense the muscle group (we will list the muscle groups and provide directions for tensing them later).

3. Ask the client to hold the tension (for five to seven seconds) and to be aware of the sensations in the affected muscles.

4. Instruct the client to relax.

5. Instruct the client to be aware of the pleasant feeling of relaxation as contrasted to the discomfort associated with tension (relaxation interval lasts about 10 seconds).

To enhance clients' awareness of varying degrees of muscle tension, we instruct them to tense and to relax each group of muscles three times, reducing the degree of tension during the second and third contractions. We also emphasize the importance of being aware of the sensations of tension and contrasting them with the feelings of relaxation, as we illustrate below in the instructions to clients.

Before actually engaging in muscle relaxation, ask clients to get into a comfortable position. Then explain that you are going to teach them to relax 16 different muscle groups. Ask them to listen closely and to follow your instructions carefully. You are now ready to begin with the muscle groups, which should be relaxed in the sequence listed. (Different authors suggest lists of muscle groups that vary slightly. The list below is the one we have found most useful.) To assist you in giving instructions, we have provided a verbatim example for the first muscle group and partial instructions for the third and fifth muscle groups. We

have also listed the remaining muscle groups together with methods of tensing them. Instructions for the remaining muscle groups are essentially the same as for those we have illustrated.

1. *Fingers and hands.* "We're going to begin with your finger and hand muscles. Clench both of your fists tightly as I'm doing but not too tightly. Keep them clenched and be aware of the tension in your fingers, the back of your hand, and your forearm. [*After seven seconds.*] Now r-e-l-a-x. Tell yourself to relax, take a deep breath, and exhale all the air. Let your hand be limp and be aware of the pleasant feelings [*After 10 seconds.*] Now I want you to make a fist again, but tense your muscles *just half as tight* as last time. Be aware of where you feel the tension. [*Pause for a few seconds.*] Now relax, breathe deeply, and think the word 'relax.' Let the tension flow out of your fingertips and enjoy the relaxation. [*After 10 seconds.*] Make a fist again, but this time tighten your fingers very lightly so that you can barely feel the tension. Hold your hand in this position and be aware that you can still feel the tension in the same places. [*Brief pause.*] Now relax, take a deep breath, and think the word 'relax.' Just savor the exhilarating feeling of relaxation for a few moments."

2. *Wrist and lower arm.* "Bend your wrists forward toward your head and point your fingers toward the ceiling so that you feel tension in the muscles in the back of your hand and forearm." [*Repeat procedure described with first muscle group, but explain that clients will need to remember to breathe deeply and think the word "relax."*]

3. *Upper arm/biceps.* "Now we're going to work with your upper arm muscles. Make your hands into fists and bring them toward your shoulders, tightening your biceps. Hold the muscles tightly and be

aware of the tension in your upper arm. [*After five to seven seconds.*] Now relax and let all the tension drain out of your arms and fingers. Be aware of the pleasurable feeling of relaxation, and just enjoy it for a few moments." [*Repeat procedure after pauses, using reduced degrees of tension as indicated for group 1.*]

4. *Shoulders.* "Shrug both of your shoulders, bringing them close to your ears."

5. *Forehead and eyebrows.* "Now that you've relaxed your shoulders, you should have a refreshing relaxed feeling down both of your arms. Notice the pleasant feeling when your arms are free of tension. Now we'll work on relaxing the muscles of the face. First, wrinkle your brow tightly. Make it furrow as though you are scowling and be aware of the tension in your forehead and eyebrows. [*Pause.*] Now relax. Smooth out your forehead until the muscles are loose. Be aware of the feeling of relaxation and enjoy it a few moments." [*Pause for 10 seconds.*] [*Repeat the preceding twice, tensing the muscles only half as tightly the second time and very lightly the third time as illustrated for group 1. Vary your words to avoid being monotonous.*]

6. *Eyes.* "Close your eyes tightly and be aware of the tension around your eyes."

7. *Jaws.* "Clench your jaws together and study the tension and discomfort in your jaws, cheeks, and temples." [*With clients who wear dentures, you may use alternate exercises of having them push their tongue against the roof of the mouth or thrust their lower jaw forward.*]

8. *Lips.* "Now press your lips together tightly and be aware of the tension all around your mouth."

9. *Back neck muscles.* "Push your head backward into the chair. Be aware of the tension in the back of your neck and in the upper part of your back."

10. *Front neck muscles.* "Now, we're going to work with your front neck muscles. Tilt your head forward so that your chin is tight against your chest. Concentrate on the tension in the front of your neck."

11. *Back.* [*Advise clients who have lower back pain or spinal difficulties to avoid straining their back.*] "Now, turn your attention to your upper back. Arch your back by sticking out your chest and stomach. Study the tension and discomfort in your back."

12. *Chest.* [*Many clients complain of tightness in the chest when they are tense and anxious.*] "Take a deep breath and hold it, thrusting your chest forward. Be aware of the tension in your chest and upper abdomen. [*Pause.*] Now exhale completely and just relax. Enjoy the pleasant feeling of relaxation."

13. *Abdomen.* "Now focus on your stomach area. Pull in your stomach and tighten the muscles of your abdomen so that they feel like a knot."

14. *Upper leg.* [*Take one leg at a time.*] "Lift your right leg and hold it. Get in touch with the tension in your upper leg." [*Repeat with left leg after alternately raising and lowering right leg three times.*]

15. *Lower leg.* "Direct your attention to your lower leg. Now flex your ankle and point your toes at your head. Be aware of the tension in your lower leg."

16. *Feet and toes.* "Arch your foot by tightening your toes and pushing them against the floor. Experience the tension in your toes and in the ball of your foot."

After tensing and relaxing each muscle group three times, the next step is to review each muscle group and to instruct the client to dispel residual tension. To accomplish this, draw attention to each muscle group as follows:

Now we're going to go over all the muscle groups again. As I name each group, be aware of any tension remaining in those muscles. If you feel tension, focus on those muscles, breathe deeply, and instruct them to relax. Think of the tension draining completely from your body. Let's begin with the toes and feet. If you feel any tension, let it drain out [*five-second pause*].

Then repeat the procedure with each muscle group, moving from the muscle groups in the legs to the abdomen, lower back, chest, shoulder, upper arms, lower arms, hands, neck, and ending with the facial muscles. After relaxing the facial muscles, instruct the client to remain relaxed from head to toes and to sit quietly and enjoy being relaxed for a few moments. Note that you instruct the client to relax each group *once* in the review.

To evaluate the extent of relaxation achieved, ask clients to relate their degree of relaxation on a scale from 1 to 10, where 1 represents complete relaxation and 10 extreme tension. If the client reports an uncomfortable level of tension, you may wish to suggest implementing an additional procedure to deepen the degree of relaxation. Akin to self-hypnosis (Lechnyr, 1980a), this procedure involves instructing the client to take 10 deep breaths as follows:

Listen very carefully to me, and shut off all other thoughts. Breathe deeply and easily [*model deep breathing*]—that's right. Now I'm going to count to 10 slowly. With each number, you will become more and more relaxed. By the 10th breath, you will be very relaxed and sleepy. Now, one [*pause*], you're becoming more relaxed. Two [*shorter pause*], still more relaxed. [*Continue counting slowly with a soft, soothing voice, suggesting deeper relaxation with each count.*]

When you have finished counting, your client should be deeply relaxed and may be in a light hypnotic trance. Instruct the client to remain relaxed for a few moments and enjoy it fully. After a pause of 20 seconds or so, instruct the client as follows:

I'm going to count backwards from five, and with each count, you will feel more alert. When I reach "one" you will be fully alert and will feel refreshed and relaxed.

When you have finished and the client is alert, explain that in the future the client can employ this procedure independently by breathing easily and deeply and counting from 1 to 10, becoming increasingly relaxed with each count. You may explain that this is a form of self-hypnosis that many people use to relax or to go to sleep.

Post-Training Follow-up   After completing the preceding relaxation training procedure, it is important to emphasize again that learning to relax, like any other skill, requires considerable practice. To master the skill, therefore, the client should practice 20 to 30 minutes daily under the conditions specified earlier. After practicing each day, the client should rate the degree of relaxation achieved using the scale described earlier, thereby making it possible to assess progress.

After clients have consistently practiced relaxing the 16 muscle groups for a week or two and report satisfactory progress in achieving relaxation, they are ready to advance to more streamlined forms of muscle relaxation. One such form involves reducing the number of muscle groups from 16 to 4 by combining the muscle groups into major anatomical parts of the body, which include the following:

1. Fingers, hands, lower arms, and upper arms.

2. Face and neck muscles.

3. Shoulders, back, chest, and abdominal muscles.

4. Upper legs, lower legs, feet, and toes.

The instructions for relaxing these four muscle groups are similar to those outlined earlier. Instruct the client to tighten and relax each of the muscle groups three different times, decreasing the degree of tension the second and third time according to the pattern described earlier. Taking a deep breath while simultaneously thinking the word "relax" is also part of the procedure. Counting to 10 while breathing deeply after relaxing all four muscle groups is optional according to the degree of relaxation reported by the client. After completing this procedure, you should again instruct the client to practice relaxing the four muscle groups daily for one week.

When the client reports success in relaxing the four muscle groups, you may employ a still more advanced procedure termed *recall* (Bernstein & Borkovec, 1973). Employing this procedure, the client relaxes the four muscle groups without first tensing them, focusing instead upon recall of the sensations experienced during the previous procedure. In introducing the client to the recall procedure, you can use an explanation similar to the following:

Now we're going to increase your skills in relaxing your muscles without the need to tighten them first. Relax the muscles in your hands and lower and upper arms, and contrast the feeling of relaxation with your memory of what it was like to release the tension in these same muscles as you practiced during the week. Just relax now and enjoy it. If any tension remains, send the message "relax" to the muscles and let the tension flow out of them.

Because muscles are not tightened in the recall procedure, muscle groups are relaxed only once. Counting to 10 while breathing easily and deeply is again optional according to the degree of relaxation the client reports.

When clients have mastered the recall procedure, they are ready to begin applying relaxation procedures as a means of coping with daily stresses. Explain to them that as they become aware of being excessively tense, they can take deep and easy breaths, think the word "relax," and consciously relax tense muscles that are not needed in given situations (e.g., the facial, chest, and abdominal muscles). By consciously practicing and employing muscle relaxation, they are developing a valuable coping tool they can use all their lives. Situations in which this tool can serve them are numerous. Some common situations in which our clients have used muscle relaxation include the following: driving under nerve-wracking conditions, waiting up for children who stay out late, taking an examination, giving a talk, managing an aversive social situation, talking to a supervisor, overcoming sexual fears, reducing self-consciousness, keeping anger under control, and mastering various types of irrational fears.

Abbreviated Muscle Relaxation Training for Crisis Situations   The procedures described in the preceding sections commonly extend across two to six weeks. When clients are overwhelmed by crisis situations, however, abbreviated muscle relaxation training often provides temporary relief from extreme tension and enables clients to reestablish emotional equilibrium. In such instances, practitioners can assist clients to achieve relaxation during a session by having them practice taking deep breaths, visualize pleasant and tranquil scenes, relax the four major muscle groups, and think appropriate cue words such as "calm," "relax," and "peaceful." Should extreme tension recur between sessions, clients can implement these same procedures. Lechnyr (1980a) has reported successful results using similar procedures with clients in crisis states. Other researchers have experimented with modifications of relaxation procedures including tape-recorded instructions, brief procedures (Marks, 1975), and use of biofeedback in tandem with muscle relaxation. Based on a review of this research, Borkovec and Sides (1979) have concluded that taped relaxation instructions are less effective than therapist-directed instructions. Lehrer (1982) has also concluded that brief procedures (often employing hypnosis) are not as effective as a full course of relaxation training and that biofeedback does not enhance the efficacy of relaxation training.

Cognitive Restructuring

Although the large majority of theories of casework, counseling, and psychotherapy acknowledge the central role of cognition (i.e., thoughts, beliefs, images, and interpretations of events) in human behavior, it has only been in recent years that theories and techniques have been developed that can be applied directly and systematically to problems of cognitive dysfunction. With the exception of Adlerian therapy, earlier therapies dealt with clients' misconceptions and mistaken beliefs only indirectly. Almost three decades ago, however, Ellis' (1962) book, *Reason and Emotion in Psychotherapy,* posited the theory of rational-emotive therapy (RET). This work proved to be seminal, and since that time, particularly in the past 15

years, cognitive therapy has burgeoned. Numerous books and articles have been published delineating the significance of mistaken beliefs and faulty patterns of thought in diverse emotional and behavioral problems ranging from childhood and adolescence (Weisz et al., 1987) to old age (Lam et al., 1987). Many of these same publications also describe the application of cognitive therapy (CT) to widely varying disorders. Perhaps most significant of these publications is *The Cognitive Therapy of Depression* (Beck et al., 1979), a book widely recognized as *the* definitive work on treatment of depression. Further, research studies have documented that cognitive/behavioral therapy is one of the two major psychotherapeutic approaches that produces outcomes equivalent to those produced by antidepressant medication. One of these studies (Elkin et al., 1986) was a sophisticated large-scale study conducted at three major universities under auspices of the National Institute of Mental Health.

Recent articles indicate that social workers have adopted CT as a major treatment modality. Cohen (1985) has reported on the use of CT with criminals; Barth (1985) has described cognitive/behavioral treatment of depression in mothers who maltreat children; and Marshall and Mazie (1987) have delineated a cognitive approach to treating depression. Schrodt and Fitzgerald (1987) present a rationale for using CT in work with adolescents. It is thus evident that CT has strong empirical support and has entered the mainstream of interventions employed by social workers.

The basic premise of cognitive theorists is that most social and behavioral dysfunction results directly from misconceptions that people hold about themselves, other people, and various life situations. To be maximally effective therefore, practitioners must become proficient in assessing cognitive functioning and in applying appropriate interventions to enhance cognitive functioning. (Recall that we focused on assessing cognitive functioning in Chapters 9 and 11 and listed examples of contrasting functional and dysfunctional beliefs.) Many cognitive theorists have also taken a multidimensional stance. Beck's "cognitive" therapy of depression, for example, embodies many elements of behavior modification as well as concepts drawn from client-centered therapy.

Uses of Cognitive Restructuring

Cognitive restructuring is a systematic intervention that is particularly useful in assisting clients to gain awareness of dysfunctional and self-defeating thoughts and misconceptions that impair personal functioning and to replace them with beliefs and behaviors that are aligned with reality and lead to enhanced functioning. Cognitive restructuring techniques are particularly relevant for problems associated with low self-esteem; distorted perceptions in interpersonal relations; unrealistic expectations of self, others, and life in general; irrational fears, anxiety, and depression; inadequate control of anger and other impulses; and lack of assertiveness. Practitioners have found cognitive restructuring to be especially useful in assisting people with problems of impulse control manifested in child abuse (Barth, 1985; Zastrow, 1981) and spouse abuse (Edleson, 1984; Neidig & Friedman, 1984; Saunders, 1984).

Cognitive restructuring is often blended with other interventions (e.g., modeling, behavioral rehearsal, relaxation training, assertiveness training, drug therapy, and desensitization) because combinations of interventions are sometimes more potent in producing change than are single interventions.

Cautions

Although cognitive theorists attribute most dysfunctional emotional and behavioral patterns to mistaken beliefs, they are by no means the only causes. Dysfunction may be produced by various biophysical problems, including brain tissue damage, neurological disorders, thyroid imbalance, blood sugar imbalance, circulatory disorders associated with aging, ingestion of toxic substances, malnutrition, and other forms of chemical imbalance in the body (Lantz, 1978). Consequently, these possibilities should be considered before undertaking cognitive restructuring.

Tenets of Cognitive Therapy

Before reviewing the major tenets of the undergirding theory of CT, it is important to note that although we have alluded to CT as a unitary entity, several therapies have in fact been termed cognitive therapies. Different authors have included rational-emotive therapy (RET), Adlerian therapy, reality therapy, transactional analysis, problem-solving therapies, and even certain phenomenological therapies under the rubric of CT. As we use the term, however, we are referring only to those therapies that employ cognitive restructuring as the primary modality— namely RET and its offshoots.

A major tenet of CT, to which we alluded earlier, is that thinking is a basic determinant of behavior. Thinking consists of statements that people say to themselves, and it is this inner dialogue, rather than unconscious forces, that is the key to understanding behavior. To grasp this first major tenet accurately, practitioners must clearly differentiate *thinking* from *feeling*. Clients (and practitioners, too) often confuse feelings and thoughts, which tends to foster confusion in communication and hinders successful implementation of cognitive restructuring techniques. The confusion is manifested in messages such as, "I feel our marriage is on the rocks," or "I feel nobody cares about me." The word *feel* is used incorrectly in these messages, which do *not* involve feelings but rather embody views, thoughts, or beliefs. Thoughts per se are devoid of feelings, although they are often accompanied by and tend to generate feelings or emotions. Feelings involve emotions, such as sadness, joy, disappointment, exhilaration, and any of the hundreds of feelings listed in the "Affective Words and Phrases" found in Chapter 5.

To assist clients to differentiate between feelings and cognitions, it is helpful to explain the difference and to provide several examples of both. Thereafter, it is important to intervene when clients fail to distinguish between these functions. It is critical that clients be able to make these distinctions, for self-monitoring of cognitions (discussed later) requires this ability.

A second major tenet of cognitive therapy is that the past is important only in identifying the origins of faulty thinking. It is the present faulty thinking, not the past, that motivates behavior. Further, new patterns of thinking can be learned and problems resolved without determining the origins of faulty thinking. Therefore, the focus of cognitive therapy is largely on the present and the future. Clients are not permitted to use the past as an excuse for present difficulties.

Still another major tenet of cognitive therapy is that to make constructive changes, people must realize that their misconceptions may produce or contribute to many of their problems, and they must assume responsibility for modifying these misconceptions. In our view, this assumption must be tempered with the recognition that many factors contribute to the problems of clients, including inadequate resources and adverse environmental conditions. Still, with clients whose problems are rooted in misconceptions and faulty logic, this tenet is valid. The thrust of this tenet is that as practitioners we must assist clients to assume maximal responsibilities for themselves.

Steps in Cognitive Restructuring

As with muscle relaxation training, several discrete steps are involved in cognitive restructuring. Different authors vary slightly in their definitions of these steps, but the similarities are far greater than the differences. The steps we have found most useful are those identified by Goldfried (1977) and Cormier and Cormier (1979). These steps together with guidelines for implementing them are as follows:

1. Assist clients to accept that their self-statements, assumptions, and beliefs largely mediate (i.e., determine or govern) their emotional reactions to life's events. Assisting clients to accept this explanation is vital, for clients are unlikely to commit themselves to procedures that they view skeptically or reject. To enhance their acceptance, we recommend that you present the rationale for cognitive restructuring and also demonstrate its relevance by citing common life experiences that document how cognitions mediate emotions. We recommend that you draw examples from your own experiences, if possible, because they will be most meaningful to you. To guide you in assisting clients to accept the rationale of cognitive restructuring, we offer the following example of an explanation provided to a client who was severely inhibited in social situations by feelings of inadequacy and social incompetence.

For you to achieve your goal of expressing yourself more openly with others, we first need to determine what happens inside you that maintains your fears. That will involve your becoming aware of thoughts you experience in social situations—in other words, what you say to yourself before, during, and after social situations. Generally, such thoughts occur automatically, and you won't be fully aware of many of them. We also want to discover assumptions and beliefs you have about social situations—beliefs you may have had much of your life. Becoming aware of self-defeating thoughts, assumptions, and beliefs is an extremely important first step in discarding them in favor of others that serve you better.

Your thoughts, or self-statements, are extremely important because what you think determines in large measure what you feel and do. For example, if a friend tells me I'm stupid because I bought a new car instead of a used one, I can make various meanings or self-statements related to that message, each of which results in different feelings and actions. Consider, for instance, the different ways I might think about this:

He's probably right; he's a bright guy, and I respect his judgment. Why didn't I think of buying a used car? He must really think I'm a clod. If I think that, I'll feel crummy about myself, probably regret buying a new car, and won't enjoy it as much as I might.

Who does he think he is calling me stupid? He's the one who's stupid. What a jerk! If I think that, I'll feel angry and defensive. I may get in a heated argument over the merits of a new car or a used one.

It's apparent that we have different ideas on that subject. He's entitled to his opinion, although I certainly don't agree with him and do feel good about what I did. I don't like his referring to my decision as stupid, though. No point getting bent out of shape over it, but I think I'll let him know I don't feel good about his putting me down that way. If I think these thoughts, I'm not going to experience negative feelings. I'll feel good about my actions despite the other person's difference of opinion and I won't be unduly influenced by his insensitivity.

There are other meanings I could make, of course, but these should make the point. To enable you to master your fears, we'll explore together statements you make to yourself and how they affect your feelings and behavior. After we've identified thoughts and beliefs that are causing difficulties, we'll begin working on developing others that are realistic and consistent with your goal of expressing yourself more openly in social situations.

When the rationale is presented in a simple, straightforward manner, the majority of clients respond positively. Nevertheless, it is important to elicit clients' reactions to your explanation and to invite discussion. It is important not to proceed with cognitive restructuring until clients manifest receptivity and commitment to implementing the intervention. Clients, indeed, tend to resist changing their beliefs if they feel they are being coerced to adopt the beliefs of someone else. Resistance under such circumstances, in our opinion, represents a healthy assertion of one's right to self-determination.

2. Assist clients to identify dysfunctional beliefs and patterns of thoughts that underlie their problems. Once clients accept the proposition that thoughts and beliefs mediate emotional reactions, the next task is to assist them to examine *personal* thoughts and beliefs that pertain to their difficulties. This step involves detailed exploration of events related to problematic situations, with particular emphasis upon cognitions that accompany distressing emotions. For example, some clients mistakenly attribute their problems to factors such as fate, inherent personal inadequacy or unlovability, and various forces beyond their control. In identifying key misconceptions, it is vital that practitioners achieve a "common conceptualization" with clients as to what problematic beliefs need to be changed (Meichenbaum, 1975). There are a variety of ways of achieving a common conceptualization, but the preferred approach, according to Meichenbaum, is to proceed so that "the client feels he is an active participant and contributor" (p. 365).

You can begin the process of exploration by focusing on problematic events that occurred during the preceding week or on events surrounding a problem the client has targeted for change. As you mutually explore these events, it is important to elicit specific details regarding overt behavior, cognitions (i.e., self-statements and images), and emotional reactions. Focusing on all three aspects of behavior enables you to assist the client to see the connections between them and to grasp the role of cognitions in mediating feeling and behavior. As clients identify their self-statements and beliefs, they become increasingly aware that automatic thoughts and beliefs they have not subjected to critical analysis are powerful determinants of their behavior. This, in turn, increases their receptivity and motivation to work on tasks involving liberating themselves from these dysfunctional thoughts and beliefs.

As you engage in explorations, it is important to identify thoughts and feelings that occur *before, during* and *after* events. To elicit such self-statements, ask clients to recreate the situation just as it unfolded, recalling exactly what they thought, felt, and actually did. If clients experience difficulty, it may be helpful to follow a procedure recommended by Meichenbaum (1977, p. 152) of having clients close their eyes and "run a movie" of the problematic event, including thoughts and feelings that preceded, accompanied, and followed the event.

Identifying self-statements and assumptions that precede events makes it possible to pinpoint cognitive sets that predispose clients to experience certain emotions and to behave in predictable ways. For example, our socially inhibited client, cited earlier, disclosed she made the following self-statements *before* a disappointing discussion with fellow workers in the lunchroom.

- "I'm not sure I want to join the others. If I do, I'll just sit there and feel left out."

- "I'll bet they'd rather I didn't join them. They probably think I'm a real bore."

- "I'd better join them, I guess. If I don't, they'll ask me where I was, and I'll have to come up with some lame excuse."

Given these self-statements, the client felt uneasy and apprehensive about joining her co-workers. As typically occurred, these thoughts predisposed her to enter the situation programmed for defeat. Moreover, she was tense and preoccupied with herself as she engaged in self-debate and finally decided to eat with her fellow workers. Such preoccupation is self-defeating because it limits involvement by dominating thinking with fears and worries about making mistakes.

Exploration of self-statements *during* events reveals how dysfunctional thoughts maintain self-defeating feelings and behavior and drastically reduce personal effectiveness. For example, clients who dwell on worries and are hypervigilant to possible negative reactions of others are unable to "tune in" fully to discussions and to express themselves in positive ways that create favorable impressions. In other words, it is difficult for them to be fully present and involved because of self-consciousness and fears of exposing their imagined personal inadequacies. To illustrate the destructive impact of such dysfunctional thoughts, let us again consider the self-statements of our socially inhibited client *during* lunch with her co-workers:

- "Well, here I am again, and it's just like it's always been. I'm just out of it."

- "I wish I had something interesting to say, but my life's such a drag. They couldn't possibly be interested in anything I might say."

- "They're probably wondering why I even join them. I sure don't add anything to the group. I wish I could just disappear."

It is apparent from these and other like self-statements that the client dwells on self-demeaning thoughts. She thinks of herself as having little or nothing to offer, behaves accordingly, and feels unwanted and unworthy to participate actively. Her preoccupation with these thoughts and assumptions about herself blocks her from engaging in ongoing interaction with her peers.

Clients' self-statements and feelings *following* events reveal the impact of earlier thoughts and behaviors on subsequent feelings, thereby highlighting further the mediating function of cognitions. Moreover, the conclusions clients draw about the outcomes of events indicate further whether they are able to focus on positive aspects of their behavior and to identify challenges for further growth or whether they merely perceive an event as the latest in a long series of failures caused by their personal inadequacies. The meanings clients make of events, of course, are powerful in shaping their attitudes and feelings toward similar future events, as illustrated by the thoughts and feelings of our familiar client:

- "I blew it again. I might as well quit trying. No use kidding myself. I just can't talk with others."

- "They didn't really try to include me. It's obvious they could care less about me. They'd probably be pleased if I didn't join them tomorrow."

- "I think I won't eat lunch with them anymore. I don't enjoy it, and I'm sure they don't either. Tomorrow I'll just eat by myself."

Clearly, this client's thoughts lead to feelings of utter failure. Without intervention into her circular self-defeating patterns of thought, she will tend to withdraw even further socially. It could be expected that she would experience further self-demeaning thoughts accompanied by depressed feelings.

As you mutually identify self-statements, it is important to assist clients to assess the degree of rationality of these self-statements. Through guided practice in critically analyzing the validity of their thoughts, clients gain experience that prepares them to engage in a similar process outside the sessions. Clients, however, may not acknowledge the irrationality of certain beliefs, especially those that are deeply embedded in their belief systems. Indeed, clients can cling tenaciously to key misconceptions and argue persuasively about their validity. Practitioners must therefore be prepared to challenge or "dispute" such irrational beliefs and to persist in assisting clients to recognize the costs or disadvantages associated with not relinquishing these beliefs. Walen, DiGuiseppe, and Wessler (1980) present and illustrate comprehensive strategies for disputing beliefs, and we strongly recommend this reference. Techniques that challenge clients to assess the rationality of their beliefs and self-statements include:

1. Asking them how they reached certain conclusions.

2. Challenging them to present evidence supporting dysfunctional views or beliefs.

3. Challenging the logic of beliefs that magnify feared consequences of certain actions.

To illustrate the applications of these techniques, we have provided three self-statements, or beliefs, followed by responses that direct clients to analyze their validity.

1. *Self-statement:* "I've got to study every available moment. If I don't get the highest score on that test, it will be just awful."

   a. "Let's just suppose for a moment you really bombed out on that test. What would it really mean?"

   b. "So if you're not number 1, it will be a catastrophe. I can agree it's nice to be number 1, but why is it such a disaster to be number 2 or number 15 for that matter?"

2. *Self-statement:* "I don't want to tend her children, but if I don't she'll be furious. I don't dare risk displeasing her."

   a. "How have you concluded she'd be furious?"

   b. "Suppose you did risk turning her down and she got furious. Perhaps a question you should answer is whether you are going to let possible unreasonable reactions on her part dictate your behavior."

3. *Self-statement:* "There's no point in talking to my teacher. She's got it in for me, and there's no way she'd believe I want to do better in her class."

   a. "How can you be so sure? What evidence do you have that she wouldn't believe you?"

   b. "Sounds like you've talked yourself into a corner. I gather things haven't gone well between you and your teacher, but how can you be sure it's hopeless if you don't put it to a test?"

Raimy (1975) maintains that clusters of misconceptions are commonly associated with dysfunctional behavior. Often it is possible to discern such patterns of thoughts even by the end of one session. By closely following feelings and eliciting accompanying thoughts, you can identify such clusters early on. Dysfunctional thoughts typically include the following clusters of misconceptions:

1. About one's self.

2. About others' perceptions and expectations of oneself.

3. Expectations of oneself.

4. Expectations of others.

Raimy has also identified clusters of misconceptions typically associated with several types of mental disorders. Space limitations preclude listing these misconceptions, but for illustrative purpose we have provided our own conception of mistaken beliefs associated with unreasonable self-expectations:

- "I must be the best in everything I do."

- "It is terrible if I am unsuccessful in any venture."

- "I am worthwhile as a person only if I am constantly working."

- "I never quite achieve the level of excellence I should."

- " When I compare myself with others, I never quite measure up."

- "I should be able to succeed in any endeavor; if I don't, it's because I'm incompetent."

- "I should be able to accept numerous assignments and perform all at a high level."

- "I don't really deserve praise for my accomplishments because they're not that significant."

- "If I'm not perfect in everything I do, it is terrible, and I'm a failure."

By identifying clusters or patterns of misconceptions, you can direct your efforts to the theme common to all of them, rather than dealing with each as a separate entity. Common to the cluster identified in the preceding is the theme of setting unrealistic expectations for oneself. By focusing on this central theme, you can conserve efforts, for the related misconceptions are merely derivatives of the central one and lose their potency when the core misconception is resolved.

By gaining practice in identifying and assessing the validity of self-statements and beliefs during sessions, clients achieve readiness to engage in self-monitoring *between* sessions. After the session in which you introduce clients to cognitive restructuring and mutually explore cognitions related to their difficulties, it is timely to negotiate a task that involves self-monitoring of thoughts and beliefs related to problematic events that occur between sessions. Self-monitoring, of course, involves taking note of one's thoughts and subjecting them to scrutiny. Through self-monitoring, clients become increasingly aware of the pervasive nature of their dysfunctional thoughts and recognize the need to cope actively with them. Self-monitoring, then, expands self-awareness and paves the way for later coping efforts. Moreover, self-monitoring alone often produces therapeutic benefits; that is, even without planned strategies, clients often begin to nip self-defeating thoughts in the bud as they realize the irrational nature and destructive impact of these thoughts.

To facilitate self-monitoring, we recommend that you ask clients to keep daily logs to record information in columns, as illustrated:[1]

---

[1]We wish to acknowledge that this schema is based on one developed by Aaron Beck et al. as presented in *Cognitive therapy of depression.* (New York: Guilford Press, 1979), appendix.

Date: Tues., Sept. 8

Situation or Event	Feelings (Rate Intensity from 1 to 10)	Beliefs or Self-Statements (Rate Rationality from 1 to 10)
1. Asked boss for a day off	Scared (7)	He'll be annoyed and critical of me (4)
2. Clerk at drugstore shortchanged me and I didn't say anything	Annoyed (4); afraid to tell clerk (8); disgusted with self (7)	I ought to tell clerk (9); she'd be displeased and I'd be embarrassed (2); it isn't worth it to risk a hassle (3)

Daily logs are valuable because they focus clients' efforts between sessions, clarify further the connections between cognitions and feelings, and provide valuable information to the practitioner about the prevalence and intensity of dysfunctional thoughts, images, and feelings. Moreover, they stimulate clients to engage in logical analysis of their thoughts. To prevent clients from feeling overwhelmed by the task of keeping a log, suggest they begin by limiting their recording to events related to those identified during the session and that they record only about three such events each day. Otherwise, clients tend to experience the task as unduly burdensome because of the host of troubling thoughts they may have during a given day. As other dysfunctional patterns of thoughts emerge during sessions, the focus of self-monitoring can be shifted as necessary.

In the preceding discussion, we have made passing references to images as an integral part of cognitions. Explorations of cognitions and self-monitoring should include images, for they may also play a key role in mediating emotions. Some clients, for example, are immobilized by terrifying images that may involve imagined rape, violence, or actual scenes that seemingly have left a permanent imprint upon their minds. After watching the movie *Psycho,* many women could not take a shower alone because of intense fear associated with vivid scenes from the movie of the stabbing and the blood draining from the bathtub. Scenes from real life may have even more powerful effects. One client found it extremely difficult to engage in sexual relations with her husband because of images and memories associated with a man who had raped her earlier.

3. Assist clients to identify situations that engender dysfunctional cognitions. As practitioners and clients review completed log sheets and continue to identify problematic feelings and cognitions associated with stressful events, it is important to note recurring situations and themes. Pinpointing the place where stressful events occur, key persons involved in them, situations that involve tearing oneself down for failing to fulfill self-expectations, and the like, enables you and your clients to develop tasks and coping strategies tailor-made for those specific situations. Clients who have difficulties controlling anger may discover that certain situations or types of persons consistently trigger their anger. Other clients may experience depression after having disputes with their husbands or with certain children. Still others may feel inadequate and demean themselves severely after interactions that have involved the slightest hint of criticism by others. Again, awareness of their areas of vulnerability often lowers clients' susceptibility to dysfunctional thoughts and feelings.

4. Assist clients to substitute functional self-statements in place of self-defeating cognitions. As clients gain expanded awareness of their dysfunctional thoughts, beliefs, and images and recognize how these produce negative emotional reactions, they generally welcome efforts to learn new coping patterns. These coping strategies consist of employing self-statements that are both realistic and effective in eliminating negative emotional reactions and self-defeating behaviors. Although functional self-statements foster courage and facilitate active coping efforts, they are not idealistic and do not ignore the struggles inherent in shifting from habitual, ingrained patterns of thinking, feeling, and behaving to new patterns. In fact, as with coping modeling, coping self-statements embody recognition of the difficulties and anxiety inherent in risking new behavior. To introduce clients to coping self-statements, we recommend an explanation similar to the following:

"Now that you've identified many of your key self-defeating beliefs and thoughts, we're going to focus on how to replace them with new self-statements. It will take a lot of hard work on your part, but as you practice new coping self-statements, you'll find that they will become more and more natural to you until they finally crowd out the old ones."

After providing such an explanation, it is desirable to model coping self-statements that can be substituted for self-defeating thoughts and beliefs. In modeling, it is helpful to explain that you are going to assume the role of the client and are going to think aloud as the client might when coping with a target situation. To illustrate the process, we return to our socially inhibited client and model coping self-statements she might substitute for self-defeating ones *before* joining her co-workers in the lunch room.

■ "I know a part of me wants to avoid the discomfort of socializing, but it's not going to get any better by withdrawing."

- "I don't have to say a lot to be part of the group. If I listen to the others and get my mind off myself, I can involve myself more."

- "I can't expect them to draw me into the conversations. It would be nice if they did, but if I'm going to be included I'll have to be responsible for including myself. I can do it even though it's going to take courage and strong effort. It's better than withdrawing and feeling out of it."

Notice in these self-statements that the practitioner models the struggle going on within the client rather than modeling "mastery" self-statements. This is important because coping self-statements lie close to clients' actual experience, whereas mastery self-statements do not. Moreover, the former convey empathy for and understanding of the client's struggle, which in turn inspires greater confidence in the process and in the practitioner.

After modeling coping self-statements, it is appropriate to ask if the client feels ready to practice similar behavior. With a little encouragement, most clients agree to engage in guided practice. To enhance the effectiveness of this practice, we recommend suggesting that clients close their eyes and picture themselves in the exact situation they will be in before engaging in the targeted behavior. When they report they have succeeded in capturing this situation, ask them to think aloud the thoughts they typically experience when contemplating the targeted behavior. Then ask them to substitute coping thoughts and coach them as needed. Give positive feedback as they produce functional statements independently and provide encouragement as they struggle with conflicting thoughts. Expect your clients to express doubt and uncertainty about their ability

to master new patterns of thinking and explain that most people experience misgivings as they experiment with new ways of thinking. Continue to practice with them until they feel relatively comfortable in their ability to generate coping self-statements. When clients demonstrate increased confidence in employing coping self-statements before entering a target situation, you can shift to a strategy for the *during* stage. Again, model coping self-statements, of which the following are examples with our same client:

- "Okay, so you're feeling anxious. That's to be expected. You can still pay attention and show interest in the others. That's it, look at the others and smile. What they're talking about *is* interesting. Ask them for clarification if you want to know more. That'll show them you're interested."

- "You have some thoughts on the subject they're discussing. Your opinions are worth as much as theirs. Go ahead, take a chance and express them, but look at others as you talk."

After modeling, ask how the client is feeling about what has happened thus far. This is important, for if clients are overly anxious, uncomfortable, or skeptical, you must first deal with these feelings before proceeding further. If they continue to respond positively, you may then ask them to rehearse coping self-statements, following essentially the same format as for the preceding phase.

When clients have demonstrated beginning ability to generate coping self-statements in the "during" phase, they are ready to enter the *after* phase. Again, it is important to model coping self-statements, of which the following are examples:

■ "Well, you did it. You stuck it out and even said a couple of things. That's a step in the right direction."

■ "No one looked down their nose when you expressed yourself. They appeared genuinely interested. Maybe I'm not so bad after all."

■ "Even though it was sweaty, it went pretty well, even better than I expected. I handled it, and that's an accomplishment. I'll join them again tomorrow and maybe do even better."

After modeling such self-statements, you should again explore the clients' reactions and feelings. If they indicate they are ready, you can then proceed to having them rehearse more coping self-statements. To assist clients to apply coping statements in actual life situations, it is beneficial to negotiate tasks that they can tackle between sessions. It is important, of course, not to rush clients, for undue pressure may threaten or discourage them. Again, we suggest using the Readiness Scale, as defined in Chapter 14, to gauge their readiness.

Continued self-monitoring by clients is essential as clients implement step 4. Maintaining a daily log, employing the format suggested earlier (but augmented with a fourth column headed with the caption "Rational or Coping Self-Statements"), facilitates active ongoing efforts by clients and requires them to attempt to place situations and events in realistic perspective by identifying coping self-statements they can substitute for self-defeating ones. Furthermore, maintaining a log and implementing tasks foster independent action by clients.

Substituting coping self-statements for self-defeating thoughts or misconceptions is the heart of cognitive restructuring. Because they tend to be automatic and deeply embedded, however, dysfunctional thoughts tend to persist and clients sometimes become discouraged when they do not achieve quick mastery of them. It is important to recognize that step 4 extends across a number of weeks. When clients express discouragement, we find they are reassured when we explain that change is only gradual and that it takes most people several weeks at least before they achieve a satisfactory degree of mastery. Nevertheless, we stress that they can hasten the process by planning at the beginning of each day to anticipate situations they will encounter that present opportunities for using their newly discovered coping skills.

Another technique that equips clients to cope with automatic dysfunctional self-statements is to encourage them at first awareness of such thoughts to nip them in the bud. We explain to clients that their first awareness of such thoughts is a flashing signal that they need to apply coping techniques. One way of coping is "to have a talk with oneself," reminding oneself that it is vital to *make a choice* not to continue thinking dysfunctional thoughts. Permitting such thoughts to continue leads to predictable undesired emotional reactions and reinforces the dysfunctional pattern. By contrast, nipping negative self-statements in the bud averts negative reactions and adds another increment of growth in the quest for mastery.

5. Assist clients to reward themselves for successful coping efforts. For clients who attend only to their failures and shortcomings and rarely, if ever, give themselves a pat on the back, this step is especially important. Aimed at reinforcing coping efforts, this step also assists clients to savor their progress in learning still another new and functional cognitive pattern.

In implementing this step, it is desirable to explain the rationale of giving oneself credit for progress. The following is an example of such an explanation:

"Louise, now that you've experienced some success in substituting coping self-statements for self-defeating ones, it's important to learn to give yourself credit for your well-deserved accomplishment. By giving yourself a pat on the back, you savor your success and encourage yourself to continue with your efforts. It's also an important way of learning to feel good about yourself. I'm going to help you learn to reward yourself by pretending I'm you and thinking aloud self-statements you might make after a successful coping experience."

After providing such an explanation, you then model several laudatory self-statements of which the following are typical examples:

- "You weren't sure you could do it, but you did."

- "You hung with it, and it came out fine! You're getting on track."

- "You didn't back off. You dismissed those negative thoughts and stayed with your game plan."

- "That was a big step. Sure, you have a long way to go, but you've made a darn good start, and it feels just great."

As with step 4, you should elicit the client's reactions to your explanation and modeling. If clients appear receptive, instruct them to recreate a recent success and practice making approving self-statements by expressing them aloud. Because positive self-statements are alien to many clients, initially they may feel awkward or self-conscious. Empathic understanding and encouragement on your part will usually prompt them to begin, and they may actually enjoy the experience. Indeed, it is vital to give consistent positive feedback, identifying the small and often subtle increments of growth clients achieve.

To facilitate the transfer of coping skills from sessions to real life, it is important to negotiate tasks with clients that involve making positive self-statements about their progress and about other accomplishments in daily living. Self-monitoring is again a valuable tool. We recommend asking clients to record in their logs all their daily successes, including small ones they may be inclined to overlook, and to record self-statements that give themselves credit for the same. This approach can be a powerful means of eliminating patterns of attending selectively to short-comings, failures, and negative experiences.

Limitations of Cognitive Restructuring

In assisting clients to make changes, practitioners must not mistakenly assume that clients can perform new behaviors solely as a result of cognitive changes. Often clients lack social skills and require instruction and practice before they can effectively perform new behaviors, such as making social overtures, expressing personal feelings, engaging in problem solving, and asserting themselves. Cognitive restructuring removes cognitive barriers to change and fosters willingness to risk new behaviors but does not equip clients with requisite skills. Consequently, cognitive restructuring is generally used in combination with practitioner modeling, behavioral rehearsal, and guided practice to assist clients to master essential skills once cognitive barriers have been removed. Another cognitive modality is also useful in assisting clients to master new skills, as we see in the next section.

Self-Instruction (SI)

In addition to being useful in modifying misconceptions, cognitive modalities can serve a guiding function in assisting clients to master *new* behaviors. Self-instruction (SI), which involves use of self-statements to direct oneself in performing given behaviors, is such a modality. Because SI embodies both cognitive and behavioral elements, it has been properly subsumed under the rubric of *cognitive-behavior modification* by Meichenbaum (1977), whose pioneering work with SI has gained wide acceptance.

Although SI is a relatively new change-oriented intervention, Meichenbaum has reported studies of its successful use in developing self-control in young, impulsive children, assisting hyperactive children to stay on task, expanding the social participation of social isolates, enhancing creativity of unimaginative college students, and improving the interpersonal functioning of schizophrenics. SI is also an integral part of stress inoculation, a modality we discuss in the next section. The potential applications of SI go far beyond those just cited, and the procedure will likely be employed with many more problems of living in the future.

SI is particularly useful in assisting clients to perform sequentially units of behaviors that are essential constituents of a larger behavioral sequence. Learning to be assertive, for example, requires mastery of numerous discrete cognitive and behavioral tasks. The same is true of many other skills, ranging from those that are relatively simple, such as listening attentively, to complex skills, such as resolving conflicts, making decisions, setting limits with children, or making social overtures. By identifying discrete tasks and instructing themselves from moment to moment as they implement a task,

clients enhance the likelihood of achieving successful results. With additional practice, they carry out the steps more easily and naturally until finally they internalize them. When they achieve this final phase, clients carry out behaviors automatically and SI is no longer necessary. In fact, when new behaviors are mastered, continued SI is distractive.

Employing SI involves seven steps, which are similar to those delineated previously in the discussion of cognitive restructuring.[2] These steps are as follows:

1. Explain the rationale of SI.

2. Model SI by thinking aloud while performing the client's task.

3. Ask clients to perform the same task under your instructions.

4. Ask clients to perform the same task again, but this time under their own verbal instructions.

5. Same as number 4, but this time clients whisper instructions.

6. Same as number 4, but this time clients give SI silently.

7. Practice self-instruction between sessions while carrying out actual tasks.

With respect to the first step, the following is an example of an explanation that clarifies the rationale for SI:

"As people attempt to learn new behaviors, what they say to themselves is critical. They may say things to themselves that make them tense or frightened and prevent them from doing their best. They may also be unsure of just what to do or get distracted by irrelevant or self-defeating thoughts. In fact, unsuccessful

---

[2]Steps 2 through 6 are based on those delineated in the following reference: D. Meichenbaum and J. Goodman, "Training impulsive children to talk to themselves: A means of developing self-control," *Journal of Abnormal Psychology,* 1971, 77, 115–126.

performance is often caused by this factor rather than by lack of ability. I'm going to assist you to learn a procedure called self-instruction that will increase your effectiveness as you perform tasks related to your goals. I'll demonstrate first how self-instruction works, and then you can practice it. I'll instruct you at first, and then you'll gradually learn to use effective self-talk independently. Do you have any questions before we begin?"

After presenting the rationale and responding to possible questions, you are ready to advance to the second step, which involves modeling of SI related to an appropriate task of the client. As with cognitive restructuring, your modeling should reflect struggles your client is likely to experience (including errors) in performing the task. To model effectively, it is vital to be thoroughly familiar with the client's typical fears and self-defeating thoughts. It is also essential that you be clear about the discrete units of behavior and their proper sequence involved in performing the task. To broaden your knowledge and perspective in this regard, we strongly encourage you to read a portion of Meichenbaum's book (1977, pp. 17–105), in which he provides several examples of self-instructional dialogue with different types of client problems.

Modeling SI ordinarily consists of the following types of self-verbalizations, as identified by Meichenbaum (p. 46):

1. What one is trying to accomplish.

2. Plans as to what one must do to accomplish the task.

3. Self-instructions and focused attention to guide oneself in performing the task.

4. Self-reinforcement to foster persistence and to reward one's efforts.

Before actually engaging in modeling, explain that you are going to pretend you are the client. Ask the client to listen to what you say to yourself as you perform the client's task. The following is an example of modeling that illustrates the four preceding ingredients. The client's task is to ask a classmate, whom he knows only by name, for a date.

Getting ready:

- "You've wanted to get better acquainted with her for several weeks. After class today would be a good time."

- "Class is over now. This is the time."

- "Don't push the panic button. The worst that can happen is that she can say no. To get to know her, you have to take a risk."

- "Remember, she's been friendly. She smiled at you today when she saw you."

- "That's it, get your courage up, there's nothing to lose and a lot you might gain."

- "She's looking this way; catch her eye and walk over to her."

- "Remember, smile and be friendly. Look her in the eyes and don't blow it by apologizing for yourself."

- "Introduce yourself and tell her you've wanted to get acquainted. Then invite her to the game and dinner afterwards. Tell her you think it could be a lot of fun."

Performing the task:

- "So far so good; she's waiting for you."

- "Don't get cold feet now. Walk through those fears of rejection."

- "Hang tough now. You've come this far. If she turns you down it's no disaster."

- "Relax, take some deep breaths. Keep cool."

- "Smile now— remember the eye contact. All right, introduce yourself now."

- "She seems friendly enough. It's going pretty well."

- "Invite her to the game now, and tell her about that neat restaurant you discovered."

- "She accepted! Make arrangements now to pick her up. Need to get her address and phone number."

Reinforcement:

- "How about that! I pulled it off."

- "She actually seemed pleased I asked her. She seems to like me."

- "Well, you finally got your feet wet, and it wasn't half as hard as you thought it would be."

- "It really worked—talking to myself. I'm going to do more of that when I take her out."

- "That calls for a celebration. I'm going to go to a show."

After modeling SI, the practitioner leads the client through the next four steps that involve practice by the client, progressing incrementally from practice under direct instructions from the practitioner in step 3, to self-administered silent instruction in step 6. Step 7 involves independent practice by the client between sessions, followed by in-session discussions of clients' experiences and additional practice as needed.

We recommend that you apply the steps differentially, depending on whether your clients are children or adults. In step 2, children who share much in common with the client(s) are the best role models. The use of films showing children interacting socially has been described by Meichenbaum (1977, p. 56) as an effective means of modeling aimed at teaching social skills to shy children. Unfortunately, such films are not readily available, and you may need to make your own or to observe children in social interaction so that you can play a believable role in properly modeling coping behavior of a child. When working with a *group* of children, it may be possible to employ other children as role models. If this is feasible, select children who closely resemble the clients and train them to model coping rather than mastery SI.

With adults or children over age 14, we also recommend eliminating step 5. Adults progress easily from giving themselves verbal instructions to doing the same silently. However, the intermediate step of whispering is essential in teaching SI to children.

Stress Inoculation Training (SIT)

It is fitting to discuss this intervention last, for it involves a blending of the interventions previously discussed—namely, relaxation training, cognitive restructuring, and self-instruction. Thus, if you have a grasp of these interventions, you possess many of the skills essential to implementing stress inoculation training (SIT).

SIT involves assisting clients gradually to gain mastery of coping skills that can be employed to deal with stressful situations. As with medical inoculations, clients' resistances to stressful situations are strengthened by teaching them coping skills and then exposing them to stress strong enough to arouse their coping defenses without overwhelming them. As clients progress in mastering coping skills, they are exposed to increasing increments of threat that require greater coping capacity. The potency of the "inoculation" thus increases gradually according to the degree of mastery attained. This systematic approach to enhancing coping skills has been termed *paced mastery* (Meichenbaum, 1977, p. 149).[3]

Indications for SIT

Stressful situations for which SIT has been employed, as reported in the literature, include those that stimulate anxiety, fear (Jaremko, 1980), and uncontrolled anger (Novaco, 1975) and conditions that cause physical pain (Hackett & Horan, 1980). Novaco (1977) has also advocated using SIT for training law enforcement personnel to cope with situations that normally generate strong anger. SIT can also be used to good effect with child or spouse abusers. In our opinion, the potential uses of SIT have hardly been tapped. For example, we have used it successfully with a limited number of sexual deviates (chiefly exhibitionists) and for other problems associated with deficient impulse control. In social work, Wertkin (1985) has demonstrated that SIT is effective in reducing stress associated with the rigors of graduate social work education.

SIT consists of three major phases: (1) educational, (2) rehearsal, and (3) application. In the following sections we delineate each of these phases. For illustrative purposes, we consider SIT as employed in anger control.

I: Educational Phase

The purposes of this phase are to provide a rationale for SIT and to present a conceptual framework in lay terms that enables clients to understand their reactions to stressful events. Ordinarily this phase lasts for only one session, and because it

consists primarily of instruction, you can employ it in a group context. It is critical to provide a plausible explanation of SIT because clients will not engage wholeheartedly in the procedure unless they understand and accept its logic.

In presenting the rationale for SIT, emphasize that emotional reactions are more than just single-phase reactions. Moreover, mastery of emotions involves being aware of what triggers them, recognizing indications of emotional arousal, and developing new ways of coping with stressful situations that permit appropriate expressions of emotions. The following is an example of such a rationale:

"You've been having difficulty in controlling anger (fear, anxiety, tension) in certain situations. To learn to control your anger, you need to understand it more fully, what triggers it, indications your anger is being aroused, and what you say to yourself and actually do when you're angry. You also need to learn new ways of coping with situations that trigger anger so that you can keep it from mounting out of control. Stress inoculation training is designed to accomplish these various tasks. Our first session will involve exploring all these matters further. Do you have any questions?"

If clients accept the rationale and appear receptive, you can proceed with presenting the conceptual framework. If they raise questions or manifest misgivings, it is important to focus on them, as favorable results depend upon gaining willing and active participation by clients. The conceptual framework you present depends upon the nature of the stressor causing difficulties. If you are seeking to inoculate clients against fears of public speaking, for example, your conceptual framework will be very different from one relevant to inoculating against stressors that arouse intense anger. For discussion

---

[3]We wish to acknowledge that much of the material in this section is based on this reference.

of conceptual frameworks that pertain to several types of stressors, we refer you to Meichenbaum (1977).

Novaco (1975) conceptualizes anger as an emotional response to stress that is shaped by three subresponses—namely, *cognitive, somatic-affective,* and *behavioral.* To grasp how each of these components relates to their anger responses, clients must first grasp the general meaning of the concepts and then discover how these concepts apply to their individual experiences.

The cognitive component relates to self-statements that clients make in the face of provocative situations. These self-statements involve appraising a situation, which includes predicting the behavior of others by gauging their intentions and motives; evaluating one's own self-expectations, personal intentions, and images; weighing the magnitude of a situation; and assessing possible outcomes. Some clients, however, exclude some of the preceding types of self-statements, which contributes to deficient anger control. Failing to consider their own intentions or the magnitude of a situation, some clients lash out wildly and impulsively when confronted with provocative situations. Such clients do not ask themselves, "How can I work this situation out?" or "What will be the consequences if I blow my stack?" What clients do *not* say to themselves is often equally important as self-statements they *do* make.

To assist clients to appreciate the importance of self-statements in provocative situations, it is efficacious to provide examples of contrasting self-statements that lead predictably to increasing anger or to maintaining self-control. The following are examples you may wish to use:

Destructive self-statements:

- "What does that rotten SOB think he's trying to pull off? I'll show him."

- "Look at that smirk on her face. She really thinks she put me down. I'll get even with her."

- "That arrogant bastard must think he can call all the shots. I'll show him a thing or two."

Constructive self-statements:

- "She's really acting like a jerk. I'll have to keep my cool, or it could really get out of hand."

- "He's doing everything he can to get my goat. But I can cope. Take deep breaths. That's right, don't let him get to you."

- "Boy, this really is sweaty. He's totally unreasonable. But I can handle it. If I lose my cool, it'll be an awful mess."

By discussing examples similar to these, clients usually readily grasp the significance of self-statements. For many clients it is a revelation, as they spontaneously realize for the first time that they make self-statements.

After illustrating the cognitive component of anger arousal, explain the somatic-affective dimension. (You should complete the explanation of general concepts before assisting clients to apply them to themselves.) This component involves the physiological and emotional manifestations of anger arousal. To assist clients to grasp the significance of this component, we recommend you explain that physical and emotional manifestations of anger serve as signals of the need to employ coping skills. By recognizing these signals, they can head off anger before it reaches unmanageable proportions. It is important to clarify further that the somatic-affective component is important also because mounting tension and emotion tend to increase the intensity of the anger response.

Physiological manifestations of anger arousal include body tension, sweaty palms, increased heart rate, rapid breathing, clenched jaws, pursed lips, gastric upset, and the like. Because people experience tension in somewhat different ways, clients need to develop awareness of their own "signals." Early emotional reactions include irritation, agitation, and feelings of resentment.

The behavioral component of anger arousal may involve withdrawal or antagonistic and aggressive behavior, either of which may produce negative consequences. For example, a person may repeatedly withdraw when a spouse makes verbal attacks, letting resentments fester and accumulate until finally even a minor provocation may trigger a violent and destructive outburst of anger. Other persons may respond aggressively to provocations by counterattacking (e.g., name-calling or counteraccusations), thereby fostering escalation of anger by both participants and culminating in heated interaction and even violence.

Phase I culminates with having clients identify their individual patterns of anger arousal and analyze situations that provoke strong anger responses. More specifically, the practitioner guides clients to determine exact aspects of situations that trigger anger, focusing particularly on self-statements and feelings that are experienced in such situations.[4] An effective way of assisting clients to pinpoint their individual patterns of anger arousal is to have them close their eyes, as though running a movie of provocative events, reporting thoughts, feelings, and reactions they experience. At the conclusion of this first session, clients are asked to carry out tasks (homework assignments)

of (1) monitoring their self-statements when angry, (2) further analyzing aspects of stressful situations that provoke anger, and (3) listing anger-provoking situations on index cards and ranking them according to the intensity of anger they provoke. These tasks facilitate consolidation of the concepts presented in the session and also set the stage for phase II.

II: Rehearsal Phase

Whereas the educational phase can be conducted in a group context, subsequent phases are generally implemented individually. The rehearsal phase consists of assisting clients to develop coping skills that involve direct action and cognitive restructuring, with special emphasis on self-instruction. Direct action involves two different aspects: (1) obtaining information about objects or situations that engender fear, pain, or anger, and (2) relaxation training. Before engaging in these activities, it is important to explain the rationale for them and to gain cooperation.

In the case of inoculation against losing control of anger, obtaining information involves analyzing the nature of stressors that provoke anger, building on the preliminary work begun in phase I. As clients report on their homework assignment related to analyzing situations that provoke anger, further analysis and discussion occur. The practitioner expands their awareness by assisting them to identify unrealistic appraisals of situations that may lead to unwarranted defensiveness and aggressiveness. Often clients' negative self-statements, according to Novaco (1975), reveal intolerance of mistakes by others, unrealistic self-expectations about the necessity of success, excessive expectations of others, hypersensitivity to criticism, and a belief that retaliation is essential when one is wronged. Emphasis is placed on meanings clients attribute to

---

[4]If situations that provoke anger responses usually involve family members, relatives, or others with whom clients have frequent contacts, you should also make efforts to involve these significant others to assist them in modifying their provocative behavior.

situations where they perceive a threat to their self-worth, which in turn often is followed by aggressive or defensive behavior that escalates the degree of negative emotionality. Clients are also assisted to analyze other options that are available (e.g., assertive but nonaggressive behavior). Obtaining information and analyzing it thus tends to neutralize the provocative potential of stressful situations.

The second aspect of direct action, relaxation training, proceeds along the lines discussed in the first section of this chapter. Before beginning relaxation training, it is important to explain that you are teaching them the procedure because relaxation is incompatible with tension and anger. Thus, when they anticipate confronting a provocative situation or recognize anger arousal manifestations, they can employ deep breathing and muscle relaxation to mitigate anger.

The cognitive restructuring component of phase II consists of *assisting clients (1) to substitute positive self-statements for their habitual negative, anger-generating self-statements; and (2) to confront provocative situations constructively.* Novaco (1975) and Meichenbaum (1977) concur that self-instruction related to provocation and anger reactions should be viewed in four stages as follows:

1. Preparing for the provocation whenever possible.

2. The impact and confrontation.

3. Coping with arousal.

4. Subsequent reflection when conflict was resolved successfully or when conflict was unresolved (Meichenbaum, 1977, p. 165).

Numerous positive, stress-reducing self-statements for each of these stages are listed by Meichenbaum and Turk (1976, pp. 6–9). We recommend that you become familiar with these self-statements. In the following, for illustrative purposes, we provide a few examples of self-statements for each of the four stages in stress inoculation for controlling anger:

Preparing for provocation:

- "This is going to be upsetting, but I can handle it."

- "If I work out a plan, I'll be prepared and won't lose my cool."

- "I've learned how to manage my anger —no need to push the panic button."

- "Remember, deep breaths and relax. Don't let it get to you."

Impact and confrontation:

- "Nothing gained by getting mad. It just makes it worse."

- "It's too bad he acts like this. I'm pleased I'm staying in control. Whatever he says doesn't matter. What really matters is that I control myself."

- "I'm staying on top of this situation by keeping under control."

Coping with arousal:

- "I can feel I'm getting tense. Need to breathe deeply and slow things down."

- "I have a right to be irritated but must keep my feelings under control."

- "Even though he's making a fool of himself, treat him with respect."

- "It takes two to have a fight, and I'm not going to let it happen."

- "Don't let him push you around. Express your views, but don't blow it by losing your cool."

- "He's really trying to get to me, but I won't let him. I'm in control of the situation."

Reflecting on the provocation:
a. When coping is successful and conflict is resolved

- "Chalk that up as a success."
- "It paid off."
- "I actually got through it without blowing my top. It sure feels good."
- "I did better than I thought I could. I really can learn to control my anger."

b. When conflict is unresolved

- "Even though it wasn't a total success, it wasn't a lost cause. It takes time to work out sticky problems."
- "Don't dwell on it. That only makes it worse. It could have gone a lot worse."
- "Can't expect success every time. You did the best you could. Simmer down, don't let it eat at you. Relax, take a deep breath."

Note that in the last stage, self-statements are included for both successful and unsuccessful outcomes. It is important to recognize the possibility of the latter and to inoculate the client for that possibility. After all, despite the best laid plans, people do not always cope successfully; moreover, forces beyond one's control (e.g., refractory behavior by another person) may produce undesired outcomes. By assisting clients to view unsuccessful outcomes as sometimes unavoidable and to construe the same as evidence of the need to persist, rather than as ultimate failure, you inoculate them against being unduly discouraged or overwhelmed by life's occasional disappointments.

After learning the coping skills discussed in the preceding, clients rehearse employing these skills by imagining themselves in the stressful situations they earlier listed on the index cards after completing their first session. They begin with the situation they ranked as least stressful, instructing themselves with coping self-statements, breathing deeply, and relaxing their muscles. The practitioner guides them as necessary. As they gain confidence in their ability to cope successfully with one situation, they advance to the next, thereby gradually increasing the potency of their inoculation. During this process, it is important for the practitioner to express approval of their progress and to encourage them to make reinforcing self-statements also. Clients continue this process until they complete the hierarchy of stressful situations. Homework assignments involving practice of the skills with the imagined stressful situation continue between sessions. Phase II thus extends across approximately three weekly sessions.

III: Application Phase

In this phase, clients apply their newly won coping skills to actual life situations and other imagined stressful situations or engage in simulated stressful situations with the practitioner playing the role of other protagonists. In this last activity, the practitioner should play the role "to the hilt," being sufficiently provocative to challenge the coping skills of clients without overwhelming them. The proof of the pudding is coping successfully *in vivo,* and clients' confidence increases as they discover they can indeed cope with situations that previously overwhelmed them.

SIT concludes with instructions to the client to continue practicing the skills indefinitely, thereby maintaining and further enhancing the potency of the inoculation. Ordinarily SIT extends across five or six sessions, although longer time can be taken if deemed necessary.

Blending Multiple Skills

In this chapter, we have delineated interventions that practitioners can employ to assist clients to work on relevant dimensions of their problems. Because most problems of clients are multidimensional, however, practitioners usually blend these and other interventions, as is true of stress inoculation training.

With socially inhibited clients, practitioners may employ (1) cognitive restructuring to identify and replace irrational thoughts and beliefs that produce fears of social participation; (2) muscle relaxation training to reduce tension before and during social situations; (3) self-instruction to manage fears and provide self-direction in relating socially; and (4) modeling, behavioral rehearsal, and guided practice to develop social skills. With a husband who abuses his wife and children in fits of anger, a practitioner may employ SIT to identify both stressors that trigger anger and dysfunctional self-statements that accompany angry outbursts. SIT would also assist the client to recognize cues of anger arousal so that he could prevent anger from mounting out of control. The client would also be assisted to learn coping behaviors consisting of self-instruction that calls for deep breathing, muscle relaxation, and positive, stress-reducing self-statements. The practitioner would also work with both marital partners to teach effective communication and perhaps independent problem solving as well. Modeling, guided practice, and self-instruction would be employed in facilitating client mastery of these skills.

19 ■ Additive Empathy, Interpretation, and Confrontation

The Meaning and Significance of Client Self-Awareness

Self-awareness is a priceless ingredient generally acknowledged as essential to sound mental health. Humans have long known of the profound importance of self-awareness as reflected by Socrates, the ancient Greek philosopher, in his often-quoted admonition, "Know thyself!" Self-awareness by clients is indispensable to the helping process, particularly during the change-oriented phase. People's efforts to solve problems and to change are effective only if they are properly directed, which in turn depends on accurate awareness of behaviors and circumstances that need to be changed. Indeed, many people experience incessant problems in daily living precisely because they lack awareness of the forces that produce these problems.

As we employ the term, *self-awareness* refers largely to awareness of forces operating in the present. Practitioners thus assist clients to expand their awareness of needs or wants, motives, emotions, beliefs, dysfunctional behaviors, and of their impact on other people. We do *not* use self-awareness to refer to insight into the remote causes or etiology of problems, for, as we have noted in earlier chapters, people can and do change without this type of insight. But on occasions, brief excursions into the past may be productive and enlightening, for example, to determine what qualities attracted marital partners to one another, to identify factors that have contributed to sexual dysfunction, to assess the chronicity of problems, to highlight previous successes, and the like. It is important in making such brief excursions, however, to relate elicited information to *present* work and *present* problems, emphasizing to clients that they can change the present, whereas the past is now history. One can alter current effects of history but not history itself.

Practitioners have at their disposal numerous tools to assist clients to gain expanded self-awareness, of which interpretation, additive empathy, and confrontation are probably employed most extensively. In this chapter, we define these techniques, specify indications for their use, present guidelines for employing them effectively, and finally, provide skill development exercises.

Additive Empathy and Interpretation

By now you are aware that empathy on the practitioner's part is critical to the helping process. In earlier chapters, we explained various uses of empathy in the initial phase of the helping process. During the action-oriented phase, additive levels of empathy are used to expand clients' self-awareness, to cushion the impact of confrontations (discussed later in this chapter), and to explore and resolve relational reactions and other obstacles to change (which we discuss at length in Chapter 20). Bear in mind that practitioners also continue to use reciprocal levels of empathy during the goal-attainment phase because the purposes of empathy in the initial phase continue throughout the helping process. The difference is that additive levels of empathy are employed sparingly in the initial phase but occupy a prominent position during the action-oriented phase.

Additive empathic responses go somewhat beyond what clients have expressed and therefore require some degree of inference by practitioners. For this reason, these responses are mildly to moderately interpretive; that is, they interpret to clients forces operating to produce feelings, cognitions, reaction patterns, and behavioral patterns. Indeed, after an exhaustive study of research involving psychoanalysis, Luborsky and Spence (1978) concluded that *interpretation*, as employed by psychoanalysts, and empathic communication are basically the same. Insight through interpretation, it should be noted, is the "supreme agent" in the hierarchy of therapeutic principles that are basic to psychoanalysis and closely related therapies (Bibring, 1954; Kubie, 1952).

Proponents of several other theories (most notably, client centered, Gestalt and certain existential theories) have eschewed the use of interpretation. Still others (Claiborn, 1982; Levy, 1963) maintain that interpretation is essential to the counseling process, regardless of theoretical orientation, and that many behaviors

of practitioners (whether intentional or not) perform interpretive functions. Semantic and conceptual confusion have contributed to the divergence in views, but recent writings have tended to sharpen concepts and to reduce vagueness and confusion.

Based on Levy's (1963) conceptualization, Claiborn (1982) posits that interpretation, irrespective of theoretical orientation, "presents the client with a viewpoint discrepant from the client's own, the function of which is to prepare or induce the client to change in accordance with that viewpoint" (p. 442). Viewed in this light, interpretation assists clients to view their problems from a different perspective, the desired effect of which is to open up new possibilities for remedial courses of action. This generic view, which emphasizes a *discrepant viewpoint*, is sufficiently broad to encompass many change-oriented techniques identified in different theories, including reframing (Watzlawick et al., 1974); relabeling (Barton & Alexander, 1981); positive connotation (Selvini-Palazzoli, Boscolo, Cecchin, & Prata, 1974); positive reinterpretation (Hammond et al., 1977); additive empathy, and traditional psychoanalytic interpretations. The content of interpretations concerning the same clinical situation thus can be expected to vary according to the theoretical allegiances of practitioners; however, research (summarized by Claiborn, 1982) indicates that "Interpretations differing greatly in content seem to have a similar impact on clients" (p. 450).

Levy (1963) classifies interpretations in two categories, *semantic* and *propositional*. Semantic interpretations describe clients' experiences according to the *practitioner's* conceptual vocabulary (e.g., "By 'frustrated,' I gather you mean you're feeling hurt and disillusioned"). Semantic interpretations thus are closely related to additive empathic responses. Propositional interpretations involve the practitioner's notions or explanations that assert causal relationships among factors involved in clients' problem situations (e.g., "When you try so hard to avoid displeasing others, you displease yourself and end up resenting others for taking advantage of you"). Claiborn (1982) presents numerous examples of both types of interpretation as well as comprehensive discussion of this important topic. Other researchers (Beck & Strong, 1982; Claiborn, Crawford, and Hackman, 1983; Feldman, Strong, & Danser, 1982; Dowd & Boroto, 1982; Milne & Dowd, 1983) have also reported findings comparing the effects of different types of interpretations.

Practitioners should avoid making interpretations or additive empathic responses (we are using the terms interchangeably) that are far removed from the awareness of clients. Research (Speisman, 1959) has indicated that moderate interpretations (i.e., those that reflect feelings that lie at the margin of the client's experiencing) facilitate self-exploration and self-awareness, whereas deep interpretations engender resistance. Because the latter are remote from clients' experiencing, they appear illogical and irrelevant to clients, who therefore tend to reject them despite the fact that such interpretations may be accurate. The following is an example of such an inept, deep interpretation:

CLIENT: My boss is a real tyrant. He never gives anyone credit, except for Fran. She can do no wrong in his eyes. He just seems to have it in for me. Sometimes I'd like to punch his lights out.

PRACTITIONER: Your boss seems to activate the same feelings you had toward your father. You feel he favors Fran, who symbolizes your favored sister. It's your father who you feel was the real tyrant, and you're reliving your resentment toward him. Your boss is merely a symbol of him.

Understandably, the client would likely reject and perhaps resent this interpretation. Though the practitioner may be accurate (the determination of which is purely speculative), the client is struggling with feelings toward his boss. To shift the focus to feelings toward his father misses the mark entirely from the client's perspective.

The following interpretation, made in response to the same client message, would be less likely to foster resistance because it is linked to recent experiences of the client:

"So you really resent your boss because he seems impossible to please and shows partiality toward Fran. [*Reciprocal empathy.*] Those feelings reminded me of similar ones you expressed about two weeks ago. You were talking about how, when your parents spent a week with you on their vacation, your father seemed to find fault with everything you did but raved about how well your sister was doing. You'd previously mentioned he'd always seemed to favor your sister and that nothing you did seemed to please him. I'm wondering if those feelings might be connected with the feelings you're experiencing at work."

In the preceding message, notice that the practitioner carefully documented the rationale of the interpretation and offered it tentatively, a matter we discuss later under "Guidelines for Interpretation and Additive Empathy."

Because we discussed, illustrated, and provided exercises related to additive empathy in Chapter 5, we shall not deal with these topics in the present chapter. Rather, we limit our discussion to uses of interpretation and additive empathy in expanding clients' self-awareness of (1) deeper feelings; (2) underlying meanings of feelings, thoughts, and behavior; (3) wants and goals; (4) hidden purposes of behavior; and (5) unrealized strengths and potentialities.

Deeper Feelings

Clients often have limited awareness of certain emotions, perceiving them only dimly if at all. Moreover, emotional reactions often involve multiple emotions, but clients may experience only the dominant or surface feelings. Further, some clients experience only negative emotions, such as anger, and are out of touch with more tender feelings including hurt, disappointment, compassion, loneliness, fears, caring and the like. Additive empathic responses (semantic interpretations) thus assist clients to become aware of emotions that lie at the edge of awareness, enabling them to experience these feelings more sharply and fully, to become more aware of their humanness (including the full spectrum of emotions), and to integrate emerging emotions into the totality of their experience.

Practitioners frequently employ additive empathic responses directed at expanding clients' awareness of feelings for several purposes, which we identify and illustrate in the following examples:

1. *To identify feelings that are only implied or hinted at in clients' verbal messages:*

CLIENT: [*In sixth session.*] I wonder if you feel we're making any progress. [*Clients frequently ask questions that embody veiled feelings.*]

PRACTITIONER: It sounds as though you're not satisfied with your progress. I wonder if you're feeling discouraged about how it's been going.

2. *To identify feelings that underlie surface emotions:*

CLIENT: I've just felt so bored in the evenings with so little to do. I went down to the bowling alley and watched people bowl, but that didn't seem to help. Life's just a drag.

PRACTITIONER: I'm getting the impression you're feeling empty and pretty depressed. I wonder if you're feeling lonely and wishing you had some friends to fill that emptiness.

3. *To add intensity to feelings clients have minimized:*

CLIENT: [*30-year-old mildly retarded socially isolated woman.*] It was a *little disappointing* that Jana [*her childhood friend from another state*] couldn't come to visit. She lost her job and had to cancel her plane reservations.

PRACTITIONER: I can see how *terribly disappointed* you were. In fact, you seem really down even now. You'd looked forward to her visit and made plans—it's been a real blow to you.

4. *To clarify the nature of feelings clients experience only vaguely:*

CLIENT: When Ben told me he wanted a divorce so he could marry another woman, I just turned numb. I've been walking around in a daze ever since, telling myself, "This can't be happening."

PRACTITIONER: It's been a crushing blow to you—you were so unprepared. It *hurts so much* it's hard to admit it's really happening.

5. *To identify feelings manifested only nonverbally:*

CLIENT: My sister asked me to tend her kids while she's on vacation, and I will, of course. [*Frowns and sighs.*]

PRACTITIONER: But your sigh tells me you don't feel good about it. Right now the message I get from you is that it seems an unfair and heavy burden to you and that you resent it.

Underlying Meanings of Feelings, Thoughts, and Behavior

Used for this purpose, additive empathy or interpretation assists clients to conceptualize or make meaning of feelings, thoughts, and behavior. Practitioners thus assist clients to understand what motivates them to feel, think, and behave as they do; to grasp how their behavior bears on their problems and goals; and to discern themes and patterns in their thinking, feelings, and behavior. As clients discern similarities, parallels, and themes in their behavior and experiences, their self-awareness gradually expands in much the same way as single pieces of a puzzle fit together, gradually forming discrete entities and eventually coalescing into a coherent whole. The previous interpretation made to the client who resented his boss for favoring a co-worker is an example of this type of additive empathic response (which also fits into the category of a propositional interpretation).

In a more concrete sense, then, practitioners may employ this type of interpretation or additive empathy to assist clients to discern that they experience troublesome feelings in the presence of a certain type of person or in certain circumstances. For example, clients may feel depressed in the presence of critical people or feel extremely anxious in situations wherein they must perform (e.g., when expected to give a talk or take a test). Practitioners may thus use additive empathy to identify negative perceptual sets and other dysfunctional cognitive patterns that can be modified by employing cogni-

tive restructuring. Clients may attend exclusively to trivial indications of their imperfections and completely overlook abundant evidence of competent and successful performance. Similarly, a practitioner may assist a client to discern a pattern of anticipating negative outcomes of relatively minor events and dreading (and avoiding) the events because of perceiving any of the negative outcomes as probable absolute disasters. One client dreaded visiting a lifelong friend who had recently sustained a severe fall, leaving her partially paralyzed. When the practitioner explored possible negative events that the client feared might occur if she were to visit the friend, she identified the following:

- "What if I cry when I see her?"
- "What if I stare at her?"
- "What if I say the wrong thing?"

Using an additive empathic response, the practitioner replied, "And if you did one of those things, it would be a total disaster?" The client readily agreed. The practitioner then further employed cognitive restructuring to assist her to view the situation in realistic perspective by discussing each feared reaction, clarifying that anyone might react as she feared reacting and that if she were to react in any of the feared ways it would be uncomfortable but certainly not a disaster. They discussed the situation further, concluding that she had a certain amount of control over how she reacted rather than being totally at the mercy of circumstances. Following behavioral rehearsal that included self-instruction, her fears of disaster gradually dwindled to manageable proportions.

Practitioners may also employ this type of additive empathy to enhance clients' awareness of perceptual distortions that adversely affect interpersonal relationships. Parents may reject children because they perceive characteristics in them that they abhor. Previous exploration, however, may have disclosed that parents abhor the same qualities in themselves and project their self-hatred onto their children. By assisting clients to recognize how self-perceptions (which may also be distorted) warp their perceptions of their children, practitioners enable them to make discriminations and to perceive and accept their children as unique individuals different from themselves.

Similar perceptual distortions may occur between marital partners, causing spouses to perceive and to respond inappropriately to each other as a result of unresolved and troublesome feelings that derive from earlier relationships with parents of the opposite sex. Hepworth (1964) has also described perceptual distortions that often occur in instances of marriages "forced" by premarital pregnancy. Because such partners enter marriage without complete freedom of choice, they may harbor doubts that they would have otherwise chosen each other, as a consequence of which they may devalue themselves and/or their partners.

Wants and Goals

Another important use of additive empathy is to assist clients to become aware of wants and goals that they imply in their messages but do not fully recognize. Beset by difficulties, people often tend to think in terms of problems and relief from them rather than in terms of growth and change; yet the latter two processes are often implied in the former. When they become more aware of the thrust toward growth implied in their messages, clients often welcome the prospect and indeed may wax enthusiastic. This type of additive empathy not only expands self-awareness but may enhance motivation, as illustrated in the interchange below.

As is apparent in the following excerpt, additive empathic messages that highlight implied wants and goals often result in formulating explicit goals and pave the way to change-oriented actions. Moreover, such messages also play a critical role in arousing hope in dispirited clients who feel overwhelmed by problems and have been unable to discern positive desires for growth manifested in their struggles. This type of message thus plays a key role in the first phase of the helping process and in the change-oriented phase as well.

CLIENT: I'm so sick of always being imposed upon. All of my family just take me for granted. You know, "Good old Ella, you can always depend on her." I'm so fed up with it all I could just chew nails.

PRACTITIONER: Just thinking about it gets your hackles up. Ella, it seems to me that what you're saying adds up to an urgent desire on your part to be your own person—to feel in charge of yourself rather than being at the mercy of others' requests or demands.

CLIENT: I hadn't thought of it that way but you're right. That's exactly what I want. If I could just be my own person.

PRACTITIONER: Maybe that's a goal you'd like to set for yourself. It seems to fit, and accomplishing it would liberate you from the oppressive feelings you've described.

CLIENT: Yes, yes! I'd like very much to set that goal. Do you really think I could accomplish it?

Expanding Awareness of Motives Underlying Behavior

Practitioners sometimes employ interpretations to assist clients to become more fully aware of basic motivations that underlie dysfunctional patterns of behavior. Other people may misinterpret clients' motives, and they themselves may have only a dim awareness of them because of the obscuring effect of their dysfunctional behaviors. Prominent among these motives are the following: to protect tenuous self-esteem (e.g., by avoiding situations that involve any risk of failing), to avoid anxiety-producing situations, and to compensate for feelings of impotency or inadequacy. The following are typical examples of surface behavior and hidden purposes served by the behavior.

1. Underachieving students may exert little effort in school (1) because they can justify failing on the basis of not having really tried (rather than having to face their fears of being inadequate) or (2) because they are seeking to punish parents who withhold approval and love when they fall short of their expectations.

2. Clients may present a facade of bravado to conceal from themselves and others underlying fears and feelings of inadequacy.

3. Clients may set themselves up for physical or emotional pain to expiate for deep-seated feelings of guilt.

4. Clients may engage in self-defeating behavior to validate myths that they are destined to be losers, to suffer, or to live out life scripts determined by circumstances beyond their control.

5. Clients may avoid relating closely to others to protect against fears of being dominated or controlled.

6. Clients may behave aggressively and/or abrasively because they thereby avoid risking rejection by keeping others at a distance.

Interpretations must be based on substantial supporting information that clients have disclosed previously. Without supporting information, interpretations are little more than speculations that clients are unlikely to accept. Indeed, such speculations often emanate from practitioners' projections and are most often inaccurate. Practitioners who engage in deep and unfounded psychodynamic interpretations might be best described as "armchair psychoanalysts." Their inept interpretations often are calculated to impress others with their erudition, but the actual effect is often quite the opposite. Clients may regard their interpretations as offensive or may question their competence. The following example illustrates appropriate use of interpretations to expand awareness of underlying motives.

The client, Mr. R., age 33, together with his wife, entered marital therapy largely at his wife's instigation. She complained about a lack of closeness in the relationship and felt rejected because her husband seldom initiated affectional overtures. When she initiated overtures, he typically rebuffed her by pulling back. Mr. R. had revealed in the exploratory interviews that his mother had been (and still was) extremely dominating and controlling. He had little warmth for his mother and saw her no more than was absolutely necessary. The following excerpt from an individual session with Mr. R. focuses on an event that occurred during the week when the R.s went to a movie. Mrs. R. reached over to hold his hand. He abruptly withdrew it, and Mrs. R. later expressed her feelings of hurt and rejection. Their ensuing discussion was unproductive, and their communication strained. Mr. R. discusses the event that occurred in the theater:

CLIENT: I know Carol was hurt when I didn't hold her hand. I don't know why, but it really turned me off.

PRACTITIONER: So you're wondering why you turn off when she reaches for some affectional contact. I wonder what was happening inside of you at the moment? What were you thinking and feeling?

CLIENT: Gee, let me think. I guess I was anticipating she'd do it, and I just wanted to be left alone to enjoy the movie. I guess I resented her taking my hand. Gee, that doesn't make sense when I think about it. Why should I resent holding hands with the woman I love?

PRACTITIONER: Jim, I think you're asking an awfully good question—one that's a key to many of the difficulties in your marriage. Let me share an idea with you that may shed some light on why you respond as you do. You mentioned you felt resentful when Carol took your hand. Based on the feelings you just expressed, I'm wondering if perhaps you feel you're submitting to her if you respond positively when she takes the initiative and pull back to be sure you're not letting yourself be dominated by her [*the hidden purpose*]. Another reason for suggesting that is that as you were growing up you felt dominated by your mother and resented her for being that way. Even now you avoid seeing her any more than you have to. I'm wondering if, as a result of your relationship with her, you could have developed a supersensitivity to being controlled by a female so that you resent any behavior on Carol's part that even suggests her being in control. [*The latter part of the response provides the rationale for the interpretation.*]

Unrealized Strengths and Potentialities

Another vital purpose served by interpretation and additive empathy is to expand clients' awareness of their strengths and undeveloped potentialities. Clients' strengths are manifested in many and varied ways, and it behooves practitioners to sensitize themselves to these often subtle manifestations by consciously cultivating a positive perceptual set. This objective is vital, for clients are often preoccupied with their weaknesses, deficiencies, and failures. Moreover, becoming aware of strengths tends to arouse clients' hopes and to generate courage to undertake making changes.

Drawing clients' awareness to strengths tends to enhance self-esteem and to foster courage to undertake tasks that involve risking new behaviors. With conscious effort, practitioners can become increasingly aware of clients' strengths, even with clients who possess marked limitations. A mildly mentally retarded and brain-damaged client, for example, lamented to one of the authors that she felt she was a total "zero." In addition to being brain-damaged, she was plagued by numerous phobias, including a fear of leaving home. She commented it had been a major effort for her to canvas the neighborhood soliciting donations for the heart fund. She believed this was a worthy cause, however, and it gave her satisfaction despite the tension and anxiety she experienced. The practitioner replied that her action was evidence of an important strength—namely, her caring about other people to the extent she would make such an effort on behalf of unknown others. He added that caring about others is a precious quality that many people lack and that she certainly was not a "zero" in light of this apparent strength. She beamed and guessed maybe she did have some good qualities. This case is but one of the countless examples that could be cited of clients' strengths manifested as they report seemingly mundane events.

Guidelines for Employing Interpretation and Additive Empathy

To employ these skills effectively requires considerable finesse. The following guidelines will assist you in acquiring this finesse.

1. Use additive empathy sparingly until a sound working relationship has evolved. Because these responses go somewhat beyond clients' awareness of self, clients may misinterpret the motives of a practitioner and respond defensively. When clients demonstrate they are confident of a practitioner's goodwill, they are able to tolerate and often to benefit from additive empathic and interpretative responses. The exceptions to this guideline involve messages that identify (1) wants and goals and (2) strengths and potentialities, both of which are also appropriate in the initial phase of the helping process. Practitioners must avoid identifying strengths excessively in the initial phase, however, for some clients interpret such messages as insincere flattery.

2. Employ these responses only when clients are engaged in self-exploration or have manifested readiness for the same. Clients or groups that are not ready to engage in self-exploration are likely to resist practitioners' interpretive efforts and may interpret such efforts as unwarranted attempts by practitioners to impose their formulations upon them. Exceptions to this guideline are the same as those cited in the preceding guideline.

3. Pitch these responses to the edge of the client's awareness, and avoid attempting to foster awareness that is remote from clients' current awareness or experiencing. Clients generally are receptive to responses that closely relate to their experiencing but resist those that emanate from the practitioner's unfounded conjectures. It is poor practice to attempt to push clients into rapidly acquiring new insights, for many so-called deep interpretations prove to be inaccurate and produce negative effects, including reducing clients' confidence in practitioners, conveying lack of understanding, or engendering resistance. Practitioners should not employ interpretive responses until they have amassed sufficient information to be reasonably confident their responses are accurate and should share the supportive information upon which the interpretation is based.

4. Avoid making several additive empathic responses in succession. Because interpretative responses require time to think through, digest, and assimilate, a series of such responses tends to bewilder clients.

5. Phrase interpretive responses in tentative terms. Because these responses involve a certain degree of inference, there is always the possibility of being in error. Tentative phrasing openly acknowledges that possibility and invites clients to agree or disagree. If practitioners present interpretations in an authoritarian or dogmatic manner, however, clients may not feel free to offer candid feedback and may outwardly agree while actually covertly rejecting interpretations. Tentative phrases include, "I wonder if . . . ," "Could it be that your feelings may be related to . . . ?" and "Perhaps you're feeling this way because . . . ."

6. To determine the accuracy of an interpretive response, carefully note clients' reactions after offering the interpretation. When responses are on target, clients affirm their validity, continue self-exploration by bringing up additional relevant material, or respond emotionally in a manner that matches the moment (e.g., ventilate relevant feelings). When interpretations are inaccurate or are premature, clients tend to disconfirm them

(verbally or nonverbally), change the subject, withdraw emotionally, argue or become defensive, or simply ignore the interpretation.

7. If the client responds negatively to an interpretive response, acknowledge your probable error, respond empathically to the client's reaction, and continue your discussion of the topic under consideration.

To assist you to expand your skill in formulating interpretive and additive empathic responses, we have provided a number of exercises, together with modeled responses, at the end of the chapter.

Confrontation

Similar to interpretation and additive empathy in that it is a tool to enhance clients' self-awareness and to promote change, confrontation involves facing clients with some aspect of their thoughts, feelings, or behavior that is contributing to or maintaining their difficulties. Practitioners employ confrontation to assist clients to achieve awareness of forces blocking progress toward growth and goal attainment and to enhance their motivation to implement efforts toward change. A potent technique, confrontation is particularly relevant when clients manifest blind spots to discrepancies or inconsistencies in their thoughts, beliefs, emotions, and behavior that tend to produce or to perpetuate dysfunctional behavior. Of course, blind spots in self-awareness are universal among human beings because all humans suffer from the limitation of being unable to step out of their perceptual fields and look at themselves objectively.

Practitioners have the advantage of viewing clients and their difficulties from an external vantage point, which makes it possible to offer fresh perspectives and corrective feedback when clients' distorted perceptions, avoidance behaviors, and other dysfunctional patterns impede progress. It is this very need for fresh perspectives and corrective input that impels people to seek help when their usual coping patterns prove ineffective.

Additive empathy and confrontation have much in common. Skillful confrontations embody consideration of clients' feelings that underlie obstacles and resistances to change. Because fears are generally involved in resistance to change, skill in relating with high levels of empathy is prerequisite to using confrontation effectively. Indeed, effective confrontation is an extension of empathic communication because the focusing on discrepancies and inconsistencies derives from a deep understanding of clients' feelings, experiences, and behavior.

It is important to bear in mind that confrontation is a *tool* to be used with discretion and not a *style* of "helping" others. Practitioners who make frequent confrontations generally have failed to master the facilitative conditions, as practitioners who use the latter skillfully foster *self-confrontations* by their clients as the helping process evolves. In other words, as clients gain expanded awareness of themselves and their problems through self-exploration, they tend to become aware of and to confront discrepancies and inconsistencies themselves. Self-confrontation is generally preferable to practitioner-initiated confrontation because the former is less risky and because clients' resistance to integrate insights is not an obstacle when they initiate confrontations themselves. Clients vary widely in the degree to which they engage in self-confrontation. Emotionally mature, introspective persons engage in self-confrontations frequently, whereas persons who are out of touch with their emotions, who lack awareness of their impact on others, and who blame others or circumstances for their difficulties are least likely to engage in self-confrontation.

Confrontation is a high-risk technique because clients may interpret confrontations as criticisms, put-downs, or rejections. Paradoxically, the risk of these reactions is greatest among the groups of clients who must be confronted most often because they rarely engage in self-confrontation. These clients tend to have weak self-concepts and are therefore prone to read criticism into messages when none is intended. Moreover, ill-timed and poorly executed confrontations may be perceived by clients as verbal assaults and may seriously damage helping relationships. Using confrontations therefore requires keen timing and finesse. Practitioners must make special efforts to convey helpful intent and goodwill as they employ confrontations. Otherwise, they may engender hostility or offend and alienate clients.

The Anatomy of Confrontive Responses

Effective confrontations embody four elements: (1) expression of concern; (2) a description of the client's purported goal, belief, or commitment; (3) the behavior (or absence of behavior) that is inconsistent or discrepant with the goal, belief, or commitment; and (4) the probable negative outcomes of the discrepant behavior. The format of a confrontive response may be depicted as follows:

          (want)
I'm concerned because you (believe)
          (are striving to)

_____
(describe desired outcome)

but your _____
      (describe discrepant action, behavior, or inaction)

is likely to produce _____
         (describe probable negative consequence)

This format is purely illustrative. You may organize these elements in varying ways, and we encourage you to be innovative and to develop your own style. For example, you may challenge clients to analyze the effects of behavior that is incongruous with purported goals or values, as illustrated in the following:

[*To male on parole*]: "Al, I know the last thing you want is to have to return to prison. I want you to stay out too, and I think you sense that. But I have to level with you. You're starting to hang out with the same bunch you got in trouble with before you went to prison. You're heading the same direction you were before, and we both know where that leads."

Notice in the preceding confrontation the practitioner begins by making reference to the client's purported goal (remaining out of prison) and expresses a like commitment to the goal. The practitioner next introduces concern about the client's behavior (hanging out with the same bunch the client got in trouble with before) that is discrepant with that goal. The practitioner concludes the confrontation by focusing on the possible negative consequence of the discrepant behavior (getting into trouble and returning to prison). Notice these same elements in the following additional examples of confrontive responses.

[*To father in family session*]: "Mr. D., I'd like you to stop for a moment and examine what you're doing. I know you want the children not to be afraid of you and to talk with you more openly. Right?" [*Father agrees.*] "OK, let's think about what you just did with Steve. He began to tell you about what he did after the school assembly, and you cut him off and got on his case. Did you notice how he clammed up immediately?"

[*To child-abusing mother*]: "Helen, I have a concern I need to share with you. You've expressed your goal of regaining custody of Pete, and we agreed that attending the parents' group was part of the plan to accomplish that goal. This week is the second time in a row you've missed the meeting because you overslept. I'm very concerned you may be defeating yourself in accomplishing your goal."

Because employing confrontation runs the risk of putting clients on the defensive or alienating them, expressing concern and helpful intent is a critical element because it reduces the possibility that clients will misconstrue the motive behind the confrontation. The tone of voice is also vital in conveying helpful intent. If the practitioner conveys the confrontation in a warm, concerned tone of voice, the client will be much less likely to feel attacked. If the practitioner uses a critical tone of voice, verbal reassurance that criticism was not intended is likely to fall on deaf ears. Keep in mind that people tend to attach more credence to nonverbal aspects of messages than to verbal aspects.

Guidelines to Employing Confrontation

To assist you in employing confrontation effectively, we offer the following guidelines:

1. Do not employ confrontation until an effective working relationship has evolved. Until clients gain trust in practitioners and perceive their goodwill and helpful intent, confrontation should not be employed because of the high risk of alienating the client and precipitating premature termination. Employing empathic responsiveness in early contacts, by contrast, conveys understanding, fosters rapport, and enhances confidence in the perceptiveness and expertise of the practitioner. When a foundation of trust and confidence has been established, clients are more receptive to confrontations and, in some instances, even welcome them.

An exception to this guideline involves highly manipulative and deceptive clients, who tend to deny problems, deliberately misrepresent facts, and maneuver practitioners for their own gain or advantage. Many of these antisocial clients openly violate laws and exploit others (including well-meaning practitioners). Confrontations are often employed to advantage early in contacts with these clients, who tend to be contemptuous of people who succumb to their manipulative tactics. In fact, they tend to respect and value persons who not only see through their devious ploys but confront them directly (although such clients typically do not convey respect). These clients tend to be provocative, and it is important not to let them goad you into responding defensively or punitively. Consistent caring and goodwill (tempered with timely confrontations) are essential to penetrate the armor of toughness these clients typically project.

2. Use confrontation sparingly. Keep in mind that confrontation is a potent technique that generally should be employed only when clients' blind spots are refractory to other less risky methods. Some practitioners use confrontation frequently, professing it to be a "high-yield" technique. Research by Lieberman, Yalom, and Miles (1973) involving groups refutes this argument. Their findings indicate that destructive group leaders tend to be highly confrontive and challenging persons who frequently attack members and pressure them for immediate change. Based on their findings, these authors concluded that this type of leadership is associated with negative outcomes. Indeed, poorly timed and excessive confrontations can inflict psychological damage on clients.

Another reason to employ confrontation judiciously is that some clients may yield to forceful confrontation for reasons that are counterproductive. Seeking to please practitioners (or to avoid displeasing them), they may temporarily modify their behavior. But changing merely to comply with expectations of a practitioner fosters passivity and dependence, both of which are anathema to actual growth. Some clients already are excessively passive, and pressuring them for compliance only reinforces their dysfunctional behavior.

3. Deliver confrontations in an atmosphere of warmth, caring, and concern. As we have previously emphasized, if practitioners employ confrontations in a cold, impersonal, or critical way, clients are likely to feel they are being attacked. By contrast, if practitioners preface confrontations with genuine empathic concern (as recommended in the paradigm presented earlier), clients are more likely to perceive the helpfulness intended in the confrontation.

4. Whenever possible, encourage self-confrontations. Recall from the previous discussion that self-confrontations have decided advantages over practitioner-initiated confrontations. Learning by self-discovery fosters independence and enhances the likelihood that clients will act upon newly gained self-awareness. Practitioners can encourage self-confrontation by drawing the attention of clients to issues, behaviors, or inconsistencies they may have overlooked and by encouraging them to analyze the situation further. For example, the practitioner may directly intervene into dysfunctional interaction and challenge individuals, couples, families, or groups to identify what they are doing. Responses that encourage self-confrontation in such a context include the following:

- "Let's stop and look at what you just did."

- "What did you just do?"

Other responses that highlight inconsistencies and foster self-confrontation are as follows:

- "I'm having trouble seeing how what you just said (or did) fits with . . . ."

- "I can understand how you felt, but how did (describe behavior) make it better for you?"

- "What you're saying seems inconsistent with what you want to achieve. How do you see it?"

Still another technique is useful when clients overlook the dynamic significance of their own revealing expressions or when their manifest feelings fail to match their reported feelings. This technique involves asking them to repeat a message, to listen carefully to themselves, and to consider the meaning of the message. Examples of this technique follow:

- "I want to be sure you realize the significance of what you just said. Repeat it, but this time listen carefully to yourself, and tell me what it means to you."

- [*To marital partner in conjoint interview*]: "Joan just told you something terribly important, and I'm not sure you really grasped it. Could you repeat it, Joan, and I want you to listen very carefully, Bob, and check with Joan as to whether you grasped what she said."

- [*To group member*]: "You just told the group you're feeling better about yourself, but it didn't come through that way. Please say it again, but get in touch with your feelings and listen to yourself."

5. Avoid using confrontation when clients are experiencing extreme emotional strain. Confrontations tend to mobilize anxiety, and when clients are under heavy strain, supportive techniques rather than confrontation are indicated. Clients who are overwhelmed with anxiety and/or guilt generally are not receptive to confrontation and do not benefit from it. Rather, confrontations may be detrimental, adding to tension that is already excessive.

Confrontation *is* appropriate for clients who experience minimal inner conflict or anxiety when such reactions would be appropriate in light of their problematic behavior as perceived by others. Self-satisfied and typically insensitive to the feelings and needs of others (whom they cause to be anxious), such clients, popularly referred to as character disorders, often lack the anxiety needed to engender and maintain adequate motivation. Confrontation, combined with the facilitative conditions, may mobilize the anxiety they need to examine their own behavior and to consider making constructive changes.

6. Follow confrontations with empathic responsiveness. Because clients may take offense to even skillful confrontations, it is vital to be sensitive to their reactions. Since clients often do not express their reactions verbally, you will need to be especially perceptive of nonverbal cues that suggest hurt, anger, confusion, discomfort, embarrassment, or resentment. If clients manifest these or other unfavorable reactions, it is important to explore their reactions and to respond empathically to their feelings. Discussing such reactions provides opportunities for clients to ventilate their feelings and for practitioners to clarify their helpful intent and to assist clients to work through negative feelings. If practitioners fail to sense negative feelings or clients withhold expressions of them, the feelings may fester and adversely affect the helping relationship.

It is to be expected that clients will respond to confrontations with a certain degree of anxiety. Indeed, confrontations are employed to produce a temporary sense of disequilibrium that is essential to break an impasse. The anxiety or disequilibrium thus serves a therapeutic purpose in impelling the client to make constructive changes that eliminate the discrepancy that prompted the practitioner's confrontation. Empathic responsiveness following confrontations thus is not aimed at diluting this anxiety but rather at resolving untoward reactions that may derive from negative interpretations of the practitioner's motives for making the confrontation.

7. Don't expect immediate change after confrontations. Although awareness paves the way to change, clients rarely succeed in making changes immediately following acquisition of insight. Even when clients fully accept confrontations, corresponding changes ordinarily occur by increments. Known as *working through*, this change process involves repeatedly reviewing the same conflicts and the client's typical reactions to them, gradually broadening the perspective to encompass more and more situations to which the changes are applicable. Unfortunately, some naive practitioners press for immediate change, sometimes inflicting psychological damage on their clients, as we noted earlier.

Indications for Confrontation

As we have previously indicated, confrontations are appropriate (1) when discrepancies, inconsistencies, and dysfunctional behaviors (overt or covert) block progress or create difficulties and (2) when other less risky approaches have been ineffective in fostering clients' awareness of these behaviors and/or attempts to make corresponding changes. Discrepancies may reside in cognitive/perceptual, emotional, or behavioral functions or may involve interactions between these functions. A comprehensive analysis of types of discrepancies and inconsistencies has been presented elsewhere (Hammond et al., 1977, pp. 286–318); therefore, we merely highlight some of those that most commonly occur.

Cognitive/Perceptual Discrepancies Many clients manifest dysfunctional behavior that is a product of inaccurate, erroneous, or incomplete information, and confrontations may assist them in modifying their behavior. For example, clients may lack accurate information about indicators of alcoholism, normal sexual functioning, or reasonable expectations of children according to stages of development. Even more common are misconceptions about the self, the most common of which, in the authors' experience, involve self-demeaning perceptions. Even talented and attractive persons may view themselves as inferior, worthless, inadequate, unattractive, stupid, and the like. Such perceptions are often deeply embedded and do not yield to change without extensive working through. Other cognitive/perceptual discrepancies include interpersonal perceptual distortions, irrational fears, dichotomous or stereotypical thinking, denial of problems, placing responsibility for one's difficulties outside of oneself, failing to discern available alternate solutions to difficulties, and failing to consider consequences of actions. We focused on these categories of dysfunction in Chapter 9.

Affective Discrepancies Discrepancies in the emotional realm are inextricably linked to the cognitive/perceptual processes, as emotions are shaped by cognitive meanings clients attribute to situations, events, and memories. For example, one may experience intense anger that emanates from a conclusion that another person has intentionally insulted, slighted, or betrayed one. The conclusion is based on a meaning attribution that may involve a grossly distorted perception of another person's intentions. In such instances, practitioners assist clients to explore their feelings, to provide relevant detailed factual information, to consider alternate meanings, and to realign their emotions with reality.

Affective discrepancies practitioners commonly encounter include denying or minimizing actual feelings, being out of touch with painful emotions, expressing feelings that are contrary to purported feelings (e.g., claiming to love a spouse or child but expressing only critical or otherwise negative feelings), or verbally expressing a feeling that contradicts feelings expressed nonverbally (e.g., "No, I'm not disappointed," said with a quivering voice and tears in the eyes). Gentle confrontations aimed at emotional discrepancies often pave the way to ventilation of troubling emotions, and many clients appreciate practitioners' sensitivity in recognizing their suppressed or unexpressed emotions. If a client appears unready to face painful emotions, the practitioner should proceed cautiously and may be wise to defer further exploration of them. Confronting the client vigorously may elicit overwhelming emotions and engender consequent resentment toward the practitioner.

Behavioral Discrepancies Clients may manifest many dysfunctional behavioral patterns or lifestyles that create difficulties for themselves and others. Even though these patterns may be conspicuous to others, clients themselves may have blind spots to their patterns or to the impact of the same on others. Confrontation may therefore be required to expand their awareness of these patterns and their pernicious effects. In Chapter 9 (Figure 9-2), we enumerated many of the myriad dysfunctional patterns that practitioners encounter. We will not repeat them here but will highlight certain pervasive categories of dysfunctional behavior.

Irresponsible behavior tends to spawn serious interpersonal difficulties for clients as well as problems with broader society. Neglect of children, weak efforts to secure and maintain employment, undependability in fulfilling assignments, failure to maintain property—these and other like derelictions often result in severe financial, legal, and interpersonal entanglements that may culminate in loss of employment; estrangement from others; and loss of property, child custody, self-respect, and even personal freedom. Irresponsible behavior often pervades the helping process as well, being manifested by tardiness, unwillingness to acknowledge problems, and failure to keep appointments or pay fees. Effective confrontations with such clients require a firm approach couched in expressions of goodwill and concern about wanting to assist the client to avoid adverse consequences of not assuming responsibilities. It is a disservice to clients to permit them to rationalize, deny, and evade responsibility for their actions or inaction. Further, the practitioner must counter their tendency to blame others or circumstances for their difficulties by assisting them to recognize that *only they* can reduce the pressures that beset them.

Other common behavioral discrepancies involve repeated actions that are incongruous with purported goals or values. Adolescents may describe ambitious goals that require extensive training or education but make little effort in school, truant frequently, and otherwise behave in ways entirely inconsistent with their goals. Spouses or parents may similarly espouse goals of improving their marital or family life but persistently behave in abrasive ways that further erode their relationships. Confrontations often must be used to assist them to desist from self-defeating behaviors. In some instances, therapeutic binds (a special form of confrontation discussed in Chapter 20) may be employed to supply additional needed leverage to motivate clients to relinquish destructive and unusually persistent patterns of behavior.

Three other common categories of discrepancies or dysfunctional behavior that warrant confrontation are manipulative behavior, dysfunctional communication, and resistance to change. Manipulative behavior involves devious maneuvering of other persons for self-serving ends with little consideration for the needs or well-being of the other persons. In groups, certain members may attempt to dominate the group, bait group members, play one person against the other, undermine the leader, or engage in other destructive ploys. The price of permitting members to engage in such behaviors may be loss of certain group members, dilution of the group's effectiveness, or premature dissolution of the group. To avert such undesired consequences, the leader may elicit reactions of other members to the manipulative behavior and may assist members to confront manipulators with their destructive tactics. Such confrontations should adhere to the guidelines delineated earlier, and the leader should encourage members to invite offending members to join with them in constructively seeking to accomplish the purposes of the group.

Because dysfunctional communication frequently occurs in individual, conjoint, and group sessions, practitioners encounter abundant opportunities to employ confrontation to good effect. Intervening during or immediately following dysfunctional communication is a powerful means of enabling clients to experience firsthand the negative effect of their dysfunctional behavior (e.g., interrupting, attacking, claiming, or criticizing). By shifting the focus to the negative reactions of recipients of dysfunctional messages, practitioners enable clients to receive direct feedback as to how their behavior offends, alienates, or engenders defensiveness in others, thereby producing effects contrary to their purported goals.

Confrontation is a vital tool in working through clients' resistance both to change and to relating openly in the helping relationship. If individual clients are left to struggle alone with negative feelings about the helping process or the practitioner, their feelings may mount to the extent that they resolve them by discontinuing their sessions. If family members or groups are permitted to resist change by engaging in distractive, irrelevant, or otherwise dysfunctional behavior, they may likewise lose both confidence in the practitioners (for valid reasons) and motivation to continue. For these reasons, practitioners must accord highest priority to focusing on and resolving resistance. Because of the importance of this matter, we have devoted the entire following chapter to it.

Skill Development Exercises in Additive Empathy and Interpretation

To assist you to advance your skill in responding with interpretation and additive empathy, we provide the following exercises. Read each client message, determine the type of response called for, and formulate a written response you would employ if you were in an actual session with the client. As you formulate your responses, keep in mind the guidelines for employing interpretive additive empathic responses. Compare your responses with the modeled responses provided at the end of the exercises.

Client Statements

1. Black female client [*to white female practitioner*]: You seem to be accepting of black people, at least you have been of me. But somehow I still feel uneasy with you. I guess it's just me. I haven't really known many white people very well.

2. Married woman, age 28: I feel I don't have a life of my own. My life is controlled by *his* work, *his* hours, and *his* demands. It's like I don't have an identity of my own.

3. Prison inmate, age 31: [*one week before date of scheduled parole, which was canceled the preceding week*]: Man, what the hell's going on with me? Here I've been on good behavior for three years and finally got a parole date. You'd think I'd be damned glad to get out of here. So I get all uptight and get in a brawl in the mess hall. I mean I really blew it, man. Who knows when they'll give me another date?

4. Male, age 18: What's the point in talking about going to Trade Tech? I didn't make it in high school, and I won't make it there either. You may as well give up on me—I'm just a dropout in life.

5. Widow, age 54: It was Mother's Day last Sunday, and neither of my kids did as much as send me a card. You'd think they could at least acknowledge I'm alive.

6. Female secretary, age 21: I don't have any trouble typing when I'm working alone. But if the boss or anyone else is looking over my shoulder, it's like I'm all thumbs. I just seem to tighten up.

7. Married female, age 26, who is five pounds overweight: When I make a batch of cookies or a cake on the weekend, Terry [*husband*] looks at me with that condemning expression, as though I'm not really trying to keep my weight down. I don't think it's fair just because he doesn't like sweets. I like sweets, but the only time I eat any is on the weekend, and I don't eat much then. I feel I deserve to eat dessert on the weekend at least.

8. Recipient of public assistance [*disabled male with a back condition caused by recent industrial accident*]: This lying around is really getting to me. I see my kids needing things I can't afford to get them, and I just feel—I don't know—kind of useless. There's got to be a way of making a living.

9. Depressed male, age 53: Yeah, I know I do all right in my work. But that doesn't amount to much. Anyone could do that. That's how I feel about everything I've ever done. Nothing's really amounted to anything.

10. Mother, age 29: [*who has neglected her children*]: I don't know. I'm just so confused. I look at my kids sometimes, and I want to be a better mother. But after they've been fighting, or throwing tantrums, or whining and I lose my cool—I feel like I'd just like to go somewhere—

anywhere—and never come back. The kids deserve a better mother.

Modeled Responses for Interpretation and Additive Empathy

1. [*To clarify feelings experienced only vaguely*]: "So I gather even though you can't put your finger on why, you're still somewhat uncomfortable with me. You haven't related closely to that many whites, and you're still not altogether sure how much you can trust me."

2. [*Implied wants and goals*]: "Sounds like you feel you're just an extension of your husband and that part of you is wanting to find yourself and be a person in your own right."

3. [*Hidden purpose of behavior, underlying feelings*]: "So you're pretty confused about what's happened. Fighting in the mess hall when you did just doesn't make sense to you. You know, Carl, about your getting uptight—I guess I'm wondering if you were worried about getting out—worried about whether you could make it outside. I'm wondering if you might have fouled up last week to avoid taking that risk."

4. [*Underlying belief about self*]: "Sounds like you feel defeated before you give yourself a chance. Like it's hopeless to even try. Jay, that concerns me because when you think that way about yourself, you *are* defeated—not because you lack ability but because you think of yourself as destined to fail. That belief is your real enemy."

5. [*Deeper feelings*]: "You must have felt terribly hurt and resentful they didn't as much as call you. In fact, you seem to be experiencing those feelings now. It just hurts so much."

6. [*Underlying thoughts and feelings*]: "I wonder if, in light of your tightening up, you get feeling scared, as though you're afraid you won't measure up to their expectations."

7. [*Unrealized strengths*]: "Paula, I'm impressed with what you just said. It strikes me you're exercising a lot of control by limiting dessert to weekends and using moderation then. In fact, your self-control seems greater than that of most people. You and Terry have a legitimate difference concerning sweets. But it's exactly that—a difference. Neither view is right or wrong, and you're entitled to your preference as much as he's entitled to his."

8. [*Unrealized strength and implied want*]: "Steve, I can hear the frustration you're feeling, and I want you to know it reflects some real strength on your part. You want to be self-supporting and be able to provide better for your family. Given that desire, we can explore opportunities for learning new skills that won't require physical strength."

9. [*Underlying pattern of thought*]: "Kent, I get the feeling that it wouldn't matter what you did. You could set a world record, and you wouldn't feel it amounted to much. I'm wondering if your difficulty lies more in long-time feelings you've had about yourself that you somehow just don't measure up. I'd be interested in hearing more about how you've viewed yourself."

10. [*Underlying feelings and implied wants*]: "So your feelings tear you and pull you in different directions. You'd like to be a better mother, and you feel crummy when you lose your cool. But sometimes you just feel so overwhelmed and inadequate in coping with the children. Part of you would like to learn to manage the children better, but another part would like to get away from it all."

Skill Development Exercises in Confrontation

The following exercises involve discrepancies and dysfunctional behavior in all three experiential domains—cognitive/perceptual, emotional, and behavioral. After reading the brief summary of the situation involved and the verbatim exchanges between the client(s) and practitioner, identify the type of discrepancy involved and formulate your next response (observing the guidelines presented earlier) as though you are the practitioner in a real-life situation. Next, compare your response with the modeled one, keeping in mind that the latter is only one of many possible appropriate responses. Carefully analyze how your response is similar to or differs from the modeled response and whether you adhered to the guidelines.

Situations and Dialogue

1. You have been working with Mr. Lyon for several weeks, following his referral by the court after being convicted for sexually molesting his teenage daughter. Mr. Lyon has been 15 minutes late for his last two appointments, and today he is 20 minutes late. During his sessions he has explored and worked on problems only superficially.

Client: Sorry to be late today. Traffic was sure heavy. You know how that goes.

2. The clients are marital partners whom you have seen conjointly five times. One of their goals is to reduce marital conflict by avoiding getting into arguments that create mutual resentments.

Mrs. J.: This week has been just awful. I've tried to look nice and have his meals on time—like he said he wanted, and I've just felt so discouraged. He got on my back Tuesday and . . . [*husband interrupts*].

Mr. J.: [*Angrily*]: Just a minute. You're only telling half the story. You left out what you did Monday. [*She interrupts.*]

Mrs. J.: Oh, forget it. What's the use? He doesn't care about me. He couldn't the way he treats me.

Mr. J.: [*Shakes head in disgust.*]

3. The client is a slightly retarded young adult who was referred by a rehabilitation agency because of social and emotional problems. The client has manifested a strong interest in dating young women and has been vigorously pursuing a clerk (Sue) in a local supermarket. She has registered no interest in him and obviously has attempted to discourage him from further efforts. The following excerpt occurs in the seventh session.

Client: I went through Sue's checkstand this morning. I told her I'd like to take her to the show.

Practitioner: Oh, and what did she say?

Client: She said she was too busy. I'll wait a couple of weeks and ask her again.

4. Tony, age 16, is a member of a therapy group in a youth correctional institution. In the preceding session, he appeared to gain a sense of power and satisfaction from provoking other members to react angrily and defensively, which tended to disrupt group process. Tony directs the following message to a group member early in the fourth session.

Tony: I noticed you trying to make out with Maggie at the dance Wednesday. You think you're pretty hot stuff, don't you?

5. The client is a mother, age 26, who keeps feelings inside until they mount out of control, at which time she discharges anger explosively.

Client: I can't believe my neighbor. She sends her kids over to play with Sandra at lunchtime and disappears. It's obvious

her kids haven't had lunch, and I end up feeding them, even though she's better off financially than I am.

Practitioner: What do you feel when she does that?

Client: Oh, not much, I guess. But I think it's a rotten thing to do.

6. You have been working for several weeks with a family that includes the parents and four children ranging in age from 10 to 17. The mother is a domineering person who acts as spokesperson for the family, and the father is passive and softspoken. A teenage daughter, Tina, expresses herself in the following excerpt.

Tina: We always seem to have a hassle when we visit our grandparents. Grandma's so bossy. I don't like going there.

Mother: Tina, that's not true. You've always enjoyed going to her house. You and your grandmother have always been close.

7. Group members in their fifth session have been intently discussing difficulties of the members in social interaction. One of the members takes the group off on a tangent by describing humorous idiosyncrasies of a person she met while on vacation, and the other group members follow suit by sharing humorous anecdotes about "oddballs" they have encountered.

8. The client is an attractive, personable, and intelligent woman who has been married for three years to a self-centered, critical man. In the fourth session (an individual interview), she tearfully says:

Client: I've done everything he's asked of me. I've lost 10 pounds. I support him in his work. I golf with him. I even changed my religion to please him. And he's still not happy with me. There's just something wrong with me.

9. The clients are a married couple in their early 30s. The following excerpt occurs in the initial interview.

Wife: We just seem to fight over the smallest things. When he gets really mad, he loses his temper and knocks me around.

Husband: The real problem is that she puts her parents ahead of me. She's the one who needs help, not me. If she'd get straightened around, I wouldn't lose my temper. Tell her where her first responsibility is. I've tried, and she won't listen to me.

10. The clients are a family consisting of the parents and two children. Terry, age 15, has been truanting and smoking marijuana. Angie, age 16, is a model student and is obviously her parents' favorite. The family was referred by the school when Terry was expelled for several days. The father, a highly successful businessman, entered family therapy with obvious reluctance, which has continued to this, the fourth session.

Mother: Things haven't been much different this week. Everyone's been busy, and we really haven't seen much of each other.

Father: I think we'd better plan to skip the next three weeks. Things have been going pretty well, and I have an audit in process at the office that's going to put me in a time bind.

Modeled Responses for Confrontation

1. [*Irresponsible and resistant behavior by the client*]: "Ted, I'm concerned you're late today. This is the third time you've been late in a row, and it shortens the time available to us. But my concerns go beyond that. I know you don't like having to come here and that you'd like to be out from under the court's jurisdiction. But the way you're going about things won't accomplish that. I can't be helpful to you and can't write a favorable report to the court if you just go through the motions of coming here for help. Apparently it's uncomfortable for you to come. I'd be interested in hearing just what you're feeling about coming."

2. [*Discrepancy between purported goal and behavior, as well as dysfunctional communication*]: "Let's stop and look at what you're doing right now. I'm concerned because each of you wants to feel closer to the other, but what you're both doing just makes each other defensive." [*To husband.*] "Mr. J., she was sharing some important feelings with you, and you cut her off." [*To wife.*] " And you did the same thing, Mrs. J., when he was talking. I know you may not agree, but it's important to hear each other out and to try to understand. If you keep interrupting and trying to blame each other, as you've both been doing, you're going to stay at square one, and I don't want that to happen. Let's go back and start over, but this time put yourself in the shoes of the other and try to understand. Check out with the other if you really understood. Then you can express your own views."

3. [*Dysfunctional, self-defeating behavior*]: "Pete, I know how much you think of Sue and how you'd like to date her. I'm concerned that you keep asking her out, though, because she never accepts and doesn't appear to want to go out with you. My concern is that you're setting yourself up for hurt and disappointment. I'd like to see you get a girl friend, but your chances of getting a date are probably a lot better with persons other than Sue."

4. [*Abrasive, provocative behavior*]: "Hold on a minute, guys. I'm feeling uncomfortable and concerned right now about what Tony just said. It came across as a real put-down, and we agreed earlier one of our rules was to support and help each other. Tony, would you like some feedback from other members about how you're coming across to the group?"

5. [*Discrepancy between expressed and actual feeling*]: "I agree. But I'm concerned you say you don't feel much. I should think you'd be ticked off and want to change the situation. Let's see if you can get in touch with your feelings. Picture yourself at home at noon and your neighbor's kids knock on the door while you're fixing lunch. Can you picture it? What are you feeling in your body and thinking just now?"

6. [*Dysfunctional communication—disconfirming Tina's feeling and experiences*]: "What did you just do, Mrs. Black? Stop and think for a moment about how you responded to Tina's message. It may help you to understand why she doesn't share more with you." [*or*] "Tina, could you tell your mother what you're feeling right now about what she just said? I'd like her to get some feedback that could help her communicate better with you."

7. [*Discrepancy between goals and behavior—getting off topic*]: "I'm concerned about what the group's doing right now. What do you think is happening?"

8. [*Misconception about the self—cognitive/perceptual discrepancy*]: "Jan, I'm concerned about what you just said because you're putting yourself down and leaving no room to feel good about yourself. You're assuming that you own the problem and that you're deficient in some

way. I'm not at all sure that's the problem. You're married to a man who seems impossible to please and that is more likely the problem. As we agreed earlier, you have tasks of feeling good about yourself, standing up for yourself, and letting his problem be *his*. As long as your feelings about yourself depend on *his* approval, you're going to feel down on yourself."

9. [*Manipulative behavior*]: "I don't know the two of you well enough to presume to know what's causing your problems." [*To husband.*] "If you're expecting me to tell your wife to shape up, you'll be disappointed. My job is to help each of you to see your part in the difficulties and to make appropriate changes. If I did what you asked, I'd be doing both of you a gross disservice. Things don't get better that way."

10. [*Resistance, discrepancy between behavior and purported goals*]: "What you do, of course, is up to you. I am concerned, however, because you all agreed you wanted to relate more closely as family members and give each other more support. To accomplish that means you have to work at it steadily, or things aren't likely to change much." [*To father.*] "My impression is that you're backing off. I know your business is important, but I guess you have to decide whether you're really committed to the goals you set for yourselves."

20 Managing Individual, Relational, and Organizational Barriers to Change

Barriers to Change

Rarely is progress smooth and steady during the goal attainment phase. Rather, the change process is characterized by rapid spurts of growth, plateaus, impasses, and sometimes brief periods of retrogression. This process varies widely according to the severity of problems, the strengths and motivation of clients, the interventions employed, the quality of the helping relationship, the responsiveness of institutions in providing needed resources, and the strengths of various forces that militate against change. Forces that impede the helping process include resistance by individuals, families, and interpersonal systems that are part of the problem configuration; difficulties in the helping relationship (relational reactions); and oppositional responses by organizations whose resources are essential to goal attainment. In this chapter we focus on these barriers to change and ways of managing them so that they do not unduly impede progress or precipitate premature termination by clients. In the final portion of the chapter we provide relevant exercises to assist you in developing skills to manage barriers to growth.

Relational Reactions

The practitioner-client relationship is the vehicle that animates the helping process; indeed, the quality of the helping relationship critically determines both the client's moment-to-moment receptiveness to the influence and intervention of the practitioner and the ultimate outcome of the helping process. Further, the helping relationship per se may be a source of positive change for many clients, who gain self-respect and feelings of worth in positive helping relationships. For clients whose previous life experiences have been void of sustained caring relationships, the helping relationship may be a corrective emotional experience in the sense of compensating for emotional deprivation experienced in earlier life.

Because of the profound importance of the helping relationship, it is critical that practitioners be skillful both in cultivating relationships and keeping them in repair. In earlier chapters, we discussed qualities and skills in cultivating sound relationships. Skills in maintaining relationships are equally vital, as feelings that influence the relationship for better or worse constantly flow back and forth between participants in the helping process.

Therefore, to maintain positive helping relationships, you must be alert to threats to such relationships and skillful in managing them. In the following sections, we discuss these factors at length.

Recognizing and Managing Threats to Helping Relationships

Helping relationships that are characterized by reciprocal positive feelings between practitioner and clients are conducive to personal growth and successful problem solving. Practitioners strive to develop positive helping relationships by relating facilitatively with high levels of warmth, acceptance, unconditional caring, empathy, genuineness, and spontaneity, as we discussed earlier. Despite these efforts, however, some clients do not respond positively for a number of reasons that we discuss later. Practitioners, too, may have difficulty responding positively to clients with certain personality attributes and types of problems. Even when a positive relationship evolves, various events and moment-by-moment transactions may pose threats to the continuing viability of the relationship. Practitioners must be vigilant to manifestations that something is going awry in the relationship. Failure to perceive these manifestations and to manage them effectively may result in needless impasses or, even worse, premature termination. In the following discussion, we focus on threats to the relationship that emanate from the client, from the practitioner, and from dyadic mixes of both.

Here-and-Now Reactions Clients often experience emotional reactions during the course of sessions that create a temporary breach in helping relationships, and if practitioners fail to recognize and handle them skillfully, the reactions may expand into major obstacles in the helping process. The following are typical examples of practitioners' behavior that may engender immediate feelings of hurt, disappointment, anger, fear, rejection, and other like negative emotions:

1. Failing to sense important feelings experienced by clients.

2. Sending messages that clients interpret as criticisms or put-downs.

3. Being inattentive or "tuning out" clients.

4. Failing to acknowledge incremental growth achieved by clients.

5. Employing inept or poorly timed confrontations.

6. Manifesting lapses of memory about important information previously revealed by clients.

7. Being tardy or canceling appointments.

8. Appearing drowsy or fidgety.

9. Disagreeing, arguing, or giving excessive advice.

10. Disapproving of a client's planned course of action.

11. Appearing to take sides against a client (or subgroup) or actually doing so.

12. Dominating discussions or frequently interrupting clients.

13. Giving advice or assignments that clients feel incapable of carrying out.

Some of the preceding events or circumstances involve "mistakes" by practitioners; others involve misperceptions by clients. Irrespective of the source, it is vital to sense and to discuss clients' feelings and thoughts as they are manifested and thus prevent them from escalating. Often clients will not initiate discussion of their negative reactions, and if you are not sensitive to nonverbal cues, the feelings and cognitions will linger and fester. To avert such a development, it is crucial to be perceptive of indicators of negative reactions including the following nonverbal cues: frowning, fidgeting, sighing, appearing startled, grimacing, changing the subject, becoming silent, clearing the throat, blushing, and tightening the muscles. When you discern these or related cues, it is important to shift the focus of the session to the clients' here-and-now feelings and cognitions. You should do this sensitively, manifesting genuine concern for the client's discomfort and conveying your desire to understand what the client is experiencing at the moment. Examples of responses that facilitate discussion of troubling feelings and thoughts are:

- "I'm sensing you're reacting to what I just said. Could you share with me what it meant to you and what you're thinking and feeling at this moment?"

- "You appear distressed right now. I'd like to understand just what you're experiencing and if I may have said or done something that caused your troubled thoughts and feelings."

Keep in mind that discussing negative feelings and cognitions toward a practitioner is extremely difficult for many clients. You can reduce the threat by being warmly attentive and accepting of clients, even though their thoughts and feelings may be entirely unrealistic. By eliciting the client's feelings and thoughts, you have the opportunity to correct a misunderstanding, clarify your intention, rectify a blunder, or identify a dysfunctional belief or pattern of thought. Indeed, some clients benefit from observing a model who can acknowledge imperfections and apologize for errors without appearing

humiliated. Moreover, clients may gain self-esteem by realizing that practitioners value them sufficiently to be concerned about their thoughts and feelings and to rectify errors of omission or commission. After productive discussions of here-and-now thoughts and feelings, most clients regain positive feelings and resume working on their problems.

On occasions, however, clients may succeed in concealing negative thoughts and feelings, or you may overlook nonverbal manifestations of them. The feelings may thus fester until it becomes obvious that the client is relating atypically by holding back, being overly formal, responding defensively, or manifesting other forms of resistance enumerated later in this chapter. Again, it is vital to accord priority to the relationship by shifting focus to what is bothering the client and responding as we recommended earlier. *After you have worked through the negative reaction of the client, it is helpful to negotiate a "minicontract" related to discussing troublesome feelings and thoughts as they occur.* The objective of this renegotiation is to avert similar recurrences in the future and to convey your openness to discussing negative reactions toward you. Learning to express negative feelings and thoughts can be a milestone for clients who typically withhold such reactions to the detriment of themselves and others. The following is an example of a message aimed at negotiating an appropriate minicontract:

"I'm pleased that you shared your hurt with me today. That helped me to understand what you've been thinking and feeling and gave me a chance to explain what I really meant last week. For us to work well together, it is important for both of us to put negative reactions on the table so that we can prevent strains from developing between us. I wonder how you'd feel about our updating our contract to include discussing immediately any troubling thoughts and feelings that might present obstacles in our relationship so that we can explore them together and work them out."

"Pathological" or Inept Practitioners
Although all practitioners commit rectifiable errors from time to time, some practitioners blunder repeatedly, causing irreparable damage to helping relationships and inflicting psychological damage upon their clients. Gottesfeld and Lieberman (1979) refer to such practitioners as *pathological* and point out that "It *is* possible to have therapists who suffer from as many unresolved problems as do clients" (p. 388). We certainly agree, based on knowledge of practitioners who are typically overbearing, abrasive, egotistical, controlling, judgmental, demeaning, rigid, habitually tardy for appointments, sexually promiscuous, patronizing, detached, and unable to tolerate clients' crying—to mention just a few "pathogenic" attributes. Practitioners with these attributes tend to lose clients prematurely (fortunately, the majority of clients discern these attributes and have the good sense to terminate such contacts), to create additional difficulties for clients, or to foster unhealthy dependency. Needless to say, these practitioners are injurious not only to their clients, but to their agencies and the profession as well. Consequently, other practitioners face a difficult situation in knowing what steps to take when they become aware of injurious practitioners. As Gottesfeld and Lieberman (1979) note: "It is painful to be a helpless observer of a situation that seems to be antitherapeutic for a client. Yet it is also painful and difficult to render a judgment about a professional colleague's competence" (p. 392).

Clearly, both individual practitioners and agencies have a responsibility to protect clients from pathological practitioners. Gottesfeld and Lieberman encapsulate this responsibility in their assertion that, "Agencies organized to help clients should not accept employee pathology that defeats the system's purpose" (p. 392). Actions to rectify such situations, however, must safeguard the rights of practitioners as well as clients, for unfair judgments may result from biased or inaccurate reports of practitioners' behavior. To protect clients' rights, "a professional's behavior must be open for review through consultation, supervision, or a peer review process" (Gottesfeld & Lieberman, 1979, p. 392). When peer review appears justified, a referral to the closest chapter of the professional organization (NASW) may be in order. Most chapters have committees formed to investigate complaints of unethical and unprofessional behavior.

Racial and Transcultural Barriers Clients may also experience adverse reactions in transracial or transcultural relationships with practitioners who either lack knowledge of the client's culture or lack experience in working with members of a given race or minority group. Members of racial or ethnic groups commonly experience fear, suspicion, and resentment toward members of majority groups who have discriminated against them. Moreover, participants in transcultural relationships may experience a mutual strangeness based on limited interaction with members of each others' culture. In such instances, "The void may be filled by stereotyped 'knowledge' and preconception, but the essential unknownness remains" (Gitterman & Schaeffer, 1972). Given these circumstances, mutual defensiveness and guardedness become an obstacle to effective communication with which the practitioners and clients must deal. Referring to transracial relationships between white practitioners and black clients, the authors just cited stress the need for "active participation directed toward reaching and touching each other" (p. 283). Active participation "sets up a demand for involvement, sharing, and feedback between white worker and black client in opposition to passive or secret observation and analysis" (p. 284).

Empathic communication is a basic skill that tends to bridge the gap often present in transracial and transcultural relationships. Empathically confronting clients' anger and suspiciousness tends to neutralize these negative feelings by demonstrating acceptance and understanding, as we have pointed out previously. Based on modest research evidence, several authors (Banks, 1971; Cimbolic, 1972; Santa Cruz & Hepworth, 1975) recommend that in preparing students to work across racial or ethnic lines, educators should train them to attain high levels of skill in the facilitative conditions of empathy, respect, and genuineness.

Even relating with high levels of the facilitative conditions may be insufficient to bridge the racial gap with certain clients. In analyzing sources of nondisclosure of black clients, Ridley (1984) has developed a useful typology that identifies "cultural paranoia" as a major barrier to transracial work involving white practitioners. Black clients who are high in "cultural paranoia" are so distrustful of whites that effective communication may not be possible; black practitioners may be required in such instances. The distrust of some black clients, of course, may be generalized ("functional paranoia") and directed toward blacks as well as whites. Ridley's article presents a cogent analysis of factors involved in black's non-

disclosure and presents highly useful guidelines to work with black clients.

Another source of negative reactions by black clients to white practitioners may be a lack of awareness by the latter to the duality of their feelings toward blacks. On one hand, as a result of a lack of adequate awareness of the effects of discrimination and oppression upon blacks, practitioners may be insensitive to a black's resentment, fear, distrust, and sense of powerlessness. Such practitioners may stereotype blacks and have a limited capacity for empathizing with them. On the other hand, sensitive white practitioners may overidentify with blacks, losing sight of clients' individual problems and erroneously attributing them to racial factors. When this occurs, as Cooper (1973) aptly puts it, "clients tend to lose their individual richness and complexity; there is the danger of no longer treating people—only culture carriers" (p. 76). Clearly then, white practitioners must empathize with blacks but not to the extent of overidentifying with them.

Given the potential obstacles that may emerge in transracial and transcultural relationships, one may well wonder if the solution is to match clients with practitioners of the same race or ethnic group. This solution is often not practicable, however, nor is there evidence that matching always works to the client's advantage. Research studies have indicated that traditional mental health services rendered by Anglo practitioners to Asian-Americans and Hispanics are markedly underutilized (Sue & Zane, 1987) and that "regardless of utilization rates, all of the ethnic-minority groups had significantly higher drop-out rates than whites" (p. 37). Further, Sue and McKinney (1975) reported dramatic increases in utilization rates by Asian-Americans when a counseling center was established specifically for this ethnic group and culturally relevant services were provided by bilingual therapists. These findings clearly illustrate that it is advantageous to match clients with practitioners of the same race or ethnicity. However, rigorous studies comparing treatment *outcomes* of racially and ethnically matched helping relationships with transcultural counterparts have not been reported. Moreover, several studies suggest that practitioners have been able to help clients of different races and ethnicity. Whether therapists of the same race or ethnicity could have been more helpful cannot be inferred because these studies lacked control or comparison groups. Based on the dearth of solid information, the most that can be concluded is that client and practitioner racial and ethnic homogeneity promote utilization of services by minority clients and that practitioners who engage in transcultural work, at a minimum, should be knowledgeable about the cultures of their clients and competent in relating with high levels of the facilitative conditions.

Difficulties in Trusting and Transference Reactions Clients vary widely in their capacity to trust. Those whose self-esteem and levels of interpersonal functioning are high may plunge into exploring their problems after only a few moments of checking out the practitioner. Yet despite the latter's goodwill and skills in imparting warmth, caring, and empathy, other clients may be guarded and test a practitioner for weeks or even months before letting down their defenses. Their reluctance to engage fully in helping relationships generally stems from previous life relationships that lacked sustained nurturance and love, a stable family life, and encouragement and approval. Aloofness and suspicion thus are defensive patterns that protect clients from imagined

hurts, exploitation, rejection, criticism, punishment, and control by others. Attempting to persuade such clients of one's helpful intent is usually counterproductive, as their distrust is deeply embedded; indeed, some clients have risked trusting in the past only to be let down and disappointed again and again.

With such clients, practitioners must exercise patience and persistence. Pushing for self-disclosure before trust and a positive relationship are established may alienate them, prolong the period of testing, or precipitate discontinuance of the helping relationship. Because these clients do not enter helping relationships readily and hence often disclose their problems only superficially during early sessions, setting time limits on the duration of the helping process is inappropriate. In fact, it may be necessary to reach out to these clients to maintain their involvement in the helping process. Often they cancel or miss appointments, and unless the practitioner reaches out by phoning them, making a home visit, or writing a letter (the last is the *least* effective), they often do not return. It is important to recognize that many of these clients urgently need help and that their failure to keep appointments may emanate more from a pattern of avoidance than from lack of motivation. Assisting them to come to terms with fears behind their avoidance behavior thus may be therapeutic, whereas letting them terminate by default contributes to perpetuation of their avoidance behavior.

Unrealistic perceptions of and reactions to a practitioner are known as *transference reactions;* that is, the client transfers to the practitioner wishes, fears, and other feelings that are rooted in past experiences with others (usually parents, parental substitutes, and siblings). Transference reactions may not only impede progress in the helping process but also create difficulties in other interpersonal relationships. A male may have difficulty trusting all women because he felt rejected and/or abused by his mother or stepmother; similarly, some people resent and rebel against all people in positions of authority, mistakenly perceiving all such people as they perceived an overbearing, punitive, controlling, and exploitative parent.

Transference reactions thus involve overgeneralized and distorted perceptions that create difficulties in interpersonal relationships. Besides being a possible impediment to progress, transference reactions in therapeutic relationships also represent an opportunity for growth. Because the therapeutic relationship is, in effect, a social microcosm wherein clients' interpersonal behavior and conditioned patterns of perceiving and feeling are manifested, in this context clients often recreate here-and-now interactions that are virtually identical to those that plague and defeat them in other relationships. The consequent challenge and opportunity for the practitioner is to assist such clients to recognize their distorted perceptions and to develop finer interpersonal perceptual discriminations so that they can differentiate and deal with the practitioner and others as unique individuals rather than as overgeneralized projections of mental images, beliefs, or attitudes.

The extent to which transference reactions occur during the course of the helping process varies considerably. In time-limited, task-focused forms of intervention, the likelihood of transference reactions is minimal. When treatment extends over a lengthy period of time, focuses on the past, and involves in-depth analysis of intrapsychic processes, transference may play a pivotal role in the helping process. Psychoanalytically oriented therapy and other long-term, insight-oriented therapies, in fact, tend to foster transference, whereas task-centered, behavioral, and crisis interventions do not. Similarly, working with marital partners conjointly tends to discourage transference reactions, whereas working with only one partner may foster transference by the client and overidentification on the practitioner's part. Smith and Hepworth (1967) have written about ways of avoiding pitfalls in working with one marital partner. Multiple transference reactions may also emerge in groups.

An individual can be experienced as a mother by one member, as a father by another, and as a sibling by still another. Similarly, that individual often "finds" parents and siblings in the group. Usually the leader is experienced as a mother or father. As the individual sees how he distorts perceptions in the group, he can begin to appreciate how he distorts other interpersonal relationships.

(Strean, 1979, p. 194)

The types of clients served also is a significant factor that determines the incidence of transference reactions. In public assistance, child welfare, and correctional settings, for example, many clients come from emotionally deprived backgrounds and have histories of ambivalent involvement with social agencies that predispose them to view social workers with fear and distrust, to react with humiliation and resentment, and to view themselves as helpless. Given these feelings, such clients are caught in a paradoxical situation, for, on the one hand, they have limited coping skills, desire to be assisted with their problems, and have dependency longings; but on the other hand, their fears and negative feelings are powerful deterrents to risking involving themselves with helping professionals. Consequently, many of these clients openly resist helping efforts or tend to relate in passive, dependent ways that block growth toward competency and independence.

To counter these inimical reactions, practitioners confront the challenge of having clients accept them and their offer of assistance. To gain acceptance of the offer to assist, it is often necessary to help clients to understand their resistance; that is, to explore their fears, resentments, and other negative feelings. Hartman and Reynolds (1987) recommend an approach that starts where the client is by focusing on the client's resistant behavior. This creates a crisis for the client and engenders anxiety and probable anger. The crisis precipitates a longing for "attachment behavior," to which the practitioner responds by interpreting the pattern of resistant behavior as an expression of distrust that derives from earlier life experiences with significant others who let the client down and could not be trusted. According to Hartman and Reynolds, clients respond to such interpretations with a sense of relief that the practitioner understands, mixed with emotions such as increased anger at being exposed, and fears as to what will happen next. In addition defensive reactions and longings may be further activated, causing the client to want to flee and cover up or to please and gain the favor of the practitioner.

To the client's reaction, the practitioner responds supportively by expressing warmth, care, and empathy related to the client's distress and fears. The client reacts to the supportive behavior with surprise and relief. The effect of the sequence of mutual behaviors and reactions is to foster affiliative behavior and trust by the client. Obviously this explanation is an oversimplification, and, as Hartman and Reynolds explain, the cycle may need to be repeated many times to penetrate clients' long-standing patterns of resistance to developing trust and forming attachments.

Managing Transference Reactions Irrespective of the agency setting and the intervention, you will occasionally encounter transference reactions and must be prepared to cope with them. For example, the authors have encountered the following:

1. A client who had great difficulty revealing her problems because the practitioner resembled her brother in appearance.

2. A client who was hostile from the outset because social workers were "a bunch of leeches who didn't know anything."

3. A client (whose father was a harsh and domineering person) who resisted becoming involved in marital therapy because she resented anyone telling her what to do. (The practitioner earlier had clarified that was *not* his role.)

4. A client who wanted the practitioner to embrace her because it was important to know he cared for her.

5. A client to whom it was important to be the practitioner's favorite.

6. A client who was sure the practitioner couldn't possibly have a genuine interest in her and saw her only because it was his job.

7. A client who misinterpreted a message of the practitioner and almost terminated as a result of feeling put down.

8. A client who accused the practitioner of being in collusion with her husband when the practitioner, in fact, viewed the husband as the major contributor to their marital difficulties.

It is evident that although such reactions derive from the past, they are manifested in the here and now. The question can be raised as to whether transference reactions can best be resolved by focusing on the past to enable clients to gain insight into their origin. We strongly maintain that exploration of the past should be undertaken only briefly, if at all. Extensive focus on the past diverts efforts from solving problems in the present and unnecessarily prolongs the helping process. Further, there is no evidence that focusing on the remote origin of unrealistic feelings, perceptions, and beliefs is more effective in modifying them than scrutinizing their validity in the here and now. Therefore, we recommend making brief excursions into the past only when it appears vital that clients understand that present feelings and reactions have not originated from mysterious forces but rather have been shaped by past experiences.

To manage transference reactions you must first be aware of their manifestations, of which the following are typical:

1. Relating to the practitioner in a clinging, dependent way or excessively seeking praise and reassurance.

2. Attempting to please the practitioner by excessive compliments and praise or by ingratiating behavior.

3. Asking many personal questions about the practitioner.

4. Behaving provocatively by arguing with or baiting the practitioner.

5. Questioning the interest of the practitioner.

6. Seeking special considerations, such as frequent changes in scheduled appointments for trivial reasons.

7. Attempting to engage practitioners socially by inviting them to lunch, parties, and the like.

8. Having dreams or fantasies about the practitioner.

9. Responding defensively, feeling rejected, or expecting criticism or punishment without realistic cause.

10. Offering personal favors or presenting gifts.

11. Behaving seductively by flirting, wearing revealing clothing, or making affectionate gestures.

12. Regressing or behaving in destructive ways when the practitioner must cancel or miss sessions.

13. Being unusually silent, inattentive, or drowsy in sessions.

14. Being tardy for appointments or striving to stay beyond the designated ending time.

15. Dressing or behaving in ways that diverge markedly from the client's usual style.

When clients manifest the preceding behaviors or other possible indications of transference reactions, it is vital to shift focus to their here-and-now feelings, for such reactions generally cause clients to disengage from productive work and may undermine the helping process. To assist you in managing transference reactions, we offer the following guidelines:

1. Be open to the possibility that the client's reaction is *not* unrealistic and may be produced by *your* behavior. If through discussion and introspection you determine the client's behavior is realistic, respond authentically by owning responsibility for your behavior.

2. When clients appear to expect you to respond in antitherapeutic ways, as significant others have in the past, it is important to respond differently, thereby disconfirming the expectations. Responses that contrast sharply from expectations produce temporary disequilibrium and force the client to differentiate

the practitioner from past figures. The client must thus deal with the practitioner as a unique and real person, rather than perpetuating fictional expectations based on past experiences.

3. Assist the client to determine the immediate source of distorted perceptions by exploring how and when the feelings emerged. Carefully explore antecedents and meaning attributions associated with the feelings. *Avoid attempting to correct distorted perceptions by immediately revealing your actual feelings.* By first exploring how and when problematic feelings emerged, you assist clients to expand their awareness of their patterns of overgeneralizing and making both faulty meaning attributions and unwarranted assumptions based on past experience. This awareness can enable them in the future to discriminate between feelings that emanate from conditioned perceptual sets and reality-based feelings and reactions.

4. After clients have discerned the unrealistic nature of their feelings and manifested awareness of the distortions that produced these feelings, share your actual feelings. This can be a source of reassurance to clients who have felt offended, hurt, resentful, rejected, or the like.

5. After you have examined problematic feelings, assist clients to determine whether they have experienced similar reactions in other relationships. You may thus assist clients to discern *patterns* of distortions that create difficulties in other relationships.

The application of these guidelines is illustrated in the following excerpt taken from an actual session (the eighth) of one of the authors with a 25-year-old female who had sought help because of loneliness and discouragement in finding a marital partner.

CLIENT: Boy, the weeks sure go by fast. [*Long pause.*] I don't have much to talk about today.

PRACTITIONER: [*Sensing the client is struggling with something.*] I gather you didn't really feel ready for your appointment today. [*Empathic response.*] How did you feel about coming? [*Open-ended probing response.*]

CLIENT: I didn't want to come, but I thought I should. Actually it has been an eventful week. But I haven't felt I wanted to tell you about what has been happening. [*Indication of a possible transference reaction.*]

PRACTITIONER: Sounds like you've had some misgivings about confiding certain things in me. [*Paraphrasing response.*] Could you share with me some of your thoughts about confiding these things in me? [*Open-ended probing response/ polite command.*]

CLIENT: OK. I've wanted to keep them to myself until I find out how things turn out. I've wanted to wait until it really develops into something. Then I would tell you.

PRACTITIONER: So you haven't wanted to risk it turning out bad and worrying about how I would feel if it did. [*Additive empathy/interpretation.*]

CLIENT: I guess I've wanted to impress you. I had a date with the fellow we talked about last week. It was wonderful. He's just the opposite of the other creep I told you about. He either has a real line or he's a super guy. I couldn't believe how considerate he was.

PRACTITIONER: You can't be sure yet what he's really like, and you want to be sure he's for real before you tell me about him? [*Additive empathy/interpretation.*]

CLIENT: [*With an embarrassed smile.*] Yes! And if it really developed into something, then I could tell you.

PRACTITIONER: And that way you could be sure I'd be favorably impressed? [*Additive empathy/interpretation.*]

CLIENT: Yes! I've felt I wanted you to know someone really good could be attracted to me.

PRACTITIONER: Hmm. Sounds like you've felt I've doubted you have much to offer a man and wanted to prove to me you do have something to offer. [*Additive empathy/interpretation.*]

CLIENT: Yes, that's true. I have wanted you to think of me as a desirable person.

PRACTITIONER: I'd like to explore where those doubts or fears that I don't see you as a desirable person come from. I'm wondering how you've concluded I don't see you as having much to offer a man. Have I done or said something that conveyed that to you? [*Probing.*]

CLIENT: [*Thinks for a moment.*] Well—no. Nothing that I can think of.

PRACTITIONER: Yet I gather those feelings have been very real to you. I wonder when you first became aware of those feelings.

CLIENT: [*After a pause.*] Well, I think it was when we began to talk about my feelings that guys are just interested in me for what they can get. I guess I wondered if you thought I was a real dud. I wanted you to know it wasn't so, that a desirable person could be attracted to me.

PRACTITIONER: You know, when we were discussing your feelings toward your mother two or three weeks ago you said essentially the same thing. [*Using summarization to make a connection between separate but related events.*]

CLIENT: I'm not sure what you mean.

PRACTITIONER: Understandably you wouldn't. I didn't make myself clear. You had said you felt your mother doubted you would ever marry because you were so cold you couldn't attract a man.

CLIENT: [*Smiles pensively and nods affirmatively.*] You know I never wanted to elope. I always wanted to marry in my hometown and have a big wedding. When I had my ring on my finger, I would turn to mother and say, "See, you were wrong!"

PRACTITIONER: So you've felt you needed to prove to her someone could love you. And that's also what you wanted to prove to me. [*Additive empathy/interpretation.*]

CLIENT: [*Nods affirmatively.*]

PRACTITIONER: I'm interested you've thought maybe I, too, didn't see you as lovable. Could you share with me how you reached that conclusion? [*Practitioner continues to explore the unrealistic nature of her perception and how it pervades other relationships.*]

By sensitively exploring the client's reluctance to attend the session, the practitioner not only resolved an emerging obstacle to productive work but also assisted her to explore further her doubts as to her lovability and to expand her awareness of how these doubts distorted her perceptions of how others viewed her—in this instance, the practitioner. As a result of the exploration, she was able to identify a basic misconception that pervaded her relationships with others and to relate more comfortably with the practitioner.

Countertransference Reactions Practitioners may also experience adverse relational reactions that can damage helping relationships if not recognized and managed effectively. Just as with clients, these feelings may be realistic or unrealistic. The latter type of reaction, which we discuss first, is the counterpart of transference and is denoted as *countertransference*. This phenomenon involves feelings, wishes, and unconscious defensive patterns of the practitioner that derive from past relationships, interfere with objective perception, and block productive interaction with clients. Countertransference contaminates helping relationships by producing distorted perceptions, blind spots, wishes, and antitherapeutic emotional reactions and behavior. Practitioners who have failed to integrate anger into their own personalities, for example, may be unduly uncomfortable when clients express anger and divert them from expressing such feelings. Other practitioners who have not resolved feelings of rejection by parents may have difficulty relating warmly to clients who are cool and aloof. Still other practitioners who have failed to resolve resentful feelings toward authoritarian parents may overidentify with rebellious adolescents and experience feelings of condemnation for their parents. Marital therapists whose spouses have been unfaithful, controlling, or sexually withholding may also overidentify with clients who have similar problems and be blind to the part these clients play in the marital difficulties they describe. And finally, some practitioners who have excessive needs to be loved and admired may behave seductively or strive to impress their clients.

Before discussing how to manage countertransference reactions, it is first important to identify typical ways they are manifest, which include the following:

1. Being unduly concerned about a client.

2. Having persistent erotic fantasies or dreams about a client.

3. Dreading or pleasurably anticipating sessions with clients.

4. Being consistently tardy or forgetting appointments with certain clients.

5. Feeling protective of or uncomfortable about discussing certain problems with a client.

6. Feeling hostile toward or unable to empathize with a client.

7. Blaming others exclusively for a client's difficulties.

8. Feeling persistently bored or drowsy or tuning out a client.

9. Consistently ending sessions early or permitting them to extend beyond designated ending points.

10. Trying to impress or being unduly impressed by clients.

11. Being overly concerned about losing a client.

12. Arguing with or feeling defensive or hurt by a client's criticisms or accusations.

13. Being overly solicitous and performing tasks for clients that they are capable of performing.

14. Being unusually curious about a client's sex life.

15. Having difficulties accepting or liking certain types of clients (may also be reality-based).

Becoming aware of unrealistic feelings toward a client or of reactions such as those just listed are signals that a practitioner should immediately take appropriate corrective measures. Otherwise, the countertransference will limit the practitioner's potential helpfulness, create an impasse, contribute to the client's dysfunction, or otherwise impair the effectiveness of the helping relationship. Ordinarily, the first step in resolving countertransference (and often all that is needed) is to engage in introspection. Introspection involves analytical dialogue with oneself aimed at discovering sources of feelings, reactions, cognitions, and behavior. Examples of questions that facilitate introspection include the following:

- "Why am I feeling uncomfortable with this client? What is going on inside me that I'm not able to relate more freely?"

- "What was I feeling when I made that response? Was I responding to the client's need or to my own?"

- "Was my message or action for my client's benefit? In what way did it benefit the client?"

- "Why do I dislike [or feel bored, impatient, or irritated] with this client? Are my feelings rational or does this client remind me of someone from the past?"

- "What is happening inside of me that I don't face certain problems with this client? Am I afraid of a negative reaction on the client's part?"

- "What purpose was served by arguing with this client? Was I feeling defensive or threatened?"

- "Why did I talk so much or give so much advice? Did I feel a need to give something to the client?"

- "What's happening inside me that I'm fantasizing or dreaming about this client?"

- "Why am I constantly taking sides with _____ ? Am I overlooking the partner's [or parent's or child's] feelings because I'm overidentifying with _____ ? Could my own similar feelings from the past be blocking my objectivity?"

Introspection often assists practitioners to achieve or regain a realistic perspective in their relationships with clients. If introspection fails to resolve problematic reactions, however, it may be helpful to discuss the situation with a colleague or another professional, which enables you to explore your feelings and to gain fresh input. Just as clients are sometimes too close to their problems to perceive them objectively and thus benefit from seeing them from the vantage point of a practitioner, the latter can likewise benefit from stepping out of the relationship and viewing it from the unbiased perspective of an uninvolved colleague or consultant.

Practitioners who repeatedly become enmeshed in countertransference reactions usually have long-standing and unresolved emotional conflicts that continue to pervade their interpersonal relationships. As such, their range of effectiveness is limited and they may cause or contribute to dysfunction in their clients. Some such "pathological" practitioners are able to work through their difficulties by obtaining professional help for themselves. Others are not suited for the profession and for the benefit of themselves, their clients, and the profession should consider making an occupational change.

Realistic Practitioner Reactions Not all negative feelings toward certain clients involve countertransference reactions. Some clients are abrasive, arrogant, or obnoxious, have irritating mannerisms, or are exploitative of and cruel to others. Even the most accepting practitioner may have difficulty developing positive feelings toward such clients. Practitioners, after all, are human beings and are not immune to disliking others or feeling irritated and impatient at times. Still, repulsive clients are entitled to service and, in fact, often desperately need help because their offensive behavior alienates others, leaving them isolated and confused as to what creates their difficulties.

When practitioners look beyond the offensive qualities of certain clients, they often discover that beneath the facade of arrogance and toughness are desirable, indeed admirable qualities that others rarely, if ever, see. Further, when they gain access to the private worlds of these individuals, practitioners often find persons who endured severe emotional deprivation, physical abuse, and other severe stresses as children and who had little opportunity to learn social skills. Being warmly accepted in spite of their annoying behavior often provides a corrective emotional experience for these clients.

Abrasive clients need far more than acceptance, however. They need feedback about how certain aspects of their behavior are offensive to others, encouragement to risk new behaviors, and opportunities to learn and practice the same. Feedback can be extremely helpful if it is conveyed sensitively and imparted in the context of goodwill. In providing such feedback, you must be careful to avoid evaluative or blaming comments that tend to elicit defensiveness. Examples of such comments are: "You boast too much and dominate conversation" or "You're insensitive to other people's feelings and say hurtful things." Clients are far more likely to be receptive to messages that describe and document their behavior and personalize the practitioner's response to it. An example of a descriptive message that embodies ownership of feelings is: "When you sneered at me just now, I began to feel defensive and resentful. You've done that several times before, and I find myself backing away each time. I don't like feeling distant from you, and I'm concerned because I suspect that's how you come across to others." This message, of course, is highly authentic and would not be appropriate until a sound working relationship has been established.

Sexual Attraction toward Clients Romantic and sexual feelings toward clients can be especially hazardous, although such feelings are by no means uncommon. Research findings (Pope, Keith-Spiegel, & Tabachnick, 1986), based on a survey of 585 psychotherapists (psychologists), revealed that only 77 (13%) had *never* been attracted to any client. The majority (82%), however, had never seriously considered sexual involvement with a client and of the remaining 18%, 87 percent had considered becoming involved only once or twice. Of the 585 respondents, about 6 percent had engaged in sexual intimacies with clients.

Most practitioners can thus expect at some point in their careers to experience sexual attraction toward a client. Managing such attraction appropriately, however, is critical. Fortunately, the data indicate that the majority of therapists manage their attractions successfully. Although 83 percent of those who experienced attraction believed the attraction was mutual, 71 percent believed that the client was not aware of their attraction. When such was the case they believed the attraction did not have a harmful impact on the helping process. By contrast, therapists who believed clients were aware of their attraction thought the impact was detrimental to the helping process. Although only 6 percent of those surveyed had engaged in sexual activities with clients, this percentage is alarming, for sexual involvement usually leads to grievous consequences for clients, who often suffer confusion and intense guilt and thereafter have great difficulty trusting professional persons. The consequences of sexual involvement may be devastating for practitioners as well, who, when discovered, may suffer disgrace, be sued for unethical practice, and be ejected from the profession. The NASW Code of Ethics on this point is unequivocal: "The social worker should under no circumstances engage in sexual activities with clients" (Article II, item 5).

Effectively managing sexual attractions for clients involves taking the corrective measures identified earlier in relationship to unrealistic feelings and reactions—namely, engaging in introspection and/or consulting with another professional person. In this regard, it is noteworthy that in the survey previously cited, 57 percent of the therapists sought consultation or supervision when they were attracted to a client. We cannot recommend too strongly that you take the same measures under similar circumstances. If allowed to mount unchecked, sexual attraction can lead to the disastrous consequences earlier discussed. Practitioners who frequently experience erotic fantasies about clients are particularly vulnerable to becoming sexually involved and probably should consider receiving treatment themselves.

A few practitioners have justified engaging in sexual activities with clients on the basis of assisting them to feel loved or helping them to overcome sexual problems. Such explanations are generally thinly disguised and feeble rationalizations for exploiting clients. Typically, such sexual activities are limited to attractive and relatively youthful clients. We have heard of no practitioners who have "assisted" unattractive, elderly, or retarded clients to feel loved by having sexual relations with them. Social workers who engage in sexual activities with clients not only render them a grave disservice but also damage the public image of the profession.

Managing Resistances to Change

Resistance has been defined as "holding back, disengaging, or in some way subverting change efforts whether knowingly or not *without open discussion*" (Nelsen, 1975, p. 587) or "as any action or attitude that impedes the course of therapeutic work" (Strean, 1979, p. 70). Some clients subvert change efforts or attempt to maintain the status quo despite pain, distress, and other costs associated with dysfunctional behavior or circumstances because change from usual patterns of functioning is at best difficult to achieve.

Resistance to change is a universal phenomenon, as anyone knows who has attempted to break long-established habits such as being unduly modest, eating excessively, smoking, talking too much or too little, being tardy, or spending freely. The pull of habits is relentless; changing, moreover, often means yielding gratifications or having to cope head-on with situations that are frightening or aversive. Making changes also often involves risking new behavior in the face of unknown consequences; although the status quo may cause pain and distress, it at least is familiar, and the consequences of habitual dysfunctional behavior are predictable.

Resistance and Ambivalence

The term *resistance* is somewhat misleading, for it appears to connote deliberate refusal by clients to cooperate. Unfortunately, social workers have often exploited this definition by attributing failure of helping efforts to clients' resistance, when, in fact, failures were often caused by inappropriate or ineffectual helping methods. Leader (1958) conceptualized resistance not as a manifestation of clients' refusal to cooperate but rather as a manifestation of ambivalence about changing. According to Leader, clients' feelings about changing are not unipolar; that is, clients seldom either want to or don't want to change. Rather, opposing feelings coexist; part of the client is motivated to change and another part strives to maintain the status quo. Despite having feelings that oppose change, many clients do change because the thrust to improve their lot in life outweighs the force to maintain the status quo. Leader argues further that social workers are overly concerned about resistance, lamenting that: "If we could only fully recognize that resistance in all phases of life is natural and healthy, perhaps we would be less concerned about its manifestation" (p. 22).

Recognizing clients' ambivalent feelings about changing enables practitioners to assist them to explore these feelings and to weigh advantages and disadvantages of making changes. Indeed, as clients think through their feelings and reassess the implications of maintaining the status quo, the scales often tilt in favor of change. Further, by accepting clients in spite of their opposition to change and by championing their right to self-determination, practitioners may similarly tilt the scales, because clients experience no pressure from the practitioner to change and are therefore free to make up their own minds. This factor is crucial, for pressure by the practitioner often engenders an opposing force or resistance from the client. Viewed in this light, recognizing and accepting oppositional feelings to change prevents such feelings from going underground where they can subtly undermine the helping process. Recognizing, openly discussing, and accepting oppositional feelings thus can liberate a desire and willingness to change.

Preventing Resistance

Resistance may emanate from sources other than ambivalence about changing. Clients may misunderstand the nature of service or of a specific intervention and may therefore be reluctant to cooperate fully. Should this occur, it is vital to explain fully the nature of the service or

intervention, clarify roles of the participants, and permit clients free choice as to whether or not to proceed. The best way of preventing this type of resistance is to be thorough in formulating contracts, clarifying roles, providing a rationale for specific interventions, inviting questions, eliciting and discussing misgivings, and fostering self-determination.

Other sources of resistance include apprehension or fear associated with engaging in behavior that is alien to one's usual functioning or having to face a situation that appears overwhelming. Such fears may be so intense that clients resist carrying out essential actions. Their difficulties may then be compounded by embarrassment over failure to implement the actions, which may produce resistance to seeing the practitioner or discussing the problematic situation further. Again, these forms of resistance can be prevented by anticipating and exploring the fears and preparing the client to carry out the actions through modeling, behavioral rehearsal, and guided practice. Because we discussed these strategies of resolving obstacles to change in Chapter 14 and because Hepworth (1979) has discussed this topic at length elsewhere, we will not discuss them further here.

Transference Resistance

Some clients become enmeshed in major transference reactions that pose an obstacle to progress. A client may idealize the practitioner and attempt to use the helping relationship as a substitute for dependency gratifications that should be obtained elsewhere; such a client may be preoccupied with fantasies about the practitioner rather than focus on goal attainment. Other clients may be disappointed and resentful because a practitioner does not meet their unrealistic expectations. Perceiving the practitioner as uncaring, withholding, and rejecting (as they likewise perceived their parents), these clients may struggle with angry feelings (negative transference) toward the practitioner, which diverts them from working productively upon their problems. Unless practitioners recognize and assist such clients to resolve these feelings by discussing them, accepting them, and placing them in realistic perspective, these clients may prematurely terminate, convinced their perceptions and feelings are accurate.

Again we emphasize that transference reactions are relatively infrequent in short-term, task-centered therapies where the practitioner takes an active role, which tends to minimize the possibility of projections. Moreover, time limits and focus on task accomplishment militate against dependency and strong emotional attachment. Long-term and insight-oriented therapies, by contrast, tend to foster dependency and transference.

Resistance with Multideficit Families

These families pose a special challenge to social workers. They may request service during times of crisis only to withdraw when acute distress is relieved, though their functioning remains submarginal. They pose ongoing problems to the community and often are involuntary clients, referred as a result of complaints from the community for recurrent incidents of child abuse and/or neglect, family violence, delinquency, and diverse forms of antisocial behaviors. Largely inaccessible to usual methods of intervention, they feel victimized by law enforcement officials, the courts, educators, and child protective services staff, whose interventions they resist as intrusions into their families.

Emotional and economic deprivation are rampant in multideficit families and

parents tend to be unstable, impulsive, and inconsistent. Parents are thus poor role models to their children, who understandably manifest gross deficiencies in coping as reflected by poor school performance, primitive social skills, behavioral problems, aggressiveness, truanting, lying, stealing, abusing drugs, and other such behaviors.

A major obstacle to assisting multideficit families is the difficulty in forming working relationships with family members, who typically view social workers with distrust, ambivalence, and hostility. Family members thus fit our earlier description of distrustful clients and the sources of the distrust are identical to those discussed earlier. The approach to developing an alliance with them is also largely the same as that delineated by Hartman & Reynolds (1987), which we discussed earlier in this chapter.

Home-based interventions are increasingly employed in work with multideficit families (Schlosberg & Kagan, 1988; Woods, 1988). Allegations of child neglect and/or abuse are frequently involved in referrals of these families and it is thus vital to assess home conditions and family functioning in the natural habitat of the family. Because a major objective of work with these families often is to prevent child placement outside the home, it is also essential to monitor home conditions and family interaction. Home visits are also necessitated by the fact that these families often have transportation difficulties and are so poorly organized that it is unrealistic to expect them to get their families to an agency at a scheduled time. Home visits also have the advantage of permitting access to all family members.

Home visits present formidable challenges, however, because multideficit families may manifest resistance through confusion or noise by having radios or television sets blaring or by permitting neighbors to walk in or out of the house during visits by a practitioner. They may also manifest resistance by preventing practitioners from observing their usual functioning (by cleaning the house and washing and dressing their children before expected visits). Parents in these families also test practitioners by frequently calling them between visits, by making impossible demands, and by expressing insatiable needs (Cowan et al., 1969).

Having worked with this type of family, we attest to the frustration and challenge they present. How do practitioners penetrate the thicket of resistance that blocks access to these families? The answer is that patience and perseverance through continuing to make regular home visits gradually becomes evidence that practitioners are really concerned about their problems. When practitioners reach this point, they can begin to discuss matters that plague clients, such as threats of eviction, fights with neighbors, and eventually problems in family relationships.

Early indications of making inroads into developing meaningful relationships are efforts by clients to quiet their babies, have older children play outside, excuse themselves from interactions with neighbors, and give up numerous distracting telephone calls. Further, clients begin to save problems for weekly discussion with practitioners rather than cope with them impulsively.

When parents manifest receptivity to assistance, interventions that address their multiple deficiencies can be appropriately employed. Prominent interventions include teaching skills in parenting, budgeting, various homemaking duties, problem solving, communication, conflict resolution, and assertion. Because these families typically are involved with many

institutions, coordination of service delivery is essential. Coordination is most effectively ensured by designating one person as a case manager (often a social worker).

Space limitations preclude a lengthy discussion of treatment of multiple deficit families. For more detailed information we refer you to the articles cited in the preceding discussion and to a book, *Working with Multi-Problem Families* (Kaplan, 1986).

Manifestations of Resistance

Resistance takes many forms, and the frequency with which clients manifest different forms varies according to the type of setting, the personality of the client, and the ethnicity and socioeconomic levels of clients. As we noted in the last section, multideficit families manifest resistance by ignoring social workers or by employing confusion and noise. By contrast, middle-class clients, who are more verbal, tend to manifest resistance in communication as, for example, by intellectualizing or discussing extraneous matters. The following are common manifestations of resistance:

1. Mental blocking (mind going blank).

2. Lengthy periods of silence.

3. Inattention or mind wandering.

4. Rambling on at length or dwelling on unimportant details.

5. Restlessness or fidgeting.

6. Discussing superficialities or irrelevant matters.

7. Lying or deliberately misrepresenting facts.

8. Intellectualizing (avoiding feelings and problems by focusing on abstract ideas).

9. Changing the subject.

10. Forgetting details of distressing events or of content of previous sessions.

11. Being tardy for or forgetting, changing, or canceling appointments.

12. Minimizing problems or claiming miraculous improvement.

13. Bringing up important material at the end of a session.

14. Not paying fees for service.

15. Not applying knowledge and skills gained in sessions in daily life.

16. Assuming a stance of helplessness.

17. Using various verbal ploys to justify not taking corrective action including:

   "I couldn't do that; it just wouldn't be me."

   "I just can't!"

   "I've tried that, and it doesn't work."

   "I understand what you're saying, but . . ."

   "I'm not so different; isn't everyone . . ."

Many of the preceding phenomena do not necessarily indicate a client is resisting change. If the client continues to work productively, the phenomenon may not warrant special handling. If, however, the client appears to have reached an impasse, it is safe to conclude that resistance is involved and to shift the focus to exploring factors that underlie the resistance.

Resistance may also emerge in family and group sessions. Individual members may manifest any of the preceding phenomena. In addition, members may form subgroups and not invest themselves in the total group process. Other manifestations of resistance in groups include scapegoating individual members, isolating oneself and not participating, attempting to force the leader to assume responsibility that belongs with the group, engaging in social banter, failing to stay on topic, and struggling for power rather than working cooperatively. It is also important to bear in mind that, "one family or group member who is showing resistance can be signaling a concern of all, or all can be cooperating in resistance due to common misunderstandings, anger, or fears" (Nelsen, 1975, p. 591). As with individuals, it is critical when impasses are reached to shift the focus of the group to the dysfunctional processes so that the group does not dissipate its energies in counterproductive activities.[1]

Managing Resistance

As we previously noted, because resistance is a universal phenomenon, it is not necessary to become alarmed about every possible manifestation of it. Moreover, focusing on trivial resistance may elicit adverse reactions from clients, such as feeling the practitioner is attempting to scrutinize and analyze their every minute behavior. Ironically, then, overreacting to presumed manifestations of resistance may needlessly engender it. A rule of thumb is that if resistance is not strong enough to impede progress, it is best ignored. Still, resistance can impede progress and, in some instances, damage helping relationships. When clients manifest resistance that blocks progress, it is imperative to grant highest priority to resolving the resistance. When clients are left to struggle with resistance alone, they often resolve it by withdrawing from the helping process.

The first step in managing resistance is to bring it into the light of discussion by

---

[1]In some instances, manifestations of group behaviors that may appear at first to be resistance consist of adjustment reactions of members to excessive changes (e.g., loss of members, canceled sessions, or a move to another meeting place), which tend to frustrate and discourage group members.

focusing on here-and-now feelings that underlie the resistance. Sensitive and skillful handling is essential because personal feelings toward the practitioner are commonly associated with resistance, and clients find it difficult to risk sharing these feelings. (Otherwise, they would have shared them already.) Empathy, warmth, and acceptance play a critical role in eliciting clients' untoward feelings because these ingredients foster a non-threatening interpersonal climate.

In exploring sources of resistance, it is important not to focus on the manifestation of resistance per se but rather to cite it as an indication that the client is experiencing troubling thoughts and feelings toward the practitioner or toward what is happening in the helping process. An authentic response that conveys the practitioner's goodwill and concern that progress has bogged down also reaffirms the practitioner's helpful intent and desire to work out whatever difficulties have arisen. At times there may be cues as to the sources of difficulties based on the content discussed in a preceding session. For example, the client may have discussed extremely painful material, disclosed personal feelings that involved shame or guilt, or bristled in response to being confronted with personal contributions to a problematic situation. In such instances, the practitioner may open discussion of the feelings as illustrated in the following: "You appear awfully quiet today, as though you're struggling with some troubling feelings. I know our last session was upsetting to you. Could you share with me what you're feeling about it *just now?*"

Notice in the preceding message that the practitioner did not inquire as to feelings the client experienced last week. Although events of preceding sessions do shape current feelings, it is the here-and-now feelings that motivate current behavior, and focusing upon them tends to be more productive than discussing feelings that have receded into history. During the course of the ensuing discussion, content regarding factors that engendered the troublesome feeling generally emerge, giving the practitioner an opportunity to correct misunderstandings, to explore feelings about a particular intervention, or to discuss events that produced a breach in the relationship. Discussing here-and-now feelings is often all that is needed to surmount barriers to change, and clients thereafter resume productive work on their difficulties. Some clients, in fact, may grow as a result of such discussions, learning that they can express negative feelings without retaliation from the practitioner. Further, by observing practitioners model mature and effective ways of dealing with interpersonal strain, clients may vicariously learn skills in dealing with interpersonal conflict.

Discussing sources of resistance often reveals fears of where exploring certain personal feelings might lead. Some clients mistakenly fear they are losing their minds and that if they share certain thoughts and feelings, the practitioner will initiate steps to admit them to a mental hospital. Other clients fear the practitioner will condemn them if they disclose hostile feelings toward a child or discuss extramarital affairs. Still other clients fear the practitioner will pressure them to obtain a divorce if they reveal their lack of love for a spouse. With respect to feelings toward the practitioner, some clients fear the former will be hurt or offended if they share negative feelings or that the practitioner will see them as ridiculous and reject them if they share warm and affectionate feelings.

As practitioners initiate exploration of the source of resistance, some clients manifest marked hesitancy about revealing relevant feelings. When this occurs, a technique often successful in cutting through the reluctance is to focus empathically on here-and-now fears about disclosing other troublesome feelings. The practitioner's sensitivity, empathy, and genuineness may well pave the way for the client to risk opening up more. The following illustrates such an empathic response:

"I'm sensing that you're very uncomfortable about discussing your feelings. I may be wrong, but I get the impression you're afraid I would react negatively if you shared those feelings. I can't say for sure how I'd respond, but I want you to know I'd do my best to understand your feelings. Could you share with me what you're feeling at this moment?"

When clients do risk sharing their feelings, it is often therapeutic to accredit their strength for risking and to express reassurance. Such positive responses further cultivate a climate conducive to reciprocal openness, obliterate the feared consequences, and reinforce the client for disclosing risky feelings. The following is an example of such a response:

"I'm very pleased you expressed the anger that has been building up inside you. That took some courage on your part. It's a lot safer to keep those feelings inside, but then they eat at you and create distance in our relationship. I can accept your anger, and your sharing it with me gives both of us an opportunity to talk things out. I'd feel badly if those feelings continued to build and I didn't even know it."

Positive Connotation

This is another technique that is useful in reducing threat and enabling clients to save face, thereby protecting their self-esteem after risking revealing problematic feelings. Positive connotation involves attributing positive intentions to what would be otherwise regarded as undesirable or negative behavior on the client's part. In using this technique, the practitioner recognizes that the meaning ascribed to behavior can be viewed both positively and negatively, depending on one's vantage point. Viewed as an obstacle to progress, resistance takes on a negative meaning. Viewed from the client's perspective, however, the same behavior may have positive intentions. The following examples clarify this point:

1. A client cancels an appointment and holds back in the following session. Exploration reveals she resented the practitioner's "pressuring her" to follow a certain course of action. The practitioner empathizes with her feelings as evidence of her determination to be her own person.

2. A client has been preoccupied with romantic fantasies about the practitioner and has digressed from working on problems. The practitioner interprets this romantic feeling as evidence he is moving away from his self-imposed isolation and is permitting himself to experience feelings of closeness that he can gradually risk in social relationships.

3. After an extended period of silence and exploration of feelings related to it, a spouse launches into a tirade over how the practitioner took sides with the partner in the previous session. The practitioner labels the client's response as a legitimate effort to be understood and to assure that the practitioner does not make the marriage worse by drawing erroneous conclusions.

The goal of positive connotation is not to condone the client's resistance or to reinforce distorted perceptions. Rather, the objectives are to minimize clients' needs to defend themselves and to safeguard their already precarious self-esteem. When using this technique, it is important to assist clients to recognize that their untoward reactions derived from distorted perceptions (if, in fact, they did) and to encourage them to express their feelings directly in the future.

Redefining Problems as Opportunities for Growth

This technique is a close relative of positive connotation because it too involves a form of relabeling. Both clients and practitioners tend to view problems negatively. Moreover, clients often view remedial courses of action as "necessary evils," dwelling on the threat involved in risking new behaviors. Therefore, it is often helpful to reformulate problems and essential tasks as opportunities for growth and challenges to gain liberation from stifling and self-defeating behaviors. Relabeling thus emphasizes the positives; that is, the benefits of change rather than the discomfort, fear, and other costs. In using this technique, it is important not to convey a pollyanna type of attitude, for the fears and threats are very real to clients, and being unduly optimistic may simply convey a lack of understanding on your part. Relabeling does not minimize clients' problems or ignore fears in risking new behaviors. It does enable clients to view their difficulties in a fuller perspective that embodies positive as well as negative factors. The following are examples of relabeling problem situations as opportunities for growth:

1. A teenage foster child who has run away because the foster parent insisted he adhere to certain deadlines in getting in at night resists returning to the foster home because the foster parents

"are unreasonable." The practitioner describes returning as a challenge to deal with a problem head-on and to work it out rather than running away from it, which has been the client's pattern.

2. A welfare mother resists seeing a doctor because she fears she has cancer. The practitioner empathizes with her fears but describes having a checkup as also being an opportunity to rule out that frightening possibility or to receive treatment before the disease progresses, should she have cancer.

3. A mildly brain-damaged, socially inhibited young adult expresses fear about seeing a counselor for vocational testing and counseling. The practitioner accepts the discomfort but depicts the situation as an opportunity to learn more about his aptitudes and to expand choices in planning his future.

4. A wife expresses intense apprehension about refusing to submit to her husband's kinky and excessive sexual demands. The practitioner empathizes with her fear but also sees an opportunity for her to gain in strength and self-respect and to present herself as a person to be reckoned with.

Confronting Patterns of Resistance

In some instances, clients fail to progress toward their goals because of the persistence of pervasive dysfunctional patterns of behavior. A client may intellectualize extensively to avoid having to experience painful emotions, such as loneliness or depression. Other clients relate in a distant, aloof manner or in aggressive ways to protect against becoming close to others and risking painful rejection. Still others may consistently place responsibility on others or on circumstances for their difficulties, failing to examine or acknowledge their part in them. Because such patterns of behavior often create impasses, practitioners must recognize and handle them. Confronting clients with discrepancies between expressed goals and behavior that defeats accomplishment of those goals is often needed to break such impasses. Because we discussed confrontation at length in Chapter 19 we limit our discussion to a special case of confrontation, namely *therapeutic binds.*

Using Therapeutic Binds Occasionally, practitioners encounter clients who stubbornly cling to self-defeating behaviors despite awareness that these behaviors perpetuate their difficulties. In such instances, placing clients in a therapeutic bind may provide the impetus needed to modify the problematic behaviors. Using a therapeutic bind involves confronting people with their self-defeating behaviors in such a way that they must either modify their behaviors or own responsibility for choosing to perpetuate their difficulties despite their expressed intentions to the contrary. The only way out of a therapeutic bind, unless one chooses to acknowledge no intention of changing, is to make constructive changes. The following are examples of situations in which the authors have successfully employed therapeutic binds:

1. Despite intensive efforts to resolve fears of being rejected in relationships with others, a client continues to decline social invitations and makes no effort to reach out to others. The practitioner confronts her with her apparent choice to perpetuate her social isolation rather than to risk relating to others.

2. A husband who, with his wife, sought marital therapy because of severe marital conflict persists in making decisions unilaterally, despite repeated feedback from his spouse and the practitioner that doing so engenders resentment and alienates her. The practitioner confronts him with how he has apparently decided it is more important to him to wield power than to improve his marital relationship.

3. An adolescent persists in truanting, violating family rules, and engaging in antisocial acts despite his assertion he wants maximal freedom. The practitioner counters that he appears unready to use freedom wisely, because being a law unto himself will only result in the court placing controls on him until he demonstrates a capacity to set limits for himself.

4. A wife constantly harps on her husband's previous infidelity despite seeking marital therapy to strengthen their relationship. His response to her constant reminders is to withdraw and disengage from the relationship. The practitioner faces her with the contradiction in her behavior, stressing that it is apparently more important to her to punish her husband than to enhance their relationship.

In using therapeutic binds, it is vital to observe the guidelines for confrontation, thereby avoiding "clobbering" and alienating the client. A therapeutic bind is a potent but high-risk technique, and practitioners should use it sparingly, being careful to temper its jarring effect with empathy, concern, and sensitive exploration of the dynamics behind the self-defeating patterns. Above all, practitioners should be sure they are employing the technique to assist the client and not to act out their own frustrations about the clients' resistance.

Organizational Barriers

Attainment of clients' goals often requires services provided by social agencies and other community organizations and institutions that are vital strands in the network of resource systems. Unfortunately, however, helping organizations sometimes fall short of delivering fully and effectively the services and resources intended for target populations. Social workers are in a strategic position to identify ways in which these organizations can enhance their responsiveness to clients' needs. In discharging this responsibility social workers sometimes play the roles of *mediator* and *advocate* in:

1. Increasing accessibility of service.

2. Promoting service delivery in ways that enhance clients' dignity.

3. Assuring equal access and quality of services to *all* people eligible to receive them.

In the following sections, we discuss each of these activities.

Increasing Accessibility of Services

Social workers have a responsibility to work with administrators within their own agency or with responsible staff of other organizations when services are not accessible to clients. Agencies that offer services only from 8 A.M. to 5 P.M. may make it virtually impossible for working adults to avail themselves of their services. Adopting flexible scheduling practices in agencies that serve families may result in involving increased numbers of working parents, which in turn may produce better outcomes. Providing staff coverage on weekends also makes it possible to respond to clients' crises when they occur, rather than waiting until the following week. Timely intervention provides support when people need it most and are optimally receptive to services.

Another example involves modifying scheduling procedures in health care centers so that patients do not have to wait several hours to be seen. Some clients' conditions or circumstances are such that they are unable to wait for long periods of time. Others become disgusted and leave, failing to receive treatment they vitally need. Still others may pay private fees (which they can ill afford) to be seen where waiting periods are shorter.

Services are not accessible to other people because agencies are not located in proximity to them. Difficulties in arranging transportation and child care may make such services virtually inaccessible to many clients. For these reasons, many family service agencies and community mental health centers have located satellite offices throughout communities rather than having only a central office. Where this is not feasible, it may be necessary to work closely with appropriate public officials to arrange for transportation of clients.

Providing for home visits to large families may circumvent problems of child care, although young children in the home can make it nearly impossible to conduct a productive interview. Some agencies have tried to solve the problem by locating an office in the heart of the area served and providing space for children to play while they wait for their parents.

In locating offices that serve the elderly, as well as other groups who are physically frail, it is important not to place them in areas that have high crime rates. Bendick (1980) has reported that agencies located in these areas are not accessible to the elderly because they fear for their safety and will not risk entering such areas.

Promoting Service Delivery in Ways That Enhance Clients' Dignity

It is unfortunate but true that some people who need services decline to use them because they have been degraded or humiliated by the actions of staff persons, by breaches of confidentiality, or by demeaning procedures. Some large public agencies, for example, make inadequate provisions for privacy, so that interviews are conducted in view of or within earshot of others. Even worse, some staff persons may be either openly or subtly judgmental of clients, making invidious remarks about their morality, veracity, character, or worthiness to receive public aid. Still other staff members may be brusque or rude or intrude unjustifiably into deeply personal aspects of clients' lives, thereby needlessly subjecting them to embarrassment and humiliation. Such behaviors are not only inhumane but unethical, and practitioners who become aware of such behavior by staff persons should call it to their attention. If the behavior persists, discussing it with responsible administrators or filing a complaint with the local professional organization may be justified.

Another circumstance that strips clients of their dignity may involve requiring them to go to unreasonable lengths to establish eligibility for concrete aid or services. Clients' dignity may also be hurt if practitioners are habitually tardy for appointments, cancel or change scheduled appointments frequently, or don't extend common courtesies.

Assuring Equal Access to and Equal Quality of Services to Eligible Persons

People may be denied resources to which they are entitled or receive services that are of lesser quality than others receive for at least seven different reasons: (1) institutional racism, (2) discrimination by socioeconomic level, age, or ethnicity, (3) arbitrary decisions of practitioners, (4) lack of knowledge of resources, (5) inability to assert rights, (6) failure of authorities to develop resources mandated by laws, and (7) dysfunctional policies and procedures. In the following sections, we consider each of these factors.

Institutional Racism Embedded in the fabric of our society to the extent that many people fail to recognize its manifestations, institutional racism often affects service delivery and availability of resources and opportunities in subtle ways. It is therefore vital that practitioners be sensitized to its manifestations so that they can liberate themselves and others from its pernicious effects. The effects of institutional racism range across the entire developmental span beginning with prenatal care and ending with care of the elderly or even burial arrangements. Racism pervades our educational, legal, economic, and political institutions, as well as employment opportunities and health care services.

Social workers have an ethical responsibility to work toward obliterating institutional racism, which is a worthy but formidable challenge. The first step toward meeting this challenge begins with developing awareness of possible traces of racist attitudes within oneself. Practitioners must also analyze policies, procedures, and practices of social agencies and other organizations to assure that all people are treated equitably. Prunty, Singer, and Thomas (1977) have described efforts of mental health practitioners who were assigned to a large integrated public school with the task of assisting school personnel to reduce racial friction and eliminate discriminatory practices. They found subtle evidence of institutional racism, including a disproportionate number of suspensions of black children and frequent assignments of children to instructional groups based on skills (resulting in groups that consisted of either predominately black or white children). Research projects with other institutions would doubtless disclose similar hitherto unrecognized practices that deny minorities equal access to environmental resources.

Discrimination by Socioeconomic Level, Age, or Ethnicity Other forms of discrimination may also restrict accessibility of services or result in inferior services. For example, Schofield (1964) and others have shown that psychotherapists (the large majority of whom are middle-class Caucasians) prefer to work with young, attractive, verbal, intelligent patients of the opposite sex. Patients who are poor, less gifted intellectually, elderly, unattractive, and lacking in verbal facility may therefore be assigned to staff of lesser rank or trainees who have little say about patient assignments. Moreover, such patients may be seen less frequently and for shorter periods of time. Irrespective of whether the outcomes are favorable or unfavorable, the fact is that some patients do not have equal access to the resources of such agencies or mental health centers. The same could probably be said of many other human service organizations.

Other clients may have unequal access to resources because of ethnicity. We have previously cited evidence (Sue & Zane, 1987) that Asian-Americans and Mexican-Americans are underrepresented in the use of mental health services in the United States. The most plausible explanations for this underuse of service are that mental health centers tend to be unresponsive to the needs of these minority groups and that language barriers may be a major deterrent to seeking service. Research by Aguilar (1983) has, in fact, verified that the predominant predictor of low utilization of health care by Mexican-American women

was the characteristics of the health care system. Sue and McKinney (1975) report similar findings concerning underutilization of mental health services by Asian-Americans.

Characteristics of service delivery systems that impede utilization by ethnic minority persons include:

- Geographic locations of centers that limit accessibility.

- Few or no staff persons of clients' ethnicity.

- Language barriers.

- Lack of knowledge about and/or insensitivity to clients' values, beliefs, and lifestyles.

- Lack of respect for clients' beliefs in the efficacy of indigenous folk healers.

- Failure to take the time needed to establish rapport and gain confidence of clients.

- Failure to explore clients' beliefs regarding the causes of their problems.

- Failure to reach out to people who are unable to or fail to take the initiative in seeking needed services.

- Excessive red tape or complex procedures that confuse clients.

- Failure to adapt treatment to expectations of clients.

To adapt service delivery systems to the needs of ethnic minority clients, administrators should include representatives of ethnic groups in the process of shaping policies, procedures, and staffing to the unique needs of ethnic minority persons. Moreover, they should develop systems of feedback that assure ongoing input from the ethnic groups they serve by having representatives of ethnic groups on agency boards and by employing periodic follow-up contacts with clients to assess the impact of agency policies and of the service provided. Enlisting volunteers from ethnic groups to serve as translators, facilitators, case finders, and investigators can also reduce barriers to service delivery and maintain liaison with ethnic groups. Further recommendations for developing delivery systems that are responsive to health and mental care needs of Hispanics and Native Americans have been made by Guendalman (1983) and Marburg (1983) respectively. Sue and McKinney (1975) also provide convincing information about the potent effects of developing culturally relevant mental health services for Asian-Americans.

An Asian-American Counseling and Referral Service was . . . established in Seattle, and this agency has in one year seen nearly the same number of Asian patients as did the 17 community mental health facilities over a period of three years. The greater responsiveness of Asians to this agency appears to be due to widespread publicity, the use of bilingual therapists and the ability of the therapist to understand the needs and life styles of Asians in the community.

(p. 117)

Arbitrary Decisions to Deny Resources to People

This is another factor that restricts the access of some people to resources for which they are eligible. It is an unfortunate reality that some human service workers are punitive and wield their authority to the detriment of certain clients. One of the authors, for example, learned that a high school counselor, upon being told by his counselee that she was pregnant, gave her a stern reprimand and rejected her in future contacts. Other "horror stories" have been reported of public assistance workers whose mindsets predispose them to search for reasons to deny resources rather than to grant them. Still others have arbitrarily excluded certain items from the needs budgets of public assistance recipients even though the latter were clearly entitled to those items. Similar incidents of clients being denied medical care for which they were eligible have been reported in the literature. When clients are arbitrarily denied services or resources, practitioners have a responsibility to serve as an advocate for the client in securing those resources (a role we discussed at length in Chapter 16).

Clients' Lack of Ability or Skills to Assert Their Rights

Some clients lack the physical and/or mental ability to assert their rights and therefore have unequal access to benefits and services. Because they are at a distinct disadvantage in asserting their rights, many such individuals tend to acquiesce to injustices that deprive them of badly needed resources. For example, mentally retarded persons lack the intellectual capability essential to plan appropriate remedial measures.

Disabled persons (particularly those who are homebound) are also likely to need special advocacy services to obtain resources to which they are entitled. Many disabled people lack the ability to stand in lines, move from office to office, fill out multiple forms, and engage in other activities typically required to gain services from public clinics or offices. Moreover, homebound persons usually lack access to communication networks that provide inside information about how to remedy some of these problems. Still another obstacle for many disabled persons is that they lack clout and find it difficult to disagree with professionals concerning their rights. Weinberg (1983) has described how the rights and dignity of physically disabled persons are typically violated and has recommended remedial interventions social workers can make.

Immigrants and minorities also typically are limited in their ability to assert their rights and historically have tended to submit to injustices rather than to risk becoming embroiled in difficulties. The frustrations of these people have been graphically described by Cameron and Talavera (1976):

When non-English-speaking people attempt to locate services, they often end their search in anger and frustration. From the client's point of view, concrete difficulties interfere with their gaining access to services from agencies; arbitrary denial of services; institutional inflexibility; red tape with long delays and silences; undignified or callous treatment; complex forms and procedures of eligibility; long waiting lists; inaccessibility by telephone or in person; a runaround from agency to agency; lack of simple clear directions and explanations. . . . This list of problems is multiplied many times when the person who needs help cannot speak English.

(p. 247)

To assist Spanish-speaking immigrants to cope with the difficulties enumerated above, the Family Service Agency of San Mateo County (California), which serves a substantial population of immigrants from Mexico, established an advocacy program that performs the following services for these people: translates documents, assists in filling out forms, provides information about and makes referrals to social service programs, and mediates problems between clients and other agencies (Cameron & Talavera, 1976, p. 429). Other immigrants and minorities, including Native Americans and Cuban and Asian refugees, sorely need similar services. Because funding for such programs often is unavailable, it usually falls on individual practitioners to perform these advocacy roles.

With respect to immigrants, Golan and Gruschka (1971) have described a model for integrating new immigrants based on extensive experience in Israel. Viewing immigration as a transition state that produces disruption and possible crisis, these authors delineate tasks for immigrants to integrate themselves into new communities, regions, or nations and parallel tasks for communities to absorb them. These tasks embody two dimensions—namely, "material-arrangemental" and "psychosocial" for both the immigrant and the community. The role of the social worker within this model is that of an enabler or catalyst in assisting both immigrant and community to accomplish their respective tasks, thereby minimizing stress and disruption for both parties. Brown (1982) and Rubin (1982) have also delineated the many needs of refugees and discussed ways that social workers can respond to these needs.

Lack of Knowledge About or Failure to Use Available Resources. This factor obviously precludes many clients from receiving services they need. Immigrants and minority group members who do not speak English are at a particular disadvantage in this regard, as they are not privy to information about services that tends to circulate by means of gossip networks in broader society. By no means are these the only groups who lack access to information about resources. People who live in rural or geographically isolated areas or have limited reading skills or visual or hearing impairments are also at a distinct disadvantage.

To enhance the accessibility of resources to all persons, both public and private human service organizations often engage in *outreach efforts* aimed at people who are unaware of or do not voluntarily seek services or resources that could improve their life situations. Toseland (1981) defines *outreach* as "a social work practice method that attempts to identify clients who are in need of services, alerts these clients to service provisions and benefits, and helps them to use services that are available" (p. 227). Whereas clients commonly take the initiative in contacting social service agencies, practitioners take the initiative in outreach efforts, actively striving to locate, contact, and engage potential clients.

Outreach activities typically involve distributing posters and leaflets, publicizing through mass mailings, advertising in various media, appearing on radio or television, publishing stories in local newspapers, locating information booths in public places, speaking at club meetings, and even canvassing door to door (Bendick, 1980). Effective outreach appears to require personal interaction with potential consumers, for the mass media methods often fail to draw attention of eligible clients most in need of service, many of whom have limited reading skills. As a means of generating face-to-face interaction, Bendick (1980) recommends directing outreach campaigns to other social service professionals, who can subsequently disseminate information about available services and benefits and can refer prospective clients. In rural areas, outreach efforts should also be directed to indigenous caregivers and local officials, for word of mouth through informal communication channels tends to be much more restricted in rural than in urban areas.

Practitioners who engage in outreach efforts must be sensitive to clients' rights to privacy and self-determination. Outreach involves informing people about available services and benefits and striving to enhance their motivation to avail themselves of needed services, but certainly not attempting to impose services upon people.

When employing outreach efforts with minorities who do not have command of English, it is highly preferable to communicate in the native tongue of potential clients. When this is not possible, using indigenous case aides as intermediaries is the next best choice. Potential clients are far more likely to understand explanations of resources, to be receptive to proferred services and benefits, and to ask questions when they can communicate in their own language.

To assist practitioners in implementing outreach services, Toseland (1981) has developed a model consisting of six discrete steps. Toseland delineates each step at length, and we strongly recommend you read his article.

Case Management Services   Certain vulnerable groups do not receive essential resources and services because they lack the physical mobility, mental ability, knowledge of resources, language facility, experience, maturity, or assertiveness to avail themselves of needed resources. In recent years the role of case manager has evolved to enable social workers and other professionals to respond to the pervasive and often unmet needs of these vulnerable groups. Because we discussed these groups and this role at length in Chapters 2 and 16 we will not elaborate further here.

Failure of Authorities to Develop Resources Mandated by Law   Sosin (1979) has written a cogent article dealing with this matter in which he points out that enactment of new legislation or regulations does not assure implementation of the same. Ignoring new laws, in fact, is a widespread phenomenon. Thus, advocacy and social action must sometimes continue even after new laws are enacted as a result of earlier successful efforts.

Because new mandates that involve social welfare issues alter social priorities, resistance by powerful individuals who oppose such changes commonly occurs. Those who bear responsibility for implementing the mandates may minimize social change by ignoring, evading, or subverting a new law, thus denying benefits intended by the law to potential beneficiaries. Sosin illustrates these forms of resistance and suggests strategies for overcoming them. These strategies are of three types: (1) increasing receptivity to the changes on the part of those who hold the authority for implementing the changes, (2) enhancing the ability of authorities to implement changes when their capacity to do so is deficient for any of several reasons, and (3) exploiting the vulnerability of authorities to sanctions for not implementing the mandates. For each of these remedies Sosin provides guidelines and cautions that will be of value to practitioners.

Dysfunctional Policies and Procedures

Rigid, outdated, and otherwise dysfunctional policies and procedures may also have the unintended effects of limiting access to resources for some clients. For example, clients who are illiterate or have limited reading skills are at a decided disadvantage when they must complete numerous forms and procedures to qualify for an agency's services or benefits. Given the fact that 75 percent of the poverty population read at an eighth-grade level or lower, this skill deficiency is a major problem as "about 90 percent of the documents drawn from public welfare agencies required more than an eighth-grade level [Bendick & Cantu, 1978], and one third . . . required college-level read-

ing skills" (Bendick, 1980, p. 272). Paradoxically, resources are least accessible to those who need them most. The obvious implications of this situation are that administrators should reduce red tape to a minimum, simplify forms, and provide aid in completing forms to clients who lack reading skills.

Other procedures cited by Bendick that limit accessibility include the number of visits required to the agency. For rural clients who must travel long distances to agency offices, the numbers of visits required can severely limit accessibility, especially with the current high cost of transportation. For clients who are handicapped or bedridden, the problem is even more severe. To accommodate such persons, either home visits or telephone applications for services or benefits are essential.

Policies may also altogether exclude some needy persons from obtaining resources. Bendick cites instances in which migrants have been denied food stamps because they could not verify their incomes. Their crew bosses, who were cheating them out of wages and stealing their social security contributions, were reluctant to provide pay stubs that could be used to uncover their schemes. Obviously, more flexible policies are needed to remedy these situations, together with advocacy aimed at eliminating the cheating.

Still another factor that may curtail access to services for some clients involves policies related to fee charging. In times of highly limited resources, agencies may give top priorities for service to clients who can pay larger fees when fee schedules are graduated according to people's incomes. Voluntary agencies, such as family service agencies, may thus exclude the poor from services, even though such agencies were originally conceived to serve clients without regard to financial status. Administrators of such agencies thus find themselves on the horns of a dilemma, for their survival requires an adequate funding base. To resolve the dilemma involves reviewing the agency's purpose with the advisory board and exploring measures that assure continued access of services to the poor. Mobilization of increased external funding may be the only realistic remedy in such situations.

Skill Development Exercises in Managing Relational Reactions and Resistance

The following exercises will assist you in expanding your skills in responding therapeutically to relational reactions and resistance. Study each client message and determine whether a relational reaction or resistance is involved. Then write the response you would give if you were the practitioner. Compare your response with the modeled response provided at the end of the exercises. Bear in mind that the modeled response is only one of many possible appropriate responses.

Client Statements

1. Client [*has been discussing feelings of rejection and self-doubt after his fiancee broke their engagement; suddenly he looks down, sighs, then looks up*]: Say, did I tell you I got promoted at work?

2. Female client, age 23 [*to male practitioner, age 25*]: I've been feeling very close to you these past weeks. I was wondering if you could hold me in your arms for just a moment.

3. Male client, age 27 [*with irritation*]: I've been coming to see you for eight weeks, and things haven't changed a bit. I'm beginning to question your competence.

4. Delinquent on probation, age 16: I think it's ridiculous to have to come here every week. You don't have to worry about me. I'm not getting into any trouble.

5. Female welfare client: Sure, you say you want to help me. All you welfare workers are just alike. You don't have the slightest idea what it's like to try to raise children on $500 a month. If you really want to help, increase the dole I get.

6. Client, age 27 [*to male practitioner*]: I've just never been able to trust men. My old man was alcoholic, and the only thing you could depend on with him was that he'd be drunk when you needed him most.

7. Male client [*to female mental health practitioner*]: Sometimes I really felt I was cheated in life, you know, with parents who didn't give a damn what happened to me. I think about you—how warm and caring you are, and—I know it sounds crazy—but I wish I'd had you for a mother. Sometimes I even daydream about it.

8. Client [*after an emotion-laden previous session, the clients yawns, looks out the window, and comments*]: Not much to talk about today. Nothing much has happened this week.

9. Male client, age 24 [*in fifth interview*]: I have this thing where people never measure up to my expectations. I know I expect too much, and I always end up feeling let down.

10. Middle-aged Native American: It's important to me that you do not think of me according to the usual stereotype. I'm ambitious and want to do right by my family. I just need a job right now.

Modeled Responses

1. "No, but before you do, I'd like to know more about what you were feeling just a moment ago when you were discussing your breakup with your fiancee. I was sensing that was painful for you to talk about. Could you share what you feel as you think about it?"

2. "I'm complimented you would want me to hold you and pleased you could share those feelings with me. I want you to know I feel a closeness to you too, but if I were to let myself feel romantic toward you, I'd be letting you down. I couldn't be helpful to you if I were involved in that way. I hope you can understand."

3. "I can see you're anxious to get things worked out, and that's a plus." [*Positive connotation.*] "But you're pretty ticked off with me, as though I haven't been doing my job. I'd like to understand those feelings more. What do you feel I should be doing different?" [*Exploring feelings and expectations.*]

4. "You sound pretty angry about having to report to me each week. I can't blame you for that. Still the judge ordered it, and neither of us really has any choice. How do you suggest we make the best of the situation?"

5. "I'm sorry you feel I'm not really interested in helping you. I gather you've had some bad experiences with other caseworkers, and I hope our relationship can be better. I do want you to know, though, that a number of us have been meeting with legislators to help them see the need to increase the amount of grants. I marvel that you do as well as you do on the amount of your grant."

6. "I can understand then that you might find it difficult to trust me—wondering if I'm really dependable."

7. [*With a warm smile*]: "Thank you for the compliment. I gather you've been experiencing my care for you and find yourself longing for the love and care you didn't receive as a child. I can sense your feelings keenly and appreciate your sharing them."

8. "Somehow that doesn't fit with what we talked about last week. You expressed some very deep feelings about yourself and your marriage. I'd like to hear what you've been feeling about what we discussed last time."

9. "I wonder if that's what you're feeling just now in our relationship—that I haven't measured up to your expectations in some way. Could you share with me what you've been feeling in that regard?"

10. "I appreciate your sharing those feelings with me. I gather you've wondered how I do see you. I see you as an ambitious and responsible person, and I want you to know I appreciate those qualities in you."

Part 4
The Termination and Evaluation Phase

21 ■ The Final Phase: Termination and Evaluation

The third and final phase of the helping process involves termination. Although it has received less attention in the literature than the beginning and middle phases, it is nevertheless a vital phase, for the manner in which the helping relationship and process are concluded strongly influences whether clients maintain the progress they have achieved and continue to grow following formal termination. It is important that practitioners plan for this phase and handle it sensitively and skillfully. In this chapter, we focus on various matters that bear on the termination process, identify relevant tasks for both practitioners and clients, and discuss skills essential to managing termination effectively.

Termination, Separation, and Loss

Inherent in termination is separation from the practitioner (and group in the case of growth groups). Separation typically involves mixed feelings, which vary in intensity according to the degree of success achieved, the intensity of the attachment to the practitioner, the type of termination, and the previous experiences of the client with separations from significant others. When clients successfully accomplish their goals, they experience a certain de-

gree of pride and satisfaction as the helping process draws to a close. If they have grown in strength and self-esteem, they may even optimistically view the future as a challenge for continued growth.

Clients and practitioners alike commonly experience a sense of loss during the termination process. Indeed, a sense of loss is a universal reaction to the many endings that are a part of life itself (e.g., leaving parents to attend school, advancing from one grade to another, graduating, moving from one home to another, and losing loved ones). This loss may be a deeply moving experience involving the "sweet sorrow" generally associated with parting from a person whom one has grown to value. Clients who have become excessively dependent on a practitioner experience little of the sweetness of termination, however, and view separation as the loss of an irreplaceable person. We discuss emotional reactions associated with various types of separation later in the chapter.

Tasks Embodied in Termination

Successful termination involves preparing clients adequately for separation from the practitioner and/or group and accomplishing other tasks that enhance the transition from being a client to being on one's own. These tasks include:

1. Determining when to implement termination.

2. Mutually resolving emotional reactions commonly experienced during the process of separation.

3. Evaluating the service provided and the extent to which goals were accomplished.

4. Planning to maintain gains achieved and to achieve continued growth.

The significance of these tasks and the extent to which they can be successfully accomplished are determined in great measure by the type of termination involved, which we next consider.

Types of Termination

There are essentially five different types of termination, which are as follows:

1. Premature, unilateral terminations by clients.

2. Planned termination determined by temporal constraints associated with an agency's function.

3. Planned termination associated with time-limited modalities.

4. Planned terminations involving open-ended modalities.

5. Termination precipitated by the departure of a practitioner.

As we explained earlier, certain of the tasks identified in the preceding section are irrelevant to some types of termination and highly relevant to others. Deter-mining when to implement termination, for example, is highly relevant to type 4 (above), is of lesser significance to types 2, 3, and 5, and does not apply to type 1. The differential significance of the tasks will become further apparent in the following sections concerned with each type of termination.

Premature, Unilateral Termination

Generally, the preferred way of terminating is for the participants in the helping process to plan the termination mutually because they have accomplished their goals. Unfortunately, some clients terminate by default, simply failing to appear for appointments, offering perfunctory reasons for termination, and refusing to return to discuss the matter further. Other clients announce at the conclusion of a session that they will not be returning and give the practitioner little opportunity to explore the basis of their decision. In such instances, it is desirable to explain that deciding to terminate is a major decision that should not be made abruptly and that you would like the opportunity to explore with the client factors that led to the decision.

Premature and unilateral terminations may be expressions of unresolved resistances that can be resolved given the opportunity to do so. If there are indications the client may be experiencing negative feelings toward you, it may be productive to share your concern that you may have offended the client and express your desire to discuss the matter further. Should the client be amenable to your invitation, you can attempt to resolve the feelings by following the guidelines discussed in Chapter 20.

Some clients attribute decisions to terminate after one or two sessions to having benefited sufficiently and no longer needing assistance. Recent research (Presley, 1987; Toseland, 1987) has, in fact, indicated that such is often the case and that practitioners have erred in assuming that "premature" terminations generally indicate dissatisfactions by clients and negative outcomes. It is also true, however, that claims of some clients of miraculous improvement may derive from denial of problems or wishful thinking. When there is no basis for believing that actual improvement has occurred, we recommend being candid with clients but exerting no pressure upon them to continue and offering service should they decide to return in the future. A practitioner thus respects the client's right to self-determination but also fulfills a professional obligation to offer expert opinion. The following is a condensed illustration of such a message.

"I wish I could honestly agree with you that you've worked out your difficulties. As I see it, however, you've made no basic changes, and I see no reason to believe that the improvement is more than temporary. I frankly am disappointed you've decided to stop this early because I believe it's possible you can yet make a great deal of progress. Still, I respect your right to decide for yourself. I hope you'll feel free to return if you'd like to work further on your difficulties in the future. I'm here to help, and I want you to know I'm still very much interested in you."

The preceding message is authentic, conveys respect and concern, and places responsibility on the client—where it belongs. When we have handled premature terminations in this manner, a number of clients have later returned for additional service, more highly motivated than before. Several clients have even expressed gratitude for our earlier frankness.

Groups may also experience adverse effects from the premature termination of a member, who may or may not reveal intent to terminate or give the group an opportunity to deal with the loss. In either case, individual members may experience anger toward the "recalcitrant" member who is, in their view, abandoning the group, thereby devaluing the group experience. Other feelings experienced by members toward the departing member may include guilt over their anger, hurt over being "rejected," disturbing doubts that perhaps the group isn't worth their investment after all, a wish to accompany the person who is leaving, and sadness over the loss of a valued relationship. Feelings experienced by the departing member may be similar, including ambivalence about leaving the group, anger at being pressured to remain in the group, guilt over leaving the group, and feelings of loss.

If granted the opportunity to work through the reactions of members, the group can usually absorb the shock of the termination of one member without threat to survival of the group. However, when the group is deprived of this opportunity, premature termination of a member can be devastating to group morale, particularly if the member departed after a negative encounter with others in the group. Likewise, if the group has experienced the loss of other members in a relatively short time, the group's survival may be jeopardized. When a member terminates without discussion, it is imperative to discuss the event with the group (sharing personal feelings in doing so), determine members' perception of the meaning of the event and its impact on the group, and decide with the group whether it wishes to reach out to the absent member. If the group declines, it is important for the practitioner to assume this role.

Feelings similar to those just described may also prevail when a group experiences extended absences of individual members or of the group leader, when a group suffers the loss of a member through death or discharge from an institution, or when a member goes AWOL from an institution. Sometimes the group in question is not a formed therapeutic group but rather consists of members who live together in institutions, such as nursing homes or hospitals that provide extended care. Nevertheless, members may experience acute losses when members leave or die, and it is vital for practitioners to assist groups to work through such losses.

Planned Termination Determined by Temporal Constraints

In organizations or agencies whose function involves providing service according to fixed time intervals, termination must be planned accordingly. In school settings, for example, services are generally discontinued at the conclusion of an academic year. In hospitals and other institutional settings, the duration of service is determined by the length of hospitalization or confinement. Service may thus extend from several days to several months. Temporal factors are also central in termination when service is provided by social work students, who leave a given practicum setting at the completion of an academic year.

Termination under the circumstances specified in the preceding involves certain factors peculiar to these settings. First, the ending of a school year or of a training period for students is a predetermined time for termination, which reduces the possibility that clients will (1) interpret time limits as being arbitrarily imposed or (2) perceive the practitioner's leaving as desertion or abandonment. Knowing the termination date well in advance also provides ample time to resolve feelings about separation.

Another factor common to termination determined by temporal constraints re-lated to agency function is that clients' problems may not have been adequately resolved by the ending of a fixed time interval. The predetermined ending time may thus prove to be untimely for some clients; consequently, clients may react intensely to losing service and the helping relationship in midstream. Practitioners are therefore confronted with the dual tasks of working through feelings associated with untimely separation and referring clients for additional services when indicated. We discuss both of these matters in later sections.

A difficulty involving predetermined endings imposed by the close of a school year or training period is that such endings do not convey the same expectations of a positive outcome as do time limits that are imposed by practitioners. In other words, to say "I will see you for eight sessions because that is sufficient time," conveys a far more positive expectation than "I will see you for eight sessions because that is all the available time before school ends." To employ time effectively as a dynamic, it makes good sense to convey a belief that the remaining time *is* all that is needed, assuming, of course, that such a belief is justified. In the majority of cases this belief *is* justified, for research indicates that outcomes of interventions ranging from 6 to 10 interviews generally are comparable to those obtained from long-term treatment.

In alluding to termination that coincides with the completion of practicum training, we have made the assumption that students have earlier explained their role as supervised learners and have apprised clients of the date of their departure from the host agency or institution. In making this assumption, we support the position taken by Germain and Gitterman (1980) that students have an ethical responsibility to disclose their role to clients. Aside from purely ethical factors, there are compelling pragmatic reasons for openly sharing this information. First, we have stressed repeatedly in this book the importance of relating genuinely and fostering trust in helping relationships. Concealing one's student status hardly fosters trust or permits one to be fully authentic in a relationship. (Most clients would learn about the student's role in time, anyway.) Further, as the practicum period draws to a close and one must introduce termination, it is most awkward to explain one's reason for leaving an agency without letting the cat out of the bag. Having to reveal (or further conceal) one's actual role during this critical time may drastically erode trust and credibility and create irreparable damage to the helping relationship.

Planned Termination Associated with Time-Limited Modalities

Negotiating time limits in advance strongly affects the termination process. Knowing the ending time from almost the beginning tends to limit the degree of emotional attachment and dependency and hence also limits the degree of loss experienced by clients as a result of termination. And by assuming an active role and by focusing on here-and-now task accomplishment, practitioners further minimize dependency and intense emotional attachment, as we have noted earlier. The emotional reaction to separation thus generally tends to be far less intense than for open-ended service. Nevertheless, clients do form attachments and experience losses in time-limited modalities, and practitioners should be sensitive to termination reactions, which we discuss at length later.

Reid (1978) recommends that practitioners initiate formal termination in the next-to-last scheduled interview by formulating the last set of tasks to be addressed, which ideally "should be repetitions or modest extensions of previously successful tasks" (p. 179). After reviewing the results of efforts on this set of tasks in the terminal interview, the practitioner then shifts the focus to (1) evaluating clients' accomplishments in relationship to target problems, (2) planning for continued work on the problems, if such is needed, (3) assisting clients to discern how they can apply the problem-solving methods they have learned generally to problems of living, and (4) planning for follow-up sessions. These activities apply to other modalities as well, and we therefore consider them later. Engaging in these activities, however, may lead to reasons for deviating from continuing with the usual process of termination. Making other arrangements may be appropriate if both client and practitioner believe that special disposition is indicated. Other possible dispositions include the following:

1. *Limited extensions of service* can be made to accomplish agreed-upon tasks if it appears that additional time would make it possible for the client to achieve *decisive progress*. There may be legitimate reasons for recontracting for additional sessions, such as not identifying key problems until late in the helping process or anticipating transitional events that bear on the clients' problems (e.g., getting married, being discharged from an institution, regaining custody of a child). The mere expectation that further progress can be achieved by extending the sessions is not a legitimate reason for recontracting nor is the lack of progress. As Reid (1978) indicated, "If little was accomplished during the regular period of service, it is not likely that a few more sessions will add much. Aside from being a waste of the practitioner's and client's time, they may increase the client's sense of failure" (p. 184).

Either clients or practitioners may propose extensions, and if the former make an unsolicited request, Reid recommends usually granting the request, being careful to establish the rationale for the extension. For most clients, the regular contracted period of service suffices, and Reid discourages practitioners from routinely asking clients if they wish additional sessions. Only if practitioners have grounds for believing additional service would accomplish a vital purpose should they suggest extending service.

2. *A successive contract* the same length as the original contract can be negotiated if major problems surface near the end of the contract or were identified earlier but had to be set aside in favor of more pressing problems. In either event, the client may not have had opportunity to tackle a major problem, and a new contract may be warranted, especially if the client achieved substantial progress on other problems during the initial contract period. Reid cautions, however, that practitioners must be careful to ascertain that the interest in the problem emanates from the client, not the practitioner. If practitioners are sensitive to clients' perceptions and motivation, successive contracts, according to Reid (1978), are very much the exception.

3. *Terminating in the context of continued care* may also be a disposition when the client has been involved in long-term care and the practitioner's involvement has been but one segment of an overall treatment program. In an institutional setting, for example, a practitioner may be one member of a clinical team, having circumscribed responsibilities for assisting clients to accomplish certain tasks that are a part of a broader treatment program. Other staff members may carry responsibility for coordinating continued efforts of the entire team when the practitioner's role is discharged.

In other situations, a practitioner may carry sole responsibility for working with a client (e.g., in child welfare) in long-term service but may negotiate a task-centered contract for addressing certain problems (e.g., a particular aspect of home management). The task-centered contract thus becomes a subset of a more comprehensive contract. Even though the helping person is the same following completion of the task-centered contract, the practitioner does a terminal interview, evaluates results, and discusses implications of the client's experience for future direction in the ongoing efforts.

4. *Converting from a time-limited to an open-ended modality* is another option open to the practitioner. Although research cited by Reid argues against using this option frequently, there are circumstances in which converting to open-ended treatment is warranted. Although large-scale research studies in the United States (Parad & Parad, 1968) and Britain (Gibbons, Bow, & Butter, 1979) indicate that time-limited interventions (i.e., 12 sessions or less) are preferable for the majority of clients, these same studies indicate that from 15 to 18 percent of the clients require a longer time. According to Gibbons et al., the clients "who developed into longer term cases tended to have a wider range of problems, usually of great complexity, and to resist the limited focus of the task-centered approach" (p. 209). Further, after the completion of a predetermined number of sessions, some clients request continued services without the limits. In such instances, if another client would not be deprived of service as a result, it may be prudent to respect the client's request rather than to refuse continued service. In any event, the practitioner should conduct an evaluation interview before changing to open-ended service.

While time limits per se are precluded by definition when changing to open-ended service, we recommend, as does Reid, retaining other elements of the task-centered format, including specifying additional goals, formulating a new contract, working on task accomplishment, maintaining focus and continuity, and monitoring progress—elements that are characteristic of all effective helping methods. By continuing to incorporate these elements, practitioners avoid one major hazard of open-ended service—namely, drift or wandering.

5. *Referring the client elsewhere* for additional assistance is a final option. Locating appropriate resources for specialized assistance, in fact, may be a central task to be accomplished in the context of time-limited modalities. We discuss skills in referring clients in the last section of this chapter.

Planned Termination Involving Open-Ended Modalities

Determining when to terminate is the first major task of termination involving open-ended service. Theoretically, humans can grow indefinitely, and determining when clients have achieved optimal growth is no simple task. The difficulty of the task is compounded when service has been lengthy (more than six months), because long-term service tends to foster dependency and some clients are reluctant to relinquish the gratifications they gain in the helping relationship. Common expressions of their wish to cling to the helping relationship include fears of being unable to cope with their life situation independently and failing to engage in change-oriented activities outside the therapeutic sessions. Both forms of expressions are manifestations of resistance to change and may be artifacts of poor treatment (e.g., fostering dependency, failing to focus on change-oriented tasks, neglecting to accredit client strengths, and otherwise not cultivating self-efficacy on the client's part). Some clients, of course, have extensive personality deficiencies and, irrespective of how the helping process is conducted, may manifest marked dependency all their lives.

Ordinarily it is appropriate to introduce termination when the client has reached the point of diminishing returns; that is, when the gains from sessions taper off to the point of being minor in significance. When practitioners believe that clients have made marked progress, they should be sensitive to expressions indicating the latter share that perception. If the client states that things have been going well for some time and has been wondering about discontinuing, the practitioner may concur and reflect the fact that the client apparently may be feeling ready to consider termination in the near future. If the client affirms that such is the case, it is appropriate to suggest beginning to plan termination together.

Often, clients are hesitant about expressing thoughts about termination, and the practitioner will need to introduce the matter based on impressions gained from indirect manifestations. A client may report having little to talk about and indicate relative freedom from stress. If the client's report is consistent with evidence of marked progress, it is appropriate to suggest reviewing the client's functioning in relationship to extant goals. If the client expresses satisfactory attainment of the goals and the practitioner concurs, the latter can channel the discussion in a natural manner to the topic of termination.

Dealing with emotional reactions related to separation is also of special significance in terminating in the context of open-ended service (Webb, 1985). Because the practitioner has played a significant role in the client's life over an extended period of time, the client may approach termination with considerable reluctance. Clients may perceive termination as traumatic and may manifest one or more of several forms of resistance to termination. Levinson (1977) has identified the following termination reactions sometimes encountered in open-ended service and, to a lesser extent, even in time-limited service:

1. *Clinging to Therapy and the Practitioner* As we previously noted, some clients tend to use the helping process as a substitute rather than a means to learn how to gain greater fulfillment from life in outside relationships and activities. To avoid fostering such reactions, it is imperative that from the beginning practitioners stress the goal of achieving independence within the shortest possible time and foster maximal independence by clients. Practitioners who are oriented to this perspective rarely have clients who perceive termination as a major trauma. Other practitioners report the majority of their clients experience severe difficulty in terminating, and one must wonder to what extent they nurture the difficulties by clinging to clients and by focusing on weaknesses, deficiencies, and "pathology" rather than strength and opportunities for growth.

It is noteworthy that group members in *open-ended* groups also frequently resist termination. As Garvin (1981) has pointed out, "Members are more likely to deny that they are ready for termination, and they will raise questions as to why the worker has decided to terminate. They must adjust to an event whose timing was, at least initially, ambiguous or unknown" (p. 208). For this and other reasons, Garvin favors using time limits with groups.

2. *Reporting Recurrence of Old Problems* Some clients tend to panic as treatment approaches closure and experience a return of difficulties that have been under control for some time. Other clients whose best functioning is submarginal may manifest more severe reactions by resorting to drastic behaviors, such as attempting suicide. Such actions, however, are infrequent and generally occur only with people who are extremely unstable. When clients manifest recurrences of old problems, it is important not to focus on the problems but rather on the client's fears and uncertainties concerning their lives after termination. After exploring these feelings and empathizing with them, it is helpful to review again the progress the client has made and to accredit the strength and personal resources from which the client can draw. By thinking through their fears and concluding anew that their progress is real, clients often regain a sense of self-efficacy and courage to face the future independently.

3. *Introducing New Problems* As a ploy to continue the helping relationship, some clients introduce new stresses and problems during the terminal sessions and even during the final scheduled session. Further, clients who normally communicate minimally may suddenly open up, and other clients may reveal confidential information they have previously withheld. Although the practitioner should not minimize the importance of new problems or information, it is vital not to grasp the bait without first exploring feelings about termination. Placed in context, new information and problems often are relatively insignificant.

4. *Finding Substitutes for the Practitioner* Although finding one or more persons to replace the practitioner may be a constructive way of developing social resources, it may also be a way of locating a person on whom the client can become dependent, thereby compensating for the loss of the practitioner. Clients who seek a nurturing, parental type of confidante are likely attempting to perpetuate dependency at the expense of growth. Should this appear to be the case, the practitioner should assist the client to recognize the pertinent dynamics and to consider the consequences of making such a choice.

Group members may also seek to compensate for losses of group support by affiliating with other groups and never actually developing enduring social support systems. We have known of individuals who have become "group bums," moving from one group to another as each group ends. Such persons resist change and seek the safety and protection afforded in a group context. When leaders are aware that a person is motivated to join a group for this reason, they should consider negotiating a goal to use the group as a vehicle for exploring and resolving fears of relating to others outside growth groups.

Termination Precipitated by Departure of a Practitioner

On occasions, practitioners must terminate their work with clients or groups because of departure precipitated by reassignment or change of employment. Termination under these circumstances is difficult for both clients and practitioners because many clients need continuing assistance. Emotional reactions are often intense, and time for working through these reactions is often inadequate. Clients who have previously been rejected or abandoned by parents are particularly vulnerable and may experience the prac-

titioner's departure as the latest in a series of painful rejections, each of which has damaged their tenuous self-esteem and constituted further evidence of their lack of worth. Aware of this possible reaction by clients, practitioners too may experience intense emotions, including guilt associated with a sense of failing the client. Because of these feelings, a practitioner may delay introducing termination or may overcompensate for guilt by being overly apologetic, solicitous, and reassuring, thereby making it difficult for clients to express and to resolve their negative feelings.

The primary tasks to be accomplished when a practitioner terminates service because of leaving involve assisting clients to work through their emotions to the extent that time permits and preparing them to transfer to another practitioner. We discuss these tasks in the next section.

Resolving Emotional Reactions to Termination

Because of the loss associated with separation, clients (and practitioners too) typically experience some degree of sadness as they approach the terminal session. The degree of sadness varies from client to client and is most intense when helping relationships have been long and emotionally deep and when clients have few or no other close relationships. (Emotional reactions are relatively minor by comparison when modalities have been time-limited and task-focused.) Mixed with sadness may be satisfaction over having successfully resolved burdensome difficulties and relief over seeing the emotionally stressful (and perhaps expensive) helping process draw to a close.

Managing Emotions Produced When Practitioners Leave

When termination occurs because a practitioner leaves an agency, clients often manifest other reactions before experiencing sadness. Because the termination is not planned and occurs with little forewarning, reactions are sometimes similar to those that involve other types of sudden crises. A client may thus respond by shutting off thoughts of the impending loss (denial) and relating as though nothing has happened. It is a mistake to interpret the client's business-as-usual demeanor as an indication the client is taking the termination in stride, for the unruffled exterior may represent the calm before the storm. The client's temporary denial of feelings is an attempt to ward off psychic pain associated with a distressing reality that must be faced.

To assist clients to get in touch with their emotions, it is helpful to reintroduce the topic of termination and to express your desire to assist them in formulating plans to continue working toward their goals after your departure. As you bring up the topic of termination, it is critical to be sensitive to nonverbal cues that manifest emotional reactions. We also recommend employing empathic communication that conveys understanding of and elicits the hurt, resentment, and rejection clients commonly experience when a practitioner leaves. It is vital, however, not to empathize to the extent of over-identifying and losing your capacity to assist the client with negative feelings and to engage in constructive planning. The following is an example of a message that expresses genuine concern, conveys empathy, and invites the client to express feelings about termination:

"I can sense that you're having a real struggle with feelings about my leaving. I want you to know how badly I feel about leaving, especially since you still have a way to go before you accomplish your goals. I know it wasn't easy for you to confide in me, and I can understand you'd feel angry over my not seeing you through your difficulties. At least that's how I'd feel if I were in your situation. You've shared a lot with me to this point in your sessions. Could you share with me what you're feeling at this moment?"

When these clients do get in touch with their feelings, anger, resentment, hurt, a sense of betrayal, and feelings of rejection and of worthlessness often emerge. Clients with low self-esteem and a history of being rejected and abandoned experience these feelings most frequently and keenly. Children or adolescents in groups often deal with such feelings by ignoring them or by indirectly attacking or demeaning the practitioner in messages to other members that insinuate the practitioner doesn't really care about them or by directly accusing the practitioner of abandoning them. When these behaviors occur, the practitioner should accept the feelings, empathize with them, and assist the group members to express their feelings directly and to weigh the feelings against the totality of the group's experience to that point. The group practitioner may also respond authentically, highlighting reality factors that foster a more realistic appraisal of the situation, as illustrated in the following message:

"I can understand your being upset and resentful over my leaving. We've grown close over our sessions, and it's hard for me too to lose that closeness. Still, I have a lot of pleasant memories about each one of you that I'll take with me. My leaving can't destroy that nor the progress you've made as a group. Though I'll be gone, you still have each other, and I'm arranging for another leader who can pick up where I leave off."

It is to be expected that members will ventilate additional anger, and the practitioner will need to stay with such negative feelings until they have dissipated. Typically, as they ventilate their anger and are still accepted by the practitioner, members gradually are able to shift to examining their feelings more thoughtfully and to conclude (1) that the practitioner's leaving is not a personal rejection and (2) that though the loss is painful, life must go on. As they resolve these negative feelings, they are then able to express and to bear their sadness and to reexperience positive feelings toward the practitioner.

Occasionally, clients express their anger and hurt over a practitioner's leaving by rejecting a practitioner before the latter can reject them. Members of adolescent groups who either ignore or profess no longer needing the practitioner are, in effect, employing the strategy that the best defense is a good offense. Individual clients often do the same by failing to keep appointments after learning of the practitioner's imminent departure. When clients thus reject the practitioner, it is critical to reach out to them; otherwise, they tend to interpret the failure to do so as evidence the practitioner never really cared about them at all. In reaching out, a personal contact by telephone or home visit is essential, for there must be an opportunity for interaction in which practitioners reaffirm their concern and care and convey empathy and understanding of the client's emotional reaction. Reaching out often succeeds in reengaging the client and averting a devastating termination experience. Some clients, however, will resist the practitioner's overtures and "will steadfastly deny or openly devalue the therapist and the therapy as not having had any influence on their lives" (Levinson, 1977, p. 486).

As members of growth groups move beyond their negative feelings, practitio-

ners empathize with members' desires to continue the group (e.g., "I know you have grown to care about each other and can understand your desire to keep the group going"). Garvin (1981) further recommends being firm on plans for ending, indicating groups will then usually develop more effective means of coping with anger over termination.

Terminations with Unsuccessful Outcomes

Practitioners must occasionally impose termination on clients in open-ended service when clients are hopelessly stalemated despite vigorous and persistent efforts by practitioners to surmount the impasse. Groups also occasionally end with unsuccessful results, and members may be frustrated, disappointed, or angry toward the leader or toward other members. When the helping process ends unsuccessfully, termination should include discussion of (1) factors that prevented achieving more favorable results and (2) clients' feelings about seeking additional help in the future. Managing any of the preceding emotional reactions involves utilizing essentially the same skills and attitudes identified earlier—namely, empathic communication, acceptance, warmth, accreditation of strengths, understanding, genuineness, and gentle confrontation. To work through negative feelings successfully, practitioners will need to maintain focus on the feelings until clients are able to move beyond them.

Practitioners will gain enhanced understanding of clients' emotional reactions to termination and be maximally effective in assisting them through these reactions by considering both the nature of previous separations in their lives and their patterns of coping with them. As we have previously noted, clients who have experienced repeated rejections may mistakenly interpret termination as rejection by the practitioner. Being aware of previous experiences and patterns can assist the practitioner to respond sensitively to clients' feelings and to assist them to recognize how these factors can color current perceptions and feelings. Gaining awareness of their reactions to separation can be extremely valuable to clients, sometimes enabling them to achieve their first nontraumatic separation—a milestone for some clients that prepares them for dealing more effectively with the inevitable separations of the future.

Positive Termination Reactions

Most clients in individual, marital, family, and group therapy experience *positive* emotions in terminations that more than balance negative emotions. Benefits of the gains achieved usually *far outweigh* the impact of the loss of the helping relationship. Indeed, clients often report an increased sense of mastery, and both practitioners and clients are likely to experience joy over such accomplishments. This is especially true when practitioners have employed a strength-oriented, problem-solving approach. Furthermore, the participants have experienced mutual enrichment from the deep, personal, and authentic human encounter, and, in a very real sense, the self of each person has been expanded by the contacts with the other.

Termination Activities with Groups and Families

In effecting termination with groups, practitioners must attune their antennas to emotional reactions manifested by both the group as a collective and by individual members as well. When the group as a whole manifests negative feelings, it is important to utilize group process to focus upon and to work through these feelings. When individual members appear to be struggling with a termination reaction, the practitioner should assist them to express their feelings to the group so that the latter can provide emotional support and assist such members to understand and resolve their troubled feelings.

Because termination involves letting go of valued relationships with practitioners and/or group members, planning often involves arrangements that dilute the intensity of the helping relationship and weaken the cohesiveness among group members. The objective thus is to mitigate the impact of the loss by weakening the emotional bonds among participants (which is the exact opposite of the objective in the beginning phase). Practitioners and clients should mutually plan the number of remaining sessions and may space them further apart. Tapering off the sessions permits clients to try their wings for longer periods of time and to demonstrate their ability to function independently.

To weaken cohesiveness in groups during the termination phase, practitioners often plan activities that involve a low degree of group interaction and cooperation. Forms of "parallel" activities, such as crafts projects, hiking, or other activities that involve minimal sharing, are appropriate during the concluding group sessions. Wayne and Avery (1979) have identified a number of activities that can be employed as tools to facilitate termination of groups.

Because ceremonies or parties are often used to highlight transitions in social institutions, practitioners may similarly employ them with families and formed groups to acknowledge accomplishments and to demarcate the status of being a client from the status of being independent (Garvin, 1981, pp. 217–218). Such events provide opportunities for members to present accolades, to express sentiment, and to express farewells. To achieve a full measure of meaning for such ceremonies, it is vital that all or some of the members, together with the practitioner, plan the ceremony, making provisions for spontaneity and surprises.

The elements that have been included in ceremonies . . . include special refreshments, gift giving, "mock" diplomas, opportunities for members to say "last words," taking a group picture, short speeches by the worker, "rituals," or singing a beloved song together.

(Garvin, 1981, p. 218)

Although many of these activities would not be appropriate for families, holding a party to celebrate successful results of family therapy may be a fitting way of marking termination. A party, which should be planned by the entire family, fetes the newly won solidarity among family members. (Termination for families involves far less loss than for individuals or growth-oriented groups because the family emerges with its natural support system intact and, in fact, with an even stronger support system if therapy has been successful.)

Evaluation

Evaluating outcomes of the helping process has assumed ever-increasing significance in recent years. Clients tend to respond positively to evaluation if practitioners explain the rationale and mutually involve clients in planning and implementing the process. The following is a brief example of an explanation you might give to a client:

"An important part of termination is to assess the results we have achieved and to identify what helped you most and least during our work together. As an agency, we're committed to improving the quality of our services, and I'm likewise interested in improving my services. Feedback from you, therefore, is most important. Your feedback will be of greatest value if you're open and frank in presenting your views. Do you have any questions about evaluation?"

Evaluation consists of three different dimensions: (1) outcome, (2) process, and (3) the practitioner. We consider each of these dimensions in the following sections.

Outcome

Evaluation of outcome involves assessing the results achieved against the goals formulated. If measures were made of the incidence of problem or target behaviors during the assessment process (as suggested in Chapter 13), evaluation is straightforward, consisting of comparing baseline measures against the latest measurement. This type of evaluation has the marked advantage of being objective.

An additional advantage of having quantifiable baseline measurements of target behaviors is that the process of evaluating progress and outcome can be aided by use of a computer. Nurius and Hudson (1988) have described the use of a computerized clinical assessment system "that interactively enables workers and their clients to assess client problems and monitor progress over time" (p. 358). According to these authors, computers can eliminate much of the time and effort involved in various aspects of the evaluation process.

Where baseline measures were not made and instruments of measurement were not stipulated in advance, evaluation is more subjective and, hence, far less rigorous. Client and practitioner (or group members) generally review each goal and discuss the extent to which the client achieved that goal. Although it is unwise to challenge clients' perceptions, subjectivity can be reduced by asking clients to provide actual examples of recent events that illustrate their attainment of goals. Discussing such events briefly also provides an opportunity for the practitioner and/or group member to accredit accomplishments, which tends to heighten confidence and satisfaction.

In addition to clients' perceptions of their progress, evaluation should include other criteria where practicable. The judgment of the practitioner, other group members, and significant others may provide a more balanced and accurate assessment.

Process

Another aspect of evaluation relates to clients' perceptions of aspects of the helping process that were useful or detrimental. Feedback about techniques and incidents that enhanced or blocked progress enables practitioners to hone certain skills, eliminate others, and use techniques with greater discrimination. A technique that is useful with an assertive client, for example, may produce an opposite effect with a depressed client. In our opinion, an important aspect of ethical practice is to seek constantly to upgrade one's effectiveness by obtaining and applying systematic feedback about clients' perceptions of the practitioner's implementation of interventions.

On occasions, such feedback can be highly informative, confidence-building,

or perhaps humbling. A practitioner may have attributed a positive outcome to a masterfully executed technique only to find the client was helped far more by the former's willingness to reach out and maintain hope when the latter had virtually given up. Group members likewise often identify certain aspects of group process or behavior by other members that were particularly helpful—factors the practitioner may have overlooked. Often, it is these subtle or *nonspecific* factors (Yalom, 1980, pp. 1–2) that likely produce change rather than the precise and calculated interventions of practitioners. The point, of course, is that as we expand our knowledge of nonspecific factors, we can knowingly incorporate them into practice, thereby enhancing our therapeutic effectiveness.

The Practitioner

By soliciting feedback regarding how their own behaviors, attitudes, and attributes may have affected the helping process positively or negatively, practitioners invite criticism, and if requests are genuine, clients are likely to be candid. Practitioners must welcome criticism and be prepared to respond to it constructively. The resultant feedback can be extremely valuable. Clients typically cite positive factors more than negative ones. In addition to the "stroking" value of positive feedback, this feedback enables practitioners to be more aware of their strengths and perhaps to tap these strengths more frequently in the future. Negative feedback, although sometimes painful, can also be extremely helpful in bringing to awareness behaviors, attitudes, and mannerisms that may be distractive or antitherapeutic. Just as clients have blind spots, so do practitioners, and criticism illuminates the pathway to growth. Practitioners may thus learn from consistent feedback that drawing premature conclusions, tuning out, giving too much or too little advice, clearing their throats excessively, frowning, jiggling the foot, being overly formal or familiar, and other like behaviors detract from their effectiveness. As with clients, awareness precedes change.

Consolidating Gains and Planning Maintenance Strategies

The aim of the helping process is not only to assist clients to develop solutions to their current problems but also to strengthen them so they can cope with the inevitable difficulties that will beset them in the future. Similarly, a major aim of work with groups is not only to assist members to interact successfully within the group context but also to transfer their newly developed interpersonal skills to the broad arena of social relationships. Toward these ends, other vital tasks involved in termination are to assist clients to consolidate the gains they have achieved and to develop plans to maintain these gains. In recent years, these tasks have commanded increasing attention as a result of alarming follow-up research findings indicating that many clients do not maintain the gains they achieve during the formal helping process. Failure to maintain gains has been variously attributed to a natural tendency to revert to habitual response patterns, pressures from the environment (e.g., pressures on adolescents to conform to the peer group and recurrences of dysfunctional behaviors in families), insufficiently established new behaviors, and a lack of reinforcement for functional be-

haviors. It follows that in planning maintenance strategies, practitioners must anticipate these forces and prepare clients for coping with them. In this section, we define relevant strategies.

An important aspect of assisting clients to consolidate gains is to review their problems and to analyze the steps they followed in resolving them. The practitioner's role in this review and discussion is to assist clients in grasping the principles of effective problem solving, which involve the basic steps of independent problem solving as defined in Chapter 15. The practitioner then assists them to understand how these principles can be applied to general problems of living. If clients learned independent problem solving and the practitioner guided them to apply this intervention to various problem situations, these clients already have potent and transferable coping skills at their disposal. In termination, the practitioner merely reviews how they applied this process to discrete problems and reinforces how they can use the process in coping with diverse problems in the future. Other discrete skills that have general application, such as muscle relaxation, cognitive restructuring, self-instruction, and various interpersonal skills, should be similarly reviewed and practitioners should challenge clients to consider how they can continue to apply these skills to problems of daily living.

Another method of preparing clients to cope with future stresses involves anticipatory guidance, as we discussed in Chapter 14. This approach enables clients to anticipate stresses and negative forces and to plan appropriate countermeasures. Former delinquents, for example, may anticipate being teased, dared, and mocked by delinquent peers and can plan to employ self-instruction and self-reinforcement to resist these forces. In some instances, practitioners may need to actively assist clients to identify forces that militate against maintaining change.

Relapse Prevention

Because of disturbingly high relapse rates following apparent treatment successes, maintenance strategies are especially crucial in work with clients who have addictions and/or habits of excessive drinking, smoking, overeating, and engaging in unacceptable sexual behaviors. Despite successful treatment, these persons experience cravings and urges after termination. The meanings they attach to continued cravings and impulses and the ways they cope with them determine in great measure whether they will maintain control or will revert to yielding to cravings and urges.

Strategies of relapse prevention (RP) have been developed by practitioners and researchers over the past decade. Multidimensional in nature, these strategies involve self-management processes that consist of cognitive, emotional, behavioral, and lifestyle components. Daley (1987) has discussed various factors that contribute to relapse, identified beliefs and myths associated with addictions, and delineated a model for relapse education and treatment. In addition, Marlatt and Gordon (1985) have contributed to and edited a comprehensive and superb book concerned with relapse prevention. Practitioners who work with addicted and impulse-disordered clients will find these references to be exceptionally helpful.

Using Support Systems

When clients' problems involve limited social skills and when their social environments are deficient in natural support systems, practitioners may explore the availability of social and recreational programs, such as senior citizens' centers. Practitioners may encourage mental patients to affiliate with Recovery Incorporated, single parents with Parents Without Partners, child-abusing parents with Parents Anonymous, and so on. Practitioners may also encourage clients to return for additional help should problems appear to be mounting out of control. Although it is important to express confidence in clients' ability to cope independently with their problems (as usually is justified), it is equally important to convey your continued interest in them and to invite them to return should they need to do so.

Booster Interviews

Still another strategy of facilitating transition to independent status and of maintaining change is to employ *booster* interviews. This involves holding additional sessions several weeks after termination at the client's discretion. Our experience has been that most clients are receptive to booster interviews, which assure them of the practitioner's continued interest and provide an extended "test" period and an opportunity for brief "clean up" work when needed. Some may argue that booster interviews needlessly foster continued dependency, but our experience does not bear this out. When we began to employ booster interviews, we suggested that clients phone us in a few weeks to schedule a booster interview, but the majority "forgot" to do so. We therefore changed to scheduling booster appointments but called clients a few days in advance to remind them. We were careful to inquire as to clients' desires for booster interviews and found the majority were getting along fine and felt no need for them. Others who kept the appointments used them to good advantage, but we have had few clients seek to resume sessions on a regular basis.

Finally, we recommend that practitioners emphasize to clients that to maintain change (and to continue to grow), they will need to develop appropriate strategies. We know one practitioner who asks clients, "How long do you want to maintain the changes you have made?" Clients invariably respond, "Indefinitely," which provides an excellent opening to stress the need for developing appropriate strategies of maintaining changes. We find clients are impressed when we stress that change is not maintained by chance factors and that people who continue to progress do so by continuing to set personal goals and to monitor their progress regularly. One couple, seen by one of the authors, purchased a journal, which they used as a log for their marriage. This couple schedules regular times with each other to review their progress and to set additional goals to improve their marital relationship. Practitioners could well advise other clients to do likewise.

Follow-Up Sessions

Clearly related to evaluation and maintenance of change is the use of a follow-up session from two to six months following termination. Wells (1981) recommends that follow-up sessions be included as an integral part of practice with all clients, and we concur with his recommendation.[1]

---

[1]We wish to acknowledge that the content of this section is largely based on material generously provided the authors by Richard A. Wells, who discusses this subject in Richard A. Wells (1981), *Planned Short-Term Treatment*. New York: The Free Press.

Practitioners who routinely employ follow-up sessions may not need to use booster interviews, for follow-up sessions can serve the same purpose and additional purposes as well.

Follow-up sessions provide benefits to both clients and practitioners. Many clients continue to progress after termination, and practitioners can accredit such gains and encourage clients to continue their efforts. Practitioners can also provide brief additional assistance for residual difficulties during a follow-up session. Follow-up sessions also enable practitioners to assess the durability of changes; that is, to determine whether clients maintain gains beyond the immediate influence of the helping relationship. An additional benefit for clients of planned follow-up sessions is that the impact of termination is cushioned by knowledge of the practitioner's continued interest in them.

To assure that clients view the follow-up session as an integral part of the helping process, practitioners should introduce the matter early in the helping process and thereafter remind them of the plan from time to time. Presenting the plan in this manner averts the potential pitfall of clients later viewing the follow-up session as an intrusion into their private lives or as an attempt to satisfy the practitioner's curiosity.

Wells recommends that in arranging for the follow-up session, practitioners not set a specific date but rather explain they will contact the client after a designated interval. The practitioner further clarifies that the interval offers the client an opportunity to test out and further consolidate the learning and change achieved during the formal helping period. To enhance clients' positive expectancies, Wells refers to the follow-up session as "a chance to check on your *progress*."

In the follow-up session, the practitioner generally relates more informally than during the period of intervention. After appropriate social amenities, the practitioner guides the conversation to the clients' progress and obtains postintervention measures when appropriate. The follow-up session also provides an excellent opportunity for further evaluation of the practitioner's efforts during the period of intervention. In retrospect, what was most helpful? What was least helpful? Further efforts can also be made to consolidate gains. What was gained from treatment that the client can continue to use in coping with life? And finally, the practitioner can contract for further help if this appears necessary. Follow-up sessions thus enable practitioners to arrange for timely assistance that may arrest deterioration in functioning. For additional guidelines to conducting follow-up interviews, we recommend an article by Bernard (1985) concerned with follow-up interviews with psychotherapy patients.

Making Referrals

As we have previously indicated, termination sometimes involves assisting clients to receive services from other resources. Further, goals of time-limited service often involve connecting clients with essential resources not provided by the given agency or practitioner. Referring clients to other resources requires careful handling; otherwise, clients often do not follow through in seeking resources they need. The following are guidelines that will assist you in making referrals:

1. Ascertain the client's readiness for a referral by eliciting his or her feelings, which may involve doubts, apprehension, and misconceptions about seeking service elsewhere. Remember that the *client* must perceive a need for a referral. Although it is appropriate to explain the rationale for making a referral, it is unwise to "sell" the client on the need for it. If clients are not ready for a referral, they are unlikely to follow through though they may express intentions of doing so.

2. Determine together what resource best matches the needs of the client. To accomplish this, you must be knowledgeable about various resources within your community. You must also be familiar with agencies' policies and procedures as well as the quality of service provided by both agencies and private practitioners. Implementing this guideline presupposes you have developed a list of resources and maintain ongoing liaison with agencies so that your knowledge about their operations is current. It is your obligation to share relevant information with clients so that they can render informed judgments.

3. As you explore possible options for referral, respect the client's right to self-determination but offer your recommendation as to which resource is likely to be most beneficial. As Weissman (1976) has indicated, "Throwing the decision back on the client is an abrogation of professional responsibility under the guise of 'participation'" (p. 52).

4. Avoid making false promises or conveying *unrealistic* reassurance about what another agency can do in assisting the client. It is realistic, however, to express optimism about clients' potential to benefit from the services of another agency or practitioner. It is also helpful to allay clients' apprehension about entering a new helping relationship by reminding them that they were also initially apprehensive about you and that they can develop a positive relationship with another

practitioner as they did with you. Emphasize the client's responsibility for developing that relationship by sharing problems, feelings, and needs as openly as possible.

5. Although you should clarify the function and methods of the agency selected, avoid specifying what the next practitioner will do. Practitioners have different styles and employ different methods. If you prescribe what other practitioners should do, you impose a handicap upon them and set clients up for disappointment.

In addition to the preceding guidelines, practitioners can enhance the rate of achieving successful connections between clients and resources in the community by following five discrete steps. Weissman (1976) has defined these "connection techniques" and has reported impressive findings on the rate of successful referrals. These steps are as follows:

1. Write out the necessary facts about contacting the resource, including such information as name and address of the resource, how to obtain an appointment, how to reach the resource, and what the client may expect upon arriving. The initiative in making an appointment and following through resides with the client.

2. Provide the client with the name of a specific contact person. To avoid disappointment and discouragement if the contact person is not available, provide alternate names.

3. If the client's problem is complex, provide the client with a brief written statement, addressed to the resource, detailing the problem and the services desired by the client. Involve the client in composing the statement.

4. Have the client call the resource *from your office* to make an appointment. You may choose to place the call to assure that the client reaches the contact person and then turn the conversation over to the client.

5. When clients manifest apprehension or diffidence about going to the resource alone, it may be advisable to arrange for a family member or friend to accompany the client. In exceptional circumstances, you may wish to accompany the client yourself. Behavioral rehearsal may also be employed to prepare the client.

After following the preceding steps, your responsibility to facilitate the referral does not end. You may ask the client to report back after making the contact or may personally initiate a contact to secure a progress report. Your continued interest and efforts may make the difference between a successful and unsuccessful referral.

A ▪ Appendix: The NASW Code of Ethics*

Preamble

This code is intended to serve as a guide to the everyday conduct of members of the social work profession and as a basis for the adjudication of issues in ethics when the conduct of social workers is alleged to deviate from the standards expressed or implied in this code. It represents standards of ethical behavior for social workers in professional relationships with those served, with colleagues, with employers, with other individuals and professions, and with the community and society as a whole. It also embodies standards of ethical behavior governing individual conduct to the extent that such conduct is associated with an individual's status and identity as a social worker.

This code is based on the fundamental values of the social work profession that include the worth, dignity, and uniqueness of all persons as well as their rights and opportunities. It is also based on the nature of social work, which fosters conditions that promote these values.

In subscribing to and abiding by this code, the social worker is expected to view ethical responsibility in as inclusive a context as each situation demands and within which ethical judgment is required. The social worker is expected to take into consideration all the principles in this code that have a bearing upon any situation in which ethical intervention or conduct is planned. The course of action that the social worker chooses is expected to be consistent with the spirit as well as the letter of this code.

In itself, this code does not represent a set of rules that will prescribe all the behaviors of social workers in all the complexities of professional life. Rather, it offers general principles to guide conduct, and the judicious appraisal of conduct, in situations that have ethical implications. It provides the basis for making judgments about ethical actions before and after they occur. Frequently, the particular situation determines the ethical principles that apply and the manner of their application. In such cases, not only the particular ethical principles are taken into immediate consideration, but also the entire code and its spirit. Specific applications of ethical principles must be judged within the context in which they are being considered. Ethical behavior in a given situation must satisfy not only the judgment of the individual social worker, but also the judgment of an unbiased jury of professional peers.

This code should not be used as an instrument to deprive any social worker of the opportunity or freedom to practice with complete professional integrity; nor should any disciplinary action be taken on the basis of this code without maximum provision for safeguarding the rights of the social worker affected.

*Passed by the 1979 Delegate Assembly, implemented July 1, 1980.

The ethical behavior of social workers results not from edict, but from a personal commitment of the individual. This code is offered to affirm the will and zeal of all social workers to be ethical and to act ethically in all that they do as social workers.

The following codified ethical principles should guide social workers in the various roles and relationships and at the various levels of responsibility in which they function professionally. These principles also serve as a basis for the adjudication by the National Association of Social Workers of issues in ethics.

In subscribing to this code, social workers are required to cooperate in its implementation and abide by any disciplinary rulings based on it. They should also take adequate measures to discourage, prevent, expose, and correct the unethical conduct of colleagues. Finally, social workers should be equally ready to defend and assist colleagues unjustly charged with unethical conduct.

I. The Social Worker's Conduct and Comportment as a Social Worker

A. Propriety—The social worker should maintain high standards of personal conduct in the capacity or identity as social worker.

1. The private conduct of the social worker is a personal matter to the same degree as is any other person's, except when such conduct compromises the fulfillment of professional responsibilities.

2. The social worker should not participate in, condone, or be associated with dishonesty, fraud, deceit, or misrepresentation.

3. The social worker should distinguish clearly between statements and actions made as a private individual and as a representative of the social work profession or an organization or group.

B. Competence and professional development—The social worker should strive to become and remain proficient in professional practice and the performance of professional functions.

1. The social worker should accept responsibility or employment only on the basis of existing competence or the intention to acquire the necessary competence.

2. The social worker should not misrepresent professional qualifications, education, experience, or affiliations.

C. Service—The social worker should regard as primary the service obligation of the social work profession.

1. The social worker should retain ultimate responsibility for the quality and extent of the service which that individual assumes, assigns, or performs.

2. The social worker should act to prevent practices that are inhumane or discriminatory against any person or group of persons.

D. Integrity—The social worker should act in accordance with the highest standards of professional integrity and impartiality.

1. The social worker should be alert to and resist the influences and pressures that interfere with the exercise of professional discretion and impartial judgment required for the performance of professional functions.

2. The social worker should not exploit professional relationships for personal gain.

E. Scholarship and research—The social worker engaged in study and research should be guided by the conventions of scholarly inquiry.

1. The social worker engaged in research should consider carefully its possible consequences for human beings.

2. The social worker engaged in research should ascertain that the consent of participants in the research is voluntary and informed, without any implied deprivation or penalty for refusal to participate, and with due regard for participants' privacy and dignity.

3. The social worker engaged in research should protect participants from unwarranted physical or mental discomfort, distress, harm, danger, or deprivation.

4. The social worker who engages in the evaluation of services or cases should discuss them only for professional purposes and only with persons directly and professionally concerned with them.

5. Information obtained about participants in research should be treated as confidential.

6. The social worker should take credit only for work actually done in connection with scholarly and research endeavors and credit contributions made by others.

II. The Social Worker's Ethical Responsibility to Clients

F. Primacy of clients' interests—The social worker's primary responsibility is to clients.

1. The social worker should serve clients with devotion, loyalty, determination, and the maximum application of professional skill and competence.

2. The social worker should not exploit relationships with clients for personal advantage, or solicit the clients of one's agency for private practice.

3. The social worker should not practice, condone, facilitate, or collaborate with any form of discrimination on the basis of race, color, sex, sexual orientation, age, religion, national origin, marital status, political belief, mental or physical handicap, or any other preference or personal characteristic, condition, or status.

4. The social worker should avoid relationships or commitments that conflict with the interests of clients.

5. The social worker should under no circumstances engage in sexual activities with clients.

6. The social worker should provide clients with accurate and complete information regarding the extent and nature of the services available to them.

7. The social worker should apprise clients of their risks, rights, opportunities, and obligations associated with social service to them.

8. The social worker should seek advice and counsel of colleagues and supervisors whenever such consultation is in the best interest of clients.

9. The social worker should terminate service to clients, and professional relationships with them, when such service and relationships are no longer required or no longer serve the clients' needs or interests.

10. The social worker should withdraw services precipitously only under unusual circumstances, giving careful consideration to all factors in the situation and taking care to minimize possible adverse effects.

11. The social worker who anticipates the termination or interruption of service to clients should notify clients promptly and seek the transfer, referral, or continuation of service in relation to the clients' needs and preferences.

G. Rights and prerogatives of clients—The social worker should make every effort to foster maximum self-determination on the part of clients.

1. When the social worker must act on behalf of a client who has been adjudged legally incompetent, the social worker should safeguard the interests and rights of that client.

2. When another individual has been legally authorized to act in behalf of a client, the social worker should deal with that person always with the client's best interest in mind.

3. The social worker should not engage in any action that violates or diminishes the civil or legal rights of clients.

H. Confidentiality and privacy—The social worker should respect the privacy of clients and hold in confidence all information obtained in the course of professional service.

1. The social worker should share with others confidences revealed by clients without their consent only for compelling professional reasons.

2. The social worker should inform clients fully about the limits of confidentiality in a given situation, the purposes for which information is obtained, and how it may be used.

3. The social worker should afford clients reasonable access to any official social work records concerning them.

4. When providing clients with access to records, the social worker should take due care to protect the confidences of others contained in those records.

5. The social worker should obtain informed consent of clients before taping, recording, or permitting third-party observation of their activities.

I. Fees—When setting fees, the social worker should ensure that they are fair, reasonable, considerate, and commensurate with the service performed and with due regard for the clients' ability to pay.

1. The social worker should not divide a fee or accept or give anything of value for receiving or making a referral.

III. The Social Worker's Ethical Responsibility to Colleagues

J. Respect, fairness, and courtesy—The social worker should treat colleagues with respect, courtesy, fairness, and good faith.

1. The social worker should cooperate with colleagues to promote professional interests and concerns.

2. The social worker should respect confidences shared by colleagues in the course of their professional relationships and transactions.

3. The social worker should create and maintain conditions of practice that facilitate ethical and competent professional performance by colleagues.

4. The social worker should treat with respect, and represent accurately and fairly, the qualifications, views, and findings of colleagues and use appropriate channels to express judgments on these matters.

5. The social worker who replaces or is replaced by a colleague in professional practice should act with consideration for the interest, character, and reputation of that colleague.

6. The social worker should not exploit a dispute between a colleague and employers to obtain a position or otherwise advance the social worker's interest.

7. The social worker should seek arbitration or mediation when conflicts with colleagues require resolution for compelling professional reasons.

8. The social worker should extend to colleagues of other professions the same

respect and cooperation that is extended to social work colleagues.

9. The social worker who serves as an employer, supervisor, or mentor to colleagues should make orderly and explicit arrangements regarding the conditions of their continuing professional relationship.

10. The social worker who has the responsibility for employing and evaluating the performance of other staff members should fulfill such responsibility in a fair, considerate, and equitable manner, on the basis of clearly enunciated criteria.

11. The social worker who has the responsibility for evaluating the performance of employees, supervisees, or students should share evaluations with them.

K. Dealing with colleagues' clients— The social worker has the responsibility to relate to the clients of colleagues with full professional consideration.

1. The social worker should not solicit the clients of colleagues.

2. The social worker should not assume professional responsibility for the clients of another agency or a colleague without appropriate communication with that agency or colleague.

3. The social worker who serves the clients of colleagues during a temporary absence or emergency should serve those clients with the same consideration as that afforded any client.

IV. The Social Worker's Ethical Responsibility to Employers and Employing Organizations

L. Commitment to employing organization—The social worker should adhere to commitments made to the employing organization.

1. The social worker should work to improve the employing agency's policies and procedures, and the efficiency and effectiveness of its services.

2. The social worker should not accept employment or arrange student field placements in an organization which is currently under public sanction by NASW for violating personnel standards or imposing limitations on or penalties for professional actions on behalf of clients.

3. The social worker should act to prevent and eliminate discrimination in the employing organization's work assignments and in its employment policies and practices.

4. The social worker should use with scrupulous regard, and only for the purpose for which they are intended, the resources of the employing organization.

V. The Social Worker's Ethical Responsibility to the Social Work Profession

M. **Maintaining the integrity of the profession—The social worker should uphold and advance the values, ethics, knowledge, and mission of the profession.**

1. The social worker should protect and enhance the dignity and integrity of the profession and should be responsible and vigorous in discussion and criticism of the profession.

2. The social worker should take action through appropriate channels against unethical conduct by any other member of the profession.

3. The social worker should act to prevent the unauthorized and unqualified practice of social work.

4. The social worker should make no misrepresentation in advertising as to

qualifications, competence, service, or results to be achieved.

N. Community service—The social worker should assist the profession in making social services available to the general public.

1. The social worker should contribute time and professional expertise to activities that promote respect for the utility, the integrity, and the competence of the social work profession.

2. The social worker should support the formulation, development, enactment, and implementation of social policies of concern to the profession.

O. Development of knowledge—The social worker should take responsibility for identifying, developing, and fully utilizing knowledge for professional practice.

1. The social worker should base practice upon recognized knowledge relevant to social work.

2. The social worker should critically examine, and keep current with, emerging knowledge relevant to social work.

3. The social worker should contribute to the knowledge base of social work and share research knowledge and practice wisdom with colleagues.

VI. The Social Worker's Ethical Responsibility to Society

P. Promoting the general welfare—The social worker should promote the general welfare of society.

1. The social worker should act to prevent and eliminate discrimination against any person or group on the basis of race, color, sex, sexual orientation, age, religion, national origin, marital status, political belief, mental or physical handicap, or any other preference or personal characteristic, condition, or status.

2. The social worker should act to ensure that all persons have access to the resources, services, and opportunities which they require.

3. The social worker should act to expand choice and opportunity for all persons, with special regard for disadvantaged or oppressed groups or persons.

4. The social worker should promote conditions that encourage respect for the diversity of cultures which constitute American society.

5. The social worker should provide appropriate professional services in public emergencies.

6. The social worker should advocate changes in policy and legislation to improve social conditions and to promote social justice.

7. The social worker should encourage informed participation by the public in shaping social policies and institutions.

References

Abramson, M. (1985). The autonomy-paternalism dilemma in social work practice. *Social Casework, 66,* 387–393. .

Aguliar, I. (1972). Initial contact with Mexican-American families. *Social Work, 20,* 379–382.

Aguliar, M. (1983). *Patterns of health care utilization of Mexican-American women.* Unpublished doctoral dissertation, University of Illinois, Urbana-Champaign.

Aguilera, D., & Messick, J. (1982). *Crisis intervention: Theory and methodology* (4th ed.). St. Louis: C. Mosby.

Akabas, H., Fine, M., & Yasser, R. (1982). Putting secondary prevention to the test: A study of an early intervention strategy with disabled workers. *Journal of Primary Prevention, 2,* 165–187.

Albert, R. (1983). Social advocacy in the regulatory process. *Social Casework, 64,* 473–481.

Alberti, R., & Emmons, M. (1970, 1974). *Your perfect right: A guide to assertive behavior.* San Luis Obispo, CA: Impact Publishers.

Alcabes, A. & Jones, J. A. (1985). Structured determinants of clienthood. *Social Work, 30,* 49–53.

Allen-Meares, P., & Lane, B. A. (1987). Grounding social work practice in theory: Ecosystems. *Social Casework, 68,* 515–521.

Altman, H. (1982). Collaborative discharge planning. *Social Work, 27,* 422–427.

American Psychiatric Association. (1987). *Diagnostic and statistical manual* III-R. Washington, D.C.: American Psychiatric Association.

Anderson, J. (1979). Social work with groups in the generic base of social work practice. *Social Work with Groups, 2,* 281–293.

Anderson, L., & Shafer, G. (1979). The character-disordered family: A community treatment model for family sexual abuse. *American Journal of Orthopsychiatry, 49,* 436–445.

Anderson, S., & Grant, J. (1984). Pregnant women and alcohol: Implications for social work. *Social Casework, 65,* 3–10.

Andolfi, M. (1980). Prescribing the families' own dysfunctional rules as a therapeutic strategy. *Journal of Marital and Family Therapy, 6,* 29–36.

Aponte, H., & Van Deusen, J. (1981). Structural family therapy. In A. Gurman & D. Kniskern (Eds.), *Handbook of family therapy* (pp. 310–360). New York: Brunner/Mazel.

Arnowitz, E., Brunswick, L., & Kaplan, B. (1983). Group therapy with patients in the waiting room of an oncology clinic. *Social Work, 28,* 395–397.

Aronson, H., & Overall, B. (1966). Treatment expectations of patients in two social classes. *Social Work, 11,* 35–41.

Asimos, C. (1979). Dynamic problem solving in a group of suicidal persons. *International Journal of Group Psychotherapy, 29,* 109–114.

Attneave, C. (1982). American Indians and Alaska native families. In M. McGoldrick, J. Pearce, & J. Giordano (Eds.), *Ethnicity and family therapy* (pp. 55–83). New York: Guilford Press.

Auerback, S., & Moser, C. (1987). Groups for the wives of gay and bisexual men. *Social Work, 32*, 321–325.

Auslander, G. K., & Litwin, H. (1987). The parameters of network intervention: A social work application. *Social Service Review, 61*, 26–29.

Bagarozzi, D., & Kurtz, L. F. (1983). Administrators' perspectives on case management. *Arete, 8*, 13–21.

Balgopal, P., & Vassil, T. (1983). *Groups in social work: An ecological perspective.* New York: Macmillan.

Ballew, J. (1985). Role of natural helpers in preventing child abuse and neglect. *Social Work, 30*, 37–41.

Bandura, A. (1977). Self-efficacy. Toward a unifying theory of behavioral change. *Psychological Review, 84*, 191–215.

Bandura, A., Lipsher, D., & Miller, P. (1960). Psychotherapists' approach-avoidance reactions to patients' expressions of hostility. *Journal of Consulting Psychology, 24*, 1–8.

Banks, G. (1971). The effects of race on one-to-one helping interviews. *Social Service Review, 45*, 137–144.

Banks, G., Berenson, B., & Carkhuff, R. (1967). The effects of counselor race and training upon Negro clients in initial interviews. *Journal of Clinical Psychology, 23*, 70–72.

Barker, P. (1981). *Basic family therapy.* Baltimore: University Park Press.

Barozzi, R., & Engel, J. (1985). A survey of attitudes about family life education. *Social Casework, 66*, 106–110.

Barth, R. P. (1985). Beating the blues: Cognitive-behavioral treatment for depression in child-maltreating mothers. *Clinical Social Work Journal, 13*, 317–328.

Barth, R. P., & Berry, M. (1987). Outcomes of child welfare services under permanency planning. *Social Service Review, 61*, 71–92.

Barth, R., & Schinke, S. (1984). Enhancing the supports of teenage mothers. *Social Casework, 65*, 523–531.

Bartlett, H. (1970). *The common base of social work practice.* New York: National Association of Social Workers.

Barton, C., & Alexander, J. (1981). Functional family therapy. In A. Gurman & D. Kniskern (Eds.), *Handbook of Family Therapy* (pp. 403–443). New York: Brunner/Mazel.

Bassuk, E. L., Rubin, L., & Lauriat, A. S. (1986). Characteristics of sheltered homeless families. *American Journal of Public Health, 76*, 1097–1101.

Bates, M. (1983). Using the environment to help the male skid row alcoholic. *Social Casework, 64*, 276–282.

Bauman, M. (1981). Involving resistant family members in therapy. In A. S. Gurman (Ed.), *Questions and answers in the practice of family therapy* (pp. 16–19). New York: Brunner/Mazel.

Bean, G. J., Stefl, M. E., & Howe, S. R. (1987). Mental health and homelessness: Issues and findings. *Social Work, 32*, 411–416.

Beavers, W. (1977). *Psychotherapy and growth: Family systems perspective.* New York: Brunner/Mazel.

Beck, A. (1974). Phases in the development of structure in therapy and encounter groups. In D. Wexler & L. Rice (Eds.), *Innovations in client-centered therapy.* New York: John Wiley & Sons.

Beck, A., Kovacs, M., & Weissman, A. (1979). Assessment of suicidal intention. *Journal of Consulting and Clinical Psychology, 47*, 343–352.

Beck, A., Resnik, H., & Lettieri, D. (Eds.). (1974). *The prediction of suicide.* Bowie, MD: Charles Press.

Beck, A., Rush, A., Shaw, B., & Emery, G. (1979). *Cognitive therapy of depression.* New York: Guilford Press.

Beck, A., Ward, C., Mendelson, M., Mock, J., & Erbaugh, J. (1961). An inventory for measuring depression. *Archives of General Psychiatry, 4*, 561–571.

Beck, J., & Strong, S. (1982). Stimulating therapeutic change with interpretations: A comparison of positive and negative connotation. *Journal of Counseling Psychology, 29*, 551–559.

Becvar, D. S., & Becvar, R. J. (1988). *Family therapy: A systemic integration.* Boston: Allyn and Bacon.

Bell, J. (1963). A theoretical framework for family group therapy: Theory and practice. *Family Process, 2*, 1–4.

Bender, C., & Wiley, T. (1982). Vocational rehabilitation-therapeutic group: A cooperative venture. *Social Work, 27,* 185–186.

Bendick, M. (1980). Failure to enroll in public assistance programs. *Social Work, 25,* 268–274.

Bendick, M., & Cantu, M. (1978). The literacy of welfare clients. *Social Service Review, 52,* 56–68.

Berenson, B., & Mitchell, K. (1974). *Confrontation: For better or worse!* Amherst, MA: Human Resource Development Press.

Berg, R. A., Franzen, M. D., & Wedding, D. (1987). *Screening for brain impairment: A manual for mental health practice.* New York: Springer.

Bernal, G., & Flores-Ortiz, Y. (1982). Latino families in therapy: Engagement and evaluation. *Journal of Marriage and Family Therapy, 8,* 357–365.

Bernard, H. S. (1985). Follow-up interviews with psychotherapy patients. *Psychotherapy, 22,* 22–27.

Bernstein, A. (1972). The fear of compassion. In B. B. Wolman (Ed.), *Success and failure in psychoanalysis and psychotherapy* (pp. 160–176). New York: Macmillan.

Bernstein, A. G. (1981). *Case managers: Who are they and are they making any difference in mental health service delivery?* Unpublished doctoral dissertation, University of Georgia, Athens.

Bernstein, B. (1977). Privileged communications to the social worker. *Social Work, 22,* 264–268.

Bernstein, D., & Borkovec, T. (1973). *Progressive relaxation training: A manual for the helping professions.* Champaign, IL: Research Press.

Berry, M. (1988). A review of parent training programs in child welfare. *Social Service Review, 62,* 302–323.

Berwick, D. (1980). Nonorganic failure to thrive. *Pediatrics in Review, 1,* 265–270.

Beutler, L. E. (1983). *Eclectic psychotherapy: A systematic approach.* New York: Pergamon Press.

Bibring, E. (1954). Psychoanalysis and the dynamic psychotherapies. *Journal of the American Psychoanalytic Association, 2,* 745–770.

Biegel, D., & Naparstek, A. (Eds.). (1982). *Community support systems and mental health.* New York: Springer.

Biestek, F. (1957). *The casework relationship.* Chicago: Loyola University Press.

Biggs, D. A., & Blocher, D. H. (1987). *Foundations of ethical counseling.* New York: Springer.

Blechman, E. (1974). The family contract game: A tool to teach interpersonal problem solving. *Family Coordinator, 23,* 269–281.

Blechman, E., Olson, D., Schornagel, C., Halsdorf, M., & Turner, A. (1976). The family contract game: Technique and case study. *Journal of Consulting and Clinical Psychology, 44,* 449–455.

Bloom, M. (1975). *The paradox of helping: Introduction to the philosophy of scientific practice.* New York: John Wiley & Sons, 231–232.

Bloom, M., & Fischer, J. (1982). *Evaluating practice: Guidelines for the accountable professional.* Englewood Cliffs, NJ: Prentice-Hall.

Bonkowski, S., Bequette, S., & Boomhower, S. (1984). A group design to help children adjust to parental divorce. *Social Casework, 65,* 131–137.

Bonkowski, S., & Wanner-Westly, B. (1979). The divorce group: A new treatment modality. *Social Casework, 60,* 552–557.

Bookin, D., & Dunkle, R. (1985). Elder abuse: Issues for the practitioner. *Social Casework, 66,* 3–12.

Borkovec, T., & Sides, J. (1979). Critical procedural variables related to the physiological effects of relaxation: A review. *Behavior Research and Therapy, 17,* 119–125.

Boszormenyi-Nagy, I., & Spark, G. (1973). *Invisible loyalties: Reciprocity in intergenerational therapy.* New York: Harper & Row.

Bowen, G. L. (1987). Single fathers in the Air Force. *Social Casework, 68,* 339–344.

Brehm, S. S., & Brehm, J. W. (1981). *Psychological reactance: A theory of freedom and control.* New York: Academic Press.

Breton, M. (1984). A drop-in program for transient women: Promoting competence through the environment. *Social Work, 29,* 542–546.

Briar, S. (1964). The family as an organization: An approach to family diagnosis and treatment. *Social Service Review, 38,* 247–255.

Bribitzer, M. P., & Verdick, M. J. (1988). Home-based, family-centered intervention: Evaluation of a foster care prevention program. *Child Welfare, LXVII,* 255–266.

Brickner, P. W., Scharer, L. K., Conanan, B., Elvy, A., & Savarese, M. (1985). *Health care of homeless people.* New York: Springer.

Brindis, C., Barth, R. P., & Loomis, A. B. (1987). Continuous counseling: Case management with teenage parents. *Social Casework, 68,* 164–172.

Brown, G. (1982). Issues in the resettlement of Indo-chinese refugees. *Social Casework, 63,* 155–159.

Brown, J. L. (1988). Domestic hunger is no accident. (Guest editorial) *Social Work, 33,* 99–100.

Brown, L., & Levitt, J. (1979). A methodology for problem-system identification. *Social Casework, 60,* 408–415.

Bruckner, D. F., & Johnson, P. E. (1987). Treatment for adult male victims of childhood sexual abuse. *Social Casework, 68,* 81–87.

Bucell, M. (1979). *An empirically derived self-report inventory for the assessment of assertive behavior.* Unpublished doctoral dissertation, Kent State University, Kent, OH.

Budner, S., Chazin, R., & Young, H. (1973). The indigenous nonprofessional in a multiservice center. *Social Casework, 54,* 354–359.

Butcher, J., & Koss, M. (1978). Research on brief and crisis-oriented psychotherapies. In S. Garfield & A. Bergin (Eds.), *Handbook of psychotherapy and behavior change* (pp. 725–767). New York: John Wiley & Sons.

Butler, R. (1975). *Why service? Being old in America.* New York: Harper & Row.

Butz, R. A. (1985). Reporting child abuse and confidentiality in counseling. *Social Casework, 66,* 83–90.

Cameron, J., & Talavera, E. (1976). An advocacy program for Spanish-speaking people. *Social Casework, 57,* 427–431.

Canda, E. (1983). General implications of Shamanism for clinical social work. *International Social Work, 26,* 14–22.

Caplan, G. (1964). *Principles of preventive psychiatry.* New York: Basic Books.

Carasquillo, C., Ing, L., Kuhn, S., Metzger, J., Schubert, R., & Silveria, G. (1981). Group counseling with persons with developmental disabilities. *Social Casework, 62,* 486–490.

Carkhuff, R. (1969). *Helping and human relations: Practice and research.* New York: Holt, Rinehart & Winston.

Carter, E., & McGoldrick, M. (1988). *The changing family life cycle.* New York: Guilford Press.

Castle, N. (1980). A group experience with physically handicapped children. *Child Welfare, 59,* 235–241.

Chandler, S. (1985). Mediation: Conjoint problem solving. *Social Work, 30,* 346–349.

Celune, G. J. (1979). Measuring openness in interpersonal communication. In G. Chelune & associates, *Self-disclosure.* San Francisco: Jossey-Bass.

Cherbosque, J. (1987). Differential effects of counselor self-disclosure statements on perception of the counselor and willingness to disclose: A cross-cultural study. *Psychotherapy, 24,* 434–437.

Chesler, J., & Davis, S. (1980). Problem pregnancy and abortion counseling with teenagers. *Social Casework, 61,* 173–179.

Cimbolic, P. (1972). Counselor race and experience effects on black clients. *Journal of Consulting and Clinical Psychology, 39,* 328–332.

Cingolani, J. (1984). Social conflict perspective on work with involuntary clients. *Social Work, 29,* 442–446.

Claiborn, C. (1982). Interpretation and change in counseling. *Journal of Counseling Psychology, 29,* 439–453.

Claiborn, C., Crawford, J., & Hackman, H. (1983). Effects of intervention discrepancy in counseling for negative emotions. *Journal of Counseling Psychology, 30,* 164–171.

Cohen, B.-Z. (1985). A cognitive approach to the treatment of offenders. *British Journal of Social Work, 15,* 619–633.

Cohen, C., & Adler, A. (1986). Assessing the role of social network interventions with an inner-city population. *American Journal of Psychiatry, 56,* 278–288.

Cohn, A. (1979). Effective treatment of child abuse and neglect. *Social Work, 24,* 513–519.

Collins, A., & Pancoast, D. (1976). *Natural helping networks: A strategy for prevention.* New York: National Association of Social Workers.

Compher, J. (1983). Home services to families to prevent child placement. *Social Work, 28,* 360–364.

Conklin, C. (1980). Rural care-givers. *Social Work, 25,* 495–496.

Connell, S. (1987). Homelessness. In *Encyclopedia of social work,* Vol. 1 (pp. 789–795). Silver Spring, MD: National Association of Social Workers.

Constantine, L. (1978). Family sculpture and relationship mapping techniques. *Journal of Marriage and Family Counseling, 4,* 19–25.

Conte, J. R. (1987). Child sexual abuse. In *Encyclopedia of social work, Vol. I.* (pp. 255–260). Silver Spring, MD: National Association of Social Workers.

Cook, R. (1988). Trends and needs in programming for independent living. *Child Welfare, LXVII,* 497–514.

Cooley, R., Ostendorf, D., & Bickerton, D. (1979). Outreach services for Native Americans. *Social Work, 24,* 151–153.

Cooper, S. (1973). A look at the effect of racism on clinical work. *Social Casework, 54,* 76–84.

Coplon, J., & Strull, J. (1983). Roles of the professional in mutual aid groups. *Social Casework, 64,* 259–266.

Corcoran, K., & Fischer, J. (1987). *Measures for clinical practice.* New York: Free Press.

Cormier, W., & Cormier, L. (1979). *Interviewing strategies for helpers: A guide to assessment, treatment, and evaluation.* Monterey, CA: Brooks/Cole.

Coudroglou, A., & Poole, D. (1984). *Disability, work, and social policy.* New York: Springer.

Coulton, C. (1979). A study of the person-environment fit among the chronically ill. *Social Work in Health Care, 5,* 5–17.

Coulton C. (1981). Person-environment fit as the focus in health care. *Social Work, 26,* 26–35.

Cowan, B., Currie, M., Krol, R., & Richardson, J. (1969). Holding unwilling clients in treatment. *Social Casework, 14,* 146–151.

Crotty, P., & Kulys, R. (1985). Social support networks: The views of schizophrenic clients and their significant others. *Social Work, 30,* 301–309.

Curran, J. P., Sutton, R. G., Faraone, S. V., & Guenette, S. (1985). Inpatient approaches. In M. Hersen & A. S. Bellack (Eds.), *Handbook of clinical behavior therapy with adults* (pp. 445–483). New York: Plenum Press.

Cutler, D., & Madore, E. (1980). Community-family network therapy in a rural setting. *Community Mental Health Journal, 16,* 144–155.

Dahl, A. S., Cowgill, K. M., & Asmundsson, R. (1987). Life in remarriage families. *Social Work, 32,* 40–44.

Daley, D. C. (1987). Relapse prevention with substance abusers: Clinical issues and myths. *Social Work, 32,* 138–142.

D'Andrade, R. (1974). Sex differences and cultural institutions. In. R. LeVine (Ed.), *Culture and personality: Contemporary readings.* Chicago: Aldine.

Dane, E. (1985). *Professional and lay advocacy in the education of handicapped children.* New York: Routledge and Kegan Paul.

Danish, J., D'Augelli, A., & Hauer, A. (1980). *Helping skills: A basic training program.* New York: Human Sciences Press.

Davenport, J., & Reims, N. (1978). Theoretical orientation and attitudes toward women. *Social Work, 23,* 307–309.

Davis, I. (1975). Advice-giving in parent counseling. *Social Casework, 56,* 343–347.

Davis, L. V. (1987). Battered women: The transformation of a social problem. *Social Work, 32,* 306–311.

De Anda, D. (1984)). Bicultural socialization: Factors affecting the minority experience. *Social Work, 29,* 101–107.

De Anda, D., & Becerra, R. (1984). Support networks for adolescent mothers. *Social Casework, 65,* 172–181.

Deffenbacher, J. L., Story, D. A., Stark, R. S., Hogg, J. A., & Brandon, A. D. (1987). Cognitive-relaxation and social skills interventions in the treatment of general anger. *Journal of Counseling Psychology, 34,* 171–176.

Deighton, J., & McPeek, P. (1985). Group treatment: Adult victims of childhood sexual abuse. *Social Casework, 66,* 403–410.

Delgado, M. (1977). Puerto Rican spiritualism and the social work profession. *Social Casework, 58,* 451–458.

Devore, W., & Schlesinger, E. (1981). *Ethnic-sensitive social work practice.* St. Louis: C. V. Mosby.

Doherty, W. J. & Baird, M. A. (1987). *Family-centered medical care.* New York: Guilford Press.

Doster, J., & Nesbitt, J. (1979). Psychotherapy and self-disclosure. In. G. Chelune & associates, *Self-disclosure* (pp. 177–224). San Francisco: Jossey-Bass.

Doster, J., Surratt, F., & Webster, T. (1975, March). *Interpersonal variables affecting psychological communications of hospitalized psychiatric patients.* Paper presented at meeting of Southeastern Psychological Association, Atlanta.

Dougherty, N. (1983). The holding environment: Breaking the cycle of abuse. *Social Casework, 64,* 283–290.

Dowd, E., & Boroto, D. (1982). Differential effects of counselor self-disclosure, self-involving statements, and interpretation. *Journal of Counseling Psychology, 29,* 8–13.

DuBray, W. (1985). American Indian values: Critical factors in casework. *Social Casework, 66,* 30–37.

Dudley, J. R. (1987). Speaking for themselves: People who are labeled as developmentally disabled. *Social Work, 32,* 80–82.

Duehn, W., & Proctor, E. (1977). Initial clinical interactions and premature discontinuance in treatment. *American Journal of Orthopsychiatry, 47,* 284–290.

Duvall, E. (1977). *Marriage and family development* (5th ed.). Philadelphia: J. B. Lippincott.

Dyer, W. (1969). Congruence and control. *Journal of Applied Behavioral Science, 5,* 161–173.

D'Zurilla, T., & Goldfried, M. (1971). Problem solving and behavior modification. *Journal of Abnormal Psychology, 78,* 107–126.

Edleson, J. (1984). Working with men who batter. *Social Work, 29,* 237–242.

Edwards, A. (1982). The consequences of error in selecting treatment for blacks. *Social Casework, 63,* 429–433.

Edwards, E. (1983). Native-American elders: Current issues and social policy implications. In R. McNeely & J. Colen (Eds.), *Aging in minority groups.* Beverly Hills, CA: Sage.

Ehrenkranz, S. (1967). A study of joint interviewing in the treatment of marital problems. *Social Casework, 48,* 570–574.

Elkin, I., Shea, T., Watkins, J., & Collins, J. (1986). "Comparative treatment outcome findings," presentation of the NIMH Treatment of Depression Collaborative Research Program, made at the annual meeting of the American Psychiatric Association.

Ellis, A. (1962). *Reason and emotion in psychotherapy.* New York: Lyle Stuart.

Ely, A. (1985). Long-term group treatment for young male schizopaths. *Social Work, 30,* 5–10.

Falicov, C. (1982). Mexican families. In M. McGoldrick, J. Pearce, & J. Giordano (Eds.), *Ethnicity and family therapy* (pp. 134–163). New York: Guilford Press.

Farina, A., Burns, G. L., Austad, C., Bugglin, C. & Fischer, E. H. (1986). The role of physical attractiveness in the readjustment of discharged psychiatric patients. *Journal of Abnormal Psychology, 95,* 139–143.

Fauri, D. P., & Bradford, J. B. (1986). Practice with the frail elderly in the private sector. *Social Casework, 67,* 259–265.

Feinstein, B., & Cavanaugh, C. (1976). *The new volunteerism: A community connection.* Cambridge, MA: Schenkman.

Feldman, D., Strong, S., & Danser, D. (1982). A comparison of paradoxical and nonparadoxical interpretations and directives. *Journal of Counseling Psychology, 29,* 572–579.

Fine, M., Akabas, S., & Bellinger, S. (1982). Cultures of drinking: A workplace perspective. *Social Work, 27,* 436–440.

Finkelstein, N. (1980). Family-centered group care. *Child Welfare, 59,* 33–41.

Finn, J., & Rose, S. (1982). Development and validation of the interview skills role-play test. *Social Work Research and Abstracts, 18,* 21–27.

First, R. J., Roth, D., & Arewa, B. D. (1988). Homelessness: Understanding the dimensions of the problem for minorities. *Social Work, 33,* 120–124.

Fischer, J. (1978). *Effective casework practice: An eclectic approach.* New York: McGraw-Hill.

Fisher, L. (1976). Dimensions of family assessment: A critical review. *Journal of Marriage and Family Counseling, 2,* 367–382.

Folberg, J., & Milne, A. (1988). Divorce mediation: Theory and practice. New York: Guilford.

Fortune, A. E. (1985a). Treatment groups. In A. E. Fortune (Ed.) *Task-centered practice with families and groups* (pp. 33–44). New York: Springer.

Fortune, A. E. (1985b). *Task-centered practice with families and groups.* New York: Springer.

Framo, J. (1970). Symptoms from a family transactional viewpoint. In N. Ackerman, J. Leib, & J. Pierce (Eds.), *Family therapy in transition.* Boston: Little, Brown.

Frankle, H., & Gordon, V. (1983). Helping Selma: A report on a therapist-volunteer relationship. *Social Casework, 64,* 291–299.

Fraser, M., & Hawkins, J. (1984). Social network analysis and drug misuse. *Social Service Review, 58,* 81–87.

Fredman, N., & Sherman, R. (1987). *Handbook of measurements for marriage & family therapy.* New York: Brunner/Mazel.

Freed, A. (1978). Clients' rights and casework records. *Social Casework, 59,* 458–464.

Freed, A. (1988). Interviewing through an interpreter. *Social Work, 33,* 315–319.

Friedman, D., & Friedman, S. (1982). Day care as a setting for intervention in family systems. *Social Casework, 63, 291–295.*

Froland, C., Pancoast, D., Chapman, N., & Kimboko, P. (1981). *Helping networks and human services.* Beverly Hills, CA: Sage.

Gagliano, C. K. (1987). Group treatment for sexually abused girls. *Social Casework, 68,* 102–108.

Galanter, M. (1988). Zealous self-help groups as adjuncts to psychiatric treatment: A study of Recovery Inc. *American Journal of Psychiatry, 145,* 1248–1253.

Gallo, F. (1982). The effects of social support networks in the health of the elderly. *Social Work in Health Care, 8,* 65–74.

Gambrill, E., & Barth, R. (1980). Single-case study designs revisited. *Social Work Research and Abstracts, 16,* 15–20.

Garbarino, J. (1980). Meeting the needs of mistreated youth. *Social Work, 25,* 122–126.

Garbarino, J., Schellenbach, C. J., Sebes, J., & Associates (1986). *Troubled youth, troubled families: Understanding families at risk for adolescent maltreatment.* Hawthorn, NY: Aldine de Gruyter.

Garbarino, J., Stocking, S., & Associates (1980). *Protecting children from abuse and neglect.* San Francisco: Jossey-Bass.

Gardner, R. A. (1971). *Therapeutic communication with children.* New York: Science House Press.

Garfield, R. (1981). Convening the family: Guidelines for the initial contact with a family member. In A. Gurman (Ed.), *Questions and answers in the practice of family therapy* (pp. 5–9). New York: Brunner/Mazel.

Garfield, S. (1971). Research on client variables in psychotherapy. In A. Bergin & S. Garfield (Eds.), *Handbook of psychotherapy and behavior change: An empirical analysis* (pp. 271–299). New York: John Wiley & Sons.

Garfinkel, I., & McLanahan, S. S. (1986). *Single mothers and their children.* Washington, DC: Urban Institute Press.

Garland, J., Jones, H., & Kolodny, R. (1965). A model for stages in the development of social work groups. In S. Bernstein (Ed.), *Explorations in group work.* Boston: Milford House.

Garvin, C. (1981). *Contemporary group work.* Englewood Cliffs, NJ: Prentice-Hall.

Garvin, C. (1985). Practice with task-centered groups. In A. E. Fortune (Ed.), *Task-centered practice with families and groups* (pp. 45–57). New York: Springer.

Garvin, C., Reid, W., & Epstein, L. (1976). A task-oriented approach. In R. Roberts & H. Northern (Eds.), *Theories of social work with groups.* New York: Columbia University Press.

Gaylord, M. (1979). Relocation and the corporate family: Unexplored issues. *Social Work, 24,* 186–191.

Gendlin, E. (1967). Therapeutic procedures in dealing with schizophrenics. In C. Rogers, E. Gendlin, D. Kiesler, & C. Truax (Eds.), *The therapeutic relationship and its impact: A study of psychotherapy with schizophrenics.* Madison: University of Wisconsin Press.

Gendlin, E. (1974). Client-centered and experiential psychotherapy. In D. Wexler & L. Rice (Eds.), *Innovations in client-centered therapy.* New York: John Wiley & Sons.

Germain, C. (1973). An ecological perspective in casework practice. *Social Casework, 54,* 323–330.

Germain, C. (1977). An ecological perspective on social work practice in health care. *Social Work in Health Care, 3,* 67–76.

Germain, C. (1979). Ecology and social work. In C. Germain (Ed.), *Social work practice: People and environments* (pp. 1–2). New York: Columbia University Press.

Germain, C. (1981). The ecological approach to people-environmental transactions. *Social Casework, 62,* 323–331.

Germain, C., & Gitterman, A. (1980). *The life model of social work practice.* New York: Columbia University Press.

Ghali, S. (1982). Understanding Puerto Rican traditions. *Social Work, 27,* 98–102.

Giannandrea, V., & Murphy, K. (1973). Similarity of self-disclosure and return for a second interview. *Journal of Counseling Psychology, 20,* 545–548.

Gibbons, J., Bow, I., & Butter, J. (1979). Clients' reactions to task-centered casework: A follow-up study. *British Journal of Social Work, 9,* 203–215.

Gilbert, N. (1977). The search for professional identity. *Social Work, 22,* 401–406.

Gilbert, N., & Specht, H. (1976). Advocacy and professional ethics. *Social Work, 21,* 288–293.

Gilbert, N., & Specht, H. (1979). Title XX planning by area agencies on aging: Effects, outcomes, and policy implications. *Gerontologist, 19,* 264–274.

Gilbert, N., & Specht, H. (1987). Social planning and community organizations. *Encyclopedia of Social Work, Vol. 2* (pp. 602–619). Silver Spring, MD: National Association of Social Workers.

Gingerich, W. (1979). Procedure for evaluating clinical practice. *Health and Social Work, 4,* 104–130.

Giordano, N., & Giordano, J. (1984). Elder abuse: A review of the literature. *Social Work, 29,* 232–236.

Giovannoni, J., & Billingsley, A. (1970). Child neglect among the poor: A study of parental adequacy in families of three ethnic groups. *Child Welfare, 49,* 196–204.

Gitterman, A., & Schaeffer, A. (1972). The white professional and the black client. *Social Casework, 53,* 280–291.

Glick, I., & Kessler, D. (1974). *Marital and family therapy.* New York: Grune & Stratton.

Golan, N. (1978). *Treatment in crisis situations.* New York: Free Press.

Golan, N. (1980). Intervention at times of transition: Sources and forms of help. *Social Casework, 61,* 259–266.

Golan, N. (1981). *Passing through transitions: A guide for the practitioner.* New York: Free Press.

Golan, N., & Gruschka, R. (1971). Integrating the new immigrant: A model for social work practice in transitional states. *Social Work, 16,* 82–87.

Goldenberg, I., & Goldenberg, H. (1980). *Family therapy: An overview.* Monterey, CA: Brooks/Cole.

Goldenberg I., & Goldenberg, H. (1985). Family therapy: An overview (2nd ed.). Pacific Grove, CA: Brooks/Cole.

Goldfried, M. (1977). The use of relaxation and cognitive relabeling as coping skills. In R. Stuart (Ed.), *Behavioral self-management* (pp. 82–116). New York: Brunner/Mazel.

Goldstein, H. (1983). Starting where the client is. *Social Casework, 64,* 267–275.

Gomez, E., Zurcher, L. A., Farris, B. E., & Becker, R. E. (1985). A study of psychosocial casework with Chicanos. *Social Work, 30,* 477–482.

Gordon, J. (1978). Group homes: Alternative to institutions. *Social Work, 23,* 300–305.

Gordon, T. (1970). *Parent effectiveness training.* New York: P. H. Wyden.

Gordon, W. (1962). A critique of the working definition. *Social Work, 7,* 3–13.

Gordon, W. (1965). Toward a social work frame of reference. *Journal of Education for Social Work, 1,* 19–26.

Gordon, W., & Schutz, M. (1977). A natural basis for social work specializations. *Social Work, 22,* 422–426.

Gottesfeld, M., & Lieberman, F. (1979). The pathological therapist. *Social Casework, 60,* 387–393.

Gottlieb, B. (Ed.) (1981). *Social networks and social support.* Beverly Hills, CA: Sage.

Gottlieb, B. H. (1985) Assessing and strengthening the impact of social support on mental health. *Social Work, 30,* 293–300.

Gould, K. (1988). Asian and Pacific Islanders: Myth and reality. *Social Work, 33,* 142–147.

Green, J. (1982). *Cultural awareness in the human services.* Englewood Cliffs, NJ: Prentice-Hall.

Greenbaum, L., & Holmes, I. (1983). The use of folktales in social work practice. *Social Casework, 64,* 414–418.

Greif, G. L. (1985). *Single fathers.* Lexington, MA: D. C. Heath.

Griffiths, K. (1976). Social work practice with groups: Decade 1965–1975. In P. Boss & J. Crawley (Eds.), *Social work in Australia* (pp. 214–226). Melbourne, Australia: Australia International Press.

Grinnell, R., & Kyte, N. (1974). Modifying the environment. *Social Work, 19,* 477–483.

Grunebaum, H. (1986). Harmful psychotherapy experience. *American Journal of Psychotherapy, XL,* 165–176.

Guendalman, S. (1983). Developing responsiveness to the health care needs of Hispanic children and families. *Social Work in Health Care, 8,* 1–15.

Gurman, A. (1977). The patient's perception of the therapeutic relationship. In A. Gurman & A. Razin (Eds.), *Effective psychotherapy: A handbook of research.* New York: Pergamon Press.

Gurman, A. (Ed.), (1981). *Questions and answers in the practice of family therapy.* New York: Brunner/Mazel.

Gwyn, F., & Kilpatrick, A. (1981). Family therapy with low-income blacks: A tool or turnoff? *Social Casework, 62,* 259–266.

Hackett, G., & Horan, J. J. (1980). Stress inoculation for pain—what's really going on? *Journal of Counseling Psychology, 27,* 107–116.

Hackney, H., & Cormier, L. (1979). *Counseling strategies and objectives* (2nd ed.). Englewood Cliffs, NJ: Prentice-Hall.

Haeuser, A., & Schwartz, F. (1980). Developing social work skills for work with volunteers. *Social Casework, 61,* 595–601.

Hagen, J. L. (1987a). The heterogeneity of homelessness. *Social Casework, 68,* 451–457.

Hagen, J. L. (1987b). Gender and homelessness. *Social Work, 32,* 312–316.

Haley, J. (1963). *Strategies of psychotherapy.* New York: Grune & Stratton.

Hall, M. (1978). Lesbian families: Cultural and clinical issues. *Social Work, 23,* 380–385.

Hammond, D., Hepworth, D., & Smith, V. (1977). *Improving therapeutic communication.* San Francisco: Jossey-Bass.

Haney, M., & Rabin, B. (1984). Modifying attitudes toward disabled persons. *Archives of Physical Medicine and Rehabilitation, 65,* 431–436.

Haney, P. (1988). Providing empowerment to the person with AIDS. *Social Work, 33,* 251–253.

Hanrahan, P., & Reid, W. (1984). Choosing effective interventions. *Social Service Review, 58,* 244–258.

Harris, E. (1966). Parents Without Partners, Inc.: A resource for clients. *Social Work, 11,* 92–98.

Harris, M., & Bergman, H. C. (1987). Case management with the chronically ill. *American Journal of Orthopsychiatry, 57,* 296–302.

Hartford, M. (1971). *Groups in social work.* New York: Columbia University Press.

Hartman, A. (1981). The family: A central focus for practice. *Social Work, 26,* 7–13.

Hartman, C., & Reynolds, D. (1987). Resistant clients: Confrontation, interpretation and alliance. *Social Casework, 68,* 205–213.

Harvey, Y., & Chung, S. (1980). The Koreans. In J. McDermott, Jr., W. Tseng, & T. Maretzki (Eds.), *People and cultures of Hawaii* (pp. 135–154). Honolulu: University of Hawaii Press.

Hawley, N., & Brown, E. (1981). Children of alcoholics: The use of group treatment. *Social Casework, 62,* 40–46.

Haynes, K. S., & Mickelson, J. S. (1986). Affecting change: Social workers in the political arena. White Plains, NY: Longman.

Henderson, S. (1982). The significance of social relationships in the etiology of neurosis. In C. M. Parkes & J. Stevenson-Hinde (Eds.), *The place of attachment in human behavior* (pp. 205–231) New York: Basic Books.

Henderson, S., Duncan-Jones, P., Byrne, D., & Scott, R. (1980). Measuring social relationships: The interview schedule for social interaction. *Psychological Medicine, 10,* 723–734.

Hepworth, D. (1964). The clinical implications of perceptual distortion in forced marriages. *Social Casework, 45,* 579–585.

Hepworth, D. (1979). Early removal of resistance in task-centered casework. *Social Work, 24,* 317–323.

Hepworth, D. H., Farley, O. W., & Griffiths, J. K. (1988). Clinical work with suicidal adolescents and their families. *Social Casework, 69,* 195–203.

Herz, F., & Rosen, E. (1982). Jewish families. In M. McGoldrick, J. Pearce, & J. Giordano (Eds.), *Ethnicity and family therapy* (pp. 364–392). New York: Guilford Press.

Hess, P. (1982). Parent-child attachment concept: Crucial for permanency planning. *Social Casework, 63,* 46–53.

Hill, B., Rotegard, L., & Bruininks, R. (1984). The quality of life of mentally retarded people in residential care. *Social Work, 29,* 275–281.

Hirayama, H., & Cetingok, M. (1988). Empowerment: A social work approach for Asian immigrants. *Social Casework, 69,* 41–47.

Ho, M. (1976). Social work with Asian Americans. *Social Casework, 57,* 195–201.

Ho, M. K. (1987). *Family therapy with ethnic minorities.* Newbury Park, CA: Sage.

Hoehn-Saric, R., Frank, J., Imber, S., Nash, E., Stone, A., & Battle, C. (1964). Systematic preparation of patients for psychotherapy—I. Effects on therapy behavior and outcome. *Journal of Psychiatric Research, 2,* 267–281.

Hollis, F. (1964, 1972). *Casework: A psychosocial therapy.* New York: Random House.

Holmes, K. (1981). Services for victims of rape: A dualistic practice model. *Social Casework, 62,* 30–39.

Holmes, S. (1978). Parents Anonymous: A treatment method for child abuse. *Social Work, 23,* 245–247.

Holmes, T., & Rahe, R. (1967). The social readjustment rating scale. *Journal of Psychosomatic Research, 11,* 213–218.

Homma-True, R. (1976). Characteristics of contrasting Chinatowns: 2. Oakland, California. *Social Casework, 57,* 155–159.

Honey, E. (1988). AIDS and the inner city: Critical issues. *Social Casework, 69,* 365–370.

Hudson, W. (1982). *The clinical measurement package: A field manual.* Homewood, IL: Dorsey Press.

Hudson, W., & Ricketts, W. A. (1980). A strategy for the measurement of homophobia. *Journal of Homosexuality, 5,* 357–371.

Hull, G., Jr. (1982). Child Welfare Services to Native Americans. *Social Casework, 63,* 340–47.

Hunt, G., & Paschall, N. (1984). *Volunteers: Forming effective citizen groups.* Lanham, MD: University Press of America.

Hurvitz, N. (1975). Interactions hypothesis in marriage counseling. In A. Gurman & D. Rice (Eds.), *Couples in conflict* (pp. 225–240). New York: Jason Aronson.

Hutchinson, E. D. (1987). Use of authority in direct social work practice with mandated clients. *Social Service Review, 61,* 581–598.

Hutchinson, W., Searight, P., & Stretch, J. (1986). Multidimensional networking: A response to the needs of homeless families. *Social Work, 31,* 427–430.

Ivanoff, A., Blythe, B. J., & Briar, S. (1987). The empirical clinical practice debate. *Social Casework, 68,* 290–298.

Jackson, D. (1965). Family rules: Marital quid pro quo. *Archives of General Psychiatry, 12,* 589–594.

Jacob, T., Ritchey, D., Cvitkovic, J., & Blane, H. (1981). Communication styles of alcoholic and nonalcoholic families when drinking and not drinking. *Journal of Studies on Alcohol, 42,* 466–482.

Jacobson, E. (1929). *Progressive relaxation.* Chicago: University of Chicago Press.

Jacobson, N. (1978). A stimulus control model of change in behavioral couples' therapy: Implications for contingency contracting. *Journal of Marriage and Family Counseling, 4,* 29–35.

Jacobson, N., & Margolin, G. (1979). *Marital therapy.* New York: Brunner/Mazel.

Janis, I., & Mann, L. (1977). *Decision making: A psychosocial analysis of conflict, choice, and commitment.* New York: Free Press.

Jaremko, M. E. (1980). The use of stress inoculation training in the reduction of public speaking anxiety. *Journal of Clinical Psychology, 36,* 735–738.

Jason, L. A., & Burrows, B. (1983). Transition training for high school seniors. *Cognitive Therapy and Research, 7,* 79–92.

Jayaratne, S., & Levy, R. (1979). *Empirical clinical practice.* New York: Columbia University Press.

Jefferson, C. (1978). Some notes on the use of family sculpture in therapy. *Family Process, 17,* 69–75.

Jenkins, S. (1981). *The ethnic dilemma in social services.* New York: Free Press.

Jennings, H. (1950). *Leadership and isolation.* New York: Longmans Green.

Johnson, C. (1974). Planning for termination of the group. In P. Glasser, R. Sarri, & R. Vinter, *Individual change through small groups* (pp. 256–265). New York: Free Press.

Johnson, E., & Stark, D. (1980). A group program for cancer patients and their family members in an acute care teaching hospital. *Social Work in Health Care, 5,* 335–349.

Johnson, P., & Rubin, A. (1983). Case management in mental health: A social work domain. *Social Work, 28,* 49–55.

Jones, R. (1983). Increasing staff sensitivity to the black client. *Social Casework, 64,* 419–425.

Joseph, M., & Conrad, A. (1980). A parish neighborhood model for social work practice. *Social Casework, 61,* 423–432.

Joyce, K., Diffenbacher, G., Greene, J., & Sorakin, Y. (1983). Internal and external barriers to obtaining prenatal care. *Social Work and Health Care, 9,* 89–93.

Jung, M. (1976). Characteristics of contrasting China-towns: 1. Philadelphia, Pennsylvania. *Social Casework, 57,* 149–154.

Kaduchin, A., & Martin, J. A. (1988). *Child Welfare Services.* New York: Macmillan.

Kantor, D., & Lehr, W. (1975). *Inside the family: Toward a theory of family process.* San Francisco: Jossey-Bass.

Kaplan, L. (1986). *Working with multi-problem families.* Lexington, MA: D. C. Heath.

Kaslow, F. (1981). Involving the peripheral father in family therapy. In A. Gurman (Ed.), *Questions and answers in the practice of family therapy.* New York: Brunner/Mazel.

Katz, D. (1979). Laboratory training to enhance interviewing skills. In F. Clark, M. Arkava, & Associates (Eds.), *The pursuit of competence in social work* (pp. 205–226). San Francisco: Jossey-Bass.

Kazdin, A. (1979). Imagery elaboration and self-efficacy in the covert modeling treatment of unassertive behavior. *Journal of Consulting and Clinical Psychology, 47,* 725–733.

Kazdin, A., Esveldt-Dawson, K., French, N. H., & Unis, A. S. (1987). Problem-solving skills training and relationship therapy in the treatment of antisocial child behavior. *Journal of Consulting and Clinical Psychology, 55,* 76–85.

Kelen, J. (1980). *The effects of poetry on elderly nursing home residents.* Unpublished doctoral dissertation, University of Utah, Salt Lake City.

Kelly, J. A., & Lamparski, D. (1985). Outpatient treatment of schizophrenics: Social skills and problem-solving training. In M. Hersen & A. S. Bellock (Eds.)., *Handbook of clinical behavior therapy with adults* (pp. 485–506). New York: Plenum Press.

Kennard, W., & Shilman, R. (1979). Group services with the homebound. *Social Work, 24,* 330–332.

Kifer, R., Lewis, M., Green, D., & Phillips, E. (1974). Training predelinquent youths and their parents to negotiate conflict situations. *Journal of Applied Behavior Analysis, 7,* 357–64.

Klein, A. (1970). *Social work through group process.* Albany, NY: School of Social Welfare, State University of New York at Albany.

Klier, J., Fein, E., & Genero, C. (1984). Are written or verbal contracts more effective in family therapy? *Social Work, 29,* 298–299.

Kolko, D. J., Dorsett, P. G., & Milán, M. A. (1981). A total assessment approach to the evaluation of social skills training: The effectiveness of an anger control program for adolescent psychiatric patients. *Behavioral Assessment, 3,* 383–402.

Krona, D. (1980). Parents as treatment partners in residential care. *Child Welfare, 59,* 91–96.

Kruger, L., Moore, D., Schmidt, P., & Wiens, R. (1979). Group work with abusive parents. *Social Work, 24,* 337–338.

Kubie, L. (1952). Problems and techniques of psychoanalytic validation and progress. In E. Pumpian-Mindlin (Ed.), *Psychoanalysis as science* (pp. 74–89). Stanford, CA: Stanford University Press.

Kulys, R., & Tobin, S. (1980). Older people and their responsible others. *Social Work, 25,* 138–145.

Kumabe, K., Nishida, C., & Hepworth, D. (1985). *Bridging ethnocultural diversity in social work and health.* Honolulu: University of Hawaii Press.

Kutchins, H., & Kutchins, S. (1978). Advocacy in social work. In G. Weber & G. McCall (Eds.), *Social Scientists as Advocates* (pp. 13–48). Beverly Hills, CA: Sage.

Laing, R. (1965). Mystification, confusion, and conflict. In I. Boszormenyi-Nagy & J. Framo (Eds.), *Intensive family therapy: Theoretical and practical aspects.* New York: Harper & Row.

Lake, R. Jr. (1983). Shamanism in Northwestern California: A female perspective on sickness, healing and health. *White Cloud Journal of American Indian Mental Health, 3,* 31–42.

Lam, D. H., Brewin, C. R., Woods, R. T., & Bebbington, P. E. (1987). Cognition and social adversity in the depressed elderly. *Journal of Abnormal Psychology, 96,* 23–26.

Lamaze, F. (1958). Painless childbirth. *Psychoprophylactic method.* London: Burke.

Lamb. H. (1982). *Treating the long-term mentally ill.* San Francisco: Jossey-Bass.

Lamb, S. (1986). Treating sexually abused children: Issues of blame and responsibility. *American Journal of Orthopsychiatry, 56,* 303–307.

Lane, F. E. (1986). Utilizing physician empathy with violent patients. *American Journal of Psychotherapy, XL,* 448–456.

Lange, A., & Jakubowski, P. (1976). *Responsible assertive behavior.* Champaign, IL: Research Press.

Lantz, J. (1978). Cognitive theory and social casework. *Social Work, 23,* 361–366.

Larsen, J. (1975). *A comparative study of traditional and competency-based methods of teaching interpersonal skills in social work education.* Unpublished doctoral dissertation, University of Utah, Salt Lake City.

Larsen, J. (1980). Accelerating group development and productivity: An effective leader approach. *Social Work with Groups, 3,* 25–39.

Larsen, J. (1982). Remedying dysfunctional marital communication. *Social Casework, 63,* 15–23.

Larsen, J., & Hepworth, D. (1978). Skill development through competency-based education. *Journal of Education for Social Work, 14,* 73–81.

Larsen, J., & Mitchell, C. (1980). Task-centered, strength-oriented group work with delinquents. *Social Casework, 61,* 154–163.

Lazare, A., Eisenthal, S., & Wasserman, L. (1975). The customer approach to patienthood. *Archives of General Psychiatry, 32,* 553–558.

Leader, A. (1958). The problem of resistance in social work. *Social Work, 3,* 19–23.

Lechnyr, R. (1980a). Hypnosis as an adjunct in crisis intervention. *Behavioral Medicine, 7,* 41–44.

Lechnyr, R. (1980b). Tuning-in patients: Biofeedback instrumentation in clinical practice. *Behavioral Medicine, 7,* 13–23.

LeCroy, C. W. (Ed.). (1983). *Social skills training for children and youth.* New York: Haworth Press.

LeCroy, C. W. (1986). Social competence training. In R. Feldman & A. Stiffman (Eds.), *Advances in adolescent mental health* (pp. 101–114). Greenwich, CT: JAI Press.

LeCroy, C. W. (1987). Teaching children social skills: A game format. *Social Work, 32,* 440–442.

LeCroy, C. W., & Rose, S. (1986). Evaluation of preventive interventions for enhancing social competence in adolescents. *Social Work Research and Abstracts, 22,* 8–16.

Lederer, W., & Jackson, D. (1968). *The mirages of marriage.* New York: W. W. Norton.

Lehrer, P. (1982). How to relax and how not to relax: A reevaluation of the work of Jacobson. *Behaviour Research and Therapy, 20,* 417–425.

Lemmon, J. A. (1985). *Family mediation practice.* New York: Free Press.

Lester, L. (1982). The special needs of the female alcoholic. *Social Casework, 63,* 451–456.

Levick, K. (1981). Privileged communication: Does it really exist? *Social Casework, 62,* 235–239.

Levine, B. (1967). Fundamentals of group treatment. Chicago: Whitehall.

Levinson, H. (1973). Use and misuse of groups. *Social Work, 18,* 66–73.

Levinson, H. (1977). Termination of psychotherapy: Some salient issues. *Social Casework, 58,* 480–489.

Levy, C. (1973). The value base of social work. *Journal of Education for Social Work, 9,* 34–42.

Levy, C. (1979). *Values and ethics for social work practice.* Washington, DC: National Association of Social Workers.

Levy, L. (1963). *Psychological interpretation.* New York: Holt, Rinehart and Winston.

Lewis, J., Beavers, W., Gossett, J., & Phillips, V. (1976). *No single thread: Psychological health in family systems.* New York: Brunner/Mazel.

Lewis, K. (1980). Children of lesbians: Their point of view. *Social Work, 25,* 198–203.

Lewis, R., & Ho, M. (1975). Social work with Native Americans. *Social Work, 20,* 379–382.

Lieberman, M. (1980). Group methods. In F. Kanfer & A. Goldstein (Eds.), *Helping people change* (pp. 470–536). New York: Pergamon Press.

Lieberman, M., & Videka-Sherman, L. (1986). The impact of self-help groups on the mental health of widows and widowers. *American Journal of Orthopsychiatry, 56,* 435–449.

Lieberman, M., Yalom, I., & Miles, M. (1973). *Encounter groups: First facts.* New York: Basic Books.

Lindemann, E. (1944). Symptomology and management of acute grief. *American Journal of Psychiatry, 101,* 141–148.

Lister, H., & Lazar, A. (1974). Group work with disabled young men. *Social Work, 19,* 489–492.

Lister, L. (1987). Contemporary direct practice roles. *Social Work, 32,* 384–391.

Long, K. A. (1986). Cultural considerations in the assessment and treatment of intrafamilial abuse. *American Journal of Orthopsychiatry, 56,* 131–136.

Lopez, D., & Getzel, G. S. (1987). Strategies for volunteers caring for persons with AIDS. *Social Casework, 68,* 47–53.

Lorion, R. (1978). Research on psychotherapy and behavior change with the disadvantaged. In S. Garfield & A. Bergin (Eds.), *Handbook of psychotherapy and behavior change* (pp. 903–938). New York: John Wiley & Sons.

Lott, J. (1976). Migration of a mentality: the Pilipino community. *Social Casework, 3,* 165–172.

Lovell, M. L., & Hawkins, J. D. (1988). An evaluation of a group intervention to increase the personal social networks of abusive mothers. *Children and Youth Services Review, 10,* 175–188.

Low, S. (1984). The cultural basis of health, illness, and disease. *Social Work in Health Care, 9,* 13–23.

Luborsky, L., Singer, B., & Luborsky, L. (1975). Comparative studies of psychotherapies. *Archives of General Psychiatry, 32,* 995–1008.

Luborsky, L., & Spence, D. (1978). Quantitative research on psychoanalytic therapy. In S. Garfield & A. Bergin (Eds.), *Handbook of psychotherapy and behavior change* (pp. 331–368). New York: John Wiley & Sons.

Lukton, R. (1982). Myths and realities of crisis intervention. *Social Casework, 63,* 275–285.

Lum, D. (1982). Toward a framework for social work practice with minorities. *Social Work, 27,* 244–249.

Mackelprang, R., & Hepworth, D. H. (1987). Ecological factors in rehabilitation of patients with severe spinal cord injuries. *Social Work in Health Care, 13,* 23–38.

Mallory, L. (1984). *Leading self-help groups: A guide for training facilitators.* Milwaukee: Family Service of America.

Maluccio, A. (1979). Perspectives of social workers and clients on treatment outcome. *Social Casework, 60,* 394–401.

Maluccio, A. N., Fein, E., & Olmstead, K. (1986). *Permanency planning for children: Concepts and methods.* New York: Tavistock.

Mann, B., & Murphy, K. (1975). Timing of self-disclosure, reciprocity of self-disclosure, and reactions to an initial interview. *Journal of Counseling Psychology, 22,* 304–308.

Marburg, G. (1983). Mental health and Native Americans: Responding to the biopsychosocial model. *White Cloud Journal of American Indian Mental Health, 3,* 43–51.

Maretzki, T., & McDermott, J. (1980). The Caucasians. In J. McDermott, W. Tseng, & T. Maretzki (Eds.), *People and Cultures of Hawaii* (pp. 23–52.). Honolulu: University of Hawaii.

Marks, I. (1975). Behavioral treatments of phobic and obsessive-compulsive disorders: A critical appraisal. In M. Hersen, R. Eisler, & P. Miller (Eds.), *Progress in Behavior Modification* (pp. 65–158). *1.*

Marlatt, G. A., & Gordon, J. R. (1985). *Relapse prevention: Maintenance strategies in the treatment of addictive behaviors.* New York: Guilford Press.

Marshall, T. K., & Mazie, A. S. (1987). A cognitive approach to treating depression. *Social Casework, 68,* 540–545.

Mass, A. (1976). Asians as individuals: The Japanese community. *Social Casework, 57,* 160–164.

Masserman, J. (1965). Historical-comparative and experimental roots of short-term therapy. In L. Wolberg (Ed.), *Short-term psychotherapy* (pp. 44–66). New York: Grune & Stratton.

Masson, H., & O'Byrne, P. (1984). *Applying family therapy.* New York: Pergamon Press.

May, P., Hymbaugh, K., Aase, J., & Samet, J. (1983). The epidemiology of fetal alcohol syndrome among American Indians of the Southwest. *Social Biology, 30,* 374–387.

Mayadas, N. (1983). Psycho-social welfare of refugees: An expanding service area for social work. *International Social Work, 26,* 47–55.

Mayadas, N., & O'Brien, D. (1976). Teaching casework skills in the laboratory: Methods and techniques. In *Teaching for competence in the delivery of direct services* (pp. 72–82). New York: Council on Social Work Education.

Mayer, J., & Timms, N. (1969). Clash in perspective between worker and client. *Social Casework, 50,* 32–40.

McCarty, P., & Betz, N. (1978). Differential effects of self-disclosing versus self-involving counselor statements. *Journal of Counseling Psychology, 25,* 251–256.

McCreath, J. (1984). The new generation of chronic psychiatric patients. *Social Work, 29,* 436–441.

McGoldrick, M. (1982a). Ethnicity and family therapy. In M. McGoldrick, J. Pearce, J. Giordano (Eds.), *Ethnicity and family therapy* (pp. 3–30). New York: Guilford Press.

McGoldrick, M. (1982b). Irish families. In M. McGoldrick, J. Pearce, & J. Giordano (Eds.), *Ethnicity and family therapy* (pp. 310–339). New York: Guilford Press.

McIntyre, E. L. G. (1986). Social networks: Potential for practice. *Social Work, 31,* 421–426.

McNeely, R., & Badami, M. (1984). Interracial communication in school social work. *Social Work, 29,* 22–25.

Meichenbaum, D. (1975). Self-instructional methods. In F. Kanfer & A. Goldstein (Eds.), *Helping people change* (pp. 357–391). New York: Pergamon Press.

Meichenbaum, D. (1977). *Cognitive-behavior-modification.* New York: Plenum Press.

Meichenbaum, D., & Goodman, J. (1971). Training impulsive children to talk to themselves: A means of developing self-control. *Journal of Abnormal Psychology, 77,* 115–126.

Meichenbaum, D., & Turk, D. (1976). The cognitive-behavioral management of anxiety, anger, and pain. In P. Davison (Ed.), *The cognitive-behavioral management of anxiety, anger, and pain* (pp. 1–34). New York: Brunner/Mazel.

Mercer, S., & Kane, R. (1979). Helplessness and hopelessness among the institutionalized aged. *Health and Social Work, 4,* 90–116.

Merton, R. (1957). *Social theory and social structure.* Glencoe, IL: Free Press.

Meyer, C. (1970). *Social work practice: A response to the urban crisis.* New York: Free Press.

Meyer, C. (Ed.). (1983). *Clinical social work in the eco-systems perspective.* New York: Columbia University Press.

Milinsky, T. S. (1987). Stagnation and depression in the elderly group client. *Social Casework, 68,* 173–179.

Miller, G. (1983). Case management: The essential service. In C. J. Sanborn (Ed.), *Case management in mental health services.* New York: Haworth Press.

Miller, J. L., & Whittaker, J. K. (1988). Social services and social support: Blended programs for families at risk of child maltreatment. *Child Welfare, LXVII,* 161–174.

Miller, K., Fein, E., Howe, G., Gaudio, C., & Bishop, G. (1984). Time-limited, goal-focused parent aide service. *Social Casework, 65,* 472–477.

Miller, K., Moore, N., & Lexius, C. (1985). A group for families of homicide victims. *Social Casework, 66,* 432–436.

Miller, M. (1977). A program for adult foster care. *Social Work, 22,* 275–279.

Miller, W. R. (1983). Motivational interviewing with problem drinkers. *Behavioral Psychology, 11,* 147–172.

Milne, C., & Dowd, E. (1983). Effect of interpretation style and counselor social influence. *Journal of Counseling Psychology, 30,* 603–606.

Milofsky, C. (1980). Serving the needs of disabled clients: A task-structured approach. *Social Work, 25,* 149–152.

Mindel, C. H., Habenstein, R. H., & Wright, R. (1988). *Ethnic families in America.* New York: Elsevier.

Minuchin, S. (1974). *Families and family therapy.* Cambridge, MA: Harvard University Press.

Mitchell, J. (1969). The conceptual use of networks. In J. Mitchell (Ed.), *Social networks in urban situations.* Manchester, CT: Manchester Press.

Mitchell, M. (1986). Utilizing volunteers to enhance informal social networks. *Social Casework, 67,* 290–298.

Mizio, E. (1974). Impact of external systems on the Puerto Rican family. *Social Casework, 55,* 76–83.

Mondykowski, S. (1982). Polish families. In M. McGoldrick, J. Pearce, & J. Giordano, *Ethnicity and family therapy* (pp. 393–411). New York: Guilford Press.

Montero, D., & Dieppa, I. (1982). Resettling Vietnamese refugees: The service agency's role. *Social Work, 27,* 74–81.

Montiel, M. (1973). The Chicano family: A review of research. *Social Work, 18,* 22–29.

Moore, J. (1983). The experience of sponsoring a parents anonymous group. *Social Casework, 64,* 585–592.

Morgan, R. (1961). Is it scientific to be optimistic? *Social Work, 6,* 12–21.

Moroney, R. M. (1987). Social planning. *Encyclopedia of Social Work, II,* (pp. 593–602). Silver Spring, MD: National Association of Social Workers.

Morrison, B. (1983). Physical health and the minority aged. In R. McNeely & J. Colen (Eds.), *Aging in minority groups.* Beverly Hills, CA: Sage.

Moynihan, D. (1965). *The Negro family: A case for national action.* Washington, D.C.: U.S. Department of Labor, Office of Policy, Planning and Research.

Moynihan, R., Christ, G., & Silver, L. G. (1988). AIDS and terminal illness. *Social Casework, 69,* 380–387.

National Association of Social Workers. (1973). *Standards for social service manpower.* New York: National Association of Social Workers.

National Association of Social Workers. (1977). 1977 Delegate assembly policy statement—Volunteers and the social service systems. *NASW News, 22,* 39.

National Association of Social Workers. (1980). NASW code of ethics. *NASW News, 25,* 24–25.

National Association of Social Workers. (1981). NASW working statement on the purpose of social work. *Social Work, 26,* 6.

Neidig, P., & Friedman, D. (1984). *Spouse abuse: A treatment program for couples.* Champaign, IL: Research Press.

Nelsen, J. (1975). Dealing with resistance in social work practice. *Social Casework, 56,* 587–592.

Nezu, A. M. (1985). Differences in psychological distress between effective and ineffective problem solvers. *Journal of Counseling Psychology, 32,* 135–138.

Nezu, A. M., & Carnevale, G. J. (1987). Interpersonal problem solving and coping reactions of Vietnam veterans with posttraumatic stress syndrome. *Journal of Abnormal Psychology, 96,* 155–157.

Novaco, R. (1975). *Anger control: The development and evaluation of an experimental treatment.* Lexington, MA: Heath.

Novaco, R. (1977). A stress inoculation approach to anger management in the training of law enforcement officers. *American Journal of Community Psychiatry, 5,* 327–346.

Nulman, E. (1983). Family therapy and advocacy: Directions for the future. *Social Work, 28,* 19–22.

Nurius, P. S., & Hudson, W. W. (1988). Computer-based practice: Future dream or current technology. *Social Work, 33,* 357–362.

Occhetti, A., & Occhetti, D. (1981). Group therapy with married couples. *Social Casework, 62,* 74–79.

O'Connell B., (1978). From service to advocacy to empowerment. *Social Casework, 59,* 195–202.

Office of Policy Development (1988). Report to the president on the family. Washington, DC: The White House.

O'Leary, K., Shore, M., & Wieder, S. (1984). Contacting pregnant adolescents: Are we missing cues? *Social Casework, 65,* 297–306.

Orlinsky, D., & Howard, K. (1978). The relationship of process to outcome in psychotherapy. In S. Garfield & A. Bergin (Eds.), *Handbook of psychotherapy and behavior change* (pp. 283–329). New York: John Wiley & Sons.

Palmer, B., & Pablo, S. (1978). Community development possibilities for effective Indian reservation child abuse and neglect efforts. In M. Lauderdale, R. Anderson, & S. Cramer (Eds.), *Child abuse and neglect: Issues on innovation and implementation* (pp. 98–116). Washington, DC: U.S. Department of Health, Education and Welfare.

Panitch, A. (1974). Advocacy in practice. *Social Work, 19,* 326–332.

Panzer, B., Wiesner, L., & Dickson, W. (1978). Program for developmentally disabled children. *Social Work, 23,* 406–411.

Papp, P. (1976). Family choreography. In P. Guerin (Ed.), *Family therapy* (pp. 465–479). New York: Garner Press.

Paquin, M. (1981). Self-monitoring of marital communication in family therapy. *Social Casework, 62,* 267–272.

Parad, H., & Parad, L. (1968). A study of crisis-oriented planned short-term treatment. *Social Casework, 49,* 346–355.

Parlee, M. (1979). Conversational politics. *Psychology Today, 12,* 48–56.

Parloff, M., Waskow, I., & Wolfe, B. (1978). Research on therapist variables in relation to process and outcome. In S. Garfield & A. Bergin (Eds.), *Handbook of psychotherapy and behavior change* (pp. 233–282). New York: John Wiley & Sons.

Patterson, S. L., Germain, C. B., Brennan, E. M., & Memmott, J. (1988). Effectiveness of rural natural helpers. *Social Casework, 69,* 272–279.

Pearlman, M., & Edwards, M. (1982). Enabling in the eighties: The client advocacy group. *Social Casework, 63,* 532–539.

Pelham, A. O., & Clark, W. F. (1985). *Managing home care for the elderly.* New York: Springer.

Perlman, H. (1957). *Social casework: A problem-solving process.* Chicago: University of Chicago Press.

Perlman, H. (1968). *Persona: Social role and responsibility.* Chicago: University of Chicago Press.

Phillips, M. H., DeChillo, N., Kronenfeld, D., & Middleton-Jeter, V. (1988). Homeless families: Services make a difference. *Social Casework, 69,* 48–53.

Pike, V., Downs, J., Emlen, A., Downs, G., & Case, D. (1977). *Permanent planning for children in foster care: A handbook for social workers* (No. 77–30124). Department of Health Education, and Welfare Publication. Washington, DC: U.S. Government Printing Office.

Pinderhughes, E. (1982). Afro-American families and the victim system. In M. McGoldrick, J. Pearce, & J. Giordano (Eds.), *Ethnicity and family therapy* (pp. 108–122). New York: Guilford Press.

Pinderhughes, E. (1983). Empowerment for our clients and ourselves. *Social Casework, 64,* 331–338.

Polansky, N. A., Ammons, P. W., & Gaudin, J. M., Jr. (1985). Loneliness and isolation in child neglect. *Social Casework, 66,* 38–47.

Ponce, D. (1980). The Filipinos: The Philippine background. In J. McDermott Jr., W. Tseng, & T. Maretski (Eds), *People and cultures of Hawaii* (pp. 155–163). Honolulu: University Press of Hawaii.

Pope, K. S., Keith-Spiegel, P., & Tabachnick, B. G. (1986). Sexual attraction to clients. *American Psychologist, 41,* 147–158.

Prager, E. (1980). Evaluation in mental health: Enter the consumer. *Social Work Research and Abstracts, 16,* 5–10.

Presley, J. H. (1987). The clinical dropout: A view from the client's perspective. *Social Casework, 68,* 603–608.

Promislo, E. (1979). Confidentiality and privileged communication. *Social Work, 24,* 10–13.

Prunty, H., Singer, T., & Thomas, L. (1977). Confronting racism in inner-city schools. *Social Work, 22,* 190–194.

Puryear, D. (1979). *Helping people in crisis.* San Francisco: Jossey-Bass.

Queralt, M. (1984). Understanding Cuban immigrants: A cultural perspective. *Social Work, 29,* 115–121.

Quinn, M. J., & Tomita, S. K. (1986). *Elder abuse and neglect.* New York: Springer.

Rabin, C., Blechman, E. A., Kahn, D., & Carel, C. A. (1985). Refocusing from child to marital problems using the Marriage Contract Game. *Journal of Marital and Family Therapy, 11,* 75–85.

Raimy, V. (1975). *Misunderstandings of the self.* San Francisco: Jossey-Bass.

Rapoport, L. (1961). The concept of prevention in social work. *Social Work, 6,* 3–12.

Rapoport, L. (1970). Crisis intervention as a mode of brief treatment. In R. Roberts & R. Nee (Eds.), *Theories of social casework.* Chicago: University of Chicago Press.

Rapp, C. (1982). Effect of the availability of family support services and decisions about child placement. *Social Work Research and Abstracts, 18,* 21–27.

Rapp, C. A. & Chamberlain, R. (1985). Case management services for the chronically mentally ill. *Social Work, 30,* 417–422.

Reamer, F. G. (1982a). Conflicts of professional duty in social work, *Social Casework, 63,* 579–585.

Reamer, F. G. (1982b). *Ethical dilemmas in social services.* New York: Columbia University Press.

Red Horse, J., Lewis, R., Feit, M., & Decker, J. (1978). Family behavior of urban American Indians. *Social Casework, 59,* 67–72.

Reid, W. (1970). Implications of research for the goals of casework. *Smith College Studies in Social Work, 40,* 140–154.

Reid, W. (1975). A test of the task-centered approach. *Social Work, 22,* 3–9.

Reid, W. (1977). Process and outcome in the treatment of family problems. In W. Reid & L. Epstein (Eds.), *Task-Centered Practice*. New York: Columbia University Press.

Reid, W. (1978). *The task-centered system*. New York: Columbia University Press.

Reid, W. (1985). *Family problem solving*. New York: Columbia University Press.

Reid, W. (1987). Task-centered research. In *Encyclopedia of Social Work, Vol. 2*. (pp. 757–764). Silver Spring, MD: National Association of Social Workers.

Reid, W., & Epstein, L. (1972). *Task-centered casework*. New York: Columbia University Press.

Reid, W., & Hanrahan, P. (1982). Recent evaluations of social work: Grounds for optimism. *Social Work, 27*, 328–340.

Reid, W. J., Kagan, R. M., & Schlosberg, S. B. (1988). Prevention of placement: Critical factors in program success. *Child Welfare, LXVII*, 25–36.

Reid, W., & Shaprio, B. (1969). Client reactions to advice. *Social Service Review, 43*, 165–173.

Reid, W., & Shyne, A. (1969). *Brief and extended casework*. New York: Columbia University Press.

Remine, D., Rice, R. M., & Ross, J. (1984). *Self-help groups and human service agencies: How they work together*. Milwaukee: Family Service of America.

Reynolds, C., & Fischer, C. (1983). Personal versus professional evaluations of self-disclosing and self-involving counselors. *Journal of Counseling Psychology, 30*, 451–454.

Reynolds, W. M., & Coats, K. I. (1986). A comparison of cognitive-behavioral therapy and relaxation training for the treatment of depression in adolescents. *Journal of Consulting and Clinical Psychology, 54*, 653–660.

Rhodes, M. L. (1986). *Ethical dilemmas in social work practice*. London: Routledge and Kegan Paul.

Rhodes, S. (1977). Contract negotiation in the initial stage of casework. *Social Service Review, 51*, 125–140.

Ridley, R. (1984). Clinical treatment of the nondisclosing black client: A therapeutic paradox. *American Psychologist, 39*, 1,234–1,244.

Riskin, J. (1963). Methodology for studying family interaction. *Archives of General Psychiatry, 4*, 343–348.

Roberts, A. R. (1981). *Sheltering battered women*. New York: Springer.

Roberts, A. R. (1984). *Battered women and their families: Intervention strategies and treatment programs*. New York: Springer.

Roberts-DeGennaro, M. (1987). Developing case management as a practice model. *Social Casework, 68*, 466–470.

Rogers, C. (1957). The necessary and sufficient conditions of therapeutic personality change. *Journal of Consulting Psychology, 22*, 95–103.

Rogler, L. H., Malgady, R. G., Costantino, G., & Blumenthal, R. (1987). What do culturally sensitive mental health services mean? The case of Hispanics. *American Psychologist, 42*, 565–570.

Rooney, R. H. (1988). Socialization strategies for involuntary clients. *Social Casework, 69*, 131–140.

Rooney, R. H. (In press). *Strategies for work with involuntary clients*. New York: Columbia University Press.

Rose, S. M., & Black, B. (1985). *Advocacy and empowerment: Mental health care in the community*. New York: Routledge and Kegan Paul.

Rosen, A. (1972). The treatment relationship: A conceptualization. *Journal of Clinical Psychology, 38*, 329–337.

Rosen, A., Proctor, E. K., & Livne, S. (1985). Planning and direct practice. *Social Service Review, 59*, 161–177.

Rosen, P., Peterson, L., & Walsh, B. (1980). A community residence for severely disturbed adolescents: A cognitive-behavioral approach. *Child Welfare, 59*, 15–25.

Rosenfeld, J. (1983). The domain and expertise of social work: A conceptualization. *Social Work, 28*, 186–191.

Rosenstein, P. (1978). Family outreach: A program for the prevention of child neglect and abuse. *Child Welfare, 57*, 519–525.

Roth, W. (1987). Disabilities: Physical. In *Encyclopedia of Social Work, Vol. 1* (pp. 434–438). Silver Spring, MD: National Association of Social Workers.

Rothman, J., Gant, L. M., & Hnat, S. A. (1985). Mexican-American family culture. *Social Service Review, 59*, 197–215.

Rotunno, M., & McGoldrick, M. (1982). Italian families. In M. McGoldrick, J. Pearce, & J. Giordano (Eds.), *Ethnicity and family therapy* (pp. 340–363). New York: Guilford Press.

Rounds, K. A. (1988a). AIDS in rural areas: Challenges to providing care. *Social Work, 33*, 257–261.

Rounds, K. A. (1988b). Responding to AIDS: Rural community strategies. *Social Casework, 69*, 360–364.

Royfe, E. (1960). The role of the social worker in a big brother agency. *Social Casework, 41*, 139–144.

Rubenstein, D., & Timmins, J. (1978). Depressive dyadic and triadic relationships. *Journal of Marriage and Family Counseling, 4*, 13–24.

Rubin, A. (1985). Practice effectiveness: More grounds for optimism. *Social Work, 30*, 469–476.

Rubin, B. (1982). Refugee settlement: A unique role for family service. *Social Casework, 63*, 301–304.

Rubin, S. (1978). Parents' group in a psychiatric hospital for children. *Social Work, 23*, 416–417.

Rueveni, Uri. (1979). *Networking families in crisis.* New York: Human Sciences Press.

Sager, C., Brayboy, T., Waxenburg, B. (1970). *Black ghetto family in therapy: A laboratory experience.* New York: Grove Press.

Saltzman, A. (1986). Reporting child abuse and protecting substance abusers. *Social Work, 31*, 474–476.

Salzberger, R. (1979). Casework and client's right to self-determination. *Social Work, 24*, 398–400.

Salzinger, S., Kaplan, S., & Artemyeff (1983). Mothers' personal social networks and child maltreatment. *Journal of Abnormal Psychology, 92*, 68–79.

Samit, C., Nash, K., & Meyers, J. (1980). The parents' group: A therapeutic tool. *Social Casework, 61*, 215–22.

Sander, F. (1976). Aspects of sexual counseling with the aged. *Social Casework, 58*, 504–510.

Santa Cruz, L., & Hepworth, D. (1975). Effects of cultural orientation on casework. *Social Casework, 56*, 52–57.

Sarri, R. (1987). Administration in social welfare. *Encyclopedia of Social Work, Vol. 1* (pp. 27–40). Silver Spring, MD.

Satir, V. (1967). *Conjoint family therapy.* Palo Alto, CA: Science & Behavior Books.

Sauer, W. J., & Coward, R. T (1985). *Social support networks and the care of the elderly.* New York: Springer.

Saunders, D. (1984). Helping husbands who batter. *Social Casework, 65*, 347–353.

Schilling, R. F. (1987). Limitations of social support. *Social Service Review, 61*, 26–29.

Schilling, R. F., Schinke, S. P., & Weatherly, R. A. (1988). Service trends in a conservative era: Social workers rediscover the past. *Social Work, 33*, 5–9.

Schinke, S. P., Blythe, B. J., & Gilchrist, L. D. (1981). Cognitive-behavioral prevention of adolescent pregnancy. *Journal of Counseling Psychology, 28*, 451–454.

Schinke, S., Blythe, B., Gilchrist, L., & Smith, E. (1980). Developing intake-interviewing skills. *Social Work Research and Abstracts, 16*, 29–34.

Schlosberg, S. B., & Kagan, R. M. (1988). Practice strategies for engaging chronic multi-problem families. *Social Casework, 69*, 3–9.

Schneider, L., & Struening, E. (1983). SLOF: A behavioral rating scale for assessing the mentally ill. *Social Work Research and Abstracts, 19*, 9–21.

Schofield, W. (1964). *Psychotherapy: The purchase of friendship.* Englewood Cliffs, NJ: Prentice-Hall.

Schopler, J., & Galinsky, M. (1974). Goals in social group work practice: Formulation, implementation and evaluation. In P. Glasser, R. Sarri, & R. Vinter (Eds.), *Individual change through small groups.* New York: Free Press.

Schotte, D. E., & Clum, G. A. (1987). Problem-solving skills in suicidal psychiatric patients. *Journal of Consulting and Clinical Psychology, 55*, 49–54.

Schrier, C. (1980). Guidelines for record-keeping under privacy and open-access laws. *Social Work, 25*, 452–457.

Schrodt, G. R., & Fitzgerald, B. A. (1987). Cognitive therapy with adolescents. *American Journal of Psychotherapy, XLI,* 402–408.

Schroeder, H. E., & Black, M. J. (1985). Unassertiveness. In M. Hersen and A. S. Bellack (Eds.), *Handbook of clinical behavior therapy with adults* (pp. 509–530). New York: Plenum Press.

Schwartz, F. (1984). *Voluntarism and social work practice: A growing collaboration.* New York: University Press of America.

Schwartz, M. (1975). Situation/transition groups: A conceptualization and review. *American Journal of Orthopsychiatry, 45,* 744–755.

Seltzer, M. M., & Bloksberg, L. M. (1987). Permanency planning and its effects on foster children. *Social Work, 32,* 65–68.

Selvini-Palazzoli, M., Boscolo, L., Cecchin, G., and Prata, G. (1974). The treatment of children through brief therapy of their parents. *Family Process, 13,* 429–442.

Serber, M. (1977). Teaching the nonverbal components of assertive responses. In R. Alberti (Ed.), *Assertiveness: Innovations, applications, issues.* San Luis Obispo, CA: Impact.

Shelton, S. & Nix, C. (1979). Development of a divorce adjustment group program in a social service agency. *Social Casework, 60,* 309–312.

Sherman, S., & Newman, E. (1979). Role of the caseworker in adult foster care. *Social Work, 24,* 324–328.

Shimkunas, A. (1972). Demand for intimate self-disclosure and pathological verbalization in schizophrenia. *Journal of Abnormal Psychology, 80, 197–205.*

Simonson, N. (1976). The impact of therapist disclosure on patient disclosure. *Journal of Transpersonal Psychology, 23,* 3–6.

Siporin, M. (1975). *Introduction to social work practice.* New York: Macmillan.

Siporin, M. (1979). Practice theory for clinical social work. *Clinical Social Work Journal, 7,* 75–89.

Siporin, M. (1980). Ecological systems theory in social work. *Journal of Sociology and Social Welfare, 7,* 507–532.

Slater, J., & Depue, R. (1981). The contribution of environmental events and social support to serious suicide attempts in primary depressive disorder. *Journal of Abnormal Psychology, 90,* 275–285.

Sluzki, C. (1975). The coalitionary process in initiating family therapy. *Family Process, 14,* 67–77.

Smaldino, A. (1975). The importance of hope in the case-work relationship. *Social Casework, 56,* 328–333.

Smith, V. (1979). How interest groups influence legislators. *Social Work, 24,* 234–239.

Smith, V. G., & Hepworth, D. (1967). Marriage counseling with one marital partner: Rationale and clinical implications. *Social Casework, 48,* 352–359.

Solomon, B. (1976). *Black empowerment: Social work in oppressed communities.* New York: Columbia University Press.

Sonkin, D. J., Martin, D., & Walker, L. E. (1985). *The male batterer: A treatment approach.* New York: Springer.

Soricelli, B. A., & Utech, C. L. (1985). Mourning the death of a child: The family and group process. *Social Work, 30,* 429–434.

Sosin, M. (1979). Social work advocacy and the implementation of legal mandates. *Social Casework, 60,* 265–273.

Sosin, M., & Caulum, S. (1983). Advocacy: A conceptualization for social work practice. *Social Work, 28,* 12–17.

Speisman. J. (1959). Depth of interpretation and verbal resistance in psychotherapy. *Journal of Consulting Psychology, 23,* 93–99.

Spiegel, J. (1982). An ecological model of ethnic families. In M. McGoldrick, J. Pearce, & J. Giordano (Eds.), *Ethnicity and family therapy* (pp. 31–51). New York: Guilford Press.

Spivack, G., Platt, J., & Shure, M. (1976). *The problem-solving approach to adjustment.* San Francisco: Jossey-Bass.

Stedman, J. M., & Murphey, J. (1984). Dealing with specific child phobias during the course of family therapy: An alternative to systematic desensitization. *Family Therapy, XI,* 55–60.

Stein, T., & Gambrill, E. (1977). Facilitating decision making in foster care: The

Alameda project. *Social Service Review, 51,* 502–513.

Steinberg, R., & Carter, G. (1983). *Case management and the elderly.* Lexington, MA: Lexington Books.

Stempler, B., & Stempler, H. (1981). Extending the client connection: Using homemaker-caseworker teams. *Social Casework, 62,* 149–158.

Strean, H. (1979). *Psychoanalytic theory and social work practice.* New York: Free Press.

Stuart, R. (1977). Self-help group approach to self-management. In R. Stuart (Ed.), *Behavioral self-management* (pp. 278–305). New York: Brunner/Mazel.

Stuart, R. (1980). *Helping couples change.* New York: Guilford Press.

Sue, S., & McKinney, H. (1975). Asian Americans in the community mental health care system. *American Journal of Orthopsychiatry, 45,* 111–118.

Sue, S., & Moore, T. (1984). *The pluralistic society: A community mental health perspective.* New York: Human Sciences Press.

Sue, S., & Zane, N. (1987). The role of culture and cultural techniques in psychotherapy. *American Psychologist, 42,* 37–45.

Sugarman, S. (1981). Convening the family for experiential group therapy. In A. Gurman (Ed.), *Questions and answers in the practice of family therapy* (pp. 40–45). New York: Brunner/Mazel.

Surber, R. W., Dwyer, E., Ryan, K. J., Goldfinger, S. M., & Kelly, J. T. (1988). Medical and psychiatric needs of the homeless—A preliminary response. *Social Work, 33,* 116–119.

Taube, P. A., & Barrett, S. A. (Eds.). (1983). DHHS Publication No. ADM 83–1275. Washington, DC: U.S. Government Printing Office.

Taussig, I. M. (1987). Comparative responses of Mexican-Americans and Anglo-Americans to early goal setting in a public mental health clinic. *Journal of Counseling Psychology, 34,* 214–217.

Taylor, J. (1980). Using short-term structured groups with divorced clients. *Social Casework, 61,* 433–437.

Thomas, E. (1977). *Marital communication and decision making: Analysis, assessment, and change.* New York: Free Press.

Thomas, E. (1978). Research and service in single-case experimentation: Conflicts and choices. *Social Work Research and Abstracts, 14,* 20–31.

Thomlison, R. (1984). Something works: Evidence from practice effectiveness studies. *Social Work, 29,* 51–56.

Timberlake, E., & Cook, K. (1984). Social work and the Vietnamese refugee. *Social Work, 29,* 108–114.

Tisdelle, D. A., & St. Lawrence, J. S. (1988). Adolescent interpersonal problem-solving skill training: Social validation and generalization. *Behavior Therapy, 19,* 171–182.

Tomm, K. (1981). Circularity: A preferred orientation for family assessment. In A. Gurman (Ed.), *Questions and answers in the practice of family therapy* (pp. 84–87). New York: Brunner/Mazel.

Toseland, R. (1977). A problem-solving group workshop for older persons. *Social Work, 22,* 325–326.

Toseland, R. (1981). Increasing access: Outreach methods in social work practice. *Social Casework, 62,* 227–234.

Toseland, R. (1987). Treatment discontinuance: Grounds for optimism. *Social Casework, 68,* 195–204.

Toseland, R., & Hacker, L. (1982). Self-help groups and professional involvement. *Social Work, 27,* 341–347.

Toseland, R., & Rivas, R. (1984). *An introduction to group work practice.* New York: Macmillan.

Toth, A., & Toth, S. (1980). Group work with widows. *Social Work, 25,* 63–65.

Tripodi, T., & Epstein, I. (1980). *Research techniques for clinical social workers.* New York: Columbia University Press.

Truax, C., & Carkhuff, R. (1964). For better or for worse: The process of pyschotherapeutic personality change. In *Recent advances in the study of behavior change* (pp. 118–163.). Montreal: McGill University Press.

Truax, C., & Carkhuff, R. (1967). *Toward effective counseling and psychotherapy: Training and practice.* Chicago: Aldine-Atherton.

Truax, C. & Mitchell, K. (1971). Research on certain therapist interpersonal skills in relation to process and outcome. In A. Bergin & S. Garfield (Eds.), *Handbook of psychotherapy and behavior change* (pp. 299–344). New York: John Wiley & Sons.

Tsui, P., & Schultz, G. L. (1985). Failure of rapport: Why psychotherapeutic engagement fails in the treatment of Asian clients. *American Journal of Orthopsychiatry, 55,* 561–569.

Tsui, P., & Schultz, G. L. (1988). Ethnic factors in group process: Cultural dynamics in multi-ethnic therapy groups. *American Journal of Orthopsychiatry, 58,* 136–142.

Turner, J. (1984). Reuniting children in foster care with their biological parents. *Social Work, 29,* 501–506.

VandeCreek, L., Knapp, S., & Herzog, C. (1988). Privileged communication for social workers. *Social Casework, 69,* 28–34.

Van Hook, M. P. (1987). Harvest of despair: The ABCX model for farm families in crisis. *Social Casework, 69,* 273–278.

Vattano, A. (1972). Power to the people: Self-help groups. *Social Work, 17,* 7–15.

Vattano, A. (1978). Self-management procedures for coping with stress. *Social Work, 23,* 113–119.

Vattano, A. (1984, October). *Teaching professionals to work with self-help groups: A multimodal learning approach.* Paper presented at the Sixth Annual Symposium on the Advancement of Social Work with Groups, Chicago.

Videka-Sherman, L. (1987). Research on the effect of parental bereavement: Implications for social work intervention. *Social Service Review, 61,* 102–116.

Vigilante, F. W., & Mailick, M. D. (1988). Needs-resource evaluation in the assessment process. *Social Work, 33,* 101–104.

Vincent, J., Weiss, R., & Birchler, G. (1976). A behavioral analysis of problem solving in distressed and nondistressed married and stranger dyads. *Behavior Therapy, 6,* 475–487.

Visher, E. B., & Visher, J. S. (1988). *Old loyalties, new ties.* New York: Brunner/Mazel.

Vogel, E., & Bell, N. (1960). The emotionally disturbed child as the family scapegoat. In N. Bell & E. Vogel (Eds.), *A modern introduction to the family.* New York: Free Press.

Walen, S., DiGuiseppe, R., & Wessler, R. (1980). *A practitioner's guide to RET.* New York: Oxford University Press.

Walker, J., & McLeod, G. (1982). Group therapy with schizophrenics. *Social Work, 27,* 364–367.

Walker, L. E. (1984). *The battered woman syndrome.* New York: Springer.

Watzlawick, P., Weakland, J., & Fisch, R. (1974). *Change: Principles of problem formulation and problem resolution.* New York: W. W. Norton.

Wayne, J., & Avery, N. (1979). Activities as a tool for group termination. *Social Work, 24,* 58–61.

Weaver, D. (1982). Empowering treatment skills for helping black families. *Social Casework, 63,* 100–105.

Webb., N. B. (1985). A crisis intervention perspective on the termination process. *Clinical Social Work Journal, 13,* 329–340.

Weick, A., & Pope, L. (1988). Knowing what's best: A new look at self-determination. *Social Casework, 69,* 10–16.

Weil, M., Karls, J. M., & associates (1985). *Case management in human service practice.* San Francisco: Jossey-Bass.

Weinberg, N. (1983). Social equity and the physically disabled. *Social Work, 28,* 365–369.

Weiss, R. (1974). The provisions of social relationships. In L. Rubin (Ed.), *Doing unto others* (pp. 17–26). Englewood Cliffs, NJ: Prentice-Hall.

Weiss, R., & Parkes, C. (1983). *Recovery from bereavement.* New York: Basic Books.

Weissman, A. (1976). Industrial social services: Linkage technology. *Social Casework, 57,* 50–54.

Weissman, H. H., Epstein, I., & Savage, A. (1983). *Agency-based social work: Neglected aspects of clinical practice.* Philadelphia: Temple University Press.

Weissman, H. H., Epstein, I., & Savage, A. (1987). Exploring the role repertoire of clinicians. *Social Casework, 68,* 150–155.

Weissman, M., Geanakopolos, E., & Prusoff, B. (1973). Social class and attrition in depressed outpatients. *Social Casework, 54,* 162–170.

Weisz, J. R., Weiss, B., Wasserman, A. A., & Rintoul, B. (1987). Control-related beliefs and depression among clinic-referred children and adolescents. *Journal of Abnormal Psychology, 96,* 58–63.

Wells, C. C., & Masch, M. K. (1986). *Social work ethics day to day.* White Plains, NY: Longman.

Wells, R. (1975). Training in facilitative skills. *Social Work, 20,* 242–243.

Wells, R. (1981). *Planned short-term treatment.* New York: Free Press.

Wertkin, R. A. (1985). Stress-inoculation training: Principles and application. *Social Casework, 66,* 611–616.

Wetzel, J., & Redmond, F. (1980). A person-environment study of depression. *Social Service Review, 54,* 363–375.

Whittaker, J. (1979). *Caring for troubled children.* San Francisco: Jossey-Bass.

Whittaker, J., Garbarino, J., & associates (1983). *Social support networks: Informal helping in the human services.* Hawthorne, NY: Aldine.

Wile, D. (1978). Is a confrontational tone necessary in conjoint therapy? *Journal of Marriage and Family Counseling, 4,* 11–18.

Wilkes, J. (1980). Separation can be a therapeutic option. *Child Welfare, 59,* 27–31.

Wilson, Anne (1984, July 27). U. doctor says mental, physical problems plague Asian refugees. *Salt Lake Tribune,* p. 18B.

Wise, F. (1977). Conjoint marital treatment. In W. Reid & L. Epstein (Eds.), *Task-centered practice* (pp. 78–88). New York: Columbia University Press.

Wisniewski, J. J., & Toomey, B. G. (1987). Are social workers homophobic? *Social Work, 32,* 454–455.

Withey, V., Anderson, R., & Lauderdale, M. (1980). Volunteers as mentors for abusing parents: A natural helping relationship. *Child Welfare, 59,* 637–644.

Witkin, L. (1973). Student volunteers in a guidance clinic. *Social Work, 18,* 53–57.

Wolberg, L. (1965). The technique of short-term psychotherapy. In L. Wolberg (Ed.), *Short-term psychotherapy* (pp. 127–200). New York: Grune & Stratton.

Wolpe, J. (1958). *Psychotherapy by reciprocal inhibition.* Stanford, CA: Stanford University Press.

Wong, W. (1983). *Present-day American Samoan family life: A training resource.* University of Hawaii School of Social Work.

Wood, K. (1978). Casework effectiveness: A new look at the research evidence. *Social Work, 23,* 437–458.

Woods, L. J. (1988). Home-based family therapy. *Social Work, 33,* 211–214.

Wright, R., Saleebey, D., Watts, T., & Lecca, P. (1983). *Transcultural perspectives in the human services: Organizational issues and trends.* Springfield, IL: Charles C. Thomas.

Wyers, N. L. (1987). Homosexuality in the family: Lesbian and gay issues. *Social Work, 32,* 143–148.

Wynne, L., Ryckoff, I., Day, J., & Hirsch, S. (1958). Pseudomutuality in the family relationships of schizophrenics. *Psychiatry, 21,* 205–220.

Yalom, I. (1980). *Existential psychotherapy.* New York: Basic Books.

Yalom, I., & Lieberman, M. (1971). A study of encounter group casualties. *Archives of General Psychiatry, 25,* 16–30.

Yankelovich, D. (1981). New rules in American life: Searching for self-fulfillment in a world turned upside down. *Psychology Today, 15,* 35–91.

Young, B. (1980). The Hawaiians. In J. McDermott, W. Tseng, & T. Maretzki (Eds.), *People and cultures of Hawaii* (pp. 5–24). University Press of Hawaii.

Yuker, H. E. (Ed.). (1988). *Attitudes toward persons with disabilities.* New York: Springer.

Zastrow, C. (1981). Self-talk: A rational approach to understanding and treating child abuse. *Social Casework, 62,* 182–185.

Zastrow, C. (1987). *Social work with groups.* Chicago: Nelson-Hall.

Zborowski, M., & Herzog, E. (1952). *Life is with people: the culture of the shtetl.* New York: Schocken.

Zeiss, A., Lewinsohn, P., & Munoz, R. (1979). Nonspecific improvements effects in depression using interpersonal skills training, pleasant activities schedules, or cognitive training. *Journal of Consulting and Clinical Psychology, 47,* 427–439.

Zimmerman, Shirley S. (1980). The family: Building block or anachronism. *Social Casework, 61,* 195–204.

Zingale, D. P. (1985). The importance of empathic responding in the psychotherapeutic interview. *International Social Work, 28,* 35–39.

Zipple, M., & Spaniol, L. (1987). Current educational and supportive models of family intervention. In A. B. Hatfield & H. P. Lefley (Eds.), *Families of the mentally ill.* New York: Guilford Press.

Zung, W. (1965). A self-rating depression scale. *Archives of General Psychiatry, 12,* 63–70.

Zwick, R., & Atkinson, C. C. (1985). Effectiveness of a client pretherapy orientation videotape. *Journal of Counseling Psychology, 32,* 514–524.

Author Index

Subject Index